GATEWAYS THROUGH LIGHT AND SHADOW

Gateways Through Light and Shadow

A True Relation of What Transpired Between Frater Ashen Chassan, His Scryer Benn mac Stiofán, and the Spirits

BRYAN GARNER ✠ FRATER ASHEN CHASSAN

2019

First Paperback Edition
published 2019 Azoth Press
ISBN 978-1-935006-98-5

First Limited Hardcover Edition
published 2016 Azoth Press

Azoth Press
Portland, OR
USA
www.azothpress.com

Printed in the United States of America.

Acknowledgements

FIRST AND FOREMOST I must acknowledge my deep debt of gratitude to my closest friend and long-time fellow explorer into magic and the spirit world, Benn mac Stiofán (Ben Willman). Benn has been with me through countless magical, mysterious, and bizarre events the extent of which we would never have believed if it weren't for each other's verification. He has been there for me during some of the harder times in my life and I for him. In many instances, he was the only other person to witness the most amazing experiences in and out of the magical circle.

Benn is quite possibly one of the most talented and powerful seers, druids, and mystics alive today. I believe his humble and completely honest approach has led to our achieving what few others have in the modern world. Despite his amazing talents, Benn exhibits a rare and genuine humility the likes of which I have not known. He never ceases to amaze me no matter how often we get together, whether to conduct magical operations or to simply share life's experiences. At the beginning of the events of this book, neither of us had any idea just what to expect or what would be in store. Looking back now, we both agree that neither would have believed the sights, interactions, accomplishments, and successes to which we would be privy.

This book would not have come to its full potential without the input of a few talented magicians who readily offered their assistance and advice whenever I reached out to them. First of all, enduring gratitude is extended to Adam Grossheider for his timely and numerous efforts to create clear and expert drawings based on my scribbling to provide the editor and illustrator with a clear understanding of my sigils, talismans, and implements. Next, a huge thank you to Gal Sofer, whose expertise in ancient Hebrew and magical lore lead to some of my greatest success and experiments in Hebrew folk magic. Finally to Magus,

Dr. Stephen Skinner, who has been an unparalleled support and encouragement since I began publishing my work in the Great Art, as well as taking his personal time to review my work before its publication. The support from the esoteric community is second to none, and speaks to the excellence of the individuals who truly pursue this Great Work.

This acknowledgement extends quite infinitely to the most divine and glorious Archangels of the celestial choruses. Quite obviously, without them and their allowance for us to put this into print, this book could never have been. Their wisdom, knowledge, and insight is beyond what I could have ever imagined. The great Archangels' continued willingness to appear and speak with my scryer and me reflects a generosity I will never fully comprehend. My life's work and direction is indebted to them, and I cannot glorify the Creator, the incomprehensible Father, enough to express my sincere gratitude.

Also, certain peril, distraction, and misdirection would have been evident if it were not for my cherished house Spirit and magical mentor, who made himself known to me and my scryer early in this work.

Finally, that these events are related herein is only made possible by the unfathomable Grace of the Most High in allowing His creations to assist me in presenting this work to you.

Contents

Acknowledgements v

List of Illustrations & Tables xi

Foreword xix
Dr. Stephen Skinner

Preface xxv

I • Since First Sight of the Seven 1

My Working Past the Events of *Gateways Through Stone & Circle* ∞ The Art of the Magician's Voice ∞ The Art of Rhetoric: Learning to Use the Three Main Rhetorical Styles ∞ A Magician's Perspective on Aristotle's Appeals ∞ The Conjurations ∞ "In the Beginning Was the WORD" ∞ Hypnosis: Trance as a Catalyst for Scrying and Spiritual Awakening of the Senses ∞ Recommendations on Qualities to Search for in a Scryer ∞ Steps for Induction for the Scryer Before Magical Operations

II • Working with a Talented Scryer 25

Hand-to-Face Hypnotic Induction Method ∞ Forehead-Tapping Deepening Technique ∞ Astral Projection Formula ∞ Scryer's Experience

III • The Four Great Elements of Creation 35

The Elements in Hermetic Magic ∞ Magical Elemental Implements ∞ The Tattwas ∞ The Tarot ∞ Traveling the Elemental Planes ∞ Elemental Fire Experience ∞ Traveling in the Elemental Plane of Fire ∞ Elemental Water Experience ∞ Traveling in the Elemental Plane of Water ∞ Elemental Air Experience ∞ Traveling in the Elemental Plane of Air ∞ Elemental Earth Experience ∞ Traveling in the Elemental Plane of Earth ∞ "Elemental" Spirit

Experience ꕤ Necromantic Evocation Experiment: The Hospital Ghosts

IV • Beyond the Elemental Implements 125

The Implements ꕤ The Lamen ꕤ The Solomonic Miter or Crown ꕤ The Holy Lamp ꕤ The Candles ꕤ Implement Box and Linens ꕤ The Book of Spirits ꕤ Unique Method for Talisman Consecration Using the Book of Spirits

V • Considerations for Scrying in Classical Evocation 135

Begin at the CIRCLE ꕤ A Latin Prayer to Assist You in Seeing Spirits ꕤ Errors in Practice

VI • Revisiting the Archangels of the Seven Spheres: Part One • New Lessons from the Divine Seven 147

Of Michael and the Office of Sol ꕤ Michael Operation ꕤ Of Raphael and the Office of Mercury ꕤ Raphael Operation ꕤ Of Sachiel and the Office of Jupiter ꕤ Sachiel Operation ꕤ Of Anael and the Office of Venus ꕤ Anael Operation ꕤ Of Samael and the Office of Mars ꕤ Samael Operation

VII • Revisiting the Archangels of the Seven Spheres: Part Two • Grimoric Necromancy Formula 237

Necromancy: The Skull Spirit Intelligencer ꕤ Of Cassiel and the Office of Saturn ꕤ Cassiel Operation ꕤ The Preparation of the Skull for the Familiar Spirit ꕤ Of Gabriel and the Office of Luna ꕤ Gabriel Operation

VIII • The Conjuration of the Supercelestial Angels 303

Of Archangel Uriel ꕤ Uriel Operation ꕤ Sandalphon Operation ꕤ Creating the Implements of the Directional Rulers • Part 1 ꕤ Of Metatron ꕤ Metatron Operation

IX • The Four Kings of the Cardinal Directions: Part One • The Round of Evocations 347

On the Four Cardinal Kings ꕤ Creating the Implements of the Directional Rulers • Part 2 ꕤ Oriens, King of the East ꕤ Operation of Oriens ꕤ Amaymon, King of the South ꕤ Operation of Amaymon ꕤ Paymon, King of the West ꕤ Operation of Paymon ꕤ Egyn, King of the North ꕤ Operation of Egyn

X • The Four Kings of the Cardinal Directions: Part Two • Learning and Redoing 449

Second Conjuring of Oriens ∞ Hiram Consultation ∞ Second Conjuring of Maymon

XI • The Olympic Planetary Spirits of the *Arbatel* 477

Hagith, the Olympic Spirit of Venus ∞ Hagith Operation ∞ Bethor, the Olympic Spirit of Jupiter ∞ Bethor Operation ∞ Phaleg, the Olympic Spirit of Mars ∞ Phaleg Operation ∞ Aratron, the Olympic Spirit of Saturn ∞ Aratron Operation ∞ The Knife of Cassiel • Part 3 ∞ Och, the Olympic Spirit of Sol ∞ Och Operation ∞ Ophiel, the Olympic Spirit of Mercury ∞ Ophiel Operation ∞ Phul, the Olympic Spirit of Luna ∞ Phul Operation

XII • A Further Archangelic Mystery: Raziel, The Secret of God 591

Of Raziel ∞ Invocation of the Archangel Raziel ∞ Afterthoughts on the Raziel Operation

Afterword • The Path of the Scryer 617
Benn mac Stiofán

Conclusion 621

Appendix A • A Cautionary Warning Regarding Grimoric Ingredients 625

Appendix B • The 62 Angels of the Fifth Encampment by Whose Names Qriphoriya Is Evoked 626

References 627

About the Author 636

About the Publisher 637

List of Illustrations & Tables

Fig. III-1. Section of Circle for Drawing Djinn into the Crystal 37

Fig. III-2. Portrait of Djinn/Ifrit as beheld in Vision 63

Fig. III-3. Section of Circle for Drawing Nichsa into the Crystal 71

Fig. III-4. Portrait of Nichsa as beheld in Vision 75

Fig. III-5. Section of Circle for Drawing Paralda into the Crystal 87

Fig. III-6. Portrait of Paralda as beheld in Vision 93

Fig. III-7. Section of Circle for Drawing Ghob into the Crystal 103

Fig. III-8. Portrait of Ghob as beheld in Vision 107

Fig. III-9. Section of Circle for Scrying the Realm of Spirit in the Crystal 115

Table VI-1. Evocatory Correspondences for Michael 150

Fig. VI-2. Lamen of Michael in the manner of *DSIC* 153

Fig. VI-3. Section of Circle with *Heptameron* Correspondences for Drawing Michael into the Crystal 157

Fig. VI-4. Portrait of Michael as beheld in Vision 159

Fig. VI-5. The Fourth Pentacle of Solomon from *The Key of Solomon the King* (Mathers edition) 165

Fig. VI-6. Lion and Hexagram beheld in Vision as Sign or Character of Michael 167

Table VI-7. Evocatory Correspondences for Raphael 169

Fig. VI-8. Lamen of Raphael in the manner of *DSIC* 170

Fig. VI-9. Section of Circle with *Heptameron* Correspondences for Drawing Raphael into the Crystal 173

Fig. VI-10. Portrait of Raphael as beheld in Vision 175

Fig. VI-11. Mercurial Talisman of Raphael as described by the Archangel in Vision 182

Table VI-12. Evocatory Correspondences for Sachiel 186

Fig. VI-13. Lamen of Sachiel in the manner of *DSIC* 187

Fig. VI-14. Section of Circle with *Heptameron* Correspondences for Drawing Sachiel into the Crystal 195

Fig. VI-15. Portrait of Sachiel as beheld in Vision 197

Fig. VI-16. The Face of the Jupiter Tin Mirror 203

Fig. VI-17. The Seal of Jupiter on the Qamea of Jupiter 203

Fig. VI-18. The Sigillate Back of the Jupiter Tin Mirror 203

Table VI-19. Evocatory Correspondences for Anael 205

Fig. VI-20. Lamen of Anael in the manner of *DSIC* 206

Fig. VI-21. Section of Circle with *Heptameron* Correspondences for Drawing Anael into the Crystal 207

Fig. VI-22. Portrait of Anael as beheld in Vision 209

Table VI-23. Evocatory Correspondences for Samael 217

Fig. VI-24. Lamen of Samael in the manner of *DSIC* 219

Fig. VI-25. Section of Circle with *Heptameron* Correspondences for Drawing Samael into the Crystal 222

Fig. VI-26. Portrait of Samael as beheld in Vision 223

Fig. VI-27. The Secret Seal of Solomon which binds the Fallen Spirits in the Brazen Vessel 231

Fig. VII-1. Hebrew Agla Seal from *Maphteach Shelomo* 248

Fig. VII-2. Agla Seal in Archaic Hebrew inside *DSIC* Circle of Divine Names 248

Fig. VII-3. Portrait of the Spirit Hiram as beheld in Vision 253

Table VII-4. Evocatory Correspondences for Cassiel 257

Fig. VII-5. Lamen of Cassiel in the manner of *DSIC* 259

Fig. VII-6. Section of Circle with *Heptameron* Correspondences for Drawing Cassiel into the Crystal 260

Fig. VII-7. Portrait of Cassiel as beheld in Vision 263

Fig. VII-8. The peculiar Crystal-handled 'Sword' from *Clavicula Salomonis de Secretis* 276

Fig. VII-9. The Skull Vessel prepared to receive the Spirit Hiram 279

Table VII-10. Evocatory Correspondences for Gabriel 289

Fig. VII-11. Lamen of Gabriel in the manner of *DSIC* 291

Fig. VII-12. Section of Circle with *Heptameron* Correspondences for Drawing Gabriel into the Crystal 292

Fig. VII-13. Portrait of Gabriel as beheld in Vision 295

Fig. VII-14. Names and Characters for the Solomonic Trumpet 300

Table VIII-1. Evocatory Correspondences for Uriel 304

Fig. VIII-2. Lamen of Uriel in the manner of *DSIC* 305

Fig. VIII-3. Section of Circle with Correspondences for Drawing Uriel into the Crystal 307

Fig. VIII-4. Portrait of Uriel as beheld in Vision 309

Table VIII-5. Evocatory Correspondences for Sandalphon 317

Fig. VIII-6. Lamen of Sandalphon in the manner of *DSIC* 319

Fig. VIII-7. Section of Circle with Correspondences for Drawing Sandalphon into the Crystal 320

Fig. VIII-8. Portrait of Sandalphon as beheld in Vision 321

Table VIII-9. Evocatory Correspondences for Metatron 332

Fig. VIII-10. Lamen of Metatron in the manner of *DSIC* 333

Fig. VIII-11. Section of Circle with Correspondences for Drawing Metatron into the Crystal 336

Fig. VIII-12. Portrait of Metatron as beheld in Vision 337

Fig. IX-1. The Holy Table as described in *The Art of Drawing Spirits into Crystals* 348

Fig. IX-2. The Magic Circle and Seals of the Four Kings from *Cypriani Clavis Inferni* 351

Table IX-3. Initial Table of Correspondences for the Four Cardinal Kings 359

Table IX-4. Evocatory Correspondences for Oriens 360

Fig. IX-5. Lamen of Oriens with Sigil from *Fasciculus Rerum Geomanticarum*, and Thwarting Archangel from *Clavis Inferni* 360

Fig. IX-6. Pentacular Plaque of Oriens with Seal from *Clavis Inferni* 361

Fig. IX-7. Image of Indra as Oriens in *The Old Book of Magic* 362

Fig. IX-8. Section of Circle for Drawing Oriens into the Crystal 368

Fig. IX-9. Portrait of Oriens as beheld in Vision 369

Table IX-10. Evocatory Correspondences for Amaymon 380

Fig. IX-11. Lamen of Amaymon with Sigil from *Fasciculus Rerum Geomanticarum*, and Thwarting Archangel from *Clavis Inferni* 380

Fig. IX-12. Pentacular Plaque of Amaymon with Seal from *Clavis Inferni* 381

Fig. IX-13. Mammon Rex from *Book of Invocations of the Demons Vercan, Maymon, Suth, Samax, Sarabotres, Mediac or Modiac, and Arcan* 382

Fig. IX-14. Section of Circle for Drawing Amaymon into the Crystal 388

Fig. IX-15. Portrait of Amaymon as beheld in Vision 389

Table IX-16. Revised Table of Correspondences for the Four Cardinal Kings 396

Table IX-17. Evocatory Correspondences for Paymon 397

Fig. IX-18. Lamen of Paymon with Sigil from *Fasciculus Rerum Geomanticarum*, and Thwarting Archangel from *Clavis Inferni* 397

Fig. IX-19. Pentacular Plaque of Paymon with Seal from *Clavis Inferni* 398

Fig. IX-20. Character or Sigil of Paymon from the *Goetia* 399

Fig. IX-21. Section of Circle for Drawing Paymon into the Crystal 404

Fig. IX-22. Portrait of Paymon as beheld in Vision 405

Table IX-23. Evocatory Correspondences for Egyn 419

Fig. IX-24. Lamen of Egyn with Sigil from *Fasciculus Rerum Geomanticarum*, and Thwarting Archangel from *Clavis Inferni* 419

Fig. IX-25. Pentacular Plaque of Egyn with Seal from *Clavis Inferni* 420

Fig. IX-26. Portrait of Egyn from *The Old Book of Magic* (1918) and *The Astrologer of the Nineteenth Century* (1825) 421

Fig. IX-27. A Magic Circle for Evocation of Egyn (or any of the Four Cardinal Kings) from *The Old Book of Magic* and *The Astrologer of the Nineteenth Century* 422

Fig. IX-28. Section of Circle for Drawing Egyn into the Crystal 432

Fig. IX-29. Portrait of Egyn as beheld in Vision 435

Table IX-30. Further Revised Table of Correspondences for the Four Cardinal Kings 447

Table X-1. Evocatory Correspondences for the Second Evocation of Oriens 450

Fig. X-2. Portrait of Oriens as beheld in Second Vision 451

Table X-3. Evocatory Correspondences for the Second Evocation of Maymon 463

Fig. X-4. Portrait of Maymon as beheld in Second Vision 465

Table X-5. Table of Possible Associations for the Four Cardinal Kings 475

Fig. XI-1. 112-rayed Circle of the Sigillum Secretorum from the *Arbatel* 480

Fig. XI-2. 32-rayed Compass Circle from the *Theurgia Goetia* 481

Table XI-3. Evocatory Correspondences for Hagith 485

Fig. XI-4. The Talisman of Hagith in the manner of *DSIC* 485

Fig. XI-5. An alternative Greek Talisman of Hagith in the language of the Papyri Græcæ Magicæ 486

Fig. XI-6. Section of Circle for Drawing Hagith into the Crystal 487

Fig. XI-7. Portrait of Hagith as beheld in Vision 489

Table XI-8. Evocatory Correspondences for Bethor 498

Fig. XI-9. The Talisman of Bethor in the manner of *DSIC* 498

Fig. XI-10. An alternative Greek Talisman of Bethor in the language of the Papyri Græcæ Magicæ 499

Fig. XI-11. Section of Circle for Drawing Bethor into the Crystal 500

Fig. XI-12. Portrait of Bethor as beheld in Vision 501

Table XI-13. Evocatory Correspondences for Phaleg 513

Fig. XI-14. The Talisman of Phaleg in the manner of *DSIC* 513

Fig. XI-15. An alternative Greek Talisman of Phaleg in the language of the Papyri Græcæ Magicæ 514

Fig. XI-16. Section of Circle for Drawing Phaleg into the Crystal 515

Fig. XI-17. Portrait of Phaleg as beheld in Vision 517

Table XI-18. Evocatory Correspondences for Aratron 526

Fig. XI-19. The Talisman of Aratron in the manner of *DSIC* 526

Fig. XI-20. An alternative Greek Talisman of Aratron in the language of the Papyri Græcæ Magicæ 527

Fig. XI-21. Section of Circle for Drawing Aratron into the Crystal 528

Fig. XI-22. Portrait of Aratron as beheld in Vision 529

Fig. XI-23. The Crystal Knife of Cassiel 541

Table XI-24. Evocatory Correspondences for Och 547

Fig. XI-25. The Talisman of Och in the manner of *DSIC* 547

Fig. XI-26. An alternative Greek Talisman of Och in the language of the Papyri Græcæ Magicæ 548

Fig. XI-27. Section of Circle for Drawing Och into the Crystal 549

Fig. XI-28. Portrait of Och as beheld in Vision 550

Table XI-29. Evocatory Correspondences for Ophiel 560

Fig. XI-30. The Talisman of Ophiel in the manner of *DSIC* 560

Fig. XI-31. An alternative Greek Talisman of Ophiel in the language of the Papyri Græcæ Magicæ 561

Fig. XI-32. Section of Circle for Drawing Ophiel into the Crystal 561

Fig. XI-33. Portrait of Ophiel as beheld in Vision 563

Table XI-34. Evocatory Correspondences for Phul 574

Fig. XI-35. The Talisman of Phul in the manner of *DSIC* 574

Fig. XI-36. An alternative Greek Talisman of Phul in the language of the Papyri Græcæ Magicæ 575

Fig. XI-37. Section of Circle for Drawing Phul into the Crystal 575

Fig. XI-38. Portrait of Phul as beheld in Vision 577

Fig. XI-39. Three Variants of the Olympic Sigil of Phul 579

Table XII-1. Evocatory Correspondences for Raziel 592

Fig. XII-2. Section of Circle for Drawing Raziel into the Crystal 594

Fig. XII-3. The corrupted name and character of Raziel in the Abognazar *Veritable Clavicles of Solomon* 595

Fig. XII-4. The rectified name and character of Raziel 595

Fig. XII-5. The Lamen of Raziel in the manner of *DSIC* 596

Fig. XII-6. Section of Circle for Drawing Raziel into the Crystal 598

Fig. XII-7. Portrait of Raziel as beheld in Vision 599

Foreword

Frater Ashen Chassan's previous book, *Gateways Through Stone and Circle*, gave very full descriptions of the preparations and equipment needed for successful traditional skrying, invocation, and evocation. In this volume, he describes in careful detail many of the results of these experiments, not fantasy but actual recorded results. Taken together, these two volumes cover the most important elements of ceremonial skrying and a wide range of visions generated by it. The first book is the most thorough examination of Trithemius' method: its completely practical outlook would no doubt have gladdened the heart of the Abbot of Spanheim. The present text takes this practice another huge step forward.

The literature of classical Western ritual magic has progressed in leaps and bounds over the last 25 years. In the late 1990s a number of authors such as Joseph Peterson, David Rankine, Daniel Driscoll, Jake Stratton-Kent, and myself strove to publish the key texts of practical Western magic, such as the *Goetia*, *Key of Solomon*, *Hygromanteia*, Agrippa's *Fourth Book*, *Janua Reserata*, and *Grimorium Verum*, many of which still resided only in manuscript form. These efforts echoed a similar resurgence in the 1890s when S. L. MacGregor Mathers and A. E. Waite also published a number of grimoires which had previous been hidden away in manuscripts in repositories like the Bodleian Library or British Library (or British Museum, as it was then). This made the methods of ritual magic available to a much wider range of people.

It is surprising that despite a lot of discussion and activity on the internet over the last 20 years, few folk were brave enough to record and publish their work in this field and the results that they obtained. This would seem to be the next logical step. This book contains just that, a series of detailed accounts of evocations and invocations of archangels, angels, spirits, Olympic spirits, and

Demon kings spread over a three-year period. It is almost unique in that it chronicles the methods and results of a magician and his skryer, rather than being a source text or merely a commentary on one. I say 'almost unique' because Dr. John Dee, Elias Ashmole, and Aleister Crowley also kept such detailed records of their workings. Like those magicians, the results published in the present book record failures as well as successes, and demonstrate the repeatability of these methods. Amongst the published occult writings of the current period such a record of results is rare and needs to be commended. A key ingredient of these records is the information that was passed via the skryer as answers to key historical and practical questions posed by the magician through the skryer.

Unlike Dee, Ashmole, and Crowley, Frater Ashen Chassan's work is both contemporary and ongoing, and has a lot of value to those of us, myself included, who are most interested in the results of such experimentation, rather than just the history and attributes of intercourse with spiritual creatures (a term which embraces gods, goddesses, archangels, angels, daimones, demons, and spirits). This work develops our understanding of these spiritual creatures way beyond the currently surviving magical records.

The book opens with a short survey of passive skrying as applied to the Tattwas, the Tarot, and sigils as was used by the Golden Dawn, but it rapidly moves on to active evocationary skrying where the magician directs the direction the skryer takes.

This volume also anchors the skrying practices more firmly in the practice of the Golden Dawn, but clearly showing how this has been evolved and extended considerably. The author makes some fascinating connections between hypnosis, astral travel, and skrying. He also dwells on the equipment used for this practice, and revisits the previous book with its delineation of actively skrying the seven archangels of the planetary spheres.

This book is not an oversimplified 'how to' textbook so beloved of New Age practitioners, but the accurate and scientific records of an experienced magician and his skryer. Frater Ashen Chassan treats the original texts of the grimoires respectfully, initially not deviating from them. But, as any experimental magician will confirm, it is only a matter of time before improvements are suggested, even by the spirits themselves. These improvements however are not the result of the 'intuition' of armchair magicians or the result of a disinclination to work strictly according to the book, but developments grounded firmly in magical experience.

In addition to the records as transmitted, the book contains some interesting comments by the skryer, Ben Willman, in which he acknowledges the self-doubt experienced by all skryers. Edward Kelley regularly refused to believe the transmissions of the words of the spiritual creatures purporting to be angels. So also in my own experimentation with lamp and bowl skrying drawn from the London and Leyden Papyrus[1] in the mid-1970s, my skryer stated that he believed that he was 'making it up,' whilst producing material which he could not possibly have known, some of which I have only managed to decode and verify four decades later.

The detailed description of the invocation of the four Demon Kings (or directional Governors of the four corners of the Earth) is something that has not been more than alluded to in published material in the past, but is here laid out in detail. No other source, ancient or modern, gives more detail. An important inclusion is the correction of the directional attributions, something that has been totally confused in the past.[2] The knowledge and conversation with these kings is often considered a necessary first step before calling the demons over which they reign. These evocationary skrying records also take in the Olympic spirits (about which too little was known until now). The tools from the Malchus *Book of Turiel* are introduced, and the talismans from the *Key of Solomon* are also skryed.

One intriguing section breaks new ground but also goes back to the practices of the *Hygromanteia* or *Magical Treatise of Solomon* (the forefather of the *Key of Solomon*), where it deals with the necromantic procedure of preparing a skull which will later act as a receptacle for a familiar spirit. Material such as the commissioning of the semi-physical familiar skull spirit is unique amongst current magical records, the like of which has not been recorded since the manuals of the Byzantine magicians of the 15th century, or in the lost notebooks of Robert Grosseteste (early 13th century).

One of the things I really like about this work is the systematic approach. It was not sufficient to just invoke and skry one angel, one demon king, or one Olympic spirit, but Frater Ashen Chassan and his skryer systematically worked

1. *PDM* xiv.1–92, 150–334.

2. See *The Complete Magician's Tables* (Tables M62 and M63) for tables of the 11 different sets of attributions (mostly wrong) ranging from Agrippa, Solomon, the *Goetia*, and Honorius to the *Clavis Inferni*.

their way through all four demon kings, all seven Olympic spirits, and all the major Archangels, even the supercelestial ones.

At all times the emphasis is upon magical tools, all of which were constructed from scratch to the highest standard. Methods used started with experiments with Trithemian crystal-gazing, recorded by Francis Barrett as *The Art of Drawing Spirits into Crystals (DSIC)*, but as they progressed took more from the skrying methods recorded in the *PGM* and *Hygromanteia* and the invocations of the grimoires.

Some of the most valuable inclusions are the methods of invocation or evocation revealed by the spirits themselves. The procedure of asking spirits how to contact or bind other spirits is as old as King Solomon, who used this method to interview all 60 demons, beginning with just one (Ornias), who then safely introduced him on to the other 59 spirits.[3] The benefits of this approach are that it is then more likely that the spirits themselves will appreciate and respond to the procedures provided by themselves. This is effectively the creation of a new grimoire, but one recorded in a much more systematic and scientific way than older grimoire texts which have been redacted by many hands, some of which may not have been practitioners.

One interesting piece of enlightenment provided by these workings is that mental states such as belief, piety, centredness, or Will do not make very much difference to the outcome. Crowley's assertion that Will is an essential ingredient of magic is partly contradicted by these results, although "without lust of result" seems to have been an important and beneficial frame of mind. The spiritual creatures show themselves as largely independent of the mind or mood of the magician and act as they truly are: independent beings. They do however respond to statements made aloud, but appear not to make a practice of reading the mind of the magician. Smoothness of practice, with none of the awkwardness of the first few tries is also important. Such smoothness comes from hard work, from memorising the conjurations rather than reading them from a script, from knowing what to expect and moving correctly around the circle.

Invoking regularly so the procedure becomes second nature rather than a slightly awkward play act is also important. The New Age insistence upon imagination and visualisation of the outcome is not just unnecessary but also unproductive. The experience should be experienced and its outcome should

3. In the 2nd/3rd-century *Testament of Solomon*. Interestingly, Ornias is reputed to be the offspring of the archangel Uriel, and it is Uriel (rather than Michael) who is able to bind Ornias.

not be forced—the spiritual creatures should be encountered on their own terms. Creative visualisation then becomes no more necessary than it might be for performing a chemical reaction. At all times the attitude and outlook in these records has been one of scientific enquiry. Rituals which did not meet the standards imposed by the experimenter were repeated in an effort to learn more.

This book also underlines the necessity of keeping a magical diary just as any scientist worth his salt will keep a journal of all of his experiments, both good and bad, to be mined at a later date for data which will enable theories or concrete methods to be tested, consolidated, and built upon.

This book is a major contribution to the study and practice of Western ceremonial ritual magic. This is a book that no serious practitioner of magic should be without.

Dr. Stephen Skinner
Singapore
January 2016

Preface

IN THE SUMMER OF 2011, I attempted to replicate a system of traditional Angelic evocation as an experiment to share with a few other ceremonial magicians. Little did I know that this art form attributed to a 16th-century abbot would catapult me into the most profound experiences of magic and the Spiritual world that I would ever encounter. Looking back, I could never have imagined the extent of the manifestations and the depth of the conversations which I have been privileged to experience through the Archangels, Angels, and Spirits I have encountered through this magical art. This grace has been extended not only to me but to a fellow partner in magic as well. Although I attempt to do so in this book, I know that it is impossible to communicate fully the wonder of these encounters or the entirety of the repercussions they have had on me and my life.

In the honor of my continuing practice in magical evocation of Spirits, I decided to present this second volume as a detailed record and personal relation of the numerous encounters and experiments evoking spiritual beings to visual and auditory presence. The majority of the contents of this volume are the actual records and testaments of magical experiments, and come directly from the words and experiences of my scryer and myself.

The full breadth of these occurrences happened only after first guiding my scryer through a series of what might be considered mystery initiations. Certain magical and hypnotic experiments seemed to open the doors which allowed us to gain audiences with the beings of the celestial hierarchies. As you will read, many of the events that transpired are quoted from my scryer's direct relation and experience.

However, in nearly every relation, I beheld, heard, and experienced much of the phenomena if not the same directly, and include my perspective as well. My scryer's relations could be considered successful examples of guiding someone to spiritual contact via methods of classical ritual magic, namely invocation/ evocation. I offer them as truthful records and examples for other aspiring magicians who may wish to conduct their experiments if they have not already done so. Regardless, none of this work would have been possible were it not for the enlightened magicians, mystics, philosophers and clergy, all who were and are my forbears and paved the way for me and gave me a structure from which I was able to contact these beings in clarity.

The framework for the vast majority of our magical evocations is primarily from the system of the magic and philosophy of Trithemius of Spanheim best known as *The Art of Drawing Spirits Into Crystals* (which I often abbreviate as *DSIC*), translated from the Latin by Francis Barrett for inclusion in *The Magus.*[1] Without a doubt, this system has become my forte, long experience having established it as my tried and proven method for getting Spirits to appear for myself and others with the greatest reliable level of success. The magical format adheres closely to the other classical Solomonic magical procedures with which I have become familiar over the years.

Besides the aforementioned method of classical conjuration, I also utilize a number of other esoteric methods to which I have become accustomed and with which I have achieved a notable level of success. Many of these methods are a mixture of what could be considered traditional grimoric magic, more modern lodge-style (Golden Dawn) ceremonial magic, plus techniques I've developed using my abilities as a hypnotherapist to introduce my scryer to experiences and beings of the occult world.

This volume will definitely speak to those who have accomplished the successful evocations of the seven Planetary Archangels and have been initiated through their celestial spheres of influence. The confirmation of these initiations will have happened naturally as a result of successful contact and conversation with these incredibly powerful beings. This is a process whose results are

1. The attribution of *The Art of Drawing Spirits into Crystals* to Trithemius is generally considered spurious, but it is worth noting that he definitely wrote *De Septem Secundeis*, that the condemnatory *Antipalus maleficiorum* shows his familiarity with many magical and grimoric texts (probably written to appease his ecclesiastical superiors when rumors of his practice of magic began to circulate), and that he was a teacher and mentor of both Paracelsus Heinrich Cornelius Agrippa, who probably conducted some of the research for *De Occulta Philosophia* in the famous library at Trithemius' abbey. —APF

only attainable by direct experience and in no way by mere armchair imagining or intellectual theorizing.

Readers attempting to replicate the spells, magical formulæ, and tools presented herein without first succeeding in operations such as were presented in my first volume may find the practices to be either confusing or incredible. Furthermore, I caution the reader against attempting the unique rituals contained in this volume until completing the cycle of evocations of the seven Planetary Archangels. Calling up the more chaotic sublunary Spirits that are associated with the seven celestial bodies will undoubtedly bring either no results or unfavorable ones for those who do not take this advice seriously. Consider yourself duly warned.

This work will not only delve into personal encounters with the seven planetary archangels who were introduced in my first volume but also introduce the reader to many more beings as well as magical experiments outside the realm of grimoric tradition. In the chapters that follow, the reader will be privy to the direct experiences of powerful Spirits listed in various magical texts of antiquity: the powerful, supercelestial Archangels; the seven Olympic Planetary Spirits; the mighty rulers of the Elemental Spirits; the four great Directional kings or princes over the cardinal points of the compass; as well as other Spirits and ghosts who operate under the major rulers of the seven heavens and beyond. You will behold descriptions and particular offices of Spirits never previously revealed in such detail. This comprehensive work will undoubtedly shed new light on previously ambiguous beings of the Spiritual world, and will hopefully give aspiring magicians further aspects to consider when attempting to contact these beings on their own.

The magical records include the methods and formulas described to me by the Spirits themselves and also many of the remarkable results which followed. This book is indeed a grand opus of experiential magic, one which unfolded into deeper and more complex revelations with each new spirit we contacted. Each Spirit is part of a puzzle, a strand in a grand design which only begins to be more fully comprehensible when the whole is woven together and studied.

Although I have practiced traditional forms of grimoric magic for many years and largely adhere to the methods given within the various manuscripts of medieval and renaissance magic, the knowledgable reader will notice places where I have deviated from the classical text to explore new techniques of working and contacting these spiritual beings. The justification for this is that I worked diligently and deliberately within the strict parameters of classical magic many times before deciding to alter any detail. I do not recommend that anyone begin their magical experiments utilizing my modified forms, but instead keep them for reference and possible later use after first working through the original texts. I state this not to impose difficulties or lead one through unnecessary antiquity, but to give the appreciation and background required to move into establishing your own system of magic.

There is no question for me that magical working and procedure must evolve naturally to embrace the evolving philosophies, knowledge, and spiritual interests of our time. While grimoric texts are the foundation of tried and tested methods of spiritual interaction and represent formats that the Spirits themselves acknowledge and recognize, the replication of ancient rituals is utilized primarily to establish a confirming contact and introduction. Through interaction building upon that successful contact, we naturally learn new methods of conversing by experience and through the instruction of the Spirits themselves. This is not to say that vital elements from the historic texts are to be discarded or overlooked. If anything, my practices still appear strikingly like what is given in the classical texts; however, certain elements or invocations have evolved after years of continued practice.

My practice of the art of *Drawing Spirits into Crystals* is designed as an experimental laboratory to initiate successful contact with Spiritual Intelligences and hold audience with them. The understanding under which I operate is that I am setting a space of ritual formality in which universal standards since the particulars of the Spirit are not yet known or assumed. In fact, the entire operation is designed around the assumption that the only reliably known information is the Spirit's name, seal, general office, and Planetary alignment. The experienced magician may be able to call up beings with even less description, and thus record new information that has yet to be included in any known book of magic. New sigils may be discovered as well as offices, procedures, and magical methods. I daresay this is among the eventual goals of the ceremonial magician who begins to venture out from the strict replication of grimoric texts of Spirits already known.

Regardless, in order to authentically and safely venture out beyond the classical methods, discerning magicians should be well-versed in traditional magical procedures before any such attempts are even considered. One should be a veteran conjuror of skill and experience, who has learned from previous errors and developed a reliable and sound practice. Although the methods and processes I utilize in many of these unique rituals are shared in detail, they do not guarantee complete success as some other modern books of magic claim. Many of my rituals are experiments I tested with my scryer and which luckily brought about the desired results. There are many factors and variables which led to the success of our operations, least of which this book is definitely not an introduction to evocation or invocation or a "how to" manual. This is a record of experiments accomplished by myself and my companions who were involved, and is best suited for magicians already involved in the practice of magical invocation.

If you have been working with an assistant or scryer for the majority of your operations up to this point, you both should be intuitively developing familiarity with the various spheres of the Archangels as well as integrating many of the corresponding benefits of each ruler within your psyches. It is quite probable that you experienced greater success with one or two of the Angelic beings than the others. This tends toward selective working with one or a couple of the major ruling Intelligences and their subordinates. It is perfectly acceptable to move on to the other beings of the spheres in which you have been most successful, but I would not attempt similar operations with the lesser entities of Planetary spheres in which you have not yet successfully contacted or worked with the ruling Archangels. In essence, such work should be undertaken by advanced practitioners who have achieved veritable contact with the highest forces in each sphere and have achieved repeated and consistent results from their experiments.

Besides our astrological birth charts, which indicate our alignments toward certain stars and planets, the timing and state of our lives may also determine how compatable some Spirits are with us. There are times in our lives when certain beings may not be able to communicate clearly with us if at all due to any number of internal or external variables which inhibit our perceptions and abilities for interacting harmoniously with a particular type or frequency of energy. It may be that there is only enough time and aptitude to become familiar with one or two of the denizens of the Planetary spheres at this point in your life. This should not be discouraging in the least, as it may cause you to explore your chosen area more deeply than anyone else who has simply visited the sphere at select times. Forming bonds and relationships with certain Spirits and Angels who work harmoniously with us is more the rule than the exception in classical magical practice. On the other hand, efforts should be made to balance out the spheres of influence when possible to avoid fixation or obsession.

With every active force or power, you will by definition need an equal and opposing force or power. The nature of these countereffects goes beyond the scope of our religious or ethical judgments and exists as a natural course in the workings of the universe. Despite the sterile knowledge of this, there is still a danger to overexposure or exposure to the inharmonious effects of these powers. The Planetary Demons that make up one type of resounding effects of the celestial Intelligences are not the opposite of the higher celestial beings, but rather the manifestation of the same energies in forms which are unbalanced or at least unbalancing for human beings.

A magus who has completed a series of the primary Planetary evocations such as are outlined in *Gateways Through Stone and Circle*[2] will be well aware that the object of Planetary Spirit communication is more about explorations into the nature of existence and the psyche than it is about the childish pursuit of riches and glory. The magician who is ready to conjure Planetary Olympic Spirits, Sublunary beings, and Demons to visible and auditory presence should know full well that it will not be for the fulfillment of basic wants and desires. The conjuror magician is an explorer and diplomat in the esoteric realms of the Spirit and mind to better understand the nature of himself as well as the universe of the unseen. Responsibility to use such gifts and experiences wisely should naturally become a major theme of one's work.

An inexperienced magician may ask, "Well, then, why call up this demon if it will not produce the pot of gold that is alluded to in so many grimoires?" The answer is both simple and involved. In the most basic sense, the reason for communing and conversing with such a being would be to better understand the more severe manifestations of the universe, perhaps revealing some hidden aspect of the true nature of ourselves and others in the process. Such contact could also be for the dispelling of fears or false assumptions we hold about aspects to which we have been attached. Perhaps our thought patterns or another's could be freed from previously unseen prisons to explore a world and life we or they would have otherwise never known.

Be forewarned that while these Spirits are not simply aspects of the human consciousness or projections of the mind, such areas are the mediums through which these Spirits often relate and interact with us. From this point of interac-

2. Of course, if the magician does not have ready access to *Gateways Through Stone and Circle*, the volume in your hands contains records of a complete successful series of such invocations of the Planetary Archangels in chapters VI and VII, and *The Art of Drawing Spirits into Crystals* is readily available in many inexpensive print and ebook editions of *The Magus*, and online at Joseph H. Peterson's priceless *Twilit Grotto—Esoteric Archives* website at http://www.esotericarchives.com/tritheim/trchryst.htm.

tion, great and fantastical events and results can be achieved, but often not in the basic sense which our reasoning will try and predict. The occult sometimes remains "that which is hidden" even to the magician as each exploration and experience reveals yet another level of potentiality which is concealed until a future working. Knowledge and revelation are sought for their own sakes as worldly comforts come easier but are not as important as they once were.

The Demons of the Planetary spheres are as objective and self-willed as the Celestial beings but do not be fooled by the illusion of separation for they will most certainly play to your imbalances and limitations. There is no mind reading or intentional malice in this, for they are merely communicating naturally with the patterns and tendencies of your nature which are closest to their own. The aspects of ourselves we assert are most hidden are the loudest signals for these beings. However, the clever and balanced magus may indeed obtain the service of the viable offices explained by the grimoires through dedicated work and continual interaction with various Spirits. For these reasons, I do not always share accounts of these conjurations where I feel the information may be misleading or potentially harmful to the inexperienced or unwary reader.

Throughout every experiment, I paid particular attention to my mental and emotional states, the weather, Lunar phases, astrological alignments, and anything else that might impact the success of the operation. The irony is that the results have proven to have been largely independent of most of these factors. Particularly, my mood, feelings of piety, centeredness, and even concentration scans the sincere motivation to conduct the magical ceremony, have not appeared to affect the outcomes of the operations to the best of my knowledge. The seeming ease of many operations may have been due to the fact that I have never considered the art of *DSIC* to be tedious, taxing, or anything but a successful means of performing what the art is intended to do. Even during times of distraction or unfavorable moods, I was genuinely excited about conducting these ceremonies. Positive results seemed to occur without hesitation, especially when I brought to the working sincerity combined with a lack of attachment to outcome.

Proper mindset is a topic brought up in the occult community often for those experimenting with evocation and other forms of classical magic. It is a state of being which simply cannot be feigned in any way, as the source lies at a deep level of consciousness and simply trying to push through or past in a logical, reasoning way will not work. Part of the paradoxical problem is that there will always be some level of doubt or misgivings as to the reality or success of the ritual until one actually has a confirmed and veritable experience.

Magic, including the arrival of and communication with Spirits, has occurred during times I thought my attempts were doomed to failure because of my lack of will, intention, passion, etc., as well as details missed during the ceremony. Then, at other times when I thought all would go as planned, I received zero results. There is still an undeniable level of uncertainty and unpredictability in this art or "technology." After all my years of study and practice, I still don't always understand why rituals sometimes work and at other times do not.

Extravagant expectations of results in the early phases of practice are a potential source of disappointment in the actual results, and in some cases can even block successful evocation. The reality is that evocation will need to be practiced repeatedly until certain parts of the process fall into place, and that expectation of success is one of the prerequisites for success. That is, all of this must be done with the expectation that the Spirit will manifest, but without discouragement if it does not. In this way, expectations are a catch-22 and one of the reasons why many would-be conjurors give up on evocation as a serious practice. Magicians conduct serious evocation rituals with the expectation and belief that the system will work and that the Spirit will appear in some fashion, but we do not always have the correct assumptions about how the ritual will go and what our state of mind and perceptions will be once we are in the midst of it. Herein lies the need for conducting the rituals, even at the very beginning of one's practice, not as dry rehearsal *per se*, but as actual experience in attempting evocation. In essence, going through the steps of the ceremony successfully, regardless of results, will integrate the unfamiliar and fairly complex procedure so that it becomes familiar and personal, freeing the new practitioner from feelings of awkwardness, and making possible the confidence and power in working that lead to successful evocation. If you are just starting out but determined to be successful in this area of magic, I would begin a regimented scrying practice.

In the meantime, prayers and petitions to see and contact the Angels more clearly should be a continual practice. I cannot reiterate enough the importance of petitioning for assistance in this endeavor; voice your desire aloud to the Creator and any assisting Spirits that you feel may help. This time is geared toward honing the multitude of intellectual, mental, imaginative, and sensory patterns to one cohesive orientation. It is something which cannot be forced, only pursued earnestly and with integrity. This is simple to explain, but more difficult to put into practical application.

I am confident in stating to the reader that your rate of success in evocation and scrying will increase after your first undeniable encounter, which encourages you to push past the 'shock-and-awe' stage. Although an Archangel's appearance and presence never lose their intensity, you will realize you are able to maintain a sense of centered concentration. At my best, I simply do the operation, and in that doing, the events and magic unfold exactly as they are meant to without expectation, attachment to outcome, or consideration of failure. I'm not sure if the state of mind which is best suited for these experiments can be created artificially outside of the experience or even practiced to the degree that someone can assume it without initial trial and error.

Observation and receptivity without assumption or expectation is a state of consciousness unfamiliar to many Westerners. In the East, lifetimes are spent trying to achieve this state of continual wakeful meditation. For Western magic, it is a particular aspect of Spiritual communication which may seem like a struggle to many. Ironically, when achieved, just the opposite is true; there is a release and shedding of the burden of built-up imaginings and projected attachments to enjoy the reality of the actual event. There is certainly no forcing any visualization or experience; it must unfold in its own way and own time. A sincere and continual seeking despite initial difficulties or seeming failure appears to be the determining factor.

There is also an element of faith that the Angels and Spirits will assist by coming their half of the way when you are ready to perceive them. There are also levels or degrees at which they not only become perceivable, but where communication becomes clearer and more fruitful. It may be likened to learning a new language and experiencing a new culture, where there are many frustrations initially, but the longer you spend immersed in the situation and initiate communication with an open heart for understanding, the more benefits you will reap.

I always began the communication by asking each Spirit a handful of questions stipulated in *The Art of Drawing Spirits into Crystals*. In Barrett's translation, these read:

1. In the name of the holy and undefiled Spirit, the Father, the begotten Son, and Holy Ghost, proceeding from both, what is thy true name?
2. What is thy office?
3. What is thy true sign or character?

4. When are the times most agreeable to thy nature to hold conference with us?
5. Wilt thou swear by the blood and righteousness of our Lord Jesus Christ, that thou art truly NN?[3]

I then asked a further series of questions of my own devising which I felt were pertinent and relevant for best understanding their identity and natures. These questions are:

1. What are your views on humanity, and what are your roles and interactions?
2. In what ways can your office directly affect and manifest assistance for me?
3. What allowances are there to intercede in human affairs? How are interventions decided and done by angels?
4. Do you have your own recollection of your creation and origin? Where do you come from? What is your purpose?
5. What advice can you give us to work and speak with you in the most beneficial ways?

I asked the above questions of nearly every Spirit we encountered. Certainly there are other relevant questions I could have put to these beings, but these were the ones in which I was most interested at the time, and that I thought would most help to distinguish the nature of the individual Spirits by providing answers which could be compared with those of the other Spirits. Indeed, once I encountered each Spirit, it seemed that thousands more questions popped into my mind (and I did ask a few additional questions of many of the Spirits, that were either based on particular issues of concern to me which were relevant to the Spirit's office, or were suggested by statements or visionary imagery communicated by the Spirit at the time), but I was forced to keep the operations within a reasonable timeframe. This is the nature of meeting, becoming more familiar with, and learning from an entity of vast influence, expereince, and intelligence; even more than most things, it cannot be accomplished instantly, but is an ever-evolving mystery that requires frequent involvement and interaction to understand in more depth.

---

3. NN here and throughout the book is a variable name to be replaced by a particular name appropriate to the circumstances of a given evocation or other event.

Most of the magical operations described here lasted up to an hour but often went over. The time actually spent in conversation with the Spirit followed the initial ritual procedures and invocations beginning at the summoned being's hour of office. Once the arrival of the Spirit was certain, the ceremony continued for the allotted time, which was intended to be just under an hour, which was nearly all my scryer and I could handle in one sitting. As I said, we sometimes went beyond an hour, but during the lengthier invocations, it was difficult to maintain the level of concentration needed while being bombarded by an array of intense sensations and emotions. Regardless, an extravagant amount of information was gathered in almost every working which I think the reader will find interesting at the very least. As for my scryer and myself, the events and information were often illuminating and sometimes life-altering. Every time I go back over our operations, I find more gems of wisdom, insight, and reflection than what were first apparent when transcribing the recordings.

In some instances, our evocations were not completely successful by my standards, so these beings (notably two of the Directional Kings) were conjured a second time to receive further information and confirmation of their identities and offices. In such cases, greater information was garnered through further grimoric research as well as consultation with other Spiritual beings to increase the likelihood of better contact the second time, sometimes resulting in implenting missing components for the following operation which seemed to be the needed ingredients for the outcome we sought.

Regardless of our successes in achieving the visual and audible presence of the Spirits, we are still far from achieving a full understanding of their natures, identities, offices, and purposes. In many instances, their mystery was only enhanced after their arrival and interaction. It has become my belief that anyone truly wishing to apprehend the benefits, powers, and offices of these beings must take on a lifelong journey of frequent interaction and exchange before the full mystery of the Spirits will be revealed.

The initial conception for this book was to present a complete and detailed account of the events which transpired between a broad array of Spirits, my scryer, and myself, with the intention of inspiring the reader who may be considering or already pursuing a similar path and wishes to explore the world of classical magic for himself. In this, I believe it will be successful and hope it leads many to experience the same wonders as have my scryer and I. However, I believe that, with the aid of the Spirits, much more was accomplished than simply presenting a collection of experiments in reproducing the magic of the grimoires. It may be that in some portions this volume carries with it the weight of magical revelation and knowledge never before recorded. The answers, lessons, and insights given to us by the beings recorded herein have undoubtedly changed the lives of all who were involved. It will be fascinating to see if the written words of this book will carry a similar impact and resonance.

✢

I

Since First Sight of the Seven

The Continuing Work Since the Events of Gateways Through Stone and Circle

I CANNOT RECALL EVER FULLY DOUBTING the existence of Angels, having encountered a variety of Spiritual beings early in my life. However, I had never encountered what I considered to be an Angel face to face before experimenting with Angelic grimoric magic. For myself, it was the process of the *Ars Almadel* which first gave me the experience I had been seeking, which was to directly see and hear an Angel. My assumption until that time was that Angels, as ascended beings of vast power, were rather reserved in their dealings with human beings, preferring to converse with only the most pious and spiritually pure of the human race.

Since my initial successes and frequent audiences with these luminous beings, my perceptions and considerations of them have shifted considerably. What began as an experiment of curiosity blossomed into a lifelong interest and pursuit. I reached beyond what I thought was possible to achieve in the realms of invocation and evocation as a magical discipline, yet the bar continues to rise with each new discovery. With evocations often being performed once a week for several years, I learned valuable lessons with each working regardless of success. The continued interactions and experiences have left me humble but continually wondering in which ways I should share these gifts and experiences.

In an effort to make the most out of these encounters and to share the wisdom these Spirits imparted to my scryer and me, I have decided to reveal the majority of the results and workings which at one point I intended to keep private. As a classical magician, I often compare the findings of my operations to those of the classic texts which describe these beings. In several cases, there have been instances in which my findings seem to contradict a historical grimoire. Rather than regard this as a frustration or a sign of illegitimacy on the part of the Spirit, Angel, myself, or my scryer, I simply recorded the operations for what they were. It is not my intention to prove the validity of my experiments through historical and textual comparison, only to present what occurred during actual ceremonies, and perhaps reveal the Angels themselves as they have not been for some time.

In the research and study I did on angelology, I discovered that the majority of historic, biblical, and recent New Age texts on the Angels are filled with comparative analysis of the same texts referring to this or that Angel, historical reference and nature, and their supposed abilities and traits as Messengers of God. Although several of these books are well written and researched, very few contained any personal accounts of contact with these beings revealing results that were worth sharing. My speculation was that either others who did claim to have interaction with these beings were keeping the results to themselves because they were of a strictly personal nature, or possibly that their encounters and experiences were not as fruitful as they led others to believe.

In my first volume, *Gateways Through Stone and Circle*, I stated that the *Drawing Spirits into Crystals* system is intended to evoke an Angel into your presence so that you can see and hear it clearly. I also stated that the process worked and that I had succeeded in it several times. In that first volume, I included only my first experience evoking the Archangel Cassiel, which was a cornerstone for me, but looking back, was nowhere near as phenomenal as the experiences that were to follow. Magic, like any skill, can and should be honed and sharpened. I know that I am not the only one capable of this feat, although I have seldom come across other accounts that seemed revelatory. The records in this volume are the shared ventures since my first undertaking of invoking the seven Planetary Archangels.

As I said in the preface, the descriptions here are direct records of the magical operations, and are predominately transcribed from audio recordings of the rituals. As became apparent very shortly after conducting the first of these experiments, I found I simply could not write quickly and legibly enough while I was receiving messages from the Archangels and Spirits either personally or through the voice of my scryer. I wanted to record everything as accurately and authentically as I could without missing the slightest detail in case it became relevant later on. As an added benefit, while reviewing the recordings, I've found that I catch new and crucial information which I simply brushed over the first time listening to the audio. It seems the Angel's teachings stretch beyond time and space and offer further benefits as new circumstances arise.

I developed a newfound respect for the tireless work of John Dee and magical operators before and after him. I respect Dee particularly, not only in his scholarly and thorough approach to magic but for the immense skill and endurance it must have taken to quill down the vast amount of notes, diagrams, and knowledge which was dictated to him by Edward Kelley. I was not very successful using modern day pens and pencils, let alone quill and ink. So modern recording devices were relied upon, while jotting down notes of important points at the same time in case the voice recorder malfunctioned. With no small measure of pride, I can declare that what you read are the actual words spoken during our invocations of the Archangels and other Spirits.

As I mentioned previously, the answers given by the Angels do not always adhere strictly to biblical scripture or lore concerning their natures and duties. You will notice points where I question what is said about them in biblical and other historic texts that mention their names and offices. The Angel's (scryer's) responses are without doubt quite interesting and bring up many other questions. I urge the reader to take what they will from these accounts, but do not be surprised if you find some of the accounts to be confusing or contrary to what you may have studied, since these were sometimes my reactions as well, and left me with much to consider.

The full nature and purpose of Angels remains mysterious despite their answering of my inquiries put to them. For the inquisitive magician, I still encourage the research and study of Spiritual beings in history and lore from whatever reliable sources you are able to find. I will include a list of some of my favorite sources in the back of this book for further study. It's very difficult to claim to be any sort of authority on Angels since several others have put far more time, energy, and research into them than I have. I do my utmost to not claim anything about a Spiritual being whom I have not directly encountered and with whom I have not communicated.

I have not known anyone else to undergo the number of encounters and results I've had from personally calling the Archangels and conversing with them at length. Neither have I read detailed accounts of any results prior to my own workings. I assure you that such vagueness will not be the case with this volume. Whether seen as insightful or fantastical, the results are what they are. I include every question and response which does not involve the identity or situation of a friend or client. Ultimately I will not be able to confirm or deny the factuality of some of the Spirit's responses concerning past events. Some verification of historical happenings is lost to both history and legend. Historic reference to Angels is unsurprisingly found to vary from text to text and from culture to culture across time. Such is the mystery and occult nature of this work which lends to its ever present fascination and intrigue for me.

The Choirs and Hierarchy of Angels and Diversity of Spiritual Creatures

For a magician seeking to explore and understand the celestial hierarchy through experimentation and actual encounter, I can honestly state that the experience of it is not so clear cut as some of the historical models lead us to believe. For instance, the identity and names of the seven major Archangels differ widely depending upon which text you are reading. The Angels associated with the planetary aspects are mostly found in classical texts relating to astrology and magic. Also, the exact natures and ranks of various Angels seem to blur and blend at some points. I am willing to bet that this has to do with erroneous attempts to fit a celestial paradigm of Spiritual intelligences and powers into an understandable human format.

The orders of Malachim[1] are vast networks of powerful causality, intermixed as beings of divine light and instruction coming forth as Spiritual ambassadors of an ultimate Source. Their functions and purpose seem auspicious for the event and situation at hand, especially if they appear and converse of their own accord. It has been suggested to me by some of the Angels that their rank and number are not nearly so important as their function, whatever that might be at a given time or prompt from the Creator. They have no hesitation in relating their nature and office to those who inquire, but add that our (human beings') conception of how those function and interact are skewed by ideals and concepts which only exist in various cultures of humanity. When acting on behalf of celestial dictates, they interact and communicate with us in the ways most suited to their purpose.

A misconception found among many modern people, but especially the New Age crowd, is the interpretation that Angels are just like people but with strange celestial powers. Although Angels typically communicate and appear in anthropomorphic form, it would be naive to assume that this is their appearance or form in their natural state. Likewise, it is quite foolish to think that any Spirit need look like anything with a physically recognizable form. As aspects of creation and divine cosmic power, their natures and abilities transcend any physical location, personification, or other limiting aspect that we think to place

1. Hebrew for "Angels."

on them. In this, their true nature in totality is still a mystery, if not completely beyond human understanding. After interacting with them, I have come to realize that even the magician's perception of them is largely based on his comprehension of what an Angel is and what sort of celestial creature is defined as one.

Interaction with Spiritual beings is limited to the effects and changes they cause within our own perceptions, our surroundings, our psychology and physiology, and events which may transpire in our lives. These effects follow the subtle or dynamic course of the universe in most situations as to allow the continual coordination of working energies that make up the whole of existence. Interaction with Angels is about coming in tune with their frequency of existence. Knowledge, ability, and insight are in fact gained more from the total interaction with these beings than from simply the verbal responses or the granting of requests. For this reason, to ask anything that is counter to the nature of the Spirit or Angel is often useless and will likely end in confusion. The mind of the accomplished magician formulates the perceived information and hopefully processes it into useful data. In this constant exchange, it's not so much the appearance and interaction with Spirits which is the magician's greatest accomplishment but the continual translation of celestial data into practical terms and concepts, which in turn manifest favorable results.

The reason the thorough magician does not rely solely on Angels (or any other Spiritual creature) for aid and information is due to his understanding of paradigms of influence. In dealing with other beings such as earthbound Spirits and Elementals, more practical responses and results which influence the physical world can be assured. For example, if a magician is consulted to investigate a haunting, communicating with a Spirit which is closer to the physical realm will sometimes be of more practical value than with an Archangel whose existence is preoccupied with more celestial or macrocosmic matters. Not that certain Spiritual creatures are too "busy" in the limited, physical sense to know or care about such matters; it comes down to the designated purpose of their office.

My conception of the learned magician is one who appreciates the diversity and immensity of Spiritual intelligences within the vast ocean of creation. There is an enigmatic yet observable harmony to existence, and the magician is able to sense its ebb and flow, and imagine the function and variety of creatures which must live in its embrace. However, unlike the mystic or Spiritual seeker who simply basks in the beauty and awareness of the universe, the magician is one who peers into its depths and risks traveling into the unknown, seeking to harness the strengths of the individual dwellers therein. The Spirits which the magician successfully uncovers and comes to know will make considerable alterations in his life and destiny. Although incomplete in a vast sense, the magus takes each experience and bit of knowledge from these experiences and utilizes their aspects to better the world in which he exists.

Sacred magic is not a sterile and objective recording of data by uninvolved observers. Each interaction and operation left its mark upon my scryer and me, as well as the persons nearest to us during these involvements. I vastly changed my own outlook on spirituality, the role of certain religious and spiritual paths, and many other ideals due to these experiments. Although of an intensely personal nature, it must be stated that nothing in this book is meant to sway the reader toward any particular spirituality, religion, or philosophy; it is simply the results of what transpired during these experiments. I still find that from time to time I question the exact meanings and messages which came across without being attached to their implications.

As a person who has a passion for the field of psychology with its attempts to understand the human psyche, I can appreciate an almost existential study of my own mental faculties as I attempt to integrate many of these experiences into my everyday life. The path of the magician is one I continue to explore but not a role I display outwardly in my other professional settings. I often feel the burden of trying to follow the teachings and advice received from these mighty beings while still meeting the obligations of family, profession, and society, and although there have been times of extreme challenge, nothing has prevented me from being able to give proper attention to each faction of life. Throughout the years, both my scryer and I have had to take some weeks away from the experiments to tend to family and other personal issues just like most people. However, we both find we are eager to return to our work as soon as we have a spare moment.

The events which transpired after acting on many of the Archangels' lessons have validated their words. Personal exploration, betterment, and often challenge resulted from fashioning new talismans, invoking the Archangels through their suggested means, and following their advice for healing, wisdom, power, and living in a sacred fashion. I've in no way come near to living like a saint or even a devout priest, but I am mindful of so much more than I was previously, seeing each thought and deed as an active choice.

Besides wanting to leave a solid record of some of the most incredible experiences I have witnessed, I also hope to inspire the readers in pursuing their own interactions with these mighty beings by providing a clear example of what can be achieved and in what fashion through using these ancient practices of Spiritual communication. I have no desire to present a body of magical dogma that will dictate presumptions of mystical guarantees, only to encourage the seeker to persevere in their own pursuit of knowledge and experience. I encourage the reader to consider or discard whatever you wish in these writings but hopefully never settle for second-hand experience. Discover the beauty of beholding these beings through your own senses. I am an advocate of sacred tradition and proven practice, but not for blind adherence without firsthand accounts and perceivable results.

In the planetary categories of the Archangels, a different aspect of the complete human can be explored and strengthened. Just as the Tree of Life in the Kabbalistic tradition shows the pathways of creation and emanation from a singular divine and unknowable godhead, so too the deep enigma of yourself can be uncovered by heeding the wisdom and knowledge of the mighty Archangels. Each will be able to communicate in words, feelings, and visions how to better manifest the full spark of your inner divinity, the strength of your concealed, perfected self.

Magic discipline is a roadmap through the astral which has no bounds or physical limits of separation or order. The entire network is quite beyond comprehension as it relates to each individual mind. The exploration of the Spiritual is immense and tradition is just a road map to follow to experience parts of this expanse in any singular conception.

Also, in the meantime, it is strongly recommended that you address prayers and petitions to God, and to any assisting Spirits or Angels that you feel may help, to see and contact the Angels more clearly. A Spiritual mediator and assistant can greatly help with contact and assist you to enter the states necessary for communication. All is about honing the multitude of intellectual, mental, imaginative, and sensory patterns to one cohesive orientation and directive. This is, simply explained, more difficult to put into practical application.

Unforeseen results from evoking each of the seven masterful Angels of the cosmos have indeed permitted me to become privy to knowledge and insight as well as benefits from each of their planetary aspects. There are potentialities to be gained by properly integrating their teachings and attributes in a multitude of ways. Even when not evoking or invoking them directly, a magician can harness their aspects via simple recollection of their energies after they have made successful contact with them and assimilated a portion of their nature into themselves.

One example of properly applying the knowledge and understanding gained from this initial contact has to do with the creation of magical talismans. The process of creating planetary talismans and seals is nothing new to magicians familiar with The Key of Solomon or similar grimoires that list amulets for various assistance and effects. The largest missing step for most modern crafters is not how the talismans are made, but how they are directly empowered by the Spirits to which they correspond. After experimenting and rereading the Veritable Key of Solomon, I became convinced that none of the mentioned talismans were intended to be constructed or used unless a successful evocation/invocation of the planetary Archangel was first achieved. In this fashion, the Angelic being or Spirit directly activates the talisman, causing it to be a functioning implement of magical power.

The diligent magician will explore several areas of working and manners of Spirits throughout their career. They will integrate and perfect their craft with all the experiences and lessons they undergo while further exploring the realm of mysteries whether they be within the furthest cosmos or ether to the deep dwellings of nature. Dealing with Angels and integrating their positive aspects will guide the mage correctly to explore the many denizens of the astral realms. Interactions with various Spiritual creatures which would be termed Elementals, Fey, Spirits of every sort known and unknown will be more likely. The wise magician does not place immediate judgment and value on any Spirit or potential contact, but instead learns to discern and communicate with those Spiritual entities that are of the most benefit to his work.

How the magician successfully perceives and interacts with the Spirit world is the secret of their craft. It is without hesitation that I state that a particular faculty of the mind is required for this to occur. In order to be able to see, hear, and interact with beings who are typically regarded as invisible, one must have the ability to perceive the unseen. The ancient methods utilized to accomplish this are not as different as ones used currently, and just as effective as they were in ancient times. Most importantly, having the faculties or utilizing someone who has the proper faculties to perceive, hear and see Spirits is required to be successful in this art. The nearly vital second component is having the proper methods and technology to call forth proper Spirits to appear. Fortunately, having skills in the latter can greatly assist developing skills in the former. This technology begins and ends with the authority and power of the magician's voice.

The Art of the Magician's Voice

The power of a magician can most certainly be assessed by the impact their spoken words have on others and their environment. The importance of the power of words combined with intention cannot be overemphasized. A magician's voice is not only heard but felt, reverberated through the air and ether when they are working their craft. The effort is not forced or artificial but resonates through practiced use in precise function. The use of focused influence through speech and causing a direct change in atmosphere as well the disposition of human begins and animals alike are essential. It's a voice to which everyone automatically gives their full attention.

When the magician speaks during ritual, his voice is filled with purpose, directed passion, and unwavering certainty in every aspect. The power of the word is the bread and butter of the ceremonial magician. One should speak the litanies and invocations with such intention and power that the very air vibrates to manifest the speaker's goal. There is a level of charisma developed from this authority that can capture the emotions and interest of an entire audience. Such aptitude should definitely be incorporated into the magician's speaking skills. The overall reactive psychology of the listeners depends on delivery and the way sounds are interpreted and "felt." The frequency and pattern of song and music can inspire and heighten certain emotions as well as recall memories or sensations in the body.

In classical magic, most of the written invocations are lengthy, arcane, often repetitive and full of religious and wordy allegories. A majority of neophytes eager and initially excited about classical magic quickly abandon following the text after they see the length and complexity of the invocations. At the first couple of readings, it is indeed difficult to recite them with any sort of cohesive attention. Even for those who get into a good flow with the classical translations and pronunciations of Hebrew and Greek holy names, they may not identify with the words they are reciting unless they come from very devout and traditional Judeo-Christian backgrounds. This can cause immediate jumps to alternate and personalized invocations which may be missing some vital components in the evocation and which the Spirits may not recognize or acknowledge. The proficient magician should rehearse and integrate classical magical formulæ into his consciousness to better apprehend the nature and intention of such rituals and thus being able to utilize the invocations with effectiveness before altering them.

Within western religions as well as western magic, King Solomon is often the icon of magical prowess, wisdom, presence, and divine authority. In the midst of invocation, a classical magician often declares the position and authority of King Solomon, Jesus, and other Biblical figures that were renowned for their ability to command Spirits. It is likely that many historical magicians attempted to embody the demeanor of these famous figures, literally assuming their archetypical positions and renown. The Greek Magical Papyri (PGM) preserve a technique where Solomon is mentioned by name for a certain phenomenon where the young boy scryer will literally fall over as a result of the magician invoking behind him. The phenomenon was termed "Solomon's Fall" and as Stephen Skinner tells us in his book *Techniques of Greco-Egyptian Magic*:

> One interesting PGM procedure (one of the few directly attributed to Solomon) explains how the magician should throw the skryer into a trance before he begins skrying, a trance so deep that the skryer will actually fall down as if in a faint. (PGM IV 850–929) ...In fact, the extended meaning (of the Greek translation which describes this phenomena) is "Solomon's invocation which causes the skryer to fall down in a trance." This interpretation is confirmed by a passage further on in the same rite:
>
> > Then say the formula 7 times into the ear of the NN man or little boy [skryer], and right away he will fall down [in a trance]. (PGM IV. 910–911)
>
> Then the passage states, with a touch of pride, that it "works both on boys and on adults." The magician planning to use this procedure is specifically made to swear not to disclose it to anyone else.[2]

Never before had I read where ancient magic accredited spoken trance induction so directly and completely. The papyrus clearly refers to the power and influence the Magician had not only on the scryer but on the Spirits and intention of the ceremony itself. This is a feat of no small mentioning, but likely a closely guarded secret in its actual use.

A study of why others respond to a certain kind of tone, inflection, and delivery is an entirely unique area of study and one beyond going into complete detail in this volume. In the area of hypnosis, students attend a multitude of seminars and classes learning how to properly engage the power of their voice to effectively place their subjects in deep trances. The magician's voice must

2. Stephen Skinner, *Techniques of Greco-Egyptian Magic* (Singapore: Golden Hoard Press, 2014), p. 255.

embody this authority and prowess absolutely without the slightest hint of pretense or forced assumption.

The Art of Rhetoric: Learning to Use the Three Main Rhetorical Styles

Perception plays a primary role in understanding and absorbing what is being conveyed by the speaker. Spiritual beings seem to respond to the same subtle and sublime effects which cause humans to become enraptured by a speaker. Tone, frequency, inflection, and pitch all seem to be universal means for conveying a more complete message to whatever or whoever it is we are speaking to. It is important that the magician is fully conscious and capable of conveying their intention (will) exactly as intended to the recipient.

The traditional grimoric invocations as well as ancient Greco-Egyptian ones often read like a persuasive argument or statement using the same principles one would use in a speech or debate with another to push their stance. Many of the invocations in the Key of Solomon texts read like legal documents, as the magician grounds themselves in divine authority and position, often reciting passages from their religion's myths, history, miracles, and lineages. Invocations are lengthy by design, making sure all the authoritative names are spoken along with reasons why the Spirit should appear and also that the Spirit should behave in such and such a way under penalty of pain.

In magical ritual, our voice, octave, and words should match perfectly with our intention. This is to say that there should be no schism between thought and word, and aptly no separation between thought, word, and deed (manifested action). In the case of evocation, the deed is the full appearance and presence of the Spirit that is conjured. The magician, who intends to place their scryer into a trance which is beneficial to scrying, must be able to manifest this action through their voice. Part of having a truly powerful hypnotic voice is having your full attention on what you are saying and to whom or what you are saying it. This means there is absolutely no other concern, consideration, distraction, or other thought in your mind while you are speaking. You are fully present with every word. During that level of communication, you are one with what you are communicating and there is absolutely no difference between what you are saying and who you are and what is happening.

Proper pitch: I learned how to properly project my voice and find the most powerful resonance while practicing in an acoustic environment where my voice would echo back right after speaking or singing. I really became aware to how some sounds and ways of saying certain words truly impacted the environment while others did not. The Hermetic Order of the Golden Dawn stresses the importance of "vibrating" certain names and words of power but the exact practice did not translate over well to many practitioners who simply do their best to mimic what the texts explain and what they observe from their teachers and fellow adepts. The closest examples of powerful song in voice have come from the western religious institutions which have several years of chant or singing within structures that echo back a melody that is truly inspiring. I'm not talking about the general mass and church proceedings which blend together an entire congregation of inharmonic voices. The classical choirs and Gregorian chants of the early church seem to best match what I have come to appreciate as a well suited voice for evocation. Invocations do not need to be sung and attempting to do this would often be a distraction, but the voice should be powerful, melodic with pacing, pitch, tone and cadence.

In evocation, you are not only identifying yourself with the highest authority or authorities, you are speaking through the mouths of every exalted magician whose voice rang with the authority to call the Gods and Spirits of any order. This is a complete assumption embodied by the magician without any need to "imagine" or think about such correlations. To develop the ability to harness true, powerful, and charismatic speech, further training may be necessary beyond a typical magical curriculum. Training as a hypnotist specifically will enhance such abilities in several aspects. Every word that is uttered during the evocation ritual should be purposeful and powerful, whether to the Spirit, a scryer, or both. Words are sacred manifestations of magical manifestations. Hypnosis or trance is established by a narrowed and focused attention which absorbs the subject into whatever holds their attention. These same principles are vital for a scryer to get the richest experience and relevant details of an operation.

A Magician's Perspective on Aristotle's Appeals

Effective and powerful communication in both speaking and writing is a necessity for the classical ceremonial magician. Besides incantations and invocations spoken to Spirits and scryers, written incantations and charges are often formulated by the classical mage. Rhetoric was a skill trained in the learned class and one known for ritual magicians and priest from the ancient world through medieval Europe.

According to Aristotle, rhetoric is "the ability, in each particular case, to see the available means of persuasion." He described three main forms of rhetoric: *Ethos*, *Logos*, and *Pathos*. Rhetoric and speech were abilities not lost on magicians, and ones in they sought to achieve a greater aptitude. In fact, many of the Goetic Spirits are credited with teaching or confirming rhetorical abilities within the magician.

Ethos (credibility), or ethical appeal: The ethos could also be considered a level of authority that a magician presents which may not always go over on intelligences who know you are presenting a façade. Many classical invocations read that the magician presents the highest authority and Spiritual ambassador, often invoking names of saviors or exalted magicians along the names of the Most High. There is an instance in the New Testament where a Jewish priest attempts to perform an exorcism of a demon, but the demon does not acknowledge his authority:

> Some Jews who went around driving out evil spirits tried to invoke the name of the Lord Jesus over those who were demon-possessed. They would say, "In the name of the Jesus whom Paul preaches, I command you to come out." Seven sons of Sceva, a Jewish chief priest, were doing this. One day the evil spirit answered them, "Jesus I know, and Paul I know about, but who are you?" Then the man who had the evil spirit jumped on them and overpowered them all. He gave them such a beating that they ran out of the house naked and bleeding.[3] -Acts 13-16

Although this is an obvious inclusion to show and support the "rightful" spiritual authority of Jesus and his followers, it gives us an example of how exorcisms and thus evocations were performed. Many medieval grimoirists were at least inducted into the minor orders of the clergy if not full priesthood, so this established authority and credibility would be adopted quite easily into their evocations. Likewise, clergy had ample practice being in front of a multitude of people during mass and performing duties as an intermediary between the divine and humanity. Experience follows tone and tone follows emotion.

Pathos (Emotional) was a skill which was used to persuade a reader or listener by appealing to their emotions and ability to imagine themselves in your situation. In speaking empathy, the utilization of intuition is to get at the deepest part of a sentient being. Allow your own emotions to assist you in forming not only your words and phrases but your tone and inflection. Your scryer will

3. *Acts of the Apostles* 19: 13–16 (NIV translation).

respond instantly and completely as long as you carry your message with this sincere and deep feeling. Although Spiritual beings are not human beings and often have dispositions that are foreign and confusing to us, they do seem to respond well to those who are genuine and sincere in their speech. So although this is a skill which can be developed, it is not easily feigned. In my experience this is not something that can be feigned or pretended, as stated before; there can be no separation between the truth of your intentions, your thoughts, feelings and your words. Your voice has to have enough emotional appeal to hold your listener transfixed. No one will listen to a monotone for very long. Also your voice should dictate the initial atmosphere of the ritual, setting the tone, the emotion, the feeling.

Logos (Logical) is Aristotle's appeal signifying persuasion by the use of reasoning. The importance of this commutative skill cannot be overemphasized as it dictates to the Spirits exactly why you are calling them and why it is justified for you to do so. You must be clear and concise, and assured of your purpose and reasoning. Many Spirits such as those in the *Goetia* are rather skilled in logic and rhetoric and will often question the magician's motives and intentions if they are not well thought out or confirmed. You must know why you are asking something of a Spirit. The power of your Logos (logical wording) will also be apparent through your knowledge and apprehension of the material of the evocation and what it entails. Also, this section is concerned with perfecting your clarity and enunciation, making sure that each word is spoken clearly and distinctly so that no misunderstanding will result.

A ceremonial magician who has had ample experience seeing his voice literally cause dynamic change in the consciousness and perceptions of others will be confident in his ability to project their intentions through that same medium towards the Spiritual world and its denizens.

The Conjurations

Being aptly familiar with if not memorizing conjurations has some beneficial if not vital advantages for classical magicians. For one, it keeps the mind and intentions completely in the present and focused on the purpose of the ceremony. Once learned, the invocations can more easily build to a harmonious crescendo in the flow of the ceremony, ever increasing the potency of the intention underlying the ritual. The mind can only focus on so many things at once. If your concentration is focused on pronouncing unfamiliar words correctly, attempting to understand what is meant by the archaic English of the conjurations, while determining if you really believe every word you are speaking while speaking them, your will and concentration will be fractured. The conjuration will be working against instead of for you if this occurs.

Luckily, in the *Art of Drawing Sprits into Crystals*, the invocations and an entire spoken portion of the ritual is dramatically shorter compared to those typical in other texts of the Solomonic evocation arts. However, the conjurations as given in the *Goetia* of the *Lemegeton*, The *Heptameron*, or *The Key of Solomon* are very complete in that they cover all the vital parameters and areas where major loopholes could be exploited, and use the most powerful names to bind the conjuration as a sealing contract. You won't have to make last-minute adjustments or become distracted with wondering if your ad-libbed or personally constructed conjuration was complete if you use the established invocations.

Another reason for reciting the conjurations from memory as opposed to reading them is the direction of will and intention. Think for a moment and remember the last time you heard someone speak to an audience while reading from a book. A few small-town ministers and teachers might still do this as they are not held to the same public speaking standards of more visible individuals. If you are younger, perhaps you can remember the last time you heard a book report from a fellow student in class and all they did was read from their paper. There is a disconnection which occurs in which the audience no longer feels as if they are being spoken to. This is a sure way to lose the attention and respect of your audience—a very bad idea when your audience is a powerful Spirit.

There are not many sources one can turn to which deal with the subject of training the magical voice. This is not the same as "vibrating" words of power, such as in the Golden Dawn's Banishing and Invoking Rituals of the Pentagram, the Middle Pillar, and Opening by Watchtowers. Perhaps the best examples I have come across concerning this all-important function are found in Jason Miller's *The Sorcerer's Secrets*. In this work, the author provides excellent explanations of how to utilize one's voice, appearance, presence, and gaze to influence the people in the world around one. Every magician should be adept (at least moderately skilled) in this area if he plans on being any source of real power or authority in the world. If you cannot at least sound confident during a conversation, you have no business trying to persuade a Spirit to do anything for you. If you cannot get people to acknowledge you as having authority, you are fooling yourself in thinking that a Spirit will do so. You will need training in how to transform your voice into one that will make the cosmos take notice.

Magical voice practice and the memorization of conjurations can be combined in the same step. Get a tape recorder and record yourself reciting the entire conjuration, word for word. However, classical grimoric conjurations are typically one big run-on sentence, so before you make your recording, write or type out the conjuration, and organize it into sentences and paragraphs. Speak every word clearly, purposefully, and directly. There is no reason to shout or vibrate unless you absolutely feel the need to do so for the "barbarous" names. Put as much intention as you can into your practice. When I was doing this exercise for the invocations in the *Goetia*, I would omit the Spirit's name so I did not draw its attention. As a developed skill, rehearsal will make the invocation quite powerful. The atmosphere would become eerily still once I got going.

When you are finished, listen to the entire recording as often as you can. Go to sleep while listening to it, implanting it in the deepest reaches of your unconscious. If you are like me, you will begin picking up sections of the conjuration quickly, memorizing more and more each time. Be patient, and listen to your recording as often as possible, saying the words in your mind or aloud while listening. A neat thing about this exercise is that you are doing more than memorization here. With every recitation, you are integrating the meaning of the words within your psyche and will. Bit by bit, the invocation becomes yours through the process of memorization and integration, and is no longer just something from a book. You penetrate deeper into the meaning of the words, and start to realize that the invocation covers very specific parameters as a matter of binding and contract. The Spirit is under the terms of the ceremony to fulfill its end of the bargain without any tricks or deceptions. Grimoric conjurations are designed with specific intent and purpose, binding them with the most potent of names.

Make the recitation of the holy and barbarous names with as much reverence and power as you can muster. Speak them as you would a prayer of invocation. The more you recite in this manner, the stronger the words will become for you.

If you follow this example, you may find that your flow and speaking improve to such a degree that you will want to re-record over your original attempt. When you record the conjurations again, you'll notice how much you've improved. Pay attention to where your voice sounds strongest. Are there any points where you hit a snag or can tell where you've broken concentration? Do you sound like you are confident in what you are saying? If you were an objective listener, does the speaker sound like they believe what they are saying? Do they sound powerful, authoritative, and certain? You should be striving for all of these elements.

Beyond getting a Spirit to appear, these vocal practices will cause your mundane conversation to have more power and impact. People will listen and take better notice of what you say and respond accordingly. This formula is the magical instruction given by Spirits as "eloquence or rhetoric." If you still have difficulty, seriously consider taking a speech or public speaking class in college or wherever you are able.

"In the Beginning Was the WORD"

Hypnosis is a fantastic practice in regard to the magical voice, in the sense that you are able to observe instantaneous results in how your voice affects another person. Further exploration of the voice can be conducted through the study of music and song, which is by far one of the most powerful and influential creations ever invented. In the utilization of our voices for ritual magic, however, speaking to a being that is initially invisible can be more challenging than one might think. The Spirit you are evoking must be spoken to directly. Not spoken at, or spoken about (remember the kid giving his book report). There are huge differences between these actions and intentions. Do not assume the Spirit will know what you mean. The Spirit must acknowledge that it is being spoken to directly and that the entirety of the evocation is directed at it. This may seem obvious, but is more difficult than you may initially assume. Your words, focus, intention, and purpose are all focused on the Spirit. This will continue to be a perplexing conundrum until you have an actual audience with a Spirit, after which your subconscious will recall the feeling of its presence and voice and associate the name with it directly.

Practice until you have the conjurations not only memorized, but internalized and energized in your innermost being with proper meaning and intention. After listening to the recordings numerous times you will know the conjurations like your own name. When you perform a magical ceremony, you speak the age-old words fluidly and powerfully. You know exactly what you are saying and why you are saying it. Your words, filled with proper intention and supported by tradition and ceremony, will speak to the Spirit directly. If you accept that there is a being out there whose name you evoke to appear with the intensity described above, if the being is there, by the names and by the art, it will appear. By training and knowing the power in your voice, you will not be disarmed by the actual appearance of the Spirit but able to continually and skillfully communicate with an authoritative voice.

Hypnosis: Trance as a catalyst for scrying and spiritual awakening of the senses

Before I go into the examples of utilizing hypnosis to assist others to experience the Spiritual and magical, let me begin by stating that it does not work for everyone who you try it on or who would wish it to work. I have been hypnotizing people since I was fourteen years old and I've witnessed some remarkable, almost unbelievable events, and I've learned some valuable lessons. Not everyone is intended or able to experience the Spiritual or supernatural. Some people simply will never be able to do so, even if they wish it otherwise with their entire being. For one reason or many, some are simply not designed to have an interaction of this sort under any circumstances. It just isn't their time to know.

Hypnosis through the use of the magician's voice and gestures is an invaluable tool for magic as it requires a sublime confidence and willpower which is laced in every utterance and even in mannerisms which have direct effects on another person's psyche and behavior. A talented hypnotist can effect change in another person no matter the environment or circumstances and use his will and understanding of human consciousness to cause all manner of changes utilizing hypnotic suggestion.

Regardless of your subject's suggestibility, you will first want to be sure they are suitable for becoming your magical partner, or more directly, your scryer. Your scryer is first and foremost the contact and translator with the beings you are evoking. I do not recommend using a scryer as a substitute for developing your own abilities and experiencing the Angels and Spirits directly. It is imperative that a magician has as much initial and personal exposure and contact with these beings for their own development and understanding rather than relying on a second party for all of your information.

However, before you decide to work with a magical partner, it is highly recommended that you use discretion and consider a few points.

The traditional choice for a scryer in classical times was a youth, a virgin, someone innocent and impressionable. The reasons for this can be best surmised by the importance and mystical qualities which were placed on purity, innocence, and chastity in those times. Within the pages of grimorical texts you can find several such references to the magical qualities associated with virginity or chastity (purity) which Angels and demons alike seem to appreciate. There are arguably reasons why adolescents were considered to be the most successful scryers. The openness that children display for novel experiences without judging or rationalizing them allows for a more genuine experience. Children often seem to simply accept what they witness. Perhaps the shortage of a multitude of predisposed perception filters which would be an inhibiting factor is the key.

If using a scryer, whether they be young or not, you will be required to take what is related without trying to force them to conform to your consciously constructed ideals. If they are actively participating within a ritual framework with you, then the chances are that they are already integrating at least some of the factors of the tradition within their perception senses. Whether or not they understand the full spectrum of the ritual or the means of the symbols and natures of the Spirits, their highly perceptive state will automatically incite much of the intended corresponding patterns and frequencies.

Despite the obvious qualities and benefits a young scryer might bring, modern day situations being what they are, it is likely inappropriate to expose young children to such practices unless they are your own children and exhibit obvious talent and interest. It is not my recommendation one utilize minors as scryers in any case which may prove to be disturbing or confusing for them. My intentions in mentioning classical considerations of a suitable scryer is for the modern day magician to look for some of these qualities in a scryer of appropriate age and disposition.

Recommendations on Qualities to Search for in a Scryer

1. A person who is believed to have had genuine encounters with the supernatural but ideally has not studied or trained in the occult and if possible, not been overly exposed to and influenced by media portrayals of the supernatural or occult, which might distort their ability to comprehend or perceive Spiritual beings. This will be a bit of a conundrum if they have a genuine interest in the occult or supernatural. However, you are likely to get a "purer" account from someone who does not have an overabundance of predisposed assumptions about Spiritual creatures.

2. Someone who proves to be trustworthy, not given to flights of fancy, and is shown to be a person of honest, discrete character as well as levelheadedness. They should have a natural trust and respect for your work and intentions and be able to follow your lead as a Magus Operator. Imaginative, creative, and sensitive individuals can make good scryers, but it is important to weed out the pretenders.

3. A person who is not rife with emotional, mental, or personal unrest, stress, strife, and personal discord. Such a person, regardless of scrying talent, could likely make your magical workings more difficult and may actually cause more problems than benefits for both of you. The magical workings, though often challenging, should result in beneficial outcomes for all involved.

The above qualifications are ideal, but often the scryer who is best suited for our work does not always match the above criteria. In the case of John Dee, Edward Kelley had the reputation of being something of a scoundrel and not the most innocent, trustworthy, or chaste of individuals, yet he had a rare acute ability for scrying. It is often that the correct magical partner will present himself to the magician who is ready to work with one.

A magician should choose a scryer with discretion and careful consideration regardless of personal preference. As stated, it is highly recommended that your scryer have noteworthy talent and aptitude for scrying beforehand. Having previously witnessed what might be termed paranormal or Spiritual phenomena is a good sign that their minds are prewired for this type of experiment. This is important for a number of reasons, but primarily for the purpose of protecting your scryer. Many people are not well suited to observe Spiritual phenomena, being that they lack the proper mental blueprints and psychological framework to perceive them properly.

Steps for Induction for the Scryer Before Magical Operations

I urge the prospective evoker not to attempt to force paranormal experiences or use the following hypnotic techniques forcefully on one who is not well-suited to be a scryer. Forcing such situations, even if the potential scryer is adamant and consciously enthusiastic to go through with it, may lead to psychological, mental, and emotional issues which could become even more problematic over time. Even if problems do not ensue, the very best you will get is a person who is psychically shut down and even less sensitive than when they began. For many, their deep mind may not be prepared or suited to such an encounter and trying to bypass these safeguards will inevitably lead to the opposite of what you are attempting to achieve. It is entirely possible that encounters with Spiritual beings are simply too distracting or possibly even detrimental for most people to handle as a fact in their day-to-day lives.

The basic process I describe is not only intended to use modern hypnotic techniques to allow the scryer's mind and sub-conscious to be more accepting and receptive to Spiritual phenomena, but to ask for blessings and allowance to do so from a higher power. The steps below should be done well before any attempt at an evocation is made and would be beneficial to do several times before an actual operation.

1. Before beginning, I recommend creating a magical but comfortable space for your would-be scryer. Have them sit in a comfortable chair or couch in the center of the room with enough space for you to move around them. If they are comfortable, fashion a circle around them and light a number of candles around them. Begin by reciting prayers, intermixed with positive reinforcing suggestions to open the scryer's mind to be receptive to Spirits, being able to see and hear them with clarity and understanding. The prayers should also be the vehicle with which you assume the correct state of mind, emotion, and purpose. Never recite prayers or invocations which stir no emotion within you. The litanies of the grimoires are designed to inspire the magus to the point of Spiritual ecstasy and passionate expression as well as a desire for union with the divine. It is to no avail to recite words and prose which have no effect on your own being. If you have never "enflamed" yourself with prayer, then I discourage you from expecting too much out of classical evocation arts as a whole.

2. Implant triggers or anchors that the scryer will immediately respond to. Anchors for the scryer may include actions like anointing their forehead with oil, placing hands on their shoulders in blessing. Doing this while giving them a lamen or image of the sigil to gaze upon for an upcoming evocating is beneficial as well. The triggers/anchors should consist of the scryer responding a certain way which tells you it's appropriate to proceed and that the induction was successful. These methods should be compounded to induce heightened awareness and perceptive albeit passive receptors, silencing of the conscious mental chatter which rationalizes, judges, and classifies the experience.

3. The primary induction should include establishing/reinforcing that every part of the ritual: the vesting, invocations, lighting of incense and candles, etc. enhances the scryer's ability and increases the depth of trance dramatically. The induction should contain layered references to being able to see and hear the Spirit clearly and effectively as well as all other senses being open and receptive to communication. Do not neglect to include smell, feeling, taste or any other sense in this. Encourage the scryer to be able to

experience the arrival and communication of the Spirit with all senses/faculties available to them.

Refrain from any suggestions or leading phrases concerning how or as what the Spirit should appear. Suggest only that if and when the Spirit arrives, the scryer will be able to perceive and communicate with it clearly and effectively. State that comprehension, understanding, and perception will not be interrupted during the entire session until you (the operator/magician) tell them otherwise, or when the ritual has come to a close. This is important since there is the rare possibility that an incorrect Spirit will be contacted and the scryer might be vulnerable to disturbing images and sensations as the Spirit tried to manipulate and possibly harm the scryer. Such ritual devices such as the lamen, magic ring, vestments and other defensive articles should be worn during these experiments. It will be up to the discretion and judgment of the operator to decide if an operation needs to be terminated and the Spirit dismissed if things apparently go awry.

4. Positive, reaffirming suggestions should be repeated and ingrained in the consciousness of your scryer before and after the session suggesting that scrying abilities and perceptions increase incrementally from that time forth, regardless of being in a magical operation or not. Make sure to suggest that each experiment, each operation only increases abilities and creates positive and beneficial results in their life. Also, it's vital that you give the suggestion that the scryer remembers the operation in explicit detail, recalling all that transpired upon its completion. Many times after a hypnotic session or magical experience, the scryer will experience an effect similar to sleep amnesia when coming back to full waking consciousness. The shift between the two levels of perception and consciousness often make it difficult for one to connect to the other smoothly. If you fail to establish that the entire session is recalled perfectly, your scryer may come out in a bit of a daze, recalling bits and pieces or possibly not remembering much at all. I've experienced this personally as well as with my own scryer. It was like having the most intense experience of my life, then like something siphoning the experience away from my conscious retention.

In the successful application of the above hypnotic-magical techniques, you can guide your scryer through the first levels of initiation into the Mysteries, wherein their perception is more appropriately geared toward beholding, speaking, and interacting with nonphysical beings. This initiation will have effects on their personality and disposition, some subtle and others more dynamic, but a palpable shift will occur if the above processes are successful. You should be sensitive and aware of your scryer's changes and invite them to discuss and share any transitions they may be experiencing to get a better idea of how things are progressing.

It is my firm opinion that trained hypnotists and hypnotherapists are utilizing an area of magic, regardless of what they or psychologists declare. The projection of intention through voice and frequency are the very factors one uses to manifest his will through space. Spells, chants, invocations, and evocations are all accomplished through intentions expressed through the word. All begins and ends with the voice.

II
Working with a Talented Scryer

HE MAJORITY OF THIS BOOK contains the cooperative efforts of myself and my scryer Benn Mac Stiofán. No better person could have filled the role of my scryer. He and I met over thirteen years before the writing of this book, and have been close friends ever since. We met during a time when we shared a common passion for magic and the Celtic spiritual path. Although our spiritual paths and particular interests have somewhat diverged over time, we maintain a similar integrity of pursuit and openness to experience the spiritual world as it presents itself and not as we would fantasize it to be. Each of us has been diligent in our spiritual practices, endlessly striving to better our gifts, perceptions, and connections to the divine in its myriad of aspects.

After having successfully evoking each of the Planetary Archangels as listed in the *Art of Drawing Spirits into Crystals*, I was motivated to find others who could share in the same experiences I was having and perhaps see and hear the spirits to the capacity I was. I was certain I was not singularly gifted or the only one fortunate enough to be able to perceive the celestial intelligences, and that there were others who could be guided through this system and see and hear them just as well as I could.

Before ever considering that my closest friend could scry for me and would become one of my closest confidants in magic, I simply planned to utilize my talents as a hypnotherapist and magician to assist him in experiencing the Astral or Spiritual world for himself. I simply wanted him to discover what possibilities might be in store for him and to have a wonderful spiritual experience.

In actuality, the following hypnotic method was more or less intended to be used one time for my friend to further explore his own particular spiritual path. I was altogether sure he would encounter and converse with one of the Celtic gods or heroes, since that would be in line with his spiritual pursuits and interests. If not one of the Celtic deities, I considered he might meet with one of his ancestors or Spirit guides. For this combination of hypnotic induction and magical technique, I use a formula for assisted Astral projection. This process has allowed me to assist a number of people to experience the very real phenomena of leaving the physical world behind to explore other worlds and perceptions.

For readers who wish to experiment with this method themselves or would like to attempt it with others, I give the basic hypnotic script below.

For this beginning part of this particular exercise I used a "rapid induction technique." There are several techniques and methods in hypnosis under the heading of "rapid inductions" but I give the one I utilize most and in this case in particular:

Hand-to-Face Hypnotic Induction Method

This is a technique which works quite well and one that I've had great success utilizing. It gets a person to a deep level of hypnosis or trance rather quickly. The technique is based on a distraction/diversion method where you interrupt a rather automatic response to get their subconscious attention. Hypnosis is a skill much like magic and requires training, practice, and unwavering confidence and know-how. Particular people seem to have talent with hypnosis and not everyone will be predisposed to excel at this practice. Regardless, I give the basic outline or "script" here for those eager to try.

First have the person you are hypnotizing relax on a comfortable chair, recliner, or couch. I recommend you do this while they are at least slightly in the sitting up position. However, it can work with them lying down as well. After you hypnotize them, you can have them lie down if needed, but I find sitting works perfectly well for this.

Hypnosis begins or at least can begin well before having them sit down and become "relaxed."

First, if they have never been hypnotized before, give them a few words on what to expect, letting it be all positive, and remove any doubts, fears, or expectations. Say something to the effect of:

"You will be totally aware of my voice and feeling relaxed and wonderful and you'll follow my instructions, simply because it will feel enjoyable to do so. You will know you will have the option to stop at any time but realize that you are rather enjoying the whole experience and that every moment you feel like you are gaining further and deeper understanding of yourself and the spiritual world."

Take as much time as is needed and be sure the person is receptive and comfortable with undergoing the experience. When ready, move directly in front of the person and tell them that they will shortly be going into a very deep, deep trance very quickly. Ask them if they are fine with this and ready to begin. When they give their consent, say that you will begin with a handshake while instructing them to continue looking at your face or eyes the entire time.

Make the gesture of beginning to shake their hand, but instead of grasping their hand as they (automatically) raise their hand to yours, take the hand they offer in your other hand quickly and place it about a foot or so away from the front of their face. Immediately begin telling them to stare at the very center of their hand and keep their gazed fixed on that point. Say that by the power of their own will and mind they are entering into a deep, relaxed state of consciousness and this is indicated by their hand moving toward their face. Continue to repeat this notion stating, "As you relax even deeper and deeper into a relaxed state, your hand naturally and easily drifts closer to your face, sending you down, down, deeper and deeper into relaxation. The closer your hand gets to your face, the heavier your eyelids become; you feel all the muscles in your body completely relax as your hand drifts closer and closer. Know that as soon as your hand touches your face, you will be able to close your eyes and immediately drop down into the deepest state of relaxation in which you have ever been."

As soon as the person touches his face with his hand, his eyes should close and you should witness a visible and obvious response. His body should relax so much it slumps, you should see the face assume a relaxed expression like sleep, and his breathing should be deep and even. His hand may stay glued to his face as he sits there relaxed and breathing deeply; you can instruct him or guide his hand down to his lap or the arm of the chair in this case. If he touches his face and somehow opens his eyes and looks at you, it is still possible to get him into a deep trance, but it takes a clever and quick-minded hypnotist to immediately distract and redirect him using another method. I have not yet had this happen to me, as everyone I've performed this on directly goes into a relaxed hypnotic state, but I immediately follow it up with what is referred to as a "deepening" technique.

Forehead-Tapping Deepening Technique

Begin by giving positive, affirming suggestions such as, "Good, excellent. Relaxing more and more, deeper and deeper with each breath that you take. Each breath, inhale and exhale simply relaxes you even further, and further, deeper and deeper into relaxation." As I say this, I bring my right index finger up near his "third eye" or forehead and I begin to tap ever so lightly, and follow with:

"As you continue to relax even further and further into relaxation and hypnosis, notice how the tapping brings your total focus to this area and sends you into the deepest trance and form of relaxation imaginable. Each tap, each breath, sends you ten times deeper than you are now, ten times deeper. The relaxing and deepening sensation causes your unconscious mind to come forward as the conscious mind slips deeply, further and further into a trance.

"I'm also going to count backward from ten to one, and when I reach the number one you will be in the most relaxed state imaginable, you will feel as if you are so relaxed, you could not open your eyes or move your body even if you tried. Any attempt only causes you to slip further and further, deeper and deeper into relaxation. You are doing perfectly. Focus solely on the sound of my voice and the sensation on your forehead which is sending you even deeper and deeper into a complete state of relaxation and trance."

Continue to tap lightly on his forehead, but altering to pause a half second or so slower. At this point say, "I'm going to count back now from ten to one. When I reach one, you will be in the deepest level of relaxation and hypnosis where nothing can disturb you, nothing can distract or inhibit your ability to enter into a deep level of trance."

ASTRAL PROJECTION FORMULA

Golden White Light

After successfully bringing your subject or prospective scryer into a deep state of hypnosis, you can continue with the actual Astral projection formula of the hypnosis session by saying the following:

"Now imagine a gold and perfect stream of light coming down from the heavens above you and entering through the top of your head. Just imagining this, you can feel the sensations as a pleasant feeling comes all across your body. Let every muscle and every nerve grow so loose and so limp and so relaxed. Arms limp now, just completely relaxed and at ease in every way. That's good. This light moved through every part of your being, through every fiber, cell, and muscle, sending a pleasant wave of relaxation over and through your entire body, from the top of your head to the tips of your toes. Just let every muscle and nerve grow loose and limp and relaxed.

"You are feeling more relaxed with each easy breath that you take. Droopy, drowsy, and sleepy. So calm and so relaxed. You're relaxing more with each easy beat of your heart... with each easy breath that you take... with each sound that you hear."

My method for inducing the effects for Astral projection is to have the subject experience the deepest level of trance and relaxation they are able and to physically experience the sensations of pre-Astral travel before the actual experience occurs. They are led to feel the quick vibration or hum of the energy moving about them, the experience of rocking or spinning, losing their sense of direction and gravity, and the sensation of lifting out of their body. Continue on with:

"This light is so profound it envelopes you in a perfect casing, a shell of protective divine light that continues to send you into the most euphoric state imaginable. You notice the light like a frequency throughout your entire being, sending wave upon wave of relaxing energy which seems to vibrate every fiber of your being. The vibration intensifies and you may notice you are completely losing any sense of your body. Direction, gravity, and position may vanish. You may feel a spinning or swaying sensation, and this is perfectly fine, and also a positive sign that you are achieving exactly what you set out to do. So allow these sensations to continue and even grow in intensity. "

Lifting Out

Some level of intuition is needed to know when to initiate or trigger the Astral projection sequence. The subject should be completely relaxed. There should be no movement or spontaneous adjusting from them at all; they should look almost paralyzed except for their deep, even breathing. When you feel they are ready, say the following induction:

"As the spinning, rocking, or vibrating evens out you may feel a pulling or a raising sensation as if you are effortlessly floating upwards. Continue to feel this sensation of effortlessly floating upwards. Up, up, upwards and out of your physical body. You are lighter than air, free, relaxed, perfectly safe and secure in this ethereal form, effortlessly floating upwards. Weightless, lighter than air, you feel yourself drawn upwards about three feet out of your physical body. Your body is safe, relaxed, completely secure, and you now have complete freedom and weightlessness to explore completely new ways of perceiving and moving. Look back for a moment at your physical form, resting quietly, peacefully. Now look about the room, noticing how easy it is to see and move and look in any direction. For a moment become accustomed to this new sensation and experience and realize how wonderful and relaxing the entire sensation is."

The Astral Doorway

The next stage is when you guide the person through the astral travel experience and then through an astral doorway. I always make sure to bring them back through the doorway and back into their bodies before bringing them fully out of hypnosis. I don't believe anyone's spirit can get "stuck" necessarily, as there are other safety measures which are automatically put in place; however this is not a theory I would care to test on someone or myself. When your intuition has told you the person has successfully achieved an out of body experiences (OBE), continue with the guided induction.

"Now I want you to feel and see yourself floating upwards. Up higher, at the ceiling, easily passing through the ceiling, through the roof, and up into the sky. Take a moment to marvel at the scene all around you as you rise higher and higher. See the building you were in become small until it is barely a perceivable speck far below, see the city, houses, town and land start to drift further away as you ascend high and higher, effortlessly floating upwards through the sky into the atmosphere. Relaxing and enjoying the feeling of complete weightlessness, and perfect security you drift even higher up out of the earth's atmosphere into the black of space.

"Although you notice the stars all around you, you feel yourself instantly surrounded by complete darkness on all sides. Complete black, empty space surrounds you. For just a moment there is absolutely no sense of direction, no sense of time or anything, just empty, black, floating space. However, a portal to another world, another realm where you can meet and interact with amazing beings, relatives, ancestors, or any manner of benevolent being that can assist you, will be opened. At first all you see is a small speck of white light in the distance, through the blackness ahead of you. You move toward it easily and effortlessly, and as you do the light grows larger. The nearer you get the larger the light becomes, and as it becomes even bigger, the blackness which once surrounded you is replaced by light, sheer, brilliant white and pure light. The light surrounds you now on all sides as you move through this astral gateway. In a moment, the brilliant light will fade and you will find yourself in new surroundings with other beings there and you will be able to perceive and hear them easily and clearly. See yourself there now; let the images and surroundings become clearer and clearer, and enjoy the experience as it unfolds."

At this point, I allow the person to experience whatever he will and try to give him at least ten to fifteen minutes to enjoy the experience, but have gone on longer when it felt right to do so. The subject's form should remain in its perfect, still state and rhythmic breathing. I notice there isn't a lot of REM (Rapid Eye Movement) or other body movements which you find when dreaming or deeply asleep; rather the body looks like it's almost paralyzed.

Give as long as needed or as long as you feel is necessary, then say:

"Alright, it's now time to return. If you have met with any being, relative, or Spirit, thank them for taking the time to share with you or teach you, remember everything that they say, and bid them farewell.

"Once again see the light before you and allow the pure white light to surround you, blocking out everything around you and once again encapsulating you in its brilliance so that all you see on all sides is this pure white light. Enjoy being in this light a moment, again remembering easily everything you experienced, down to each detail, and once again see the light begin to fade, and once again the black of space is all around you, and the stars, constellations, and planets begin to come into view.

"You feel yourself descending back down now, back down toward earth, through the atmosphere, through the brilliant sky, and back down to the city, and the building you came from. Allow yourself to drift down easily and effortlessly back through the roof and ceiling, and then gently back into your physical body, relaxing here gently and perfectly.

"Enjoy this wonderful feeling for just a moment longer and recall your experiences perfectly and easily. In just a moment, I'm going to count from one to ten, and when I reach the number ten, you will be wide awake, feeling wonderful and refreshed and remembering everything from your experience just a moment ago. Starting from number one now: One, two, three, four, five, starting to feel yourself completely back in your body and beginning to wake, six, seven, starting to move and stretch, number eight, nine, and ten, wide awake, feeling refreshed!"

The above technique is interesting in that if it is successful, the person will literally feel himself being pulled out of his physical body and won't necessarily feel as if he were in a trance or under hypnosis at all. He should recount to you later how very real and physical the sensation felt and how vivid the experience was and what he saw. If the subject remarks on how it was dreamlike or vague, it may have been a bust for an authentic Astral experience and you will have to try again.

You will notice from the above induction that I reiterated the point for the person to "remember" quite a few times. Otherwise, he may experience a bit of "post-hypnotic amnesia" in which the conscious mind has difficulty recalling the events of the other mind state and will forget it as we often do with dreams upon awakening.

The above hypnotic method was the one I used on my scryer to have him experience an Astral journey of sorts. What transpired was directly recorded after his experience, and is presented below. It is a very good idea to have someone record his experiences right afterwards for the best account and detail as well as the emotion of what transpired.

Scryer's Experience

SCRYER: First, the sensation of rising was gentle but palpable. I was very aware of your voice during the entire experience. Before leaving the room, which I could not see very well, I was suddenly rising through the floor of a hospital room in the midst of a surrounding privacy curtain, around a bed that contained a man whose face was in very bad shape; bloody, swollen, he looked to be completely unaware. The vision quickly faded and I was back rising through the roof of the house.

The sense of relaxation was very intense now, the vastness of the blue sky was high, very high above me. I saw for a moment a bird, a black bird, crow or raven flying above me. Again that vision faded and I was back in a dark, relaxed state with lights moving before my vision. Moving into space was unsettling, but not debilitating so. The light grew before me and as I moved into it, it became totally encompassing. Again there was a brief vision of a room, totally white, like light infused cream, with table and chairs also white. Again this faded but the feeling of the room was still there.

As you directed me to behold a Spirit guide, I saw a face before me, very androgynous in appearance, but beautiful and kind, in a stoic way. There were no words exchanged at first, only impressions. The first impression was of frequent visitations by his kind to our planet, conveyed with some humor but some gravity as well. I felt his energy encompass

> me, almost like wings, an energy exchange or communication, perhaps both.
>
> When I asked how I could easily contact him, he pointed to my forehead and heart and said, «Through these places.» Next there were strong impressions of needing to work closely with you as if we had important task or tasks to do. When I asked his name there seemed to be a moment of consideration on his part. My impression was that he had many, but eventually he said, «Bazaleel.» As I was returning saw a very detailed vision of a long rod of aquamarine filled with energy, and pearled white light. Coming back was very comforting and the feeling or dropping back in was not bad in any way, like a feather falling on a windless day.

Naturally I found the above relation interesting and exciting, but not at all what I was expecting. Also, to hear mention of a particular Angel's name was most fascinating, and I wasted no time beginning a search for its origin. I had never previously come across the name to my knowledge, but I decided to see if I could find any similarity or mention of such an Angel in any classical texts. To my amazement, I discovered the name in *Exodus*:

> Then the LORD said to Moses, "See, I have chosen Bezalel,[1] son of Uri, the son of Hur, of the tribe of Judah, and I have filled him with the Spirit of God, with wisdom, with understanding, with knowledge and with all kinds of skills—to make artistic designs for work in gold, silver and bronze, to cut and set stones, to work in wood, and to engage in all kinds of crafts."[2]

After this experience, my friend and I talked at length about the meaning of his experience. There was agreement that we should do some magical work together, but what sort of work and by exactly what method was not initially apparent. Benn seemed fascinated by Angels after this encounter and wanted to learn more about what I had experienced and discovered, so I thought that I would try to bring him through a series of experiences and exercises I had undergone before summoning the Archangels of the seven Planets into a crystal scrying sphere. Who knows? Perhaps my friend would have more interesting experiences which we could share and discuss. Little did I know at the time that

1. Hebrew בצלאל (*Betzalel*, "In the Shadow [*i.e.*, under the Protection] of God"), written as *Bezalel* in many English translations, and Bezaleel in the King James Version. —APF

2. *Exodus* 31:1–5 (NIV translation).

Benn was to become my scryer and partner in some of the most spectacular experiences of my esoteric career.

Within a couple of weeks following the interesting Astral experience with the Angel Bazaleel, I scheduled some magical rituals designed to take Benn through a series of Spiritual introductions and possibly initiations that I had gone through when I began my magical experiments. I reasoned that I should introduce him to Western ceremonial magic by way of the Hermetic foundations of the magical world, the four primary Elements of Greek philosophy.

✣

III
The Four Great Elements of Creation
Invocation and Astral Travel Through the Four Realms

> There are then, as we have said, four Elements, without the perfect knowledge whereof we can effect nothing in Magick.
>
> Agrippa, *Of Occult Philosophy*[1]

The Elements in Hermetic Magic

I N DECIDING TO GUIDE BENN through the rich world of Western Esotericism, I settled firmly on introducing him to the occult aspects of the four Elements and their correspondences within Hermeticism. When setting forth on the path of Hermetic magic, most begin with the Elements and their correspondences. It allows the neophyte to develop a proper sense of mystical relationship and focused practice.

A magician must formulate a cohesive and accessible assortment of interrelating concepts and patterns through which to understand themselves and the universe. For many Western occultists, this foundation is represented by the four primary Elements of Creation postulated by ancient Greek philosophy. The Elements contain within themselves symbolic references to coincide with every human being, every aspect which constitutes an action. The Elements both in physical manifestation and metaphoric concept are the praxis from which the ritual magician moves from their center of being. It is the basis for understanding the complex network and matrix that is the microcosm of the

1. Heinrich Cornelius Agrippa, *Of Occult Philosophy*, Book I, Chapter IV, "Of a Three-fold Consideration of the Elements."

human being. Only from a point of self-actualization and "knowing thyself" can one hope to achieve the greatest manifestation of his desired end.

I knew of no better way to establish an intimate connection with the four Elements than to directly experience the Astral Elemental planes. In my early explorations and self-initiation into the Golden Dawn system, I had first been successful in Astral projecting through the Elemental Tattwas. The exercises of scrying the Tattwa cards led to amazing experiences, including distinct sensations of entering into what appeared and felt like another world. My senses after I felt myself move through the symbols were oddly acute, feeling and beholding many incredible experiences. Likewise the things I learned directly from the beings that appeared to me there were valuable beyond compare.

By encountering the Spiritual denizens which dwell within the Astral equivalent of the physical manifestations of each Element, the exposure to the Astral realms is intense and invigorating. It is also highly saturated by the singularity of its Elemental energetic makeup and thus not suitable for extended exposure by any creature—such as a human magician—whose nature contains a delicate balance and mixture of all the Elements. In dealing with the Elements, the magician begins at the most basic yet powerfully primal level of existence. The four pillars of energetic creation, moved by the underlying fifth power, consititutes the ceremonial magician's mode of primal function.

I have an enduring fondness for Spirits of the natural world. That is to say, I appreciate those Intelligences which appear to inhabit or are at least connected to particular places or conditions of nature. My senses became more aware of the Spiritual world early on while out in nature, particularly in the forests and mountains of my homeland. Long before my involvement in ritual magic, I had encounters with what many might consider to be Spirits of the Elements. The diversity I encountered seemed to be as rich as the personalities found in human beings. Apart from their obvious Elemental natures, I found that these Spirits seemed to have individual attitudes in regards to human interaction. There were alarming and malevolent apparitions which seemed determined to frighten or harm, perhaps having a particular disdain for human beings in general (or at least me in particular) which influenced their actions. I would catch glimpses of anthropomorphic forms darting behind trees and bushes and hear disembodied voices which would echo off into the trees. Many of these apparitions seemed skittish, reserved, preferring not to be seen and not interested in conversing with people. I dare say that it is naive to think that most of these types of beings would have any taste for interacting with human beings and that such cases are even more rare nowadays.

We get many examples of dealing with Spirits of the Elements from folklore and legends. The modern magus would do well to become familiar with such accounts, for they often play significant roles in magical formulæ and methods that prove to work well when called for by the situation. For instance, in dealing with Water Spirits such as Undines or Nixies, if a Spirit seems potentially hostile, legend says that throwing a piece of steel into the water before entering it can keep the dangerous Spirit at bay. Anyone familiar with such stories will instantly recognize steel as being anathema to many Spirits, especially Færies and Nature Spirits.

The magician who wishes to encounter the reality of Elementals or Spirits of nature should earnestly pursue time out in the wild in places where one particular Element predominates. Seek out areas of true natural beauty and power far removed from civilized habitations. For those not used to spending periods of time in isolation in the wilderness, such prospects might seem uncomfortable at best. However, no magus will truly come to either appreciate or behold the presence of nature Spirits by attempting to contact and summon them only in the safety of the artificial envirnment of his own home. Do not expect any mastery over the Water Element if you are uncomfortable being in a boat at sea or diving beneath the surface of a lake. You have to go where the Elementals are if you want to increase your chances of encountering an actual nature Spirit. Expect long hours and perhaps the better part of a lifetime if you truly wish to form a genuine relationship with and understanding of them.

In ancient and medieval folklore, each Spirit or Elemental was named and classified based on what type of environment it was observed to inhabit. Streams, mountains, wastelands, valleys, and so forth each had its own particular Spirit or *Genius loci* ("Spirit of the place"). Folklore and legend developed out of the stories of interactions between people and these Spiritual beings. The nebulous dividing lines between what was classified as an Elemental, a Spirit, a Fæ, an Angel, or a God varied with cultural interaction and interpretation of them.

As with many Spiritual beings, a researcher will find a rich history of names which local cultures coined for Spiritual beings of a particular nature. In the case of the Elementals, there is a rich diversity of names for Spiritual creatures which may, in fact, be the same classification of Spirit.

The same is true with the Elemental Kings or rulers, who have been considered everything from lesser Angels to Demon princes. For some ceremonial magicians, the Elemental kings are known by the Hebrew names Seraph, Cherub, Tharsis, and Ar(i)el, which are the singular forms of the names of Angelic types.

Terms and titles for the Spirits classed Elementally according to the categories of Earth, Air, Water, and Fire were relatively unknown until the publication of a work by Paracelsus entitled *Liber de nymphis, sylphis, pygmæis et salamandris et de cæteris spiritibus.*[2] This text was first printed in 1566, after Paracelsus' death, and not only gives the names which would become the standard magical terms for the beings of the four great Elements, but also archetypical forms for these forces. In *Liber de nymphis*, the classification of Elementals as Undines of the Water, Salamanders of the Fire, Sylphs of the Air, and Gnomes of the Earth was firmly established, building upon other sources of natural philosophy, contemporary living folklore, and classical myths dealing with the often invisible inhabitants of the Elemental world.

Of Earth, we are given several names which correspond to the Elemental nature of some Spirits, but Paracelsus' *Gnomi* or Gnomes is the title used predominantly in ceremonial magic. In the range of Western lore, there are countless names for the Spirits of Earth. From elves to dwarves, brownies, dryads, and pygmies, each seems to share characteristics with the other in being found in deep natural dwellings such as caves and forests, or unnatural depths such as mines. The *Pygmaioi* or Pygmies of Greek mythology are described in much the same way as dwarves or goblins in northern folklore. In spite of the large varieties of names, these Earth dwellers seem to share striking similarities in appearance and mannerisms. Many, for example, have a marked love for treasure.

The name for the Elemental King of Earth, Ghob, is derived from the medieval French *gobelin*, obviously related to the English goblin.[3]

Water Elementals have just as many names as they do appearances throughout the Western cultures. The term established by Paracelsus and adopted widely by ceremonial magicians is Latin *Undinæ* (Anglicized as Undines), from *unda*, "wave." The other predominant name for these creatures stems from Greek and Latin, and is *Nymphai*, *Nymphæ*, or Nymphs. Nereids are young

---

2. Latin, *"A Book concerning nymphs, sylphs, pygmies, and salamanders, and other spirits."* —APF

3. Also cognate to Welsh *coblyn* and probably German *kobold*. All likely derive through Latin *cobalus* from Greek *kobalos*, a type of mischievous Spirit said to lurk near altars looking for opportunities to steal offerings. *Kobaloi* are also invoked in expletives by human rascals and tricksters in Græco-Roman comedies. —APF

feminine Water Nymphs of the sea. As Walter Burkert, the noted scholar of ancient Greek religion, remarks, "The idea that rivers are gods and springs divine nymphs is deeply rooted not only in poetry but in belief and ritual; the worship of these deities is limited only by the fact that they are inseparably identified with a specific locality."[4]

In the range of Western folklore, the image of a Water Elemental took on many forms, including those of a magnificent horse, a water serpent or wyrm like a dragon, a beautiful nude woman, a man playing a fiddle in a stream or waterfall, and a half-fish, half-human form like the classical mermaid or merman.

Folkloric Water Elementals are notorious for trying to drown humans. In the form of water horses, they lure humans into climbing on their backs and then gallop away to bear them beneath the waters. In human or merfolk form, they may enchant humans into the water by their music, either sung or played on instruments. They may also serve as death portents, crying or singing at a spot where someone will soon drown.

The Water Elementals are also said in folklore to teach humans who bring offerings to them. For example, one Scandinavian Water Spirit, the *Nøkk*, plays exotic music which he will teach to a supplicant in return for offerings of blood, liquor, or tobacco.

The Paracelsian name of the Elemental King of Water, Nixa or Nichsa, has an obvious derivation from the German word *Nix* or *Nixie*. The Nixies are portrayed as malicious in some stories but harmless and friendly in others. In the 19th century, Jacob Grimm mentions the Nixie among the water-sprites who love music, song, and dancing. Female Nixies are typically described as river maids who are as notorious for attempting to drown the unwary as they for seducing hapless youths into marriage, sometimes appearing wholly human and sometimes with the tail of a fish like the classic mermaid. When they are in human form, they can be recognized by the wet hem of their clothing. The males can assume many different shapes, including those of a human, a fish, and a snake. Nichsa's name is also, like Nixie and Nix, related to other Northern European names for Water Spirits. In England we encounter the *Neck* and the *Knucker*, and in Scandinavia the *Näck* and *Nøkk*, derived from more ancient forms such as *nykr, nikk,* and *nicor*.

---

4. Walter Burkert, *Greek Religion* (Cambridge, Massachusetts: Harvard University Press, 1985), p. 174.

Of the Air Element, the Sylphs are the Elemental beings of the winds, storms, and invisible Air. In modern folklore, the *Sylph* or *Sylphide* has taken on almost a synonymous archetype with the winged fairies of popular legend. The word *Sylph* is believed to stem from combining the Latin *Sylvestris* ("woodland being," another term Paracelsus used to refer to a particular type of Air Elemental) with the ancient *Nympha*. In *Liber de nymphis*, Paracelsus describes these Air Elementals as being "rougher, coarser, taller, and stronger" than humans. According to Paracelsus, Air Elementals are the most closely related to humans, as we share the air as our natural place and medium.

Air Elementals seem to be the most sublime of all magical creatures, since it could be said that all Spirits are made of the air. It then becomes difficult to distinguish them from other Spiritual creatures and understand their unique roles and order. However, the manipulation of breezes, winds, and sound, as well as mental facilities, are the powers most closely associated with these beings. In many instances, any shape given to Air Elementals is simply a glamour or illusion and not the true semblance of the Elemental, who by definition is without directly visible form.[5]

In the kingdom of Air, the name or title of the Elemental King *Paralda* stands as the most difficult term for which to discover the origin. It can be assumed that, like the names of the other three Elemental Kings, this name originally referred more to a class of beings rather than a single figure. In Franz Bardon's *The Practice of Magical Evocation*, there is a Sylph queen named Parahim, which has the closest resemblance to the name of Paralda, although we don't know of any evidence for that name being older than Bardon's use of it. It has been proposed that the unfamiliar name may be unlike the other three, and may have originated from a single, specific Sylph which either Éliphas Lévi or his source encountered.

The Salamanders are the Elemental beings of the intense realm of Fire. As first described in detail by Pliny the Elder, the creature in question was undoubtedly a very real and commonly known amphibian. The creature's reputation as a creature of Fire continued to spread, and the *Talmud* (*Ḥagiga 27a*) records two beliefs. The first is that anyone who is smeared with its blood will be immune to harm from flame. The second is that a salamander is produced when someone burns a fire in the same place for seven years. It is generally

5. Bear in mind that we only see air indirectly by its effects. When we speak of 'seeing' the wind, we in fact are seeing the movement of leaves, clouds, trees, and other visible materials moved by the invisible currents of air.

believed that the popularity of the reptilian-looking amphibian as a creature of Fire was due to its appearing from rotting logs which, once set on fire, caused the animal to attempt to escape and thus reveal itself in the flames.

Djinn is the name generally accepted as that of the Elemental King of Fire, but as seen with the beings of Earth and Water, *Djinn* is more a classification of a particular type of Spirit or Elemental rather than a personal name. The djinn are said in Arabic lore to be Spiritual beings of "smokeless fire" who have considerable magical abilities. The *Ifrīt* is a species of infernal Djinn known known for its cleverness, cunning, and strength to accomplish mighty feats. They are depicted as enormous winged beings of Fire, often to be found in deserted buildings or in caves. They have male and female genders, and (like Western Spirits, often said to be led by kings, dukes, and earls) are described as having a social structure parallel to ancient and medieval Arabic tribal societies. Like European lore of melusine Water Elementals, there are stories of *Afarīt* (plural of *Ifrīt*) marrying and copulating with humans.

Care must be taken when working with the Elemental Kings, powerful constructs of the fundamental building blocks of the universe. In many ways, the mind of the magician or scryer will simply perceive such beings and experiences as contained within the experiential boundaries of his own psyche. I admit that I fell into this mode of thinking when I took my scryer through the Astral journeys which are described below. The experiences were intense, vivid, and very informative. After each operation, my scryer and I could feel the particular nature and energy of the Element saturate the magical chamber as well as our own beings. The Elementals themselves seem to draw out the particular natures and qualities that resonate with them from within the magician and the scryer. There is no other experience quite like this and if done carefully, such experiences can strengthen the fundamental aspects of the magician to unimaginable degrees.

As I mentioned before, one should use caution and not make the mistake of considering such experiences as being isolated to the mind, magical chamber, and magicians themselves. The Elemental beings will seek to encourage their own nature in whatever aspect and capacity they are allotted, especially if given a conduit in which to focus that nature. When a magician opens a clear link or passage between the Astral realms and the physical realm, often what follows can be surges in physical reality which may not have occurred under "normal" circumstances.

Magical Elemental Implements

The process of harnessing the purest energies of the Elements and Elementals without unnecessary distortions created by our own minds requires the aid of divine assistance connected with each Element but also in harmony with human nature. The Elemental Angels are the reliable intelligent mediators between the raw, primal power of the Elements and the human being who interacts with them. The processes by which we may contact and communicate with these Elemental Angels are through a ritual of gateway openings to connect our minds and wills to those of the Angelic realms. To further concentrate and balance the effort between each of the Elemental realms, tools of deeply archetypical and symbolic form are constructed, consecrated, and used in order to connect the wellspring of the magician to that of a particular Elemental realm. The Order of the Golden Dawn constructed a regimented training which is intended to accomplish all of the above results.

The secret, if it ever was a secret, to successful contact and clear communication with Spirits is decisive and dedicated immersion to the point of temporary exclusion of other forms and practices of magic, other traditions and concepts. The human mind can be debilitated for powerful experiential achievement by its tendency to grasp at several conflicting paradigms at once.

The first set of Elemental tools I created was in the tradition of the Golden Dawn with their brilliant flashing colors and archetypical shapes. These classical tools, however, did not seem to reflect my personal connection to what each Element embodied so I went on to design and craft a whole new set of tools. It took several years to develop the visualization of what I wanted these Elemental implements to embody, and then to design and construct them. From the materials of which they were made to their shape, look, and feel, I wanted my Elemental implements to resonate as perfectly as possible. It is possible that the very process of imagining, meditating on, drawing, and visualizing each implement led to the discovery of how to open the gateways to the Elemental planes.

I took my time studying and reading about the traits and offices of the Elemental Angels, and meditating on their sigils and names until I had the feeling of a connection to each and every one of them before inscribing their names and sigils upon my Elemental tools. The Angels and sigils should be treated and considered as alive and actively aware beings of intention and purpose. Begin by integrating correspondences for each Element, deciding on direction, day, time of day, time of year, and so forth, and seeking to communicate with each of them in turn.

The Tattwas

Perhaps one of the greatest tools for discovering the nature and reality of the Elemental planes is the set of Indian *Tattwa* or *Tattva* symbols, brought to the attention of Western occultists in the 19th century by the Theosophical Society and then by the Golden Dawn. Within their basic shapes and colors are found established and ancient concepts of the five Elemental natures, the fifth being *Akasha* or Spirit. These archetypical symbols actually serve as the Elemental gateways through which able magicians can project their consciousness or Astral body in order to dynamically experience the realm. The ones employed and expounded upon by the Golden Dawn also use complementary "flashing" colors which create astonishing optical effects when looked at for a long period of time. The symbol of *Akasha*, the Spirit Tattwa, is typically a black or indigo vesica piscis or egg shape, and is sometimes placed on a lime-green background. The *Tejas* Tattwa represents Fire as a red equilateral triangle, typically placed on a bright green background. The Element of Air or *Vayu* is symbolized by a blue circle on an orange background. *Apas* is the Water Tattwa, and is a silver crescent against a black background. Finally, Earth or the *Prithivi* Tattwa, is a yellow square against a purple background.

There are enough published works on the Tattwas concerning their use or potential misuse in magic and the ways in which to scry them that I will not go into detail here, particularly as the discerning reader will be able to apprehend the formula for scrying the Elemental planes from the accounts which follow of guiding my scryer through the Elements.

Tarot

There are countless books and references on the Tarot and their use and meaning. Most magicians will be at the very least familiar with their symbolism and meaning, as they are typically a fundamental aid in most Western occult practices. If the reader is as yet unfamiliar with their use and meaning, I strongly suggest taking several months to a year just focusing on learning the cards. Become proficient in knowing how they are used and their meaning to properly integrate many important correspondences and energetic patterns into your psyche. The Tarot will link visual symbolic archetypes to interpretations that will impart the ability to discern the meaning of images which are encountered in Astral voyages. This is crucial, because correspondent imagery is the medium by which the magician moves and operates in the nebulous world of the Astral. Imagination is the vehicle which translates the multitude of energetic frequencies into understandable and maneuverable symbolic images. Understanding various patterns and images that arise during your evocations or other magical work will allow you to discern the occult nature behind many things not only in the Astral but the physical world as well.

The number of choices for a tarot deck has reached an almost ridiculous proportion. On one level, we can appreciate the diverse creativity and distinction that artists and magicians and card readers have put into creating their own decks. On the other hand, such diverse and sometimes absurd variation can simply confuse the unconscious to be able to powerfully and clearly establish important forms of archetypical correspondence. I strongly recommend that you choose one of the classical and well-established decks that agrees with your magical paradigm and training.

Consider all the "positive" and "negative" aspects of each Element as you study the Tarot. Strongly consider which cards represent your particular or overall strengths and weaknesses. Are you able to discover which Element you are lacking in the positive qualities or perhaps have an overabundance in? The most efficient sort of psychoanalysis and personal empowerment can be actualized through a critical and detailed investigation into the self in this matter. Moving past constructed justifications, defensive emotions and excuses, the aspiring magician can take complete ownership over his or her person and delve into the practice of mastery.

The four or five Elements create a strong yet flexible framework in which to move past the ambiguous jungle of the personality, to strengthen attributes and lessen vices, as the magician consciously chooses. The beauty of the Tarot is that its use can greatly organize the magician's thoughts and considerations when faced with a dilemma or complex situation. I do not claim to be a great card reader or teller of fortunes, but I am always pleasantly surprised how readings turn out. It seems as though every sincere Tarot spread I've done for myself or others has hit directly on specific points of the overall issue and has often led to resolutions and insightful decisions based on the cards' symbolic references. Through the use and familiarization of the cards comes a more detailed assimilation of various patterns at work both internally and externally in the world. More than simply an oracle or fortune telling cards, the Tarot are a wealth of information and pattern aligning to better connect the magician to the subtle strands of influence and energetic frequencies which make up the whole of existence. With practice, we recognize more and more the patterned responses to our decisions and intentions which we extend out into reality.

The Elements and their denizens form the foundations of Spirit interaction and understanding in the realm of occult correspondences. It is by these archetypical expressions and manifestations in nature that we find attributes most closely linked with our own systems and functions.

In the practice of ritual magic, ritual tools or implements are an ancient and lasting tradition. They can be found in astonishing number and frequency, forever aiding the will of the magus to achieve his desired result. In classical lodge-style ceremonial magic such as that of the Golden Dawn, the four Elemental implements or weapons are a familiar set of tools closely matching the symbolism found in the major suits of the Tarot.

The Elemental implements are for the most part based on common tools created to harness, manipulate, or contain the Elements to which they correspond. Think of a wooden stick or poker for tending a fire as a most ancient and primitive tool connected to Fire. Sticks or branches also became torches, allowing humans to carry and use fire to light their way. Vessels have been shaped from wet clay or molten glass to hold liquid. Blades exist because of the Airy intelligence and technology that achieved their forging, and fly through the air in order to cut whatever stands before them or open holes in the solid. The disk's range of Earthy symbolism includes the metal currency of material gain, the plate on which rests the solid nourishment for physical survival, and the shield which protects the body from injury.

Whether or not you choose to create or obtain a set of Elemental implements, I encourage the beginning magician to establish the veritable foundation of theses archetypes within your practice. Both Eastern and Western magical traditions have expounded on this notion to masterful ends. If you decide to create your own Elemental tools, consider how they will harness and direct the energies in ways you would consciously choose for them. When crafting your Elemental implements, consider their symbolism and purpose and how they relate to the suits of Tarot. As you learned about the distinct nature and office each card represents inside its Element, consider what personality traits they might represent in the associated Elemental Angels or Demons.

Are Elemental or magical tools really needed? The better question is what purpose do these implements really serve? Experience teaches us that with time and infrequency of exposure to events anyone, even the master magician, may gradually forget the direct knowledge of what an experience was like and eventually may find that such perceptions have diminished almost entirely. Elemental tools are designed to contain and amplify the energy of those expereinces, and maintain direct conduits of energy between the Elemental realms and beings and the clear and concise perception and will of the magician. That is, if properly constructed and consecrated, the Elemental tool acts as a channel of focused intent toward that specific line of energy which was contacted during the event of its consecration. It weeds out all unnecessary, scattered energies and thought processes which may have clouded the perceptions and intentions of the magician over time and directly links back into the core source of knowledge and power for which the implement was crafted.

The realization of this struck me when I observed that, regardless of my mood or intention, the moment I gaze upon or especially hold one of my Elemental tools, I am immediately reconnected to that exact moment in time and space when my Elemental tool became consecrated to its purpose. I also immediately recall the intensity and clarity of visiting that Elemental plane and what all of my senses experienced as if it happened just a moment ago. I also sense in my being the clearest forms of being able to call up that energy singularly in my being and bring it to the verge of my magical expression. It's not that these abilities are dormant or absent without the presence of my magical tools, but the difference between the focus and level of energy is extremely considerable.

Can magical actions be done without the use of such tools? Of course they can. For me, however, the magical experience can be likened to that of driving. If magic were to be the experience of vehicular travel, a working with the use of the tool versus one without would be like the difference between driving a motorcycle down the highway versus sitting in the back of a bus, being driven through a suburban neighborhood. Both may be experiences of riding on a vehicle, but one is much more involved and powerful.

An additional consideration for magical tools is that their "battery" life seems to be determined by their frequency of use and "recharging." I find that the more dynamic and powerful the consecration, the longer the implement will hold a discernible charge of its intended power. Likewise, the more the implement is used for its intended purpose, the stronger it becomes and the more charge it will hold. Physical items definitely do pick up energies and sometimes memories of certain individuals who seem to leave an imprint behind, especially during times of strong emotional or energetic release. Imagine an implement holding the magical, emotional, and intentional imprint and record of your most profound magical experiences in detail and one you can experience every time you place it in your hands.

No magical tool will ever be able to exceed the abilities and intentionality of the magician. However, a properly consecrated implement combined with the veritable presence of the involved Spirits lending their own energy and power of office to the implement will provide a skillful magus with all the proper support for effecting change on a grand scale. The dynamic and successful result of such a combination is the embodiment of a true magical working. Might others be able to tap into its power and energy as a similar experience? This is hard to confirm since your individual nature, language of frequencies, and purpose will definitely be unique to you and may not directly translate, at least in all ways, to another person who may come in contact with your magical implement. Great care should be taken to prevent this from accidently happening, and magical tools should be kept carefully secured when not in use.

Besides the listed benefits of having magical implements at hand, each designated for a particular function in ceremony, the creating, consecrating and use of implements is an essential skill for any ceremonial magician. Anyone who claims there is little use in crafting or using magical paraphernalia will not be well-suited to making talismans, charms, or anything of use in a magical sense for themselves or others. The making of magical tools has a history as long as that of the human race and transcends Western and Eastern cultures. Magic itself is definitely a crafty act of creation. Regardless of one's artistic talent, the exercise of one's skill to craft and create is inseparable from the practice of magic.

A talented magus will be able to demonstrate the power of the four Elements before another, whether they be a student, an inquirer, or another adept. The appropriateness or need for this will of course be left to the discretion of the magician. They should be able to demonstrate the singular nature of one of the Elements both as an expression of power from the inside of their being, and also as an experiential display outside of themselves where others involved will be able to witness a measure of the Element's power and presence. The power of a magician is renowned for being able to influence and alter the course of physical reality. Due to the very occult nature of these abilities, the occurrences may go unrealized by the casual observer or those unaware of the multitude of subtle energies all around them. By the very nature of his occult craft, the adept will tend keep all operations concealed and known only to himself while working his intentions through the focused labor of his trained abilities.

A magus may use his knowledge and abilities to bring an Elemental energy into a particular area or person to influence them toward some sort of action or result which coincides with the magician's intentions. The subject of this type of magic will most likely be unaware of external influences upon his thoughts, emotions, or physical disposition at the time, and may consider such sudden changes as occurring within his own being in isolation. Basic magical activities such as these can be formulated with little time and preparation if the magician has a clear link and proximity to the subject at hand.

For the purposes of initiation and instruction, however, the adept is attempting to link both conscious and unconscious awareness to what is taking place for the neophyte and uninitiated to assist them with building experiential bridges between the worlds of matter and spirit. It is my experience that it is the Spirits and Angels themselves who assist the magus in formulating the proper and clear channels of communication and directed intention to not only achieve their desired ends but to become aware of them in the first place. Without their aid and ability to communicate back to the human mind which has difficulty conceptualizing that which is beyond physical reality, there would be no perceivable results to the incantations and methodologies of the magician.

The experiments involving the four Elements and their denizens have led me into better understanding and appreciation for the conscious world around me. In some cases I've noticed where I've developed better sensitivity for my surroundings and the subtle energies that exist all around. There is an almost indescribable awareness to subtle Spiritual energies which seem to exist like an ever fluctuating network of electricity, bringing up new currents with each working I perform, no matter what the category or intention.

My Elemental implements were not consecrated in the traditional way as found in the Golden Dawn. I utilized parts of their rituals, but also went out in nature to places where I felt the associated Elements and Elementals were strongest. I believe that the usage of a focal point where the Elemental energies are naturally strongest is indispensable for truly tapping into their power during evocations and invocations. The Elemental tool is used as a storehouse, a magical recorder or memory drive for the energetic exchanges of the Elemental beings who arrive through the process of evocation. Just as a seal or sigil of a Spirit becomes linked with that being after an evocation is successful, so too does an Elemental Spirit's essence become imprinted on an Elemental tool during a successful conjuration. Such magical tools and talismans become a receptacle and a battery for the types of energies that they are designed to embody. It is not so much the tool that gives the magician his power, but it serves as a direct and uninterrupted line to a very specific source of power. Just as Spirits are meant to arrive swiftly once they have been successfully invoked, so too do the energies and beings of a specific Element arrive quickly once an Elemental tool has been consecrated. This consecration only occurs once the beings of that realm have been properly conjured forth to the intermediary of the physical and spiritual realms where their essence can combined with the base material of your implement. Simply undergoing the Opening by Watchtower ceremony or a similar rite will not make your Fire wand a tool for commanding the forces of Fire. If the magician is clever, he will construct a tool that has as many corresponding materials as possible to the Element's natural realm. Stones, metals, plants, trees, and herbs, symbols, design, colors, all of these provide sympathetic links to the energies meant to link them. He will fashion the tool in the most potent semblance representing the Element which agrees with his deepest understanding of and relationship to the Element. The more the subtle Astral levels and your mind agree on, the more potent and dynamic the connection. The Elemental tools used needn't be the classical weapons of the Golden Dawn or Tarot. The weapons do have significant historical lines of fixed intention despite any preferences of particular orders or individuals. They can be statues of attributed beings or gods or goddesses, pictures, household items, or whatever you prefer given that the symbolic significance makes sense to both your deep unconscious and the Astral archetype they embody. Although of different cultural and mystical tradition, the four weapons or treasures of the Tuatha de Danaan, of the Celtic mythos, resemble these archtypes perfectly. There is a cauldron, spear, sword, and stone that have enormous magical reference in use and purpose as well as corresponding with the traditional Elements associated with them.

Knowing that the magical implement is charged—consecrated and imbued with the power of its purpose for maximum effect—should be easy to distinguish. For one, whenever the item is looked at or held, the energies associated with it should be instantly felt in every aspect. The level of success in empowering the item as well as your personal initiation through the Elemental realms should cause instant physical, emotional, and mental shifts which are geared toward that specific Element without conscious effort. Such should be the level of power in your Elemental tools that if anyone else were to gaze upon them or hold them in person, they should instantly experience these shifts as well. Herein lies the true meaning of being cautioned against displaying your magical implements or allowing anyone else to handle them. If they have been crafted and consecrated correctly, they should be in fact "possessed" items, which is to say they are utterly pulsing with the same energy as the Elemental realms themselves with all associated beings. The nature of the ritual is designed to properly pattern them with the Elemental energies of divine influence, so that the work that is used with them is energetically balanced or within control of the magician, according to your will extended through the godhead. Only your consciousness through the crucible of experience and personal connection is meant to work with the perceptibly chaotic Elemental forces that are linked into your Elemental implements. Although others should be able to feel and respond to the energetic signatures and imprints upon them, they should not be allowed to handle your Elemental tools for the very reason that they will eventually and inevitably unbalance their own energetic makeup.

A word should be said here that working with the Elemental forces will not be dependent on your having a set of customized "Elemental weapons." Indeed if you have successfully been initiated through the Elemental realms and have conjured the Elemental rulers and other beings to appear and converse with you, you will be able to tap into any of their currents quite effectively. The tools are an added benefit if the forces agree to consecrate them in your favor.

Creating a veritable magical tool is simply a feat of the accomplished magician. If you can possess an item with a particular energy and have that item exude that energy over time without dissipation, it is a testament to not only your personal ability of energy direction, but of your successful relationship and correspondence to the entities who empowered the implement to begin with. Such a magician would never be reliant on such a tool in order to achieve the same ends he would without it. The implement is simply a mechanism of convenience and energetic categorization. As the wizard becomes familiar with more and more strands of Spiritual energy, (i.e., Spirits and entities) it becomes difficult to organize the applicable associations with each in his consciousness. The wide array of energetic patterns tends to blur and become intertwined, much as they are in the relative matrix of patterns found in the universe. Magical implementation is another way of keeping energetic bodies separate and organized for specific use. This is another reason why magical items are not handled or gazed upon casually as the mindful mage keeps all points of symbolic energetic reference for times when he wishes to connect dynamically to that strand. The clearer the channel, the more potent the working.

Traveling the Elemental Planes

The first time I attempted to guide another person through an Astral plane was with my scryer and friend Benn Mac Stiofán. It was to be our first official ceremonial magic working together in which I wanted him to see and explore the Astral planes as I had but in a way of not only scrying the Tattwas but using a method of Astral projection I had come to develop. In this fashion, the experience wasn't limited to just "scrying" and seeing the Astral plane, but completely being immersed in it.

I was fortunate that I began this experiment with someone who had already been developing their Spiritual sight and practice consistently for many years prior to these events. My friend's dedication for daily meditations, rituals, and following his path is impressive by anyone's standards. We had known each other for over a decade and working together turned out to be far smoother and more successful than I could have imagined. Benn had not, however, been through any of the initiations, exercises, or lessons concerning the four classical Elements and their correspondences. Although I'm sure he knew of some of the correlations, much of the material was new to him and I was excited to participate in his experience of how these Elemental realms would appear to him and what sort of things he would learn as a result.

The idea of taking Benn through similar magical experiences was an exciting proposal for me as it allowed me to recreate practices I had delved into during the earlier stages of my magical training and discovery. My foundations for ritual/ceremonial magic were based on integrating and balancing the symbolic Elemental archetypes and correspondence from the Greek Hermetic philosophy of antiquity. This model of cosmology and physio-psychic association along with their esoteric principles seemed perfect for introducing my magical partner to the world of ceremonial magic. The practice also gave me a chance to come full circle and acknowledge just how much my abilities and methods had evolved over the years. In this sense, I could better gauge how my practices, magical implements, and methods affected others during the ritual, and how similar or dissimilar the experiences would be.

In the early stages of my exploration of ceremonial magic, I had created a set of Elemental "weapons" or implements in the tradition of the Golden Dawn. The crafting of these four magical tools was for my personal initiation into the philosophy and practice of lodge-style ceremonial magic. However, the GD's traditional brightly colored tools never quite felt adequate for me so I spent a number of years designing and crafting my own set of Elemental implements, ones I felt could truly harness the powers of the Elements and Elementals with which I sought to work. In each case, I wanted to combine as many corresponding materials that would harmoniously and skillfully blend together as possible to create a truly magnificent and awe-inspiring implement. I stuck with the primary images and archetypes of the implements which are associated with the Tarot as well as the Golden Dawn, but in their particular aspects I took the liberty of combining my own knowledge of Elemental correspondences.

Elemental Fire Experience

The Elemental Fire wand was the third implement that came into my possession years ago when I began. I had considered replacing the wand with a dagger or another implement which I felt could equally or perhaps better represent the Element of Fire. However, due to years spent using the Tarot and basing much of my early work on the system of the Golden Dawn, the wand was the Elemental weapon I most associated with Fire. An artisan and long-time friend helped bring about the physical reality of the wand based on my instructions and did a superb job in its crafting. The shaft is carved from aromatic cedar, which seemed the best corresponding wood for a Fire wand as cedar is the wood associated with Mars according to Agrippa. I had filled the center of the cedar handle with a Fire mixture I created that consisted of carefully selected herbs, oils, incenses, metals, stones, and other materials corresponding with the Element of Fire. A 24k gold plated dragon was molded to wrap around the width. The wand is studded with rubies, garnets, and fire opals. I had inscribed the wand with the names and sigils associated with each of the Fire Elemental Angels as in the Golden Dawn design, but I also included the names and sigils of the Elemental kings and rulers.

I consecrated the Fire wand on the Sunday nearest the Summer. The first part of the ritual was based on the Opening by Watchtower formula that Israel Regardie created, but with a few additions. This was conducted in the midst of a desert environment, far removed from the likelihood of anyone passing by and interrupting my ritual. I drew out my circle in the sand and used large stones to create an altar in the center of the circle as well as one in the south outside the circle with a triangle traced around it. On each of the two makeshift stone altars I placed a bright red and orange cloth. Also at the three points of the triangle outside the circle I set metal braziers which contained cedar wood, dead wood I collected from the desert, plus large quantities of a Fire incense mixture. On top of the altar I formed another triangle from three red beeswax candles in brass candlesticks which were engraved with sigils, names, and symbols associated with Fire Elemental beings.

I worked the ritual during the hour of Mars nearest to noon. I began with the ceremonial procedures from the Opening by Watchtower, invoking the Holy

Names of God as well as each of the Elemental Angelic rulers as they were given by Regardie. The ritual flowed nicely and I was able to concentrate fully on what I was doing since I had spent several months becoming familiar with the ritual. After the first phase of the consecration was complete, I placed my Fire wand on the altar within the triangle, using two long sticks to balance it. I lit the end of another stick and used it to light the three braziers and the three red candles, then stepped back to the center of my circle.

The second part of the ritual was to be the evocation of a Fire Elemental strong enough to consecrate my Fire wand with the capabilities I would dictate to it. When the fires in the braziers were going as well as the candles, I began my evocation. I called forth the ruling Spirits of Fire I had previously invoked to send forth a powerful emissary who could grant my request to empower the wand which now lay at the center of the triangle surrounded by burning candles and braziers. After the first spoken invocation, I extended my senses and intuition to determine when I should proceed. At some point, I recall that the sun became intense, piercing through the clouds of incense smoke billowing up from the triangle and combining with the light of the candles, causing a rather interesting optical effect. At this point I recited the Prayer of the Salamanders, followed by a poem I had written which spoke of the passionate, creative, and energetic power of Fire.

To my appreciation, the air right above the triangle became active with swirling waves of heat distortion visibly moving rapidly and directly over the Fire wand, optically distorting the background scenery. I took this to indicate the possible presence of a Fire Elemental Spirit. I spoke directly to it, giving a welcome followed by a clear petition of what I wished the Fire wand to be able to perform and to be capable of assisting me to achieve. I never heard a "voice" respond back or received any clearer indication that the ritual was going according to plan other than a continual building of energy, excitement, and gratitude for the whole undertaking. I never once felt like I was speaking to the empty air and thanked the perceived Spirit in the triangle above my wand. I sat in a meditative and focused stare at the wand and heat waves which continued for several moments until the sun moved a bit higher in the sky and the rite seemed to naturally draw to a close. I stood, giving a final and formal thank you to the energies, Spirits, and beings in attendance and then closed the ceremony in the fashion of the Golden Dawn. I exited the circle and extinguished the candle flames, and as I reached for the Fire wand on the southern altar, any doubts I may have had as to the overall success of the ceremony were abandoned.

I wanted the wand to resonate with a frequency which the Elementals of Fire would recognize immediately and to which they would respond powerfully. The wand was created to be able to call forth Fire Elementals at will as well as endow me with all of the positive aspects of the Element of Fire whenever I held it in my hands. To this end I believe the consecration ritual was successful beyond my initial imaginings. To this day, each time I hold the wand I instantaneously feel a tremendous surge of power, heat, and activity. The question of how much of this "power" is actually contained in the wand itself, and how much is the product of my deep unconscious associating all those powerful correspondences of Fire when I hold the wand, is a matter of speculation.

Regardless, this wand was to be my primary ritual implement in opening the doorway to the Elemental plane of Fire to hopefully allow my friend and newly appointed magical partner to experience the majesty of this realm.

Experiments in Traveling the Elemental Planes

The operations described below originated in a careful blending of traditional magical methods from various sources. When it comes to conducting magical operations in a particular tradition, I am averse to mixing and matching aspects of any kind simply to suit the comforts of the practitioner. However, to my knowledge, there was no direct traditional method for Elemental Astral travel to the degree I sought. So in the experiments described below, I combined a set of magical methods in which I had become proficient to formulate a working procedure. As the records of the experiments demonstrate, it appears to be an effective mode of working.

The Fire Elemental plane experiment was my first attempt to see if I could effectively lead another human being through experiential, esoteric initiation. It was my intention that this could be achieved utilizing process via a ritual of combined esoteric paradigms. I was excited at the prospect of accompanying another while he experienced magical phenomenon, sensations, and intelligences of which he did not otherwise have the integrated corresponding knowledge. In this experiment it was also my intention to saturate the ritual environment, as well as the participants, with the corresponding nature of the Elemental energy. I attempted to do the above while hopefully not short-circuiting or overcomplicating the ritual for myself and the scryer.

Traveling in the Elemental Plane of Fire

For the Elemental Astral voyage of Fire I selected a Tuesday in the summer which seemed to have all beneficial aspects conducive to setting the stage for this experiment. I used the magic circle from my *DSIC* experiments, which is a ring of foot-wide canvas fabric painted with four hexagrams and three sacred names of the Creator plus an empty section for the appearance of the Spirit which in this case I positioned toward the south. I placed a comfortable chair in the south end of the circle also facing south. Behind the chair was a small altar which holds my magician's wand and dagger, along with my consecrated Fire wand, consecrated Fire oil (a strong cinnamon oil with ingredients similar to the Oil of Abramelin), and also a small Tejas Tattwa card of the Fire Element.

In the blank area on the circle reserved for the Spirit's name and sigil, I placed parchment sheets of alchemical and grimoric symbols for the Element of Fire as well as the name of the Elemental king. Just beyond the magic circle in the south, I placed an altar table. This altar was covered with a scarlet silk cloth, and on it were a Fire wand, a brass censer, a container of Fire incense, and three red beeswax candles, as well as a few other objects corresponding to Fire magic and workings which I felt already resonated with the appropriate energies. My personalized Fire altar tablet created the backdrop to the altar.

Prior to this operation, I had created a set of large Tattwa cards, each of which was about 24 × 24 inches. The Fire or Tejas card consisted of the traditional bright red and green symbol pasted in the center of a large background photograph of a blazing fire. The idea was to have a large enough 'gateway' image that anyone looking at it could not help but have his eye drawn to focus on the Elemental imagery before him. The background photograph of the physical Element acts to compound and assist the subconscious to focus on the appropriate archetype as well. The large card was placed on the face of an antique mirror that I had long used for scrying and Spiritual or Astral voyages of all kinds.

Ritual items for this experiment:

1. Magician's wand and dagger.
2. Fire Wand.
3. Two altars: One for inside the circle, one for outside as the main Fire altar. Red altar cloths for each.
4. Consecrated Fire oil: Olive oil infused with essential oils of dragon's blood, cedar, rue, peppercorns, ginger, cinnamon, galangal, and myrrh.

5. Three red candles, preferably beeswax, with brass or iron candleholders.
6. Brazier, charcoal, and lighter.
7. Optional: A ruby or rubies; iron, brass, or bronze statue(s) or icon(s) of dragon, salamander, serpent.
8. Fire Elemental incense: Frankincense, dragon's blood, red cedar, black peppercorns, benzoin, gum Arabic, small powdered lodestone, tiny amounts of sulfur, hellebore, and tobacco.

Hypnotic Induction of Scryer while staring at the Tattwa

Before beginning with the vocal invocations of the ceremony, I went around and lit the charcoal and the candles, while reciting a grimoric consecration blessing:[6]

I conjure thee, O thou creature of Fire! By Him Who created all things both in heaven and earth, and in the sea, and in every other place whatever, that forthwith thou cast away every phantasm from thee, that no hurt whatsoever shall be done in anything. Bless, O Lord, this creature of Fire, and sanctify it that it may be blessed, and that they may fill up the power and virtue of their odors; so neither the Enemy nor any false imagination may enter into them; through our Lord Jesus Christ. Amen.

When the charcoal was ready, I poured a fair amount of the Fire incense mixture on the coals and observed as the clouds of perfume billowed upward.

After everything was lit and prepared, I reentered the circle and circumambulated it clockwise blessing the working space, saying, "In the name of the blessed Trinity, I consecrate this piece of ground for our defense, so that no evil Spirit may have power to break these bounds prescribed here, through Jesus Christ our Lord. Amen." When that was complete, I picked up the smaller Tattwa card from my altar within the circle and gave it to my friend in the chair. I instructed him to gaze and focus on the card while relaxing. I guided him through a few more hypnotic induction exercises and a breathing exercise to deepen his concentration as he stared at the card.

I then picked up my consecrated Fire wand as well as the consecrated Fire oil and placed a bit of oil on the end of the wand. I then drew Fire signs on his fore-

---

6. I always recommend blessing and consecrating any charcoals, incense, and lights used in rituals, following forms such as the ones given in *DSIC* or *The Key of Solomon*.

Fig. III-1. ***Section of Circle for Drawing Djinn into the Crystal***

head with the wand and Fire sign portal (upside-down V) drawn on his third eye with consecrated Fire oil. The act of using the Fire wand and oil seemed to have a particularly startling reaction on my friend, but he continued to gaze down intently at the Tattwa card. I once again walked around behind him in the center of the magic circle and placed my Fire wand back on the table while retrieving my magician's wand and dagger. With three taps on the small altar, I began with the first part of Opening By Watchtower:

Declaring in a firm voice, I uttered, "HEKAS, HEKAS, ESTE BEBELOI!"[7] I then used my dagger to perform the Banishing Ritual of the Pentagram. I will not be giving the instructions for this ritual or the Banishing Ritual of the Hexagram, which I performed after, as these rituals can easily be found in several sources. After those opening rituals, I set my wand and dagger back down on the altar and once again picked up my Fire wand, this time with the intention of opening the door to the Fire Astral Plane. Walking clockwise I moved directly in front of the Fire altar and made three striking motions in front of it in the shape of a triangle with its apex at the top.

I then held the wand above my head and walked clockwise around the inside of the circle, saying, "And when, after all the phantoms have vanished, thou shalt see that holy and formless Fire, that Fire which darts and flashes through the hidden depths of the Universe, hear thou the Voice of Fire!"

When I returned to the south end of the circle, I once again made three striking motions with the wand forming an upright triangle. Afterward, I traced a large circle in front of the altar, then an invoking Pentagram of Fire within it, then the Fire Kerub (sign of Leo) in the center, saying: "OIP TEAA PEDOCE[8]. In the names and letters of the Great Southern Quadrangle, I invoke ye, ye Angels of the Watchtower of the South."

7. Pronounced *hay-kahs, hay-kahs, ess-tee bee-ba-loy*.

8. Pronounced *oh-ee-pay tay-ah-ah pay-doh-kay*.

The chamber area should exhibit a distinctly different atmosphere when a conjuration or magical operation is successful and currently underway. There should be no requirement for imagination or sensitivity testing to sense this change. It should be welcomed and expected as a sure sign of a successful operation.

Perception in the circle and magical room immediately changed to take on a statically charged sensation and I again moved behind my scryer with my Fire wand still in hand and directed him to stare straight ahead at the large Apas Tattwa on the Fire altar. I turn to the scryer/subject and guide him to Astral travel state as he continues to stare, I find the right time and have him close his eyes, knowing he's able to see the inverse Tattwa image on his retina. Hypnosis used with the effects of the Magician's Voice to draw others into a shared mystical experience has been an excellent tool. I find that if I can just get the person there, the rest of the ceremony will follow suit without me having to paint the picture of what experiences should be like. The person will witness what they will use their own perceptions and capacity to comprehend.

Standing directly behind my scryer, I begin to speak using my hypnotic voice and saying something similar to the following:

"As you continue to stare into the very center of the triangle, you may notice how the colors have seemed to flash or change in color, causing a light to form around them that was not there previously. Allow this effect to draw you deeper and deeper into the image. As you gaze comfortably at the image, you relax even deeper and find your complete focus, your complete attention drawn even deeper into the magical image. Let the triangle and colors fill your every perception, your entire focus and attention, so that each breath allows you to enter into an even deeper state of consciousness. Now, allow your eyes to close gently and easily. You should easily see the image of the triangle before you, imprinted on your eyes past the blackness of your eyelids. The triangle should appear green and the background red. Do you see it?"

After a brief pause, my scryer nodded his head slightly and I continued.

"You will hear me count from ten to one. As I do so, see the green triangle growing larger and larger. Instead of the image moving toward you, you feel as if you are being drawn like a magnet toward it. You continue to move closer and closer and the triangle grows larger until it becomes the size of a doorway. Ten, drifting easily and effortlessly toward the Elemental gateway of Fire. Nine, drifting closer and closer. Eight. Seven. Six. Five. Four, the triangle is now large enough to step through without even touching the sides. Three, stepping all the way through the triangular door to the Elemental Plane of Fire. Two. One, you now find yourself completely through the door."

With a steady inhalation and long exhalation, I could practically sense my friend's perception move out toward the south and the Fire Tattwa and through the other side. At this point, I chanted the Divine name YHVH Tzabaoth followed by the Archangel name Michael, and the Angel name Aral. After I did this, I assisted my friend further, saying, "Allow your senses to be completely aware of your surroundings, being able to see, hear, feel, and interact with your environment in this new plane of existence. As you explore, images and perceptions will become sharper and you will easily recall and remember every detail upon returning to this plane."

After this I stood motionless behind my scryer with my Fire wand pointed at the Fire altar and large Tattwa in front of us. I then recited The Prayer of the Salamanders:

Immortal, eternal, ineffable, and uncreated Father of all things, who art born upon the ever-rolling chariot of worlds which revolve unceasingly; Lord of the ethereal immensities, where the throne of Thy power is exalted, from which height Thy terrible eyes discern all things, and Thy holy and beautiful ears unto all things hearken, hear Thou Thy children, whom Thou didst love before the ages began; for Thy golden, Thy grand, Thy eternal majesty shines above the world and the heaven of stars! Thou art exalted over them, O Glittering Fire! There dost Thou shine, there dost Thou commune with Thyself by Thine own splendor, and inexhaustible streams of light pour from Thine essence for the nourishment of Thine infinite Spirit, which Itself doth nourish all things, and forms that inexhaustible treasure of substance ever ready for generation, which adapts it and appropriates the forms Thou hast impressed on it from the beginning! From this Spirit the three most holy kings who surround Thy throne and constitute Thy court derive also their origin, O Universal Father! O Sole and Only Father of blessed mortals and immortals! In particular Thou hast created powers which are marvelously like unto Thine eternal thought and Thine adorable essence; Thou hast established them higher than the Angels, who proclaim Thy will to the world; finally, Thou hast created us third in rank within our Elemental empire. There our unceasing exercise is to praise Thee and adore Thy good pleasure; there we burn continually in our aspiration to possess Thee, O Father! O Mother, most tender of all mothers; O Admirable Archetype of Maternity and of Pure Love! O Son, Flower of Sons! O Form of all Forms, Soul, Spirit, Harmony, and Number of all things! Amen.

I remained silent afterward, allowing my scryer to experience whatever he would in the moments that followed. As for myself I remained fixed in the sensations of the magical ceremony, feeling the continual currents of energy and vitality radiating through me the entire time.

Scryer's Experience:

SCRYER: As Frater Ashen's voice began to direct me through the Tattwa, I could easily see the reversal of the red and green colors. The triangular doorway being green at first seemed to contradict my logical associations with color, but I put them aside and let the experience unfold as it would. I felt and saw myself stepping through the triangle and it led me into a scene of rich foliage. Immediately I could see pulses of light zipping through leaves, vines, and branches of the plant life. The idea of communicating life force was very evident, with an energetic, almost electrical bright spark delivering patterns, frequencies, and messages of life throughout. All of a sudden, my vision faded out again and I was unable to see anything. After a moment, I was faintly able to make out a city formed of shining brass and black and red marble, with towers and spirals of shining gold. The city seemed alive as if its very structure moved a circulation of energy within it and exuded its own light. Above it all a great burning presence of life as if multiple suns next to one another was shining, overpowering in light and heat. This was when Frater Ashen invoked the Archangel Michael. There was so much movement, and activity I was unable to take it all in and perceive it properly. I remember thinking that I was terrible at multitasking and that it was hard to follow the beings as they flashed and moved everywhere. Forms and lights moved with such rapidity of motion and speed that it took me a long time to get my bearings in all the perceived chaos.

I had to consciously shut my sight down for a few seconds and ask for a being to stop and converse with me. As my vision returned, I saw only a face of flame directly in front and very intent on me.

When I asked his name and who he was it responded by crying out, «IFRIT!!!» It raised its arms and suddenly the scene behind came flooding into vision. A red plain of smooth lava appeared and on the lava sat what appeared to be thousands of brass vases. Out of the vases shot pillars of thin Fire straight into the sky. Where the Fires touched the ether, above them formed stars, thousands of them. All brilliant and flashing in the sky.

> The being which called itself Ifrit spoke of purification and that it was that energy which connected it with the Element of Water. It went on to explain that healers must bring the presence of Fire with them when healing themselves and others to burn away what was most harmful and unneeded. He talked of a method of connecting one's self into the Element of Fire to energize and push through obstacles of all kinds. Although I was unsure if I completely understood, the being instructed on how to utilize the power of its Element and its energy linked to all four of the forces that fuse the golden key. That Fire had many forms: Heating and expanding, some cooling, some destructive, purifying, but all was passionate energy.

The session was concluded by a hypnotic command to do an about face and once again see the Astral doorway of the Fire Tattwa in front of him (the Scryer) and have him once again step through the portal back into the room while I counted from one to ten. For some reason, the energy filled the room and I decided not to do a Closing by Watchtower of the Fire portal or a banishing pentagram. No Lesser Banishing Ritual of the Pentagram was done, and the room remained *energized* for a time. Both my scryer and I were excited and related what we had experienced. Very positive and amazing energy flowed through both of us the entire remainder of the day and evening. After the operation, I left to run 3 miles and teach my martial arts class with plenty of energy left to burn!

When the experiment was concluded, I decided to close down the session with a simple prayer of thanks instead of the "banishing" and reversal methods of closing used by the Golden Dawn in the Opening By Watchtower. I did not retrace and close down the Fire portals I had opened, since after the experience, both my scryer and I were absolutely teeming with energy and vitality. I ended up running a 5k just an hour afterward quite spontaneously and ran the entire thing without exhausting the exhilarating vitality that had filled me since the experiment. My scryer reported similar reactions and enjoyed the feelings of seemingly endless energy.

Some of the greatest testaments to magic working I have witnessed were due to mistakes I've made. Many of these examples were made under the assumption I was doing everything correctly or that various omissions would not cause any serious repercussions. It still is logically debatable whether any of the Elemental operations had any relation to events which occurred in my community, but the Fire operation did happen to coincided with some of the more devastating natural disasters which befell my city shortly after the experiment. Coincidentally (or not), each Elemental experiment happened to foreshadow a display of a related Elemental power and destruction that was visited on my city.

A week or so after the experiment involving the Elemental plane of Fire, my city experienced one of the worst natural disasters in its history. A fire burned out of control from a mountain trail which ended up spreading down the better part of the mountain range, covering nearly 19,000 acres. The fire caused the evacuation of over 32,000 residents and resulted in insurance claims totaling nearly half a billion dollars. The ensuing blaze destroyed more than 300 homes and claimed the lives of two people.

During the valiant attempts to contain the wild fire, it was reported that the fire broke past a containment road when a flaming deer leaped across the road and made it difficult for firefighters to manage the fire. A record high temperature of 101° F was also recorded during that day, which is a rarity for a high mountain environment. It was the most destructive fire in the state's history, as measured by the number of homes destroyed, until another forest fire the following summer surpassed it.

This time the evacuation area covered 94,000 acres, 13,000 homes, and 38,000 people. 14,000 acres were burned, more than 500 homes were destroyed, and two people perished.

It was a very difficult time for people during those hot days, and the smoke seemed to choke the throats and irritate the eyes of everyone for miles in every direction. For days and days, the smoke was so thick that it covered the sky completely. It was not until a week or so after the second fire that I planned on taking my scryer through the Water Elemental experience. My motivation this time was to put a stop to the devastating fires and heal the land which was parched, burned, and devastated both physically and emotionally and so were the people, vegetation, and wildlife. It seemed like a perfect opportunity to affect some magical change in our area as well as explore the Astral realm and Element of Water.

Elemental Water Experience

The first Elemental implement I obtained in my search was the Water chalice. As a precursor to the events of the catastrophic fires, I had spent several years previously hunting for the perfect representation for the Element of Water, however commonplace a chalice might seem. In my travels, I eventually came upon a shop near the gulf which sold exquisite works of silver and I spotted a chalice which instantly took my breath away. It was a silver goblet that was

Fig. III-2. ***Portrait of Djinn/Ifrit as beheld in Vision***

expertly upheld by three abalone-scaled fish supported by a silver base with another ring of abalone shells that encircled the bottom. To add to this, a tiny turquoise fish was welded to one side.

If any chalice ever displayed the embodiment of Water and the ocean, it was the lovely work of art I beheld. I purchased the chalice and took it home and eventually decided to add some personalized touches. Near the rim, I added aquamarine stones which separated the sigils and names in ancient Hebrew of the associated Angels and Elemental Ruler of Water. I also added moonstones and mother of pearl. Silver and abalone moon-shaped stones were also mounted on the base. I was very pleased with how it came out, as the ornamentation looked as though it had been part of the chalice since it was originally made.

I knew that consecrating this Elemental treasure would have to be done carefully and particularly, so I took my time in planning it.

I consecrated the Water Chalice on a Monday under a waxing gibbous Moon. I decided to conduct the ceremony at dusk near a mountain lake that was often clear of people during the onset of autumn. The air was crisp, but not yet cold enough to be uncomfortable. I cast my magical circle, carving it in the sand using a willow branch directly near the shore of the lake which was perfectly enclosed in a highly scrubbed inlet, allowing me ample privacy. The shore's edge was perfectly positioned with the water opening up towards the west with a trickling stream flowing from the opposite side. The setting sun could be seen through trees on the opposite shore, casting shadows on the rippling water of the lake.

The lake itself had several feet of shallow water leading out into the deeper center. I decided to build an altar in the shallows using stones I gathered in and around the lake. I formed a sort of ring of small stones supporting a larger flat stone. Over the flat stone I draped a blue silk cloth on which I set a silver bowl of sweet white wine as an offering. I had also brought some sea shells I collected years ago, and I arranged them on the altar. This magical ritual setting looked particularly fascinating with my circle drawn in the sand directly in front of the lake while the Water altar appeared to be floating just beyond the circle, surrounded by its Element.

At the hour of the Moon, I began with the Water portion of the ritual for Opening by Watchtower, clearing the space of any negative influences and inviting in the pure Spirits of Water to attend. I picked up my silver chalice and invoked the holy names of God as well as each of the Elemental Angelic Rulers. This ritual seemed pleasant but one I recall having difficulty focusing as I felt my mind drifting off at times and entering into a sort of euphoric daydream during the invocations. Although I had spent time becoming familiar with the ritual during the prior several months, I found myself having to repeat the invocations. After the OBWT phase of the consecration was completed, I used the willow stick with which I had created my circle to carefully place the silver chalice on the altar in the shallows. The task was a bit more daunting than I expected and I ended up dropping the chalice into the water twice before finally bringing it to rest securely on the altar.

By the time I was ready to begin the second part of the consecration, the sun had already dipped behind the trees and mountainside at the far end of the lake and everything was beginning to be covered in deep shadows. Regardless I steadied myself in the center of the lake shore circle and called forth the Elementals of Water I had previously invoked to send forth a powerful emissary that could grant my request of empowering and consecrating my implement of Water. I remember my voice echoing a bit louder than I anticipated over the lake and for a moment was worried that I might be overheard by a lakeshore visitor of whom I was unaware but who might become aware of me. Regardless, I carried on with my evocation and sent my voice steadily out across the still water of the lake.

After a brief silence following my evocation, I heard a distant splash which I assumed was a fish leaping from the lake to catch an insect that had dared too near the surface. The splash, however, was soon followed by more noises in the water which seemed to be drawing steadily closer. I strained my eyes trying to discern the source of the noise, but I was unable to detect anything. In the dying light, all looked as still as it did before with no indication of what was causing the splashing noises. My rational mind was reasoning that the sounds were amplified due to the acoustics of the lake and that the noise was not near enough for me to see the source but the motion in the water continued to grow in volume.

After a time the noises abruptly stopped and all I could hear was the water lapping faintly against the shoreline. I was uncertain how to proceed since I had very little clarity on whether or not my invocations and petitions had been answered.

I recited the Prayer of the Undines, followed by a poem I had devised which spoke of the deep mystical and emotional power of the Waters, along with dreams, and the ebb and flow of the Spiritual world around us. In the distance, a faint, silvery light appeared either on the far side of the shore or somewhere in the midst of the lake. It was so dark I couldn't be certain of the exact position nor could I be certain of its source. The light seemed to appear out of nowhere and remained motionless for a time. It captured my attention and held it for several long moments. I tried desperately to decipher its origin and nature but was unable to settle on anything. It could have been a reflection off some material in the Water from the moon. However, the light did not bob or appear to move that often. It could have been a person who turned on a light of some sort and set it down near the water's edge.

Regardless of the origin, the light interested me to such a degree that I lost track of what I was doing and continued to stare at it. Unexpectedly the light sank downward out of sight and I lost all track of it. I stayed motionless for quite a while, hoping to see it reemerge. Thinking back now I don't know why I was so fascinated by the light, as it did not appear that unusual. It did not appear again, but an evening wind picked up and the sound of the water seemed to increase across the lake. Splashing sounds increased in volume and intensity as the water lapped against my makeshift altar which was barely discernible. I became concerned that the whole thing would be knocked over and that I might lose my precious chalice.

Intuition prompted me to turn my attention from the altar and extend a formal greeting to the Water Elemental which I somehow knew was directly in front of me though not visible. I spoke to it as if I could see it clearly before me in the waters. As soon as I did, the winds subsided but the activity in the waters continued unabated. Besides being filled with the magical correspondences of the Water Element, I asked that the chalice resonate with a frequency to which the Elementals of Water would respond and recognize instantly. I stated that it was my desire for the chalice to be able to call forth Water Elementals at will as well as endow me with all of the positive aspects of the Elemental kingdom whenever I held it in my hands. I also asked that the chalice have the ability to bless and sanctify whatever liquid that was placed inside to have healing qualities as well as assist with Astral journeys of all sorts. I spoke from my heart and my desire for it to connect with the physical object I had personalized. A lovely effect of the rising moon happened to reflect off the surface of the chalice after I completed my invocation and petitions and the object appeared to glow with an Astral light. The sight and nebulous beauty of it filled me with a sense of accomplishment, gratitude, and wonder.

I bowed deeply, placing my hand across my chest, and spoke a heartfelt appreciation for the experience. I closed the ceremony in the fashion of Opening by Watchtower and rubbed out the circle in the sand. Retrieving my Water chalice from the water suspended in the shallows of the lake, I was confirmed that the lovely object was now a consecrated treasure of the mystical depths. Upon arriving home that evening, I sat and stared at it for nearly an hour before finally cleaning the surface and wrapping it in sheets of blue and silver silk.

O Thou Who art from everlasting, Thou Who hast created all things, and doth clothe Thyself with the Forces of Nature as with a garment, by Thy Holy and Divine Name EL whereby Thou art known in that quarter we name MEARAB, I beseech thee to grant unto me strength and insight for my search after the Hidden Light and Wisdom.

I entreat Thee to cause Thy Wonderful Archangel GABRIEL who governeth the works of Water to guide us in the pathway; and furthermore to direct thine Angel TALIAHAD to watch over our footsteps therein.

May the ruler of Water, the powerful Prince THARSIS by the gracious permission of the Infinite Supreme, increase and strengthen the hidden forces and occult virtues of my chalice so that I may be enabled with it to perform aright those magical operations for which it has been fashioned. For which purpose I perform this mystic rite of Consecration in the Divine Presence of EL.

In the Three Great Secret Holy Names of God borne upon the Banners of the West, EMPEH ARSEL GAIOL, I summon Thee, Thou Great King of the West, RAAGIOSEL, to attend upon this ceremony and by Thy presence increase its effect, whereby I do now re-consecrate this Magical Cup. Confer upon it the utmost occult might and virtue of which Thou mayest judge it to be capable in all works of the nature of Water, so that in it I may find a strong defense and a powerful implement with which to rule and direct the Spirits of the Elements.

Ye Mighty Princes of the Western Quadrangle, I invoke you who are known to me by the honorable title and position of rank of seniors. Hear my petition, and be this day present with me. Bestow upon this Cup the strength and purity whereof ye are Masters in the Elemental Forces which ye control, that its outward and material form may remain a true symbol of the inward and Spiritual force.

O Thou Powerful Angel HNLRX, Thou who are Lord and Ruler over the Fiery Waters, I beseech thee to endow this Cup with the Magic Powers of which thou art Lord, that I may with its aid direct the Spirits who serve thee in purity and singleness of aim to hasten the arrival of forceful waters to parched land.

O Thou Powerful Angel HTDIM, Thou who are Lord and Ruler over the pure and fluid Element of Water, I beseech thee to endow this Cup with the Magic Powers of which thou art Lord, that I may with its aid direct the Spirits who serve thee in purity and singleness of aim to bring copious and continual water to heal this land.

O Thou Powerful Angel HTAAD, Thou who are Lord and Ruler of the Etheric and Airy qualities of Water, I beseech thee to endow this Cup with the Magic Powers of which thou art Lord, that I may with its aid direct the Spirits who serve thee in purity and singleness of aim to move large clouds to deposit healing waters upon this land.

O Thou Powerful Angel HMAGL, Thou who are Lord and Ruler of the more dense and solid qualities of Water, I beseech thee to endow this Cup with the Magic Powers of which thou art Lord, that I may with its aid direct the Spirits who serve thee in purity and singleness of aim to bring showers of healing waters to my land and area here presented.

Traveling the Elemental Plane of Water

The event for this magical experiment was set on a Thursday evening only a week after the second fire mentioned above was still burning. I began setting up my ritual room as soon as I arrived home from work and arranged a Water altar in the west containing all of my corresponding tools, plus my personal Water chalice and a large posterboard-size Apas Tattwa. I also had a printed map of my city and the surrounding areas, an oil diffuser with Water-corresponding essential oils, a large silver bowl filled with water, and another sealed container filled with rain water I had collected last year, various sea shells, and other Water-corresponding items.

My magical partner arrived, and after a purification and blessing we entered the magical chamber. We began during the hour of the Moon.

Ritual items for this experiment:

1. Ritual magician's wand and dagger
2. Consecrated Water chalice
3. Two altars: One for inside the circle, one for outside as the main Water altar. Blue and silver altar cloths for each
4. Consecrated Water Oil: Olive oil, jasmine, lotus, sandalwood, and anise essential oils
5. Four blue aor silver candles, preferably beeswax, with glass or silver candleholders.
6. Charcoal and lighter.

7. Optional: Aquamarine and clear stones like quartz, fish, sea shells.
8. Water Elemental plane incense: Sweet myrrh, anise seed, camphor, white poppy, white rose, orris root, storax, white sandalwood, lignum aloes, jasmine, willow.

As with the Fire Elemental realm experience, I had my friend relax in a chair and begin to stare at the silver crescent-moon Tattwa for Water. He performed his own breathing and deepening techniques this time to enter into a trance state while he gazed at a smaller version of the Apas Tattwa card. I performed the section of Opening by Watchtower dealing with the Water Element, with the intention of opening the door to the Water Astral Plane, using my consecrated Water chalice while my scryer focused on the Apas card.

After the opening rituals, I circumambulated the circle clockwise to the west and picked up my consecrated Water Chalice. I then faced the Elemental Tablet of Water and altar and sprinkled droplets of consecrated Water from the chalice before it three times. I then raised the chalice above my head, and walked clockwise around the circle saying, "So therefore first the priest who governeth the works of Fire must sprinkle with the lustral Water of the loud resounding sea!" When I returned to the west, I again sprinkled the Water altar in front of the tablet. Then with the chalice I traced a large blue Invoking Pentagram of Water in blue energy. Enunciating "MPH ARSEL GAIOL," I then traced the Water sigil in the center. I presented my chalice to the center of this pentagram and said, "ALEPH LAMED EL," then finished with, "In the names and letters of the Great Western Quadrangle, I invoke ye, ye Angels of the Watchtower of the West."

As before, I used the hypnotic induction method to assist the scryer with Astral projection. I then chanted Lévi's Prayer of the Undines from the Conjuration of the Four Elements:

Terrible King of the sea! Thou who holdest the keys of the floodgates of heaven, and who enclosest the subterranean Waters in the hollow places of Earth! King of the Deluge and the rains of the springtime! Thou who openest the sources of streams and fountains! Thou who commandest the moisture, which is like the blood of Earth, to become the sap of plants! We adore and invoke thee! Speak to us, ye moving and changeable creatures! Speak to us in the great commotions of the sea, and we shall tremble before thee. Speak to us also in the murmur of limpid Waters, and we shall desire thy love! O immensity in which all the rivers of being lose themselves, whichever spring up anew in us! O Ocean of Infinite perfections! Height which beholdeth thee in the depth! Depth which breathes thee forth in the height! Bring us to the true life through intelligence and love! Lead us to immortality through sacrifice, in order that one day we may be found worthy to offer thee Water, blood, tears, for the remission of sins. Amen.

After I completed the prayer and directions for my scryer to project completely through the Water portal, I followed with other prayers and invocations, chanting the Holy name Elohim Tzabaoth, the Archangel Gabriel's name, and finally that of the Angel of Water, Taliahad.

My Astral senses opened further and began to experience my own sensations of the Water realm in lighter context while keeping an active hold on the flow of the ritual. The area beyond the circle appeared to ebb and flow with a cool sense enveloping the ritual chamber. My consecrated and empowered Water chalice glowed and seemed to pulse in my hands. My scryer was moving, his expressions tensing and relaxing, obviously having an intense experience as I conducted the rituals to hopefully bring rains back and quench the fires.

O Spirits of the Watery realms, Thy who brings forth life in abundance, O Undines, O Great Elemental Beings of the oceans, seas, rivers, ponds, lakes, streams, pools, fountains, and all other abysses of Water, O Spirits of the blood of life, O unstable ones who constantly move, Whose grace flows upon all things, O Sustainers, O Spirits who speak in movements, flowing within the emotions of life, O Regenerating ones, who washes away all impurities, Who hast brought forth the floods of the Heavens, O Healing Suave, O Giver of the Gift of Life, Thy whose depths reflects thy heights, Thy whose sacrifice brings forth life, O Spirits of Water, O Spirits of the west, we call Thee forth, Rain upon us, and come as the four rivers that flow forth from Eden, bringing unto us the seeds from the Tree of Life, come forth, come forth, we invoke Thee, come in Thy Gentle Guise, O come Magnificent ones. Amen.

O King of the Divided Waters, O Lord of the Four rivers of Eden, O Emperor of the four rivers of the Infernal Realms, O Regenerating King of Life, care holder of the Elixir of Immortality, Bestower of Gifts, Granter of Blessing, Lord of Beauty, O Lord of the Vengeful Waters of the flood, O Great King of the Sea, come as the rain, and water our circle with the Heavenly Dew of Wisdom, Grace us with your presence, Bless us with Your Beauty, O Nichsa, come forth from Thy depths and grace us with Thy conversation. Amen.

On my altar was a map of our city which was inscribed with several Angelic sigils associated with the Element of Water, plus other Water-corresponding symbols drawn on the reverse side. At the height of the invocations to the An-

Fig. III-3. Section of Circle for Drawing Nichsa into the Crystal

gels of Water, the King, Ruler, and associated Archangel, I asked that rains come to wash the burning flames and restore the hearts of those involved. I unsealed the rainwater gathered from last year and poured it into my consecrated chalice.

Scryer's Experience

SCRYER: The Water realm was so different compared with the Fire Elemental plane. Fire was so energetic, so noisy and quick, and everything passed very quickly. This experience was so different than that. What was interesting when I first stepped through the Water Tattwa portal was it began looking like a bowl way before you mentioned it, that image was already coming to me and looking like that and I sped over and through that image, over the top and into water.

The very next thing I recall was feeling like being in my mother's womb again. It felt like I was floating in embryonic fluid...that was the feeling throughout the midst of this: A calm loving, moving, presence but that could shift really quickly and adapt into so many different forms, to whatever was needed. In fact at this point, the word adaptation, adaptation, adaptation kept repeating in my mind.

When you invoked the guide to lead me through this experience, it felt like someone was holding my hand and I felt that my blood was flowing from their hand to mine. Things then went black for a moment, but when my vision returned I looked down at my hand and all I could see was ocean, but there was light coming from everywhere. At first it was really disorienting since I couldn't tell which direction was up. I then looked to who was holding my hand and noticed it was a woman. I first noticed her hand, and...her skin was shimmering and moving...When she would breathe in, all of her body would go from flesh to scales, and it shimmered all over her body as if she was breathing in through every pore, pulling everything in, and then the scales would flatten back into regular looking human skin, and she would exhale. It was so amazing to witness, and I just became captivated by looking at her. She felt so comforting. She was so kind so very kind and curious, really, curious, and was never not touching me throughout the entire experience. It seemed like she wanted to just feel me and look at me as if I was the most interesting thing she had ever seen. It's funny because I was completely fascinated watching her; watching her breathe and watching how she moved and looked back at me. She was studying me so intently, looking at my hair and face, looking just as interested in me as I was in her. It was like seeing a child study something fascinating. She seemed so much like a child, just like a child looking at me, that was incredible...Time seemed to stop while we were looking at each other, floating in this endless sea of light and comfort.

Some time after, we began moving, a gentle floating current...I was holding on to her hair which was incredibly long; it was twice as long as she was. We were flowing through endless water till we came to point where it looked like the water suddenly stopped and formed into a wall. We both stepped through this wall into a vast open space which looked like an enormous stone basin but where you couldn't see any structure, just thousands of waterfalls cascading far down to this where there was a giant whirlpool churning at the bottom. I remember being in awe hearing the roar of the multitude of waterfalls, feeling the cool mist on my face and breathing in the fresh spray and it felt so good. It felt so good that I remember thinking to myself that I didn't want to leave this place.

The next thing I recall was hearing you invoke the Water Elemental King, Nichsa, and as I looked up and I could see from rise up where I was standing on the edge of all of those waterfalls, that even more cascaded in from all around. It was if I suddenly was looking at all the water on the planet. I then saw this enormous figure in the midst of all that water, and it was somehow moving toward him and away from him at the same time. This magnanimous being looked immensely powerful and stood proud like a king. He stood in the midst of a massive column of Water, and I couldn't understand where it was all going or coming from. I then saw it was following at and from the center of his huge torso as if he were somehow absorbing it all and sending it all back out again. The power of it was completely overwhelming; there was just so much Water. As I was looking up at him, I noticed there were three other Kings, sitting and looking in other directions behind him, but I could barely make them out from where I stood. However, I knew that these were the Kings of Earth, Air, and Fire, and they all together seemed like four legs of a throne.

When you began reading the Prayer of the Undines, I felt this intense need to call out to them and repeat them aloud to the king. I remember your voice and it felt like the intention was so perfect. It was not just the words, it was your intention and message; you had so much reverence in what you were saying, along with humility and real respect. From where I stood, a feeling washed over me that it just really needed to be said.

After that point, though, things quieted down and the Water Elemental King stood and gazed down at me while remaining still and unspeaking. It felt as if he was waiting for something, and I became rather nervous as the moments passed by and nothing happened. I began thinking that I may have done or said something wrong or forgot to do or say something. Then my guide said, «I will add my voice to his,» and as soon as she said that, it felt like things just opened up like a floodgate. It felt like my guide needed to say those words, that she needed to match her voice with mine, for things to continue. And the response from the Elemental King was a nod of recognition, as if to say, «That was what I was waiting for.»

I then began to dialog with him, repeating your questions and requests for rains to help with the severe drought and dangerous fires. When you began asking and petitioning the Water Elemental King to assist us with the fires, his face took on a very serious expression.

He replied, «When you ask this of me, you must know that you cannot ask just for men. You ask for the worms, trees, moss, bacteria, birds, everything. You are assuming you speak for the needs of all. In fact, you were created to *be* the voice for all created life, but this tremendous gift and responsibility have been lost on humanity, and that is a major reason why so many things are out of balance. You do realize you two are introducing a tremendous amount of imbalance which is not easily reversed, and that you are injecting these forces into the fabric of life that will have consequences by altering all these things?»

There was a very clear feeling and realization of the immense responsibility and severity of our actions. I felt really small, *really* small. I had the sense that I had no real conception as to the power that was truly in play here and our actual part in it. All of a sudden I felt out of my league, I felt like a fool. It wasn't that the Elemental King was being mean, cruel, or condescending, but he was being very clear and made sure I understood the weight of what we were asking.

He continued by saying, «All these things function together and you need to take your place in creation by speaking for other forms of life. When you speak for other forms of life and consider the needs of all, your needs will be met, because that's what you were created for. When you fulfill that role, you will be taken care of. You were created for a great purpose, you just need to fulfill it.»

The massive King seemed to regard me intently, his expression impossible to read, but I got a sense that he knew me on the deepest of levels. He spoke again to drive home his point.

«For those of you who do have this consciousness, you have to use it responsibly and to the benefit of others. Most people do not. Most people are not yet able to see beyond the surface of things and that is okay. That's where they are. But if you are...you are responsible for doing something with it. Your awareness is used for the service of others. For those of you who reach a place of consciousness where you are aware of us and the role you play, you must act accordingly, you now have a responsibility to be mindful.»

I felt a tremendous responsibility and also that I needed to do so much more beyond what I had currently been doing up to that point. I didn't get a sense that he disliked human beings, but that he hoped we would fulfill our purpose and become actively aware of the important role that we played.

I asked more about his power and nature and he spoke again of the Waters: He said the movement of Water was the blood of the Earth, its cycles and circulations doing much more to nourish the land and its many life forms. The Waters are the connecting agent to all matter, and he could feel all through it.

He said, «Water is conscious. I can see through it, I can hear it, I can feel through it wherever it is.»

I was somehow able to feel myself passing through the cycles of great bodies of water in an instant, to the great underground rivers, to the deepest ocean, to minute points of dew, and vapor rising up to form massive thunderheads in the sky. I literally felt how the water flows from the mountain down to the lands below, and I was part of the process. Right after this image, I got the feeling of being in this huge anvil-shaped cloud,

Fig. III-4. ***Portrait of Nichsa as beheld in Vision***

miles and miles across, as if an entire continent was formed of cloud. I saw below me the fires that had us so worried. I knew instantly that to this power I was in, the fires were nothing, to this tremendous force and power and movement of massive Water: it could put out the flames as if they were embers in a whirlpool.

The experience left me disoriented but feeling empowered at the same time. I then asked King Nichsa about harnessing the magic of Water.

He said, «When you are making the incantations for Water, or doing any magic involving Water, feel the blood flowing through your body and I will be there.»

Directly after he spoke these words, I could feel the blood flowing and pulsing through my veins and all the physical sensations of the blood inside my body. This sensation took me aback but was also quite interesting.

The conversation and experience of talking to the great Elemental Ruler of Water were overwhelming and humbling to say the very least. I inquired a bit further of how I could harness my gifts and live my life more adequately. The king's response seemed to center around love, and that if I wanted to achieve something individually, I had to make a point to be to be as open and loving to everyone I met. If I sincerely chose to remain openhearted and treat all who I encountered with sincere compassion, I would be able to release blockages that had been constructed over time. It wasn't until he spoke those words that I realized how much I had built up walls, and closed myself off from others. I had closed them off from my real feelings and awareness. It honestly felt wonderful to suddenly feel connected again, as if certain internal walls were breaking down the dams of the heart, releasing the floodgates. The King of Water was saying that when people give and take care of each other, when they help each other like this, that it brings the rains.

He seemed to reflect on this and continued, saying, «Most people are not even aware of this concept, that such things could ever be connected. Some are even doing the work and are not aware that their choices are benefiting more than just those around them. Be aware of the flow and connection to all. Feel the flow; adapt; try not to hold on to a particular way of life so hard. Adapt. Pain comes from those who remove themselves from the ebb and flow of creation.»

I reflected on the immense importance of the King's words before thanking him for his guidance and council, and I returned through the

> wall of Water as if we faded back into an enclosure of peace and tranquility. After I went back behind the wall, everything faded and my guide and I were again floating, and it was blissful, calm, and wonderful as if being in my mother's womb again. My guide continued to look upon me with interest and attentiveness and was right there with me, our blood merging and pulsing and flowing back and forth. I floated with her a while longer as we moved back the way we had come.
>
> I reached the Water Elemental Tattwa portal as before, starting to move nearer and back through, however, my guide didn't come with me. She came right to the doorway with me and said, «I am always with you, I am in your blood, all the time.»

After the working was concluded, we spent some time speaking inside the magical circle. There were many remarks on the immense complexity and detail to this particular experiment. The detail and imagery that was related was quite remarkable.

In reflection, my scryer also commented that "The more we do this, the differences between the planes stand out even more. The contrast becomes apparent."

After I brought my scryer back from the Water Elemental plane and back through the Tattwa doorway, I had him ascend to a celestial realm of Sachiel/Zadkiel/Jupiter as soon as the Jupiter hour came upon us. I guided my magical partner using the same Astral projection formula I used for going through the Tattwas, only this time I had him travel out through the sky into the heavens and darkness of space, surrounded by the stars of the cosmos. I directed him to move toward the light of Jupiter and eventually envision a royal blue door, with gold trim, having symbols and sigils of Jupiter.

At this time I intoned a prayer to Jupiter saying:

Oh, salutary and benevolent Zadkiel who are covered with honors and who are pleased to distribute wealth and bounty with a liberal hand, open your abode to us by the prayer I am making to you at this hour through your well-loved and favorite Maaguth, Gutriz, Sachiel, Suth, and give my venture a happy outcome so that we may render glory unto you!

I then chanted a Secret Invocation learned from the Jovial Angel himself.

When I directed my scryer through this door, he was to meet the embodiment of the Archangel Tzadkiel as expressed through the Archetype of Jupiter/

Zeus. I again let this experience unfold without direction till I felt it was time to end the experiment.

Scryer's Experience:

SCRYER: Then when we went up, and when I saw the doorway I was breathless. The doorway was amazing! It looked Babylonian to me, decorated with those lions with the male heads and the wings and braids. All was covered with gold and lapis lazuli, colored royal blue. I gazed upon it, and it seemed so amazingly old. It was ancient, past anything of memory. However, the door was flawless and perfectly crafted. It somehow appeared like wood and lapis at the same time and was unlike anything I've ever seen before. I saw the symbol of Jupiter clearly near the top, and then when the doors began to open a light came through that was at first blinding.

When the doors were fully opened, I found I was already kneeling. I felt this enormous presence of complete power and royalty. I mean my knee literally went to the ground on its own. When I finally lifted my gaze, the first thing I saw was his feet. They had sandals on which also seemed, very Babylonian in style. I'm not sure if it fits in with lore or tradition, but when I finally gazed up at the image of this being, I felt I beheld the true forms of Zeus, Jupiter, Marduk, which were archetypes, or just all layers, masks of him, and I was in awe. He was the defining image of sovereignty: very kingly, and also happy.

He looked to be almost a perfect mix of Babylonian and Greek imagery with a beard that came down to his chest in tightly curled braids, which ended with gold rings on the bottom of each one. Not a hair was out of place; all was very perfectly manicured. He appeared tall, healthy, and robust, with a distinct sparkle in his eye. He was wearing a white tunic, with knee length white bottoms, all trimmed in that classic Greek box-spiral pattern. His hair was thick, dark brown, and was tied back coming straight down to his back.

It was just amazing to behold a being that was so immensely powerful but lighthearted. His demeanor was confident and welcoming as if to say to me, «Come on in!» I truly hadn't expected this at all. As I moved into his great hall and gazed upon him, I had an instant realization that this was the fountainhead of civilization. I somehow knew that so much of what we've become as human beings, the fact that we build cities, that we began making roads, came from here! That so much of our accomplish-

> ments in civilization somehow extended through him, was inspired by him. It was amazing to be in the midst of this realization, in front of him, in front of the source.
>
> I felt somewhat ridiculous in his presence, but he smiled at me warmly and seemed to regard me with interest. I began again speaking of our need for rain and water to help quench the fires and droughts. He immediately smiled and said not to worry so much about it. He actually suggested that we have some laughter about it, and a little bit more of a carefree attitude, and it would work itself out. He then rose up from a mighty throne and began to walk confidently around it, gliding his hands along it as if it were a habit formed out of thousands of years. He said that the more people worry and fret over a matter, the more it would create more difficulty and strife. It was refreshing to be there...it feels like it invokes that in you...that he calls that part of him that is in you, as if «you can handle it,» as if to say, «Part of me is in you; invoke that and you'll be fine!»
>
> When I asked him if there was something we could do further to bring the rain storms he showed me an image of a silver cup or bowl filled with water that had a bit of the mountain rock submerged. The mountain granite was completely immersed in water.

When it felt time, I directed my scryer to thank the mighty being and depart back through the Astral doorway of Jupiter and descend back down into the magical chamber. When I brought him out of the experience, he was exuberant but also had a look of awe on his face.

Benn remarked that there was "such an amazingly powerful presence...when the door opened..it was like, wow! Like walking into a person's life you've respected all your life like a celebrity. When the experience ended, the message was, «Heed the balance. Bring all these intentions you've heard back with you. Everything will be okay...*You two need to start taking your place in creation.*»"

The image that the Jupiter Spirit showed to my scryer was one I had received almost exactly during a previous night's meditation. In the vision I had, I also saw a drawn or printed map of the afflicted area with sigils relating to Water and Sachiel written on the back. I was thoroughly excited to see such a similarity between our two experiences and figured that the images were an important method for bringing the rains we so desperately needed.

I recited a final prayer and also asked the powers of Tzadkiel to bring rain storms. I closed the ceremonial space and grabbed one of the silver bowls I used in the ceremony for the altar space. I filled the bowl with water from a sink then returned to the magical chamber. Then taking a silver bowl I had I also took out the map and granite stone I had in one of my boxes from a hike years ago. Next, I removed a sealed glass vial in which I had collected rainwater during a magical working the previous year. As I poured the rainwater over the map and then submerged it in the silver bucket of water, I placed the stone directly on the center of the map to keep it submerged.

Rains arrived the following day and actually showered the exact spot of the fire. Rains of increasing strength fell each consecutive day afterward.

The experience was incredible, and my scryer talked for more than half an hour after coming out of his vision trance, recounting everything he and I had experienced. My excitement with his relation was that he described the beings he witnessed in great detail that perfectly matched what I had witnessed. Also, he is not well-versed or knowledgeable about Spirits and archetypes in western ceremonial magic, so it was fascinating to hear such correlation from one who did not have built-up images and expectations.

The following autumn, approximately a month and a half after the Water Elemental experience, a cold front crept slowly over the entire area my map represented and collided with the warm and moist monsoonal air from the south. With my area experiencing such intense drought and fires previously, the land was unable to handle the enormous amount of water it received all at once. The flood waters spanned a range of almost two hundred miles from north to south, and that spread through seventeen counties. At least eight deaths were reported, with two more missing and presumed dead and hundreds remaining unaccounted for. More than 11,000 people were evacuated. When the rains came and the floods began stripping things away, and when a mountain town nearly washed away, I witnessed the powerful and devastating force of water. I realized that I had not properly gauged the magnitude of what the Elemental King of Water and Tzadkiel had warned.

After witnessing the continual flooding, I wondered just how much of the responsibility might have been ours. Sure, many people had been praying for rain and perhaps other magicians had done what they could to call the rains. I dreaded to think such devastation could be placed squarely in our hands. The Astral experience my scryer and best friend was recounting was spectacular, but how much bearing and impact could it truly have on the physical world? These were events the magnitude of which I had never before considered.

Elemental Air Experience

For reasons which only revealed themselves much later in my magical career, I was always drawn to the archetypical phenomena associated with the Element of Air. I had an absolute love of storms, lightning, the sound of thunder, and the energy it created. I also enjoyed feeling the rushing mountain winds on my face and would become very uncomfortable in areas of the world that had no moving air.

The Air Elemental dagger was the third of the four Elemental weapons I completed. I settled on the Air implement being a dagger or sword, although magically it equally had Fire qualities. The dagger had direct correspondences to the Air Element for me as in the Tarot. The mind and intellect with the swiftness of thought could pierce any haze. A realization beginning in the unmanifest could cut like an icy mountaintop wind. The weapon not only slices through the murkiness of ignorance, but it also demands focus to be used without injuring one's self.

The design I settled on came from the inspiration of the same craftsperson that made my Fire wand. The shape was in a perfect *avis* ("bird") form. The guard made up the front part of a bird with its wings spread wide on either side. The pommel was gold-plated bronze, the tail feathers fanning out. For this implement, I commissioned that the blade be etched with several wind-patterned symbols. I also wanted the All-Seeing Eye as an absolute divine force, giving recognition to the intellect of Air. Purple amethyst and gold citrine cabochons were added. The dagger came with its own handle, but I felt I needed to personalize the piece more, and carved a handle myself.

I could say that the ritualized consecration for this implement was done in two parts. The first consisted of driving up to one of the higher mountains in my area to a secluded aspen grove. I wanted to find an aspen tree with particular properties that I felt would endow the Elemental weapon with powerful Air correspondences. I spent time asking the Spirits of the forest and trees directly if I could use one of the younger trees to fashion my handle in exchange for an offering. I took my time selecting and considering several of the young aspens, using my intuition, and passed up several trees that looked ideal but did not feel appropriate to cut down. Finally, I spotted one young tree in the midst of towering adults which seemed to beckon me closer. I arranged an altar in front of the young aspen, and brought forth offerings of honey and milk and spring water, as well as mastic incense to burn in a small brazier.

After meditating a while on the tree, attempting to connect with this aspect of life, its sensations in the Earth, reaching up to the sky where the topmost leaves danced in the continual breeze and seemed to touch the blue of the sky just beyond, I asked permission to take this particular tree from the clearing. The sapling continued to sway as the other surrounding large aspens remained still. I withdrew a long sword that I reserved for magical purposes. In the traditional fashion of making wands and other wooden tools of magic, I wanted to make one swift, clean, and powerful stroke to sever the sapling. I stood in front of the tree, which was about the thickness of the handle of a baseball bat.

I recited the prayer of the Sylphs along with a personalized prayer to the trees of the mountain and asked that the tree be filled with the most potent aspects of Air, and that all its interaction and play with the sky would come into the tree and reside there. I raised my sword and made a very swift and precise diagonal cut near the base. The sword passed completely through the aspen with ease, and I quickly retrieved the tree before it fell over to the ground. The action might sound amazing, but interaction of the leaves with those of the neighboring trees slow the descent of the lightweight young trunk.

At last I had the wood for my handle, but I would have to let it dry for some time before carving it and making it the hilt of my dagger.

I had more than enough wood in the young sapling for the handle and I did not want to waste any of the excess so I decided to try my hand at carving another Air magical implement in the form of a caduceus. I'd never whittled or carved anything of note, but I always wanted a staff of Hermes and this seemed like an ideal opportunity to try. I bought a new whittling knife and got to work one afternoon. I worked for hours and the piece seemed to come alive in my hand. I attached a Herkimer diamond and birth feathers below in the shape of wings. I showed a few magical friends my creation and everyone seemed impressed by the work. I've kept the item in my possession ever since and use it for both Air Elemental magic as well as Mercury and Raphael Planetary evocations.

I started the work on my dagger hilt on a Wednesday morning and it took me several hours to complete. Drilling and shaping the central hole for the tang of the blade was the most challenging aspect. I engraved the traditional Golden Dawn Angelic and sacred sigils into the handle, along with the names in ancient Hebrew. The handle was painted a bright canary yellow and the sigils and words a bright purple. I also ordered some fine blue topaz gems in diamond shapes and embedded them in the handle. I also made a matching wooden sheath which I painted the same colors and on which I engraved alchemical Air sigils as well. I was very pleased with the product as it represented my ideal Air dagger and the essence of the handle could be felt and added to the effect of the implement.

For the full consecration of the Air dagger, I chose a Wednesday morning during a favorable aspect of Mercury. The setting would be on top of a mountain summit I had hiked many times before and over which I had always felt the winds come sweeping. I had experienced a couple of great thunderstorms from that place as well and reasoned it to be a perfect location. The eastern face of the mountain looked over the whole city and the rising sun would be a spectacular view from this place. It also had parts that were covered enough with foliage that I would not likely be seen even if someone else decided to hike here to see the sunrise in the middle of the week. I decided to be a bit creative in the magical setup for this ceremony and wanted both the Air dagger and the Air altar to be suspended between trees for the consecration.

For the Air altar to mimic the aspects of the Element as much as it was able, I surmised it should be surrounded by Air as much as possible. This approach had seemed to work well for the Water chalice, so a suspended Air altar seemed appropriate for the Air dagger. I decided I wanted the dagger itself to be suspended with strands of silk ribbon between trees that were near each other on the eastern end of the mountain summit. The altar I designed for this consecration was a round wooden disk with four eye screws or eye bolts at the quarters. I planned to set the incense and necessary items for the consecration on the suspended table, and the Air dagger suspended just above the altar.

I had everything packed in a carry satchel about four hours before dawn. I had woken up, taken a ritual shower saying prayers of intent and consecration and hopped in my car toward the mountains. I arrived at the base of the trail leading up the mountain and grabbed my pack of supplies. Something about being out in the mountains and wilderness at night with magical intent always filled me with excitement. The hike was quiet but a bit slower as the satchel of ritual equipment became cumbersome and I was breathing hard and sweating quite profusely when I finally arrived at the summit.

Everything on the mountaintop was still with only a slight predawn breeze blowing just enough to cool me. I spent some time hunting around for the spot I thought would work. Finally, I spotted a nice clearing between trees and scrub oak I knew would work perfectly. The area overlooked the entire city below from the eastern part of the mountain.

I set down my pack and began taking out items. I positioned the circular wooden disk of the altar first about three feet off the ground. It took me longer than I expected to get it right, but I threaded yellow string through the eye bolts and attached them to the two main trees, and the other to two scrub oaks to the front and sides of the trees.

The setup wasn't quite as I had planned and it was difficult to get the altar even and steady in the near dark of the predawn. I felt a bit anxious as I hurried to set everything up so I wouldn't miss the rising of the sun and the first hour. I carefully took my newly fashioned Air dagger from its sheath and tied the yellow silk ribbons around the hilt and around the section of the tree trunks about a foot above the suspended Air altar. I wove a sort of wreath out of flowers, pine boughs, and feathers I had collected and brought with me for this ritual to attach to the strands of silk as a last-moment bit of inspirational decor.

As soon as the dagger and altar were tied securely between the trees and scrub oak, the morning breeze began to pick up and I could make out the steely gray color of the sky as the sun was beginning to make its way to the eastern horizon. A circle was carved out in the dirt in front of the altar which was moving and swaying much more than I had imagined. The Air dagger itself was making little twirling and swaying motions as the wind continued to grow in strength. I arranged a small incense burner and placed a measure of galbanum, lavender, mastic gum, and benzoin on a lit charcoal.

As the first yellow rays of the sun streaked across the sky in the east, I began with the rituals for Opening by Watchtower, followed by a declaration for the Spirits and Angels of Air to attend upon my ritual. I leaned forward, picking up the Air dagger in my hands as I invoked the sacred names from the Opening by Watchtowers as well as each of the Elemental Angelic rulers as they were given. When it was ended, I slowly allowed the dagger to dangle once more from the silk ribbons keeping it floating between the two pines which looked like dark sentinel pillars framing the rising sun.

For the second part of the consecration ritual, I performed the invocations and names, recited the Prayer to the Sylphs, followed by a poem I devised which consisted of my personal affinity and love for winds, and storms, moving air and the freedom of flight and quickness of thoughts. The sun was beginning to rise and everything was coming into clear view. The morning winds steadied and everything was peaceful and serene.

The Air dagger unexpectedly stopped spinning and swinging in the breeze and reflected brightly from the morning sun as it held its position at an angle from me. I had a sense that my invocation had been acknowledged and that the summoned Elemental had arrived. The incense on the suspended altar table which a moment ago had simply dispersed in the growing breeze now sent tendrils of smoke in a straight line up toward the dagger and enveloped it. I could clearly see an anthropomorphic shape form from the incense clouds as if a humanoid stood just behind the suspended dagger and regarded me. It was truly an awesome and unexpected sight and I stared at it for several moments.

The morning light continued to reflect off the blade of the dagger and the rising incense was somehow able to recreate its outline of a humanlike figure which moved and shifted. I spoke a formal greeting to the Air Elemental and recall having a very pleased smile on my face as I did so. I requested that the suspended implement be filled with the magical correspondences of its kingdom and Element and that it resonate to the frequency that the Elementals of Air would respond and recognize instantly. I stated that it was my desire for the dagger to be able to call forth Spirits and beings of the Air when I desired and endow me with all of the positive aspects of the Elemental kingdom whenever I held it in my hands. I paused for a moment extending my senses of the Elemental's intent. I then continued to ask that the dagger be able to beckon forth wind and storms as well as be able to divide the energies of aerial beings which posed a threat. I spoke from my heart and my desire for it to connect with the physical object I had personalized. I wanted this particular weapon to guide, draw and cut energies equally with the Elemental aspects of Air, intellect, and electricity.

I bowed deeply placing my hand across my chest and spoke a heartfelt appreciation for the experience. I closed the ceremony in the fashion of Opening by Watchtower and rubbed out the circle in the sand. The Air dagger was spinning steadily when I went to retrieve it and as soon as I placed my fingers around it, I felt an almost electrified current within it. A gentle breeze rose up, cooling my skin that had heated with the excitement of the operation. The odd but meaningful occurrence stopped as soon as it had come leaving me grinning broadly at the consecrated implement I held in my hand. I had always wanted one of these.

Traveling the Elemental Plane of Air

For the Air Elemental Astral voyage with my scryer, I selected a Wednesday in the summer following more long rains, storms, and floods that had arrived late in spring. I constructed the ceremony indoors like the previous two operations, using my magic circle from my DSIC experiments. The scryer's chair was placed in the east end of the circle facing the east. Behind the chair, the small altar held my magician's wand and dagger and a small vial of Air anointing oil. The small Tattwa card of Vayu sat next to my primary magician's implements. In the blank area on the circle reserved for the Spirit's name and sigil, I placed parchment drawings of alchemical and classical symbols for the Element of Air as well as the angels, ruler, king, and Spirits associated with the Element. Just beyond the magic circle in the east I placed an altar table.

The altar was covered with a bright sky blue silk cloth and other objects corresponding to Air magic and workings which I felt already resonated with the appropriate energies. My personalized Air altar tablet created the backdrop to the altar. The Vayu Tattwa card was two feet square. The card was done on a background photograph of the sky with clouds. The bright blue circle and orange square was pasted in the center and immediately drew the eye. As with the previous two, the large card was placed against the face of the antique mirror that I used for scrying.

Ritual items for this experiment:

1. Ritual magician's wand and dagger.
2. Consecrated Air dagger.
3. Two altars: One for inside the circle, one for outside as the main Air altar. Sky blue altar cloths for each. Air altar tablet in the Golden Dawn system.
4. Consecrated Air Oil: Olive oil, benzoin, clary sage, eucalyptus, lavender, lemon balm, star anise, and hyssop.
5. Four blue and yellow candles preferably beeswax with tin or glass candleholders/candlesticks.
6. Brazier, charcoal, and lighter.
7. Optional: Agate, diamond, yellow or blue topaz, serpentine stones; feathers, bird or eagle statues.
8. Air Elemental plane incense: Galbanum, storax, lavender, lemongrass, mace, mastic, cloves, marjoram, white sandalwood, gum mace, cloves, storax, lemon peel, benzoin.

Hypnotic Induction of Scryer while staring at Tattwa

Before beginning with the vocal invocations of the ceremony I again went around and lit the charcoal for the incense, as well as the candles while recit-

Fig. III-5. Section of Circle for Drawing Paralda into the Crystal

ing a grimoric consecration blessing. When the charcoal was ready, I poured a fair amount of incense mixture on the coals from a container on the altar and observed as the clouds of perfume billowed upward. After everything was lit and prepared, I reentered the circle and walked around it clockwise blessing the working space saying,

In the name of the blessed Trinity, I consecrate this piece of ground for our defense; so that no evil Spirit may have power to break these bounds prescribed here, through Jesus Christ our Lord. Amen.

I then picked up the smaller Tattwa card from my altar within the circle and gave it to my friend in the chair. I instructed him to gaze and focus on the card while relaxing. By this time, my scryer was accustomed to the ritual and entered very quickly into a trance as he stared at the card. I picked up my consecrated Air dagger and made an equilateral cross right over his head. I once again walked around behind him in the center of the magic circle, placed my Air dagger on the altar, and retrieved my dagger and retrieved my magician's wand.

With three taps on the small altar, I began the first part of Opening By Watchtower. I stated powerfully: "HEKAS, HEKAS, ESTE BEBELOI!" I then used my dagger to perform the Banishing Rituals of the Pentagram and the Hexagram. I then set my wand and dagger back down on the altar and picked up my Air dagger, this time with the intention of opening the door to the Astral plane of Air. Walking clockwise, I moved directly in front of the Air altar and made three striking swirling motions in front of it in the shape of a circle. I then held the Air dagger above my head and walked clockwise around the inside of the circle, saying, "Such a Fire existeth, extending through the rushing of Air. Or even a Fire formless, whence cometh the image of a voice. Or even a flashing light, abounding, revolving, whirling forth, crying aloud!"

When I returned to the east of the circle, I once again made the three slashing motions with the wand forming a circle or spiral in front of the Air altar. Afterwards I traced out a large circle in front of the altar and Tattwa, then an invoking Pentagram of Air within it, then the Air Kerub (sign of Aquarius) in the center, saying: "ORO IBAH AOZPI.[9] In the names and letters of the Great Eastern Quadrangle, I invoke ye, ye Angels of the Watchtower of the East."

The air about us seemed to take on an electrical static nature and directed him to stare straight ahead at the large blue circle on the Tattwa card. I again used the hypnotic methods as before to guide him through the Tattwa symbol as an Astral doorway. When my intuition told me he had succeeded in this, I chanted the Divine name Shaddai el Chai, followed by the names of the Archangel, Raphael, and Angel, Chassan.

After I did this, I assisted further saying, "Allow your senses to be completely aware of your surroundings, being able to see, hear, feel and interact with your environment in this new plane of existence. As you explore, images and perceptions will become sharper and you will easily recall and remember every detail upon returning to this plane."

After a moment of allowing his Astral senses to adjust, I again focused on using my magician's voice and said the Prayer of the Sylphs:

Spirit of Light, Spirit of Wisdom, whose breath gives and takes away the form of all things; Thou before whom the life of every being is a shadow which transforms and a vapor which passes away; Thou who ascendeth upon the clouds and dost fly upon the wings of the wind; Thou who breathest out and limitless immensities are peopled; Thou who breathest in and all which came forth from Thee unto Thee returneth. Endless Movement in Eternal Stability, be Thou blessed forever! We praise Thee and we bless Thee in the fleeting empire of created light, of shadows, of reflections, and images, and we aspire without ceasing towards Thine immutable and imperishable splendour. May the ray of Thine Intelligence and the warmth of Thy Love descend upon us. Then what is volatile shall be fixed, the shadow shall become a body, the Spirit of Air shall receive a soul, and the dream shall be a thought. We shall be swept away no more before the tempest, but shall bridle the winged steeds of the morning, and guide the course of the evening winds that may flee into Thy presence. O Spirit of Spirits, O Eternal Soul of Souls, O Imperishable Breath of Life, O Creative Sigh, O Mouth which dost breathe forth and withdraw the life of all beings in the ebb and flow of Thine eternal speech, which is the Divine Ocean of Movement and of Truth! Amen.

---

9. Pronounced *oh-roh ee-bah-hay ah-oh-zohd-pee.*

Scryer's Experience:

SCRYER: In contrast to Water, which was such an emotional experience, this was clear and direct. Very clear, very instructive is the best way to put it. The experience and messages were rather straightforward but of a multitude. The experience of entering through this Tattwa was totally different as well. It was sort of disorienting but interesting at the same time. Instead of going through the central circle, when the Tattwa expanded, the space around it expanded and the circle got smaller. When I reached toward the circle, it became even smaller to the size of a small point, then it opened really quickly, I went through then it shut again behind me. The sensation of going through this Tattwa was expansiveness coming out then stepping through it really quickly and then a sphere closed around me.

After I felt myself first stepped through, I got the sense of being extremely high up. I felt as if I were way up above the clouds. It was incredibly expansive as if there was no end to it whatsoever. At times through the entire experience, I was able to see clouds move by and then sometimes I would see leaves flying through the air. It was difficult at first since I was unsure of where to rest my awareness or attention. Everything looked like endless air all around me. I wasn't sure what I should be looking at since all about me was this endless expanse.

Then I heard you invoke the Elemental guide. I couldn't see anything or anyone at first but shortly after I heard a male voice. I couldn't see where it was coming from and couldn't place even a direction to its source. I asked if it could put some form to itself because it was hard for me to know where or how to communicate with him. The being complied and all of a sudden there was this falcon before me.

The voice of the Spirit returned and was very clear about the fact that the being of the falcon wasn't him. He said, «I am just picking a form that you can understand but know this is not what I look like.» The Spirit did indeed sound male though.

I recall seeing thunderheads and clouds, but they were those types of clouds that get blown into very smooth shapes, elongated, but without billowing or rough edges...stratus clouds.

During the beginning of the journey, I remember saying, "Wow this is just really different!"

The Spirit replied, «That's the point! That's what Air is. It needs to be open and clear and all about possibility and potential. It needs to be empty, free and open, because it contains the intention of all creation, the dream of creation, the design, and also where it's headed.» There was an Element of pride in the voice of this Elemental. To me its inflection seemed to convey that «Air is sort of the best Element.» However, it also did say, «Earth has its own power, Earth is the exception.» His view of Fire and Water was that they (Spirits of Air) direct where those Elements go because it's something directly from the 'dream of creation', and began with the intention of Air. It was really interesting to hear of his views on the Element of Earth. There was a lot of respect but also a sense of it being foreign or possibly disturbing to him.

As our conversation and the experience continued, it became rather difficult because it felt like so much information was coming in at me all at once. There wasn't so much going on visually as compared to the Fire realm experience but there was much more potentiality and raw information as well as ideas that it became difficult to know what to focus on or remember. I recall thinking that I really needed to focus on something or I was going to lose all sense of focus or direction. There was so much to take in; I had to figure out what I truly wanted to learn from this experience. I tried to focus on what I wanted to ask and focus on. When I voiced this concern to the Air Elemental guide, the Spirit said, «There is a lot here; what do you want to know? Simply let me know of your intention and we can work from there.»

I asked him how we could clear our minds and be open and also how we could see, hear, and converse with Spirits better.

The Elemental guide replied saying, «Okay, those are two different questions with a common source but I would have to address each differently. As for clearing the mind and seeing Spirits, Meditation is the key for both.» The Spirit continued stating, «To achieve these abilities you have to clean things out. You have to be completely open like this space you're in, totally open to perceive things without expectation of results.»

Next the guide said, «Okay, you need to remember this: Clear statement of intent. Open to instruction with faith in potential.» The Elemental had me repeat this phrase again and again until I had it correct. It made sure that I remembered it word for word.

Periodically the Elemental guide would disappear once and I would say, "Whoa, where did you go? I'm just hearing your voice now."

He then would say something like, «Oh, yes, I forgot that you need this,» and immediately appear as the falcon again. It seemed almost like it was a distraction for him to maintain a visible form.

The guide went on to instruct that beginning with proper intention was paramount for achieving not only the desires I expressed but nearly everything as well. «For improving the ability to hear Spirits better it should begin with a perfectly open and clear space of meditation,» the Elemental instructed. «Intention begins everything, it is like the wind that blows the storm to you, the wind is what pushes it there. So after you've made a clear space, set a pure and direct intention of ‹I wish to hear, see, or communicate with Spirits better.›» The guide said that to hear Spirits clearer, you need to practice remaining open to whatever way they chose to communicate with you. To not have a preconceived notion of how they were going to communicate. He said, «You have to let them communicate to you on their own level. Whether through words, omens, or signs, are open to instruction of how they prefer to communicate to you. Not having a preconceived belief of how this is supposed to take place.»

Then you invoked Raphael, and suddenly we were moving *very* fast. I felt like I was taken in the wake of this enormously powerful and swift being and as we were rushing along, all of these beings were being drawn along behind him. To me it seemed sudden, almost violent and chaotic as we flew through the air at top speed. The Elemental guide however seemed rather nonchalant about it, and said something along the lines of «Oh, so he's here now and we are following him.» It seemed perfectly normal for him, not disturbing him in the least.

I was still caught off guard and said, "Whoa! Where are we going now?"

The Spirit replied for me to relax, just let it happen, and enjoy the experience. After this rushing and sudden experience, I found myself looking at very distinct and intense images of tornados, and witnessing them as they descended toward earth. They were devouring all in their path and moved with such force and determination. What the Spirit said to me next would be very difficult to relate to anyone who has ever experienced a tornado, lost a home or loved one in because it stated that these were all deliberate acts. The Elemental guide explained that none of the tornados were a random occurrence, but that they deliberately pick places to change, or lives to alter. The destruction or violent occurrence of a cyclone is a very deliberate choice. This is why when people wonder how a tornado destroys one home, misses another, and hits yet another on the other side, the reason is this intentional act which human beings do not quite comprehend. The Elemental alluded that there were very particular reasons why a place will get destroyed.

All I could reply with was, "Oh, okay, wow."

The Spirit said that this is «part of the unfolding of the dream.»

Shortly after viewing all this, we came upon an enormous tornado that eclipsed all the others I had just witnessed. This colossal tornado moved and seemed to face me directly and I could tell that it was obviously a powerful Spiritual being. It appeared alive and conscious and I was informed that this was Paralda, the Air Elemental King.

The massive, cyclonic Spirit was breathing in and breathing out. It revealed that it was breathing out the «dream of creation,» then breathing in the individual beings that were created along with the experiences they were having. All the experiences the beings contained was being breathed back in by the Elemental king and that breath was returning back to «the dreamer» to inform it. It was an endless cycle of giving forth and drawing back in. The Elemental king's every exhalation was based on the experiences these beings were having, giving forth, taking in, all this activity all this thought, all this intention, all these things that were being brought forth. Each cycle of breath was also an act of redirecting everything. I was in awe in seeing it all. There was so much activity, so much thought, intention, so many things going on all at once. My mind seemed really out of sorts as the experience of time and order of which things transpired seems all mixed together. There was all this thought, intention, ideas that were flowing through the king, continually being cycled, absorbed and then redirected.

The Air Elemental guide went on to explain that, «Air really likes to break through barriers. We really like to destroy orthodoxies. We don't like orthodoxies. Our nature is if we see something too codified, too stable, we like to go in and tear it apart, to break it open. That's the only way for things to breathe. It needs to have movement, that's the only way 'Spirit' can get in and out. If you are presented with something or if society tells you that something can only be done one way, you have to look at it and see if there is another way. Think, is there a better way? If you have something in your life that you feel is limiting you or you need to get rid

Fig. III-6. ***Portrait of Paralda as beheld in Vision***

of, you need to have the intention that ‹I don't want this, I'm ready to get rid of it,› put the intent that you want it removed.»

Time is really different there; it's somehow altered or out of order as I'm used to. It was all a bit confusing for me, I remember more than once thinking, "Where am I now and what am I doing?" I definitely feel different after this experience. I'm much more in my head, much clearer and able to think. Not like I was with the Water Realm experience, which was all about touch, emotion, and sensation. The Air Realm is much more direct and information-based. I admitted to the Air Elemental guide that I was having a hard time fitting everything together.

The Spirit reminded me, «Just remember what I told you: Statement of intent, open to instruction, and faith in potential. The faith in potential was the component which wrapped it around to the beginning again.» It said that, «you needed the faith that you have greater potential in order to make the intention in the first place and you would go full circle between those three things. The faith would lead you to another intention where you would be open to instruction and the faith in potential would make it all possible to happen.» The Spirit said if you had all those three things—a clear statement of intent, are open to instruction, and have faith in potential—that your desires would come to fruition.

The Spirit also mentioned that when learning through the Element of Air there is a lot coming in at once and you will be receiving a lot more than you are able to remember. However, the information will be unlocked and remembered when you need it. He said, «That is the faith of potential. You don't have to take it in all at once since some will initially be forgotten. It will return when it is needed.»

Toward the end of this journey there was this intensive expansive open feeling, like an endless sky. The guide imprinted upon me that the expansiveness represented the enormity of choice. Choice was found in this expanse and also the consequences of choice.

It's odd that much of my memory of the beginning now comes back to me toward the end of this relation. In the beginning, all I saw first was a sort of gray, silvery expanse; there was nothing really defining in it. Then I started to hear things first. I first heard a horn, this call of a horn, from really far away, but really strong. There were different sounds of wind in the leaves, voices, song, echoes, and lots of sound in the beginning. Sound seemed to be a major introductory part to the Element of Air. It was really amazing but difficult to put into a linear pattern of events, too.

When the Spirit talked about Air, he said, «I cannot comprehend Earth, you'll have to go somewhere else for those answers. We help the Earth to breathe but it has its own power which is not within my understanding.» When the Spirit was talking to me about the Earth Element, it showed me a vision of looking at the Earth from the outside; I could clearly see this layer of air on the outside, the atmosphere, but then there was this sphere of Earth beneath it, and things are locked and dark and still and quiet, completely stable. In some ways I got the feeling that this Air Spirit thought this concept made it uncomfortable. I found that rather amusing.

Afterthoughts on the Air Elemental Operation

Scryer and operator felt what was sensing, the air changed, the air got bigger, and the incense it felt really open and cool during the summer hour. When Archangel Raphael was invoked I felt a huge channel of air move quickly through the circle.

SCRYER: This was such a different experience, and I feel totally different after each time we do this. After traveling through this realm I remember how I felt when I was in college. I wanted to read books, I wanted to think about things, I wanted to get into debates. It's very Aquarian; no wonder Aquarius is an Air sign.

OPERATOR: The Aquarius sign is the sign in the opening pentagram.

SCRYER: That whole feeling pulls me in.

As with the previous two Elemental experiments, an interesting event occurred soon after the Astral voyage. A tornado appeared on the side of the highest mountain that overlooks my entire city. A rare, high-elevation funnel cloud was reported and photographed as well as videotaped. My scryer also saw it in person not three days after our working!

Photos of the distinct funnel cloud were captured near the 14,110-foot summit of the largest mountain in our area Saturday afternoon. There were several sightings reported of at least one funnel cloud over the mountains. Tornados on mountains are very rare and the occurrence happened only days after the experiment. Again, coincidence could have been at play, but I found the occurrence quite interesting if not auspicious indeed.

Elemental Earth Experience

The final Elemental implement I created was the Earth disk. As with the other three Elemental implements I wanted this one to symbolize the full power and authority of the Element it symbolized with as much corresponding materials as I could tastefully place into the object. First I wanted the combined material of wood and stone to create the main material of the Earth disk. I commissioned the aid of a talented wood whittler to help me create the main carvings which was a Celtic knotted style pentagram on one side and the tree of life hexagram or Star of David on the other. On both sides I set a blue colored stone with the ancient Celtic triskelion or triskele engraved on the stone. On one side the triskele was spiraling out to the counterclockwise direction, and on the opposite, it spiraled clockwise. On the side with the pentagram I engraved the Theban letters to spell "Earth." I also included the triangular images for the major directions. Five gems of peridot were fixed to the pentacle and six green jade stones were fixed to the hexagram side.

Around the outside of my Earth disk I inscribed an excerpt from a famous poem from the Celtic tradition which still has a lot of power and meaning for me. The poem is by Amergin or Amhairghin ("Birth of Song"), the famed bard of the Sons of Míl, who fought with the Tuatha Dé Danann (Celtic Gods or Færy race) for possession of Ireland. The inscription is the last few lines of *Amergin's Challenge*, a poem which had the power to control the Elements of the land and thus the storm that the Tuatha Dé Danann conjured to sink the ships of the Sons of Mil. The inscribed disk reads thus:

Am úagh gach uile dhóich dhíamaíní
Cía fios aige conara na gréine agus linn na éisce
Cía tionól na rinn aige, ceangladh na farraige,
cor i n-eagar na harda, na haibhne, na túatha.

Translated:

"I am the grave of every vain hope
Who knows the path of the Sun, the periods of the Moon,
Who gathers the divisions, enthralls the sea,
sets in order the mountains, the rivers, the peoples."

The poem states clearly the power of the Earth as expressed through poetic inspiration from the land. It states the finality and inevitability of the Earth's power to control and bring everything together.

My experiment for consecrating this Earth implement was planned to take place in the most "Earthy" place of which I could conceive, which was a cave, or in this case more of a tunnel. The man-made structure was about twenty feet high to the stone ceiling and about the same distance wide at the main entrance. It extended some hundred feet back and had an odd shape consisting of branch tunnels which appeared to be attempts to dig into the mountain further which had been abandoned for some unknown reason. The large cave, which had been used for mining trains, sat empty year round except for curious hikers, explorers, and sometimes transients who utilize it for shelter. I was a bit apprehensive about using this location, as it always had a rather eerie feel about it and any manner of animal or person could stumble upon me even in the middle of the night, which was when I planned to do this consecration. A few days before the scheduled operation, I hiked up to the tunnel to inspect its condition and to be sure it didn't seem like it was being frequented by people or animals. To my dismay, there were traces of trash, and discarded furniture from when someone had last utilized it for shelter. However, everything appeared as if it had not been used in a while, and since it was during the colder months, few cared to venture into the chilly cavern. I spent some time clearing away the trash and discarded makeshift furniture, settling on a spot near the center of the large tunnel to one side. It seemed this area was least occupied or disturbed and had an ideal space for a circle and altar near to the cave wall.

Hauling everything up to the cave entrance was considerably more laborious than the other three Elemental consecrations. It took a couple of trips, as I had made sure to bring extra clothes and a large cloak to keep me from being distracted by the cold during the invocations. I prayed that no one would notice me parking my car and hauling a large sack up the mountainside in the middle of the night. Maintaining secrecy and privacy was always a challenge for these types of workings, and nothing could distract the magical mind more than being halted and questioned right before an operation. Luckily, I was unchallenged the entire way, with no other people or vehicles in sight. The early winter night was still and quite cold.

When I arrived at the cavern entrance, I felt a rising sense of apprehension. It was pitch black two feet within the cave. It sat open and silent, and the feeling of a tomb could not escape the forefront of my thoughts. I turned on my headlamp and ventured in to find the cave as empty as when I had left it. Nothing moved or stirred as I made my way toward the far wall of the abandoned tunnel where I planned to evoke the Elementals of Earth.

I worked quickly, removing all the necessary items from the packs once I had everything within the cave. I was excited but didn't want to spend longer than I needed to within this place. I measured out my circle using a stick to carve the circumference in the packed dirt of the cave floor. When I was done, I took out a can of salt and sprinkled a solid white line inside the traced circle in the Earth. I spent some time finding suitable stones to serve as the Earth altar, and ended up leaving the tunnel a few times to collect the right size and shape of stones to support the candles and large Earth disk. The altar ended up being more or less a pile of stones, arranged in such a way that it was level enough to support an incense burner and the Earth disk. Four candles and candlesticks surrounded the altar at the corners. Afterward, I decided to gather ten more stones a bit larger than my fist to place around the outside of my magical circle. The result had a very Celtic pagan feel, like the standing stone rings in Ireland and Britain, even though on a small physical scale.

It was my desire to be able to contact a powerful but benevolent Earth Elemental in this place who could empower my Earth disk with the properties I desired. I couldn't shake my uneasiness in the cavern, however, and hoped such benevolent Spirits could be found here.

I lit my coals and candles. I recall the interesting smells of earth and cold stone as they mixed with the pungent mixture of my incense wafting through the cave. When I began my invocations, I became instantly aware of the acoustic power of the cavern as each verse I spoke reverberated off the stone walls. Never before had I been able so fully to appreciate the effects my voice could have on the environment until I experienced the spoken conjurations in that space, even while lowering the volume of my words, as I was concerned that I could easily be heard if someone ventured too near to the cave. I pushed that thought aside and focused completely on the invocations and the intentions behind them.

The candles on the altar began to flicker wildly, casting all sorts of eerie shadows and lights on the cavern wall, and I felt a sense of stirring awareness, as if something were waking up. While I wanted my mind and senses to be open to perceive any Spirits, I tried to restrain my imagination from running away with the sensations I was experiencing. I concluded the initial invocations in the center of my stone circle and waited expectantly.

A deafening silence settled over the cave after a few long moments of waiting in the circle. I noticed that I could no longer hear the breeze or any noises outside of the tunnel. The only thing I recall hearing was my heartbeat in my ears. In the heavy stillness, my feelings of uneasiness increased with each passing moment. If a Spirit of Earth were going to arrive it would be soon, I reasoned. I did my best to remain calm and waited in the silence for what seemed like an eternity. The stillness never shifted, never changed, and no light revealed what was about to happen. After the extended time standing and attempting to perceive something, a scratching and then a tapping noise occurred as if an animal were steadily picking at one of the tunnel walls. No matter where I looked, though, I could not find the source of the noises as everything remained visually still except for the flickering candlelight. Then I realized that there was also a breathing sound. I remained perfectly still, keeping the hood of my cloak pulled far over my head as if it warded against anything which might try to startle me.

A cold wind gusted through the tunnel and extinguished all of my ritual candles on the altar. The only light source left was a small black lantern with a small tea light. The darkness immediately closed in around me. The tea light's illumination was enough to barely make out the shadows within my own circle and nothing beyond. My heart quickened and my mind raced with wild ideas about what might be going on in that deep darkness. My headlamp was tucked in my bags outside the circle and I dared not venture out in the middle of an evocation.

I deepened my breathing and pushed down the rising fears, refocusing my magical intention for being here. I settled my gaze once more in the direction of the altar outside my circle, although I could see no hint of it. After a moment's concern, I figured if anything were to appear it would be Astral anyway, so the physical sight of the altar was not necessary. After a moment I thought my eyes were playing tricks on me as I glimpsed colored lights dancing around where I knew my altar stood in the blackness. I strained to see any clear movement or image, but it was simply impossible to make out anything definable.

Then my breath caught as my intuition and magical sense informed me that a presence—a very old and very sullen Spirit of Earth—had formulated right before me in the darkness, just behind the stone altar where my Earth disk rested. I began the formal greetings. I spoke to the perceived Spirit in front of me and asked that the Earth pentacle be imbued with its power for protection, for stability, for growth, and strength. I asked that it be able to ground, stabilize, and center me when I held it. I asked that it fill me with deep wisdom when I meditated with it. I asked for it to have the properties to call forth the powers of the Earth, the Elementals of forest and stone and mountain. I asked that medicines or food eaten from its surface would receive true blessings and profound positive effects. When the requests and invocations were finished, I thanked the presumed Earth Elemental Spirit and gave it the license to depart. For a long moment, there was no change in the atmosphere or my sense of the being before me. Then, slowly, its presence dissipated and melted away. Suddenly I could feel a slight cold breeze and hear distant sounds coming from outside the tunnel. It was as if a vacuum or pressure had lifted which allowed the air to move and vibrate freely once more.

When I went to retrieve the Earth disk from the altar outside the circle, I noticed that the face of the disk with the hexagram and tree of life was cool to the touch, but the other face was not. I thought this was interesting since the entire cave and area was cold but the Earth disk seemed to maintain a difference in temperature to each side.

The consecration for my Earth disk ended up consisting of two parts. The first consecration in the cave seemed to be an acknowledgment as well as a formal immersion into the Earth realm which was more underworld and subterranean. The "darkly splendid world" saturated at least half of the pentacle with the still, cool, and immovable forces of Earth which represent its unchanging (or incomprehensibly slowly changing) state of stone, the stillness of death and winter, and the inevitability of mortality in unchanging return. The other aspect I wanted my implement to be consecrated with was the more active, expanding forces of life on earth, to imbue it with the promise of life and return, support and nourishment. For this operation, I settled on an isolated forest grove I had gone to many times in my teenage years and considered the place quite sacred and filled with these fertile Earth energies in abundance.

I used the same invocations as I had in the tunnel, but this time made a particular call to the Earth Elementals which supported and nourished life, growth, and fertility. The invocations echoed off the trees of the dense vegetation of the clearing and I felt an encompassing sense of security and peace. I spoke to the land, to each variety of plant and insect as well as stone and soil and invited all the positive dwellers of Earth to attend the ceremony. I asked that the Elemental guardian of this place arrive and agree to participate in this operation.

Each of my Elemental implements now had gone through a unique and considerable consecration. Each had particular memories and feelings associated with their consecrations and I was confident in their usefulness to tap into the Elemental powers as they were designed and consecrated to do. With each evocation of an Elemental, none appeared solidly or spoke in the clarity I have come to require of classical evocations. Regardless, due to the events which followed their consecration and use, I have been given ample evidence of their successful consecration and Elemental connection. Each implement has proven to be a powerful vessel of Elemental power and correspondence.

Traveling the Elemental Plane of Earth

The Elemental Astral voyage of Earth was conducted on a Saturday evening in the late fall. This experiment was to be the first conducted in a new house I had just moved into with a newly arranged and consecrated magical ritual room. I was unsure how well magic would work in this new location compared to my previous one where some of the earliest and most fascinating experiments had been undertaken.

The scryer's chair was placed in the north end of the circle facing north in the smaller magical chamber. Behind the chair was the small altar which held my magician's wand and dagger, along with my consecrated Earth disk, consecrated Earth oil, and a small Prithivi Tattwa. In the blank area on the circle reserved for the Spirit's name and sigil, I placed parchment drawings of alchemical and classical symbols for the Element of Earth as well as the Elemental King. Just beyond the magic circle in the north, I placed an altar table. This altar was covered with dark green silk cloth and other objects corresponding to Earth. My personalized Earth altar tablet served as the backdrop. As with the previous three operations, I placed a large Tattwa symbol against the face of an antique mirror. For the Earth Tattwa, the background was a 24-inch-square image of a myriad of stones and rich green forest, with the Prithivi Tattwa's bright yellow square with purple background pasted in the center.

Ritual items for this experiment

1. Ritual magician's wand and dagger.
2. Consecrated Earth disk.
3. Two altars: One for inside the circle, one for outside as the main Earth altar. Green, dark brown, or black altar cloths for each, Earth altar tablet in the Golden Dawn system if you choose.
4. Consecrated Earth oil.
5. Four green and black candles, preferably beeswax, with stone candleholders.

6. Brazier, charcoal, and lighter.
7. Optional: Emerald stones.
8. Earth Elemental plane incense.

Hypnotic Induction of Scryer while staring at Tattwa

After lighting the charcoal for the incense, as well as the candles while reciting a grimoric consecration blessing, I had my scryer stare at the Tattwa card for Earth. When the charcoal was ready I poured a fair amount of incense mixture on the coals from a container on the altar and observed as the clouds of perfume billowed upward. After everything was lit and prepared, I reentered the circle and walked around it clockwise blessing the working space, saying, "In the name of the blessed Trinity, I consecrate this piece of ground for our defense; so that no evil Spirit may have power to break these bounds prescribed here, through Jesus Christ our Lord. Amen."

When that was complete, I picked up the smaller Prithivi Tattwa card showing a yellow square on a violet background from my altar within the circle and gave it to my friend in the chair. I instructed him to gaze and focus on the card while relaxing. By this time my scryer was accustomed to the ritual and entered very quickly into a trance as he stared at the card. I picked up my consecrated Earth disk pentacle and held it near my chest for a moment to feel the centeredness and stability. I once again walked around behind him in the center of the magic circle and placed my Earth disk back on the table while retrieving my magician's wand and dagger.

With three taps on the small altar, I began the first part of Opening By Watchtower:

I stated powerfully: "HEKAS, HEKAS, ESTE BEBELOI!" I then used my dagger to perform the Banishing Ritual of the Pentagram and Banishing Ritual of the Hexagram.

After those opening rituals, I set my wand and dagger back on the altar and picked up the Earth disk, this time opening the door to the Astral plane of Earth. Walking clockwise, I moved directly in front of the Earth altar and made three motions, drawing the top part of a square in front of it. I then held the disk above my head and walked clockwise around the inside of the circle, saying, "Stoop not down in that darkly splendid world wherein continually lieth a faithless depth and Hades wrapped in gloom, delighting in unintelligible

Fig. III-7. ***Section of Circle for Drawing Ghob into the Crystal***

images, precipitous, winding: a black ever-rolling Abyss, ever espousing a body unluminous, formless, and void."

When I returned to the north, I used the Earth disk to draw an encircled Invoking Pentagram of Earth. Within the star I drew the sign of Taurus. Pointing to the center of the pentagram, I said, "EMOR DIAL HECTAGA, in the names and letters of the Great Northern Quadrangle of the North, I invoke ye, ye angels of the Watchtower of the North." Then I replaced the pentacle on the altar, moved to the west, and faced east behind the altar.

An interesting sensation came over me as I reached this part of the ritual. I felt like I was entering a cool cavern with rich, damp, earthy smells and it felt comforting and enveloping.

I directed my scryer to stare straight ahead at the large Prithivi Tattwa on the altar until I felt he was ready to be guided through the Astral projection formula and travel through the symbol. After guiding my scryer once more out of his physical body and through the Elemental gateway, I chanted the Divine name Adonai ha-Aretz, followed by the names of the Archangel Uriel and the Angel Phorlakh. I again encouraged the scryer to be completely aware of his surroundings, to be able to see, hear, feel, and interact with his Astral environment. After allowing him to become accustomed to this fourth Elemental realm, I recited the Prayer of the Gnomes:

King invisible, Who, taking the Earth as a support, didst furrow the abysses to fill them with Thine omnipotence; Thou Whose name doth shake the vaults of the world, Thou Who causest the seven metals to flow through the veins of the rock, monarch of the seven lights, rewarder of the subterranean toilers, lead us unto the desirable air and to the realm of splendor. We watch and we work unremittingly, we seek and we hope, by the twelve stones of the Holy City, by the hidden talismans, by the pole of the lodestone which passes through the center of the world! Savior, Savior, Savior, have pity on those who suffer, expand our hearts, detach and elevate our minds, enlarge our entire being! O stability and motion! O day clothed with night! O darkness veiled by splendor! O master Who never keepest back the wages of Thy labourers! O silver whiteness! O golden splendor! O crown of living and melodious diamonds! Thou Who wearest the heaven on Thy finger like a sapphire ring, Thou Who concealest under the Earth, in the stone kingdom, the marvelous seed of stars, live, reign, be the eternal dispenser of the wealth whereof Thou hast made us the wardens! Amen.

The feeling of being within a cavern intensified and I noticed how perfectly silent it was within and without the circle. I could practically smell rich, damp stone and hear far-off droplets of water echo. It was so odd but I craved to be deep within a cave and just sit and enjoy the silence.

Scryer's Experience

SCRYER: At the beginning, I really felt like the soil and the stones around the house, that the vibration of them are changing by you all living here, and that it would be interesting on how it would affect your neighbors actually and then I noticed when you spoke at the very beginning that a dog started to bark and that it was recognizing that something very odd was going on, like something that had not happened here before. Then with the tattwa, I noticed as you were counting down it started to look like a hallway going into this opening with a floor and ceiling and two walls, and it was just dark when I stepped through, dark and quiet and it had a feeling of cool moisture in the air. There was a deafening silence. I was amazed that I didn't feel stifled, or uncomfortable...it was like a living darkness. And when you started to sing the prayer of the Gnomes, I noticed crystals sticking out of the walls and they started to light up, and the longer the song went on, the more steady the light became and the more there were, or the more that there were or the more I could see. I really had the sense that this was a place that was created for me, that it was a space that was made for me to interact with Earth, because it's so dense and different than our experience in a lot of ways, dark dreaming quality to it, when the guide came, it was this face that just came out of the wall. It reminded me of my wife actually because Earth has no rush, at first I didn't know if it was going to interact with me. At first I wasn't sure what to do or what to say, then you started to do that prayer and I started speaking that prayer to the guide face on the wall. And it was so interesting, I felt the guide really responded to it, almost as if it was happy at what was being said, next thing I knew it beckoned me over to this place where I was looking down this shaft, there was like a wall, and I peered over and it went down, down into a bottomless abyss. It was all lined with crystals as if they were lined perpendicular to the shaft and they were all lit up and it was beautiful, eventually it was just black below, the face appeared on the other side of this shaft, and I asked what's down there face: well that's where everything comes from, that's where the dream of the Earth comes from and you're not ready to go down there yet son, I cannot stop you from jumping in but I don't recommend it.

We did another prayer and I spoke down the shaft and way, way down there I saw this flash of blue light like it heard the prayer. Then we turned around and what had been that cavern of crystals when I turned around it became this cave with stalactites and stalagmites...and the face appeared to my left said that the power of Earth could really be seen here...because all of those formations had created drop by drop, grain by grain and that Earth was patient and it was in no hurry and because of that it could create flowing forms with incredible strength and that is the attitude I should have toward my enlightenment which is to not be in such a hurry to get it done, and let it form, be steady and patient, that it takes place in the dark. That it is slow, was not meant to be a fast process, it was made to be a slow process since that is the only way things are made to last. The only process which things that can last for a long, long time. And then I flashed back to the last time I was in Carlsbad caverns to a stalactite that is enormous, it's like 50 feet across, the mind-boggling time, from drops of water, the time, put in perspective that sort of age and patience was overwhelmingly powerful, incomprehensible. Then you invoked the Angels of Earth and I felt one was in front and one was behind and they lead me down a spiral staircase right in the chamber...it felt so solid but could instantly change or morph into something else....the staircase was turning downward to the right always turning to the right. I got down to the bottom of this staircase which lead out onto a ledge and the angels said, behold the cavern of Ghob, and at first I couldn't see anything, all I could see was stone, then I realized I was looking at a forehead of this huge being, and then when I peeked my head over, I could see down his body and it was going all the way down and it was all filled with mist...greenish blue mist, and there were all these vines and things growing out of the side of the cavern...I was looking at his forehead. He suddenly backed up and I could see more of the cavern and I could see more of head and face he stretched and reached his hand above him and he placed his hands on the stones and his hands up and his fingers literally merged with the stone and I could tell when he did that merged with the cavern like that, that he could feel everything, everything that was touching it, all the soil, everything, he could be aware of it, all he had to do was stretch out and touch it, he could be aware of everything, completely connected.

He looked at me and said «EVERYTHING is REMEMBERED.»

It just hit me with this flash that there are realms underneath our feet, every culture, every language, everything that the Earth has experienced is remembered inside of it and that we can go there at any point and that in death, that is what you can experience, everything that has happened. And not only in death but in life, if you have the ability and allow yourself and believe you can do that. I felt this immense gratitude as I realized that things are always changing, but nothing is ever lost, that it's preserved, but the dream is still unfolding, but that everything that has happened is protected, remembered, saved. It's always going to change, continually moving forward.

And then in the caverns of the Gods, Ghob moved back even further and the cavern just got bigger and bigger, and just like in the other realms, in the others I couldn't see who were on the throne I could see the other three thrones, and I could see one of the legs of this huge throne was Cernunnos. I could tell on the other realms that there were pillars to the thrones but couldn't see but on this one I could. The cavern was there and there was forest there, and all sorts of different forests—tropical, deciduous, rainforests, baobab trees, and trees I didn't even recognize and couldn't tell you what they were.

And then it was a totally different experience of feeling how much bigger the unfolding dream is than me, and how much bigger it is even than humanity, that we are important to it, and an aspect of it, but in no way remotely being the center of it and that one day, the active time of humanity will end and something new will begin. But that we would be preserved, that we would move to a different state. That the Sidhe would move into a deeper state than they are now and they will move even deeper into the Earth, deeper into memory and one step closer back to the Source.

When you spoke about the vitality of life, I was like, yes, the tenacity of life comes from Cernunnos; it's his spirit that is when you get knocked

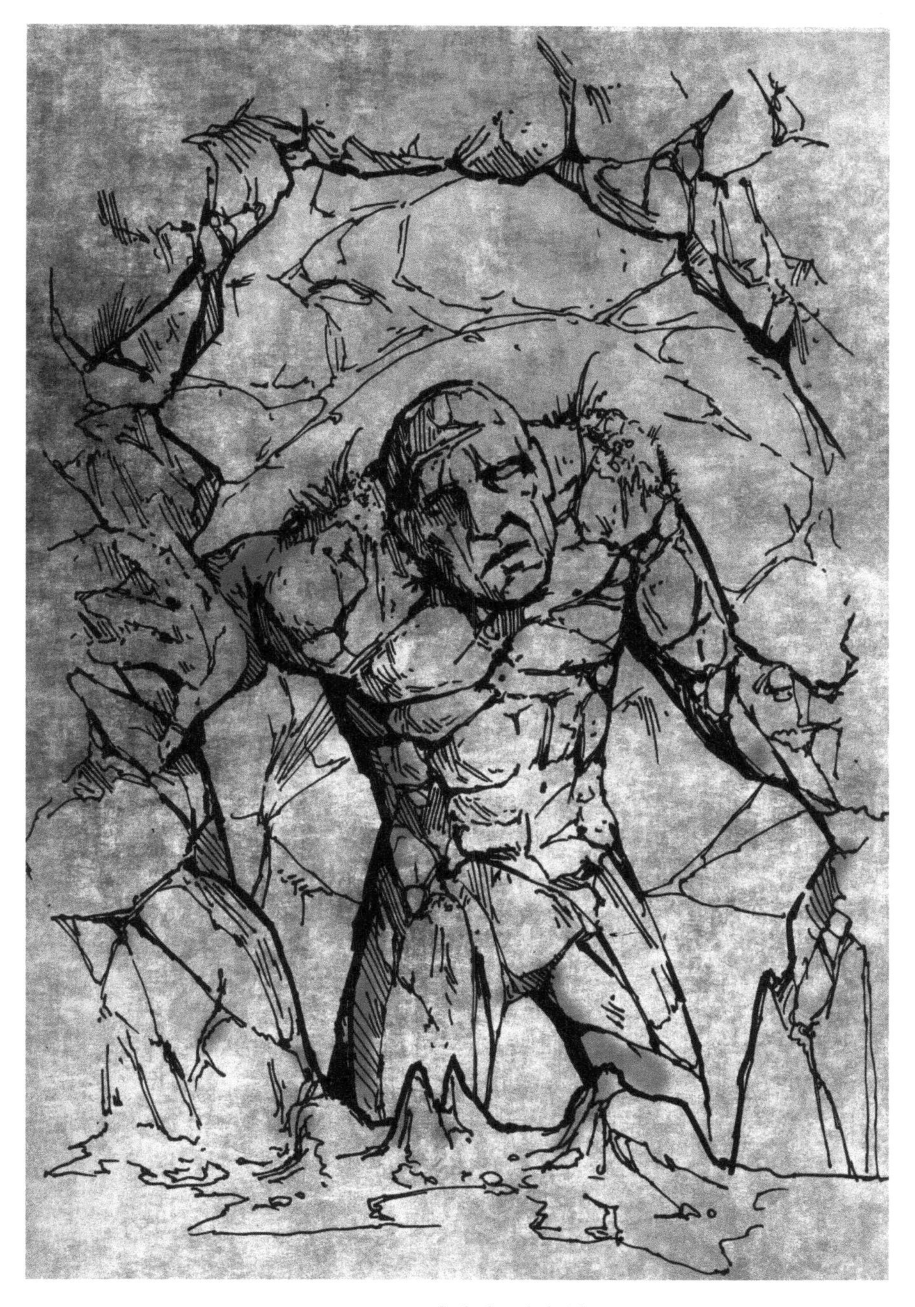

Fig. III-8. ***Portrait of Ghob as beheld in Vision***

down and life beats you up, but you get right back up, you're connecting into his spirit and that aspect of life, faith.

At one point, I said to him, "It's so good to have that pressure taken off, that things can radically alter but it's okay." And how good it was to be an aspect of the dream, but being okay at not being the center of it.

Connecting to magic of the Earth: Finding a place underground, find a stone attached to the bedrock, holding onto it, praying into it, holding onto it, praying into it, that it would be a powerful means of communicating with the planet or Earth, or being in a cave and putting your hands on the wall...being present and still and connecting that way.

When you asked about the Spirits to protect the home and property and people, the Spirit guide said, «Yes, as long as they are fed in a stone bowl, given offerings in a stone bowl once a week. A part of the give-and-take.»

When asked about wealth and prosperity, coming of wealth and preservation of our resources, the Spirit said, «You all are on a different level, you have crossed into a different plane of human existence. So your relationship to wealth is to steward it, but always make sure you're okay with giving it away, it has to be used for the benefit of others. As long as you're doing that it will create a vacuum that will bring more to you, but it has to flow through you. Some people have a totally different relationship of wealth. They're in a lifetime where they need it. Their fascination is with the accumulation of it and the use of the power of it, but no one can stay in that place and still progress.» And that you or we could have large accumulations of wealth, but the responsibility we would have would be much greater if that were the road we started to follow and would be for others' sake and if we ever stopped doing that we would lose it.

The sign said there would be a movement of the Earth. And I was like "*Really*?" And when I questioned it, that candle fizzed, and that corresponded to him saying, «You asked and I'm answering.»

When I said goodbye to the Spirit guide, I was like, "Thank you, because this one was more impactful, there was something that coalesced everything, bringing it all together. And I can see now why that Air Elemental acknowledged Earth. There was so much contained there, and the feeling of looking down that shaft was like looking directly into Spirit and the home of the stars.

Afterthoughts on the Earth Elemental Operation

As far as "movements in the earth" promised by the Earth Elemental, there was not a singular significant event which seemed to match the previous three, but possibly more cumulative effects in ways I was not directly expecting. There was a 3.6-magnitude earthquake reported shortly after the evocation, but being born and raised in California, this hardly seemed anything noteworthy since very few even felt it. However, due to the intense rains and previous Elemental disturbances, earth was indeed moved by the water with severe erosion, mudslides, and sinkholes which appeared to pop up all over the city. Massive flooding caused numerous structural and vehicular damages, lifting homes from their foundations, littering the streets with debris, and pushing vehicles off the highways. People were injured as well as some animals.

There was much more of a palpable feel and shift in atmosphere within the magical working room during this experiment. It seemed that we were both going into vision, and shared a similar vision of the crystal cave. A pleasant feeling of encompassing, deep, presences pervaded the ritual chamber. Although it was early evening, it was dark and quiet. I swore I could hear droplets of water echoing within a cave. All around was expansive silence. It was like an awakening of the land there that something was being done that hadn't been done there before.

My scryer said it seemed to him that the magical work was like powering a battery, creating resonances in the stones and soil with the magic. At one point in the midst of the operation I sensed myself in forests and remembering exploring in the deep woods, I started speaking invocations spontaneously, poetry and litany of prayers to the Earth. My scryer recalled that and commented on how they seemed to correspond with what exactly was going on in his experiences. I really wanted to be in a cave just then, something drawing and desirable to connect that way. Connect with that ancient familiar.

SCRYER: Every one of these seems like more and more pieces of a puzzle, I've been dreaming again too. I went through a long lull of not dreaming...was freaking me out but since this work I'm dreaming again.

At the time of completing this book, it has been three years since this Earth Elemental experience with my scryer. I have since honored the advice given by the Elemental King, and have faithfully delivered offerings within a stone bowl once every week with a prayer. I begin by placing the food offerings in a bowl and making an invoking Earth pentagram with my finger right above it. I follow with another Earth sign and reminder of the promise for the Earth Spirits to watch over and protect my home, the property, houses, and belongings and people therein. I spend a moment with my hands above the offering, blessing and consecrating toward this end. I love feeling the awareness of Spiritual beings come near in a recognizable fashion. To me they appear rather tall, lengthy, and shadowed; they seem to be beings who have existed on and near the earth for a very long time.

The Elemental Astral voyages resulted in far richer experiences than I could have imagined. I was overjoyed at being able to assist my friend and scryer to experience these realms which very few actually enter. The detail, information, and experience of each yielded far more than what could have been imagined initially. For many it seems such experiments still take place solely in the mind and are more or less psychological explorations of the psyche in measures of archetypical understanding and categorization. With these experiments, however, it felt as if both of us were stepping into new territory of esoteric endeavor where the experiences and wonders could be appreciated in tandem with rich encounters and also a clear record of events.

Traveling through the celestial realms and spheres can be like reforming the makeup of your consciousness. The symbolism, energy, and programming which occurs happens at so many subtle levels of your being that it will be difficult to distinguish the particulars of what has been altered about you. A flood of energetic pattern, knowledge, frequency and cosmic connection will all occur simultaneously without the ability to directly comprehend the immensity and direct purpose of all of these realignments and integration of new data. Such are the aptitudes and capabilities of the Malakhei Elohim as they are the direct relays of the intentions of creation in consciousness. Depending on your route of travel and intentionality for moving through these heavenly bodies of consciousness, you may find yourself disoriented or being forcefully compelled to rearrange your awareness and lifestyle. This process can be quite upsetting to the explorer who was not prepared for the dynamic shifts which inevitably occurred as a result of being in proximity to such heavenly celestial movers.

Within the framework of cultural spirituality as it relates to our magical practice, we can understand the similitude of images and symbols being displayed in a wide array of powerful imagery and experiential metaphor. That is not to say that these powerful metaphors are strictly imaginary and referral but that our minds and senses depict them as such.

After the initiation through the four primary Elemental realms I felt it was time to explore the other Astral realm of Spirit and Æther. Being able to enter into the nebulous Spiritual realms just adjacent to the physical is of particular importance to many magical traditions.

"Elemental" Spirit Experience

Implements for this experiment:

1. Large 13-inch black obsidian scrying mirror.
2. *DSIC* magic circle.
3. Two white, black, or silver candles.
4. A magical journal containing invocations, prayers, questions to Spirits, etc., and pen or pencil for recording findings and feedback if working with a scryer.
5. Ritual wand (myrtle wood in this case) and/or dagger is recommended but not required.
6. Akasha Tattwa card in proper colors. Two-toned "flashing" is best.
7. Astral Earthbound Spirit Summoning incense mixture.
8. Brazier, charcoal, and burner.

Necromantic Evocation Experiment: The Hospital Ghosts

It so happened that a situation came to my attention that not only sparked my curiosity to explore a magical method but also gave my scryer and me the perfect opportunity to explore the "Elemental" realm of Spirit or Akasha in a dynamic form. Coincidently, the wife of my scryer came to me asking if I would be able to discover the truth behind paranormal occurrences which were reported as going on for several years at the hospital in which she worked. She explained that several of the hospice nurses, as well as the patients, reported seeing children. In a purely Elemental sense, the realm of Spirit or Akasha does not coincide with the nebulous Astral realms wherein we find a plethora of Spiritual beings including the ghosts and Spirits of those who have passed on. The truer aspect would be the deep Spirit or Astral where all things come into being, perhaps the page of the Creator on which thoughts are put into divine words to eventually manifest in existence. Regardless, the various Astral realms are indeed connected to this more unfathomable realm of Spirit and the Tattwa representing this aspect seemed like a perfect doorway to access the realm in which these Spirits resided.

More than simply experiencing the Astral and possibly communicating directly with some ghosts of people who had passed on, I thought it would be a perfect opportunity to see if we could get any relevant information on the occurrences at the hospice center at which my scryer's wife worked. I thought about the ways in which we could do this and quickly reasoned that trying to perform any sort of magical operation involving Spirit contact at the hospital would be out of the question. Instead, I devised a layered ritual involving scrying and Astral travel, as well as Spirit communication and retrieval.

After planning everything out and concocting my blend of Spirit-seeing incense, I set up the experiment on a Saturday evening during an hour of Saturn.[10] The Moon was in an Earth sign and waxing. The magical chamber was arranged with the *DSIC* protective circle with the blank space facing toward the west. Just beyond the circle, in the west, an altar stand with a black cloth and large black obsidian mirror was positioned at eye level to the scryer. The mirror was large enough to be perfectly visible for both the seer and operator magician. Two candles were placed on either side of the mirror, far enough away so that no reflection of the flames appears on the surface of the mirror.[11] It is also perfectly fine to light other candles around the chamber for extra illumination in case the operator or magician is taking notes during the ceremony. For my experiment, I also placed two small silver bowls containing water as extra Spiritual-conduit correspondences. I performed opening prayers to bless the working spaces.[12] I also blessed the circle with holy water.

The summoning mixture I used is as follows: I add few small shavings from a wild mushroom I had collected in the forest. Mushrooms represent well the threshold of the light and dark worlds, growing from damp, dark places as neither a plant or mineral. The mushroom needn't be psychedelic in any regard, although that may have interesting effects, but it should be found in the wild and kept in a jar till needed. Only a small quantity, about a third of a gram is required for the mixture. 3 parts wormwood, 1 part mugwort, 1 part myrrh, 1 part dark musk, and 1 part Solomon's Seal. Mash and mix all into a powder for burning incense.

Lunar Necromantic Fluid Condenser, based on a recipe in *The Veritable Key of Solomon*:

- A base of white sandalwood powder
- Orris root and myrrh in equal parts

---

10. Although, if you ever need to work this ritual, a Monday or Wednesday during a Saturn or Mercury hour would also suffice quite well.

11. White, black, or silver candles can be used.

12. If you so desire, the Lesser Banishing Rituals of the Pentagram and Hexagram are perfectly suited here.

- Jasmine flowers (optional)
- Dried skin of a frog
- A small pinch of refined camphor
- White poppy seeds
- Small amounts of moonstone & silver shavings (extra addition)

Blend together the sandalwood, myrrh, and orris root, and crush them into a powder. True, refined camphor can be hard to come by, but if you should find some, add a pinch to the powdered base. Also, mix in the poppy seeds and, if procured appropriately, skin of a frog. Put this mixture in an air-tight jar. Let these sit until the next full Moon. On the evening of the full Moon, mix together, in a silver or crystal bowl if possible, olive oil and the powder base, meditating on the purpose for scrying into the Spirit world. Recite this prayer for intention as you do:

Dominus sors partir meæ, et calieis mei; tu sustententabis sortem meam. Funes ceciderunt mihi in jucundia, insuper hæreditas praeclara mihi.[13]

Once gathered, the herbs are placed in a pot with distilled water or rainwater. There should be about an ounce of each herb and enough water in the pot to cover the contents completely. Bring this mixture to a boil, and then turn down the flame and let it simmer for an hour with the pot lid on. When this is done, let the mixture cool and strain it through an unbleached coffee filter or muslin cloth. Put the liquid back into the pot and simmer without the lid until only a quarter of the original amount is left. When this is cool, add small amounts of fine silver shavings, if you have them. Then, add the shavings of moonstone, again if you have them.

When you have combined all the fluid-condenser ingredients together, add an equal amount of wood or isopropyl alcohol to preserve the mixture. Store the condenser in an air-tight glass container. Keep it with the rest of your scrying equipment.

After you have all the necessary equipment in order, and the magical room arranged, the next vital Element is to be able to enter the trance state for Astral soul travel. If you are working with a scryer/seer, you will need to be able to guide them through this process while they contact the correct Spirits via use of

---

13. The Vulgate Latin translation of *Psalm* 15:5–6. The *Psalm* is numbered 16:5–6 in the Hebrew Tanakh. Should the magus prefer the Hebrew to the Latin, it is *YHVH menath-chelqi ve-kosi; Attah tomikh gorali. CHhavalim naphelu-li banneimim; aph-nachalath shapherah alai.* —APF

Fig. III-9. Section of Circle for Scrying the Realm of Spirit in the Crystal

the proper conjurations. In the below experiment, I ask questions of the Spirits and scryer directly, recording information by hand. It is important to maintain control of the experiment at all times, especially if you are contacting these Spirits directly. If working with a scryer, do not allow them to become engaged in any disturbing or negative reactions triggered by the Spirits they contact.

My magical room was all arranged for the Spirit experiment. I had my herb and ingredient shelves turned into a temporary altar in the west where a black cloth was draped over it along with silk cloth used to wrap the large black obsidian mirror when it was not in use. An elegant iron bookstand now propped the large circle of volcanic glass up so that anyone standing or sitting in front of it could see within its dark, semi-reflective surface with ease. Placed directly against the mirror was a Tattwa card about three inches square which had a deep indigo oval on it with an almost lime-green background. If you stared at the card for any length of time, the colors would seem to flash and draw you in. Two white candles were arranged to the sides as well as two small silver bowls containing water. In front of the makeshift altar I also had a metal tripod stand that was originally made to hold a glass and candle holder but instead served to hold my small brass chafing dish containing charcoals which were already lit and beginning to glow with a hint of scarlet beneath the hot white ash.

The cut-out magic circle bearing four hexagrams in the cardinal direction as well as holy names of God in Latin, standard Hebrew, and archaic Hebrew took up the majority of the working room with a comfortable chair and small table placed within. Upon the small table were a small leather journal and a pen for jotting down any notes or images I witnessed during the ceremony that I wanted to keep an accurate record of.

It was already dark outside in the new autumn evening. The hour of Saturn was approaching on the day of Saturn and I was anxious to begin. Benn would be over soon so I made haste in mixing the incense blend that would be conducive to our workings.

I shaved off a bit of a wild mushroom I had collected years earlier in the forest into a bowl. I then added three parts of wormwood herb, Solomon's seal, mugwort, orris root, and cardamom. The mixture was meant to assist with manifesting earthbound souls or Spirits. It was also intended to balance the powers of the Moon, which was not in the most ideal phase for the experiment. I ground and mixed all of the particularly odorous herbs together, saying very pointed prayers and litanies of intention for its use. When I felt it was suitable, I funneled the entire mixture into a small ebony wood jar and placed it on the altar next to the dark obsidian mirror.

Next I went over to my main altar and retrieved my wand and holy water sprinkler. I stood within my circle, gathered my will about me, and recited a prayer to bless the working space. Candlelight danced around the walls as I felt the reassuring resonance of my will gather to a single focus. I began to walk around the perimeter of the circle, tracing it with my wand as I went and also sprinkling the circle and ground with the holy water.

I heard my magical companion arrive shortly after and my wife answered the door to let him in. I continued to make sure the magical working room was all in order while they talked upstairs. When I was sure everything was ready to begin, I went upstairs and greeted Benn. He knew that we planned to contact some Spirits that his wife had asked us to investigate, but he had no idea how we were going to attempt this.

My scryer and his wife had worked at a hospital that was first founded in the late 1800s as a tuberculosis sanatorium. The hospital soon grew and functioned as a unique center for cancer treatment before eventually converting to house patients with mental and emotional disorders as well as having a floor serving as a hospice center. Both my scryer and his wife eventually became privy to stories that were kept strictly between the close hospital staff and the hospice patients who informed them. There were alleged haunting activities that much of the staff and many of the patients recounted during their time in the hospital.

Basically, we were investigating claims from several hospice patients and many nurses who said they had seen "ghost children" who came around when patients were near to death at the St. Francis hospitals. Patients would inform the hospice nurses that "two small children" would visit them although they were not related. Also the nurses said they kept finding windows open after the patients passed away but were closed before and they were still alive.

My scryer and I entered the magical chamber and my scryer took a seat within the magic circle. I had him begin with his breathing and meditative exercise he has perfected since his training and our numerous workings. I retrieved an ebony jar of incense from the table and lit the candles to the right and left of the scrying mirror. I poured a copious amount of incense mixtures on the hot coals of the small brazier and the pungent aroma and smoke began to curl up in front of the black mirror and Tattwa card, causing lights and shadows to dance even more. Before the scrying mirror I did a very intense Opening of the Veil gesture with my hands, a technique I adopted from Jason Miller's *Sorcerer's Secrets.*[14] I had been practicing the technique for some time and found it extremely effective. I next intoned the final blessings on the working space and sealed the circle.

Come forth, you who are behind the hidden veil which lies beneath the mundane senses and world of form, who see beneath perspective sights to the world here but beyond what we may touch and capture. Hidden eyes of light and shadow, enclosed within the silky gray mists of memories, dreams, and lingering visions; stirred within stillness the breath from deep abodes, fills the air and speaks of mysteries still recalled. Let your images appear, and voices be heard now they ever were before, unbroken by conceptual time and minds of forgotten yearnings.

I maintained my focus as I went from holding my wand and dictating the questions to grabbing the small journal and pencil to write down the answers to my questions as Benn would speak them back to me.

Scryer's Experience

SCRYER: The first thing that I remember was going through the Spirit Tattwa gateway, which felt odd. I really wasn't seeing much at all, but there was this intense green space that I passed through when I traveled through the doorway itself. It was this striking green color that filled my vision for a moment and then all of a sudden I was on the other side and it was really open. I still wasn't seeing much of anything; it was just a feeling of being in a really open and different sort of space, really big, really wide open and I felt light and movable. I recall you sending me out again through my body and through the roof and I was amazed at how clearly I could see the intersection of the nearby streets and that big power transformer over there and I was like, wow. As I was moving toward the hospital, I could trace my route perfectly as I was moving over everything.

14. Jason Miller, *The Sorcerer's Secrets: Strategies to Practical Magick* (Franklin Lakes, NJ: New Page Books, 2009).

OPERATOR: The sensations in the magical chamber were interesting and I could definitely feel the veil between the worlds being lifted completely. The scrying mirror remained black for the first part, but as soon as I sent my scryer through the Akasha Tattwa it took on a milky white haze appearance.

SCRYER: When I got to the hospital, I went in through one of the windows on the old unit floor. That was odd for me since my mom died upon that very floor. I was in a different section, however, and I was looking down at the nurse's station and that is when I saw the little girl and the older boy.

They were both standing on top of the nurse's station counter looking friendly. The girl looked to be around five years old, having blond hair with big curls, wearing white tights or socks with black shoes and a blue linen-looking dress. The dress looked rather old-fashioned in style but was a nice blue color.

I could also see the boy that just stood there near the girl who was looking at me. He looked like he was in his teens, had sandy blond hair and freckles, and was wearing jeans and a flannel shirt. The shirt he wore looked like a typical one seen in the seventies to me. When you asked what his name was, he said it was Matt. The little girl said her name was Julia.

I saw a third apparition, but it was barely visible in the background but not in full view. She appeared misty or foggy the entire time and I could never quite see her clearly and she never spoke to me. Julia stated, "Her name is Alice and she is scared of men because men treated her badly in life." From what Julia said, Alice didn't like being around men at all and when I tried to talk to her, she didn't say anything. She wouldn't talk the whole time, Julia would just sort of speak for her when I asked questions but I didn't get much more information. Julia seemed a very nice and smart little girl, but it was like talking to a child, to a five-year-old.

As we began talking about why they were there and if they wanted to leave, right in the middle of the conversation, this lady comes out of nowhere in a hospital gown with long gray hair running out of the hallway furious, scaring the crap out of me.

She just started screaming "GET OUT! GET OUT! GET OUT! Go Away! Leave. Get out of here!" She was really agitated and it freaked me out. I did my best to try and speak with her, got the name Roberta, but she didn't like us being there at all and definitely not talking to the children.

Roberta didn't like answering any questions I asked and afterward clung to Alice saying, "Come here! Don't trust this strange man. You don't want to be around men like that, do you?" Roberta proceeded to take Alice back into the hospital room that I remember the other staff saying was paranormally active. I didn't really see Alice the rest of the time.

After that, I asked the questions you told me to ask.

Julia said she was born on March 4th, 1902, and died in 1907 of scarlet fever. She shows herself getting really hot. When asked, she said her mother's name was "Alice" like the other little girl's name, and that her father's name was "Caleb."

When you questioned Matt, he said his birthday was November 14th, 1965, and that he had died of Leukemia in 1977. Matt said his mother's name was Janice, but did not seem to know his father's name. When asked how he came to be at this hospital he replied, "I don't know, I just woke up here." He mentioned that he and Julia became friends since he didn't have many friends when he was alive and she was always nice to him.

When you asked if they were stuck or noticed seeing a light, Julia said that she has seen the light and the tunnel and likes to "guide others to it when the Angel comes." Julia said, "We miss all the people who used to be here." I got the impression that Julia had been there a long while and was there before Alice or any of the others arrived as well.

When you asked Matt if he wanted to leave, he responded with, "No, I like being around Julia. I didn't have a lot of friends growing up and it's nice to have a friend."

Julia had gotten attached to Alice. Julia liked talking to the people who were dying, and she liked leading them toward the tunnel. She told me that the 'Angel' told her that was what she was supposed to do.

When I asked about the Angel, Julia started describing what she looked like. She said she was a tall woman with long blonde hair that was full of light. I thought this was interesting but a bit cliché, and then all of a sudden Julia gestured over to the window. I looked toward the window and there was the Angel!

OPERATOR: I heard my scryer take a sharp inhale like a gasp and shiver.

SCRYER: She was floating outside of the window and just looking at her I could feel her presence. It was overwhelming. I could feel her presence was all around me. My body was literally tingling. At first it really surprised me but it actually felt really good. It took my breath away.

I then walked over to the window where this luminous being was just floating, and the Angel smiled and gestured in Roberta's direction. In almost a joking way the Angel ran her finger across her neck and then grabbed her neck and made a choking expression as if to say, "Don't worry about her, she's dead, or a pain?" I'm really not sure what to make of it, but it sort of made me chuckle and seemed so out of character.

The Angel was amazing, and I got the sense that this was a being that guided souls to the other side and was very comforting about the entire process.

I remember that shortly after this exchange with the Angel, you encouraged the Spirits, including Roberta, to cross over if they so wished with your promptings, if Roberta wanted to move on and you explained to her that she could.

Julia said she could go as well, encouraging her, but Roberta became argumentative and started speaking to Julia, saying, "How do you *know* what's on the other side of that tunnel? You don't know what's on the other side of that tunnel, none of you do!"

And Julia responded, "Can't you hear the laughing? Can't you hear how joyful they sound, they are having fun! Can't you hear that?"

Roberta responded, "I don't hear a damn thing!"

Matt said, "Yeah I can hear them laughing and so can Alice, but for some reason Roberta cannot hear them." She is not able to trust that there is going to be something good on the other side. She can't trust it.

Then you said, "Well, maybe Alice can lead Roberta through the tunnel, through the light.

That's when Julia replied, looking sad, saying, "Yeah, she probably could, but I don't want Alice to go. Alice is the only real friend that I have who's a girl. I like leading the people through the tunnel, but I don't want to be here by myself."

I found this a really interesting situation. All of these Spirits have particular attachments to one another and that is why they are all still there.

Roberta seemed really attached to Alice and didn't want her to leave and like the daughter she never had? I'm not sure. Not a very happy existence; if you take her away now, it will be miserable in this afterlife.

Then you said, "If Alice wants to leave and go through the tunnel, it is not right of you to force her and keep her from making that decision."

After you said that, that was the only time I saw Roberta's demeanor or expression change, and it looked like she felt a little guilty. She no longer looked angry, mad, but just sad, and didn't want to dwell on this. She said, "I can't deal with this right now," and then she left.

Then you asked if you would like us to return and bring a woman back with us, and they seemed agreeable to this since Julia and Matt both seemed to think that a woman was needed to come ask Alice if she wanted to leave or go somewhere else.

Julia said she's afraid of men with beards and she's not going to go with you and won't do what you say. However, both Julia and Matt seemed like they wanted us to come back. There was also talk of the new hospice and Julia mentioned interest in going there but unsure how. Matt seemed like wherever Julia went that he would go too, regardless.

Then you asked if any of them would be willing to return with me and visit us both in the magical chamber for a moment.

OPERATOR: I then said, "Bring the Spirits with you. When you are ready, allow yourself to float back out of the hospital and return here and ask them to appear in the dark mirror."

SCRYER: When we brought them back, what was really interesting was when Julia got out this big ball of gray string, and she tied one end of the string around one of the pillars there, and then handed the rest of the ball of string to me. It seriously looked like gray yarn or something and I held onto it as I was returning to the magical chamber. As I was coming back, I looked behind me and they were holding on to the string. Then as I felt myself come back to the circle, I saw the ball of gray yarn sitting in front of the mirror. I remember saying, "That's it." When I opened my eyes back in the circle, I looked into the mirror and it looked really deep, big, black space. I was amazed how deep it looked, and I saw these pinpricks of light all over the place. After a time of that I noticed a quick glimpse looking at a negative of a photo of Matt's face. It seemed to take them a while to appear. He was definitely there in the room.

At one point, I also saw Julia in the mirror turning till her profile and the back of her hair was visible. The image of her appeared and was there, then it was gone. For whatever reason it seemed like the two of them were there and then they just faded back.

You then had me return to the hospital and they reappeared there and seemed somewhat confused by the experience.

You had me ask if there were any other entities or Spirits, occurrences that were notable in the hospital, and they brought up that they knew of a black shadow figure that was really evil or harmful that was in the basement and sometimes on the first floor, but seemed isolated to those areas. She had only seen it on the second floor once, and that was when people were fighting. I asked her what they were fighting about and Julia replied, "I don't know, it looked like two doctors screaming and yelling at each other," but that it was around there when that happened; it was in the corner watching. That creeped me out actually, and I felt like I didn't want to know any more.

Julia said that the black shadow thing was "mean and cold." I got the impression that it was cold temperature-wise, but that "The Angel lady said that it wouldn't bother us and go near us as long as we stayed out of the basement and stayed away from it." It felt like talking to a five-year-old. It came up a couple times that she wanted to go over to the new place she mentioned. "I don't want to stay here anymore, it's too lonely." Before, there was so much activity and they saw a lot of people pass on, almost like a train station, and that it was interesting and interactive for them, but now it was too slow and empty. They enjoyed talking to all sorts of different people. I got the feeling that they had all become a bit lonely due to the new hospital and not many people being around there anymore.

OPERATOR: When the Spirit arrived, I knew it instantly. There was a very palpable shift in the room's atmosphere which happened quickly. The candles that had been flickering went completely rigid and the air cooled. I immediately focused my attention on the obsidian mirror. Although my intuition was telling me that Spirits were indeed there, I got the sense that they were moving about the room and not settling in any one location.

I then heard Benn say aloud, "Right there in front of me, in the mirror." I instantly knew that the Spirit was inquiring exactly where it was supposed to go and how to present itself. There seemed to be a bit of confusion, and as my scryer and I both looked into the mirror, there appeared a few bright sparks or tiny flashes in the upper right-hand section of the mirror, accompanied by the usual smoky white haze of the ethereal plane. I then saw the distinct photonegative image of a figure walk from the left to right, as if I was looking out a window at someone a bit off in the distance. There were a few waves and wisps of smoky images, but then it subsided. The Spirits seemed to have as much difficulty seeing us as we were trying to see them at that moment. Perhaps there was a bit of confusion about exactly how they were supposed to interact with us through the mirror. I swore I saw the old woman Roberta looking in on us and looking very suspicious and seeing what we were up to.

SCRYER: Yes! I saw that as well. Wow, the exact same experience.

OPERATOR: I finished the experience with sending them well wishes, and extending blessings. My goal was not to try and force any of the beings to do what they don't want to do or perhaps are not ready for but to extend help and assistance if they should so desire it and at least know that it is available. I wanted to make sure there was no needless suffering and that they did have a choice still.

SCRYER: That blessing seemed to resonate there. I remember hearing it but somehow felt it in the hospital and the children seemed to be aware of it as well. The children didn't say anything in particular, but they seemed really grateful for that. That was really powerful; it truly echoed throughout that entire space.

The part of this experiment that centered on evocation was the attempt to bring back the Spirits or ghosts from their residing place at the hospital to the magical chamber. Though it was not completely successful, I'm certain that the process could be refined and perfected to guide Spirits of the departed to appear clearly within a black scrying mirror or other device, or possibly to appear in the air outside the circle itself. The process coincides with techniques described by Franz Bardon, by which the scryer or magus first projects to the Spirit and brings the Spirit back with them to appear before the magic circle.

Research into the results of the operation was done, but unfortunately, neither myself or an acquaintance who is a paranormal researcher was able to find any information regarding the identity or existence of the Spirits my scryer encountered. I was truly hoping to find more corroborating evidence for the entire encounter, but thus far have not been able to do so. At the time of this writing, I have plans to contact these Spirits or others to see if more evidence can be gathered to match historical records.

✣

IV
Beyond the Elemental Implements

EFORE PROCEEDING to the experiments for conjuring the seven great Planetary Archangels, I think a few words need to be said concerning the nature of magical ritual items beyond what was covered concerning the Elemental Implements in the previous chapter.

The Implements

Magical working is tactile, expressive, passionate, exhilarating, and sometimes terrifying. It is in no way sterile, objective, or removed from the exciting sensory perceptions which are inherent in human beings. Magic is an art best suited to experience. If conducting magical experiments does not excite some of the deepest responses of your being, then you are not doing it correctly. When encountering a true Spiritual phenomenon, the conglomerate of sensations will tell you more about the results of your ceremony than any rational data you received. When getting to know an aspect of your craft, you must explore each element of its construction and consider them with every vibrant sensation available to you.

This is why reading about a piece of magical implementation and considering its use is but the smallest imaginary tip of the iceberg. If you truly want to know the implement, physically fashion it. Gather the materials you need, and manifest the implement. Feel it in your hands, and only then will you sense the subtle and almost untranslatable meaning in its purpose. A true magician is open and receptive to each sense and intuition, aware that he is gathering information on both the conscious and unconscious levels. Open to that harmony in both crafting and using the implement, and you will harness the corresponding energetic purposes of the implement each time you reach for it and grasp it in your hands or have it near your person.

The other overlooked aspect of magical paraphernalia is their function as powerful conscious anchors while the magician's mind drifts into the nebulous unknown. Even the most adept Astral travelers often find themselves in experiences of uncertainty, going into aspects of consciousness or Astral dimensions that were not intended. If your primary objective is contact and interaction with one particular Spirit, then drifting off into some mystical parallel universe is not conducive to your immediate goal. Likewise, if working with Goetic or possibly dangerous Spirits, the magician will want as many protective measures in place as possible so he can allow himself to enter into the deep spaces of Astral consciousness without fear of being heavily influenced by these chaotic forces. Powerful implements of his chosen path and alignment will allow the magician to travel between the worlds undistracted by the innumerable irrelevant frequencies, energies, Spiritual intelligences, and the mere Astral junk that moves throughout the unseen worlds.

A realization which may or may not have occurred to the modern traditional magician is that nearly all of the implements and vestments employed in ritual are of an unfamiliar nature. That is to say, unless you are an ordained priest accustomed to donning vestments on a regular basis and handling various instruments used when conducting religious ceremonies, the items used will not be natural to you. The irony is that this fact will initially detract from your magical success rather than aid in it. In the beginning, the unfamiliar robes will cause your conscious mind to be constantly aware of your movements so as not to step on your hem or pass your sleeves through open candle flames. The unfamiliarity of handling wands, lamens, swords, pentacles, and other magical implements will initially frustrate the subtle consciousness, and cause you to focus more on the mundane tasks of moving unfamiliar objects around, rather than focusing your will on the one supreme goal of the ceremony.

But with experience, the unfamiliar vestments and implements will become familiar and your use of them will become powerful and graceful. They will no longer be distractions, but instead cues to your mind at both conscious and unconscious levels that when you wear these vestments and wield these implements, you are a magus engaged in the practice of magic.

The Lamen

In grimoric magic, the single most widely used magical piece of equipment would arguably be the Spirit lamen. Few classical grimoires fail to instruct the magician to craft the lamen or medallion to be worn upon the breast, on which is typically inscribed the sigil of the particular Spirit to be summoned.

The lamen is the magician's foremost measure of protection and linked control to the Spirit he intends to call. The parchment or metal lamen is secured above his chest and around his neck, and the invoker can feel it at all times. It is usually the first symbol that is focused on during an evocation.

In *The Art of Drawing Spirits into Crystals*, the primary lamens are those of the seven Planetary Archangels. The four lower pentagrams are all that are needed for the Archangels' seals; they work perfectly.

I find that the introduction to contacting the Angels seems to begin with the construction of their seals. The timing and focus of carving or painting the seal, name, and symbols of the Angel brings its attention to you.

In my experience, I have found that any manner of chain, ribbon, or cord for suspending the lamens will suffice. I always wear the lamen outside of my robe so that it is clearly visible.

Although it must have occurred to other practicing magicians, the intensity with which lamens may or should be crafted was communicated to me by allowing me to observe in vision such an activity while being able to feel the intensity of emotion which the sorcerer put into his handiwork. I scryed the vision of a magician of old who handled the piece of metal upon which he was to inscribe the sigil with such reverence and attention as if nothing else existed in the world. As he began to trace out the pattern of the sigil from his personal handbook of magic onto the metal disk, he began to chant deeply at a barely audible but intense level. He prayed, asking the divine to bind to this lamen the nature and essence of the Spirit, to have it appear and be constrained by it. He then spoke aloud to the Spirit itself, demanding that it recognize and adhere to the image as well. The tool with which he worked seemed to come alive in his hand as it carved the array of lines, circles, and crosses into the metal, the contact of steel tool on metal lamen being charged by his full attention and chanting directly at his creation.

The use of the magician's mind as the smelting crucible to bind the nature of the Spirit to its sigil is the secret to powerfully connecting the lamen and Spirit and having the intelligent being acknowledge and respond to its use during evocation. This is why purchased or readymade seals are fairly ineffective and of little to no value. Today, there are even T-shirts being sold with Goetic Demon seals on them that are—thankfully—no more talismanic than a blank T-shirt.

To get a further understanding of how a medieval magus consecrated or activated the Spirit lamen, I urge you to attend a mass, and pay close attention at the point where the priest turns the bread wafer into the sacramental Eucharist by prayer, ceremony, and divine grace. The priest is not the one who transforms the material; it is the divine Spirit itself, and the priest knows it is so. The same reverence for and grasp of transformative ritual must be integrated into your psyche for this effect to occur in your workings. It will occur not by reverence for the Spirit, but by the conviction that through you the divine Creator can transmute a seemingly mundane material into an active Spiritual representation or physical embodiment of the Spirit itself! Regardless of your personal belief system, I encourage the sincere ritual magician to study the methods, techniques, and feelings used by a sincere and devoted priest who is willing to express his personal feelings and comprehensions of the rituals performed and how he feels they are conducted.

Another part of this method is to not try and imaginatively "create" what the Spirit will look and be like while charging the symbol but to know that its presence is real. You could liken it to the experience of reading the signature of someone you never met and getting a feeling of what their personality might be like by looking at the way they wrote their signature.

Other Grimoric Items

For the magician interested in completing his or her inventory of magical vestments and implements, I present instructions for a few other items.

The Solomonic Miter or Crown

The classic grimoires of *The Key of Solomon* and the *Goetia* call for a headpiece to be worn during magical evocation. Such ritual attire is noted elsewhere, but the most detailed instructions are found in the *Key*, which says that the magus should write (with the ink and pen of Art) four divine names upon a crown of virgin parchment: יהוה (YHVH, or JEHOVA) in front, אדני (ADONAI) behind, אל (EL) on the right, and גבור (GIBBOR) on the left.

The *Goetia* simply mentions a cap or miter, which can be your standard linen Catholic miter (*mitra simplex*), the Jewish turban of the High Priest, or probably any significant clerical headdress, granted that it's white and should be of a similar material to the robe.

To create this magical headpiece, you should first select a piece of parchment and consecrate it to its use. Then measure the circumference of your head and allow a small amount of extra space and get an idea of where you would like the crown or miter to sit on your head. You can experiment a bit with this by using regular paper to get it right before cutting the parchment. Once you have the length, space out the holy names to your liking so they evenly reflect the front, back, and two sides of your head. For my miters, I use the red cinnabar ink that is used for magic sigils and holy names in my Book of Spirits, separated by black crosses with the black ink. This forms a nice little magic circle directly around your most centered magical tool. You'll obviously want a bit of extra material so you can attach the ends of the parchment together, making small holes and using a bit of white or red silk thread. However, if you're adding the silk or linen headdress piece, don't sew it together quite yet.

The next part will be to decide what sort of wizard hat you want to have. The classic cone shape is easiest and can be seen with good examples of the "conjures" in the front of Joseph Peterson's *Lemegeton* at his Esoteric Archives website.[1] It's your classical wizard's hat with the conical shape and buffer brim near the forehead. There are two basic ways to make this one:

1. Simply cut out a triangle with the base measuring just past (enough to sew) the measurement of the length of your crown parchment. The length can be about any you desire, although I honestly think it looks silly if it is too tall. Five to seven inches is plenty, and will give it more height than you initially think. Once you have this, simply fold the fabric in two and stitch up one side of the length.

2. Cut two pieces of fabric the base of which measures half the length of your original parchment and sew up the two sides of the length.

Another version you can use is almost like the chef's hat or *toque blanche* which puffs out on the sides. This one can be a bit more complicated to sew in order for it to look nice, but the best way I've found is to cut several small triangles together so that they form a natural dome around the top and once that is done, sew the top together. For those of us not used to sewing, don't forget to turn the fabric inside out so that the proper shape can be seen with the rough sewn edges hidden inside the hat.

Once the basic pattern for the linen or silk is sewn, you'll want to attach it to the parchment crown in two ways. First, you'll want to sew or otherwise attach

---

1. http://www.esotericarchives.com/solomon/lemegeton.htm

the crown with a small part of the fabric of the hat showing at the bottom. Next, you'll want to sew the top fabric part together, do one more check on how it will fit on your head, mark it and then sew the fabric and crown "ring" together. The last part will be to sew or attach the small piece of fabric around at the very bottom part of the sharp parchment crown to create a soft buffer.

If you so desire, you can also attach lappets or strips of material 2 to 3 inches wide and roughly a foot long on the back. To do this, you want to sew them directly to the parchment and fabric if possible. Tassels can be added on the end of the lappets for the complete fancy show. As many of you have seen, I added the All-Seeing Eye to my first miter and also the planetary and astrological sign symbols to my lappets on the underside, and additional Hexagrams of Solomon to the backs. All those personal touches are not needed. I advise consecrating the magical hat when it is completed in addition to anointing the forehead before serious magical operations as these further sacraments will only further the "fire in the head" that is generated by the ceremonial magician.

The Holy Lamp

During a *DSIC* ceremony, I will begin by lighting the ritual holy lamp which is normally kept on my altar and bring it to the center of the magic circle. The lamp of course serves a primary function of adding additional illumination to the space, which is very useful when reading from the Book of Spirits. I also use the flame from the lamp to light any candles used in an operation. The lamp is particularly helpful in lighting the charcoals for the censer, since they can be held over the flame as long as you need using tongs, which is quite useful since the charcoals can be difficult to get started. Having the candles and charcoals lit from the holy lamp adds another level of sacredness to the entire ritual.

There are a variety of ancient and modern models used for the olive oil lamp; you'll want to select something appropriately designed, since regular oil lamps don't typically burn olive oil that well and the light has a tendency to go out quickly. Personally I have a large brass oil lamp with four wicks. For fuel, I use blessed virgin olive oil with additions of consecration oil fragrance and a drop of holy water.

Candles

I now consecrate my colored beeswax candles for each operation in the following manner: During the day and hour appropriate to them, I take a bit of the consecrated incense mixture I will use for the evocation plus a small amount of consecrated virgin olive oil and rub it along the length of the candle and wick. I also use my *Key of Solomon* burin to etch the sigil of the Angel on the candles. The practice resembles folk magic candle charging, but I have come to appreciate the effects.

Implement Box and Linens

I keep the majority of my equipment stored in a latching wood box. All of the items are wrapped in white linen, except the Planetary lamens, which are stored in linen colored according to their Planets. After making a stole for each Planetary Archangel, I've had colored linen left over in which to wrap the lamen and also to drape as an altar cloth over my Altar of the Stars.

The Book of Spirits

In *Gateways Through Stone and Circle* I went into depth on how one can create a *Liber Spirituum* or "Book of Spirits" as described in the instructions of *DSIC*. I also shared a few different methods I developed in its creation and use that I still utilize today. Upon experimenting more with this iconic item of ceremonial magic, I have discovered a few more ways it can be put to good use.

Although the invocations are memorized, I have found that I enjoy using my Liber Spirituum, as the very object contains a good measure of the powerful workings my scryer and I have done. Each time it is opened and used for the specific purpose of calling forth the mighty Archangels or Spirits, or recording their images, the book seems to increase in power. The words and images written within have a power and presence all on their own. If calling one of the Archangels or other beings I have recorded, simply turning to its page and revealing the iconographic image while reciting its particular invocation will bring the Spirit before the circle quickly. The Book of Spirits is a treasured tool that contains a measure of the office and imprint of each Spirit that is contained within its pages. The book acts as a direct link to each of them if they are recorded under the proper circumstances and the Spirit agreed to "sign" the page of the book with its "signature" of office. The signature is both metaphorical and actual, as you will be able to have a traceable imprint of a sigil or character you can permanently record but also have a permanent energetic one as well, so long as the book is kept in proper reverence.

There is a culmination of visual and expectant mental cues as well, which assist in bringing about the quicker arrival of the Spirit. The imagery will naturally spark instant recognition and memory within the magus and scryer who beheld the Spirit in that form. The captured image also provides a consistent example of how the spirit may appear. The expectancy is the acknowledgment that the Spirit promised to bind a part of its essence to the image and invocations on the page itself and recognize them when utilized with proper intention.

In the course of an evocation, the image of the Angel on the page has seemed to stir and a pressure within my head has begun to form as I read the invocations just opposite the Angel's image. At this point, a phenomenon may confirm the connection being formed with the Angel, such as the light intensifying in the area of the altar. As I continue to invoke and call toward the direction where the Angel is to appear, I face the page of my book toward that direction as well. After the initial traditional invocation, I place my open right hand or hold the wand directly above the page with the image of the spirit, close my eyes, and speak a personal prayer and invocation to the Angel directly. The connection is often instantaneous and my scryer will begin speaking with the Angelic being not a moment afterward.

At the conclusion of the rite I thank the Spirit, once again placing my hand above its image, and issuing a personalized prayer before reciting the license to depart. When the Spirit departs, I recite the thanks to God and then close the book.

With each evocation and continued use, the images in the Book of Spirits draw more meaning, power, and association with the Spirit directly. The information in the book also increases, as on the pages after the Spirit's image and initial invocations, I add records of important phrases and things they have said concerning themselves and their office.

Utilizing the book during evocation can be considered a compounded art form of layered symbolism and measures to securely call forth the presence of a Spirit or Angel. The Book of Spirits contains the name, sigil or sigils, the actual invocations, and after successful contact will contain the very portrait of the Spirit as it was seen by the magus or scryer or both. The magus speaks the name and invocations in the book, while the lamen, the section of the circle, the direction, and possibly the altar all repeat the name and sigil from the book, and create a compounded pull for the Spirit to acknowledge. No article should be abandoned or considered redundant as each has a specific call and signal to the Spirit as well as the magus on a different level, all focused at calling the Spirit from its proper direction and place in the universe to arrive right before the circle, symbol of complete universal authority and perfection.

Unique Method for Talisman Consecration Using the Book of Spirits

Make a talisman out of clean parchment under the name, hour, and day according to one of the Planetary Archangels and ask for their direct blessing to consecrate it. For one week, beginning on that day and hour, place the parchment sigil directly on the page of your Liber Spirituum with the angel's image and invocation. Wrap the book back up in linen or silk and keep it in your altar and pray over it twice each day (once in the morning, once in the evening) until the same day and hour on the following week. As an act of reverence for both the Spirit of the page and the talisman, remove the talisman from the page without opening the book fully, and retrieve it using linen, being careful not to touch the talisman with bare hands. Then wrap the consecrated talisman in a square piece of silk that corresponds to the Planet.

V
Considerations for Scrying in Classical Evocation

HE REALITY OF WHETHER OR NOT we are able to behold Spirits is a conundrum of the human psychological condition. If we once again look to classical texts of magic for methods of conjuring Spirits, we will find many references to utilizing children as the seers or scryers. The Abramelin operation requires a young boy to be the assistant as well as the initial observer of your Holy Guardian Angel. Many of the operations in the *Hygromanteia* describe using such youthful assistants. The varieties of *Key of Solomon* texts also describe using such seers in many of the operations.

The modern would-be evocator would do well to ask why the idea of the child scryer has had some persistence over the centuries. The appeal of these young seers goes beyond their innocence and purity of heart, mind, and Spirit which are indeed virtues that well support Spiritual contact of any sort. A child has not yet been as bound by culturally developed filters which inhibit the witnessing of such beings as Angels and Spirits. That is to say, the scryer who is most successful will have the least amount of conscious assumptions and preconceptions about what a Spiritual encounter should be and look like, including notions that the interaction will be upsetting in any way.

The limiting factors of our pre-existing framework are counter to the nature of the Spiritual world which by very definition is counter to our usual merely sensory perceptions.

The human being—magician or otherwise—has continually anthropomorphized every unknown power he does not comprehend. Indeed, he is frustrated by the very idea of something being beyond his sensory capabilities. If there are indeed entities, powers, and energies beyond the physical world, surely they must have some relatable context to the human condition. This is where we get Gods, Angels, and Demons that seem to exhibit human traits, appearances, emotions, or motivations.

I dare say that after all of my experiences I am quite aware of my conscious mind perceiving such beings within the framework of a limited understanding. I am sure I do not perceive nor comprehend any being (physical or otherwise) exactly as they are just from my human perspective. It could be truly stated that we do not perceive ourselves or one another without the clouded judgment, cultural framework, and labels our conscious mind has developed over time. We can easily assess someone to be good, bad, friendly, hostile, and any hundreds of simplifying descriptive terms that are but a fraction of the reality of the person.

One way we can get out of our prejudicial frames of perception and into this "state of innocence" is through an altered state of mind, such as hypnotic or other light trance. A scryer should be in a passive, neutral, and receptive state of consciousness. Any conscious attempt by the scryer to judge, criticize, analyze, or evaluate the process will disrupt the chance of useful communication or exchange.

Grimoric magic designs and creates a particular paradigm of corresponding elements, behaviors, and reactions which by the law of causality result in exchanges of a particular (albeit limited) nature, unique unto the art. It is made up of perceived workings and interactions of higher celestial intelligences and infernal beings experienced by the perceptive faculties of the participants. Without a doubt, the nature of summoned Spirits will most definitely be colored by the deepest unconscious constructs of our comprehension as well as the contextual framework of the ritual we are utilizing.

The Angels, Spirits, ghosts, and demons may not be just coming from your mind, but that doesn't mean that you perceive them beyond the context of the personal filters, perceptions, context, and unconscious judgments which exist in your mind. The practice of magic is not a sterile experiment in objectivity. In actuality, it is probably the furthest thing from it. Imagination is the tool used to bridge the gaps where human reasoning breaks down. It colors and forms an emotional and intellectual link to patterns, energies, and ideas which may be beyond the known framework of human conceptualization. Usual ways of thinking and reasoning will do a partial reboot and you'll be able to have access to new areas of your consciousness. This is not without its risks of course, and could be just as potentially hazardous as taking too many psychedelic drugs. Adventure and discovery are not without their risks.

We often speak of the mind or brain as if it were one simple, unified, and perfectly functioning organ. Thoughts are complicated and ever-shifting enough as they are and even they are not "the mind," just a small part of it. When you have no vested expectations, labels, judgments, and psychological frameworks about what is supposed to be, then your ability to accept what actually *is*, is greatly enhanced. It takes a lifetime of continual practice and dedication to remove oneself from the constructed paradigms of modern social structure.

The steps of research, complete immersion, contemplation, planning, and ritual tool construction establishes the power behind your chosen tradition in ceremonial magic. The purpose of these steps is to integrate and construct a "magical universe" or working model wherein semi-structured experience and comprehension may occur. Successful undertaking and completion of these steps could be dubbed an initiation.

Initiation is a term widely used in the occult community, especially in magical lodges such as those of the OTO and the Golden Dawn. Initiation can refer to the simple stepping in, "shedding the old" and then "donning the new." It is an initial dedicating of oneself to a particular practice, system, or method of working and being. It can be a willful declaration and firm decision to proceed in a specific manner. Fasting, retreat, prayer, and focus were the methods to initiation most mystical practices of the classical era used. To willfully surrender comfortable surroundings and habitual ways of behaving is perhaps the greatest method of transforming the self. The degree of societal and habitual programming of our conscious and unconscious assumptions is the main inhibitor of a mystical mindset. The removal of any lingering distractions or anxieties surrounding your purpose is the first step. The importance of this realization in the mystical, magical, spiritual process cannot be overstated. This state has yielded the most significant spiritual experiences recorded by the founders of the world's top religions and philosophies. The most intense practices of yoga and meditation deal fundamentally with removing all artificial constructs and conceptions from the mind in order to experience life and consciousness in the purest way possible; that is to say, with the least social, psychological, cultural, judgmental, ethical, or other limiting labels as possible. This is getting closer to the truth of a thing, which is intensely difficult for any person to do.

Questions to consider might be: If you had no idea of what an "Angel" was, how would you perceive it? What is something perceived for which we have no label, frame of reference, nor societal standard? Spontaneous encounters with Spirits have no preconceived expectations or framework; they are encounters perceived in conscious innocence, which is to say, when the person experiencing the entity is not consciously attempting to manipulate the encounter nor force it to respond as they expect. Although unconscious and subconscious factors are surely coming into play to interpret preconceived entities, they are working from paradigms already constructed instead of new, actively created ones. Spontaneous encounters have the benefit of calling up raw reactions from the perceiver. Unfortunately, these deep-dwelling emotions are typically fear and uncertainty. I've witnessed what appears to be a built-in defense mechanism which warns when situations or perceptions are outside the bounds of typically accepted reality. This defense mechanism is what causes adults to become more terrified than young children who have not built fearful associations of the unknown.

Adjusting the senses and levels of perception and comprehension will be vital for those seeking to truly experience what the art of magical evocation has to offer. This can be achieved without the use of psychedelics or substitutions of any sort. In my own experience, the most successful methods for improving faculties for achieving successful Spiritual interactions were:

1. The HGA retreat.
2. Ritualistic shock.
3. Maintaining a specially dedicated room for practice.

Human beings can cling so tightly to these beliefs and paradigms that any tampering by conflicting thoughts or actions can sometimes be met with violent hostility. Here is the paradox: In the attempt to expand awareness and perceive new entities, encounters, and truths of the "unknown," there is the potential to inadvertently also create a prison of isolated fantasy. Anyone whose deep unconscious does not shut down from conflicting paradigm models may well experience the intense presence of the Spirits as he has. However, the resulting consequences of such frameworks may also exhibit undesirable circumstances in day-to-day life. Where these magicians may simply lay the effects at the hands and feet of the fallen, my assessment is that more will be due to their own subconscious considerations.

Early religious and social programming is highly effective and continues to be so in this day and age. Its methods can lead a college graduate of considerable intelligence to firmly believe that people of dissimilar faiths are destined to have their immortal souls doomed to an eternity of painful torture. No matter what arguments are presented to him that would suggest otherwise, his early social programming and resulting construct is such that his mind will simply refuse to acknowledge such possibilities.

A magician will become familiar with a multitude of Spiritual beings, correspondences, and specific powers to better organize his practice and level of understanding. In learning to harness his will and intellect into one clear channel of effort and causality, the more specified and directed the focus, the better the magician will be able to cause the intended change. The more general the topic and focus, the more diluted the effort becomes in trying to effect change in any veritable sense. This is why a magician with a singular tradition and focus may have more insight and effect in a certain area than a mystic who only ponders the phenomena from a broader and more reserved position. The same situation can be likened to an anthropologist who decides to immerse himself within a foreign culture for a time to garner knowledge of the social and cultural traditions of the peoples. He may gain considerable insight and respect for the people he studies, but in many ways he will always be an outsider, unable to completely comprehend and view the world from the perspective of the people he is studying.

To have any sense of harmony and productivity, a magician should continually work within a paradigm and system which is empowered by his subconscious constructs as well his conscious belief system. It should challenge and expand his awareness to new heights rather than constrict him into dangerous cages of self-constricting dogma. Cyclic practices of building up and breaking down should be perused with careful consideration allowing for time of strict, regimented practices of arcane arts without fanciful folly or deviation. And then time for complete abandonment of structure and tradition in favor of passive calm and stillness of mind.

To better gauge a magical operation, I will typically reflect on a few points which have become a guide to what I consider a successful evocation: If I can answer in the affirmative to the questions below, my scryer and I usually consider the operation an overall success.

1. Did the ceremony produce a noticeable, environmental change and/or alterations in mental, emotional, or sensory states when the Spirit arrived? That is, could the Spirit be seen and heard and its presence felt?

2. Did the Spirit we conjured resemble its classical form or what is known about it from classical sources, matching at least to some degree its ascribed office and correspondences? Did it speak with the authority of its office? Could it answer questions correctly and informatively?

3. After the ceremony was completed, did results occur that showed evidence that the desired working was being fulfilled in purpose and intention? If the Spirit promised to fulfill certain tasks, were they done?

After an operation is concluded, I often find myself doing more research to find if there are any recorded parallels with what the Spirit said or how my scryer experienced it that I was unaware of previously. If it is a Spirit I contacted myself previously in private, I consider in what ways the operation with my scryer felt and appeared the same and where it differed. With the combined results and recalled transmissions from Spirits as well as any newfound occult knowledge, I determine if the ritual was indeed fruitful.

Here are some factors to keep in mind:

1. No matter how many times a magical operation is undertaken, you are dealing with invisible forces and concepts, so it will always be dealing with the unknown.

2. Applying laws that are sound in the physical world of matter to the non-physical worlds of Spirit will continually fail due to a false assumption. While analogies may be sometimes be fairly drawn between matter and Spirit, Spirit is not matter.

3. Be open to allowing magic to work in manners which do not match your expectations. As an example, Trithemius apparently contacted Angelic beings in hopes of securing a method to magically send messages from one person to another in complete secrecy. Instead of the Angels granting him and his intended recipients telepathic abilities or a Spirit servitor to deliver audible messages back and forth, history shows that Trithemus instead discovered ingenious methods of cipher and coded writing. The *Steganographia* would become one of Trithemius' most famous and influential writings. It is an extensive work of three volumes which contains meticulous instructions for the evocation of Spirits, particularly Angels, in order to transmit messages over long distances. It was eventually realized that these volumes contained the codes to decipher the extensive cryptic messages hidden throughout his writings. It is purely speculation that any of these methods were taught to him by the Angels, but it is an interesting and entirely plausible idea.

Begin at the CIRCLE

When a ritual magician is starting out and even after his thousandth evocation, he comes full circle, so to speak, back to basics. Forming of the point of the cause of all creation, the place wherein you stand in totality, the witness to the ultimate mysteries.

In our very senses exist the construct of total perception beyond which lies the fabric of reality and the cosmos. In evocation, we draw forth the realm beyond dreams, beyond imagining, and behold it with senses foreign to its very evoked nature. The magus ventures beyond perceptive barriers and laws of logical reason, beyond the dictates of learned knowledge, to the source of origin for every collected atom. In this sense of complete unknown and alien experience is the most similar states of existence.

Never is there more intense reaction in the psyche than in the moment of manifestation from the unmanifest, of perception of a form from the formless. There is realization where before there was nought but unknowing. The mind of the magus must be able to surgically divide the curtains of accepted reality and fully conjoin the undefined ether with the world of form.

Through the experiences related in the following chapters, I share what I have learned in my own workings. I also share with you the intuitive discoveries I've made concerning some aspects of ritual magic and the purposes and mechanisms thereof. More than anything, though, I wanted to share what has transpired and bring the knowledge and gifts I have received from the beings with whom I've personally interacted so that they may assist or inspire other magicians in their own personal workings.

The beings who fill the pages of grimoires as well as other magical, mystical, and religious writings are as mysterious as ever. Even with the encounters with the Spirits which have changed my life and reshaped my consciousness indefinitely, I am little closer to understanding the complete nature of their existence than when I began. Each explanation, definition, and conclusion I come up with seems always to be lacking in the full comprehension of them, as their existence, in fact, does lie beyond my comprehension of them.

My experiments through *DSIC* and other grimoric systems are the foundation of my magical experience, but are only a part of my continued experience outside of the magic circle and in my daily life. In this volume I am happy to share with you some of the many instances where the Spirits, Angels, and the very magic itself interplayed with everyday working and experiences, to put quite a magnificent spin on my life's journey. How wondrous it is when you see that the magic and mystery does not simply end at the close of the ceremony and the visual departure of the evoked Spirit. Magic, true magic, is a holistic undertaking that is set in motion by your actions and intentions but is not defined by them. The reason magic is wondrous is that it exists beyond your perceptions and your desire for control, no matter how much you try to define it.

The body of this work covers many specific and detailed instructions within the scope of traditional grimoric magic and the calling of Spirits within crystals and mirrors. However, it also blends practical application with techniques acquired by revelation and more so by experience due to encounters with celestial beings. The process is ongoing as the adventurous magician will see, with new situations and experiences creating new dynamics for working your developing will in the world.

Without romanticizing it in any way, I can state that magic becomes a theme in the life of one who utilizes it on a continual basis. The manner in which it threads its workings into your circumstances will depend largely upon the particular entities and energies which are most compatible with you and intermingle with your own destiny.

In the chapters which follow, you will share in the encounters as well as the words of instruction and wisdom from the celestial rulers who are under the supreme Creator and Source. The operation with each Archangel was one of considerable impact and change for not only my scryer and myself, but for our families as well. In each case, I felt there was vastly more to learn and discover, even after an operation with an Archangel whom I had contacted numerous times. My personal assessment is that the more time spent with a particular Angel, the more attuned to its sphere of influence you will become. However, I must caution the newcomer to this work that coming into proximity with the Archangels and other potent beings may be more upsetting than expected, so I warn against any casual invocation without careful consideration. Some of their offices or particular natures may be in opposition to parts of your psyche and this may initially invite more strife and conflict than understanding.

A Latin Prayer to Assist You in Seeing Spirits

Mitte lucem Tuam et veritatem Tuam, Domine, quæ nos ducant et perducant ad montem sanctum Tuum, et ad cœlestia Tua tabernacula.[1]

1. "Send Thy light and Thy truth, O Lord, that they may lead us and guide us to Thy sacred mountain and to Thy celestial tabernacles." This first part of the prayer is a paraphrase of the Vulgate Latin translation of *Psalm* 42:3 (43:3 in the Hebrew Bible) as employed by John Dee to seek to be granted vision in the crystal, as recorded in his Magical journal for 5 September 1607. —APF

Qui tollis peccáta mundi
miserere nobis;
Qui tollis peccáta mundi,
súscipe deprecatiónem nostram.
Qui sedes ad déxteram Patris,
miserere nobis.[2]

Angele Dei,
Qui custos es mei,
Me tibi commissum pietate superna,
Hodie (vel hac nocte) illumina, custodi, rege, et guberna.
Amen.[3]

Errors in Practice

As it is human nature to err in perception and comprehension, so will there be errors in magical workings. It's forever a learning and refining process of accurately recording and following up on experiments. Although magical ritual is experienced through the sensational and enigmatic, it is pertinent that we be as thorough and discriminating as possible in the examination of the results. To experience any useful singularity in magic, we have to understand it from a perceivable framework. As I mentioned before, the ritual framework of *Drawing Spirits into Crystals* is the structure which is used and described in my first publication. The subsequent workings were not to be my first 'initiation' into the calling of Angelic beings, but it was my first initiation into the dynamic planetary Archangels and their spheres, far beyond any visualizations or invoked petitions I had done previously. In all my practice, I really do find it is the Angels themselves who guard us from the repercussions of many possible oversights and false conceptions. They also seem to have attuned my perceptions to be able to experience further evocations of Spirits from other systems and paradigms.

---

2. "Thou Who taketh away the sins of the world, have mercy on us. Thou Who taketh away the sins of the world, receive our prayer for pardon. Thou Who sitteth at the right hand of the Father, have mercy on us." This second part of the prayer is from the Latin Mass. —APF

3. "O Angel of God, Thou who art my guardian, me having been entrusted unto thee by supernal compassion, on this day (or night) enlighten, guard, rule, and govern me. Amen." If the prayer is being said during the day, say *hodie* ("this day"); if during the night, say *hac nocte* ("this night"). This traditional Catholic prayer for the guidance and protection of the Holy Guardian Angel is mediæval in origin, and was formerly attributed to Anselm. —APF

In the course of several years working intensively with the *DSIC* system, I have definitely personalized some of the components to coincide with what I've found to be beneficial and more conducive to successful operations. Success in this case being the contact with the intended Spiritual beings, any adaptations to the ceremony are geared toward establishing and getting the most out of the interaction.

Despite some of my personal adaptations, I continue to recite the invocations as given in the grimoire, as I feel a sense of purpose and honor in their use. The recitation of the written invocation during the early part of the ceremony sets the tone and specifications for the proper exchange between human and Spirit. However, after achieving contact, I will often go right into very spontaneous and willful discourse. Before the invocations are memorized and integrated, while they remain strange and unfamiliar, they may seem to distract from developing your connection and interaction, but as you memorize and deepen your understanding of the invocations, you will find that they grow more and more effective in deepening your receptive state of awareness for the evocation. By the way, it is worth noting that the conjurations in *DSIC* are almost certainly designed for the use of an operator who is not also the scryer, since "we" is used and the words to be spoken are those of someone who is not in a trance or other altered state of perception. I recite the conjuration before sitting down to scry, and when the Spirit arrives, I typically forgo the additional prayer of thanks and instead go with a personal remark of welcome and gratitude.

No later than a few days before evocation I will receive communion and undergo at least a Solomonic (*Key of Solomon*) confession, and use prayers from the *Ars Novum* and *Ars Nororia* as well as ones given in the *Key*. I typically recite these prayers for most if not all evocations because they deal specifically with conversing with Spirits through the strength of the Most High. Naturally I use the prayers and requests from the particular grimoire with I am working, but have become accustomed to the above methods due to the Solomonic nature of the practice.

Three days before the ritual, I abstain from sugars, coffee, sex, alcohol, and any other activity prohibited for Solomonic magic, gearing my mind and body toward magical working. I don't go overboard when I still have to function in my day-to-day life. I simply make conscious efforts to put my energy, will, and thoughts into conscious control and decisions that works toward the outcome of the ritual.

Recently I've conducted *DSIC* operations more spontaneously, preparing only a few days ahead of the operation, but I believe this is a privilege earned after initial invocations and initiations by the Angels, and the building of relationships with them. It's not something I can claim will work for everyone. My fasting will not be too abrupt or drastic for these operations, but I will not eat any meat or heavy meal for at least eight hours leading up to the invocation. Water and good healthy greens and foods prior seem good.

I still take a ritual shower or bath, reciting the *Psalm* and then anointing with holy oil right before the ritual.

In my first volume, I did not go into personal ritual alterations since I believe it is important for others to try out the system first without making any changes and then see what needs to be done. I don't wish to assume my unique adaptations are useful for everyone working from this text either. I include my adaptations in this work in order to assist those who may have encountered similar challenges and are looking for advice and examples.

Even after repeated success, it's still possible that some experiments will fail where absolutely nothing occurs and no Spirit arrives. This can be rather disconcerting, especially after having achieved some consistency with success. It becomes easy trying to wrack your brain attempting to discover every variable which might have gone wrong. This happened for me during both *Almadel* invocations as well as *DSIC*. Sometimes operations just fail for no apparent reason. It is equally mysterious how some rituals also sometimes work perfectly for unknown reasons. In my experience, the best answers for why certain operations fail or succeed have been revealed by the Spirits themselves during a consecutive successful operation.

There is a tried and tested process of approaching Spiritual contact in a humble yet pragmatic way, whereby the magician and the scryer are assisted by the Spiritual beings who are beseeched to help them. This lengthy process usually involves going through several initiations and introductions where various Spiritual concepts are integrated by the very process of evocation/reflection (prayer), etc. The result seems to allow for the more ambiguous contacts and Spiritual explorations to be allowed.

The magical and mundane worlds scarcely appear to line up in a cohesive way that makes sense. The magician's and seer's roles of mediator and communicator with the Spirit world determines the level of effectiveness in the exchange. Positive result from change typically depends upon built (initiated) relationships between the higher intelligences that have some understanding about the workings of human beings and the physical world.

VI

Revisiting the Archangels of the Seven Spheres

Part One • New Lessons from the Divine Seven

THE EXPERIENCES THAT LED to the writing of *Gateways Through Stone and Circle* comprised an immersion in a world that has endless possibilities. As a system of magical evocation within the Solomonic strain of Western Esotericism, *The Art of Drawing Spirits into Crystals* has proven to be reliable in continual application, resulting in more successful contact with Angels and other Spirits than any other system with which I have experimented. This is likely due to the system's flexibility; the magical formula, though simple, is highly adaptive, allowing for alternate methods in its execution without ruining or discarding any of the vital components of the ritual.

The Planetary superpowers (Planetary Archangels) of the Western world are an enigmatic wonder to behold. Witnessing them in the midst of ceremony, one is flooded with multiple sensory impressions received through vision, hearing, touch, and even smell, which I came to realize I am not fully able to comprehend or appreciate in its totality. Initially all the operations were solitary, with my mind struggling to maintain conscious, focused attention so that I could respond in the present moment while simultaneously trying to maintain a sense of rational recall so that I could quickly and coherently record the incoming stimuli. I believe I accomplished what I set out to do within the extent of my abilities during my initial evocations, all while struggling to maintain these two functions.

However, to better understand and possibly perceive these Messengers of celestial origin, I surmised that having another gifted seer within the magic circle with me was possibly a superior way to conduct these experiments, perhaps resulting in better responses and questions while in the midst of the evocation. I have come to believe that no one involved in authentic conversation with visible and audible Spirits can interact with them in a purely sterile and objective manner. So much of their presence and communication reaches people on emotional and subconscious levels, despite the boundaries of the magical circle. The process of evocation creates a more complex and thus more complete system of communication than the usual, and the heights to which it can take us seems to be limited only by our own mental and perceptual ceilings. When more than one mind is responding to the presence of these beings, a wider perspective is possible. This is not always the case, but if the two or more minds are in harmony as well as in allowance to observe such phenomena, undoubtedly a richer perspective on the actual occurrence is probable.

The magical experiments presented in the following sections were conducted for a set of specific reasons. Among these was to gain a clearer understanding of the offices or purposes of these Archangels in their relation to humanity and their ability to actually fulfill or demonstrate what that entailed. The opportunity that working with my scryer allowed was for him to fully immerse himself in the experiential aspect of communicating (scrying) with these Spirits while not being concerned with any other ritual functions or duties. It left me the opportunity to record his experiences as well as the responses to each of the questions I posed to the Spirit in question.

In none of the operations presented here did I ever reveal to my scryer in advance the questions I planned to ask the Spirits. In many cases I didn't even reveal the name or nature of the Spirit we were going to contact, nor show the scryer the image of the Spirit in my personal Liber Spirituum. Often the only instruction I gave him was that he needed to be ready at such and such a date and time to take part in a magical evocation. My reason for this was to test the ability of the operation as well as the particular Spirit to produce authentic experiences that were to some extent consistent for my scryer and myself. I took such measures not primarily to prove or disprove what was being experienced to anyone else, but to verify it for myself. I was also particularly excited to see what would truly come through to someone who was not a trained and learned Hermetic magician, and who had not been raised in Catholicism or any other Judeo-Christian sect which has a tradition steeped in Angelic lore.

I was fully aware of the fact that my scryer was by no means a "pure subject"; undoubtedly he had come across the names and natures of some of these Archangels. However, to my knowledge it has never been an interest nor an area of study for him. After several operations, he remarked that many of these Angels and Spirits were completely foreign to him, and that he had never encountered even their names in literature or other media. His spiritual interest and passion are dedicated to the Celtic traditions and pantheon. In spite of or even because of this fact, he is quite possibly the best candidate I know for proving the objective existence of Angelic beings. If anything, his lack of personal attachment to who and what these Spirits are supposed to be is an ideal state of mind for a scryer. Nothing distorts or destroys a scrying session more than the mind attempting to color and dictate what will transpire.

Our first operation was to be with the great Archangel of the Sun, Michael.

The Archangel of the Sun
Michael

✠	Day and time	On Sunday, during hour of Sol or Midday
✠	Name and meaning	Hebrew מיכאל *(Michael* or *Mikhael),* "He who is unto the likeness of God"
✠	Pronunciation of name (as spoken by the Spirit)	«Me-kah-el»
✠	Planet	☉
✠	Materials for lamen	Parchment, gold, brass
✠	Sigil	[sigil]
✠	Direction for Invocation	West, South
✠	Incense mixture	Frankincense, red sandalwood, saffron, amber, musk, aloes wood, balm wood, laurel seeds, cloves, benzoin, storax, galbanum.

Table VI-1. ***Evocatory Correspondences for Michael***[1]

Of Michael and the Office of the Sun

There can be seen in Greco-Egyptian magic evidence of conjurors assuming the authority of solar deities such as Apollo in the evocation of other spirits. In spiritual traditions across the globe it seems that ghosts, demons, and even darker gods are held in check by sun deities. Nowhere is this solar power more prevalent in the grimoires than when Archangel Michael assumes this role. Some scholars see Michael as the Hebrew adaptation of the Mideastern Sun God Shamash. As Michael would come to be in later times, Shamash was widely viewed as a dispenser of justice, shining light into dark places both physically and metaphorically. Hammurabi's famous law code was secured and recorded in the name of Shamash. The oppression and injustice from which the ancient sun god was invoked to deliver suffering people included the torment of demonic possession. Records remain where he is called upon to exorcise demons and dark entities as well as illnesses from people. In this aspect Shamash was also a

1. Please see the Cautionary Warning Regarding Grimoric Ingredients in Appendix A. —APF

god of healing and salvation. In Greek magical texts, Rē-Hēlios the Sun definitely held his position as the ruler, life-giver, and authority in the Heavens. The Sun is continually perceived as the power that dispels the darkness of night and gives life and light to all. As I stated at the beginning of this section, in Greek magical texts it is Apollo who is often invoked for the controlling of other, usually darker Spirits.[2] It is difficult to dismiss the parallels between these being and the mighty Archangel of the Sun, Michael. However, while it is worthwhile for the learned magus to be aware that in many cases Spiritual beings have assumed different roles and names depending on the culture and people who adopted them, it is equally important to be cautious of making assumptions lightly. As practicing magicians, we should verify the true nature of these beings on our own.

Magic paraphernalia and vestments for the controlling of Spirits appear largely based on Solar symbolism as well. I suggest that this Solar dominance over infernal or sublunary Spirits may have a connection with the much-discussed lion-skin belt of the Lemegeton's *Goetia*. The exact purpose of this particular piece of ritual attire is debated by magical scholars and practitioners alike. Many assume the belt to be simply a piece of bravado to intimidate unruly Spirits by showing them that the magician is not even afraid of slaying lions. However, I strongly suspect that the association of the lion with the powers of

2. Apollōn is called upon in the Papyri Græcæ Magicæ (PGM) in both His oracular and (by the time of the Papyri) Solar aspects. It may surprise readers who are as yet unfamiliar with the PGM to learn that in its multicultural, syncretic texts Michaēl is also invoked in many places (though nowhere near as often as Apollōn). In some cases, Michaēl is in fact linked with Apollōn. In an invocation of Apollōn in PGM I (Papyrus Berolinensis inv. 5025), lines 262 ff., there is a metrical hymn in which Apollōn is called "First Angel of great Zeus Iaō," immediately followed by "and I invoke Thee, Michaēl, controlling the heavenly cosmos." In PGM II (Papyrus Berolinensis inv. 5026), lines 64 ff., a rite invoking the Solar Apollōn at sunrise, the mage inscribes the name of Michaēl upon the doorpost of the chamber in which he prepares himself for seven days before the invocation. Michaēl is also identified with a Solar Osiris in the Papyri. In PGM IV (the Great Magical Papyrus of Paris), in the invocation at lines 2241 ff., we find reference to Hēlios-Osiris, later in the same rite further described as "Lord Osiris, the Path-Illuminating God, Michaēl, Archangel of Angels." In PGM VII (Papyrus Londinensis 121), lines 255 ff., a brief rite to receive a vision by means of a magic lamp, the lamp is addressed as the very tool which Osiris-Michaēl uses to illuminate the way: "O Lord, I wish Thee well, Lamp, the one lighting the path for Osiris, and lighting the path for Osir-Chentechtha and for my Lord Michaēl." Another version of the same lamp ritual in PGM XXIIb (P. Berolinensis inv. 13895), lines 27 ff., unambiguosly says that the lamp is the one lighting the path for "the Great [Fa]th[er] Osiris Michaēl." —APF

the Sun may be more relevant, particularly as it corresponds to powerful Solar deities of magic like the Egyptian Sekhmet. As Stephen Skinner states:

> The skin of any big cat, especially a lion, was held in awe, as it related to the fierce goddess Sekhmet. Sekhmet also has associations with magic. High Priests of Sekhmet were often associated with magic, such as Heryshefnkht, who was both Chief of Magicians and High Priest of Sekhmet.[3]

It is understandable that such a lion-skin belt or girdle was adopted into later evocation practices to assist with having direct control over spirits and demons. Exactly when and where this article of attire in its particular form (three inches broad, inscribed with the same words as the magic circle) was first included in the practice of the *Goetia* is still a mystery. It's entirely possible that the belt was suggested to a practicing magician by an Angel or Spirit as an added defense against the machinations of chaotic, sublunary Spirits. In other words, in my assessment, it is far more likely that the lion-skin continues to be employed in magic as a potent correspondence of a creature of Solar power and spiritual authority rather than merely as a boastful hunting trophy.

Regardless of his planetary association, Archangel Michael is viewed as a champion for mankind and for the faithful, a protector against wicked Spirits or other enemies. Michael is the one who aids those who have seen great peril and overwhelming odds. In Roman Catholic angelology, Michael holds four principal offices:

- To fight against Satan.
- To rescue the souls of the faithful from the power of the enemy, especially at the hour of death.
- To be the champion of God's people, the Jews in the Old Law, the Christians in the New Testament; therefore he was the patron of the Church, and of the orders of knights during the Middle Ages.
- To call away from earth and bring men's souls to judgment ("signifer S. Michael repraesentet eas in lucam sanctam", Offert. Miss Defunct. "Constituit eum principem super animas suscipiendas", Antiph. off. Cf. *The Shepherd of Hermas*, Book III, Similitude 8, Chapter 3).[4]

---

3. Stephen Skinner, *Techniques of Græco-Egyptian Magic*, p. 134.

4. Frederick Holweck, "St. Michael the Archangel," in *The Catholic Encyclopedia*. Vol. 10 (New York: Robert Appleton Company, 1911).

The very first known written reference to the Archangel Michael is in the book of *Daniel* in the Old Testament. Daniel sees an Angel in a vision after a devout period of fasting, and others who are present during the occurrence cannot see the Spirit. The passage, when looked at from a magical and mystical standpoint, is very understandable to those have experienced the presence of these mighty beings. Many accounts of Angels describe their appearance as shining, brilliant beings, but even so there are particularly Solar-related details in Daniel's description of the Angel sent by Archangel Michael:

Fig. VI-2. ***Lamen of Michael in the manner of DSIC***

> I lifted up mine eyes, and looked, and, behold, a man clothed in linen, whose loins were girded with pure gold of Uphaz: his body also was like the beryl, and his face as the appearance of lightning, and his eyes as flaming torches, and his arms and his feet like unto burnished brass, and the voice of his words like the voice of a multitude. And I, Daniel, alone saw the vision; for the men that were with me saw not the vision; but a great quaking fell upon them, and they fled to hide themselves. So I was left alone, and saw this great vision, and there remained no strength in me; for my comeliness was turned in me into corruption, and I retained no strength. Yet heard I the voice of his words; and when I heard the voice of his words, then was I fallen into a deep sleep on my face, with my face toward the ground.[5]

The Angel mentions to Daniel that Michael is a "chief prince" there to defend Israel against attacks.

---

5. *Daniel* 10:5–9 (American Standard Version).

> But I will tell thee that which is inscribed in the writing of truth: and there is none that holdeth with me against these, but Michael your prince.[6]

And again:

> And at that time shall Michael stand up, the great prince who standeth for the children of thy people; and there shall be a time of trouble, such as never was since there was a nation even to that same time: and at that time thy people shall be delivered, every one that shall be found written in the book.[7]

After this there is a passage describing Michael acting as the judge or at least witness during the final days of all those who "sleep in the dust." Again, these are offices reminiscent of the Sun God Shamash.

In the Rabbinic Midrash, Michael is described as fighting against Samael,[8] who in later magical lore becomes the Archangel of Mars but in other texts is seen as the great Accuser.[9] The two dispute over the land of Israel and, according to one tale, even over the soul of Moses.[10]

The most well-known description of Michael in the Christian New Testament is without doubt in *Revelation*:

> And there was war in heaven: Michael and his angels going forth to war with the dragon; and the dragon warred and his angels; And they prevailed not, neither was their place found any more in heaven. And the great dragon was cast down, the old serpent, he that is called the Devil and Satan, the deceiver of the whole world; he was cast down to the earth, and his angels were cast down with him. And I heard a great voice in heaven, saying, Now is come the salvation, and the power, and the kingdom of our God, and the authority of his Christ: for the accuser of our brethren is cast down, who accuseth them before our God day and night.[11]

---

6. *Ibid.*, 10:21.

7. Ibid., 12:1.

8. Due to his role of accuser, Samael is given over as being an evil Angel, possibly even the Dragon of *Revelations* and the first fallen Angel—an issue about which I planned to ask Archangel Samael directly in another evocation.

9. The "Accuser" is in Hebrew שטן (*Satan*), translated into the Greek of the New Testament as Διάβολος (*Diabolos*), which eventually mutated into the English *Devil*. The evolution of language is a strange process which makes the platypus seem nearly reasonable. —APF

10. Midrash *Deuteronomy Rabbah* or *Devarim Rabbah* 11:6. Also in the *Epistle of Jude* 1:9. —APF

11. The *Revelation* or *Apocalypse of John* 12:7–10 (ASV). —APF

In the Greek Magical Papyri, Archangel Michael is invoked along with five other Angels in order to force a group of 13 demons to appear before the magician.

There are several legends and accounts of people seeing the Archangel Michael in locations around Medieval Europe up to the Renaissance.

The founder of anthroposophy, the esoteric teacher Rudolf Steiner, in a November 1917 lecture on Michael, taught that in 1879 the Archangel achieved a victory over "the Dragon," clearly a reference to the war in the book of *Revelation*:

> In 1879, in November, a momentous event took place, a battle of the Powers of Darkness against the Powers of Light, ending in the image of Michael overcoming the Dragon.[12]

In several systems of Kabbalistic and magical correspondences, Archangel Michael rules the fourth Heaven called Machen, the sixth Sphere on the Tree of Life called Tiphereth, and the Sun. However, in some systems, Michael is ascribed to the Sphere of Hod and to Mercury, while Raphael rules Tiphereth and the Sun; and in still others, Michael rules both Sephirotic Tiphereth and Planetary Mercury. I wanted to question the Archangel in reference to this topic and possibly clear some of the confusion.

---

12. Rudolph Steiner, "Behind the Scenes of External Happenings," in Rudolph Steiner and Christopher Bamford (ed.), *The Archangel Michael: His Mission and Ours: Selected Lectures and Writings* (Hudson, NY: Anthroposophic Press, 1994), p. 76.

In his claim in that lecture that Louis Claude de Saint-Martin, Franz von Baader, and Éliphas Lévi had all spoken of this event, Steiner seems to be laying a thumb on the scale to gain important endorsements for his statement, which would have constituted prophecies by the three luminaries, as all were dead before 1879 (in 1803, 1841, and 1875 respectively). However, the event to which they may well have referred was not a future victory of Michael over the Dragon in November 1879, but a somewhat different though related significance attributed to that date by the Abbot Johannes Trithemius. In his well-known *De Septem Secundeis*, Trithemius set forth a cycle of Ages under the revolving governorship of the seven Planetary Archangels in the interesting order ♄, ♀, ♃, ☿, ♂, ☽, ☉ (*i.e.*, the reverse of the order of the Planetary rulerships of the days of the week). Each of these Planetary periods lasts 4252 months, or 354 years and four months. Trithemius catalogued the cycles from the beginning of the world (in his calculation having occurred a little more than 5200 years BCE) until the end of the cycle following the Martial age of Samael in which he himself lived. The next Planetary period, that of Gabriel Archangel of Luna, would last from June 1525 until—insert drumroll here—November 1879, which was the beginning of the next cycle, the Solar period governed by the Archangel Michael, a significant Æonic shift in energies which would certainly be in harmony with many of Steiner's statements, but nothing relating to the Archangel once more overcoming the Dragon. Lévi, for example, put his hopes for November 1879 in a New Age of Michael bringing peace to the world under the universal political and religious dominion of an enlightened France.—APF

It was my plan to use the invocation from *The Art of Drawing Spirits into Crystals* with which I had invoked the Archangels before:

In the name of the blessed and holy Trinity, I do desire thee, thou strong and mighty Angel, Michael, that if it be the divine will of Him who is called Tetragrammaton, the Holy God, the Father, that thou take upon thee some shape as best becometh thy celestial nature, and appear to us visibly here in this crystal and answer our demands in as far as we shall not transgress the bounds of the divine mercy and goodness by requesting unlawful knowledge, but that thou wilt graciously show us what things are most profitable for us to know and do, to the glory and honour of His divine Majesty Who liveth and reigneth, world without end. Amen.

Lord, Thy will be done on earth as it is in heaven; make clean our hearts within us, and take not Thy Holy Spirit from us.

O Lord, by Thy name we have called him; suffer him to administer unto us, and that all things may work together for Thy honour and glory, to whom with Thee, the Son, and blessed Spirit be ascribed all might, majesty, and dominion. Amen.[13]

Preparing for the Invocation of Michael

The ritual was set to take place on a favorable Sunday during the hour of the Sun nearest midday. The entire day was beautiful and I was excited by what my scryer might be able to behold and if he would truly be able to see the Archangel as I had seen him. There was an odd mix of yearning and apprehension to once again be in the presence of this awesome being. If we were to be successful, today was a perfect day, reflecting the nature of this most mighty Archangel.

If we made successful contact, I very much wanted to see what the responses would be from this great Archangel to my scryer. I was very curious as to how he would appear and what he would tell my scryer through the questions I put to the Angel directly. Among other questions, I wanted to get a direct account from the Archangel himself of how he considered his purpose and role against the backdrop of traditional stories told of him. I hoped to learn what he thought about his notorious nemesis, the Devil, and about Demons. Also, of course, I was curious to see what sort of aid and consideration he had for a magician who dared to call him forth.

13. Closely following Barrett's translation in *The Magus*.

Invocation of the Archangel Michael

Fig. VI-3. Section of Circle with Heptameron Correspondences for Drawing Michael into the Crystal

Appearance of the Spirit

SCRYER: I see a figure is appearing in three-quarter profile with a sort of golden lion metal headdress on. He looks rather masculine; a stern-faced, beautiful Angel with a lion headdress that looks like metallic gold. He opens his mouth and it's as if stars and the whole cosmos can be seen. His face is so bright and shining like the Sun itself. He looks at me and his mouth opens and it is like I am looking into the universe, seeing a multitude of stars. The universe is in his mouth...looking out through him. Although I am seeing this clearly, it feels like this is a being that you can't completely see, or it wouldn't be a good idea to even if you could. My instincts tell me that I would not be able to be completely in the presence of him because we would be completely useless and wouldn't be able to function... or even *be*. There is a lot of golden light. I just tried closing my eyes but it is still there. It's like looking at the Sun and feeling it shine on my whole being.

(At this point, the magical chamber became filled with light, which I at first attributed to a curtain being moved aside and the light of the noonday Sun streaming in. During the entire operation, the room remained warm and unusually bright.)

Opening Questions[14]

OPENING QUESTION 1: In the name of the holy and undefiled Spirit, the Father, the begotten Son, and Holy Ghost proceeding from both, what is thy true name?

14. The Opening Questions are the probationary queries specified by *The Art of Drawing Spirits into Crystals* as those proper to begin the conversation with any evoked Spirit. The administration of the Oath constitutes the fifth Opening Question. —APF

(Scryer's voice, although just above a whisper, assumes a very authoritative, strong, deliberate tone.)

SPIRIT: «I am the Fierce Love of God. The greatest loved by the Father. I am Michael.»

OPENING QUESTION 2: What is thy office?

SPIRIT: «I am the Fierce Love of God that lays low the obstacles that stand in the way of *His* light, *His* music. When obstacles arise, I break them down. I teach mankind by slaying the dragon within. I am the roar of the lion that, upon hearing, no evil can withstand.»

OPENING QUESTION 3: What is thy true sign or character?

SCRYER: An Image appears of a lion. Its mouth opens and a six-pointed star is within.

OPENING QUESTION 4: When are the times most agreeable to thy nature to hold conference with us?

SPIRIT: «When the Sun is at its highest and the days and nights are of equal length, and when the day is longest. When the sunrise is bright and red and orange, when it pulls the breath from your lips. When you look upon the Sun and you feel God.»

OATH: Wilt thou swear by the holy blood of Jesus Christ that thou art truly the Archangel of the Sun, Michael?

MICHAEL: «I do. I can swear by the Tetragrammaton, Who is my Father and Mother, Whose love pervades the universe, Whose voice is the thunder, Whose eye is the Sun, that I am Michael. My understanding will shine through the crystal of yours.»

Further Questions

QUESTION 6: What are your views on humanity, and what are your roles and interactions with humanity?

Fig. VI-4. ***Portrait of Michael as beheld in Vision***

Michael: «Humans are shards of God who have forgotten they are of God. They chose to be apart, so that when reunion comes, the love for the Father will astound even me. All that I do and all that I am is for that day, the day when my love will be eclipsed for the love shown by my Father to humanity, then I will know what love is and the depth of my Father's love. I teach mankind to subject their ignorance with faith, that they and the Father are one. To forget is Lucifer, and that is his role.»

Question 7: Do Angels have any measure of free will? Have any Angels fallen from grace as many stories have led us to believe? What are the true natures of Demons and their role?

Michael: «Angels have fallen from grace, like an apple falls from the tree, like the wave crashes on the shore. By some measure of their own will, they have fallen from grace, even at their unawareness of the direction of the Father; for no grain of sand, no drop of rain moves or comes into being or fades away without His knowing. Demons are the lust and frenzy of this forgetfulness, of separation; and my Father loves all of them. He loves them in the same way, and with the same truth as he loves me and all the blessed saints.»

Question 8: What allowances are you and other Angels given to intercede on human affairs? How are interventions decided and done by Angels?

Michael: «We decide by feeling the will of God that moves through us. Whatever His feeling, it becomes our action. His leeway is ours. We each fulfill His will in a different way. One like a hammer, one like a knife, one like a mantle, one like the maker of music; in these ways do we speak and act.»

Question 9: Do you have your own recollection of your creation and origin? Where do you come from? What is your purpose?

Michael: «I remember light. I remember song. I remember the love so intense that I awoke with tears in my eyes with the love of my Father for me. I am blessed among all beings in the universe, and that makes me humble. My role is to be the fierce love of God.»

QUESTION 10: What advice can you give us to work and speak with you in the most beneficial ways?

MICHAEL: «Fight your battles, first, inside. Do *not* call on me until you have done this first. In the continual struggle in your soul, I will be your ally. Awaken your fellow man to the knowledge that all struggles are within. And when peace is made on that battlefield, all of mankind will sing with the joy and love together. That is the True image of the Christ and that will be His second coming.»

QUESTION 11: Can you explain the confusion between you and Archangel Raphael whereby your offices are mixed between Mercury and the Sun?

MICHAEL: «The Sun is like the raw power of God, and Mercury is like the looking glass. If God were to not look or speak through this glass, His creation would be destroyed. Imagine a father who wishes to embrace his son, but knowing that he would crush it if he did. In this is the difference between Raphael and myself. The ambiguity of this answer has its purpose. Through its ambiguity, and the contemplation thereof, wisdom of understanding will blossom.»

QUESTION 12: What instruction and insight can you give us concerning exorcism? How should we banish or dispel evil Spirits in times of need?

MICHAEL: «The exorcist must know that he or she is God. When they speak, authority must resonate with their voice. In that authority, the exorcist *must* find love for the Demon in his heart. They must see and understand it as a child of God, but a child that is in the wrong place. They must be astute, focused, determined, and filled with faith. Without the sincere, divine love for the Demon, a piece of that Demon can break off and take root in the exorcist. After this is done, you must perform a blessing for three days following, in complete privacy in a protective circle. Perform a strong cleansing and clearing ritual afterward. There is no need to conjure the Demon forth to do this blessing.»

QUESTION 13: Are there any special conjurations we can use to call you for assistance?

MICHAEL: «When I awoke with tears in my eyes and saw the light of my Father and heard his music, I became as I am. Remember this thought, recall this memory while singing my name, and my blessing will come unto you.»

QUESTION 14: Are there any unique magical methods you can give us to benefit from the positive powers of your office and the Sun? Do you have any other advice for us individually and together in our continued work and lives?

MICHAEL: «Work together, write, and share. Do all with the goal of bringing peace to all you meet, human and otherwise. Do all in the glory and in the love of your Father. Revel in the love of your Father. Every working with the goal of unifying the living Christ of His most perfect and blessed Son. When conflict arises, I will get word first; this is a miracle.»

QUESTION 15: Are you able to bestow upon us greater authority and strength to conjure and evoke the Goetic Spirits to manifestation?

MICHAEL: «Yes. You only need what I have already shown you.»

QUESTION 16 *(on behest of the scryer)*: What is the history with you and Skellig Michael of Ireland? In which ways is it best to connect with you there?

MICHAEL: «The men who went there came because I called them there. They went to specifically subjugate their own ignorance. They answered the call to suffer like Christ. They suffered starvation, demons, doubt, and agony. In that place I stood by them. Because of their work, many transgressions, many sins, and the suffering of thousands was avoided and purified. That is the work of a real and true monk. To take on the sufferings of the world so that the world does not have to feel it. The island is like the head of the dragon; whatever is whispered in its ear is heard all the way to Jerusalem.»

(At this point in the operation I had difficulty standing, feeling overwhelmed by the presence in the room and the strain of speaking with the being for an hour, so I decided to conclude the evocation.)

OPERATOR: We thank thee, mighty and most powerful prince, great Archangel of the Sun, Michael. We ask for your continued blessings and favor, and praise be always to the highest.

(License to Depart given.)

Afterthoughts on the Michael Operation

SCRYER: This was unbelievably intense. I felt like my body was curling over in on itself. Somehow I felt like I was becoming the scrying crystal itself, like a globe. I had trouble remembering what was going on during the evocation. I couldn't feel the Archangel very distinctly, but I could see and hear him clearly, which was really unusual. In the other experiences, it was much more emotional, a feeling of connection, but this was beyond me. After this experience, though, I realized how from my/our perspective, creation looks really messy and chaotic, but there is actually a lot of order and purpose behind it. The parts I remember from Archangel Michael was that allowances to intercede on human affairs all came from God. Human perspective on how or why or in which way God should interfere is naive and moot. Man's perspective is so limited and cannot contemplate its reasons. It's like saying sunlight cannot shine in two places at once. I swear I felt like I was in a different place the whole time during the operation, almost like being a medium while I was sort of observing from somewhere far off.

OPERATOR: There was no doubt as to the power and awesomeness and authority of this mighty Archangel. However, Michael totally surprised me with his position on the treatment of other beings, Spirits and especially Demons. More than a warrior and an oppressor of Demons or destroyer of infidels, the Archangel stressed the divine compassion for all created beings, both physical and spiritual. The Archangel's remarks on Demons and thus all forms of life was truly interesting to me. So many assumptions of the nature and persuasions of Angels and God from classical sources and modern belief were examined and found wanting. I realized just how much human beings assume about the natures of these mighty vehicles of creation. There was no hatred, no cosmic battle or conflict—at least as

> human begins understood it—between good and evil. Rather, it appeared that all efforts, whether by celestial or physical beings, were at work exactly according to their purpose and design. Even the most destructive and loathsome beings are loved equally by the Creator who manifested them.

Another fascinating part was how Michael mentioned that nothing is beyond God's awareness or control, even if particular created beings are not aware of being connected to Him. This first Archangelic operation with my scryer confirmed some lessons I had learned during my initial contacts with them. Angels are not human beings with human needs, fears, persuasions, and conflicts. They have their own agendas and perspectives which are quite removed from the understanding of human beings in many regards. Despite these very alien differences, the celestial Messengers nonetheless have a vested concern for humanity and offer to lend their assistance and wisdom in some astonishing ways.

The "Sunday School" model of what and who Angels are became even more a ridiculous concept than before as I realized that even the perceptions and contact my scryer and I had was severely limited in relation to what the entirety of these beings must be. In no way did I feel that our efforts discovered the full identity and purpose of this Archangel.

This fascinating experience shed further light on many of Archangel Michael's qualities. It is little wonder that he is first among the Angels called to assist with defeating evil, controlling Demons, and performing exorcisms. His Solar nature is amply displayed by theses offices. His authority and presence is absolute. Nothing can withstand or refute the very light shining from his presence. There was a distinct and palpable power felt during this ceremony that was so great in magnitude that it seemed to dispel any notion of anger or fear, beyond hatred of anything. The interaction definitely revealed a more divine perspective of what true justice entails, and one beyond human assumptions.

The expereince also inspired me to reflect on another aspect of Solar magic that we find emphasized in the Solomonic grimoires, that of sight. This is expressed via the description of Solar talismans being able to cause Spirits to become visible or to allow the magician to become invisible to his enemies. The esoteric powers of the Sun are claiming to cause things to be seen or to be unseen, the presence or the absence of sight being wholly dependent on light. In this there is an obvious correlation to the presence of our most abundant dispenser of light, the Sun, in being able to see and perceive things, revealing what may otherwise be hidden from us.

Likewise, having control over Solar influences does not mean an overabundance of light is always desirable. Too much Sun is not a good thing for people or land, so at times the removal of light and thus sight may be a necessary ability as well. A magician may wish, for non-malefic purposes, to conceal himself by removing light. To have the option to hide from one's enemies or to hide from the sight or attention of harmful Spirits is a prudent magic for any working magician to have.

Fig. VI-5. ***The Fourth Pentacle of the Sun from* The Key of Solomon the King *(Mathers edition)***

Visibility or sight also comes into play when harnessing other positive aspects of the offices of the Sun. To be "seen in a certain light" or noticed, or shining like a luminary or star, is to charismatically draw support, as people are naturally drawn to those who generate that type of Solar light.

As an additional tool for the magician who wishes to increase his own ability or that of another person to see Spirits properly, I would like to offer the Fourth Pentacle of the Sun from the *Key of Solomon* (Fig. VI-5). This particular pentacle

> serveth to enable thee to see the Spirits when they appear invisible unto those who invoke them; because, when thou hast uncovered it, they will immediately appear visible.[15]

Mathers notes:

> The names IHVH, Adonai, are written in the center in Hebrew; and round the radii in the mystical characters of the "Passing of the Riv-

15. S.L. MacGregor Mathers (ed. and trans.), *The Key of Solomon the King: Clavicula Salomonis* (London: George Redway, 1889) , Book One, Ch. 18. —APF

> er." The versicle is from *Psalm xiii. 3, 4:—"Lighten mine eyes that I sleep not in death, lest mine enemy say, I have prevailed against him."*[16]

This talisman should be made using the same timing as that to evoke the Archangel Michael himself. If you make it on parchment, be sure it is blessed in frankincense smoke ahead of time, use gold and bright yellow colored inks to draw the image. If in metal, make it of gold. To truly empower this talisman, an evocation of a Solar Spirit, either the Archangel Michael himself or the Olympic Spirit of the Sun, should be conducted.

As far as Solar talismans, the symbol of the lion head and hexagram has become a powerful image after this encounter and further consideration of its meaning and symbolism. Although not specified by the Archangel himself, I feel this could make a potent talisman with qualities associated with his might and authority (Fig. VI-6). Perhaps aiding in both protection and authority, this may serve as a potent amulet or talisman which could be engraved with the Archangel's sigil on the reverse.

Despite the session going over an hour, I felt I had still only scratched the surface of what this being was who seemed mighty and complex beyond human comprehension. However, I feel that I did achieve a clearer understanding of what aspects and offices this most mighty being embodies in relation to mankind. A magician who has gained a level of mastery over the occult influences and corresponding offices of the Sun is one who is able to consciously control the amount of "light" he is radiating. This light is the inner Sun of his being, his charismatic nature, public visibility, and leadership qualities. It is a light he is able to dim on command as well, and conceal when prudent to do so, allowing him to become virtually invisible, unnoticed, shadowed, and hidden from all whom he wishes. There is often a suspicion of illicit clandestine intentions when this ability is invoked, but it can be recognized as a legitimate necessity by those who understand it as a technique to protect the mage from the harm resulting from overattention by opposing Spirits and, to a lesser extent, from the overexposure which can indeed be a negative result of abundant Solar energy. At the level of mastery, the magus would be able to extend these attributes and abilities

---

16. *Ibid*. Mathers provides the translation from the KJV. For those who intone or vibrate the versicle while charging or employing a Solomonic Pentacle, the Hebrew of the versicle reads *Hairah einai, pen-ishan ha-maveth, pen-yomar oyevi yekhaletio*. The Greek of the *Septuagint* reads *Mou phōtison tous ophtalmous mou mēpote hypnōsō eis thanaton, mēpote eipē ho echthros mou ischysa pros auton*. Finally, the Latin of the *Vulgate* (12:4–5) reads *Illumina oculos meos ne umquam obdormiam in mortem. Nequando dicat inimicus meus praevalui adversus eum*. —APF

to others by means of invocation or talismans.

In reviewing the advice given by the Archangel, it becomes clear that there can be no falsehood or concealment of the truth in the revealing light of this magic. The concealment only works in regard to the sight of others who may wish to do harm. However the magus requesting the help of Michael cannot hope to conceal his own truth from this most mighty of Archangels or from himself in the full light of the Sun. Shining forth with one's light means opening to vulnerability, to becoming completely visible even in the face of adversity or ridicule. It is standing in the forefront of life, exposed to all its diversity. In such mastery comes the paradoxical quality of the office of the Sun.

Fig. VI-6. ***Lion and Hexagram beheld in Vision as Sign or Character of Michael***

Finally, let me share a prayer to invoke the Office and protection of Archangel Michael:

> O glorious prince St. Michael,
> chief and commander of the heavenly hosts,
> guardian of souls, vanquisher of rebel spirits,
> servant in the house of the Divine King
> and our admirable conductor,
> you who shine with excellence
> and superhuman virtue, deliver us from all evil,
> who turn to you with confidence
> and enable us by your gracious protection
> to serve God more and more faithfully every day.
> Amen.[17]

17. This is best known as one of the closing prayers of the Chaplet of Saint Michael the Archangel, a practice revealed in 1751 by the Archangel himself to Antónia d'Astónaco, a nun in Portugal. The Chaplet invokes Michael along with each of the nine Choirs of Angels (according

This operation was to be the last time I attempted to record the results of the operation by hand. During the Michael communication I scrawled desperately, trying to account for every word my scryer repeated as coming from the Archangel. Many times my attention was fractured by sparks of golden light which seemed to flash randomly throughout the magical chamber. Not only were the sensations and visions overwhelming, but the responses my scryer dictated to me were simply more than I could keep up with by hand. I knew there had to be a better way of recording the data during the ceremony and making sure I got each detail exactly as it happened. Thus, all following operations have been preserved with an audio recorder so I would not miss a single word. It also gives us the opportunity to verbally debrief after the ceremony and accurately record any fresh reactions we have.

to the reckoning of pseudo-Dionysios the Areopagite), and involves reciting a series of Pater nosters and Ave Marias accompanying each invocation of Michael and a Choir. —APF

The Archangel of Mercury
Raphael

✠ Day and time	On Wednesday, during hour of Mercury
✠ Name and meaning	Hebrew רפאל *(Raphael)*, "Healing Power of God," "God Heals"
✠ Pronunciation of name (as spoken by the Spirit)	«Ra-fa-el»
✠ Other known forms of the name	San Rafael (Spanish), Israfil (Arabic)
✠ Planet	☿
✠ Materials for lamen	Parchment, fixed quicksilver (mercury), cinnabar, yellow brass
✠ Sigil	[sigil]
✠ Direction for Invocation	East, Northeast
✠ Incense mixture	Galbanum, aloe wood, mastic, cinnamon, cardamom, musk grain, anise, bergamot.

Table VI-7. Evocatory Correspondences for Raphael[18]

Of Raphael and the Office of Mercury

Thou true healer who senses the patterns and complex exchange of energies that fluctuate around and within us, you who by making is made aware of the ebb and flow of men's faculties, bless us with your presence. O great herald of the Father, Raphael, hear my call. Divine physician, the light of whose eyes descends on the brows of men at the very break of day, light of rejuvenation, and revitalizer, invigorate and replenish me to fulfill the tasks to which I am set.

My first encounter with the Archangel Raphael was still a distinct memory as I began to prepare for the next invocation. On that occasion, I had felt like I had instantly traveled to the upper atmosphere as I viewed him within the crystal pedestal. He appeared to me as a bright, silvery being, as if formed from the first

18. Please see the Cautionary Warning Regarding Grimoric Ingredients in Appendix A. —APF

rays of dawn. The bright yellow and violet colors blended with a silver line across a heavenly horizon that illuminated the Angel's majestic appearance. The entire crystal seemed haloed with this light. He looked to be wrapped in pale yellow and light violet robes, which folded together and unwrapped again as if blown by a wind. He held an intricate staff, adorned with scrollwork, multi-colored stones, and images too numerous to count. In his other hand he held a scroll of parchment with an endless array of letters, symbols, and pictures, which seemed to trail into infinite length behind him. His appearance was the epitome of youthful vigor. I found this Archangel's presence one of the most splendid to experience, as Raphael infuses the magus with the encompassing sensation of ease and wellness and the vitality to accomplish any goal.

Fig. VI-8. ***Lamen of Raphael in the manner of DSIC***

The earliest Biblical reference to the Archangel Raphael by name is found in the *Book of Tobit*. In this text, canonical in the Roman Catholic and Eastern Orthodox Churches, Raphael is sent to the earth in response to the prayers of Tobit, who has gone blind, and of Sara, whose seven bridegrooms have each been slain by "Asmodeus the evil Spirit"[19] before consummating their union.

> And Raphael was sent to heal them both, that is, to scale away the whiteness of Tobit's eyes, and to give Sara the daughter of Raguel for a wife to Tobias the son of Tobit; and to bind Asmodeus the evil spirit.[20]

Raphael appears disguised as a human, Azarias, and travels on a journey with Tobit's son Tobias. At the river Tigris, the disguised Raphael directs Tobias to

19. *Tobit* 3:8 (KJV).

20. *Ibid.* 3:17.

save the heart and liver and gall of a fish, and reveals esoteric knowledge to Tobias which will lead to the healing of the troubles of both Sara and Tobit:

> Then the young man said to the angel, Brother Azarias, to what use is the heart and the liver and the gall of the fish?
>
> And he said unto him, Touching the heart and the liver, if a devil or an evil spirit trouble any, we must make a smoke thereof before the man or the woman, and the party shall be no more vexed.
>
> As for the gall, it is good to anoint a man that hath whiteness in his eyes, and he shall be healed.[21]

Tobias follows Raphael's instructions, burning the heart and liver of the fish on coals in a censer at the home of Sara,

> The which smell when the evil spirit had smelled, he fled into the utmost parts of Egypt, and the angel bound him.[22]

The burning of foul-smelling substances to produce a strong, odorous smoke is found in prominent magical texts as a sure way to banish Demons from a place or person. The method was utilized in ancient Egyptian and Greek magical practices, and survives in Solomonic grimoires such as the *Lemegeton*, where asafœtida and sulfur are burned to compel Spirits into obedience.

Tobias later employs the other magical method revealed by the Archangel, anointing his father's blind eyes with the fish's gall, and restoring his sight.

The account in *Tobit* is in line with the sort of responses my scryer and I have received from these beings. In the above example, instead of simply dealing with the Demon or the blindness in a direct manner on behalf of Tobias, Raphael reveals a "technology" or method of dealing with the problems. There are other accounts of this Archangel inspiring or instructing people in the use of remedies or methods to overcome illness and hardships rather than simply performing a miracle and fixing the situation.

Raphael is also found elsewhere binding great Demons. In the *Book of Enoch*, the Archangel is sent to bind and imprison the chief Demon Azazel[23] under stones in the desert.[24]

---

21. *Ibid.* 6:6–8.

22. *Ibid.* 8:3.

23. After which the Archangel Gabriel is sent to destroy the giant offspring of the fallen Watchers and their human lovers, and the Archangel Michael to bind and imprison all of the rest of the fallen Watchers, according to *I Enoch* 10:11–13. —APF

24. *I Enoch* 10:4–6.

From the accounts in the *Book of Tobit*, Archangel Raphael takes on very similar offices or qualities to the Greek God Hermēs, which reinforces the Archangel's Mercurial Planetary correspondence. The Greek God and the Archangel share the patronage of travelers, roads, the arts, doctors and nurses, healing, the use of technology, and there is a strikingly similar emphasis on providing insight, genius, and creativity.

Preparing for the Invocation of Raphael

One of my primarily reasons for evoking the Archangel of Mercury again was to inquire about healing for a client of mine who was suffering from some fairly serious chronic ailments. I felt it would be an excellent chance for my scryer to be introduced to this wonderful being as well as accomplish tasks as a magician working for a client.

I realized I had not been introducing the seven planetary archangels to my scryer in the proper Chaldean order as I had been so insistent on when I undertook the operations myself for the first time. When I began in *DSIC*, I felt that each sphere was a descending or ascending hierarchy which I had to travel in order. Perhaps this was the case, but my scryer had not seemed to falter with one of the most intense beings of the Angelic hierarchy, so I continued with my experiments as opportunity and time allowed the both of us to prepare for another Angelic evocation.

It happened around this time that a mutual friend of my scryer and me became interested in our experiments and asked if she could serve as scryer during one of the operations. I saw this as a good opportunity to experiment with conducting an evocation with a second scryer and comparing the results. The woman, whom I had known for a few years, was raised a Catholic, although she had become interested in Celtic Druidism and had practiced "seeing" exercises with my scryer for over a year.

I had been planning for the evocation of Archangel Raphael, but my usual scryer had scheduling conflicts that did not allow him to attend the first operation. It did however become perfect timing to attempt an evocation with this new scryer. The operation was conducted in the first hour of Mercury on a Wednesday. The event turned out to be my one and only session working with a different scryer during these workings, but it did offer some perspective and different insight. I later repeated the operation with Benn.

In the transcript of the operation below, I give the responses of both scryers to the same questions I asked during both ceremonies. It was only myself and one scryer present during each evocation, but I asked the same series of questions each time, not revealing the questions to either scryer beforehand. In the responses labeled as Scryer A, I am indicating the responses received from the new scryer, and Scryer B the answers from Benn, my usual scryer.

Invocation of the Archangel Raphael

Fig. VI-9. ***Section of Circle with Heptameron Correspondences for Drawing Raphael into the Crystal***

Appearance of the Spirit

(Operator sees the face of Archangel in the crystal while Scryer B is viewing him as well.)

OPERATOR: He appears as a young man in early or mid-twenties with features not able to identify completely but appears European, possibly Romanian, in appearance, perfect dark youthful features, and silky black ear-length hair.

SCRYER B: He has wavy black hair and appears in grayish, silvery robes. He is holding a caduceus in right hand and a bolt of lightning in left hand. The caduceus is quite large, like a staff, with one of the snakes appearing gold and the other silver. Both are definitely metallic-looking. He is quite a sight to behold and I feel very humbled and invigorated in the face of such greatness.

OPERATOR: Great spirit, can you please tell us the significance the lightning bolt has in your hand?

(Scryer B's voice assumes a soft and instructive tone.)

SPIRIT (VIA SCRYER B): «It is the quickness of thought, and the speed of God's help to those in need. The arc, the energy of thought in the body, the quick illumination derived from the patience and skill and the cleverness to overcome obstacles with the power of free will.

Scryer B: As Raphael is stating this, he brings the lightning and caduceus near one another, and that causes an arc of energy between the two. The snakes on the caduceus appear to writhe and move. The gold and silver snakes seem to be animated and alive.

Scryer A: He appears as an older man with long white hair that seems to be flowing backward, away from his face. He has bare, white skin that is dressed in white, but quickly changes or shifts into another form that is difficult to distinguish, but is unto the likeness of a human figure. He is in the center of the crystal and there is light coming from it, in a circle or sphere of light which is radiating outward. The silhouette shows him with his head bent down; he has large wings, and he is holding an object in his hand. His legs are shaped almost like a number four and he appears to be suspended in air.

Opening Question 1: In the name of the holy and undefiled Spirit, the Father, the begotten Son, and Holy Ghost proceeding from both, what is thy true name?

Spirit (via Scryer A): «Raphael.»

Spirit (via Scryer B): «I am Raphael.»

Opening Question 2: What is thy office?

Spirit (via Scryer A): «To Heal.»

Spirit (via Scryer B): «Skill. Mercury. Power of the Sun in the magnifying glass. Maker of shoes. Shaper of power. Teacher of all skills. Friend to mankind, friend to all life. Teacher of men's responsibility.»

Opening Question 3: What is thy true sign or character?

Spirit (via Scryer A): «I am known by every sign of Wisdom, Compassion, and Love.»

Scryer B: He holds forth the caduceus, which arcs with the lightning bolt. I see three stars above his head.

Fig. VI-10. Portrait of Raphael as beheld in Vision

Opening Question 4: When are the times most agreeable to thy nature to hold conference with us?

Spirit (via Scryer A): «Noon on Wednesday.»

Scryer B: He shows me a sunrise. I see a flock of birds in the air. Shows a star and a constellation, which he says I should remember its shape, and I'm supposed to remember what it looks like and find it. One of the ruling stars when it is at the highest point in the sky. He then shows me what looks like a coming of age ceremony: A boy being given tools and weapons, and shown how to use them.

Oath: Wilt thou swear by the holy blood of Jesus Christ that thou art truly Raphael?

Raphael (via Scryer A): «Yes I am.»

Scryer B: He smiles and says he does.

Question 6: What are your views on humanity? What are your roles and interactions?

Raphael (via Scryer A): «To heal, to touch, and to teach others. All are children of God, a power they do not fully understand or comprehend. I teach through honesty, wisdom, compassion, and love. My purpose is to ease suffering, pain and sadness, discomfort and confusion.»

Raphael (via Scryer B): «Humans, like all things, are the children of God, Whose power they cannot comprehend. I focus that power and move it. I teach them how to shape it. To sew, to carve, to build, so that they may carry out the plan of the Creator. I teach men to heal their bodies, their spirits, and their relationships with one another through action.»

Question 7: What allowances are there to intercede in human affairs? How are interventions decided and done by Angels?

Raphael (via Scryer A): «For the good of God.»

RAPHAEL (VIA SCRYER B): «I am directed by the Creator to teach. To instruct and to guide. But I cannot interfere with how those skills are used, by the power of their free will which is a piece of the mind of God, which even I cannot comprehend. I instruct and teach men and women how to instruct. And when knowledge is lost, it will no longer need to serve them, so I take their fragments and reweave them and give them back.»

QUESTION 8: Do you have your own recollection of your creation and origin? Where do you come from? What is your purpose?

RAPHAEL (VIA SCRYER A): «Yes, but these are secret things to know, and comes from a purpose to love, a purpose to heal, a purpose to teach.»

Blessings and greatest honor and glory to the beloved Heavenly Father, wherefore I would not have the mind to know and seek Thee and Thy heavenly Angels and not have the power to do so but not for Thy endless and merciful love. O great heavenly and blessed Father Whose Love is beyond the bounds of the universe, by Thy great and endless goodness and grace, I thank Thee for Thy heavenly Messengers and continued gifts bestowed upon Thy creature. Amen.

RAPHAEL (VIA SCRYER B): «These are secret things to know; treat them with respect. I can remember springing forth from my Father's crown, as quick as the lightning, and a flash of inspiration from my Father: all His learning, His skill, His wit, His cleverness. I am blessed among all beings, and love my Father with words I cannot describe.»

SCRYER B: I perceived Raphael springing forth from the brow of God in a great golden and white cathedral. There were already several other Angels there when Raphael arrives, and he was brought forth already having his incredible wisdom and skill.

Great Father in heaven, blessings of all the ages be upon Thy name. My heart sings to Thee with the joy of having known Thee and felt Thee and for answering my prayers. Great, mighty, and endless is Thy love, power, and mercy. Thanks and grace to Thee always and forever, my loving Father of all, through the ages of ages without end. Amen.

QUESTION 9: Would you prefer we kept these words for ourselves and not commit them to being published?

RAPHAEL (VIA SCRYER B): «No. But before you write the words, write blessings on my Father at the beginning and at the end.»

QUESTION 10: What advice can you give us to work and speak with you in the most beneficial ways?

RAPHAEL (VIA SCRYER A): «Today, just today.»

RAPHAEL (VIA SCRYER B): «You have done this very well. You have crafted this room, this circle, the devices, the incense, the tools. It is in those preparations that you demonstrate your desire to know the mind of God. Find the skill, hone it, know it, and immerse yourself in it. This is one of the paths to the Father. His Son made this path as the carpenter. Unbeknownst to many, several revelations about His Father did the Son learn as a carpenter.»

QUESTION 11: What can you teach us of the true nature of healing? How can we manifest positive, healing interaction?

RAPHAEL (VIA SCRYER A): «Be good to each other. Put healing into the Earth and places you reside. God will show you the way. Call on me when you need. Sacred form. Learn to trust and be still.»

RAPHAEL (VIA SCRYER B): «The healers who go wrong spend little time in their judgment. They leap quickly to thinking they know the problem. A true healer observes, feels, communicates, and casts all his degrees aside and beholds the individual needs of the patient. The diagnosis is the most important part: Feel the pulse. Lay your hands on the body. Listen to the breath. Feel the difference in temperature on the skin on various places on the body. Listen to the quality of the voice. Smell the odor of the body. In matters of the spirit in healing, the healer is a facilitator to those who suffer. The purpose is to bring out their own strength of God that they possess. In both cases, the healer must look into the eyes of those who would be healed. He or she must love them, and recognize them as fellow children of God. All treatments should be covered under the mantle of prayer and blessing. And in the end, both healer and healed must submit to the will of God.»

QUESTION 12: What afflicts NN?[25] Are you able to provide her with any healing assistance or recovery? Can you give us any wisdom to pass on to further heal her?

RAPHAEL (VIA SCRYER A): «She is healed. She is loved, she is watched over. Patience. She appears loved, supported. She is in a sea, an ocean, and floating peacefully. It massages and comforts her. She is feeling washed over with healing. She is one with the waves; she moves with the waves, their acceptance; there are no worries or troubles. There appears to be an emerald-green colored crystal wand that was being waved over her throat. I sensed that the area of her discomfort was coming from her chest—her breasts, to be exact—and her throat.»

RAPHAEL (VIA SCRYER B): «What part of this problem do you feel is unspoken or unknown to you?»

OPERATOR: I wish to convey any other message on what would be able to assist her in her own recovery and healing, and if you have any other words directly I could pass on to her to aid her in her recovery.

RAPHAEL (VIA SCRYER B): «Yes, she must see her ailment as a gift. A gift to learn more and discover more of who she is. She must understand how she is a child of God by whatever name she calls Him. Only in envisioning the *opportunity* of disease can it be healed. She must give love to her ailment, cherish her ailment, and be at peace with her guardians who always surround her.»

QUESTION 13: What are the best ways to call on you for assistance in healing of ourselves and of others? Are there any other magical methods or other Spirits that can assist us with healing?

RAPHAEL (VIA SCRYER A): «Just have the clear thought and petition. Write the petition and ritual out, and act on it out of honor.»

25. Client's name of course anonymized for confidentiality and privacy.

RAPHAEL (VIA SCRYER B): «When doing a healing, arrange the room that the healing is taking place in with the same skill and attention that you would give to this circle. Any tools laid out with care. The smell of the room, conscious and crafted. Welcome the aliment in the same way you welcome the patient. Connect your heart to the patient before the healing begins. Place your hand on their heart and their hand on yours. Lay your forehead against theirs and pray a prayer that moves them the most. Acknowledge the fear, the sadness, the doubt, and remind them all are mortal and do not know their time; all do not know their time of passing. For in truth the healer could go to God before the sick.»

QUESTION 14: What can you teach us of better ways of communicating and seeing Spirits?

SCRYER A: There is a white blue light, and a crystal-clear sphere "ball." I see a wand, a tree branch. Now there is a wand shaped like a crystal—green emerald. The wand is multi-sided, like an octagon, just like a crystal, but longer and an emerald green in color. I see what looks like you standing next to me and placing your hands gently on the crown of my head. Your hands come together and form a circular shape. It's kind of hard to explain, but your hands also make the shape of a stop sign—an octagon.

RAPHAEL (VIA SCRYER B): «You have done this already so well; crafting your space, your tools, giving your heart to the attention of the details. When this is seen, we know your effort is genuine. And in their applications, the application of these tools, in your conversation with the Angels, always have in mind that it is subservient to the will of the Creator. Embody this in all that you do, and even the mistakes will be blessed.»

QUESTION 15: What messages of wisdom and insight can you give to us and humanity at this time?

RAPHAEL (VIA SCRYER A): «To be on your own. To be on your own way. To be of yourself. To have friends. To leave things behind. To move forward where and when there is fear. To trust, to hope, to love. To abandon the ways of men. To know that you are guided. To call on me. To be whole. To make sure all your actions are done with honor and respect always.»

RAPHAEL (VIA SCRYER B): «If the way forward is difficult, my sons and daughters, have patience. Make consistent, small efforts. Sacrifice the destination to the journey. Revel in the skills of your mind and your hands. Make all your works, all your skills, all your thoughts move towards the heart of my Father, and all will be right and perfect in *His* eyes.»

QUESTION 16: What do you share with Archangel Michael? How do you two work together? What can you tell us of other Angels?

RAPHAEL (VIA SCRYER A): «We work together as one. We are as spokes on a wheel.»

SCRYER A: I see a central object and from that center object there are spokes that came out from it. It seems to mean that there are efforts being made by all of the spokes, but that they each have a different role. I sense that if it remains together and whole, all needs are met and it serves a greater plan.

RAPHAEL (VIA SCRYER B): «We both work as one yet individually in our natures. Each fulfilling part of our Father's plan and design. Both my brother and I share the ultimate love of our Father, and at times we are called to perform a similar task. At other times, our tasks differ.»

QUESTION 17: Is there a symbol or talisman we could make to assist others with healing, protection, and recovery? What would it look like? What would it be made from? How should it be consecrated towards its proper use and function?

RAPHAEL (VIA SCRYER A): «All that is your own. It would be circular in shape. Wood or silver.»

RAPHAEL (VIA SCRYER B): «Yes, A silver Octagon with a hole in the middle, consecrated in the name of the Father, His Son, and the Holy Ghost. And on this consecration, the magician must see Mercury moving through the hole in the center. There should be three stars on the surface with the Star of David to the side. The Octagon can have a chain, preferably made of silver as well, hung so that it is flat to the chest. The talisman grows more powerful the more Mercury is glimpsed through the center. When the eye of man beholds the movement of Mercury, I will bless this talisman.»

Fig. VI-11. Mercurial Talisman of Raphael as described by the Archangel in Vision

OPERATOR: Great and wondrous Archangel of Mercury, Raphael, I thank you for your presence and attendance upon this ceremony. Blessings to the Father and His wondrous Archangels, whom He has agreed to instruct us and lead us in these matters.

(License to Depart.)

Afterthoughts on the Raphael Operation

SCRYER A: I felt, not heard or seen, that he had a sense of sadness as part of his view on humanity. It felt like there was disappointment for the way we live our mundane lives; it felt sad and soulless—and I am not sure if the feeling was his own view or if I was feeling what it feels like to our fellow humans. I hope that makes sense. Raphael's response to his roles and interactions seem to be more of how we might work to help our fellow man and ourselves to bring us from this place of despondency to a place of being more fully aligned with Spirit, even if we do not or cannot at this time fully understand the concept of Spirit or God.

When Raphael said, «For the good of God,» the response was direct but also somewhat ambiguous. So I think what I was hearing is that if they—the Angels—choose to intercede in human affairs, it is by the Will of God. If we ask them, we need to do so humbly, and with a sense that our actions and outcomes are being done to ultimately serve God, not the needs and wants of humankind. This isn't to say that we do not work to help heal the state of human affairs, as in to relieve suffering, but it is to say that what we do in interceding and assisting others needs to be done not to assist them with accomplishments in the mundane world. So much beyond what we can see at first helps people further along on their spiritual journey—to help them come closer to 'God.' The simple answer applies to the part of the question that asks how the Angels decide on interventions.

When you asked about Raphael's origin and he said, «Yes, but these are secret things to know, and come from a purpose to love, a purpose to heal, and a purpose to teach,» I feel like what he was saying was that his origin is secret—maybe not meant to be known by me at this time; I don't know. But I felt as if it is something that, in that moment, needed to be kept hidden. Perhaps meaning that some of this will be made known to some people and not to others. I'm not really sure...

When you asked, "What advice can you give us to work and speak with you in the most beneficial ways?" and Raphael responded, «Today, just today,» my impression of this answer is that the ritual operation and technique we were using is one that could be used effectively when we desire to speak and get to know him. The way you performed the operation seemed to feel to me like it worked well for him.

When Raphael said, «Be good to each other. Put healing into the Earth and places you reside. God will show you the way. Call on me when you need. Sacred form. Learn to trust and be still,» I feel like this answers the second part of the question, and not really the first. The wording is as it was presented to me. My only explanation would be on «sacred form»: This felt to me like there is a form of sacredness in the Earth that is overlooked by people, that if we work with the land, the Spirits of the land, and with him, that this question will be answered more fully. But it seems like he was suggesting that it is not enough to just have a relationship with one aspect, be that the Earth, land, God, or Angels, but that they all work together and that there is something to be gained from working with more than one modality, if one desires to.

It felt like he was suggesting we should find ways in which to be comfortable being alone, on our own. I felt like he was suggesting that we walk away from those people or activities or places in our lives which didn't or don't feel right to us, or don't serve us. To prepare ourselves for the fact that some people won't like or agree with what we do, what we have to say or how we live, but that we must continue on, in spite of what others say or think. To leave behind things that distract us or attempt to keep us from spiritual growth. To find friends who share similar beliefs and cultivate friendships with them, to work with them collectively.

SCRYER B: This Angel was a lot more personable, or approachable. He seemed a little more used to dealing with people than Michael is. It was if he was a bit closer to humanity or like he worked with people on a regular basis. He was just speaking and conversing with such enthusiasm and detail. I was able to "feel" him much better than Michael. It was very apparent that he was here...very quickly. You could recognize when he arrived instantly.

I feel like there is so much they, the Angels, can say, so much they can impart, but I sort of feel limited or am a bad filter, like my comprehension or understanding limits what they can tell me. I don't know if the information was due to my limitation, or if it is simply meant to be that way. Regardless, what comes through always astounds me. During the questions on healing, he looked really interested, and almost seemed excited himself speaking about it and in detail. I really got the impression that he enjoyed it. It was pretty amazing how clearly I could hear him while I was speaking with him. When he stopped to speak I would start to see the images in my head of what he was meaning to convey to me, then when he would begin speaking again, the images would subside and I would hear him once again. These ways of communicating seemed to alternate.

OPERATOR: In *DSIC*, I've always associated Archangel Raphael with Mercury and call on him that way, but feel no conflict about it at all when the roles are switched in other grimoires. It's my assessment that Michael and Raphael (as well as the other Archangels) are able to take on varying aspects and offices as needed. Their multidimensional aspects have really become more apparent over time, and honestly do not seem to be limited or categorized necessarily by our esoteric classifications. In my personal workings with them, Raphael is really the healer, reconciler, communicator,

> and encourager, which seems to have strong Mercury correspondences, whereas Michael definitely uplifts, encourages, restores, and protects. In this regard, the associated Planetary offices seem well suited.

It was very interesting for me to compare the results from my two scryers and see how the same questions were answered. In my evaluation, many of the responses had striking similarities. Probably due to my primary scryer's practice and experience, the answers received through him were relayed in more depth or had a few additional elements. Overall I found doing both of the operations fascinating, and was pleased by how the same presence could be felt in the room during both workings. I may conduct more experiments utilizing different scryers in the future to compare the results. It is unsurprising to me that there is variation in the responses to questions, as each scryer receives the messages through his or her individual filters and level of comprehension.

I related the information we received in the operation to my client. To be honest, I was not completely satisfied with the information I had to pass along. It seemed rather vague and general in nature, but I relayed it word for word without embellishment. To my surprise, the client seemed overjoyed and inspired by the words. I offered to assist in any way I could. She thanked me and I have not heard back from her as to her condition.

The Archangel of Jupiter
Sachiel

✠	Day and time	On Thursday, during an hour of Jupiter
✠	Name and meaning	Hebrew צדקיאל *(Tzadqiel)*, "Righteousness of God," and *Sachiel*, perhaps "Covering of God"[26]
✠	Pronunciation of name (as spoken by the Spirit)	Baktum «Bak-toommm»
✠	Other known names and forms of name	Chesediel, Hesediel; Tzadkiel, Zedekiel, Zadakiel, Zedekul
✠	Planet	♃
✠	Materials for lamen	Parchment, tin, brass, bronze
✠	Sigil	
✠	Direction for Invocation	Southwest
✠	Incense mixture	Mastic gum, cloves, saffron, lignum aloes, benzoin, allspice, star anise, juniper berries, nutmeg.

Table VI-12. ***Evocatory Correspondences for Sachiel***[27]

Of Sachiel and the Office of Jupiter

The greatest evidence I've witnessed of not only Angelic presence but action has been through the efforts of the Archangel of Jupiter. As expressed a number of times in *Gateways Through Stone and Circle*, I credit the influence of the

26. *Tzadqiel* is from the Hebrew צדק (*Tzedeq*), "Righteousness," which is also the Hebrew name for the Planet Jupiter. The name Sachiel seems to first occur in Latin (*Sachiel*) and Greek (Σαχιηλ, *Sachiēl*) texts, so we aren't sure of a correct Hebrew form. Davidson, *A Dictionary of Angels: Including the Fallen Angels* (New York: Free Press, 1967), gives "Covering of God" as a meaning of Sachiel, but I am unable to fathom a derivation meaning "covering" in either Hebrew or Greek. If there is a source name for Sachiel in Hebrew, it could be צחיאל, *Tzachiel*, from צח, *tzach*, "pure, clear." It is also very much worth bearing in mind that not all Angel and Spirit names have etymological meanings, as some are not formulated from a root, but directly transmitted by the Spirits themselves. —APF

27. Please see the Cautionary Warning Regarding Grimoric Ingredients in Appendix A. —APF

Archangel of Jupiter as significantly contributing to my advancement in magical working.

In various Kabbalistic traditions, Archangel Sachiel or Tzadkiel is assigned to either the order of Cherubim or that of Chashmalim. The office of the Cherubim is manifesting the Creator's aspects of divine mercy and benevolence. On the Tree of Life, this influence is expressed by the fourth Sephirah, called Chesed, which corresponds to God's mercy, and is also connected with the Chashmalim. In *The Magus*, Barrett explains,

*Fig. VI-13. **Lamen of Sachiel in the manner of DSIC***

> The fourth name is El, whose numeration is *Hesed* [Chesed], which signifies clemency or goodness; and likewise grace, mercy, piety, magnificence, the scepter, and right-hand; and hath its influx by the order of Dominions, which the Hebrews call *Hasmalim* [Chashmalim]; and so through the sphere of Jupiter fashions the images of bodies, bestowing clemency and pacifying justice on all: his particular intelligence is *Zadkiel*, the ruler of Abraham.[28]

The order of Chashmalim or Hashmalim are Angelic entities whose name derives from the Vision of Ezekiel:

> And I looked, and, behold, a whirlwind came out of the north, a great cloud, and a fire infolding itself, and a brightness was about it, and out of the midst thereof as the colour of amber [*Chashmal*],[29]

---

28. *The Magus*, Book II, *The Cabala; or, The Secrets of Ceremonial Magic Illustrated*, chapter IV.

29. In the Greek and Latin translations of *Ezekiel*, Chashmal is rendered as ἤλεκτρον (*ēlektron*) and *electrum*, "amber." The luminous quality of amber was anciently associated with the Heavens, and in Greek *Ēlektris* is an Orphic epithet of the Moon, and *Ēlektōr* an epithet of the Sun. Some even thought that amber was condensed from the celestial rays of the Sun. In Alchemy

> out of the midst of the fire. Also out of the midst thereof came the likeness of four living creatures [*Chayoth*].[30]

The Spirit which exists as the archetypal embodiment of Jupiter and Zeus, and indeed almost every sky and thunder God, exhibits tendencies similar to their interactions with humans. Indeed the list of sky Gods contains so many names that it becomes difficult to distinguish one from the other beyond culture and language barriers. From my workings with him, it is clear that the great Jupiter Archangel has undoubtedly assumed mantles or masks of identities and names without any hint of conflict among them. There is the possibility of error in magicians assuming that all such powerful beings are one and the same, but it is equally erroneous to assume that powerful Spirits cannot easily assume the title and visage they are given, as perceived by individuals in differing cultures.

Being Born to Storms

My fascination with and attraction to Jupiter energies and Spirits began much earlier than my explorations into Angelic magic and *Drawing Spirits into Crystals*, and indeed before formally undertaking classical magical work of any sort. As a possible relation to my love for weather phenomena and associated Jovial disposition in general, I would like to share a few accounts from my earlier life. My childhood was filled with paranormal and bizarre events which may have developed into my passion for magic.

My mother was fond of sharing a certain story with me well before my immersion in the magical arts. While she was pregnant with me, she had an interesting encounter during one of her hospital visits. At a pre-delivery checkup, she was sitting in the hospital waiting room, trying not to become lost in worry and concern about whether everything would go well with the pregnancy. A woman sat down next to her who seemed to have some psychic abilities, since she immediately knew precisely how far along my mother was as well as the sex of the baby, as she told her not long after they sat down next to one another. My mother said that the woman had an incredibly kind nature about her and that she spoke with a very soothing voice. "Your baby will be just fine," the woman

---

and metallurgy, electrum was also used as a name for an alloy of gold and silver, because it shone like the Sun and the Moon. In addition to amber's beauty, its ability to attract lightweight materials to its surface by static electricity was known to the ancients, and our modern English word electricity derives from *electrum*. *Chashmal* is likewise the word for "electricity" in modern Hebrew. —APF

30. *Ezekiel* 1:4–5 (KJV).

said. "He will be healthy and strong, having gifts few others have in the world." My mother told me that after hearing that, she did not question the woman's validity, but felt reassured and at ease after the encounter.

It was also an interesting occurrence that upon my entering into this world, lighting struck the hospital or very nearby and made for quite a disturbance, according to my mother. She said a large and violent thunderstorm had been occurring during her whole stay at the hospital, and that after I was born another bolt hit very close that made her jump with fright, but that I didn't cry or seem to be upset by it. Regardless of the significance or possible embellishment of the story by my mother, I took particular interest in it due to my fascination with lightning storms, winds, and deities associated with such phenomenon. To this day, my energy increases in the midst of a storm and I become quite "jovial."

During my early teenage years, I found my awareness and connection to the elements taking on a much more intimate involvement as I became interested in the occult. For reasons I still do not completely comprehend, the aspects of air (wind, storms, and breezes) felt particularly substantial and tangible to me. I spent hours out in the forest, feeling and listening to the wind flowing through the pines, filling me with energy I could not quite define. There was a sense of the world being awake to my presence, or perhaps it was I who was waking up and truly becoming aware of it for the first time. Perhaps it was simply that I was going through puberty. I recall feeling lonely during many of these unexplainable sensations I was having and desired to have a teacher or friend with whom to share these experiences. The attempts of trying to share or express these discoveries with friends or girlfriends previously did not go well.

I had made a close friend at the martial arts school that I had been attending, and after a couple years of friendship I revealed my fascination with the occult. He also had an interest in the subject, and over time I confided in him further about my esoteric practices. I was glad to finally be able to share my interests with someone who seemed as interested and intrigued as I was.

This friend—who has since become one of my closest confidants in matters magical—was with me during a particularly spectacular summer day as we hiked through the forest. The walk along the trails filled me with more energy as we continued to talk about magic and arcane possibilities. We hiked the full way through the forest to the connecting trails down which led to a midsize reservoir and started up the steep mountainside which eventually reached a mountain road. The steep incline was strewn with loose gravel, huge boulders, and even overturned cars that had fallen down from the road above and never been retrieved. As my friend and I made our way up the incline, the wind began to pick up and it was as if the swirling air intensified the energies that had been building inside me the entire trip.

I was breathing heavily, not only from the physical exertion of climbing the steep mountainside but also from the building energy that was nearing a bursting point within me. It seemed that I could feel every molecule of energy gathering in the clouds that were being swept by the winds over the mountains. My fingertips literally seemed to buzz with the electricity of the surrounding air. About halfway up to the road there was a rock face jutting out that could be climbed from the topside. Without speaking a word to my friend, I climbed the rock outcropping and faced toward the open sky. Before me was a perfect view of most of the city and forest below. I breathed in deeply and tasted the moisture on the air charged with energy.

The first "wand" I ever owned was simply a branch that literally fell into my hand while walking home through the forest from school. It was among the first magical experiences I would record and the simple, twisted, scrub-oak branch became my initiation into using magical implements. I carried it with me nearly every time I ventured out into the forest, never really knowing what it was suppose to do for me should the need arise. As usual, I had it with me on my hike with my freind that afternoon.

I retrieved my scrub-oak branch from my side pack and extended it to the sky with my right hand and extended my left hand in kind. I really had no plan or idea what I was attempting to accomplish, but I remember not having any feelings of doubt or hesitation. What I did next was purely through feeling. I felt the wand branch in my hand become an instrument of connecting, a clear channel or cord to the vast sky before and above me. I reached behind me with my wand and made a motion of pulling forward. The winds instantly began to howl down with tremendous force and speed. I saw before me the clouds had appeared in mass to the north and south of the main area of the city. With complete conviction, I began making gathering motions before me with my hands and wand, feeling as if I were pulling a physical substance into the area where I was looking. The clouds began to move almost immediately, drifting with steady speed toward one another to collect over the city. Time seemed in suspension as the experience encapsulated me in momentary isolation from everything else. There was no doubt anywhere in my mind as to what I was doing and what was occurring—no break in thought, no distraction about my friend, or thoughts of other viewers. There was nothing but my mind working in will with the gathering storm. My friend told me afterward that from his perspective, I seemed to be glowing and had a wild expression on my face. Storm clouds continued to gather and concentrate directly over the city, as well as all around. There was a moment's pause, where everything seemed to slow. With a deep inhalation, I raised my arms and brought them down slowly and with intensity, as if I were pushing a great weight down in front of me. Rain began to fall from the sky. It started lightly, then increased with each motion of my hands and wand pushing down from the sky toward the earth. I repeated this gesture over and over until the rain was coming down in torrents. The winds rose to a speed that seemed to be battering the very mountainside, but I don't recall feeling unsteadied by the wind any more than the rain; all I felt was just a maddening current of energy. As more clouds billowed over the mountain peaks behind me, I started to thrust the point of my wand in various places in the clouded sky. It was not instantaneous, but near where my wand pointed, bolts of lightning leaped down and struck the ground. At this point I remember coming to my senses long enough to consciously test this seemingly fantastical feat and thrust my wand in various other parts of the sky. Sure enough, after a moment, a streak of lighting would lance down from the area that I indicated with the wand. The only other lightning that was visible flashed several miles away to the north and south of me.

One of the bolts hit something in the city and a dome of blue light flared up. The storm was growing in frenzy from where I was, and the stronger it got, the more energized and frantic I became. I remember laughing and shouting at the top of my lungs, dancing on the stone spire, arms waving in seeming madness. At some point I suppose it became a little much, and I made out my friend's voice through the roaring storm, shouting at me to calm it down. I looked over at him and he was hunkered against the rocks as the wind and rain lashed at him. We were both drenched, but I hadn't really noticed before.

I took a moment to consider how I might make the storm and rain lessen. It occurred to me that if I reversed the motions I had made with my hands that seemed to make it rain, perhaps the reverse was true also. As I made the motion upward toward the sky, it actually felt like I was reversing the whole process. Sure enough, the rain and wind began to lessen with each upward sweep of my wand and hands until they stopped altogether. The clouds over the city before me remained but the lightning and dark streaks of rain dissipated.

I remember breathing heavily as I turned to stare at my friend, who was smiling as we looked at one another with amazed expressions. My fingertips still buzzed with energy and the wand felt like a conduit in my hand that still connected to the heavens above. The event remains one of the most spectacular and unbelievable experiences of my life.

During the months and years following this event, I recall continually experimenting with various acts of will and intention, until I was able to call up a breeze or winds on request for the few trusted friends who knew I was able to perform such a thing. The more I worked with the physical components of air and weather, the more I realized how others would be altered psychologically by my usage of it. Looking back, I'm amazed how little I knew of the actual practiced arts and developed magical systems that were in existence. My creative drive, however, continued to lead me to experiment with the information I had available at that time. I was content to exert the measure of control I was beginning to manifest over my environment.

My abilities to manipulate atmospheric conditions continued into my late teens. There were moments of considerable cockiness or hubris during this time, as I felt nothing was beyond my grasp. I was able to demonstrate my "Elemental talents" to others and never failed to produce a wind in a single demonstration. One of these displays transpired when I bragged about being able to control the weather to my mother, and put on a rather dramatic demonstration of stopping a rainstorm while traveling in a car. The most I got for that was, "You're freaking me out," followed by a period of silence. No one spoke about it afterwards and when I asked my mother about it years later, she only replied with, "Yeah, that was really strange."

A year or so following these events, I bet my treasured scrub-oak wand in a magical "test of the land" which I initially failed. I didn't offer up my prized implement, and even made an effort to refute my wager by pointing out technicalities to the land Spirits I had challenged. Regardless of this effort, it happened that I was sitting out in the woods one day with my wand by my side and the implement ended up being snapped in half, and then vanishing on the forest floor.

I have not since attempted to summon a tempest out of the clear blue as I once did but have continued to help bring moisture to the land when it seemed needed.

On Archangel Tzadkiel

My initial *DSIC* interaction with the Archangel Tzadqiel instilled the impression of his celestial sovereignty. Beholding the mighty Angel in the crystal pedestal for the first time was an unforgettable experience that was somehow both awe-inspiring and familiar.

There was no doubt as to the being I perceived as I beheld the Archangel, who appeared to me as a shining king with long, silky black beard and hair, adorned with gold, and sitting upon a large throne. I felt that I did not really comprehend the extent of his influence and power, but nonetheless related to it. He spoke about the evolution of humankind, of our accomplishments and rise to industry and national prestige, as if he were an aspect of each accomplishment and vision.

Part of his communication to me during that initial meeting was very profound, leaving me with much to consider. Here is a transcript from my personal journal of *DSIC* operations.

SACHIEL: «From perceived meekness, you will rise and be guided by the throne of righteous judgment. Your word and action shall be in the house of the mind of God, extended through creation and expression of excellence of creation. Know my name and work. Know my measure of council, of judgment, of design, to uplift all that you survey. Mine is the steadfast procession of expansive control. The careful wielder of wealth, influence, and artistry, the formulator of culture to its finest exhibition and portrayal. Of a people defined and exalted in their measures. Let your every action be filled with my presence and voice. Work no tasks without the excellence that is due a king during the height of rule.

«Your rights will be set by putting forth value in all that you do. From the smallest of acts to the most fleeting of thoughts, let the mantle of ruling and the scepter of sovereignty be your extension. Give attention to all that you do and it will be as the purest gold crafted into works of splendor for ages without end.

«Know that no obstacle is insurmountable to the clever. Through knowledge and power comes the mind to judge with clarity. Wealth is accrued to benefit one's will; will is not to benefit one's wealth. My hand is recalled in the stories of Solomon. It is within your nature to perfect yourself and extend that grace to others in your surroundings. The tests in life are not those which would crush nor curse you, but shape and forge you into the splendor of the skillful ruler.

«Wisdom is not gained by books or counsel alone, but more so from experience of conquering the challenges which are pitted against you. To appreciate this fully, you have to embrace life beyond fear or disappointment of idealistic and naive imaginings. Your place is at the solid chair of kingship with all that it entails. The ruling scepter extends past where your feet and hands may touch on their own. It spans to the borders of your kingdom, of your influence. Thus you uphold and govern even that which is immediately beyond your reach and control. Take heart in this fact even when your kingdom needs reshaping and you will not falter. Change and conflict exist only to strengthen the worthy ruler. A king awakened to his right of rule will never respond from anger or fear, but with the wisdom of one who sees from the skies.»

In more ways and examples than I could put into a single volume, Sachiel and the Spirits of Jupiter have had the most impact and influence on my work as a magician. The situations, graces, and accomplishments afforded me have been assisted by the archetypal powers of Jupiter in many ways, and almost certainly more than I know. To identify this connection is not so much a glorification of an Archangel, though that is well deserved, but something more personal. This great being's involvement in countless of my endeavors is quite beyond what I can understand or feel that I deserve. There are familiar aspects which cause me to believe that the current of energy which runs through and from its particular Archangel has more to do with my own making than I can as yet fully comprehend.

Preparing for the Invocation of Sachiel

The Thursday evening I settled on to call this being was set, and I was excited to reintroduce my scryer to Sachiel in a more formalized setting than the Astral experiment we had conducted during the Water Elemental experience. I had no doubts of my ability to contact this particular Archangel, who was more familiar to me than any other. Certainly I wanted to get a second account of this being's position and what specific aptitudes it had for its office and its relation to mankind. Even more, I wanted to get an outside take on how this Spirit related to me that could not stem from my personal ego.

Invocation of the Archangel Sachiel

Fig. VI-14. Section of Circle with Heptameron Correspondences for Drawing Sachiel into the Crystal

(Note: After the invocation, the light intensified so dramatically above and behind the altar that both my scryer and I can be heard gasping on the recording. The display signifying the Archangel's arrival was so undeniable that I didn't need to ask my scryer if he perceived the Spirit, but welcomed Sachiel straight away as I knew my scryer witnessed the light as well by his reaction.)

Appearance of the Spirit

SCRYER: He appears tall with curled black hair like a Babylonian king. Fine jewelry and beads of lapis lazuli adorn his beard. He wears sandals of gold. He has on knee-length breeches, white clothing, and his massive wings seemed to be formed of clouds. He is smiling confidently with a scepter in his right hand and white blazing light in his left.

OPENING QUESTION 1: In the name of the holy and undefiled Spirit, the Father, the begotten Son, and Holy Ghost proceeding from both, what is thy true name?

SCRYER: He loudly claps his hands together and pronounces what sounds like «Bak—» and pronounces something else which is lost in the roar of thunder that follows.

OPERATOR: Great Spirit, can you clarify your name and title, as my scryer was unable to make it out?

(Scryer's voice assumes a lively and authoritative tone that fills the room.)

SPIRIT: «Can you pronounce the sudden release of power and the rolling echo at the end? The sound and name that issues from what rolls across the clouds and into the heavens and speaks of my Father's rule?»

SCRYER: The closest I can tell, the name sounds like «Baktum.» (Baktoommm?)

OPENING QUESTION 2: What is thy office?

SPIRIT: «I am the confident, Jovial rule of my Father. I give the wealth of confidence. I give the bounty of action. I make a throne for all living beings that they may sit and remember the shard of sovereignty that they carry is of God—that is, of El; that is, of Elohim, Who is older than the Hebrews, older than Sumer, and what brought men out of darkness.»

OPENING QUESTION 3: What is thy true sign or character?

SPIRIT: «The scepter, curved by the wind and crossed by the sea, whose impact is the rolling thunder, the explosion of stars, and release of laughing power. I open the threshold that creates life and whose chaos creates order. I am the sovereignty of created being that longs for Elohim.»

OPENING QUESTION 4: When are the times most agreeable to thy nature to hold conference with us?

SPIRIT: «When the Sun is at its height, when the summer is at its peak. When the father returns home. When the prosperity that flows from action is given, like the hunter returning with his food for his family, for his people. When people feel a sense of victory, use that energy to call on me. It can be quick, like the flash of lightning, and it must be filled with joy and laughter. I am the father that lifts his child high above his head and laughs.»

OATH: Wilt thou swear by the blood and righteousness of our Lord Jesus Christ that thou art truly Sachiel?

SACHIEL: «I will swear by the blood of the Christ that I am Sachiel, although that is but one of many of my names.»

Fig. VI-15. ***Portrait of Sachiel as beheld in Vision***

QUESTION 6: What are your views on humanity? What are your roles and interactions?

SACHIEL: «Humanity is one of my favorites of all the Creator's children. The hot spark of His sovereignty is in each one of you. It may burn the world, or it may burn one another, but we guide you, we watch over you, and you were made for a noble purpose. Remembering this is a blessing in itself and annihilates sin. Direct your sovereignty to the service of the Creator and all His creations. Take your place among your brothers and sisters in life: male, female, plant, animal, element, rock, air, microbe, from the smallest to the greatest, your sovereignty serves one another.»

QUESTION 7: Great Archangel Sachiel, do you have any words of wisdom and guidance for my fellow Gentlemen of Jupiter? Any messages collectively and individually that would help us improve or increase or connection with you and embody the traits and strength of your office?

SCRYER: He holds forth a chest of gold; it opens and it gleams with brilliance.

SACHIEL: «Wealth is to be created by all of you and dispensed to those in need. What you give will be returned twice for a collective purpose that I will make clear to you in time. Encourage all beings to live from their sovereignty. Teach them to be unafraid, to revel in the sacredness of their humanity and laugh often.»

QUESTION 8: Do you have your own recollection of your creation and origin? Where do you come from? What is your purpose?

SACHIEL: «I was born from the Creator, from His laughter, and what you would call a fist breaking against the walls of the old. My beautiful, eternal Creator has given me His generosity, His rulership, His confidence, and I run through His creation, and call all of His children to seize their own power and revel in their will—free and not free.»

QUESTION 9: Great Archangel Sachiel, you know I call on you every Thursday. I feel your presence, your blessings, and speak with you often. Is there any other advice you would give to work and speak with you in the most beneficial ways?

SACHIEL: «I have been with you. I have picked you up in the palm of my hand and raised you above my head and shown you to God. I have called Him to see your work and the heart you have put into it. I have shouted to Him that you seek Him with your heart and your hands. And I have stood proudly to watch your works and see your understanding grow. Use these gifts with humility but with joy. When you are called on for help, you *must* answer. You *must* serve. When you feel weak, when you feel bereft or in grief, when you feel the voltage of your will is low, come to the circle and call on me, and like a laughing wind from my Father I will blow your weakness away from you. And we will laugh together at the foolishness of our darkest dreams.»

(There is a strong and personal stirring within me from hearing these words through the mouth of the scryer.)

QUESTION 10: What is the connection we have, great Archangel of Jupiter, Sachiel? Are there certain ties you and I have from the happenings since my birth? If so, what can I do to strengthen our connection further and harness the blessings of your office?

SACHIEL: «Oh, yes. When you are older, you will live in a place where you will be able to see the stars. Throughout the year, you will walk outside and you will whisper to me, and I will come to you on the wind, as I have always done to you on the wind. And I will blow the clouds away and reveal the endless creation that lies above you, around you. And in the glittering stars you will see my face. Your laughter pleases me. My blood runs through your veins and your heart will be light, proud, and oh so peacefully humble.»

(I am filled with overwhelming emotion at this response and it takes me a moment to regain my composure.)

QUESTION 11: What can you teach us of better ways of magically working with the weather? Are there certain Spirits under you who may assist with this?

SACHIEL: «Working with the weather pulls and pushes all the clouds and winds of the world. Do so with great care. For what you put on one place takes away from another. Do so under only the greatest of need. However, when done with great confidence, feel the power of the storm in your breath, or the clarity of the sky in your heart, in your, yes, in your mind. Bring all your tools to bear and explain very clearly the need for the change. And commit yourself after each work to the teaching of all men and women how to maintain the balance and to remember that dearth is just as important as wealth. One feeds the other.»

QUESTION 12: Were the great rains and floods which occurred assisted by your hand this past summer? Was any of the intense weather a sign from Spirits wishing to convey a message?

SACHIEL: «Yes. You, and many around your mountain called the rain that fell. This all came about with many different prayers in many different ways, and that collective will was answered in turn. The fire was alive and the release of a guardian of the land, the second of four. The flood was a gentle reminder to some, and deep, hard cleansing for others.»

QUESTION 13: Is there a symbol or talisman we could make to assist others and us with health, wealth, and success? What would it look like? What would it be made from? How should it be consecrated towards its proper use and function?

SACHIEL: «The lodestone, in a shape as close as possible to a coin. It should be smudged in the smoke of dried mint, sap of frankincense, the wood of Lebanese cedar, as well as the dried flashing yellow of the petals of the sunflower. It should be held aloft in a thunderstorm without fear, shouting my name when the thunder rolls, seven times.

«Use this talisman personally, and lend it only to the most cherished of your friends. If you desire to help those who may not give it back, place it secretly under the chair that they sit in and it will work just the same. This free giving of its power to those you do not understand or fully trust strengthens its draw."

«When the thunder rolls, bring the stone outside to look at the sky, even if just for a few moments, and speak my name silently to it seven times.»

QUESTION 14: Great Jovial king, Sachiel, Archangel of storms, the heavens, and might, Tzadkiel, great father and ruler, thank you for attending upon us. Are there any final words or inspiration you wish to impart before we conclude the ceremony?

SACHIEL: «Laughter and gratitude, action, confidence, and joyful use of *will*, will call me to you—every time. Laugh often. Strengthen and move your body and enjoy its strength, its vitality, and its power.»

(A lengthy and heartfelt License to Depart is intoned.)

Afterthoughts on the Sachiel Operation

(Note: This working was incredible and second to none. One of the first remarks out of my scryer's mouth after we were done was, "Did you see the intensity of the light?! I've never witnessed such an arrival before!")

SCRYER: At one point the spirit appeared so dramatically in the crystal it seemed to turn opaque white and bulge out from the ebony pedestal. At first it was all stark blackness; then I saw pin pricks of blue light like stars, then the planet Jupiter. Sachiel's face appeared suddenly in that space in vivid, vivid detail, as if peering out from behind the Planet Jupiter and coming starkly into view. Three quarters of his face became visible. I could see the detail in his braided hair and beard that was adorned with lapis lazuli beads.

He seems to have quite a connection with you. When we came to that part where you asked about your connection, there was a lot of emotion coming through from him. *(Scryer looks around the magical chamber.)* Look how the light isn't as bright anymore since he left. That light was amazing. Even the glow on the wall got brighter! That was simply incredible. I don't know if you saw, but I jolted when Sachiel clapped his hands. He looked at me for a moment, then clapped loudly, and it was like a clap of thunder. Very sudden and very loud.

OPERATOR: Another fascinating part for me was after the rite was completed, my scryer and I stayed in the circle and I turned to the page in my Book of Spirits and showed him the image I had drawn of Sachiel. My scryer was the first to ever look upon this image and had never seen it previously. We were both amazed, as the image looked exactly as my scryer had seen and described him. I had seen Sachiel and drew him the same way during one of my first evocations of him, years earlier. He held in his right hand a scepter and what looked to be a glowing ball of light in the other. The Archangel of Jupiter seemed to maintain a consistent image through the various workings I've done with him, changing only once or twice the appearance of his surroundings or background.

The operations never cease to amaze, and I felt particularly blessed and uplifted after this confirming encounter with the Archangel of Jupiter.

Operation of the Tin Mirror

For this volume I also want to share a Jovial magical device I was inspired to create after a private scrying session with Sachiel during a particularly invigorating Thursday morning.

The magical item is a scrying mirror specifically suited for drawing forth and conversing with Spirits of Jupiter. It involves creating a mirror made out of polished and consecrated tin (Fig. VI-16) in the form of the seal of Jupiter from the system of the Magic Squares (Fig. VI-17), with these sigils and symbols drawn on the back (Fig. VI-18). If you prefer to hold the mirror in the hand rather than stand it on a table, a handle of oak can be added to the bottom.

The one I designed is four inches in diameter. Its edges are bordered in copper with gold leafing at the top, and a cabochon lapis lazuli stone is fixed to each of the circles at the ends of the extending arms.

Before using the mirror to scry or call for a Jupiter Spirit, wash the surface with a mixture of spring water infused with clove and frankincense oils.

Place blue or violet candles on each side of a small table that sits at eye level. Also have a small incense burner with four legs in front of where you hold or position the mirror so that the smoke drifts up the face of it. Burn a small amount of the Jupiter incense of cedar and frankincense.

Say forth this prayer and invocation while staring into the mirror:

Come speedily, ye blessed Spirits who preside over the operation of this day. Come, incomprehensible Zebarel, Sachiel, Tzadkiel, Joviel, and all your legions, haste to my assistance and be propitious to my undertakings, be kind, and refuse me not your powerful aid and assistance.[31]

Then, still staring into the mirror, whisper the name of Sachiel seven times.

Perform the initial prayer and invocation on a Thursday in the morning, but vocalize your wish and petition in the evening. State aloud your highest aspirations, what you wish to accomplish. Then wait for a response, which may be seen, heard, felt, or a combination of any of these.

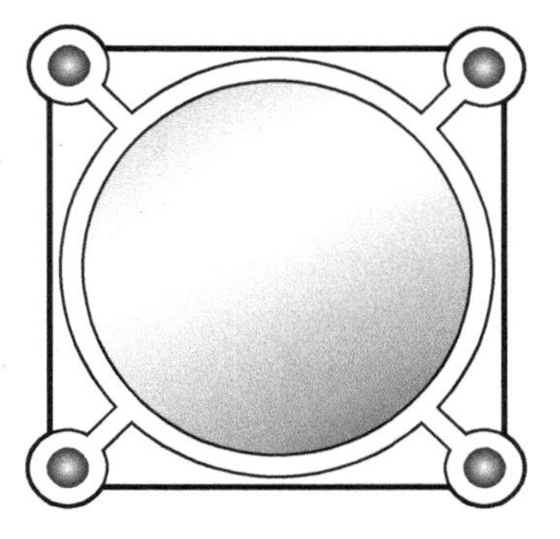

*Fig. VI-16. **The Face of the Jupiter Tin Mirror***

*Fig. VI-17. **The Seal of Jupiter on the Qamea of Jupiter***

The Lodestone Talisman

Weeks after the Sachiel operation I found myself compelled to make the talisman as instructed by the Archangel. I hunted around online for a «lodestone, in a shape as close as possible to a coin,» and finally came upon what I felt was a suitable specimen. It was a naturally disk-shaped piece of magnetite from Europe that was being sold as a geology specimen. After receiving the stone in the mail, I quickly acquired the ingredients listed for the incense and planed out a short ritual involving the points described by the Angel. It just so happened that the following week after I had gathered all the materials, a massive thunderstorm formed in my area, and on a Thursday, no less.

I quickly set out a small altar table containing a censer, four blue candles, and a bottle containing the incense mixture of dried mint, sap of frankincense, the wood of Lebanese

*Fig. VI-18. **The Sigillate Back of the Jupiter Tin Mirror***

31. Modified Invocation for the Spirits of Thursday from Hockley's 19th-century *A Complete Book of Magic Science*, published by Teitan Press in 2008.

cedar, and dried flashing yellow sunflower petals. In the center of the altar table I set my circular lodestone upon a circular diagram I had made specifically for this ritual that encompassed numerous Jupiter symbols and sigils. As a further consideration, I also put on my Jupiter ring, which is a band of white gold set with a star sapphire, that I wear only on Thursdays during my weekly Gentleman for Jupiter rites.

With the incense plumes wafting up under a porch canopy, and while rain beat down, causing an almost deafening cacophony intermixed with loud thunder, I began my ritual.

I picked up the small lodestone in my right hand and blessed it. I held it for several minutes within the smoke tendrils of the incense while intoning my personal blessings for its consecration. When this seemed adequate, I walked out into the pouring rain and awaited a nearby flash of lightning and clap of thunder I was sure would come at any second.

Admittedly, I did have the sense to be wary of the intensity of the storm and did consider the possible foolishness of raising my hand which contained a magnetic iron conductor. Regardless of this fact, I raised my face to the storm and felt the heavy droplets instantly soak the rest of my being. I felt a very familiar electrical charge run through me and fill me with an adrenaline rush that caused my skin to tingle. I remember breathing hard in anticipation as I awaited a display of lightning and following thunder. Regardless of my state, I was still surprised when it actually arrived and my first shout of Sachiel's name came as an exclamation of surprise and excitement. The following six recitations of his name were done with increased vigor as more lightning struck nearby. I held the talisman aloft, unafraid, and I felt the energy of the storm rush into the tiny object. The overall process was among the more exhilarating and energized consecrations of a talisman that I have ever done. I remember shaking for several minutes afterward, more from the continuing energy than the cold of the rain.

The effects of this talisman have been considerable. Since its consecration, I have received numerous orders from individuals wishing to commission me to make them various talismans. Each was willing to pay whatever the price to possess a magical item made by me. The number of orders continues to surprise me, and I am forever grateful for the abundance I have received from magical workings. The Jovial blessings of health, wealth, and prosperity have continued to grow.

The Archangel of Venus
Anael

✠	Day and time	On Friday, during an hour of Venus
✠	Name	Hebrew אנאל *(Anael),* Greek Ἀναηλ *(Anaēl)*
✠	Pronunciation of name (as spoken by the Spirit)	«A-na-el»
✠	Other known names and possible meanings	Hanael, Haniel, possibly "Joy of God" or "Grace of God"
✠	Planet	♀
✠	Materials for lamen	Parchment, copper, brass
✠	Sigil	
✠	Direction for Invocation	North
✠	Incense mixture	Spikenard, musk, ambergris, wood aloes, dried red roses, jasmine flowers, ylang ylang.

Table VI-19. ***Evocatory Correspondences for Anael***[32]

Of Anael and the Office of Venus

It has been stated many times in religious and spiritual literature that "God is Love." Beyond any romantic notion, there is the idea of a divine love that pervades every aspect of creation without judgment or value limitations. For every travesty, there can be seen examples of grace and apparent intervention in times of need. There is a human condition that I believe attempts to emulate the nature of this cosmic love in a very profound way. It is a love quite possibly beyond definition and certainly beyond any one religion, culture, philosophy, or social boundary. Demonstrating unconditional love without possessive or lustful intentions or attachments is rare among human beings, but if we are lucky, we will be able to experience it directly.

The Archangel of Venus, Anael or Haniel, is generally portrayed as an Angelic equivalent to the Greek Goddess Aphroditē. She is the epitome of compassion, love, attractiveness, and companionship. The Archangel is perceived

32. Please see the Cautionary Warning Regarding Grimoric Ingredients in Appendix A. —APF

as the intelligence of the Sephirah of Netzach. Netzach is the emanation of divine beauty and love on the Tree of Life. Some of the oldest surviving records we have of attempts to utilize Spirits to manipulate the world and others involve "love" spells. Truthfully the majority of these spells and magical methods involve torturing or enslaving the will of another until they submit to the magician or person on whose behalf the

Fig. VI-20. ***Lamen of Anael in the manner of DSIC***

so-called love spell was cast, fulfilling lustful desires that bring conflict rather than completion. After my initial interactions with the Archangel of Venus, it is not surprising to me that this being was not invoked more often in such spells, and you find petitions to Demons and other chaotic beings rather than Angels when dealing with these particular types of magic. Such methods are simply not her function. The Archangel Anael conveys the divine nature of love.

My first experience of Anael was intensely moving. Upon reflection, every encounter with an Angelic presence is life-changing, and leaves me in a state of awe and grateful humility. While the other Angels had all exhibited a power and expression of the Creator's divine love, this Angel embodied it in such a way that it made any attempt at rational reflection or reservation completely null and void. The Archangel's communication was that of unlimited compassion, passion, and devotion.

Our first conversations centered on looking into myself to examine the cause of many of my wants as well as past hurts. Rather than granting me any desire that surfaced from the deep churnings of my subconscious, Archangel Anael revealed the parts of my psyche that I attempted to satiate with other existential wants and distractions. With unparalleled compassion and patience, the celestial embodiment of Venus counseled me in ways that would lead to experiencing a measure of this divine love that has never left me. As a grace that manifests through every aspect, my experiences with this Angel led me to be generally more personable to all I encounter, and more attentive to the needs of my fellow man.

Preparing for the Invocation of Anael

The date for the evocation with my scryer was set on a Friday evening just as the sun was going down at the third hour of Venus. I had recently become more interested in Gnosticism and esoteric Christianity, and was excited to see how the Archangel would answer questions relating to certain scriptural figures. Stories ancient and modern relating to Biblical characters have become so much a part of western civilization that they have impacted both general society and the culture of the occult alike, regardless of their basis in fact or fiction. I had never thought previously to question the Angels about them. Beyond this, I wanted a better grasp on how to assist others magically by harnessing the wonderful gifts from this Archangel.

Invocation of the Archangel Anael

Fig. VI-21. Section of Circle with Heptameron Correspondences for Drawing Anael into the Crystal

In the name of the blessed and Holy Trinity, we invoke you, thou wondrous and blessed Angel Anael. Great and beautiful Angel of Venus, hear me. Thou who arrives with hands upon the water and showers truth in the hearts of men, great Angel, beautiful Angel, appear unto us now, visibly present to council us at this time.

Appearance of the Spirit

SCRYER: I very clearly see her standing before me. She is naked, and the Planet Venus shines over her heart. Her wings are spread out behind her, her feet close together. Behind her, a vast sky filled with gray cloud and stars. Her heart, which looks like the planet Venus... pulses.

Opening Question 1: In the name of the holy and undefiled Spirit, the Father, the begotten Son, and Holy Ghost proceeding from both, what is thy true name?

Scryer: She sings her name: The «Ahh-» at the beginning, the sound is pure longing, pure devotion. The «-N-» is almost impossible to explain, but is like the pure joining of two beings. The end of her name is the lifting of that longing, the joining, and love, lifted up to God, «-El». Her name she sings as the most beautiful song I've ever heard.

Opening Question 2: What is thy office?

(Scryer's voice takes on the most compassionate and soothing tone I've ever heard.)

Spirit: «I am most blessed and beloved of the Angels' line. I am the Love of my Father, my Husband. *Shekhinah* is my name to some, *Sophia* to others. I am the love, divine love, that shines into every corner of the universe, whose light is inescapable, unknowable, and filled with a power that the mind cannot comprehend, that only the heart receives, touches, and knows. I am the essence of Magdalene, and the longing of the Son for the Father, of the Son for the Mother, of the Son for the Lover. My name is on the lips of every lover.»

Opening Question 3: What is thy true sign or character?

(At this point in the operation, a very peculiar event occurred in which the right-hand candle on the altar crackled and went completely out for a moment, and then sparked and relit itself. I am unsure what to make of this occurrence, or if it had direct significance at all.)

Scryer: She holds her arms over her head, forming a circle. A great light appears behind her head. I now see a flaming heart before her. The flaming heart hides, masks an unknowable light behind it. Below it is a cross. I see tears on her face.

Opening Question 4: When are the times most agreeable to thy nature to hold conference with us?

Fig. VI-22. ***Portrait of Anael as beheld in Vision***

SPIRIT: «Whenever Venus shows in the sky. Whenever longing of love seizes the heart and overwhelms the spirit and feels incomplete without the other. When this occurs, whisper my name that I may midwife greater love into your heart that is the purpose of your existence. The joining of two leads with hands clasped down the road that leads to God.»

OATH: Wilt thou swear by the blood and righteousness of our Lord Jesus Christ that thou art truly Anael?

ANAEL: «I swear by the beloved Son, Whose hair I ran my fingers through when He slept; Whose tears I wiped with my fingers; Whose feet, scarred with nails and covered in blood, I kissed; Whose voice was music; Whose devotion was perfect; Whose love astounded even me. I swear by the most perfect Son of God, Whom I love still, that I am Anael.»

QUESTION 6: What are your views on humanity, and what are your roles and interactions?

ANAEL: «Ohh, you are such great beings, filled with such blessing and such terrible power. I have seen the worst of men commit the greatest acts of love. I have seen mothers give everything for their children. I have seen sons die for a cause they feel is just. I look into your hearts and I am so amazed at the turmoil, the beauty, the complexity, the music and the symphony that is the heart of man. I love each and every one of you, regardless of your actions, regardless of your ignorance and pain. Each one of you is a precious shard of God. Each one of you can tell me of my Husband, Father, something I do not even know. It is there, at the center of your heart, untouched by the past, unsullied by the actions of others, of the pain that you have endured. It is pure, it is light, and it is potent. It is not naivety; it is strength; it is true power. And it is the most precious thing you possess.»

QUESTION 7: What allowances are there to intercede on human affairs? How and in which ways do you intervene?

ANAEL: «I reach my fingers into the hearts of men and women and children and I hold the light that is within them in front of their eyes. I remind the dictator of the love he has for his daughter. I remind the torturer in his dreams that every blow, every humiliation, he has also inflicted on himself. I show him that he cannot escape his divine self no matter what atrocities he commits. I have the honor, the blessing of pulling the greatest part of humanity into the light. In this light, they astound themselves. And regardless of what they do...I love them.»

QUESTION 8: Do you have your own recollection of your creation and origin? Where do you come from? What is your purpose?

ANAEL: «The very first sound I heard was a great heartbeat surrounding me, enfolding me. Before my eyes were open, there was only the sound of that great heart...beating. Warm, powerful, undeniable, and it filled me and made me...Anael. And when my eyes opened, I saw into the future, the judgment, and all I saw was being after being after being after being, embracing one another, forgetting everything they had done to one another...and laughing in the blessing of their God. And I knew from the very first moment that that was His judgment on us. That He would lead all beings to the place where there would be nothing but embrace. And I wept. I...wept.»

QUESTION 9: Great and beautiful Angel, what instruction can you give us to work and speak with you in the most beneficial ways?

ANAEL: «I require nothing. Simple. Come to me knowing that I will never judge you. That I will accept you for who you are, where you are, no matter what you've done. Step into the circle when you are in pain and allow me to comfort you. When you kiss the forehead of your son, your daughter, your wife, your mother, your father, see me in your mind. Kiss them for me. Speak openly of your love for your family, your friends, and care not for others when they call you naïve, when they call you a well-wisher or a fool. For that power, my power, is beyond the grasp of the ignorant and those who have fallen in love with their own pain.»

QUESTION 10: Great Angel, can you tell us more of the woman known as Mary Magdalene? What was her true identity and purpose? If she existed, what part did she play with Yeshua/Jesus of Nazareth and what is the true history behind her?

ANAEL: «Her Spirit moves through the world again because she is needed. Her role is special and unique. Ask yourself: How could the Son have endured the world, its fear, its ignorance, its desperation, without nights of falling into the arms of His beloved, who did nothing else but love Him? Who could sooth His mind and His heart with her hands, with her voice?...She would sing to Him...and I would listen and sing with them. And in those moments, God was all around.

She knew the love of God with her heart, with her body...with a vulnerability that astounded the other disciples. It is a mystery of Jesus that many are not yet ready to hear.»

QUESTION 11: In what ways can we improve our lives in love and relationships?

ANAEL: «Speak your love. Express your love, and in its expression it grows. It is fed, and when fed and expressed, it runs like a river into the hearts of all you know. Don't wait; say it today. Say it tonight. Place yourself, your heart on the chest of the one you love. Take joy in seeing and experiencing the world from their eyes, with their fingers, with their ears, their tongue, and their feet, and liberate yourself in the alleviation of their burdens. And when this is done in sincerity with the wife, the son, the daughter, the father, you will find this capacity: this circle will grow to the friend, the coworker, the passerby, and eventually the enemy.»

QUESTION 12: Can you teach us how to create the most powerful talisman, blessed by you, to attract love, desire, and passion to us, or to give to a significant other to further inspire the acts, these feelings of love?

ANAEL: «There are many. There is the giving of rings. The tying of hands, dipped in the water of the spring. When Venus rises and appears in the sky, the lovers with their right hands tied together face my star with a plate of food, and a glass of wine, and in silence. After singing my name, look into one another's eyes and feed one another. Bring the bread to her lips, bring the wine to her lips, and know inside wordlessly that you feed one another your devotion, your love. And Venus, my star, will shine upon you and you will be blessed. Anoint your hearts with my oil, and it is done.»

OPERATOR: How is it that your oil is made?

ANAEL: «It is made with essence of red and white and yellow rose; flecks, dust, of red quartz; saffron; oil of the olive; and one tear of joy.»

QUESTION 13: For my wife, is there any blessing or talisman that could be given to her to further heal and open her heart?

ANAEL: «Do the ceremony that I gave you with her. And afterward when you are home, hold her in your arms, let her speak of her past, run your fingers through her hair; do not instruct, do not guide. Invoke me at the foot of your bed, and let her speak to me of her past, of her pain. Keep silent. Hold her against your chest. And just run your fingers through her hair. And if she weeps, save one of the tears for my oil in a clear flask and seal it with wax till you are ready to put it and mix it with the oil.»

QUESTION 14: For all those who may be hurting or wishing to heal the heart and emotions, memories and pains, desiring to grow closer, do you have any other methods for healing the heart, emotions, memories, pains, and bringing your divine love and power to them? A prayer, invocation, or poem of love to call you near and bring love to a place?

ANAEL: «Yes. Those who would do this carry a great responsibility for the alleviation of pain for others. First the afflicted must speak their pain and they must *know* fully that those who listen will not judge. Before they speak, all in the room must hold hands and sing together my name. The person who speaks must be given as long as is needed. No interruption, no instruction. And when it is done, when they have finished speaking, all those in the room, with warm cloths of white dipped in rose water will wash, lovingly...invoking my blessings on them by singing,

> *Anael, come, purify the pain, purify their pain, wash them in the light and love of the Creator; remind them they are unique, remind them that the light in the middle of their hearts remains pure.*

And each person in the room must speak and be washed.»

QUESTION 15 *(personal, asked by the scryer)*: In Færy lore, what is the meaning or truth behind Lucifer falling through Venus to the Earth Mother?

ANAEL: «Some will hear this spoken or hear this teaching, and may see it as naïve; as fairies traipsing on dust.

When Lucifer fell, when he fell through Venus...he fell through me. His love for 'she who could not breathe out' was so great that he severed himself utterly from the Father. I do not know his destiny; it is a mystery kept even from me. But when briefly he passed through me, I could feel his longing. The longing of a broken heart...for knowledge of the other.

For an Angel to do this it is *such* pain you humans have no conception. But I suspect that in darkness, there is something inexplicably light. This is all I can say of this for now.»

QUESTION 16: What similarities do you share with the Goddesses of history: Aphroditē, Venus, Cytherea, Ishtar, Inanna, Isis, Freya, and others? Are you all the same being, only in some aspects, or individual? Are the other Angels and the Gods the same?

ANAEL: «Inasmuch as two mountains of the same range are connected and ultimately one, whose peaks are touched by the same sunlight in the morning, but whose slopes and features are different and unique and beautiful... No...and Yes. It is a mystery that very few will feel. And this is all I will say.»

QUESTION 17: Great Angel, is there any way my wife can harness her spiritual sight? Would she be able to see and converse with you in this operation as we have?

ANAEL: «Yes, by expressing her past and speaking in the way I have given. Her heart will lead her forward from there. And I will rest her hand in mine. And when she is ready, I will feel her and she will feel me, and we shall speak...But be patient with her.»

SCRYER: She is showing me an image now...It's an icicle melting in the sun...

QUESTION 18: Great Angel of divine love and beauty, do you have any final words of teaching or advice that we may share with others or integrate into our own lives?

ANAEL: «The scryer must make his decision to love. The scryer must understand that his blockages are *love · of · self*. He must know that he is worthy of love, regardless of who may show him that love. And for the magician... touch her gently, run your fingers over her skin, her hair, and say nothing.»

OPERATOR: Great beautiful and wondrous Angel Anael, we thank thee for your attendance and council during this ritual. We ask continually for your grace and blessings upon us, and for our hearts to be opened by your light.

(License to Depart.)

Afterthoughts on the Anael Operation

Note: The session was so intense and emotional it was difficult to maintain control of the ceremony. The energy I can only describe as divine passion, love, and acceptance beyond what either of us was ready for. Both the scryer and myself had tears streaking down our faces. We were both astounded. It also touched deeply on our personal relationships and intentions to become better spouses.

SCRYER: When she first appeared, I perceived the intense light behind the flaming heart as the divine love of God that was too powerful to come through in its purity. The heart of fire seemed to allow God's love to emanate through it without overpowering that which it touched. Anael seemed to form the symbol for Venus using her body and the accompanying light.

When Anael described her birth, there was so much passion and that ancient sense theme of love and suffering together. There was such longing, like the passion of Christ. I'm glad we recorded this, because every time we do this I'm getting a bit deeper, and it's so overwhelming I think my mind has trouble keeping up with everything. Many times I can't remember what is said.

OPERATOR: We both felt so appreciative of the other and how we were able to share these life-changing experiences. We realized just how incredible and unique our experiences were, and what it meant to share them with one another. It's very humbling.

I had never heard my scryer's voice as it sounded during this operation. It was as if Anael's voice emanated through his in the most nurturing and caring tone, emanating from his true heart. I think it is nearly impossible to grasp the extent of this undertaking without hearing and experiencing the sincerity and loving-kindness which emanated through the entirety of this operation. Written words fall short, and although this is an earnest and complete record of all that was recorded during this session, it simply cannot convey the intense emotion with which each word was delivered and the impact it had on both my scryer and me.

The lessons from the Archangel lasted for weeks afterward, with several manifesting through interesting occurrences.

I believe that learning to be a living embodiment of this divine love and emanating it to others is quite possibly the most powerful level of ascending as a magician or a mystic. However, one aspect of magic is that it is practical in its purpose. In that regard, the Venus magic of love and companionship seems to have evolved in its intentions as well as application. For instance, whereas many ancient papyri and medieval grimoires contain methods and recipes for entrapping or seducing a lover, this one contains formulæ for keeping and nurturing one. Although I mainly speak from my own perspective, it seems that finding a lover or companion is perhaps not quite as difficult as it once was, but keeping one and maintaining the relationship is the real challenge in modern times.

The Archangel of Mars
Samael

✠ Day and time	On Tuesday, during an hour of Mars
✠ Name and meaning	Hebrew סמאל *(Samael),* "Venom of God"
✠ Pronunciation of name (as spoken by the Spirit)	«Ssssa-ma-el»
✠ Other known names and forms of name	Sammael, Camael,[33] Zamael[34]; Azazel?
✠ Planet	♂
✠ Materials for lamen	Parchment, bronze, iron, steel
✠ Sigil	
✠ Direction for Invocation	South
✠ Incense mixture	Cedar wood, red sandalwood, cypress, lodestone powder, gum Benjamin, camphor, costus root, a small amount of red pepper, and a small amount of sulfur.

Table VI-23. ***Evocatory Correspondences for Samael***[35]

33. The name of the Archangel of Mars, Samael, undeniably originated as Hebrew סמאל, and was transcribed into Greek as Σαμαηλ (*Samaēl*). I realized some years ago when laboriously studying Greek manuscripts (with tired eyes, bright lights, and a magnifying glass) that the variation Camael is almost as certainly a scribal error originating when some tired Mediæval scribe, unfamiliar with the Angel names, was translating texts from Greek to Latin. In Greek script after the classical era, the letter Sigma evolved from the angular *Σ* to the cursive *C*. So Samael was written in Late Antique and Mediæval Greek not as Σαμαηλ but as Cαμαηλ, and likewise in Coptic texts as ⲥⲁⲙⲁⲏⲗ. Someone copying lists of unfamiliar Angel names from either Greek or Coptic easily made the mistake of transliterating the name as Camael into a Latin list, from which it entered Western angelology. The Hebrew name כמאל (*Kamael*) found in Hermetic Qabbalistic lists is a late bit of reverse engineering from Camael. —APF

34. Zamael is an artificial variation of Samael very likely introduced to distinguish the Martial Archangel from the Qlippotic Archdemon. For years I thought it had originated as recently as the Golden Dawn knowledge lectures, but I finally noticed it in Agrippa's Book III, chapter XXIV, where the occult encyclopædist says he found it in a manuscript of his teacher Trithemius' *De Septem Secundeis*. —APF

35. Please see the Cautionary Warning Regarding Grimoric Ingredients in Appendix A. —APF

Of Samael and the Office of Mars

Samael is the most controversial Archangel catalogued in magical texts, as he is also often listed among the more ruthless demons. In several systems of Angelic magic, Samael is completely excluded, being replaced by Kamael as the Angel invoked under the auspices of Mars. There are few accounts of Samael arriving with good or helpful tidings for men. Usually his vision is the last anyone sees, with death coming swiftly on his celestial heels.

When I first decided to contact the Archangel of Mars, he arrived to greet me first. The Tuesday evening after I created Samael's lamen, I was visited by his presence in the night, accompanied by an overwhelming sensation of dread and oppression. I awoke and tried to muster all my strength and defense as a magician, as I would handle any oppressive Spirit that would dare enter my abode with hostile intentions. My efforts and mental focus were simply brushed aside as a presence of dark fire made itself known near my bedside. It seemed to mentally strip me of any pompous assumptions about myself or my accomplishments. A mental debate began between us in which I sought to defend my position, not only as a magician, but as a human being worthy to continue my existence for the short while I had. The Angel was able to deprive me of any philosophical or moral foothold by which I could justify my existence. I simply did not have a leg to stand on when implacable divine judgment was applied to my justifications. It was pathetic, I was pathetic, the Angel declared in harsh clarity. «Pathetic!»

Without hesitation, he brought up transgressions I had committed, many I had attempted to keep hidden from all others. His words and presence paralyzed me in my bed, and I felt a fear and sickness that was beyond words. I remember thinking very distinctly that my presumptuous role as a magician had finally landed me in a spiritual situation that would cost me my life.

The being at my bedside did not relent. He continued to keep my attention fixed on my deceits and failures. With each moment I seemed stripped of any worthy sense of self; death was presented in a terrifying way that I had never considered before: the complete dismantling of a consciousness. Nothing I could think of would allow me to outwit or defend against this entity's judgment of me.

There is a judgment and consideration for every conscious act that is severe. If ever there was a presence to directly embody the impact and nature of Geburah, it was this entity. This Messenger was not only fierce in all his aspects but absolute in his judgment of me. Severe in consideration, tone, and speech, he was a fire that would instantly burn and possibly completely consume the one who did not tend to it immediately.

Fig. VI-24. ***Lamen of Samael in the manner of DSIC***

I wish I could fully describe my fear of looking upon this Angel of black and red burning shadow. This wasn't an argument with a religious zealot, a human being hurling fanatical and dogmatic religious accusations. It was an inhuman celestial authority that knew every microsecond of my existence and behavior. It knew every action I had ever expressed in the world, and it recalled instances to me I had presumed long forgotten. Within the seemingly endless peeling away of my ego and sense of purpose and worth, I somehow finally stepped beyond my pain and defense of my purpose and individuality. I stopped trying to justify myself. The interaction with this Archangel at my bedside forced me to confront my faults with a critical and truthful eye. It was not self-demoralizing or self-hating, as those can be other forms of self-pitying and self-justification. Instead, I was forced to look at my transgressions as they were, accept full responsibility for them, and make a decision about how to live from then on that it seemed I had been unable or unwilling to do before. There also arose a strength and determination to overcome previous limitations and passive acceptances of unworthy behaviors and actions.

I spoke to Samael in the night through my mind, "You are right. I confess and admit all which you have said, without retort. You speak the truth of my faults and failures without embellishment. You see all that is, without mercy or falsehood. I did not call upon you to challenge you or attempt to control your nature. I do not assume for you to bestow gifts upon me as if I would be someone worthy to do so. But, as God allows, I did call you to teach me. Teach me then. If you are judge and destroyer, destroy then those aspects of my wicked nature that I no longer need and which must not be brought forth unto God. Burn up any deceitful desires for all that which is not of my intended purpose. I submit to your teachings as they are justified under God, since I know no being is beyond what God himself devises. The wickedness and fear lies within my own dissolution. Therefore I attempt not to hide from you and will submit to your judgment and council."

After this spontaneous but sincere response, the relation between the Archangel and me changed, as did the hostile feelings and oppression. The being's presence did not lack any of its foreboding nature, but it was no longer directly threatening. I daresay the change was mostly in me, but he seemed to accept my words and did not challenge me any further, but simply stated, «We will see.»

He departed without another word, and I remained awake for the remainder of the night.

In the first evocation, I remember vividly Samael's shield. It is a face screaming in fury or agony or more probably both, but somehow also pleading as if it is the face of a victim who is still trying to petition his innocence or his worthiness to live. It shows anger, horror, despair, madness, and anguish. Rather than being an implement used for protection, Samael's shield looks more like a trophy head, shown to those into whom he wishes to strike fear as a foreboding of what will soon befall them. It is a mirror into which few would ever willfully gaze.

The sword Samael carries is wicked, honed, and has the look of being frequently used for all manner of slaying and dismemberment. His eyes hold you fast, seeing and burning away all defenses and deceit. There is death there, and exposure beyond any grace of compassion and mercy. There is blinding light that exposes the truth of your darkness.

Samael's wings sometimes assume the look of intense fire and then of dried blood, occasionally brightening and then darkening once more.

I caution anyone daring to purposefully contact this Archangel. You will feel yourself to be the lowest of the low. You will experience the oppression of aggressive scrutiny directly focused upon yourself and all that you try to keep concealed from the world. This is a being who forces you to see the truth uncovered, without self-justifying philosophical excuses. How your actions have hurt others. You will know a fear that reveals itself not as fear of the Angel but fear of one's own evil, done against oneself and others. Make no mistake; this powerful Angel's office is not to assist humankind and boost us up with positive feelings and support. Quite the contrary, Archangel Samael will challenge you in every hidden corner of your being. He indeed will tempt you, displaying your weaknesses, your unbalanced desires and fears, right in front of you. After working with him, or leading up to the operation working with him, you may have vivid dreams of indulging in your own pleasures that go outside your conscious morality, or else of being confronted by them in a very accusatory way.

The self-concealing justifications we offer for ourselves as being a single drop in the vast sea of the human race will never stand while working with this Archangel. We may ask why we should be held up to such unyielding scrutiny, since we are in fact just one person and—please bear this in mind—only human after all. With Samael, this justification holds absolutely no water; we are judged as individuals and treated as if we were in full knowledge of the correct way of living, separate from the enabling leniencies and justifying statistics of our brothers and sisters.

Preparing for the Invocation of Samael

The Tuesday planned for the evocation of Samael was scheduled following some disturbing incidents that had been increasing in frequency in and around my city. Acts of violence and death seemed to be on the rise, and I began to wonder if there were any contributing spiritual energies or imbalances that were pushing people over the edge. I was apprehensive about summoning this particular Archangel before the magic circle again, as his presence was always more than I felt confident facing. However, I wanted to discover if there was some occult cause or contributing factor to the horrendous crimes and acts of violence. I also wanted my scryer to experience this intense being and for us to possibly learn further ways to positively harness the office of Mars.[36]

---

36. As with the previous workings, this operation seemed to come about at just the right time where such lessons about conflict, violence, and intensity were important. It seemed to me that the Angels themselves played an important role in arranging when these evocations would take place and what could be learned and accomplished at those times.

Invocation of the Archangel Samael

Fig. VI-25. Section of Circle with Heptameron Correspondences for Drawing Samael into the Crystal

Note: This operation commenced with intense presence and interaction. The arrival of this Angel was announced with the familiar increase of light as well as the charcoal and incense sparking loudly.

Appearance of the Spirit

SCRYER: He appears very tall, dressed in red. He has long red braids, and has a solemn expression. It is holding a sword in his right hand. The wings literally look made of fire, and he has already said he is the «Fierceness of God.» He looks almost like he is halfway between a man and a woman.

OPENING QUESTION 1: In the name of the holy and undefiled Spirit, the Father, the begotten Son, and Holy Ghost proceeding from both, what is thy true name?

SCRYER: He holds forth his hand and fire comes out of it straight up. It sounds like «SSSSSSSSSSSS, (takes on the sound of boiling sap) SSSamael.» Somehow his name takes on the characteristics of fire, difficult to pronounce.

OPENING QUESTION 2: What is thy office?

(Scryer's voice takes on a rather raspy yet hardened tone.)

SPIRIT: «I am the Fierceness of God, the sword that obeys *His* will, that cuts through injustice, ignorance, deception, lies, sloth, and arrogance. I leap like a flame through dry grass. I sing the fury of my Father, and coast upon

Fig. VI-26. ***Portrait of Samael as beheld in Vision***

the wings of flame. I open the chest of men to expose their hearts to the Creator.»

OPENING QUESTION 3: What is thy true sign or character?

SCRYER: He holds his sword aloft above his head. Suddenly he disappears and I see the planet Mars. It looks as if Mars is 'crowned' by his sword. And I see fire dance along the blade.

OPENING QUESTION 4: When are the times most agreeable to thy nature to hold conference with us?

SPIRIT: «When in need of justice. When struggling for a cause that serves the needs beyond the self. When the year is warm. When Mars is prominent in the sky or closest to the Earth. When revolutions topple kings, evoke me that I may usher in harmony through conflicts.»

OATH: Wilt thou swear by the holy blood of Jesus Christ that thou art truly the Archangel Samael?

SAMAEL: «I am Samael, The Fierceness of God, he who held the hammer to pierce the flesh of the Son on the cross, while weeping tears of fire.»

QUESTION 6: What are your views on humanity, and what are your roles and interactions?

SAMAEL: «My views on humanity run from anger to admiration to love. The power of their free will is great but often used for such terrible tyranny and destruction. Even the Father who loves His child can still become angry at the actions of the child. With the grace and precision of the sword, I sever ignorance to be cut away from humanity and the times of the greatest need, I come to burn, not out of hatred but out of love. The might of kings, presidents, and ministers should always be in service of all creation in order to be just. If this is not done, eventually I come to tear down the stones of the castles, so that the oppressed can sing.»

Scryer: I'm suddenly being shown the Pentagon of the United States, with Samael looking on with intense displeasure.

Question 7: Do you have your own recollection of your creation and origin? Where do you come from?

Samael: «Yes, I remember fire. I remember feeling my Father's hand below me, as I rested upon His palm, feeling the warmth of His skin, His blood, the flames around me, warmth of love and ferocity. I remember a great voice saying, ‹Awake, Samael.›»

Scryer: I hear his name again in the way I cannot pronounce.

Samael: «‹Awake, Samael, awake.› And I stood, sword in my right hand, wings spread in flame, and I marveled at the power of my Father that was in me.»

Question 8: What advice can you give us to work and speak with you in the most beneficial ways?

Samael: «Call on me primarily to bring justice to others. Call on me to shelter them from beneath my sword, only in the greatest of need, only as a last resort. Call on me and my sword will be with thee. Fire should be with you. Speak my name into the flames, and know with humility and responsibility that you call on the very Fierceness of God.»

Question 9: Are you the same being or have a connection with Satan, Satanael, Lucifer, the Adversary, Great Accuser, or Fallen Angel?

Samael: «I am not Lucifer, though we share the same fierceness of our Father and a decisiveness of His will. Lucifer, first son, most beloved, whose return to the Father will make all weep and sing...Such great destiny for my elder brother.»

Question 10: What can you teach us of the brass vessel of the *Goetia* and the black-hilted knife? How can we constrain and speak with certain Spirits/Demons more effectively?

SAMAEL: «The vessel is a container of passion, of suffering, fear, of anger. The knife of black is a goad for those called by it. It can be used to discern the will of those who oppose you, but beware of what those who are called say. Their truth will be cloaked in lies and they will pretend to bring forth the deepest, the most vulnerable insecurities of the magician. The black-hilted knife is a reminder of this truth.»

OPERATOR: Can you teach us a powerful method for magical attack and defense with use for this weapon?

SAMAEL: «As the goad it may threaten, it may inflict pain, the infliction of pain the responsibility of the one who wields it. Move it always in circles, accompanied by sound. At the end of the working, it may be used to cut any such connections or pathways between the magician and what is called. After the cut, the severing, call down the blessings of God on that which was evoked. It can be used to burn with the love of God.»

QUESTION 11: How can we positively harness the office of Mars? Are there any invocations, prayer, and magical method to increase strength and harness courage?

SAMAEL: «In a circle composed of Fire, anoint yourself with the oil of cinnamon when Mars is high in the sky, in a sacred place. Move and strengthen the body, churn the blood in the veins, and whisper my name again and again. Burn slightly the middle of the right palm in remembrance of my birth, wearing vestments of red, with flame in the room.»

(Operator retrieves his magical sword from within the circle and presents it toward the scrying pedestal from behind the scryer.)

QUESTION 12: Great Archangel Samael, I ask for your power and blessing on this magical sword. Do you have a method for further empowering and consecrating this weapon, which is dedicated to the heavenly Sphere of Geburah and your office?

SAMAEL: «Hold it aloft with both hands parallel to the ground above your head and it will be done.»

(Operator unsheathes the sword and raises it as instructed. He feels a pressure on his hands and head as if the Archangel's hand pressed down on the sword from above.)

SAMAEL: «When needed, take your sword outside. By pointing it straight at Mars as if you were balancing that red point of light on its tip, know that it further receives my power. Then speak my name seven times.»

QUESTION 13: The area just north of our lands here especially seems to have an affliction of young people committing more violent and deadly crimes and actions than what is found in many parts of the country. Is there a certain spirit or energy which has been infecting that area and its people since the [name deleted] shootings or before? What is the nature of this and what can be done to change or lessen it?

SAMAEL: «Yes, the configuration of the valley holds energy. Since certain tragedies occurred through deception, through confusion of the spirits of the two boys, by the feeding of beings filled with anger, and the ignorance of the brutality of all the acts of the city, this can breed a psychosis, fueled by beings and demons that cannot be seen. The souls of the boys must be liberated. The sites of the killings anointed with my oils and the oils of Michael and the blessings of the love of God called down on those who were killed and those who did the killing.»

QUESTION 14: Great Archangel Samael, Fierceness of God, do you have any final words of advice, inspiration, or teachings before we conclude the ceremony?

SAMAEL: «When teaching the use of force, the student must understand the ultimate purpose in service of the skills they possess and responsibility of wielding Fire; the Fierce Love of God. And for the scryer: Burn away expectation; submit in faith wholly to the experience.»

(License to Depart.)

Afterthoughts on the Samael Operation

SCRYER: During the invocation, the vision of Samael would fade at times, but when he returned, he seemed more and more flamelike, especially toward the end. When he was talking about the oppression of kings and presidents, I got a very clear vision of the Angel directly above the Pentagon with an expression of intense displeasure, a displeasure verging on anger.

He seemed to communicate, «These men have no idea what they are doing.»

The feeling I got the most is that force isn't necessarily a bad thing. It's how it's used and the reasons it is used for. When it stops serving people in their greater interest it turns into the "these are the people who pay us so we do what they tell us to do."

The Archangel really looked like an androgynous face with fiery features, a perfect blend between the two genders.

At the end, when he was talking about me, I felt the anointing you did on my forehead like never before, like it was almost burning. It really stood out like the feeling, like you have stuff getting in the way of you seeing, you need to stop expecting things and not expecting others, you have to open better to things. I'm always worried since I don't know the system, and wonder what would happen if something comes through that is totally outlandish or contradictory to the system. The Angel made it clear that I am to let that go and let the experience happen, and just report what I see. That can be hard.

I got the clear image of you holding the sword, of you balancing Mars on the tip of the sword. Another thing I realized when we were talking about his 'true symbol' was that his sword directly above Mars looked just like the symbol for Mars with the arrow coming out of the circle.

OPERATOR: The Angel's sigil, upon closer inspection, seems to reveal the pain and punishment of sin. Moving from left to right, the first symbol easily resembles a cross wherein a knot is tied, then arches up at a sharp angle toward the end with an arm extending out at an inward angle. The circle and line which strikes back through the initial image looks like a nail being driven through it by the hammer of the arm above. Pain, suffering, and punishment are obvious themes associated with this Angel. After the second invocation of him, when he said he was the «hammer that drove the nail through the hand of Christ to the cross with tears of fire,» I see how the part at the end of his sigil looks like a nail being driven through the rest of his sigil.

I seriously considered removing the section of the evocation pertaining to the shootings from the record to be published in this book. An infamous shooting incident occurred not far from my city which I'm sure many readers will be able to determine. Ever since this event, there have been tragedies and unusual outbreaks of violence which continue unabated. The process described by Archangel Samael to liberate the souls of those who instigated and met a violent end is an extremely delicate matter, if not obviously dangerous. It is a situation that both my scryer and I felt needed to be handled carefully as well as thoroughly planned out. There were a few aspects for completing the mentioned ritual successfully that I failed to understand before the end of the ceremony. For instance, I was unsure from what ingredients Archangel Michael's oil was made, and I had not asked during the evocation. I wasn't about to call up the Archangel of the Sun or Mars again just to ask this question, so I planned to find out another way. There were a few more details as well which I will keep hidden for the time being, as this undertaking will have to be conducted in relative secrecy.

The Sword of Geburah

My magical sword has become a weapon of considerable power with a presence all of its own. Where I had thought it beneficial to have the mighty Archangel imbue the weapon with his strength, I did not realize the extent of what that entailed.

The magical sword, fashioned after the weapon in the Mathers version of the *Key of Solomon*, was consecrated shortly after the invocation of Samael. On an auspicious Tuesday evening, I took the sword out, finding Mars to be particularly bright in the sky on that evening. As I leveled the tip directly at the light coming from the Planet, I began chanting Samael's name seven times. The chant took on a drawn-out, hissing quality, elongating the *S* in Samael's name each time. The event seemed rather uneventful, as I did not sense or witness anything particularly noteworthy during it. When it was done, I sheathed the sword and wrapped it back in its silks.

Months after the consecration and operation with Samael, my scryer's home became subject to disturbance by some haughty and unruly Spirits. He and his family asked for my assistance in ridding the house of these Spirits and I obliged. I brought the magical sword with me as a possible tool to use for banishment. However, when I unwrapped the sheathed sword from its silk coverings, the weapon became immediately active in the sense that both myself and my scryer's wife felt the power emanating from it. It had the feeling one might get in the presence of a very deadly and aggressive animal. I became wary of unsheathing the weapon simply for the sake of banishing possible ghosts. Benn's wife agreed that it seemed a bit too intense to unsheathe within the house, so I wrapped it back up. I had no trouble clearing the house without the sword, and have since not found an appropriate opportunity to draw it from its sheath.

However, the weapon has continued to be useful against bothersome Spirits without even taking it out of its wrappings. Since the consecration of it, I've had three different encounters when various Spirits gained access to my house and became bothersome or frightening to other members of the family. In these particular cases, the entities refused to leave and would not do so until I mentioned the sword. Simply describing it and who consecrated it was enough for them to depart without a further word. Interestingly, I'm not sure if they could sense the weapon nearby or if they simply didn't wish to bother testing me to see if I was bluffing. Either way, the very idea of the weapon seems to have a potent effect.

Any security or level of control aside, my one concern is this: What sort of being would dictate the need to unsheath such a weapon?

The Brass Vessel of Solomon

Like many magicians before me, The *Goetia* of the *Lemegeton* was my first passion in exploring classical magic. Next to *The Art of Drawing Spirits into Crystals* and *The Key of Solomon*, the *Lemegeton* is my go-to book for occult experiments. The implements, vestments, and magical procedures listed in the *Goetia* fascinated me since my first reading of it. I have since created each and every implement according to the written specifications. However, despite their use in a number of evocations, I was still not certain about the exact origins and function of some. I thought that the items which appeared to have some relation to the office of Mars had been perfect subjects to discuss with this Archangel.

One item in particular which has always fascinated me is the Brass Vessel of Solomon, along with its Secret Seal to trap the powerful Spirits in the container. As described in the *Goetia*:

> *The Secret Seal of Solomon.*
>
> by which he bound and sealed up the aforsaid spirits with their legions in a Brazen Vesel &c.
>
> This secret seal is to be made by one that is cleane both Inward and outward, and hath not defiled himself by any woman in the space of a Month; but hath with fasting and prayers to God desired pardon of all his sins, &c: Itt is to be made on a Tuesday or Saturday night at 12 of the Clock, written with the Blood of a Black Cock which never trode hen, on virgins parchment. Note, on those nights the ☽ must be increasing in ♍, when it so made, fume it with Allum, Raisins of the Sun, dates, Cedar & lignum Aloes, by this seal Salomon

> compelled the aforesaide spirits into a Brass vessel, and sealed it up with the same, he by it gained the love of all Manner of persons, and overcame in Battle, for neither weapon fire nor water could hurt him.[37]

In our evocation, Samael described the brass vessel as a «container of passion, of suffering, fear, of anger.» He seemed to be giving us more information about the nature of the Goetic Spirits that are bound within it than about the brass container itself. As a magical device, the jar is meant to be able to contain considerable, decisively hazardous power, and to render it into a controlled, usable form. As a sort of Demon engine, it can be utilized to constructive ends, but with high risk factors.

Fig. VI-27. ***The Secret Seal of Solomon which binds the Fallen Spirits in the Brazen Vessel***

An interesting bit of ancient Greek lore describes a brass jar which may share common origins with the Goetic brazen vessel. The Messenger God Hermēs is said in the *Iliad* to have released Arēs the God of war from a brazen vessel. The Goddess Diōnē tells her daughter Aphroditē,

> So suffered Ares, when Otus and mighty Ephialtes, the sons of Aloeus, bound him in cruel bonds, and in a brazen jar he lay bound for thirteen months; and then would Ares, insatiate of war, have perished, had not the stepmother of the sons of Aloeus, the beauteous Eëriboea, brought tidings unto Hermes; and he stole forth Ares, that was now sore distressed, for his grievous bonds were overpowering him.[38]

---

37. *Of the Arte Goetia*, in MS Sloane 3825, folio 113ʳ, following Peterson's transcription in Joseph H. Peterson and Solomon, *The Lesser Key of Solomon: Lemegeton Clavicula Salomonis: Detailing the Ceremonial Art of Commanding Spirits Both Good and Evil* (York Beach, ME: Weiser Books, 2001). —APF

38. Homer and A.T. Murray, *The Iliad* (Cambridge, MA, Harvard University Press; London, William Heinemann, Ltd., 1924), Book V, lines 385–391. —APF

The Black-Handled Knife

According to *The Key of Solomon*, the black-handled knife is used for "making the circle, wherewith to strike terror and fear into the spirits." It is constructed by the magician himself or by a blacksmith and placed "thrice in the fire until it becomes red hot in the day and hour of Saturn, and dipped in the blood of a black cat and in the juice of hemlock."[39]

Archangel Samael's reply to the questions regarding the black knife were interesting, but somewhat cryptic as well. The knife being utilized as a «goad» is understandable enough since the majority of Solomonic magic utilizes such techniques to command various spirits.

As far as it being intended to «discern the will of those who oppose you,» I should have had the Archangel clarify what he meant by this, but I failed to do so at the time. This is definitely a matter I'll have to pursue in future operations with him.

Samael's warning of being wary of «what those who are called say» and that their «truth will be cloaked in lies and they will pretend to bring forth the deepest, the most vulnerable insecurities of the magician» seems along the lines of how many of these Spirits or Demons tempt the magician. The black knife in this regard seems to be suggested as a weapon to make sure the Spirits are being truthful (perhaps in using it to draw a triangle outside the circle?).

Samael also mentioned that «as the goad, it may threaten, it may inflict pain, the infliction of pain the responsibility of the one who wields it. Move it always in circles, accompanied by sound.» I found this interesting but was uncertain if the Spirit meant to draw circles on the ground, as in magic circles, to use the knife only while in magic circles, or to use the knife by making circular patterns in the air. Again, more mysteries that would need to be clarified later, but my intuition was that it was meant to be used by making circular patterns in the air before the Spirit.

Finally the Archangel of Mars stated that «at the end of the working the knife may be used to cut any such connections or pathways between the magician and what is called.» Again, my intuition was telling me that the magus was to make a circular motion of severing with the knife after the evocation to signify the cutting of the connection between Demon and magician. A blessing was to be recited after this to ensure a positive outcome from the action.

---

39. Mathers and Solomon, *op. cit.*, Book II, ch. VIII.

Ritual Curse: Bound by Irons

This ritual was envisioned during a Tuesday evening scrying practice, and reminded me instantly of the Curse of Chains which is found in the *Goetia*. The ritual which I saw unfold in the black mirror was extremely severe and only to be used in the most dire of circumstances. This was a spontaneous vision, as I was not looking for a ritual or curse by any means. Due to the detail and complexity, I recorded what I witnessed to the best of my ability.

I have not attempted the ritual I describe below, as I have not come across a situation in which it seemed warranted. I caution the reader to attempt this experiment only with the utmost discretion.

The ritual must be performed on the day of Mars in the hour of Saturn. The magician must secure or create a chain of iron links, an iron box with the kamea of Mars engraved on it, a sword, a red altar cloth with symbols of Mars, a black candle, a red candle, spices, and parchment.

On one piece of parchment draw the sigil of Samael. On another slip of parchment, write on one side the name of the being you wish to be bound and on the reverse side whatever action they are committing which you wish to see stopped. Attach Samael's parchment to one end of the chain, and the wrongdoer's parchment to the other end.

Create a small altar in the South dedicated to the Spirits of Mars. Drape the altar with the red mars cloth, set the iron box on the center of the altar and place hot spices within it. On the left side of the altar place a black candle and on the right place a red candle.

Balance the center link of the chain on the end of an upright sword which rests against the altar. Position the red candle and black candle near but not directly under the pieces of parchment. The red candle should be nearest Samael's parchment and the black candle nearest parchment with the person or Spirit and situation to be bound. Allow the flames to heat the parchment, but do not allow it to catch fire.

Spend a moment fixated at the very point of the sword where the chain is suspended and concentrate the intention of the ritual there. When you have focused your full attention for several moments, speak aloud the invocation below:

Send me forth from the light of justice, O Lord, beyond the darkness and death of my slavery. Beyond any images and imaginings of fear and destruction will I rise and conquer all mine enemies by Your hand and word. By this chain and judg-

ment of the great Fiery One, I bind NN so that neither his actions, nor his words, nor his intention have any bearing whatsoever. Let his efforts be confounded and his will broken and constrained by these irons.

Retrieve the sword which is holding the chain and pass the slip of parchment with the description of the person and situation briefly through the flames of the red and black candles. Hold it over the iron box saying, "I seal this being, NN, here to remain without release until such a time when they are no longer able to DD and are by Divine Mercy released."

Then place the parchment in the box and close it, and wrap the chain around the box.

It is important that you break the chain for this ritual when you no longer wish for it to have effect on the being who has been bound.

The Poem of Samael

The screams of agony of man's multitude of sins, how do you realize that you carry the weight of your kind upon your mind, heart, and loins? Your spirit would remain unvexed by the multitude of transgressions, of wicked action, seemingly disposed to selfless and oblivious innocence. It shall not be hidden from me nor excused in the slightest, for I am the scourge of creation which has fouled under pretense, the accuser and dissolver of blemished morality. I am the very light that blinds the shadow of illusion, the grave of spirit in form. Do not attempt to tempt me, for my temptations far exceed your ability to resolve to the Highest, for I am the Fierce Sword of God. Be admonished to receive my wrath and judgment for the wickedness of which I know well the extent in man. I show you that which you would not see if not made to see beyond will. I rip from you the safety of comfort, of compassion, beyond your hurt of others. Who would dare face me directly and not buckle and break under my hand? You will not long escape the consumption of hell created by your own misdeeds since the beginning of man. I bring you the light which burns and sears you to truth.

One may question the benefit to be gained from evoking the embodiment of one of the most destructive forces known to exist into your life. This Archangel is a being who may well deserve some of the reputation as being the leader of the fallen Angels and a hostile adversary of mankind. The same may be said of war itself, the ultimate hell of a mass of men consumed by conflict, hatred, and fear. When all safety and shelter is stripped from you and there is no illusion to cling to for self-preservation, a great release can be achieved which dissolves the spirit of ego. For some, it is the method by which to soar beyond illusion and be released from falsehood, to release what you are and what you have done with no reservations or attachments.

The light is Truth. Truth in pure judgment is the light that exposes and roots out all illusions. When faced with this light, we see that evil is all our own, an evil that we must accept from others as part of ourselves when blame is no longer allowed to be shifted. This is truly what we all fear when pretenses are stripped away.

To descend into hell and emerge again is the accomplishment of the divine warrior. Each and every champion of mankind, the ones whose stories formed movements of faith and culture, are those who made this journey in earnest. To not shy from hell and damnation, but to face it, knowing that it faces you back, and plunge regardless is to make it past the gates of hell itself.

No one can expect to bring anything back with them once they descend into the crucible of unquenchable fire. Imagine: What sort of warrior would you be if you emerged from the place all men dread and fear, with no lingering shadows of attachment or falsehood? How would you live once all your transgression were faced without self-deception or blame or loathing? How would you do your work and exercise your true will once you realized that the responsibility for all of mankind's evils was your own, that you escaped no measure of judgment for others' hurts upon one another?

It is something entirely novel to face another human being in conflict and struggle where you realize you are fighting yet another aspect of yourself, no different and no more foreign than your own spirit. When you fight justly, you will do so without attachment to ego, or false ideals of separation. Your movements and actions will become the sword of the divine rather than the anger of one man. Yours will be the fire which "changes and reveals," forging the raw iron of your will into steel, an alloy of destructive precision, forged in the hottest fires of resolve, continually burnt, beaten, drowned, tempered and made anew.

The Archangel of Mars will indeed teach you the significance of conflict, anger, war, and the heat of battle. Your connection to divinity will determine if you keep your soul and sanity in the process. I cannot reiterate enough the profound danger that is inherent in this Archangel's presence and purpose. I cannot in good conscious recommend evocation of this being to anyone, since I cannot vouch for their safety and sanity.

My own experience with Archangel Samael is no testament to either bravery or ability. All such illusions were stripped from me. I in no way felt more powerful after my initial introduction to Samael. However, I am now familiar with the fires that grow and consume due to humanity's evils to one another and to the world. They exist because conflict, fear, and change exist, and cannot be separated from the fabric of reality.

✢

VII

Revisiting the Archangels of the Seven Spheres

Part Two • A Grimoric Necromancy Formula

In the midst of my scryer's and my experiments contacting the seven Planetary Archangels, I became quite interested in the prospect of obtaining a Spiritual helper or *Spiritus familiaris*. The initial concept was to conjure an Air Elemental Spirit as an intelligencer and Spirit fetch. As an intelligencer, its duties would include being able to inform and instruct on any matters magical, and particularly to garner information that was only obtainable in the Spirit world. As a fetch, it would ideally be able to quickly retrieve other Spirits to communicate with me.

I can easily recall the first time I learned about Spirit familiars and supernatural assistants, as I was instantly intrigued by the idea. From my numerous successful evocations and encounters with Spirits since then, I reasoned that obtaining a Spirit familiar was easily within the realm of possibility, but I had no direct example of what that would entail. I had never constructed an ancestor altar that many pagan and ancient religion practitioners use, nor had I practiced any form of ancestral worship. Nothing I had encountered up to that point would be what I considered a familiar Spirit, which would be an ever-present, disembodied Spirit whom I could see and hear, and with whom I could converse consistently with little to no preparation, timing, or lengthy invocations. The prospect of having readily on hand a powerful Spirit who was sympathetic toward my magical endeavors was too enticing to ignore any longer.

Necromancy: The Skull Spirit Intelligencer ✣ Part 1

On Familiar Spirits

It did not take long before I began researching just how a modern magician might go about securing a Spirit ally or familiar. I began this endeavor by reading through all the grimoires I knew, and then researching any Hebrew or Aramaic rituals that might be suitable to this end. It soon became clear that I would require a ritual conjuring a suitable entity and successfully binding it to a physical 'Spirit container.' My previous researches had led me to be interested in the idea of a human skull as Spirit container, which meant I needed to be aware of necromantic formulæ as well.

I went on to learn what I could of the folk traditions regarding familiar Spirits, including in the the notorious witch trials. Anthropologist Margaret Murray scoured the records of the trials and the manuals written to train the witchhunters and prosecutors for accounts of witches, including their familiar Spirits.

One 17th-century manual cited by Murray told jurists:

> These witches have ordinarily a familiar or spirit in the shape of a Man, Woman, Boy, Dogge, Cat, Foale, Fowle, Hare, Rat, Toade, etc. And to these their spirits they give names, and they meet together to Christen them.[1]

Although the popular image of the witch's familiar is as an animal, this contemporary account records the belief that familiar Spirits could be in human as well as animal form. The idea of limiting familiar Spirits to animal form was of great use to witch hunters, as anyone who happened to have a pet or domestic animal could be considered in possession of a Spirit familiar, and this often assisted in sealing the fate of an accused witch.

In the English trial records, Murray found a tradition of domestic familiars in the form of small animals being kept in a Spirit pot or bowl.

> The Domestic Familiar was always a little creature—a little dog, a small cat, a rat, a mole, a toad, or a mouse—which could be kept in

1. Richard Bernard, *A Guide to Grand-iury Men: diuided into two bookes: in the first, is the authors best aduice to them what to doe, before they bring in a billa vera in cases of witchcraft, with a Christian direction to such as are too much giuen vpon euery crosse to thinke themselues bewitched. In the second, is a treatise touching witches good and bad, how they may be knowne, euicted, condemned, with many particulars tending thereunto* (London: Printed by Felix Kingston for Ed. Blackmore, and are to be sold at his shop at the great south dore of Pauls, 1627), quoted by Margaret A. Murray, *The God of the Witches* (London: Oxford University Press, 1970 [First ed. 1931]), p. 81.

> the house in some small receptacle like a box or a pot. The creature was fed by its owner, originally that it might become tame and return to her after it had worked its magic. In the food was mixed a drop of the witch's blood so that the animal became in a sense a part of the owner. A name was always given to it, and in every way it was regarded as a creature of magical powers though under the control of its owner.[2]

Murray quoted the 1582 testimony of Ursula Kemp that one day she knocked at the door of another accused witch, and when there was no answer she looked in the window and called a greeting.

> 'And casting her eyes aside, she saw a spirit lift up a cloth lying over a pot, looking much like a ferret. And it being asked of this examinate why the spirit did look upon her, she said it was hungry'. Mother Bennet acknowledged to having Familiars, 'many times did they drink of her milk-bowl. And when, and as often as they did drink the milk, this Examinate saith that they went into the earthen pot, and lay in the wool'.[3]

Historian Emma Wilby reports that, though many witches and cunningfolk were said to use informal means of summoning their familiar Spirits, some employed more formal modes of evocation. In 1589 English witch Joan Cunny affirmed that she cast a magic circle in which she knelt to pray to summon her Spirits. 40 years earlier, cunningman William Wycherley used not only a circle, but also a magic ring and sword for evocation. In 1645, an accused witch demonstrated the summoning ritual for her familiar Spirits, which involved putting a pot of beer and bread in a magic circle by a hole in the wall and invoking, "Come, Christ, come Christ, come, Mounsier, come, Mounsier!" Other traces of more grimoric magic in the witch persecutions include Agnes Sampson's 1591 testimony that her familiar 'Devil' was name Eloa.[4]

The office of familiar Spirits was to inform and protect their masters and assist them in any manner in their craft. Accounts tell of familiar Spirits being sent to retrieve information, spy, or travel a distance where their master is unable to do so. These reports match those of the shaman of other cultures where their animal Spirits are sent to retrieve information or soul pieces to heal others.

---

2. Murray, *op. cit.*, pp. 83–84.

3. *Ibid.*, p. 85.

4. Emma Wilby, *Cunning Folk and Familiar Spirits: Shamanistic Visionary Traditions in Early Modern British Witchcraft and Magic* (Brighton: Sussex Academic Press, 2005), pp. 78–79.

Many times we find that familiar Spirits and allies are not merely servants but friends, and even highly respected guides and close confidants. in the records of a 1615 French trial at Orleans, we read the account of Silvain Nevillon, one of the victims of the witch hunts.

> 'And when they wish to go away on business or pleasure and to know if it will turn out well, they note if the familiars are joyous, in which case they go on business or pleasure; but if they are spiritless and sad, they do not budge from the house.' Gentien le Clerc, tried and condemned at the same time as Nevillon, declared that 'he had more trust in his familiar than in God, that there was more profit in it than in God, and that he gained nothing by looking to God, whereas his familiar always brought him something.'

The Romanian historian of religion Mircea Eliade wrote extensively on Siberian shamans and their rich history of interaction with familiar Spirits. He reported one particularly interesting 1924 interview of an earlier researcher with a shaman. The man told of his tutelary Spirit or *ayami*, a primary familiar Spirit who also grants the shaman lesser assistant Spirits. This particular shaman's *ayami* appeared in various forms, usually as a woman less than three feet tall, but sometimes also as a female elder, a wolf, or a winged tiger. She first appeared to him when he was sick in bed, as is often the case with tribal shamans, and explained that she was a hereditary Spirit.

> She said: 'I am the ayami of your ancestors, the Shamans. I taught them shamaning. Now I am going to teach you. The old shamans have died off, and there is no one to heal people. You are to become a shaman.'

Then she defined another aspect of their relationship:

> 'I love you, I have no husband now, you will be my husband and I shall be a wife unto you.'

It is interesting to note the similarities between this Siberian account and European stories of magicians forming intimate relationships and even lifelong marriages with their familiar Spirits.[5]

Over time, the *ayami* gave the shaman three assisting Spirits, who took the animal forms of a panther, a bear, and a tiger. The shaman described a hierarchical relationship between his tutelary Spirit and the lesser helper Spirits she gave

5. Those interested in paranormal unions should refer to a fantastic dissertation by Alexandra Nagel entitled *Marriage with Elementals: From Le Comte de Gabalis to a Golden Dawn Ritual.*

him which sounds very much like that described between greater and lesser Spirits in the grimoires.

> [The assistants] appear whenever I summon them while shamaning.
> If one of them refuses to come, the ayami makes them obey...[6]

Hebrew Familiars and Necromancy

The only necromantic episode in the Hebrew Bible occurs in *I Samuel* 28:3–25, when King Saul visits the "Witch of Endor," and has her summon up the ghost of the prophet Samuel.[7]

My further interest in this account was sparked by *Communing with Spirits: The Magical Practice of Necromancy*,[8] in which Martin Coleman theorizes that the necromancer of Endor had most likely called upon the aid of a familiar Spirit within a vessel to summon forth another ghost or spirit.

The necromancer is described as *isheth, Baalath ha-Ov*, "a woman, a Mistress of the *Ov* (אוב)." *Ov* has been translated as "a prophetic Spirit," but also as "a wineskin" (or a Spirit container made from animal skin used by a necromancer).[9] In the Hebrew Bible, *Ov* (אוב) is a feminine term for the Spirit employed by a necromancer or—as shorthand for *Baalath ha-Ov* ("Lady of the *Ov*")—for the necromancer herself, and *Yiddeoni* (ידעני) is a masculine term for

---

6. Mircea Eliade, *Shamanism: Archaic Techniques of Ecstasy* (London: Routledge & Kegan Paul, 1964), pp. 72–73.

7. The similarity of the circumstances between this episode and the famous necromantic scene in the *Odyssey*, Books X and XI, is striking, In both cases, the protagonist is using a form of double divination, *i.e.*, using necromancy to gain access to prophecy, by summoning the ghost of the most adept prophet of his culture, who has died. In the case of Odysseus, that prophet is Teiresias, and in the case of Saul, it is Samuel. —APF

8. Martin Coleman, *Communing with the Spirits: The Magical Practice of Necromancy Simply and Lucidly Explained, with Full Instructions for the Practice* (York Beach, Maine: Samuel Weiser, 1998). —APF

9. There are a few works which go into detail about spirit pots/vessels, and practicing magicians Aaron Leitch, Frater Rufus Opus, and Jake Stratton-Kent have written about this subject a number of times.

a diviner,[10] perhaps particularly a necromancer.[11] Rashi[12] stated that *Yiddeonim* put the bone of a particular animal in their mouths, and that it was (the Spirit of) the bone which spoke oracles.[13]

There is a magical ritual in the *Sepher ha-Razim ("The Book of Secrets")* entitled "To ask by *Ov*," which consists of conjuring a Spirit named Qriphoriya to bring forth the dead. It is presented thus:

> If you wish to question a ghost; stand facing a tomb and repeat the names of the angels the fifth encampment[14] (while holding) in your hand a new flask[15] (containing) oil and honey mixed together and say thus.
>
> *I adjure you O spirit of the ram bearer[16] who dwells among the graves upon the bones of the dead, that you will accept from my hand this offering and do my will and bring me the spirit of N son of N who is dead. Raise him up so that he will speak to me without fear and tell me true the things without concealment. Let me not be afraid of him and let him tell me for my question, the answer I need from him.*
>
> He should appear immediately. But if he does not, repeat the adjuration a second time and up to three times if necessary. When the spirit appears, set the flask before him and after this speak your words while holding the branch of myrtle wood in your hand. When you wish to release the spirit, strike the spirit three times with

---

10. *Yiddeonim* comes from the same root (ידע) as דעת (*Daath*, "Knowledge") in Qabbalah, in this case meaning either that *Yiddeonim* are knowledgeable in esoteric lore, or that they know hidden things by means of divination, or both. —APF

11. *I Samuel* specifies that Saul had previously banished the *Ovoth* and *Yiddeonim* from his kingdom, but when his usual Yahveh oracles (dreams, Urim and Thummim, and the prophets) went offline, he had to send servants out to covertly locate an underground *Baalath ha-Ov* for him to consult, on the divinatory black market, as it were. —APF

12. *Rashi* is the acronym (רש״י) for Rabbi Shlomo Yitzchaqi, a famous Mediæval commentator on the Torah and Talmud. —APF

13. In his commentary on *Leviticus* 19:31 ("Turn ye not to the *Ovoth* nor the *Yiddeonim*."). —APF

14. The names of the 62 Angels of the fifth encampment are given in Appendix B for those who may be interested in this working. —APF

15. The word Morgan translates as "flask" is in fact פיאלי (*phialei*), a phonetic Hebrew transcription of the Greek φιάλη (*phialē*), a shallow bowl used to pour ritual libations. —APF

16. The word translated "ram bearer" is *Qriphoriya* (קריפוריייא). This barbarous (to a Hebrew reader) Name is, as Morgan recognized, the Greek Κριοφόρος (*Kriophoros*, the "Ram-bearer"), an epithet of the God Hermēs, Who is evoked here in His function as the preeminent *Psychopompos*, "Guide of Souls." —APF

> the myrtle branch and pour out the oil and honey, and break the cup, and throw the myrtle from your hand, and return home by a different route.

This is immediately followed in the *Sepher ha-Razim* by a ritual to gain a familiar Spirit, also invoking the names of the Angels of the fifth encampment:

> If you wish to speak with the spirits, go out to "the place of the killed" and call out there in a singsong, whimpering way:[17]
>
> *I adjure you in the name of the angels who serve in the fifth encampment, and in the name of the overseer who is over them, who is 'SYMWR, that you will hear me at this time and send me the spirit of ḤGRGYRWT. She shall go accordingly to my will for whatever I send her and shall obey me in everything until such a time as I release her.*
>
> If you see opposite you a column of smoke, speak your words and send (her) for whatever purpose you wish.[18]

These rituals gave some interesting ideas and possibilities, but they weren't exactly the process for which I was looking, although I knew by this stage that I wanted to conjure the Spirit intelligencer into the skull utilizing methods and formulæ from Hebrew sources.

The Skull as Spirit Vessel

Upon further research I discovered that ancient Hebrew necromancers did sometimes use a human skull as a Spirit container. Archeologists have unearthed skulls inscribed with various spells and incantations written in Aramaic in ancient Jewish communities in Babylonia. So far, there have been over two thousand bowls and pots and five skulls[19] found inscribed with ancient Hebrew or Aramaic spells written in complex patterns.[20]

---

17. That is, in the manner of a lament. This may relate to the ancient funerary functions of a *goēs*. See Jake Stratton-Kent, *Geosophia: The Argo of Magic* ([Dover]: Scarlet Imprint/Bibliothèque Rouge, 2010), *passim*.

18. Michael A. Morgan (trans.), *Sepher Ha-Razim: The Book of the Mysteries* (Chico, Ca.: Scholars Press, 1983), pp. 38–39. —APF

19. The most recent inscribed skull to surface is contained within a case consisting of two earthenware bowls or pots. See Dan Levene, "Rare Magic Inscription in Human Skull," in *Biblical Archæology Review* (March/April 2009), Volume 35, Number 2. —APF

20. In the case of the "Witch" of Endor, the skull Spirit is what Martin Coleman alludes to as possibly being the assistant which summoned the shade of the prophet Samuel.

In Stephen Skinner's indispensible work detailing the origins and traditional lineage of Solomonic-style magic, *Techniques of Greco-Egyptian Magic*, he states:

> In the Talmud it says:
>
> > There are two kinds of necromancy (בעל אוב. Baal Aib [Aub]), the one where the dead is raised by naming him, the other where he is asked by means of a skull (הנשאל בגלגלת).
>
> The first kind of necromancy has survived through to the modern era. The second type, where a head or a skull has been kept as a sort of oracle to answer questions also has a long separate history. The most famous oracular skull was that reputed to have been owned and used by Roger Bacon.[21]

Skinner goes on to point out that the Sabians of Harrans were said to use skull oracles, and that Apuleius of Madaura refers to the magical use of skulls in his Roman-era defense of magic. He also calls attention to a ritual in the *Papyri Græcæ Magicæ* that explains how to restrain and silence a divinatory skull which is "not satisfactory."[22]

The references found in the Talmud seemed to refer to exactly what I was seeking, and although I had as yet found no specific Hebrew magical formula for achieving it, I was confident I would discover how to successfully conjure a Spirit into a skull as the ancient Hebrew necromancers had.

Beyond the *Ovoth* and *Yiddeonim* and the other examples provided by Dr. Skinner, I found a few additional significant traditions about "talking heads," such as the tales of Orpheus and Brân the Blessed.

In Greek lore, after Orpheus, the mystical musician, founder of Mystery cults, visitor to the underworld, and magus, was torn apart by Mænads in the wilds of Thrace, his head washed ashore on the island of Lesbos, where it was established in a famous shrine, and continued to give oracles for many years.

In the Celtic tradition preserved in the Welsh *Mabinogion*, the giant Brân is fatally injured in a great battle in the West,[23] and he tells the seven heroic

---

21. Stephen Skinner, *Techniques of Greco-Egyptian Magic* (Singapore: Golden Hoard Press, 2014), p. 296.

22. The rite is in PGM IV, The Great Magical Papyrus of Paris, lines 2125–2139, in the midst of a necromantic section of the papyrus, following two rites of Pitys for oracular skull cups, and being followed by Pitys the Thessalian's Query of a Corpse. Morton Smith's translation of the Restraining Seal for wayward skull Spirits may be read in Hans Dieter Betz, *The Greek Magical Papyri in Translation* (Chicago: University of Chicago Press, 1986), p. 75. —APF

23. Ireland in the legendary version in the Second Branch of the Mabinogi written down in the Christian era, but almost certainly the Otherworld in an earlier mythic version. —APF

survivors to cut off his head and bear it back to Britain. They honor his request, and Brân's living head hosts them in the Feast of the Wonderful Head for seven years at Harlech and 80 years on the island of Gwales, until someone violates a taboo and ends the idyllic spell.[24]

In the popular modern occult fiction series *The Dresden Files* by Jim Butcher, the wizard Harry Dresden has a skull named Bob that is basically a magical encyclopedia and storehouse of occult knowledge. In the novels, Bob helps Harry solve a plethora of occult mysteries and riddles with his vast occult knowledge that makes up the main function of the Spirit. I must admit that this fiction series further sparked my passion for being able to create a real version of this helpful Spirit.

The process of acquiring an actual skull and formulating the ritual to bind a Spirit within it was several years in the making. Only small pieces of the ritual came together at particular times. I had learned from the aforementioned sources that the traditional way to bring a necromantic Spirit into a vessel was by invocations adjuring the Dæmons or beings that ruled over it or over the underworld as a whole. As in many Solomonic magic texts, a Spirit is coaxed and commanded via the authority of either its ruling Spirit or Angel, the Creator, or both. There is such an experiment in the Hebrew *Maphteach Shelomoh ("Key of Solomon")*, which contains this adjuration:

> Shitrael, Malutam, Tamur, Palur, Shitrami, I adjure you and order and command you, by the name of the great God that banished you from garden of Eden, and by the name of the God that said so be it, and it was, and by the name of the God that will judge the living and the dead and the world by fire , so you—five ministers of hell—will come here in front of me, to fulfill all my wishes and desires and requests and orders. And I adjure you again, you the devils and demons, and I order you by the Lord, our God, and by the name of all the Patriarchs: Abraham, Isaac and Jacob, and by the name of the twelve tribes, and by the name of all the prophets, and by the name of all the saints that sanctified the blessed God, and by the name of all male-virgins and female-virgins, and by the name of all the servants of the superior one. And I adjure you again

24. The *Triads of the Isle of Britain* go on to relate that Brân's head was then buried in London, and it guarded Britain against invasion for centuries, until King Arthur, in his pride, had the head exhumed, claiming that he alone would defend Britain from invasion. I'm sure the subsequent waves of Angles, Saxons, Frisians, Danes, and Normans were grateful for his hubris. —APF

> with anger and wrath of hell, and by heaven and earth, and by the heavenly host and earth, and by the stars and signs and seven planets and four elements, which are Fire, wind, water <and> earth, and by the upper and lower garden of Eden, and by all the things in there, and by your hell, and by all the demons and devils inside and outside it, and by your virtue and ability, and by all the things that can bind and force you, so you are bound and forced to my desire. Come here with great humility and nice face and nice forms, to let my eye see and my ears hear, to fulfill all my desires and requests, and do not depart from here without my permission. And if you won't hear me, to do and obey to my orders, I swore to bind you in a manner that you will never get out of the great deep, of the great sea. Therefore, obey my orders and do my desires and requests, because I adjure you by Lord, God, the God of the world who is be feared above all gods, which his government rules over all forever.[25]

The operation further explains that when the Spirits arrive in front of the circle they will "get off the horses in front of you, and they will kneel in front of you and say: 'Our master! Order us whatever you wish. We are prepared to fulfill your request.' Then the Magician is to say: "I order you to swear to me that you will do anything I will order you, and (also that) you won't depart without permission", and then they will swear in the manner of the *Key of Solomon the King*.

In this experiment the magician conjures the intelligencer Spirit into a crystal, the most common medium in which to scry and converse with immaterial beings. After the Spirits swear their oath, the magician is to say,

> I order you to bring into this crystal a wise spirit that knows any wisdom and that is savant of all the seven known wisdoms, so in anytime, and whenever I want him to teach me and instruct me clearly for all the things I will ask him, and he will be enslaved for me by you, since you are his masters, to do anything I order him truly and honestly, without guile and deception.[26]

It seemed clear to me that it would be traditional to contact an otherworld/underworld Deity or powerful Spirit who could assist in bringing forth my particular familiar Spirit. I required a being who could answer questions about other Spirits and have deep occult wisdom as well. I formulated an initial bind-

25. The invocation is an excerpt from a translation of *Maphteach Shelomoh* from the Hebrew of BL MS Oriental 14759, part of an unpublished work in progress by Gal Sofer, generously made available in private correspondence with the author.

26. *Ibid.*

ing invocation which I planned to combine with a written invocation inscribed on the physical skull. I used verse style and composition similar to the above lengthy invocations to match the ritual I planned. When I was done, the invocation contained the basic elements I wanted for the Spirit and how I wanted it to be bound to the skull. The invocation I devised was based on the below:

> Spirit of Air, of Mind, of Thought, of Intellect and hidden Wisdom; Thou who art named NN and this by your sign and true character, NN be bound and kept here to be summoned forth to speak and be visible unto me clearly, for any question or task I may set to you. Be conjured and gathered within this vessel to answer in truth any question and to bring forth any other spirit wherefore ever they may be, that I may see and speak with them, and that you act as counselor, advisor, and assistant to me in the mysteries, by the Most Holy and High Lord God of Hosts. Amen.[27]

I planned to inscribe the invocation on the skull in Hebrew. I felt that the language is not only potent but relevant to the type of necromancy being performed.

> I adjure you NN by the power of the creator of heaven and earth, and by the name Adonay, and by the power of the heads of the Cherubim and the Seraphim, and by the power, ability and crowns of heaven kingdom, and ten ranks of angels above and below, I adjure you NN by all the power of the kingdom of the superior God, and by all the aerial powers, so you will hear my words and get into this skull, and tell me the truth about anything I will ask you, with an honest and true answer without any lie or deception, and bring spirits before me that will give me a true answer, without any lie or deception.[28]

In the same Hebrew *Maphteach/Clavicula* manuscript (British Library, Oriental MS 14759) which contains the preceding invocations, there is also a seal that is connected with summoning Spirits of the dead (Fig. VII-1). I decided to write the Name Agla in archaic Hebrew characters, and attune the seal to my work by placing it inside the circle of divine names from *The Art of Drawing Spirits into Crystals* (Fig. VII-2). I planned to inscribe this seal on both temples of the skull. I also decided to place a Grand Seal of Solomon on the crown of the skull, and to inscribe various verses around the eyes and mouth.

---

27. *Ibid.*

28. *Ibid.*

Fig. VII-1. ***Hebrew Agla Seal from MAPHTEACH SHELOMO***

Fig. VII-2. ***Agla Seal in Archaic Hebrew inside DSIC Circle of Divine Names***

I searched for a proper human skull vessel for quite some time, not finding anything realistically within my price range from a source which seemed clearly reputable. Many skulls which I found online were dissected and intended for medical laboratories, and most ranged upwards from a thousand dollars. I continued my search over the span of a couple of years and finally found a specimen from a source in South America which I felt was intact enough to be suitable, and also fit my budget as well as my magical needs.

Much to my delight, the skull arrived at my front door in good order and with impeccable timing on October 31st, Halloween. It was packed in all manner of wrapping and bubble tape with a few layers of cellophane which gave the parcel a rather eerie appearance.

I had worked in a hospital for a number of years and had been partially responsible for the transfer and storage of human remains so the idea of human bones did not make me squeamish, but I do admit that the unwrapping and beholding of an actual human skull in my own house had a peculiar effect on me. I understood that classical and ancient magic often utilized the remains of deceased individuals, but this was touching on an area of magical practice in which I was not well-versed. However, I treated the empty vessel with the care and respect it deserved and set it in a black pine box to await the proper time and place for it to be consecrated.

All that was left was to find a Spirit that would agree to be my assistant in magical matters as well as a fetch for other Spirits from whom I could learn. I knew that I did not want to bind a Spirit against its will to anything since, regardless of the power of the ceremonies, I felt I could never fully trust or consider the Spirit a beneficial ally under those circumstances. The spirit would have to willingly choose to be bound on its own accord in conjunction with the magical ritual and methods I used for the physical vessel.

To make initial contact with a potential familiar Spirit, I decided to once again use my scryer and guide him through the experience so that a clearer approach and thus retention of such an encounter could be recorded. I did not notify him about this intention ahead of time, but instead invited him over simply informing him that I wanted to try a magical experiment.

When my scryer arrived at my house, he had the expectation that we were going to prepare for another Angelic invocation. Instead I drew his interest by explaining that I had been reading a fascinating book entitled *The Exorcist's Handbook* by the respected author and practitioner Josephine McCarthy[29] and very much wanted to try a technique she described for entering the Astral plane very quickly.[30] The process for conducting this experiment required no elaborate ritual process or implementation. I simply erected a silver candle in a brass candlestick on a small altar table about a foot high in the western part of my magical chamber. I also arranged two sitting cushions so that both my scryer and I could stare at the candle flame from the floor level. Once we were seated before the altar, I simply applied the techniques I utilize to get his vision going and then followed the outline.

The experiment was quite interesting and turned out to be more profound than I had anticipated.

Scryer's Account

SCRYER: I remember the beginning when I stepped out onto the desert and was amazed how clear it was. The immensity of the desert swept forward and behind and on all sides. Moving through the candle flame to the desert was a quick and instant change, but there was something natural about it as well. It was an immediate change like a veil was suddenly being pulled back. When you invoked the Sandalphon Angels, I found myself walking between two beings and looked up at them. I was fascinated by their perfection in every detail; their faces and appearances were flawless. They were simply beautiful but appeared quite androgynous. I couldn't quite

29. Now also writing and teaching under her married name of Josephine Littlejohn.

30. Josephine McCarthy, *The Exorcist's Handbook* (Berkeley, CA: Golem Media, 2010), p. 18.

tell if they were male or female, which made me really wonder about that. As we walked along in the sand, I was noticing how their hair was sweeping behind them causing their footprints to disappear. I sensed there was important significance behind this, but wasn't sure about what that could be.

As we were walking, even before you said, "There is a big crack or fissure ahead," I had already seen it up ahead of me, and that's when I knew the contact and experience was really going well. The huge fissure appeared really deep. The stone it was made of was a really dark gray. There was a thick mist or fog covering the far bank and most of the sides. The light seemed to have a hard time reaching down into it, and any sound seemed like it was being purposefully muted in and around it. As we approached nearer, I looked over the edge and spotted all these ledges, which instantly reminded me of those terraced farmlands in the Himalayas. The ledges were cut and kind of smooth; there seemed to be thousands of them, dark and worn smooth. On each of the ledges were all these...people, and some were not people. It was eerie, because it looked like they were all waiting for something. For some reason their appearance and postures gave me the creeps. There was something intensely foreboding about the dark chasm and the figures. I wasn't sure if I wanted to get too close to some of them. However I did feel anchored and secure with the two Angels on either side of me. Their presence made me feel protected and somewhat at ease where I know I wouldn't be otherwise.

Suddenly, the mist parted in front of me and it looked like a figure emerged out of it. I couldn't make out who it was. At first it only looked like a silhouette or someone with dark, black skin perhaps. I then heard you speak aloud your intention about finding a Spirit who could be contacted, to become your familiar Spirit for the skull. I told the being in front of me that I was asking for you and not for myself. I asked that we be able to bring forth more knowledge from the Spirit world to help others and the planet. The being seemed pleased with this reply, and suddenly flew backward and grew. It appeared to me to sink down into the opposite side of the cliff and instantly grow, and then step out of the side of the cliff as if he had been a part of it. He was massive now, standing within the fissure and impossible to see the entirety of. He walked over and held out his hand and it was enormous, about the length of a house. After a moment, the Angels on either side of me seemed to reassure me, so I stepped out onto the tip of his finger. The enormous hand immediately started heading down into the abyss with me on it.

As I started going down, the light vanished above and that part was a little scary. I felt a bit nervous, so I walked further onto the giant Angel's hand. I then repeated your petition that "we needed someone who could tell us various things about the Spirit world and magic, etc." As you asked aloud for the certain kind of Spirit we were looking for, I thought I saw a faint light seem to flash that was way down in the fissure. Then, as you mentioned the other particulars that were needed, another light blinked as if the first one was willing to do the first part but the second was willing to do both. Somehow I knew that the second light was the Spirit we were seeking and was where we were going. Soon we were heading down to where that second light had emanated from.

The enormous hand continued to descend for a while, until finally I came to this ledge and was put down on it. In front of me I saw what appeared to be a hunched-over, Mayan-looking man. His face was really dark and weathered, and his hair was black and matted. He had this large stick in his hand as he sat in front of a fire. He was so interesting-looking and difficult to describe. I looked at him and assumed he was the being I was looking for, but he shook his head as if to say ‹no,› and turned and pointed to a door behind him. I looked to the door where he pointed and realized that's where I needed to go.

Walking up to the door in the face of the rock cliff, I noticed that it looked well made and really ancient, as if it had been there a long time but was made to stand the test of time. It was a little disorienting as I pulled the door open and walked through the door, because suddenly I was in a huge chamber with this amazing library! It had at least fifty-foot-tall shelves and stacks of books. An old sextant was lying on a nearby table and weird games that I'd never seen before. I remember distinctly that there was this marble in this glass thing and you had to hold it and keep on this certain timer, and balance it to this device; it was the oddest thing I'd ever seen. I looked up toward the top of the stacks and shelves of books, and it was all misty, and I could see Spirits zooming through it periodically. I looked back behind me on the door and it said *Hiram's Library*.

I was looking through all sorts of interesting things stacked on tables and near the bookcases when I became aware of someone standing next to me. I turned to see a figure of a man who was taller than me (over six foot), pretty robust, wearing black clothes, a dark robe, and had a completely bald head. The figure's head was smooth as if hair had never grown there, and he had dark brown eyes and a black, full, and long mustache which reached beyond his chin. He had the look of someone who was extremely intelligent.

I asked him who he was, and he responded, «I am Hiram, I am the owner of this library.» Then without me even asking, he continued, saying, «I am the one.»

You seemed to know when I made the contact with the Spirit, because I heard you ask for a symbol or sigil to contact him. The large man or Spirit calling himself Hiram smiled and walked over to a shelf, showing me a sort of plaque with a symbol on it.

(My scryer drew the sigil, which was fairly complex and took him a while. When he was finished, it appeared similar to some I had seen in the LEMEGETON, but also unique and perfect in symmetry. I am refraining from including an exact image of the sigil for reasons which I hope practitioner-readers will understand.)

He said for calling him, you place your finger on the sigil and trace it over a number of times while calling his name and finishing with, «Hiram, come from your library and speak.» He said that is all that is needed, and that you would know how he needed to be fed.

I made sure to ask if there was anything else, and he said that you have a test coming. He said that he had called for you, and that he would prove his worth to you during this upcoming test.

I remember the eyes and face of this man just exuding wisdom and an assurance that made me feel immediately at ease. After a few more words, I said my farewell and departed from the library. I passed the old Mayan man and walked back onto the enormous hand that was still waiting at the edge of the cliff. It immediately rose as soon as I stepped back on it, and a while after I could see the light near the opening to the desert. The hand came to rest neat the ledge of the desert and the two angels were still there waiting.

I looked back up to the two beautiful Angels, but they simply turned around and guided me back between them. As we were walking back, I heard you ask for any information about the journey that would help understand this way of working. The angels replied that their reason for erasing their footprints was so that nothing could follow them to the Abyss

Fig. VII-3. ***Portrait of the Spirit Hiram as beheld in Vision***

> or could follow them back from it. They stopped for a moment and asked me to hold my hands like this. *(My scryer held up his palms cupped as if he were to drink water from them)* The Angels held their hands up and then they said, «Now blow.» As we blew out, this mighty wind came up and erased their tracks completely. The Angels turned and said, «You have to do that every time...so that nothing follows you back.»

This magical experiment lasted nearly a half hour. My scryer repeatedly commented on how surprising he found the unprecedented continuity and detail of the experiment. He remarked that in his scrying sessions there were sometimes gaps where the vision and experience ebbed during the operations. The candle-flame method seemed to be a straightforward approach with extremely noteworthy results!

We then spoke at length about the identity and nature of the Spirit that called itself Hiram. The name was interesting and I wasted no time researching it. As embarrassing as it is to admit now, the name was unfamiliar to me and my scryer up until that evening. If I had come across it before, I did not recall it. Thanks to the wonders of Google, with a typed word and a quick click of the mouse, I found more than ample significance for the name.

Hiram,[31] whose name translates from Hebrew as "high-born," is mentioned in the Bible as the Phœnician king of Tyre who is credited in the books of *II Samuel, I Kings,* and *I Chronicles* with supplying building materials and craftsmen for the construction of Solomon's Temple. Hiram reigned in Tyre in the tenth century BC, and was an ally of both David and Solomon.[32]

There is a second significant Hiram in the Bible.[33] In *I Kings* 7:13–14, this Hiram is described as the son of a Tyrian bronze artisan and a widow from the tribe of Naphtali, sent for by Solomon to cast the bronze furnishings and ornate decorations for the new temple. Under the name Hiram Abiff,[34] he is also

---

31. In the Bible, the name of the king is spelled חירם (*Chiram* or *Ḥiram*), and normally written as Hiram in English translation. —APF

32. King Hiram also appears in Josephus' *Contra Apion*, which provides confirmation of the Biblical account.

33. The name of the great artisan of the bronze or brass artifacts of the temple of Solomon is found in two slightly different forms in the Bible: in *I Kings* 7, it is חירם (*Chiram* or *Ḥiram*), just like the Phœnician king, and in *II Chronicles* 4, it is given as חורם (*Churam* or *Ḥuram*). —APF

34. This name originates in *II Chronicles* 4:16, where חורם אביו (*Churam Abiv*) has often been translated as "Huram his father" (*e.g.*, in the KJV, the Vulgate [*Hiram eius pater*], the ASV,

a well-known figure in Freemasonry. Often referred to as "the Widow's Son," Hiram is the central character of an allegory presented to all candidates during the third degree in Freemasonry. In the Masonic portrayal, Hiram is presented as the chief architect of Solomon's temple, who is murdered in the temple he designed by three ruffians during an unsuccessful attempt to force him to divulge the Master Masons' secret password and the other secrets of his craft. The themes of the allegory are the importance of fidelity, and the certainty of death.

There was also a third Hiram whose story caught my eye. Hiram Page (1800–1852) was a prominent early member of the Latter Day Saints, and one of the church's first dozen officers. The interesting history about this Hiram was that he used a black (obsidian?) "seerstone" to scry visions concerning the location of Zion. Joseph Smith secured his own position as the sole receiver of prophetic revelations for the new church when he reported receiving a revelation that Hiram Page's visions were diabolically-inspired illusions. Page acknowledged Smith's prophetic superiority, and allowed his seerstone and the records of his visions to be destroyed.

I was unsure if any of these three Hirams would turn out to be the Spirit we had contacted, but I felt certain it wasn't the early Mormon scryer. As fascinating as I was finding this magical experiment, I also remained skeptical that my potential familiar Spirit would turn out to be either the fabled king of Tyre or the beloved master mason of Solomon's temple. This seemed a bit too far-fetched to take at face value. However, something about the experience of my scryer convinced me to not dismiss it out of hand.

I planned to inquire about the validity of the vision to an Archangel who would certainly know if the claims of this Spirit were truthful or not. The Archangel Cassiel of Saturn would be privy to knowledge of all Spirits, but especially those of the deceased, and would be able to decipher the true identity of the Spirit. I wanted to be sure I had contacted the correct Spirit for the job, one suitable to remain in my home and magical chamber, who would not be a burden or trickster of any kind. There were some exciting prospects in the future, but I didn't want to build my hopes up and get ahead of myself before I was certain of what I had.

Also, although I felt confident that my combination of invocations and sigils would ensure the appropriate housing, binding, and preservation of the

---

and the Hebrew Names Version). However, other versions have chosen to leave the second component untranslated, producing the name *Huram-abi* (RSV, NIV, ESV, NASB) or *Huram-abiv* (the Darby Bible). Masonic lore follows this second school of thought. —APF

skull for the Spirit, I knew it would take the instruction and knowledge of an Archangel or other powerful Spirit to know how to properly bring a familiar to reside permanently within the vessel.

Plans were made to contact the great Archangel of Saturn as soon as my scryer and I could set a date.

The Archangel of Saturn
Cassiel

✠ Day and time	On Saturday, during an hour of Saturn
✠ Name and meaning	Hebrew כפציאל *(Qaphtziel)*, possibly "Speed of God," and *Cassiel*
✠ Pronunciation of name (as spoken by the Spirit)	«Kass-ee-el»
✠ Other known names and forms of name	Kafziel, Qafsiel, Qaphziel, Tzaphqiel, Zaphkiel, Zafkiel
✠ Planet	♄
✠ Materials for lamen	Parchment, lead
✠ Sigil	
✠ Direction for Invocation	North
✠ Incense mixture	Fine quality myrrh, styrax, saffron, a small amount of sulfur, ambergris, mandrake root, spikenard, galangal root.

*Table VII-4. **Evocatory Correspondences for Cassiel***[35]

Of Cassiel and the Office of Saturn

Cassiel is the name given to the Archangel of Saturn in many Western magical texts. As with several of the other Angels, Cassiel's name is only loosely rendered from Hebrew into Latin. The Hebrew original is קפציאל, *Qaphtziel,* meaning the "Speed of God." This enigmatic being of ageless patience and stillness "is known for simply watching the events of the cosmos unfold with little interference. He is the angel of solitude and tears, and is said to preside over the deaths of kings."[36] In the Kabbalistic magical text *Berit Menuchah,* Cassiel is associated with *Qephitzat ha-Derekh,* קפיצת הדרך, the ability to travel quickly or teleport through space, or to be in several places seemingly simultaneously, which con-

35. Please see the Cautionary Warning Regarding Grimoric Ingredients in Appendix A. —APF

36. Constance Victoria Briggs, *The Encyclopedia of Angels* (New York: Plume, 1997).

nects with his name meaning "Speed of God."[37] In his connection to death, he is associated with leading departing souls to the otherworld or paradise. Amulets and talismans containing his name have been crafted in order to "cause destruction, to scatter crowds, to cause a person to wander aimlessly, or to fall from a position of power."[38]

Cassiel was the first Archangel I ever contacted using the magical system of *Drawing Spirits into Crystals*, and the system worked to a degree which moved me to conjure the rest of the celestial Planetary Angels. I was curious to follow up my first contact to see if I could get clarification of imagery which had been shown to me, as well as to obtain new knowledge regarding the proper ways to invoke a helper Spirit into a skull.

Although I was interested to speak with this Archangel once more, the prospect of being again in its presence was more than a little unnerving. It is nearly impossible to escape a sense of the vastness of death and eternity when the Archangel of Saturn arrives. Although not evil, the feeling of this somber Messenger is dark, remote, inevitable, and ancient beyond human comprehension.

If ever there was a lesson on the inevitability of death, change, and impermanence, it came ironically through this everlasting celestial being: the beauty and sorrow of so many lives, so many unique experiences, memories, desires, hopes, dreams, and fears passing away in the inevitable return to the source. The imagery of the very Creator whispering the name of each being which existed briefly in mortal flesh before passing onto the road to return struck deeply. For many, such imagery and inevitability are things to be avoided, often fueled by denial. If true wisdom is to be found in Buddhist principles, it is that release from attachment is a salvation beyond compare. Release from attachment to events, people, memories, material things, and even from one's own identity. I would say nearly every human being has had or will have this internal struggle and fear. The only cure and saving grace I have found is faith that something grander is indeed aware and working the unfolding of the dream exactly the way it is sup-

---

37. *Qephitzath ha-Derekh* in Hebrew is literally "The Leaping of the Way." The Archangelic name Qaphtziel derives from the same root as *qephitzah* (√קפץ).

 Readers of Frank Herbert's *Dune* may be interested to learn that the primary title of the Messianic figure in that work derives from *Qephitzath ha-Derekh*. Herbert translated his *Kwisatz Haderach* as "The Shortening of the Way," and in applying it to a person, as "The one who can be two places simultaneously." —APF

38. Moses Gaster, *The Wisdom of the Chaldeans: An Old Hebrew Astrological Text* (London: Proceedings of the Society of Biblical Archaeology, 1900), pp. 17–18.

pose to unfold. This faith must extend beyond our own fears and limited understanding. If we find great fear or discomfort in stillness, in death, we must look deeply into that place to understand the nature of our fear. Is it natural? Is it needed or important? What exactly do we fear? What are we grasping so tightly and why? There are important truths to uncover about the nature of our existence that is best done before we pass on from this life. The greatest fears and horrors seem not to arise from the inevitability of this process but from the unnatural horror and refusal to let go of things when they need to be released. Hauntings, Demons, and our own self-torturing thoughts are all fueled if not generated by the desperate refusal to release attachments.

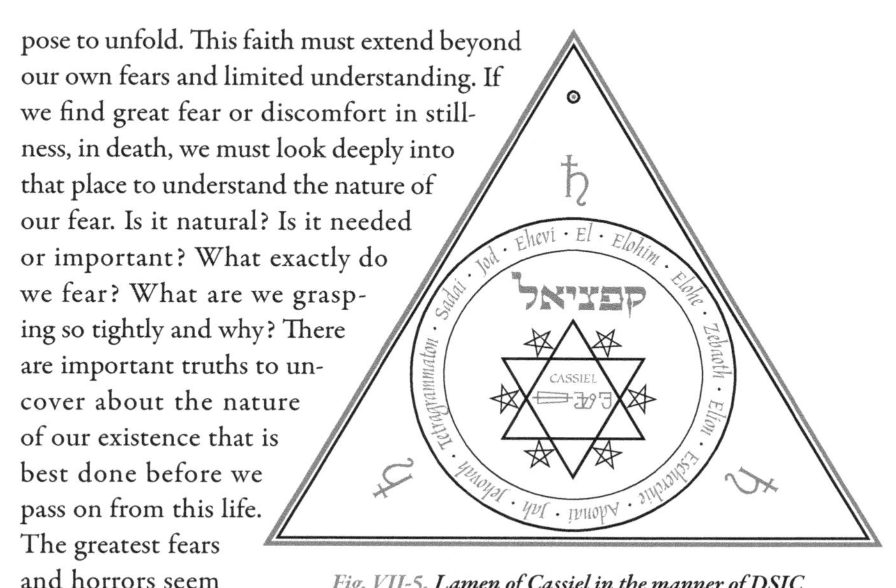

Fig. VII-5. ***Lamen of Cassiel in the manner of DSIC***

As terrifying as the Grim Reaper's scythe is to the collective unconscious and the individual human psyche, it is a symbol of divine mercy as well. It severs the bonds of the stubborn and unchanging. The blade divides the festering mass which attempts to barricade itself against the song of creation. Do not be fooled into believing the love for life is the same as attachment to unchanging illusion. The degree of pain or suffering seems to be equal to the degree of refusal to accept this process. To be truly in the presence of this Archangel without overwhelming fear and dread is to behold the truth within one's self about what we cling to in desperation. The very presence of Cassiel will challenge the fallacies to which you cling.

Invocation of the Archangel Cassiel

Fig. VII-6. Section of Circle with HEPTAMERON Correspondences for Drawing Cassiel into the Crystal

(Note: It took Cassiel quite a while to come into view and to arrive completely to speak with us. It seemed as if it was almost in his nature to take his time.)

Appearance of the Spirit

SCRYER: At first all I saw was the ring of Saturn. Then the image started to pull back and it transformed into a scythe which was held in the hands of the giant Archangel. The being is massive and a multitude of stars appears behind him. His hair is long and gray with streaks of black. His eyes are piercing, impossible to hide from. Great black wings are folded behind him. He is just huge, and he stands on a plain of snow that stretches out into the stars. His face is somewhat old but strong.

OPENING QUESTION 1: In the name of the holy and undefiled Spirit, the Father, the begotten Son, and Holy Ghost proceeding from both, what is thy true name?

SCRYER: He makes a cut with a scythe, and it sounds like the cutting of a man's throat or a blade running through wheat. It makes a *SSSSyhth* sound. And then a sigh or an out-breath, like the final breath of a dying man. Like a release.

OPENING QUESTION 2: What is thy office?

(An eerie, sharp whisper comes from my scryer.)

SPIRIT: «To tear down that which no longer serves in order for it to be remade, to be recast when beyond the ability of change of self or changing of others. The scythe severs the tie to this world. I am the judgment of my Father the Creator, harvester, reaper, breaker of disease, wielder of disease, eyes of silver in the darkness.»

OPENING QUESTION 3: What is thy true sign or character?

SCRYER: I see the crossroads, and the cross in the background. From the cross, a shadow is cast by a distant silver star that is covered in mist. The shadow of the cross runs along the earth, the snow, and is instead shaped like a sickle.

SPIRIT: «The crossroads, the place where one world meets the other. The scythe, the road that leads between them; it is the catalyst, the initiator. And the silver star, the distant light of the other shore.»

SCRYER: And I see people in the mist, like shadows, caught between the star and the crossroads and the cross. They are lost, searching. And just as quickly as they came, they're gone, there is only the mist, and the star.

OPENING QUESTION 4: When are the times most agreeable to thy nature to hold conference with us?

SPIRIT: «3:33 AM. At the crossroads, or on a bridge over running water. On the winter Solstice. At the bedside of the dying. In the silence of grief.»

OATH: Wilt thou swear by the holy blood of Jesus Christ that thou art truly Cassiel?

CASSIEL: «I swear by the blood of Jesus Christ, the Son of the Father...brave enough to hang on the cross between the worlds...that I am Cassiel.»

QUESTION 6: What are your views on humanity? What are your roles and interactions?

CASSIEL: «Humanity, though blessed, is one of only many beings, innumerable, uncountable, and I usher all things to sit again in the cauldron, the throne of the Creator. When man forgets their place with arrogance, a sickness develops inside, so they are brought to me. I receive them with truth and nothing else. I leave love to others. Truth is the ultimate purification. Truth: the final road to my Father Whose presence calms me and fills me with faith.»

QUESTION 7: What allowances are there to intercede on human affairs? How are interventions decided by you and the heavenly Father?

CASSIEL: «I intercede often in sickness and disease, in the disgust of corruption of power, or aimlessness of ignorance. These things will always exist but have a limited life here. Ignorance builds, brick by brick, stone by stone a road...that leads to me. With no more change, with no more life to give or receive, I drop the scythe.»

QUESTION 8: Do you have your own recollection of your creation and origin? Where do you come from? What is your purpose?

CASSIEL: «Yes....I remember silence...darkness, but presence....as if the Creator was all around me. Unseen and unheard, but felt. I remember a cold caress of stone, and when I stood, I felt His hands upon me, and His voice, His voice beyond description in my ear, whispering the names of all beings whom I would bring before Him. He spoke of how He loved them, cared for them, and laid upon me...the blessed responsibility of greeting them with Truth. I felt the scythe placed in my hands, and when I finally held it, the stars appeared all around me, and I knew the eternal wisdom of my Father, my Creator, was the one thing I would never see die.»

QUESTION 9: What advice can you give us to work and speak with you in the most powerful and beneficial ways?

SCRYER: He's showing me a scene of a man on his death bed who can no longer see or speak. His son and his daughter lean in at the same time, and whisper their love, their farewells in his ears. They anoint his body with oil. They hang an image of the Angel, of Cassiel, above the bed; it looks very Russian or Greek Orthodox to me. He now shows me a tomb, an open grave, and an urn of ashes. All of these he sprinkles with water and sings.

Fig. VII-7. ***Portrait of Cassiel as beheld in Vision***

QUESTION 10: Can you describe in detail how many others have contacted you and the other Angels in this manner? Can you share how their experiences and experiments were the same or different? What can you teach us of the history of contacting Angels magically in this manner? What other ways have there been?

CASSIEL: «In this manner, few, a hundred, all who have used this manner have spoken to the beings they have summoned, the Angels. I have seen the crystal crack when summoning Demons. I have seen some abuse this way and be brought to tears, and some paralyzed with fear. All confront the truth that's within them. As to the other ways, there have been countless, some at the crossroads, some at the tomb, some at death, some in fear, all when fate is about to be set.

«Your system that you use, that you are blessed with from those who worked it and created it before you, you should know that you are bound to them. They stand at the edges of your circle. Their work further fulfilled by you. You are kin. You are brothers and sisters of an Order whose name you have forgotten but will one day remember. Only together will you ascend to the next story created by the Source of all. Take time to honor their work. Speak their names and make blessings on their spirit.»

QUESTION 11: What are the most successful methods for conversing directly with Spirits of the departed? What is the proper way to receive messages from the departed?

CASSIEL: «*Hiram* and Spirits like him will be of great aid to you in this. Always use your discernment. Ignorance in life often means ignorance in death. Redemption is not a certainty but a gift upon continual purification. The redeemed of your line, of your people, of your species are with you now, but so are those who will lose themselves in their own delusions and obsessions, and for this, those mediators like Hiram will help you navigate the roads between the worlds. Make this connection with Hiram soon and he will teach you more, especially during time spent with him in private.»

QUESTION 12: Is the Spirit Hiram what he claims to be? Will he assist me in my endeavors and life positively? Will Hiram be and do as he says he will, which is to instruct me or inform me of anything magical or esoteric as well as fetch other Spirits of the departed so that I may speak with them?

CASSIEL: «He is and will indeed as you will discover.»

OPERATOR: Is there anything you can further advise on conjuring him properly into the skull and consecrating it toward its proper use and function? How should I successfully bind him to the skull? What is the best way to speak with him and call upon his Spirit properly in order to see and hear and converse with him?

CASSIEL: «The sigil is important. The care and respect of the skull, vital. The daily feeding, very important. Like a member of the family, like you: fed every day, nourished, communicated with, respected. When leaving on a trip, warn. In the invocation, whisper his name in the left ear of the skull. To show your devotion and your desire to develop a relationship with him, infuse the invocation with your own creativity and effort. He too has chosen you, and it will be a relationship you will have for the rest of your life. And when you die, he will stand at your bedside and hold your hand. You will be like brothers of an order whose name you have forgotten and will one day remember.»

QUESTION 13: What esoteric knowledge can you impart to us concerning your office and role that we may use to better live and serve others?

CASSIEL: «Yes. Speaking of truth remakes the world. The magician, the adept, the shaman, the scryer, the druid, the priest, this is their most important function. The greatest among you are the ones who in the face of the clamor and noise of the crowd are unafraid to speak what is often the opposite of what they say is the truth. In those times, when the truth is like a slave or an outlaw, call to me, anoint your chest with my sigil. In the night, whisper my name as you fall asleep and your dreams will show you the way.»

QUESTION 14: What can you teach us of Solomon's brass vessel and the beings? Are they Demons? Concerning the *Goetia*, how does it work and how do your powers interact concerning this with Mars and Samael? Do you have any further advice on how it should be constructed and used? Are there other Spirit pots and containers that we can make to house Spirits to assist us and communicate with?

CASSIEL: «The vessel is a container. The *Goetia*, a name of a throng of Spirits used to its function and attracted by its shape and in memory of its design and working. Samael is the binder, the one who marshals the Spirits into the vessel, whose fiery nature of the brass is reflected in his eyes. I, Cassiel, am the guide, the overseer who judges the heart of the magician who uses it. When not done to serve the Creator, I teach the magician through judgment. When done to serve, truth and wisdom is the result.

«As for the Spirits of the *Goetia*, each is a shard of understanding, but not the whole concept. They are full of passion, many of them, and move quickly and often. They hold keys to specific locks in the body and the mind of the magician. When worked with patiently and over time, the right keys can be fitted to the right locks, but the keys must be used only after great deliberation and care. In this working, I may guide you.»

QUESTION 15: What magical teachings and methods can you impart to us for defense against magical or psychic attack from Spirits, Demons, or people?

SCRYER: He shows me a knife. The blade is buried in the snow, on the dark of the moon, at a crossroads. A man in black, with black hair and black skin, whispers the name of Cassiel three times to the blade and fades. Now I see the magician waiting on the eastern road, perfectly silent. He picks up the blade after a period of total silence and leaves back down the eastern road.

OPERATOR: Do you have further instruction on how this blade it to be made?

CASSIEL: «Silver, pearl, clear stone. The blade etched with my sigil in whatever form you choose. I promise that when you use the blade and consecrate it as I have told you and shown you, that it will sever any tie that a Spirit may have with you—until such time as I decide you may meet again.»

OPERATOR: Do you have any other magical arts you could impart to us concerning the Spirit world or to invoke your power?

CASSIEL: «The knife I have described, excellent for protection, the severing of attack, and retribution. For calling to the departed, speak my name, bless the departed in the name of the Creator. Speak honestly and without deception to them. You may record their voices, you may see their messages in cards, or when the mind is still and open, in a protected space you may behold their image. When done to serve, my scythe will ward you. When not done to serve, my scythe will wound you.»

QUESTION 16: What can you tell us of the transition of the Soul/Spirit from life to death and beyond?

CASSIEL: «Many get lost. Not because they have sinned or offended the Creator, but because they cannot perceive anything else. Because they cannot see the road of the star laid before them. Many immediately see the star. Those who do are those who have walked the road of truth; they have purified themselves in it, and their heart is light, light as a feather, and my scythe merely a road they walk on. Some struggle, and ancestors and guardians rise and teach them, and together they walk to the other shore as one...And there are some I must cut and cut and cut...and recast.»

QUESTION 17: Great Archangel Cassiel, can you explain the images you showed me during our first meeting? What was the road with long wheat growing in fields in a rolling landscape? The human skull which was underneath a path in the foreground, and a figure that was shooting an arrow or throwing a spear back toward the right? After, I then saw a horse running backward, heading toward the left, and three riders were upon it. Can you explain all these images to me?

CASSIEL: «These horsemen: keys to your locks. The arrow: movement of your mind over the fields of your life's harvest. And the skull: a partner.»

OPERATOR: We thank you, mighty Archangel of the Crossroads, of Shadow, and Otherworld. May we always heed your words and carry out our time here as best we may. Great blessings between us through the Creator.

(License to Depart given.)

Afterthoughts on the Cassiel Operation

SCRYER: Cassiel seemed so different, very thoughtful, patient, like he had all the time in the world. Almost as if he *was* time itself. At the start of the ritual, my ear started to ring loudly, my right ear right before he appeared. At some point after the Angel appeared, it seemed to recognize that I was uncomfortable and I actually started getting a pain in my back sitting there. It was beginning to get difficult for me physically, but at one point the Angel looked right at me and said, «That is part of what you're doing here. You are learning that such efforts require carrying that burden. To understand part of my office is to sit in stillness, uncomforted and sit with the pain, that is going to help bring these things through and help communicate with me properly.»

Looking back on the images of his birth and origin, it was such an immense concept of being given a huge responsibility and burden. It really is an unfathomable weight to carry, being the one to harvest and collect the souls. I really feel the connecting energies between these beings and the Celtic Gods and Goddesses, as if they are indeed mountains of a similar range in the mist, with unique and important functions, but each serving a unique purpose.

OPERATOR: So much transpired during this invocation of Archangel Cassiel. When he mentioned that what he first showed me of the horsemen were "keys to my locks," my initial thought was that it may be a certain *Goetia* Spirit; I'll have to meditate on this. He described the *Goetia* Spirits precisely as "keys to locks," so I will need to look into which Spirit this could possibly be.

I was looking forward to this operation for a few reasons, as I have mentioned. One was for obtaining answers I had involving previous dealings with the Archangel and I received way more than I expected. My recollection of this operation was that the air was heavy throughout the entire operation and reminded me of the coolness and damp of Halloween night. Another odd occurrence was that throughout the session, cool breezes blew through the circle. Moisture was thick as well, and precipitation formed on the door and window. During the operation, the magical chamber reminded me of being in a tomb actually. My scryer and I both felt rather vulnerable and, well, aware of our mortality.

My scryer commented on how long it took for the images to arrive, as if the Archangel was in no rush. During the operation, I noticed how the Spirit seemed to take long, long pauses between questions, as if he enjoyed taking his time to answer. The Archangel continues to feel eerily steadfast. My scryer's vision and interaction with this Angel, like the others, were familiar in manner and appearance to what I experienced previously.

Also, as with previous Archangels, Cassiel's presence was felt for a long while before his appearance manifested. It was also similar to some other operations in which the Angels began to answer some of my questions before they were asked, as if they knew what was coming. Their comments and replies appeared to be making a point of blending answers together.

The area was not oppressing, but very sobering and solemn. When the Angel mentioned my elders and brothers and sisters in the Art were around my circle, I physically shivered and could feel their presence indefinitely. After that point I felt such pride and love for my forebears and wanted to acknowledge their efforts and realized how much responsibility I had to carry on their work with integrity in the most honorable way that I could.

The Ritual Litany of the Ascended Mages

The pointed statements the Archangel of Saturn made about the lineage of magicians struck a deep chord with me. It seemed to be a heritage that went beyond bloodline or any physical fraternity. I was made aware of the assistance I have received beyond simple written records of magical theory and practice. It is by the efforts of those who came before that magic continues as a living tradition.

As Archangel Cassiel stated, «Your system that you use, that you are blessed with from those who worked it and created it before you, you should know that you are bound to them. They stand at the edges of your circle. Their work further fulfilled by you. You are kin. You are brothers and sisters of an order whose name you have forgotten but will one day remember.» This, I felt, was a vitally important statement, one not given due observance in my practice up to this point. It became very important to me that I should acknowledge my forbears. I began by doing more research into magicians and occultists of the past. The more I read of their lives and works, the more I felt a connection to them. Many led astounding lives, often marked with great tragedy and trial in the midst of their achievements and abilities.

Cassiel also declared that «only together will you ascend to the next story created by the Source of all. Take time to honor their work. Speak their names and make blessings on their Spirit.» Our ancestors, our teachers, those who have gone before us still watch and lend nourishment and encouragement to our work. Ancestral veneration and even worship is a practice that is found in many ancient religions and magical traditions, but became almost nonexistent in Western culture, particularly after the rise of Protestantism, which opposed the veneration of Saints, the closest observance to these ancient traditions. I wanted to make a formal practice of honoring the magicians and occultists who had come before me on such occasions that would be appropriate to do so. In the observance and acknowledgment of the multitude of the occult and magical pioneers who paved the way for my work and that of every living magician, I created a ceremony to honor them.

Items:

1. Parchment with names, sigils and symbols, as well as titles and magical names on a decorated piece of parchment.
2. A place setting on a table or altar for offerings of food, wine, and water. If honoring one or a few names, set places for each respectively.
3. Have three candles: silver, gold, and white. Incense burner with incense used in magical workings such as Abramelin incense or mixtures in the *Key of Solomon*.
4. A lead and stone plaque with Archangel Cassiel's image and sigil.

My prayer/invocation for the lineage of magicians:

Allow us all to be worthy, O most high and absolute Creator, Father of all, to partake of the sacred order of Magi. Grant the purification of our body, our speech, and our mind, that we may attain to the holy Gnosis, having a share and inheritance with all the mystics and adepti who have pleased you since the beginning. Remember, O Lord, those you bestowed with the gifts of your Mysteries. Allow us to share in the love, glory, and sacred knowledge of all the ascended masters whom you have graced with the most mysterious and powerful of gifts.

Divine Creator, let peace be on your chosen magicians, your mystics, your wise men and women of the ages, who have paved the roads of reason, mystery, and discovery. Let your grace, mercy, and light come unto them, O Lord. Allow blessings come unto them O Lord, past any transgression, blunder, or misdeed they have committed during their mortal lives. I ask you remember them as the great adepts and teachers of the hidden arts. May all those named be blessed and my prayer be heard for them. Let any unnamed masters who have lent their Spirit to my work be blessed even though I recall not their names.

The list of my magical forbears is extensive beyond the range of this work (not to mention beyond my range of knowledge), and ever-evolving as my knowledge evolves. However, there are many occultists and magicians of whom

I know who left their mark on the tradition, some of whom have left a profound impact on my own work and in the continual practice of magic.

Beyond my full knowledge of their deeds, their virtues, their abilities, and their contributions to the Great Work, I give honor to the great seekers, occultists, and mages:

- Enoch, antediluvian seer and prophet who wrote of his visionary ascents to the heavens, who taught esoteric lore to his heirs, and who walked with Elohim;
- The Telchines, semi-divine magical artisans of the islands of Rhodes and Keos;
- Abaris the Hyperborean, legendary ancient sage, healer, and priest of Apollo;
- Hermes Trismegistos, legendary Egyptian sage, avatar of Thoth, and founder of Hermetism;
- the *Baalath-Ov* of Endor, necromancer and Spirit medium of King Saul;
- Solomon, king of Israel, wise ruler, builder of the Temple, great magus and binder of Demons;
- Hiram, Phœnician king of Tyre, who provided artisans and materials for the building of Solomon's Temple;
- Orpheus, priest of Dionysos and Apollo, descender to and ascender from the Underworld, and founder of the Orphic Mysteries;
- Pythagoras, philosopher, mathematician, occultist, founder of an esoteric school;
- Plato, founder of Platonic philosophy;
- Apollonius of Tyana, philosopher and wonderworker;
- Apuleius of Madaura, Initiate of the Mysteries, magician, and author;
- Julianus the Chaldæan and Julianus the Theurgist, the father and son magus and scryer who by their Theurgic Art brought forth the *Chaldæan Oracles*;
- Iamblichos, the great teacher of Neoplatonic Theurgy, called "the Divine Iamblichos" by his disciples;
- Zosimos of Panopolis, Egyptian alchemist, Gnostic and Hermetic mystic;

- the legendary Honorius of Thebes, magician and author of the *Liber Juratus*;
- Abraham Abulafia, writer and teacher of ecstatic Kabbalah;
- Abramelin the Mage, who in Egypt taught the Sacred Magic of the Knowledge and Conversation of the Holy Guardian Angel;
- Abraham of Worms, Kabbalist and Magus, who wrote the *Book of the Sacred Magic*;
- Christian Rosenkreuz, sage, pilgrim, mystic, mage, legendary founder of the Rosicrucian Order;
- Marsilio Ficino, philosopher, priest, astrologer, head of the Platonic Academy, and translator of Plato, the Orphic Hymns, Iamblichus, and the Hermetica;
- Count Giovanni Pico della Mirandola, philosopher, Hermetic Kabbalist, and author of the *900 Theses* and the *Oration on the Dignity of Man*;
- Johannes Trithemius, abbot, cryptographer, scholar, author of *De Setpem Secundeis*, and reputedly of *The Art of Drawing Spirits into Crystals*;
- Heinrich Cornelius Agrippa, philosopher, scholar of magic and theurgy, author of the Three Books of Occult Philosophy;
- Paracelsus, medical pioneer, alchemical master, and classifier of the Elemental Spirits;
- Giordano Bruno, philosopher, astrologer, Hermetist, poet and author, martyred by the Inquistion;
- Elias Ashmole, scholar and collector of occult manuscripts, student of Enochian magic;
- William Lilly, astrologer, translator of magical works, and author;
- Doctor John Dee, polymath, and the magus who with his scryer Edward Kelley founded Enochian magic;
- Edward Kelley, alchemist, and the gifted scryer who saw the Angels and with the magus John Dee founded Enochian magic;
- Benvenuto Cellini, goldsmith, sculptor, soldier, and participant in the evocation of Spirits;
- Robert Fludd, Hermetic philosopher, astrologer, geomancer, and author;
- Thomas Vaughan, Eugenius Philalethes, natural philosopher, alchemist, Rosicrucian, and occult author;

- Sir Isaac Newton, physicist and alchemist;
- Martinez de Pasqually, theurgist, founder of the Order of Elus Coëns;
- Louis Claude de Saint-Martin, the Unknown Philosopher, mystic, author, and inspirer of Martinism;
- Ebenezer Sibley, ceremonial magician, collector of magical texts, and author;
- Francis Barrett, ceremonial magician, author of *The Magus*, and translator of *The Art of Drawing Spirits into Crystals*;
- Frederick Hockley, scribe, scholar, scryer, and ceremonial magician;
- Éliphas Lévi, Kabbalist, Hermeticist, magus, and occult author;
- Edward Bulwer-Lytton, Baron Lytton, member of the Orphic Circle, author of occult novels;
- Elizabeth Hardinge Britten, Spiritualist leader and occult author, who in her youth was scryer for the Orphic Circle;
- Marquis Stanislas de Guaita, founder of the Kabbalistic Order of the Rose Croix, and occult author;
- Sar Joséphin Péladan, co-founder of the Kabbalistic Order of the Rose Croix, founder of the Catholic Rose Croix Order of the Temple of the Grail, establisher of the artistic Salons de la Rose Croix, and occult author;
- Oswald Wirth, occultist, artist, and creator of the Arcana of the Kabbalistic Tarot;
- Papus, Dr. Gérard Encausse, co-founder of the Kabbalistic Order of the Rose Croix, Initiate of the Golden Dawn and the Hermetic Brotherhood of Luxor, founder of modern Martinism, bishop of the Gnostic Church of France, and occult author;
- Helena Petrovna Blavatsky, co-founder of Theosophy;
- Colonel Henry Steele Olcott, co-founder with Blavatsky of Theosophy;
- William Wynn Westcott, Frater Sapere Aude and Non Omnis Moriar, co-founder of the Hermetic Order of the Golden, Hermeticist, Freemason, Theosophist, ceremonial magician, occult scholar and author;

- S.L. MacGregor Mathers, Frater Deo Duce Comite Ferro and 'Srioghail mo Dhream, co-founder of the Hermetic Order of the Golden Dawn, Chief Adept of the AO, Hermeticist, Kabbalist, ceremonial magician, author, and translator of works including *The Key of Solomon the King*, *The Qabbalah Unveiled*, *The Book of the Sacred Magic of Abra-Melin the Mage*, *The Grimoire of Armadel*, and *The Goetia of the Lemegeton*;
- Moina Mathers, Soror Vestigia Nulla Retrorsum, Adept of the Golden Dawn, Chief Adept of the AO, ceremonial magician, scryer, and artist;
- Florence Farr, Soror Sapientia Sapienti Deo Dona, Adept of the Golden Dawn, ceremonial magician, actress, and author;
- William Butler Yeats, Frater Dæmon Est Deus Inversus, Adept of the Golden Dawn, ceremonial magician, author, and Nobel laureate poet;
- John William Brodie-Innes, Frater Sub Spe, Adept of the Golden Dawn, Chief Adept of the AO, Theosophist, and occult writer;
- Arthur Edward Waite, Frater Sacramentum Regis, Adept of the Golden Dawn, founder of the Fellowship of the Rosy Cross, occult author, and co-creator with Pamela Coleman Smith of the Rider Waite-Smith Tarot;
- Pamela Coleman Smith, Initiate of the Golden Dawn, and co-creator with A.E. Waite of the Rider Waite-Smith Tarot;
- Robert Felkin, Frater Finem Respice, Adept of the Golden Dawn, and Chief Adept of the Stella Matutina;
- Aleister Crowley, Frater Perdurabo, adept of the Golden Dawn, founder of Thelema, ceremonial magician, and author;
- Paul Foster Case, Frater Perseverantia, Adept of the AO, founder of the Builders of the Adytum, and occult author;
- Dion Fortune, Soror Deo Non Fortuna, Adept of the Stella Matutina, founder of the Fraternity of the Inner Light, and occult author;
- Franz Bardon, occultist, magician, and Hermetic author;
- Francis Israel Regardie, Frater Ad Majorem Adonai Gloriam, Adept of the Stella Matutina, ceremonial magician, and author;
- Manly Palmer Hall, philosopher, occultist, collector of alchemical manuscripts, founder of the Philosophical Research Society, and author of Hermetic works including *The Secret Teachings of All Ages*;

Lord, hear our prayer:

Requiem æternam dona eis, Domine; et lux perpetua luceat eis.[39] *May their souls and the souls of all those who have trodden the path of the Mysteries by the mercy of God forever receive Your light.*

The Knife of Cassiel ☩ Part 1

By far the most intriguing part of the operation with Archangel Cassiel was the description of the knife which is made in part of «clear stone.» With the ritual at the crossroads, this weapon shown to my scryer appeared to be a magical tool of considerable potency. Although I had already fashioned a traditional Solomonic black-handled knife, and a magical sword that was blessed by the Archangel Samael himself, I was inspired to create another magical bladed weapon. I had a feeling that this particular knife would prove to be highly effective against hostile Spirits in ways I had not previously considered.

Clavicula Salomonis de Secretis ("The Clavicle or Little Key of Solomon on the Secrets"), chapter 8, "About the Sword," describes a crystal-handled magic sword. It reads: "A Sword may be obtained, [its blade] made from steel three feet in length, its hilt may be crystalline, inscribed with these characters written in human blood at the full Moon."[40]

Fig. VII-8 is a rendering of the manuscript's illustration of the sword (which looks oddly like a pruning hook or sickle of some sort[41]) with the sigils to be written on the hilt.

In research, I also came across descriptions of 17th- to 19th-century knives called *pesh-qabz* ("fore-grip") made in Persia and in the Mughal empire in India that combined exquisite steel blades with handles carved of rock crystal.

---

39. Latin, "Eternal rest give to them, O Lord; and let perpetual light shine upon them."

40. Trans. by Adam P. Forrest from the Latin of National Library of Poland MS Rps 3352 II. The *Clavicula Salomonis de secretis* is an early form or precursor of the *Grimorium Verum*. —APF

41. Also like the head of a mediæval military polearm—particularly some type of guisarme or bill hook—that evolved from the pruning hook and similar agricultural tools. In a later French manuscript of the text, *Traité Universel des Clavicules de Salomon ("Universal Treatise on the Clavicles of Solomon")*, Wellcome MS 4669, the sigils and the drawing have been further degraded, so that the sword—already bizarre in the *De secretis*—looks rather like a boxing glove on a stick. The *Universal Treatise* has been published with a translation by Paul Harry Barron in Skinner and Rankine, *The Veritable Keys of Solomon* (Singapore: Golden Hoard Press, 2010), with the sword depicted on p. 389. —APF

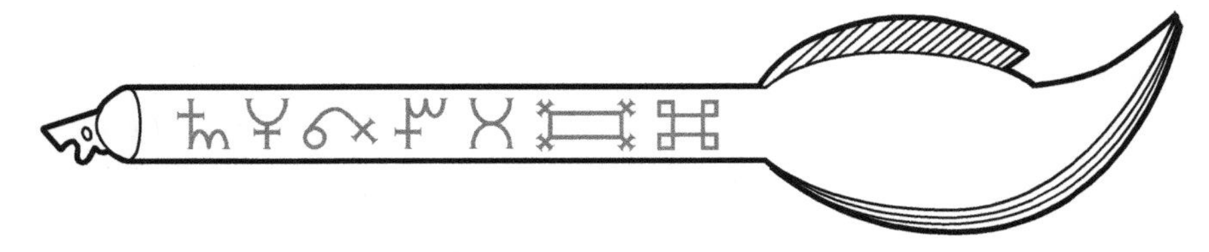

Fig. VII-8. The peculiar Crystal-handled 'Sword' from CLAVICULA SALOMONIS DE SECRETIS

After extensive online hunting, I finally found a suitable knife that represented to me what Cassiel had shown to my scryer. The next time Benn came over, I showed the knife to him and he agreed that it looked like an appropriate weapon to be the Knife of Saturn. The hilt was magnificently carved from one piece of transparent rock crystal or quartz into the shape of the head of a ram. The blade was of Persian style and unusually thick and robust with a greatly reinforced central ridge, secured to the hilt with a clear resin or gum fixing. The steel blade was deeply engraved with applied silver work in designs of flower blooms.

While I felt I had found the proper knife, I was not convinced I had all the details needed to consecrate it properly. I would wait until I felt it was the proper time to create this most potent spiritual weapon.

Necromancy: The Skull Spirit Intelligencer ✣ Part 2

The Preparation of the Skull for the Familiar Spirit Hiram

Based on the confirming replies from the Archangel Cassiel and research on the name Hiram, I felt confident that I was ready to conjure my familiar Spirit into the skull. I was eager to meet this mysterious Spirit called Hiram. The impression that I got both during the first meeting with my scryer and from historical references was that Hiram of Tyre was a very crafty and intelligent ruler who valued information, knowledge, craftsmanship, and trade. If there were celestial archetypes to which this Spirit would be linked, they would be in the aspects of Mercury and perhaps Jupiter. What made his kingdom great as well as the knowledge of his city was its productivity in trade, artisanship, and information. If the Spirit turned out to be anything like what I assumed of this great ruler, he was ideal for an intelligencer Spirit. Regardless of my initial skepticism of the conspicuous figure of the Biblical king, I decided to trust the instruction and advice received in the operations. I figured if anything went wrong, I would simply have to resort to the severe magical solution of destroying the skull and contact. It was difficult to imagine being set up for failure at this point, since the Archangels had never led me wrong and each encounter had been followed by considerable good fortune when I honored their advice.

I was also somewhat apprehensive about doing the physical work on the skull, since I knew I had only one chance and would likely not be able to acquire another one if I botched it up. Besides being rare and expensive, the skull was rather delicate, and I worried how it would hold up to engraving and painting. Regardless, I went to work gathering up all the plans and conjurations I had created or discovered, along with the array of symbols, sigils, seals, and binding diagrams. It took me a while to adjust the size and arrangement of the complex magical formulæ to arrive at a final plan of exactly how I wanted them to be arranged upon the surface of the actual skull.

I knew that creating the perfect vessel for my familiar Spirit would be a lengthy and delicate process, so I selected three days to dedicate solely to the creation, evocation, and securing of this Spirit in its new home. The first step would be cleaning and preparing the skull. I planned to bleach the skull by submerging it in a bucket that was filled with hydrogen peroxide solution plus measures of holy water and blessed salts. Since receiving the human skull on Halloween, I had kept it safely wrapped up and secured in a black pine box. The skull had arrived in fair shape but was not perfect by any means and did not appear to have been cleaned and sterilized by the usual North American standards I was familiar with from my time working in the hospital. The human skeletal remains certainly had an eerie look and I was not certain of exactly how it was procured. I did a bit of research on properly bleaching the skull, and peroxide seemed like it would be effective while not being overly corrosive. The bleaching process was also intended magically to make sure it was a pure and empty vessel for the Spirit to inhabit, and that all residual material as well as energy from the previous owner was removed prior to the operation. The process took longer than expected, nearly the entire day to let it soak and then completely air-dry. I created a protective "cage" for the skull outside and even traced a magic circle around it while it dried.

The second stage was to draw, engrave, and paint on the skull each of the multitude of magical symbols and binding conjurations I had designed. I devoted an entire Wednesday under a favorable alignment and an increasing Moon. I placed a beeswax candle on either side of my working table and I also placed a stone incense burner nearby. On the first hour of the day, I woke up, showered, and recited the same litany of prayers and *Psalms* that I use before an evocation. I took the now-bleached white skull and set it on a wooden plaque on which I had previously engraved a Grand Seal of Solomon. The wooden disk acted as a turntable so that I could easily reach all areas without having to continually pick up the skull once it had wet paint on it. I began by using a bit of white acrylic paint to repair and conceal a few broken teeth. Before I set to engraving, I was inspired to combine a mixture of Mercury, Jupiter, and Saturn incenses and intermittantly fume the skull as I worked on each engraving or painted each symbol.

Slowly and carefully I engraved and painted the skull with the sigils and seals I had decided on, as well as the binding invocations in the angular, archaic form of Old Hebrew script. In ancient letters I drew out spells around the ear canals that it would hear me and respond to my words and intentions. I wrote around the eye ridges that it would be able to show visions and instructions clearly. Around the jawbone I wrote that the Spirit would speak clearly and truthfully each time I called upon it. I constructed the Agla seals upon the temples. A Grand Seal was created on the crown, supported by the sigils of Cassiel, Raphael, and other Angelic forces. With painstaking patience and accuracy, I traced out on the forehead the sigil of Hiram that was given to me through my scryer at the first encounter. The sigil was encircled with its name, four letters in ancient Hebrew script.

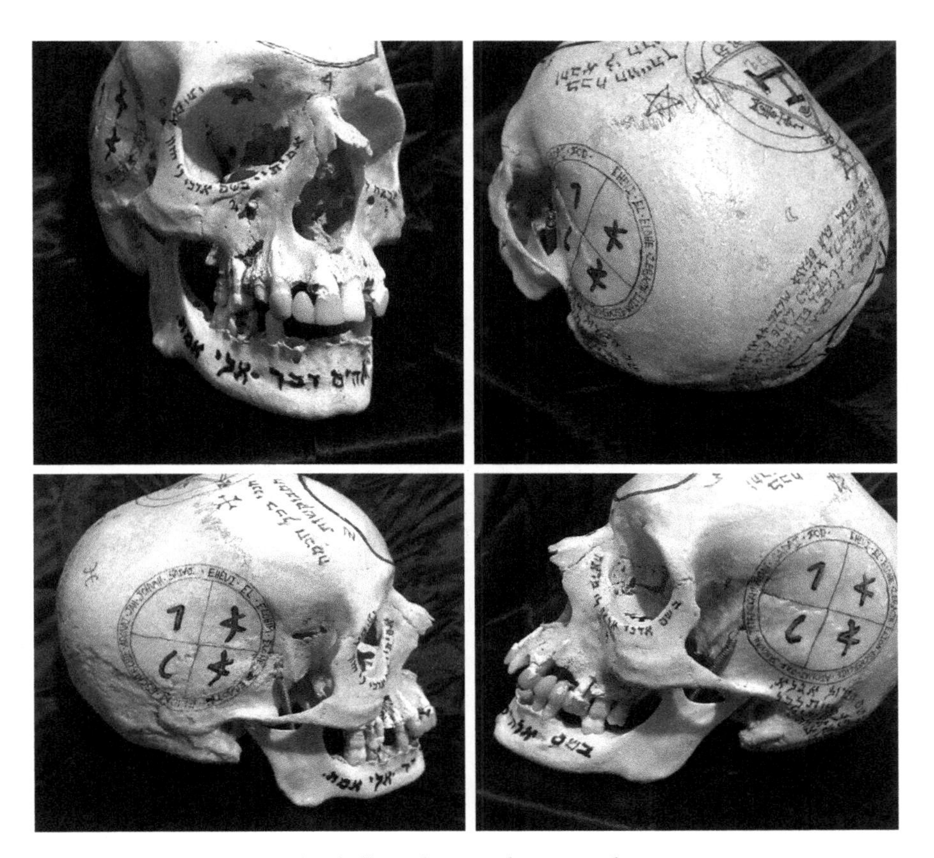

Fig. VII-9. The Skull Vessel prepared to receive the Spirit Hiram

This process lasted all day with only one short pause to eat a bowl of cereal.

After the inscriptions were completed, I looked it over several times, making sure that each word, sigil, and symbol was properly inscribed and painted, and that each section worked together in a cohesive matrix of magical formulæ focused toward the purpose of bringing about the desired effect. When I was certain the physical component of the project was completed, I submerged the entire skull in a bucket of polyurethane. I did this several times, giving it multiple coats and letting each coat dry before applying the next. The result left a smooth and shiny finish. Besides protecting the skull itself, the effort sealed in all the meticulous artistic work I had put into the inscriptions and sigils. Finally, I added a coat of clear lacquer, and then placed the skull on a stand to dry.

The ritual planned to bring the Spirit into the skull was set for the following Saturday during an evening hour of Mercury. I cleaned and arranged the magical chamber to be conducive to this event. I was eager to finally meet this being for myself and hopefully see and hear Hiram as my scryer had.

Invocation of the Spirit Hiram

Saturday evening came and a heavy freezing mist descended on the city that did not dissipate for the entire weekend. The now sealed and sigilized skull was prepared in the north section of the Magical chamber on a small altar table at knee level. On the table were three consecrated candles: one black, one blue, and one orange, corresponding to the offices and authorities of Saturn, Jupiter, and Mercury, and each engraved with the sigil of the appropriate Archangel. A brazier was placed directly beneath the altar with charcoal. Offerings of purified water, red wine, and bread were arranged to either side. My large obsidian scrying mirror was placed upright behind the skull and elevated so both my scryer and I could peer into it without obstruction. I also decided to add two oil diffusers with a mix of consecrated water, cypress, patchouli, and pine oils.

My scryer and I donned our linen robes and entered the magical circle. As I engaged in the preliminary steps of the ritual, he silently sat in the center on one of the floor cushions. I prepared the ritual similarly to the manner of *DSIC* but also sprinkled the circle and four corners with holy water. I lit the charcoal and added moderate amounts of incense. The mixture was the same I used during the engraving of the skull with the addition of a bit of Spirit summoning incense. After prayers that our efforts would be blessed and successful, I sat down to join my scryer.

We took a few moments to breathe and prepare ourselves to travel into the Astral. I again used Josephine McCarthy's candle-flame induction. I began by using my hypnotic techniques to describe the process to the scryer as before. I don't recall exactly what was said but remember not having any difficulty recalling the steps for traveling through the flame into the empty blackness. I spoke long enough to be sure my scryer was through the void, where he could find his way to the desert as before.

After my intuition told me he had arrived, I stared into the intense light of the candle flames myself and silenced all other thoughts but sending my awareness through the fire. At some point I lost any awareness of my surroundings and entered into the void. I guided my scryer and me through a doorway which appeared in the dark, to the desert of the Astral void. This experiment was the first time I attempted going in tandem with my scryer on an Astral journey. I didn't find it all that difficult as I could pretty much discern right where my scryer was in the process before I let go of trying to guide him and found my own way to the desert and then to the abyss.

As soon as I found myself looking around the desert scenery, I saw my scryer standing next to me. I intoned aloud our intention to find Hiram again and lead him back from the abyss and void to the skull located in the magical chamber. Just a moment passed, and then I beheld the Sandalphon Angels on either side of my scryer and myself. I noticed how much taller the both of them appeared than us, and they were indeed perfect in every detail. Their gender was impossible to discern and their shining white robes revealed no indication either. I spent a long while gazing at the Angels, and wondered how much of their imagery was based on Josephine McCarthy's account and how much was their natural form in any state. We walked steadily and silently while the Angels sang an eerie but familiar song in unison. The cadence of their song and the sound of their long, long hair swishing in the sand behind us, erasing all signs of travel, caused a rather disorienting feeling. It grew even more so when I looked back and ahead and saw that in the sandy waste it was difficult to tell how far we had traveled or that we were even moving.

After a while, I made out a dark spot in the distance that I knew to be the rocky fissure of the abyss. The very sight of the dark chasm filled me with an ominous sensation in the pit of my stomach. As we neared the edge of the giant gap in the desert floor, one of the twin Angels placed a hand on my scryer's chest, and an audible crack or pop was heard like static electricity. My scryer's face shuddered for a moment and he seemed surprised. I could not discern the reason for the gesture. I turned my attention out over the enormous precipice, noticing how it seemed to vanish dreamlike as the mists concealed the far side and the depths, making it impossible to discern its size. This was the first time I saw it in such stark and vivid clarity.

We stopped for a moment to gaze at the enormity of the infinite fissure in the earth that was appropriately named "the abyss." The large ledges disappeared out of view and the further you looked down, the more you felt as if you were already falling through its depths. Oddly shaped beings and forms looked up expectantly. The yawning chasm and the slowly swirling mists, along with the shapes of the beings below, imparted an overwhelming sense of foreboding.

The guardian was called, and a dark silhouetted figure appeared just as my scryer had described it. The form came to the center of the chasm and asked what our purpose was for coming. This time I spoke directly out over the chasm to the figure attempting to make clear our intentions in bringing the spirit Hiram back with us.

My scryer added his voice, saying, "To reconnect, to seek, and bring back Hiram. To aid the spirit world. To aid all life, to aid in our workings, that he may fulfill his destiny and we may fulfill ours."

Instantly, the dark body of the guardian merged with the cliff on the other side of the chasm. Its head appeared to grow out the top of the cliff. Its chest and arms became visible as the form grew to the size of a colossus. The massive being reached out with a great gray and black hand to our side of the chasm and my scryer and I walked onto its palm.

Being in the experience for the first time, I found the giant elevator hand ride down to be pretty intense. I could feel myself dropping down, down, passing a series of ledges and a myriad of odd forms, faces, and expressions. The ride seemed to take us down an impossibly long way. Eventually I heard my scryer mention the light of Hiram's ledge, and I could just make out a distant glow below on the left side. As we descended towards the source, the vague glow clarified into a flickering orange light when I again looked over the edge of the guardian's hand. As we drew even nearer, I recognized the light as a campfire with a figure squatted beside it.

The hand came to rest where we could step out onto the ledge. The person crouching by the fire appeared to be a Peruvian man with keen eyes, grizzled hair, and thin gray whiskers on his chin. He held a long, thin, perfectly straight stick in his right hand. I studied the fellow, and decided that he seemed to have the likeness of a South American shaman. All this I was seeing simultaneously as my scryer spoke of what he was seeing as well. The shaman gestured for us to continue on past the campfire to the large wooden door that looked to be very solid and intricate with overlaid panels of wood. As we reached the door, my scryer's voice described he heard multiple locks releasing as I turned the handle. The door opened toward us, and we stepped inside.

Towering bookcases and books were stacked impossibly high, as if the chamber ascended a hundred feet or more, with the tops disappearing in a mist where swirls and apparitions darted in and out. The strange place felt surprisingly comfortable, even sheltering to me. There were numerous fascinating items scattered about on tables—old games, phonographs, sextants, and quills caught my eye. It was utterly intriguing, just as my scryer had accounted when he had first journeyed here. It was impossible not to be drawn to all the sights with scientific devices as well as old and foreign-looking games and mechanisms designed to study a variety of phenomena. We both spent another moment looking around at the impossibly impressive library before we each felt a hand on our shoulder.

I heard my scryer announce in a pleasant tone, "And there he is."

I looked up at the owner of the hand resting on my shoulder, and beheld a giant of a man with the warmest expression on his face. His appearance was just as Benn had described him. He wore a scholarly-looking dark robe that covered his broad, fit frame. His head was completely bald, and he had a dark mustache and eyebrows. His dark brown, intelligent eyes held enormous warmth.

After greeting the being that could only be Hiram, my scryer became silent and for the first time I heard the deep voice of the Spirit fill the library. His voice was very distinct, with a hint of an accent and deep with intelligence and certainty, but a pervasive patience and kindness as well. He said to me, «We finally meet. I am eager to share our journey together. This will be a very studious undertaking with many lessons and challenges, but I hope to lead you to wisdom and experience previously incomprehensible.»

I remember smiling up at him and saying, "Great Spirit Hiram, I ask you to accompany us out from the abyss, to join us in the full potency of your spirit, and bring forth the vast wisdom of your library, your knowledge, and expertise."

He smiled warmly, embraced me and said, «May I embrace you, brother, and our pact be sealed, and I will go with you.»

I remember feeling his embrace very distinctly: warm, assuring, steady, and sincere. He was massive and I pretty much lost myself in the embrace as the sleeves of his large robes folded around me. I was not nervous or put off by the experience at all; it was like embracing a lifelong member of my family.

He spoke to me briefly of how he had called me, how he had known of my work, and how we shared a bond that could only be understood with time and discussion. The way in which he spoke did not make me question him, but instead caused a sense of familiar kinship to draw me towards him.

After our brief discussion, Hiram gestured for my scryer and me to lead the way. The three of us departed the library, and just before I exited the door, I made sure to glance up above the frame, where a skillfully scrolled sign read *Hiram's Library*.

I stepped again onto the huge hand of the guardian accompanied this time not only by my scryer but also the towering figure of Hiram. As we ascended both my scryer and I watched the crouched shaman look warmly up at us and wave farewell. At that moment I wondered if the man might also be a part of the same line of magicians, the order that Cassiel had mentioned, perhaps an ancient order that was beyond time, geographical location, and ethnicity.

We ascended the way we had come to the edge of the abyss where the Sandalphon twin Angels stood silently waiting. As we stepped off the hand of the Guardian of the Abyss, I declared again my intention to take Hiram with us to the physical world. The Angels responded by saying that I was taking on a significant responsibility by doing this, and that the care, interaction, and usage of Hiram would be a serious task. I responded that I understood, and reiterated that we wished to walk with Hiram back to the physical world so he may act as spiritual advisor, companion, and friend. The Angels agreed and gave council as the five of us walked back through the desert.

The Angels reminded me again that what I was attempting was a serious task, and that I would be steward to the consecrated skull as well as the Spirit, and must protect and guard it and be attentive to his fate, as it was now tied to mine. I again heard the Angels' hair erasing the steps behind us. I felt Hiram's hand on my back and saw the other on my scryer's. As I looked behind me, I saw Hiram smiling. He seemed so tall and sheltering.

We continued walking back the way we had come till the desert landscape began to fade and I felt my awareness beginning to be drawn back to the room. At some point, I became aware of myself back in the magical chamber. Before I fully regained my senses however, I spoke a personal welcome to Hiram, as I could feel him in the room with us. His presence seemed to expand, and then to contract over the area where the skull rested on the altar.

I spoke aloud the official invocation and binding spell that was written on a piece of paper in front of me. I also recited the English translation of the Hebrew inscription on the skull. I could sense that his energy was somehow being drawn through the skull directly though his sigil that was engraved and painted on the forehead. As I sensed this happening, I began uttering a personal prayer, a sealing of the Spirit to the skull as well as a deep expression of gratitude for the Spirit's agreement to become my advisor.

I heard Hiram's voice as a whisper in my head and it said, «Bryan, trace now my sigil with your hand and it is complete.»

I leaned forward and did as he asked, feeling his presence grow almost physically tangible.

When it was all concluded, I looked at the human skull in front of me. Moments ago, it was simply the decorated and slightly macabre remains of a human head. Now the skull exuded a very palpable presence, a true aura.

My scryer spoke a personal greeting and thanks to Hiram as well.

"Hiram, for my part, I want to thank you for being able speak with you and walk with you, for calling Bryan, and allowing me to help. I will always say hello to you when I walk into this home, and I will always say goodbye to you when I leave. I wish you and Bryan great success in your workings together, and I hope that you will share your insight and your wisdom with me. Blessings unto you and all your work."

Afterthoughts on the Hiram Operation

I remember that my scryer and I simply stayed seated a while, staring in awe at the skull before us, marveling at what had just occurred. There was a distinctive change in the atmosphere of not only the magical working room, but also the house in general. It was if there were now another family member or friend in residence and his presence could be sensed clearly. After my scryer and I removed our robes and debriefed a moment upstairs, I went back down to offer Hiram his first meal, consisting of honeycomb covered with chocolate, fresh dates, a honey and olive oil mix, red wine, and bread.

I attempted to speak with him, but my mind started reeling, wondering how or what I was hearing.

Distinctly I heard his familiar tone and it said, «Do not worry; our conversations and interactions will become even clearer as we work together. It will take me a time to become accustomed to this new station and surroundings. Continue with your work and do the work you need to do. I will be here but will be occupied in becoming fully adjusted to this new place.»

One of the first conversations with my new familiar and house Spirit was when he said that he wanted to introduce himself in more depth. He said that it required going into vision, so that he could show me more of who he was and from where he had come. So the following Saturday I found myself down in my working room talking with this Spirit in the skull at 3:33 AM, everything being still and me wrapped in a large hooded cloak I had made because it got cold in my work chamber... And not even a bit of "spookiness" was felt. The humor of this struck me as I realized what the scene would have looked like to anyone else, but for me the feeling was like talking to a long-familiar friend who had memories, experiences, and knowledge which I found fascinating. So I stayed down there for an hour and a half...just talking. I haven't really had a one-on-one with a Spirit like this ever before. Most has been ritualized and formal. The things I learned blew my mind, but the interaction was oddly normal.

My skull Spirit is turning out to be an amazing spiritual as well as magical teacher. I've decided I need to journal every session since I'm always learning from each of our conversations. I've never, ever had continual and impacting conversations like this. One night I was instructed on how my emotions were prodded a variety of times I had already started to forget (but was wondering why I was irritable when I came home). I was made aware of some alterations, and then given a magical technique to bring emotions and energies quickly under control, complete with gestures and words which I had to look up to understand their meaning and origin. Here he was, my advisor, my Spirit within a human skull, and a powerful Spirit from Biblical antiquity, no less. I never quite believed this was possible, and even though I am a magician, magic seen and experienced still places in me in a state of awe.

I began speaking with Hiram every night. My daily ritual took on a new practice. It begins with me lighting the olive oil lamps on my main altar which held images and objects representing balance and the ultimate divine. I then light candles around the magical chamber according to the day and purpose. I bring in food offerings as well as water and sometimes other drink for Hiram and light a candle in a lantern near his place on my bookshelf. After sitting in front of my main altar and offering prayers and doing meditation, I move to sit on a stool in front of Hiram and trace his sigil on the skull while speaking "Hiram, Hiram, Hiram, come from your library and speak." It never takes long for me to hear him greet me with that warm, intelligent voice.

Before Hiram was even conjured and invited into the skull which was to become its physical link and habitation, the Archangel Cassiel made it clear that the Spirit is to be fed and attended to every day. Hiram had no trouble declaring what sorts of offerings he appreciated and how they should be delivered. His diet remained fairly consistent with bread with olive oil and honey, along with dates and figs. I have offered my Spirit a variety of other fruits and breads and drinks, but have always selected quality foods. I'm also informed when the Spirit needs the previous offerings removed and new ones brought forth, but most of the time I do this without having to be asked. The two primary ritual offerings I attend to are Hiram's and the one I leave weekly for the Earth Spirits to protect my home and belongings.

Early in our communications, I remember asking Hiram how he and other Spirits actually "eat" food offerings. He advised me to move closer and asked if I could smell the fruit offerings I had placed in a bowl for him. I responded that I could. He said as soon as the food or liquid offerings come into being, they start to decay and parts of them begin to drift up into the air till they become «of the air» or ethereal, which we can easily detect as smell or scent. The particles of food which dissolve into air he described as the actual nourishing properties of the offerings as they undergo the «natural transformation from substance to spirit» via the process of decay and oxidation, which is a release of energy that Spirits can consume. Incenses, smoke, and vapor also offer a nourishment of a different variety. I thought this lesson from my Spirit was fascinating and pondered if other environmental factors in the area also contributed to a Spirit's nourishment. Perhaps the purported cold spots and rapid temperature fluctuations which are attributed to paranormal activity have commonalities with this phenomenon.

In the realization of the above concept, I became mindful of not leaving prepared foodstuff out in the open. The same went for glasses of water or other consumable liquids, since I didn't need any uninvited guests hanging around expecting free meals.

Tending to a Spirit familiar and its offerings is an ongoing discipline of mindfulness and attention to detail. During the times my family and I went on trips, I informed Hiram and often left larger offerings. In our house, my wife helps tend to the offerings and also speaks with my Spirit when I am away, which she finds enjoyable. Her first experience of being able to see, hear, and converse with a Spirit was with Hiram, and she has become quite fond of him as an honored guest of the house. I cannot fully express the enjoyment having him around has been for the entire family. I have a personal esoteric teacher, assistant, and confidant, and one who also takes it upon himself to be considerate of the family's overall safety and wellbeing.

A related question I put to Hiram was "What would happen if you stopped receiving offerings, and interaction of any kind?" Although I didn't plan on ever stopping my relationship with him, I wondered what would transpire if somehow I were unable to provide offerings and speak with him. If I were suddenly disabled mentally, or restrained, or even after I passed on, what would happen if his skull, his vessel were left unattended, perhaps in a storage box somewhere? The binding enchantment I engraved onto the skull was intended to be everlasting, so I wanted to make sure he would be taken care of somehow.

His reply was, «If I were to be left alone and received no more offerings, and no one was around who could see or hear me, I would simply withdraw until my connection to the physical world became dormant; still residing within the skull, but dormant. Should the skull be broken or lost, I would simply return to my place of origin within the deep ethereal.»

It seems to be the attention, care, and effort which goes into the offerings that makes the difference rather than the amount or expense of them. The interaction and attentiveness keep the relationship strong, vibrant, and relevant for the practitioner and for the familiar.

The Archangel of the Moon
Gabriel

Day and time	On Monday, during hour of Luna
Name and meaning	Hebrew גבריאל *(Gabriel)*, "Strength of God," or "Man of God"
Pronunciation of name (as spoken by the Spirit)	«Ga-bree-el»
Other known forms of name	Gavriel, Gabrielus (Latin), Jibrail and Jibril (Arabic)
Planet	☽
Materials for lamen	Parchment, silver
Sigil	
Direction for Invocation	West
Incense mixture	Euphorbia, bdellium, hellebore root, lignum aloes, camphor, myrtle leaf, clary sage, davana, geranium, wormwood, eucalyptus, rosemary.

*Table VII-10. **Evocatory Correspondences for Gabriel***[42]

Of Gabriel and the Office of the Moon

Next to Archangel Michael, Archangel Gabriel is the Angelic being of greatest renown and record. He is the messenger, the equalizer, and the sound which strips hierarchy, a cosmic sound of harmony which no being can disregard. The trumpet of judgment is the dispenser of true equality of creation before the Eyes of the Source. Fear may arise in those who refuse to acknowledge equality, who withold compassion and empathy towards other beings. True and unerring equality beyond the machinations of humankind seems to be the power of this Archangel of the Moon, whose reflected light bathes all beyond shadows.

The Moon is considered the entry and exit point between the world of manifestation and the Celestial realm of the Angels and ascendant Spirits. From the Kabbalistic viewpoint, all of the emanations of the higher Sephiroth are

42. Please see the Cautionary Warning Regarding Grimoric Ingredients in Appendix A. —APF

funneled through the sphere of Yesod. Gabriel is the Archangel responsible for ushering souls from the realm of Earth to the plane of Spirit.

In the Christian tradition, Gabriel is portrayed as sounding the trumpet on the day of the Last Judgment (1 Thes. 4.16). In Islam, Gabriel revealed the *Qur'an* to Muhammad, becoming the Angel of truth. In art and literature, Gabriel is most often depicted as the Angel of the Annunciation, in which role he often carries a lily, the symbol of the Virgin. He is often represented on churches with trumpet raised and facing east, ready to proclaim the second coming of Christ.

The *Catholic Encyclopedia* calls attention to the rarity of Angels in the Bible, only three Archangels being mentioned. Further,

> Only four appearances of Gabriel are recorded: In *Daniel* 8, he explains the vision of the horned ram as portending the destruction of the Persian Empire by the Macedonian Alexander the Great, after whose death the kingdom will be divided up among his generals, from one of whom will spring Antiochus Epiphanes. In chapter 9, after Daniel had prayed for Israel, we read that "the man Gabriel, flying swiftly touched me" and he communicated to him the mysterious prophecy of the "seventy weeks" of years which should elapse before the coming of Christ. In chapter 10, it is not clear whether the angel is Gabriel or not, but at any rate we may apply to him the marvelous description in verses 5 and 6.
>
> In the New Testament, Gabriel foretells the birth of the Precursor, to Zachary. To Mary he proclaims that she is to be the mother of the Savior.[43]

When first I conjured Archangel Gabriel, he appeared as a tall figure with long hair mixed of dark and bright white. Besides his eyes, little of his features could be discerned, as his entire face seemed to glow outward into a bright halo, which caused the crystal to shimmer. More incredible was the long silver horn he held. The detail and intricacies of the instrument was unlike anything I had ever seen. I remember thinking that "the Angel blowing a horn" was sort of cliché and was surprised to actually see the being holding it when I conjured him. Gabriel's robes appeared a majestic blue and silver, with accents that seemed to trail on forever behind him. A bright night sky filled with stars larger and brighter than what can be seen on earth created the backdrop. The Angel's voice was very melodic and reminded me of the sounds crystal glasses made when

43. Hugh T. Pope, "Gabriel," in *The Catholic Encyclopedia, Volume VI* (New York: Robert Appleton Company, 1909).

filled with water. It sent sensations of gentle pressure from my forehead to the sides of my temples as he spoke.

Fig. VII-11. ***Lamen of Gabriel in the manner of DSIC***

Gabriel has long been associated with the Astral and dream worlds, the nebulous realm between life and death. I remember that my dreams took up sharp clarity and were more vivid after encountering and conversing with him. One of the Archangel's initial messages to me was that the deeds, fears, and hopes of humanity are all heard by him and brought to the Father. His chalice or cauldron was the other great symbol he held before him and it indeed represented the deep oceans of the subconscious and the dream of creation itself. Anyone wishing for their spirit to ascend to the furthest heavens must not be afraid to be baptized in the deepest well.

Initially I had planned to evoke all of the great Archangels in order with my scryer so that he would undergo the same progression and initiation that I had. Although it had not turned out that way with the first six planetary Archangels, the ritual circuit was once again being completed with Gabriel.

Gabriel is indeed the Archangel of the celestial gateway, the divine messenger between the world of form and the spiritual realm. Through him, the communication between all the previous spheres and his own can be accomplished. The crystal sphere, which is used to descry these beings, is listed as the stone attributed to Archangel Gabriel in *The Three Books of Occult Philosophy* by Agrippa. Besides the seeing stone, I was aware that the handle for the knife Cassiel described was also made of crystal stone. Not only that but silver and pearl were also components, all of which I knew to be Lunar corresponding materials and thus within the office of Archangel Gabriel.

A Monday, early evening operation was set for the third hour of the Moon. I was excited for my scryer and me to have contacted all of the seven Planetary

Archangels successfully. Although a magical ritual was never a sure thing, our level of contact and interaction had been amplifying with each attempt so I saw no reason why the next session would not go smoothly.

By the time my scryer arrived, we had just enough time to wash and prepare for the conjuration.

Invocation of the Archangel Gabriel

Fig. VII-12. ***Section of Circle with Heptameron Correspondences for Drawing Gabriel into the Crystal***

Appearance of the Spirit

SCRYER: The Angel appears standing on a plain of silver white. The sky appears like twilight behind him and a single star is seen over his left shoulder. He has long, long black hair. The features of the Angel are sometimes male, sometimes female, as if moving slightly between the two, but always with the same characteristics. The Angel holds a silver chalice, inlaid with pearl and sapphire. His wings are gray and wrapped closely about him and his vestments. He wears a red sash and black and white vestments, with inlay on the cuffs and hem as in the Greek-style square spirals. Occasionally a shooting star shoots across the sky behind the Angel.

OPENING QUESTION 1: In the name of the holy and undefiled Spirit, the Father, the begotten Son, and Holy Ghost proceeding from both, what is thy true name?

SCRYER: The Angel sings: *(Singing:)* «Gaaa-Bree-el.» The «Ga» echoes like thunder or a trumpet call, the «Bri» feels like millions of people raising their hands to God, and the «El» surrounds all of it.

OPENING QUESTION 2: What is thy office?

(Scryer's voice takes on a melodic and pensive tone.)

SPIRIT: «The twilight and the dusk. A ring of light and dark that moves as a halo around the Earth. The place where birth and death are one. The calling of the final trumpet, echoing the cry of a child. Black and white together, woven, fused to create, to destroy, to bring forth and mold with fate. My office is to move life as a great wave around the surface of the Earth.»

OPENING QUESTION 3: What is thy true sign or character?

SCRYER: He raises the chalice overhead and above the chalice is the crescent of the moon. From the crescent moon pours water into the cup. I see a fish gleaming in the water as it falls into the chalice. Gabriel then sings... which sounds like moving water. In rolls peace and stars.

OPENING QUESTION 4: When are the times most agreeable to thy nature to hold conference with us?

SPIRIT: «The day of the Moon. When the Moon is near full and at the zenith of Pisces, Cancer, and Taurus.»

OATH: Wilt thou swear by the holy blood of Jesus Christ that thou art truly Gabriel?

GABRIEL: «I swear by my Father's most Holy Son, I am Gabriel: Who moves in the Moon. Who is the gateway for souls to enter and leave, who dances around the Earth, watching, protecting all life. My beautiful, unique, special children, all.»

QUESTION 6: What are your views on humanity? What are your roles and involvements and interactions?

GABRIEL: «I see all life as my children. I see human, plant, animal, coral, tree, lichen as my charges. I remember when a human first awoke, and beheld the life around them. In that youth, in that purity there was no hierarchy, just one being marveling at the life of another; no better than, no worse than. A life beholding life. And although many of you are cursed with the sickness of hierarchy, I see life equally, the same. And in death, which all beings come to, our ground is the same. I strip the false discernment of men from their eyes to behold life as brother, sister, and kin. This teaching is the sound of my trumpet.»

QUESTION 7: What times and instances have you interceded on human affairs? How have you intervened in the past and currently?

GABRIEL: «I have spoken to prophets in song and poetry. When the Sufi dances, he spins just as I move around the earth. I have shown men how to dance. I have cut their hearts open that they may bleed poetry. I have melted the hardness and tyranny of kings with the sight of a child. I have called the hardest of men and women out of their stone walls and into a place where they know they are the same.»

QUESTION 8: Do you have your own recollection of your creation and origin? Where do you come from? What is your purpose?

GABRIEL: «Yes. I remember faint sound, an embrace all around me, warm. I remember a glowing, growing light. Beneath me a great hand that pulsed with change, pure change. I raised higher and higher toward the light and when I broke through I saw around me a vast ocean and I beheld my Father smiling on me. Above me, the uncountable stars with their planets and their moons. Within a wind that whispered into my ears, I knew and could see the birth of all beings, all of my Father's precious children, that he would cover the universe with life, and bring them back in death. I would see and feel and know every single one. I remember the salt water on my lips, the way the starlight danced on the water and my pure, open, naked form. And together, before I spoke a word, my Father and I laughed and laughed.»

QUESTION 9: What advice can you give us to work and speak with you in the most beneficial ways?

GABRIEL: «When you behold life: the dog, the bird, the tree, remember the sameness. Annihilate the hierarchy in your mind. Drown it in the ocean

Fig. VII-13. ***Portrait of Gabriel as beheld in Vision***

of my chalice. When the moon rises, know that the light of my rays embraces all beings. that you are but one of my many beloved children. And in times of death and in times of birth in the twilight between life, death, night, day, that is my halo. When you speak in that place, I cannot help but hear. Fill your chalice with water in the twilight, blow your horns above it. When you do, my spirit rushes into the waters. Use it to heal, use it to quench thirst, use it to bless in the name of my Father, crossed with the deathbed of his son and laugh like my father and I and do not speak a word.»

QUESTION 10: How can we perceive Spirits better? In what ways can we improve our Spiritual and Astral sight? Are you able to bless us with this ability?

GABRIEL: «Use the water from the chalice from which I told you how to anoint and bless. When anointed on the forehead, it opens the eye. When anointed on the ears, it lends to the hearing of Spirits. When anointed on the nose, the scent of Spirits. When anointed on the heart, the empathy, the feel of Spirits. On this anointing, sing my name as you have heard it, *Gaaaa-BREE-el*. In the twilight facing the west, speak to your ancestors, to your friends who have gone. To those you admire who have left, openly, honestly, without deception, and this will open the way. At deathbeds and at births, remember me and know that my hand is upon them and they move simply from one state to another, world without end.»

QUESTION 11: Archangel Gabriel, are you aware of the knife which Archangel Cassiel instructed us to make that is used to cut the ties with any Spirit and visit retribution upon them? The materials he suggested were «clear crystal stone, pearl, and silver» which all seemed to correspond to Lunar qualities. Can you give us more insight?

GABRIEL: «Yes. As I bring all Spirits in, and bring all of them out, those materials cut that cord and reshape the fate that I have sewn through the will, strength and power of Cassiel who alone decides the time of reaping and harvest. As the magician wields the knife, when their hand embraces the silver and the pearl, I am called to help, to aid, in the severing, the cutting, and the reshaping of fate. Therefore, we, my brother and I, become one in the blade and in its work. It is like a scythe that cuts through time.»

QUESTION 12: How much does the Moon really affect our magical works and conversing with Spirits? In which ways? Are there phases or times to avoid or ones particularly beneficial to working with Spirits and Angels? Any to look out for and not do invocations or evocations?

GABRIEL: «When the Moon is void, I turn myself away to rest, to be at peace, to remember my purpose, my Father. When the Moon is void, do not call on me. All of my other times and phases are like the masks of the otherworld; of the place where spirits, demons, angels, devas, ancestors, and ghosts walk. Each phase is a shaped doorway through which the magician may step, lending power, lending resonance. When in the zenith of a constellation, the power is enhanced. Darker of the moon, waning to new gifts of the inside. Lighter of the Moon, from new to waxing, gifts for the outside. When you are born, when you will die, the doorway, shapes the destiny, the quality of its light and shadow, the measure of its need. The stars that uphold it, the catalyst of its story. All subject to the will of God.»

QUESTION 13: My wife consistently sees numbers in groups. She often sees 111, 333, 44, or 444; do you know the meaning if any behind this?

GABRIEL: «The numbers are doorways opening into the experience of her ancestors and to the times when her redeemed ancestors shelter her. Like tumblers in a lock, they align and open. 1, for sovereignty. 4, for stability. 3, for energy. 2, for love. Pray at these times for the quality they represent. Have her speak openly of her fears in private, when none may listen. Ask for Hiram's help, and beseech me to open the door a little wider. Those are the times of the most power for her, but she must pry her hands into the door gently and with prayer, open them.»

QUESTION 14: It is said that you revealed the *Qur'an* to Muhammad; is this so?

GABRIEL: «I sang sweetly, gently to Muhammad, peace was upon him. And the song I heard from my Father, I sang to him. Had the frail form of the prophet heard the song of the Father directly, he would have been broken. So I sang for Allah, I spoke for Allah and I knew and wept at the teachings that poured through me, like a master plays his flute. In a cave on a mountain, blessed by a single star, the Moon, me, cradling the prophet, singing to him the song of God.»

QUESTION 15: Where you indeed the great Archangel that brought news to Mary that her son would be Christ? Would you be able to share your personal account of this with us?

GABRIEL: «Yes, though it took time for her to understand. It took many visits, although she knew in her heart it was true from the very start. But a mother fears for her son. Especially when she knows that as a child of God, he cannot be sheltered, he cannot be protected, and never fully understood. I would come to her in the mornings, in the evenings, and she would turn me away. There were times when her burdens were greater than her son's. Eventually she understood, she knew, she accepted, and it was in that moment, that acceptance, one of the greatest acts of devotion to the Father that I have seen. For a mother to give her son into the uncertain hands of an unknown God, with nothing but prayer and faith as a path to walk upon is a miracle.»

QUESTION 16: Great and bright Archangel of the heavenly Moon, do you have any further instruction, insight, or wisdom to impart to us?

GABRIEL: «Listen for the call of my trumpet, in the dawn, in the twilight. Sound the horns yourself in that time, and all who hear will be reminded that they are but one among equals of all forms of life that surround them. In that blast, in that call, the deep remembrance of your sameness will flicker to wakefulness. Some for a lifetime, some for a moment. My trumpet is that call, the reminder of the end that is the beginning. The halo that spins around the earth, and is never broken. Annihilate your hierarchy.»

(License to Depart.)

Afterthoughts on the Gabriel Operation

SCRYER: It is really difficult to describe from my perspective but he was just so peaceful, so at peace, more so than all the others. It felt so good to be around especially after these last few days. It just felt so wonderful to be in his presence. You know, I'll never look at the Muslim holy symbol the same again. The moon and star, it is Gabriel, holding the prophet and singing to him. I mean, I'm not Muslim, but that was beautiful! I got a clear image of someone blowing a horn or trumpet at dusk which rang out and reminded all who heard it that there is no hierarchy in the sight of God. The sound was to remind everyone that we are all one, all the same under the heavens.

OPERATOR: He truly does seem like the Spirit involving the peacefulness and ease of transitions. Very peaceful and very pleasant to be in the presence of. The angel's responses were very poetic and somewhat mysterious but at the same time clear in the picture they painted. There was much more music emphasized, much more interwoven meaning and exchange communicated in a wonderfully harmonic way. This Archangel definitely embodies the truer aspect of moving between the worlds.

The Chalice of Anointing

After further review of the operation with Archangel Gabriel, I was able to put together the ritual involving a chalice. All the elements were related piecemeal by the Archangel in a poetic and rather mysterious manner. If the responses from our questions were put together, it reveals a detailed structure in which to perform this ceremony. The most potent time to conduct this ritual would be on a Monday when the Moon is near full and at the zenith of Pisces, Cancer, or Taurus. For this ritual I would arrange an altar in the west within a magical circle. I would set this either outside or at least visible to the sky to catch the rays of the moon. An altar arrangement similar to the one used for the Water Elemental journey would be appropriate with the themes and corresponding materials being in agreement with the Lunar aspects of the ritual. The chalice should be positioned in the center portion of the altar with a basin or pitcher of purified water or holy water nearby.

Also included would be a horn for magical purposes. The Hebrew shofar ritual horn would seem appropriate, as would the trumpet in *The Key of Solomon*. That implement it is briefly described as "a trumpet made of new wood,

Fig. VII-14. Names and Characters for the Solomonic Trumpet

on the one side of which shall be written in Hebrew with the pen and ink of the art these Names of God, ELOHIM GIBOR, ELOHIM TZABAOTH, and on the other side these characters." (See Fig. VII-14.) The magus is then instructed in its use.

> Having entered into the circle to perform the experiment, he should sound his trumpet towards the four quarters of the Universe, first towards the East, then towards the South, then towards the West, and lastly towards the North. Then let him say:—
>
> Hear ye, O spirit N, I command you. Hear ye, and be ye ready, in whatever part of the Universe ye may be, to obey the voice of God the mighty one, and the names of the Creator. We let you know by this signal and sound that ye will be convoked hither, wherefore hold ye yourselves in readiness to obey our commands.[44]

Instead of sounding the trumpet towards the four quarters of the Universe, I would sound it into the West only for this ritual.

As the Moon rises, during twilight, allow the light of the Moon to shine on the chalice and sing the name of Gabriel. Fill a silver ritual chalice (possibly beset by pearls and sapphires) with water in the twilight. The Archangel instructed to «blow your horns above it.» The Archangel stated that when the horns were blown, his Spirit «rushes into the waters.» It was also suggested that the sign of the cross should be made over the water in the chalice. The waters could be used to heal, to quench thirst, and to bless. The waters would also be used to anoint parts of the head in order to communicate more clearly with Spiritual beings The anointing should be done in silence.

The Knife of Cassiel ✠ Part 2

Although I failed to ask more pointed questions about its creation and consecration, I received a bit more insight as to how the crystal-handled knife functioned between the offices of Cassiel and Gabriel. I became increasingly fascinated with its creation, but still felt that I needed a bit more information

44.Mathers and Solomon, *op. cit.*, Book II, Chapter 7.

before attempting to create such a potent magical tool. I wanted to make sure I had all the details as clear as I possibly could. I felt either another conjuration of Archangel Cassiel was in order, or perhaps a consultation with Hiram would help me determine the proper course of action. After questioning the Archangel on the knife, Gabriel made it clear that both he and Cassiel came together to empower the function of the knife.

The responses I received from both of the Angels put in perspective just how powerful and how dangerous this knife would be when properly consecrated and empowered per the Archangels' instructions. If it could truly perform the sort of acts Archangel Gabriel was describing, a person could sever any sort of Spirit from himself as he chose. This means negative and evil Spirits, but also good and helpful ones as well. Indeed a magician could separate any Spiritual being from himself or others if the knife was utilized by a magician who understood how to use it.

The ramifications of changing fate utilizing the crystal-handled knife could be far-reaching, possibly beyond death, subsequent lifetimes, or future generations. Any number of interwoven patterns of destiny, design, and spiritual interaction might be significantly altered by its use. I daresay the improper application of this knife could likely curse or destroy a person beyond reckoning. I did not care to test the limits of what it could accomplish but planned to make it as an implement of last resort. A weapon, any weapon in the wrong hands can be a tool of destruction and horror. A weapon which is imbued with the power of the most powerful Archangels is a considerable responsibility—if not liability—that should not be taken lightly.

I set about finding two sets of three pearls that I could fix to the crystal of the Mughal-style knife I had purchased. I planned to do some more silver work to keep them in place against the crystal handle. The effect left a beautiful triangular display of three pearls on either side of the handle near the blade.

Later that evening while sitting down in my chamber to talk to Hiram, I remembered to ask him about the knife and what I would need to complete it. He said, «You will have all of the information you need after you consult another being of Cassiel's office. The knife will successfully be made and you will know when the time is right to fashion it.»

His advice was rather matter of fact and to the point, so I didn't question him further and turned my attention to the next phase of evocations I had planned.

Afterthoughts on Revisting the Seven Planetary Archangels

As if by design, my scryer and I found ourselves dealing with issues and events related to the offices of each Archangel in the period leading up to and following the evocations. The nature of these events far exceeded the simple explanation that our attention was on the Planetary correspondences, and so we were more likely to notice corresponding events. Occurrences coinciding with the aspects of each Planetary lesson unfolded in ways I will never forget.

The lessons of each successful operation continue to present themselves at intermittent times. I will recognize the benefits of newfound thought, consideration, and action. During many of the operations there were analogies of locks and keys that the Archangels described. I feel as I have access to levels of thinking and acting which were inaccessible to me before, or at least I was unaware of in the moment. Since contacting these mighty Archangels again with my scryer, I feel as if they have blessed me with access to new levels of insight and aptitude in areas both dynamic and sublime.

VIII
The Conjuration of the Supercelestial Angels

THE WORK WITH MY SCRYER felt far from complete after going through the experiences of the seven Archangels of the Planetary spheres. There were several other Spirit beings in both religious and magical traditions that I had yet to contact. Among these were the other significant Angels not ascribed to the seven Planets of that classical cosmological model. Some were considered by esoteric scholars to be "Angels of Earth," but somehow seemed to be nearer to the divine Source at the same time. It seemed to me these particular Archangels were somehow transcendent in regards to specific hierarchies or Planetary associations. The first of these Angels was Archangel Uriel, often portrayed as being a significant counselor to mankind during auspicious times.

There were still a number of other Angels from religious and magical lore that I wished to contact, but Uriel was primary among these interests. My curiosity prompted me to plan an evocation despite not having a symbol or sigil that stemmed from the same sources as the seven Planetary Archangels. I also could not locate a specific time and date associated with the Archangel. Whereas the seven Planetary Archangels are all supplied with specific gestures and symbols to call them forth, Archangel Uriel was elusive in such categories. Regardless, factors came together which allowed me to formulate the ritual with enough detail to feel confident to conduct the ritual. I honestly was unsure of what to expect due to the somewhat ambiguous accounts of those who had made contact with this being previously.

The Archangel
Uriel

✠ Day and time	On Saturday (?)
✠ Name and meaning	Hebrew אוריאל *(Uriel)*, "God Is My Light" or "Light of God"
✠ Pronunciation of name (as spoken by the Spirit)	«Uu-ree-el»
✠ Other possible names	Nuriel, Phanuel
✠ Planet	⊕/☉/♅
✠ Materials for lamen	Parchment, platinum, silver
✠ Sigils	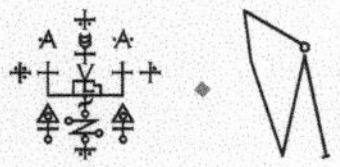
✠ Direction for Invocation	North
✠ Incense mixture	Jasmine, galangal, storax
✠ Candles	Violet-colored beeswax candles with engraved sigils and name of the Archangel.

Table VIII-1. ***Evocatory Correspondences for Uriel***[1]

Of Uriel

My only real familiarity with Archangel Uriel was through his association with being the Archangel of the Earth and the North in the Golden Dawn system of magic. Specifically, my one reference to him was in The Lesser Banishing Ritual of the Pentagram, a magical exercise I became adept in performing after practicing it twice daily for a number of years. After a time, I did perceive the presences of each Archangel and could even behold a semblance of their anthropomorphic presence in various colors and sensations. However, the experiences were never to the degree of clarity and interaction as the ceremonies of *DSIC*. It seemed to me I did not quite fully have an appreciation or knowledge of this particular being and I was curious to get to know him in a much clearer fashion.

Besides his given name and title, I did not have much practical knowledge of Uriel besides what could be found in historical texts and a few modern

1. Please see the Cautionary Warning Regarding Grimoric Ingredients in Appendix A. —APF

interpretations. There were no Planetary correspondences from which to garner a more complete record of his offices. His sometime association with the Planet Uranus was unfounded in the classical Chaldean order model of the universe. In the original text of *DSIC*, Archangel Uriel is at one point referred to as the Archangel of Venus, which later does not coincide as Archangel Anael is given that category. However, he is once again included as one of the four primarily Archangels upholding the directions along with Michael, Raphael, and Gabriel. As an Archangel of the Quarters, Uriel is typically the Angel of the North, across from Michael. In *DSIC*, the four balancing Archangels are written around the gold disk of the ebony pedestal as equally balancing and governing celestial powers.

Fig. VIII-2. ***The Lamen of Uriel in the manner of DSIC***

Archangel Uriel is not mentioned by name in the canonical books of the Hebrew or Christian Bibles, but he is named several times in *The Book of Enoch*. He serves as one of Enoch's principal guides and teachers in his vision. Uriel is one of the Archangels who asks for God to intervene to save humankind from the influence of the fallen Angels, the Watchers, and he is sent to inform Noah to build his ark in preparation for the Flood. Michael, Raphael, and Gabriel also have roles in dealing with the Fallen Angels and the Flood. Later, three more Archangels are named to make the traditional seven: Raguel, Saraqael, and Remiel.

There were unfortunately not many examples of invocations to directly call Archangel Uriel that I could find in classical texts. Although I planned to use the format given in *DSIC*, I sought prayers associated with him to perhaps get a better idea of his offices and perceived interactions with mankind.

An Anglican intercessional prayer to Saint Uriel the Archangel is as follows:

Oh holy St. Uriel, intercede for us that our hearts may burn with the fire of the Sacred Heart of Jesus. Assist us in co-operating with the graces of our confirmation that the gifts of the Holy Spirit may bear much fruit in our souls. Obtain for us the grace to use the sword of truth to pare away all that is not in conformity to the most adorable Will of God in our lives, that we may fully participate in the army of the Church Militant. Amen.[2]

Preparing for the Invocation of Uriel

Mid-April was an interesting time where a few rare astrological events and alignments were occurring or would be occurring, and with a surprising frequency that hadn't been seen in quite some time. Specifically four "Blood Moons" would be happening in the next six months, and all of them happened to be landing on Jewish holidays which seemed perfect for planning a magical working. During a total Lunar eclipse, the Moon is entirely immersed in Earth's shadow, causing it to take on a glowing rust or "blood" color. Without a certain day or time that specifically related to Uriel, and inspired by his posssible association with the Planet Uranus, corresponding to inspiration, astrology, and the unexpected, I decided spontaneously that an unusual astrological event would be an auspicious time to do the evocation. I set the day of evocation for the first of the series of four total eclipses of the Moon between April and September in what scientists were calling a Lunar-eclipse "tetrad" series. Often such times were considered to be hazardous for any sort of magical or talismanic working; however I felt somehow compelled to attempt an evocation during this time.

2. Church of St. Uriel the Archangel webite, "Our Patron Saint" (http://www.urielsg.org/our-patron-saint).

Invocation of the Archangel Uriel

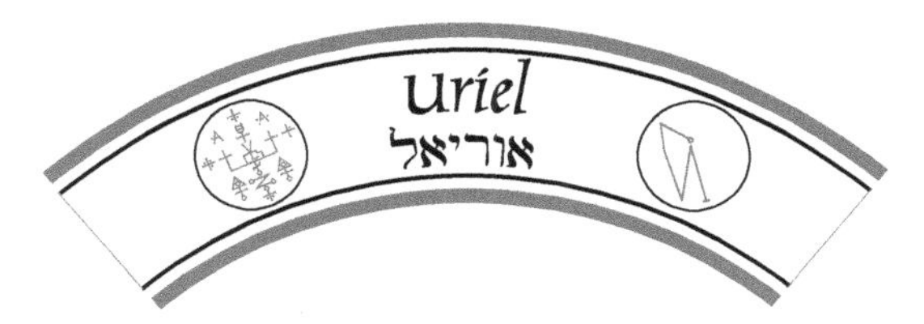

Fig. VIII-3. Section of Circle with Correspondences for Drawing Uriel into the Crystal

(Note: Whether from the unknown presence and association of the Angel, or the being itself, a very foreign, alien presence filled the magical chamber, which gave a rather eerie feeling.)

Appearance of the Spirit

SCRYER: Uriel appears as a loosely anthropomorphic cosmic formation, nebula, or a galaxy, but I only see the upper part of his torso and his head formed by the nebula and the galaxy, as if they are one in the same. He is looking away from me into the depths of the universe. His wings are so big they are nearly impossible to perceive. His mouth is slightly open. He says «I am in my Father's House.»

Opening Questions[3]

OPENING QUESTION 1: In the name of the holy and undefiled Spirit, the Father, the begotten Son, and Holy Ghost proceeding from both, what is thy true name?

SCRYER: He opens his mouth and draws me in and I see a large group of people in a circle holding hands. They are singing his name as they surround a person in the middle who is riddled with pain or possessed by some torment. I come back out of his mouth again and he sings the first two syllables, which feels like the gathering of immense power. It's very deep

3. The Opening Questions, as always, are the probationary queries specified by the *The Art of Drawing Spirits into Crystals* as those proper to begin the conversation with any evoked Spirit. The administration of the Oath constitutes the fifth Opening Question. They are worded according to Barrett's translation. —APF

and it rolls like thunder, it even seems to make the stars vibrate. His voice sounds like a Tibetan throat singer or the deeper Gregorian chant that I've heard. The «Re-el» sends out the amassed power in every direction.

OPENING QUESTION 2: What is thy office?

(Scryer's voice takes on a tone that is very difficult to describe.)

SPIRIT: «The stewardship of the house of my God, my Father. Globes of vast water, speaking and murmuring, whispering, opening of primal depths, encompassing Tiamat.[4] Holding choruses of sound. Moving like water through all things, that pulse with the fires of God. Rushing like torrents, rushing like stones, rolling with the thunder of the first word.»

OPENING QUESTION 3: What is thy true sign or character?

SCRYER: I see a distant, faint light, unified, unapproachable, unknowable. Two shadows are cast from this light forming two great crosses, one black, one white, male then female, dark, light. All spoken from within the cosmic mouth of Uriel.

OPENING QUESTION 4: When are the times most agreeable to thy nature to hold conference with us?

SPIRIT: «When time is no time. When day is like night and night is like day. Found in the quiet after the last breath, before the lights. In the murmur of oblivion, holding time in the palm of your hand as an unimportant toy to be cast aside. Open fully to the first word.»

OATH: Wilt thou swear by the holy blood of Jesus Christ that thou art truly Archangel Uriel?

URIEL: «I swear by Jesus Christ, Who became my Father manifest in the flesh, that I am Uriel.»

4. In the mythology of Sumeria, Assyria, Akkadia and Babylon, Tiamat is a mighty sea monster of primordial chaos, an ancient Goddess of destruction and reformation who is sometimes portrayed as a mighty sea serpent or dragon.

Fig. VIII-4. ***Portrait of Uriel as beheld in Vision***

Further Questions

QUESTION 6: Great Archangel Uriel what are your views on humanity? What are your roles and interactions with us?

URIEL: «Blessed as, important as humanity may be, my voice runs through all space and time. I sing the first word to enliven the fabric of eternity, rolling through gnat, house, star, comet, stone, man, and woman, all enlivened and purified by my song. Sometimes humanity feels remote, far away, and I forget. And sometimes I hear something sing back to me, sometimes one lonely voice, sometimes nations, and someday all of you will, but the time of that song has not yet come.»

QUESTION 7: Can you explain your role as the Archangel of "Fire and Light"? Do you have a Planetary or Heavenly sphere of association as do the other Archangels? What is your dominion?

URIEL: «Fire and light are the vibration, the symptom, the effect of the Word. Fire and light, the heat and the quick flashing spark of the divine Word. In every star, in every planet, reflecting again the first light, the first word, there I am. Echo upon echo upon echo of light. The divine recombobulation of my glorious Father. Beyond time, enfolding it, shaping it, bending it, creating it.»

QUESTION 8: Can you explain the relevance and information of what is said of you being one of the Four Angels of Presence? What about being "The guardian of Tartarus" as explained in *Enoch*, that God placed the Archangel Uriel in charge of the world and of Tartarus?[5]

URIEL: «Tartarus: Deep, black, void, pulling, older than the old. When standing at its gate, my voice is the key and the lock. The other three Angels of Presence are linked.»

SCRYER: He shows me a ray of light extending way off into space, and distantly it gets crossed by another ray of light like a giant crossroads or equal-

5. Tartarus or Tartaros is the dark underworld in Greek mythology where Zeus imprisoned the Titans. In *Enoch*, it is generally understood to be the place where 200 Watchers (fallen Angels) are imprisoned.

armed cross. It looks like the 'gates' are the other three terminuses of the lines...I'm beginning to hear some really disturbing sound!

(Scryer makes some startled, nervous sounds.)

SCRYER: Okay I can't stand to listen to these sounds any longer.

QUESTION 9: What allowances are there to intercede on human affairs? What evidence of your actions is there in the world? What can you teach us and assist us with concerning your role and how it relates to creation?

SCRYER: He shows me mountains lifting through seas; he shows me cracks opening and water is pouring in. He shows me pillars of ash, and the rumble of volcanoes, all of them with sound. Great rushing sound.

URIEL: «And those sounds are but minuscule echoes of the Word, to the ears of my Father, barely audible. The chanting of monks, and the drum, and the lullaby, and the thunder.»

QUESTION 10: What can you teach us of true Alchemy, of the hidden knowledge of the occult, magic and working with Spirits?

SCRYER: He shows me the image of three people holding hands sitting down together, chanting his name again and again. Now he shows me you...singing over a dagger, over a staff, over a crystal, over a fire.

URIEL: «In any ceremony when using song, chant, before the song is uttered, remember consciously that what comes from your mouth—the sound—know that it is the echo of the first Word. It is a shard of God. When resonated and sung in this manner, it is potent. It is me singing with you. The sound you must feel it vibrate all of your body, even your hair to your toenails. Feel the sound in the body chanting. And trust that I am there. Remember the Word.»

QUESTION 11: Great Archangel, do you have your own recollection of your creation and origin? Where do you come from? What is your purpose?

URIEL: «I see no beginning. I see no end. In my thoughts, the Creator forgot the Alpha and the Omega. I do not conceive time as you. Explaining it by beginning and my end will be beyond your understanding. This question I cannot answer.»

Question 12: What advice can you give us to work and speak with you in the most beneficial ways? Is there any significance to tonight's Moon and eclipse?

Uriel: «It is I who called you here tonight. In the time that is no time, the full Moon that is black, the noon Sun that is dark. In the times that cannot be recognized as time, just as my birth, just as my death, the Word is beyond time. The Word moves through me and I am one of its echoes.»

Question 13: Great Archangel, can you impart to us any further knowledge on the magical tools or talismans to best harness the benefits of your office? Can you impart to us any unique talisman or magical method to benefit from the positive powers of your office? What were the images of the tools you showed us? Were they magical Elemental tools?

Uriel: «Tools are tools, whether Elemental, Angelic, Demonic, exalted or profane, it is the Word that enlivens them. You may sing over a staff, or sing over the body of your wife. Or whisper in her ear, when remembering the Word. The song is changed. The presence of creation becomes—now—tithed together in the folding of space and the folding of time, of the Word to the moment. Opening hearts, removing barriers, cleaning souls.»

Question 14: Archangel Uriel, are you able to give us a prophecy which will be impacting for us and those near and dear to us? Do you have any other advice for us individually and together in our continued work and lives?

Scryer: He shows me a group of people of many different traditions, their uniting purpose to sing hope into the hearts of men and women. They are oriented specifically in that one purpose. He shows me a symbol of a white fire crowning a halo. Beneath it a perfect globe of gray stone. Each one understanding the power of the Word. Each consciously recognizing their voice as its shard and echo of the ultimate Divine, constantly resurrecting the Son (Sun?) with the voice.

OPERATOR: Great and powerful Archangel Uriel, we thank you for your attendance upon this operation and ask that we receive your blessings and that the power of your song resonate in our soul.

(License to Depart given.)

Afterthoughts on the Uriel Operation

OPERATOR: I seriously felt like I was in a trance myself during most of this operation. It was as if I lost sense of where I was or any sense of time passing. Although the angel is attributed to earth such as in the Golden Dawn aspect and others as the fourth primary angel, this being was unique in all respects. If anything, this archangel felt really 'alien,' quite remote and removed from humanity in many ways. When you started repeating how the people were singing his name, I started swaying and seeing lights. At the same time, my mouth opened wanting to feel the vibration that was coming from these singers. It was hard to explain but I wanted to blend or integrate his presence into myself somehow.

When you reported that Uriel showed a "symbol of a white fire crowning a halo and beneath was a perfect globe of gray stone," I thought this may be a potent symbol for him. I wonder if this is somehow combined with the "two shadows are cast from this light forming two great crosses, one black, one white," that you reported making up his true character?

SCRYER: This operation was really disorienting. Totally different, totally different than the others. This Angel was unlike anything I could even compare something to. I find that I'm having difficulty making sense or connecting the experiences together in my head. I remember I was looking at those rays of light when you asked about him being a guardian over Tartarus. I was looking down from where those rays of lights were coming from, and there was some sort of sound that absolutely frightened me. It felt and sounded like I was at the bottom of an enormous globe and right below me was that disturbing sound. The sounds were coming from something immeasurably large which I didn't want to see the origin from, I don't think I could have handled it. It was as if some ancient, primordial Gods or beings that were beyond the comprehension of man were being contained below. The noises sounded like some sort of murmuring that chilled me to the bone. I don't think the Angel was trying to scare me by showing me this, but I felt so minute and insignificant. Humanity seemed

> like such a small thing to him. However, it was fascinating when he stated that we could «sing» back to him. When you sang his name at the end, it gave me chills because it sounded eerily familiar to the sound I was hearing come from him. How did you do that? I clearly remember him saying, «Remember consciously that what comes from your mouth—the sound—know that it is the echo of the first Word. It is a shard of God.» That seemed really powerful and important. I'm not sure what to make of that, very different. There is such subtlety to their responses, but at the same time, profound and almost obvious after they answer. I won't forget this one, that's for sure!

Further research in comparative myths and legends brought me to references of a Roman sky God named Cælus, from which the English word "celestial" is derived. The God is thought to be a counterpart of the Greek Ouranos or Uranus with connections to the cult of Mithras. There are accounts of Roman writers using Cælus to describe their conception of the Jewish celestial God that resided in the highest Heavens. The description of this God is strikingly appropriate to a Spirit that would be "beyond" the seven known spheres. Cælus is a God of the upper Æther, which puts him beyond the Planetary intelligences. There is also the Greek myth of Uranus imprisoning Gaia's children the *Gigantes* or Giants in Tartarus, another place where the myths possibly crossed over. The Enochic lore of Uriel being a guardian over Tartarus leads me to think there may be more to this being than I originally considered.

Being in the presence of these mighty beings always effected more change than I could ever predict or fully understand. I wondered truly if the Archangel had indeed "summoned me" as it proclaimed. I could not seem to fathom what I could have done to draw its attention or why it would bother. However, the plan to conjure it on the Blood Moon seemed to happen quite spontaneously.

The following operations my scryer and I conducted after evoking Archangel Uriel took on an even more profound transformation when I spoke the invocations. Indeed, my voice seemed to be amplified with power as soon as I began speaking in magical ritual. Perhaps the change was needed for the following beings we were to evoke. Much of the effect and power behind the spoken word has already been covered in the section dealing with the Magician's Voice, but the "song," the music and harmony and melodic power of the Angels, is what is being referenced.

Further research into the power of harmonic frequencies led me to a theory referred to as *musica universalis* or "universal music" of the spheres. The harmony of the Spheres is an ancient philosophical concept that regards proportions in the movements of the classical Planets as harmonic movements of particular frequencies. This "music" is not usually thought to be literally audible, but a harmonic, mathematical, or spiritual concept. The idea continued to appeal to thinkers about music until the end of the Renaissance, influencing various scholars and philosophers. Apparently, many claiming to have out of body or near death experiences have heard this celestial music or singing. Previously I had considered the "choirs" of Angels and their singing toward the Father in Heaven to be a rather naive and romanticized idea. My perception of what this actually entailed was limited by semantics and rather sophomoric assumptions of what such references actually meant. After the operation with Archangel Uriel, I have no doubts as to the monumental and pervading power of sound, vibration, and song/harmonics/frequency. "Song" even beyond audible sound waves could definitely be considered as the music found in each harmonic issue from every aspect of creation.

My conception of the Angels and their communication altered dramatically with this experience as well. I felt that I grasped another fraction more of how they communicated, not only to us but how they communicated their purpose through the frequencies directed through them by the very Source of Creation itself. It lent a beauty and awe that I could not entirely wrap my mind around. The Angels' diversity of communication lent a level of sophistication which eclipses the languages and even music of mankind. Although my mind could only comprehend a small fraction of their "song," what did come through was not only words and linguistic communication, but images, colors, overwhelming sensations and emotions, all simultaneously and all with perfect intentionality. This is the song of the Angels, their language, their very being, a vibrant and active song, singing the Creator's plan, His first Word, expanding, creating, revolving, and connecting in ways too innumerable for the mind of man to comprehend.

I had previously read of similar encounters with music or song by people who experimented with psychedelics, altering the brain's chemistry and perceptions temporarily to see color in sound and vice versa. The level of perception seems to depend on a person's ability to decipher and translate the various frequencies of data that are contained in these various frequencies. All these revelations occurred after the encounter with Archangel Uriel. Likewise, when I emptied my mind of all conscious efforts and distraction, and simply sang or spoke from the deep place in my being, the sound found its way to create or call whatever it is

I desired into being. I have no doubt that if someone were to master this power alone, one would possess the highest magic available. The power of the Word is indeed ultimately expressed through this mastery.

I had a bit of difficulty settling on which Angelic being I wanted to contact with my scryer next. There was a multitude of other Angelic intelligences I wished to meet, but few which seemed to extend beyond the Planetary realms and influences with which I was familiar. It occurred to me that my scryer and I had already come in relative contact with two well-known Angels, albeit in different form and functions than what was usually ascribed to them. It seemed prudent to formally introduce ourselves and possibly acquire deeper and fuller knowledge of exactly who and what these celestial beings were that transcended the usual cosmic associations.

The Archangel
Sandalphon

✠ Day and time	On Saturday (?), at what time?
✠ Name and meaning	Hebrew סנדלפון *(Sandalphon)*, possibly from Greek *synadelphos*, "Co-Brother"
✠ Pronunciation of name (as spoken by the Spirit)	«San-dahl-fon»
✠ Other forms of the name	Greek Σανδαλφών (*Sandalphōn*)
✠ Planet	⊕/♅
✠ Materials for lamen	Parchment, iron, copper, clay, stone
✠ Sigils	
✠ Direction for Invocation	North
✠ Incense	Sandalwood.

Table VIII-5. ***Evocatory Correspondences for Sandalphon***[6]

Of Sandalphon

Two Archangels that are relatively well known in occult circles and of considerable authority and might are Sandalphon and Metatron. Among other things, these two Angels have been ascribed to the cherubs on either side of the Ark of the Covenant, in which role they are perceived as the balancing forces of terrestrial and celestial divinity and communication. The twin Angels who featured in the method[7] my scryer and I utilized to bring the Spirit Hiram into the skull were the twin aspects of the Angel Sandalphon that guide the seer from the desert of void to the abyss. For both my scryer and me, these Angels were pretty distinct and vivid, although they did not say much regarding their personal origin or offices. Likewise, Metatron was the being that grew to colossal height to guide us to the levels within the abyss itself.

I wanted to contact both of these Angels individually and get a better sense of exactly who they were and how they fit into the Angelic and esoteric work-

6. Please see the Cautionary Warning Regarding Grimoric Ingredients in Appendix A. —APF

7. As described by Josephine McCarthy in *The Exorcist's Handbook.*

ings of creation. It would be interesting to see if the Angels would appear in the same fashion they had for the Hiram experiment and if they would again appear in tandem or as a conjoined manifestation of both.

I read that Sandalphon was regarded as the twin Angel to Metatron, representing the link with mankind and the earth and thus the physical realm. There was also speculation that one or both of these Angels were the Spiritual incarnations of the Biblical prophet Elijah and the famed Enoch himself.

There appears to be some confusion as to the correct translation of Sandalphon's name. "Brother" or "Co-Brother" seem to be the most widely accepted or at least most widely used translations. Sandalphon is described as "the tall Angel" in Moses' apocalyptic journey to the third Heaven. He is seen to stand at the crossroads of Paradise and the earth, guiding righteous souls to find Heaven. In Kabbalistic tradition, Sandalphon is the guardian of the tenth Sephirah *Malkuth*, "The Kingdom," and thus the moderator of all Spiritual emanations transferred to the physical world.

There seems to just be a smattering of mention of Archangel Sandalphon, with brief descriptions and allusions being found in the Jewish and Greek texts. Gustav Davidson assembles a few more associations:

> In Mathers, *The Greater Key of Solomon*, Sandalphon is designated "the left-hand feminine cherub of the ark." In the liturgy for the Feast of Tabernacles, he is credited with gathering the prayers of the faithful, making a garland of such prayers, and then "adjuring them to ascend as an orb to the supreme King of Kings." In *3 Enoch*, Sandalphon is described as ruler of the 6th Heaven (*Makom*), but, in the *Zohar* (Exodus 202b), he is "chief of the 7th Heaven." According to Islamic lore, he dwells in the 4th Heaven.[8]

Beside the reasons mentioned above I wanted to determine if Sandalphon would be a good teacher for magicians wishing to understand the divine in the manifest or physical. As the Archangel of Malkuth, I assumed he would be intimately connected with the aspects found in nature. My other primarily interest was to inquire about the four Direction Kings, rulers, or governors. These spirits are mentioned several times throughout the gamut of classical grimoires yet remain some of the most obscure spirits in occult practice. There have been several attempts to categorize them by esoteric scholars and magicians, but few seemed to have any useful information or firsthand experience. Hopefully, with

8. Gustav Davidson, *A Dictionary of Angels: Including the Fallen Angels* (New York: Free Press, 1967).

successful contact, I could learn more about the four Kings as well as the nature and offices of the Archangel Sandaphon himself.

Fig. VIII-6. ***The Lamen of Sandalphon in the manner of DSIC***

As with Uriel, I had considerable difficulty finding an exact sigil, day and hour, or direction to conjure this being. The research I did led to a sigil created by the Rose Cross style, like one of the sigils I used for Uriel. There was also a relatively new seal of Sandalphon which is gaining increasing acceptance. These seemed to work where other more classical sigils could not be found. Settling on the two likely sigils to call forth this being plus its name written in Hebrew, I created the section to go in the circle as well as a lamen made from parchment. As to timing, I surmised that my best bet would be to associate this being with the "earthiest" natures possible, which corresponded to Saturn where the classical Planets are concerned. Saturday at a suitable hour and facing North seemed to be appropriate.

Invocation of the Archangel Sandalphon

*Fig. VIII-7. **Section of Circle with Correspondences for Drawing Sandalphon into the Crystal***

Appearance of the Spirit

SCRYER: He appears to be standing in a cave. He wears a crown carved of thin, beautiful, and even stone. Round gems of obsidian or jet are set into it. He has a thick brown beard and brown hair. In his right hand he holds a globe that is a brown stone covered in ivy. I also see obsidian or polished jet set in the hems of his garment, round and polished. He wears a cloak or mantle that looks to be made out of furs and skins. In his left hand he holds a straight staff.

OPENING QUESTION 1: In the name of the holy and undefiled Spirit, the Father, the begotten Son, and Holy Ghost proceeding from both, what is thy true name?

SCRYER: He says very plainly «Sandalphon.» When he says it, the stone around him seems to shake in his name. He smiles.

OPENING QUESTION 2: What is thy office?

SPIRIT: «The coming together of beings into a whole. Coalescing. Creation of communities. The reliance of one being on another. The flow of life from one mouth to the next. The awakening of the men of life, from bottom to top and top to bottom. To put the foundation beneath the feet of men. Beneath the roots of trees. A basin to hold oceans. Mountains to praise the Father. Fields to grow food. The people of the earth. Strength in muscles, bone, stone.»

Fig. VIII-8. ***Portrait of Sandalphon as beheld in Vision***

OPENING QUESTION 3: What is thy true sign or character?

SCRYER: He shows me many stones hovering above his hand, floating and moving around somewhat chaotically. Then they form into five, in the shape of a star. Other stones join it and pull together, surrounded by a circle. Then all slowly coalesce and then merge into one stone. It seems to glow from the very inside.

OPENING QUESTION 4: When are the times most agreeable to thy nature to hold conference with us?

SPIRIT: «When it is practical.»

SCRYER: He says he listens to the needs of men and wife, distributes abundance according to need. At all times he is at hand. Need is the key that opens his lock. He says to me, «Need equals Time.»

OATH: Wilt thou swear by the holy blood of Jesus Christ that thou art truly Sandalphon?

SANDALPHON: «I swear by Jesus Christ whose blood soaked the stones. Whose body made a bridge and set an example for men and women. I swear by Jesus Christ, that fine carpenter, that I am Sandalphon.»

QUESTION 6: What are your views on humanity? What are your roles and interactions?

SANDALPHON: «Humans are all shards and reflections of the Creator, my Father, totally beloved by the Son, Jesus Christ. Fascinated by them He was, fascinated by each and every one of them. Like Him I see every one of you as a window into the heart of my Father, into His mind, His intention, His mystery. So I care for you, cultivate you; grow your understanding and knowledge of self, so that I may see into the innermost heart of creation. It is the same with the fish and the tree, the river, the bat, the whale, all children, all windows into the innermost heart of my Father, cupped always in His praying hands, sheltered by His spirit. I place the foundation beneath the feet of humanity so that they may reach their God.»

QUESTION 7: Do you have your own recollection of your creation and origin? Where do you come from? What is your purpose?

SANDALPHON: «I remember being in many different places first, drifting, floating around a Sun. I remember slowly coming together. As I was being assembled, I could hear louder and louder, clearer and clearer, the singing of my Father, echoing through the stars and the voids. Piece by piece I was assembled, stone by stone. And as I came together, I could feel more and more clearly my Father. I could feel His hands on me, the purpose of every gesture of His fingers, every movement of His hand, and I gave myself willingly to His sculpting. And when done, I was Sandalphon. Like He did for me, He awakened in me the desire to do the same for all of His children; to help them assemble, to help them more and more every day hear their Father singing.»

QUESTION 8: What advice can you give us to work and speak with you in the most beneficial ways?

SANDALPHON: «I loved watching Jesus work with wood. The way His hands moved, the way He used the tools, the way He carved and hammered and sawed, and immersed Himself in the creation of something of use. Your souls are like this. So much of Who He was, was a carpenter. So much of His insights, His understanding of His own true Self that was and is God, came when He worked with wood. Your souls are like this as well. Work with your hands, create, immerse your mind into the act of creating, the care, and in it you will reveal your soul and be embraced by our Father. I have wondered sometimes if even He is surprised by you, all of you.»

QUESTION 9: Lore describes you as "Brother," possibly Brother to Archangel Metatron? Are you the Angelic form of the prophet Elijah?

SANDALPHON: «Better said that Elijah is the earthly form of me. The bone, the flesh, the hair, the teeth, the eyes of Metatron. Spoken on the lips of Elijah. The flute, me. The breath through the flute, Metatron. The musician, God.»

QUESTION 10: What are the most successful methods for gaining the strengths of your office? What can you do to assist us and improve this gift within us?

SANDALPHON: «So much depends on the body, the way it is nourished, the way it is moved. Consume that which is closest to its original form. Broccoli instead of broccoli soup. If meat, let it be steak instead of hot dogs.»

SCRYER: *(Laughing)* He's holding up a hot dog and pinching his nose as if it stinks. *(Laughs again.)* His expression looks as if to say, 'What is this?!'

SANDALPHON: «Moving the body, breathing, feeling the muscles in the body strain just enough but no more than needed. Stressing the bones just enough but not more than needed. To be practical in your life, to take care of those around you, to set aside your needs for theirs. To help them coalesce, to help them come together and understand themselves as if you've placed another piece of their puzzle into their soul.

«Touch your feet, your bare feet to the earth as much as possible and your hands as well. Feel it with your body, and do something with your hands—play an instrument, carve a stick, build a wall—and as you do so, just like the Son, hold in the front of your mind, the question: <How does this teach me about God? How does this reveal my heart to Him?> Hide nothing.»

QUESTION 11: What should your lamen be made from? Is there a certain metal or material which corresponds to you best?

SANDALPHON: «I like the feel and power of iron and copper. The way it rusts, the way it can be smooth and coarse all at once. I love the deep, cool density of peat, of mud, of moss, any moss. My talismans can be left in a place near the base of a tree, covered in the earth for seven days and seven nights, in the dark, left alone, quiet. And in that time I will move my hands over it, I will finger my way into its metal and imbue it with my spirit. Let it be round with the star within the circle and made from iron, copper.»

OPERATOR: Can you tell me the properties, powers, and benefits of this talisman?

SANDALPHON: «To remind the magician of the truth. It is to be worn in times when direction is needed. To remind the magician of his original purpose, his destiny. To wear and ask the question, ‹What is the ground beneath my feet; what supports me and why?› To let go of pretention and fear. To reveal yourself fully to God. To place stability under the feet of those who suffer from chaos, insanity, anxiety, or fear. To help a being coalesce and reassemble.»

Question 12: What can you tell us of the Four Emperors, Oriens, Amaymon, Paymon, and Egyn? In which ways should we conjure them? What should each of their seals be made from and what incenses are used to evoke them? Are there any other requisites important for conjuring them and what can they assist us with?

Sandalphon: «As we are the vertical, they are the horizontal. They open gates that allow the plane of experiences to converge on the circle of the magician. Associating with their direction, they pull the qualities of that space and send it to those who call in a holy matter for holy intentions, and for those who call for bad or evil intentions. They are without judgment, without morality. They give their energies forth simply to give, not to judge.

«A circle of stone, a lens, a candle, a cup can be used to summon each of the Kings. A symbol of an Element that is also a gateway make excellent talismans for them.

«An incense can be used for each of them, but only use one as dominant for the particular purpose that fits the intent of the working. To use incense of all four would bring in too much and dilute the intent of the work. Using the correspondences with the intent of the work, any energy direction of the gate correspondence can pull and amplify the energy of the gatekeeper. Use the correspondences to the direction intuitive to the magician, as these qualities are mixed and reflected differently in each of you. You will find one gatekeeper more dominant than others for you. Exploring this dominance, this hierarchy between the four, gives insight into the composition of the self.»

Question 13: What can you tell us of the ability to Spirit travel and ascend from the plane of Earth?

SANDALPHON: «I am like the surface that the body rests on so that the Spirit may travel. To travel the Astral, the magician's body must be safe, secure, protected. If the point of origin and return is unsure, the Spirit cannot fully move and explore. I shelter the body and call quietly to the Spirit as it moves. Like a roadmap or a travel back to the body. When the Spirit is assured in this way can the travel in the Astral be broader, longer, and uninhibited.»

QUESTION 14: We thank you for your teaching and wisdom to strengthen us and assist us on our path and purpose. Do you have any final words for us to help us further on this journey?

SANDALPHON: «You're both being called to set aside distraction because it's time. As you've progressed in this work like the carpenter or the sculptor, you have come closer and closer to the original self. This work can only be entertainment until it is focused for purpose; to further the plan, the song, the play, of the Creator. To be a magician, to be a druid, is to set aside distraction for the benefit of others. In many ways, your life will not be your own. Accept that truth, make decisions in that truth and your effect on the people you know and many people who you will never meet or even know exist will resonate and remain long after your physical bodies have fallen into dust. It is a choice of clear understanding to laugh at your own faults and mistakes and reveal them fully to God, without shame, with the wisdom and understanding to know, to feel, that He may have put them there for a reason.»

OPERATOR: Great and wondrous Angel Sandalphon, I thank you for your attendance upon this rite and ask for your continued blessings and involvement with our works always.

(License to Depart given.)

Afterthoughts on the Sandalphon Operation

OPERATOR: This Angel was not at all as I expected, and looked very different from the visions we saw during our journey into the desert from the void. Regardless, this Angel felt extremely familiar and seemed quite capable at communicating with us in modern terms and methods. Returning to *The Exorcist's Handbook*, I recalled that the author describes the Angels as

"Companions, brothers—the fragment angels of Sandalphon." This made sense for some reason as the familiar feeling I got from the Sandalphon Angel we just encountered felt like the Angels of the desert, although they looked quite different in appearance save for the size. The Spirit my scryer and I had just encountered had quite the sense of humor and was quite adept at modern communication.

SCRYER: He was cracking me up! I guess no more Ball Park franks. *(Scryer laughs.)*

OPERATOR: I was able to perceive this Angel quite clearly in the crystal as my scryer spoke with him. As before I did not hear what he was saying while talking to my scryer but saw him as my scryer described. I clearly saw a towering dark figure with earth-colored robes. He was tall with a thick beard, dark hair and eyes, looking Middle-Eastern, as well as like someone who is outside a lot.

SCRYER: That is how he appeared to me. What surprises me every time we do this is that you can feel the energy of the arrival of the Spirit slowly building, then you call and they are there! It's becoming expected by now, but still amazes me when they finally arrive. The light increased again, the presence and glow over the entire area is neat to see. I like how practical he was; it made it very enjoyable to talk to him. All the Angels seemed so different, with very specific traits and personalities, as well as times to speak with them, whereas this Angel said things were based on need. I wonder what «Need equals Time» means? I'll have to meditate on that for a while.

The Archangel commented that a round iron or copper talisman with a pentagram figure in the center was appropriate for its lamen and could be consecrated in a very curious fashion. It also seemed to suggest the type of environment that was most appropriate in which to bury the talisman in order for it to be consecrated. A deep wooded, forested environment in a cool, mossy area seemed appropriate. I designed a ritual and invocation to accompany the creation of this talisman that would commence out of doors far removed from civilization. After meditating on the entire procedure for several days following this operation, I devised a unique magical operation that I realized was dissimilar to what is found in most classical workings. After engraving or otherwise making the metal talisman on iron or copper on a Saturday during a favorable hour, the magician should select a very secluded and hidden forested area. The exact location may be discovered by his senses leading him to a tree which corresponds to Earthly powers or calls to him in a particular way. The tree could even be discovered through dowsing or having another Earth Spirit, Angel, or Elemental guide the magician to the tree. Once the tree is chosen, the area should be blessed and honored with spoken intentions in the nature of the ritual.

Once the location is selected, pick a Saturday during an hour of Saturn or Venus that suits you. Bring with you the created iron or copper talisman, a wand or staff consecrated for magical purposes, a simple linen robe, (optionally the Sandalphon lamen, which can be worn and is separate from the talisman), holy water and sprinkler, food offerings, a copper ritual knife or digging instrument that should be consecrated, and a candle and lantern. Carve out a large magical circle encompassing the tree at the correct hour using the copper knife or tool. The same style and names used in *DSIC* could be easily incorporated. For this ritual, I also borrowed inspiration from previous Celtic magical workings and decided to outline the circle in earth with stones found in the area. In the North, dig a small hole at least a hand's length down nearest to the tree without damaging it.

In the center, place your lantern and candle with the talisman nearby. When you are ready, remove any shoes or socks and stand barefoot on the earth. When the correct time approaches, bless the circle by sprinkling it with blessed water while moving around the tree clockwise. Light the candle in the center and recite any prayers or invocations to prepare to call the attention of the Archangel. Stand in the center facing North, toward the tree and small hole near the base. When you are ready, raise arms and staff toward the tree and recite the following invocation:

I invoke you, Great Co-Brother and ambassador of physical Creation. O great Archangel Sandalphon, guardian of the earth, of Malkuth, the Kingdom, and Mighty Twin Angel, hear me. (Pick up talisman raising it overhead.) *Let this talisman be consecrated by your divine office. Let it be a container of Truth to guide the magician so that he remembers his original purpose and destiny. Great and wondrous Archangel Sandalphon, grant that the magician who wears this, your talisman will have their path made clear. Make it to heal and rebalance any distempers in the mind, body, or soul. I invoke and adjure you, great Sandalphon, that you bless and empower this emblem of your office so that the wearer will know and feel the support of the Creator. As you have declared, let your blessings come across this talisman as it stays covered in the earth for seven days and seven nights. Let it grant stability and focus to the magician that all endeavors and goals are realized. Let your talisman focus and center the wearer so that he knows the correct action to take, removing any fear, anxiety, or distraction. This I ask by He who is everlasting, King, Master, and Creator, unto the Ages of the Ages, Amen.*

Once the invocation is complete, set the bare metal talisman in the hole in the earth. From what I gathered of the operation, the connection with bare earth seems important, and even if it were to rust slightly, it was part of this process that the Archangel finds sacred. Although not mentioned by Sandalphon, I also engraved a pentagram on a large stone and set it over where the talisman was buried. Around this stone I arranged five small stones in the shape of a pentagram around the area where the talisman was buried.

After concluding this ceremony, remove traces of the circle and stones if you used them. Clean and restore the land around the tree to how it appeared before, minus the stones over the talisman. Be sure that no one will be able to discover the location of the talisman.

Depart the area, taking everything else with you and do not return anywhere near this area for seven days and seven nights. At the end of this period, repeat the above formula but forgo the mention of burying the talisman. At the end of the invocation, dig up the talisman, cleaning it gently with a cloth, and wrapping it in a piece of black or brown linen.

The Ark Angels

Some texts describe Sandalphon and Metatron as brothers and possibly the twin Cherubim Angels represented on the Ark of the Covenant. One of the most significant meditations I experienced while taking courses on The Kabbalah under a Jewish rabbi was the visualization of the Ark of the Covenant focusing on a light directly above the golden box and between the two Cherubim where Elohim, the essence of YHVH, could be contacted. During this particular class, the rabbi took us on a guided meditation and Spiritual vision journey that involved traveling through the point between the two Angels to a light that represented supreme divinity.

This practice was only done once after two years of attending the Kabbalah class, and we were cautioned against casual experimentation afterward. The rabbi said that the exercise is one of the most powerful methods for nearing the spiritual Holy of Holies and coming nearer to understanding the deeper, sacred mysteries of the Torah and Kabbalah. To be a richer and more involved experience a deep knowledge of Jewish mysticism and the Kabbalah is required. Such efforts are beyond the scope of this work, but I share it as a further possibility to appreciate the supernal natures of the Archangels named Sandalphon and Metatron.

As Cherubim, these two Angels are indeed guardians of sacred doorways. The form and origin of the Cherubim appears to share in the myths and iconography of the Akkadian *Lamassu*. These magical creatures are normally portrayed with body of a lion or an ox, the wings of an eagle, and the head of a human. They are the gatekeepers, and it is by their authority and allowance that we are able to travel past them into new worlds. The Cherubim are the guardians securing the Angelic realms that lead nearer to the throne of divinity, to the pure manifestations of the Godhead. None do pass unto these worlds but by their leave. Possibly the true gateway to divinity is to speak with Metatron closest to seat of God.

I invite the magician who seriously plans to walk this path in earnest to explore these concepts more thoroughly than what is explained here.

Creating the Implements of the Directional Rulers ✠ Part 2

One of the most valuable pieces of information I received from Archangel Sandalphon was the instruction to make the four talismans for the Direction Kings. Sandalphon described them as the «horizontal» as compared to him and the Angels as the «vertical.» Advice for contacting each of them successfully involved the presence of four symbolic talismans, which would serve as «gateways» to contact the Kings. The prospect of such talismans being gateways in and of themselves caused me to look at them in a new way: not simply as objects that hold or draw power, but also as devices through which a magician or scryer can travel directly to the realm of the Spirit, and possibly through which that Spirit may travel to reach us here in the physical realm.

The Archangel of Malkuth specifically said «A circle of stone, a lens, a candle, a cup can be used to summon each of the kings. A symbol of an Element that is also a gateway...» The items seemed obviously related to the Elements. However, despite the Angel's inference, I would not assume that this endeavor would be comparable to summoning the Elemental Kings. The Directional Kings were known to possess power and authority far beyond those of the Elemental kingdoms and their influence seemed to have considerable sway in the Spiritual world. I reasoned that simply associating each king with a classical element was oversimplifying their significance.

It took several weeks to settle on what each Directional talisman would look like and how it would function to summon forth the associated king. I poured over the grimoires that I knew had some mention of the Directional Kings, but few agreed with one another. I reasoned that the stone ring was most certainly Earth, and likely for the Northern King. The lens seemed likely to be the Air talisman, and so situated to the East, but I was unsure. The candle was the obvious Fire symbol for the South, as was the cup for Water to the West. However, before I needed to worry about what symbol belonged where, I should find an appropriate stone, lens, candle and candlestick, and cup that would be befitting talismans of Spiritual Kings.

Archangel Sandalphon went into more detail concerning the incenses that were used. The Spirit seemed adamant on not mixing the incenses used for evoking the four Kings. He cautioned to only use one ingredient as dominant to fit the intention of the working. Beyond this, the remark that one of the Kings would be more dominant than the other three and that exploring this dominance between the four would give insight into our own composition seemed interesting. I spent quite a bit of time meditating and preparing the items needed to attempt evoking the four Directional Kings while realizing I had at least one more Angelic evocation to perform before such an undertaking.

Before moving on to the Directional Kings, I felt it was pertinent to attempt to conjure the most exalted of Archangels, Metatron, the co-brother of Archangel Sandalphon. The Angelic being regarded as the scribe to the Almighty Himself, this Archangel was about as far up the ranks of the Celestial choirs as one could go. I honestly was unsure if such a task was possible and did consider that this could be one operation that would not succeed, as the prospect seemed almost preposterous.

The Archangel
Metatron

✠	Day and time	On Saturday/Sunday (?), Dark of the Moon/New Moon
✠	Name and meaning	Hebrew מטטרון *(Metatron)*, perhaps from Latin *Metator*, "The Apportioner" or "He Who Metes Out"; Greek μετὰ θρόνος (*meta Thronos*), "[One] Beside the Throne"; or Aramaic מטרא (*Mattara*), "Keeper of the Watch"
✠	Pronunciation of name (as spoken by the Spirit)	«Met-ah-tron»
✠	Planet	⊕/Sephirah Kether
✠	Materials for lamen	Parchment, gold, meteoric metal
✠	Sigils	•
✠	Direction for Invocation	North
✠	Incense mixture	Mastic, frankincense, fir, and coltsfoot.

*Table VIII-9. **Evocatory Correspondences for Metatron***[9]

Of Metatron

There is no Biblical mention of Archangel Metatron by name; of course this is true of every Angel except Michael and Gabriel (and Raphael, if you include *Tobit* as part of your canon). However, Metatron does feature in the *Talmud* and prominently in the *Books of Enoch*, as well as in later Kabbalistic and magical works, such as *Sepher Raziel ("The Book of [the Archangel] Raziel")*. In book 3 of *Sepher Raziel*, Metatron is described as having "all the actions and power of Shaddai, of all the one power. It is proclaimed, Metatron comes from below, pure and clean,"[10] which may allude to him being the celestial form of Enoch. In

9. Please see the Cautionary Warning Regarding Grimoric Ingredients in Appendix A. —APF

10. Steve Savedow, *Sepher Rezial Hemelach: The Book of the Angel Rezial* (York Beach, ME: Samuel Weiser, 2000), p. 198. —APF

his role as the highest Archangel, he is known as the Recording Angel or the Chancellor of Heaven.

Fig. VIII-10. The Lamen of Metatron in the manner of DSIC

There has been much debate over the centuries as to the origin of the name Metatron. Several scholars have suggested an origin in Aramaic *mattara*, "keeper of the watch." A Latin origin has also been proposed from *metator*, "a measurer, a meter out of allotments, a fixer of boundaries." A Greek etymology has been suggested from *meta thronos*, the one stationed "near the Throne" of God. Hugo Odeberg even theorized that Metatron's name is a direct derivative from that of the Persian God Mithras whose cult was so popular in the Roman era.[11]

Regardless of the direct origin, the references to this archangel in the *Talmud* and *Books of Enoch* place Metatron as an Angelic being of the highest supernal station in the celestial hierarchy.

There has always been a lot of debate and disagreement as to whether or not the Archangel Metatron is actually the ascended Spiritual form of the Biblical patriarch Enoch. There are several points where the references to each differ significantly and while at one level it seems unlikely that such an exalted Spiritual being would have ever been human, according to Jewish apocrypha, Metatron is indeed Enoch, the great-grandfather of Noah, transformed into an Angel. *Genesis* 5:24 is the text which inspired the lore of Enoch's ascension into heaven: "And Enoch walked with God: and he was not; for God took him."

In *The Grimoire of St. Cyprian or Clavis Inferni*, edited and expounded upon by Stephen Skinner and David Rankine, Metatron is found as a central figure

11. Hugo Odeberg, *3 Enoch or The Hebrew Book of Enoch* (London: Cambridge University Press, 1929), pp. 1.125–126.

within the brief text, which is a rare occurence in other grimoires except in allusions to talismans and function. Skinner and Rankine say:

> Metatron is described as the Prince of the Divine Countenance (*Malach ha-Panim*) or Angel of the Divine Countenance (*Sar ha-Panim*). As the first Sephirah on the Tree of Life, Kether, represents the Divine Countenance, so its archangel Metatron is the representative of the Divine Countenance. This is seen in the *Shiur Qoma*, where it says, "This is the seat of Metatron, the Lord of the Presence which is written with one-letter [i.e. Aleph, whose numeration is one]." The same text even goes so far as to identify Metatron with Adam Kadmon, the archetypal divine man made in the image of God.[12]

Indeed, there is reference to this being as the most mighty of Angels and the nearest reflection of the Source and God of Creation. The very idea that a magician could evoke and contact this being directly seemed implausible at first, put I persisted, as access to even a measure of this mighty being could reveal extraordinary mysteries and esoteric knowledge. It was initially difficult to uncover any means or methods to invoke this Archangel directly but I eventually uncovered some examples which seemed usable in actual ceremonial practice.

Scholar James Davila has published a fragmentary text from the Geniza[13] which preserves a process for the invocation of Metatron. The process appears to be quite similar to the sort of fasting and abstaining from sexual and social activity as that is found in the *Magic of Abramelin the Mage*. It first gives a preliminary prayer:

> And hear the voice of my prayer in this hour, O magnificent and strong King, the gracious and merciful One Whose eyes are on His creatures. Turn to the prayer of your servant and answer me in a time of favor, O Lord of all the worlds, Creator of all, Unique One of the world. Let the gates of heaven be opened by my cry, for I [in]voke and seek grace before Your great, holy, pure, and blessed name.[14]

It then provides instructions and the main invocation:

---

12. Stephen Skinner, David Rankine, and Cyprian, *The Grimoire of Saint Cyprian: Clavis Inferni* (Singapore: Golden Hoard Press, 2009), p. 20.

13. The same depository for worn-out Hebrew religious texts from which Margalioth assembled the *Sepher ha-Razim*. —APF

14. James R. Davila, *Descenders to the Chariot: The People Behind the Hekhalot Literature* (Leiden: Brill, 2001), p. 113. —APF

How does he (Moses and/or the practitioner?) make use of it? He goes and sits in a house by himself, and he must be in a state of fasting all day long. He eats no bread (made by) a woman, and he gazes at neither man nor woman. When he walks around in the marketplace, his eyes are raised above all creatures, and he does not gaze at anyone, even a baby one day old. He immerses from evening to evening and recites this word after the reading of the evening *Shema*[c] every single day. How does he adjure? He begins here:

I adjure you, Metatron, Prince of the Presence; I recite over you, Metatron, angel of the Presence; I decree over you, Metatron, Prince of the Presence; I establish over you, Metatron, angel of the Presence; and I seal upon you, Metatron, Prince of the Presence. In the name of ŠQDḤ<W>ZYY, what is called by the seven names:MRGYWY'L GYWT'L ṬN'RY'L HWZH YH ŠQDḤWZY MṬRWN GNWW YH SSNGY' SSBRY' R' S', God of Israel, God of hosts, God of heaven, God of the sea, God of the dry land. BZBWRY'L HWZH YH YH YHW holy YH QDŠYH QDŠYH."

Thus far, one hundred and eleven times. He must not decrease and he must not increase. If he decreases or increases, then his blood is on his (own) head. How does he count? On every single finger ten times. And he repeats on his first finger <ten> and on his second finger one time, and they are sweet on his hand.[15]

Preparing for the Invocation of Metatron

Admittedly I was rather nervous attempting this evocation; that may have had a lot to do with my difficulties during the actual ritual. In all probability, my senses would likely have been overloaded regardless in attempting to directly communicate with such a being. Initially, I didn't quite believe such a thing was possible or even beneficial for a human being to attempt. Regardless, I spent over a week fasting, abstaining and preparing for this operation and advising my scryer to do the same.

I studied the process and evocation from the Genizah fragment, adapting some of the invocation to use along with my usual conjurations from *DSIC*.

I conjure thee, Metatron, Prince of the Presence; I recite to thee, Metatron, Angel of the Presence; I decree for thee to appear, Metatron, Prince of the Presence; I invoke thee, Metatron, Angel of the Presence; and I conjure thee Metatron, Prince

15. *Ibid.*, p. 114. —APF

of the Presence, to appear. In the name of Shaqadchoziai, who is called by the Seven Names, Margiziel Giyutael Tenariel Huzah Yah Shaqadchozi Metatron Ganavu Yah Sesnagiya Sesbariya Ra Sa, God of Israel, God of Hosts, God of Heaven, God of the sea, and God of the dry land, Bazburiel Huzah Yah Yah Yahu Qadoshyah Qadoshyah Qadoshyah Qadoshyah, that you attend unto us and appear before this circle within this crystal.

Invocation of the Archangel Metatron

Fig. VIII-11. ***Section of Circle with Correspondences for Drawing Metatron into the Crystal***

(Note: During the Invocation I felt an indescribable pressure and presence that nearly made me lose consciousness. There were several times I had to pause and consider abandoning the operation, as overwhelming sensations continued to flood through me which I could not seem to comprehend.)

Appearance of the Spirit

SCRYER: He stands upon a web or network of light drawn between stars. I can see his shape but it's see-through at the same time. His skin is black like space; his muscles, his eyes shimmer slightly like silver. His hair when he is still is black, but if he moves it ripples and shines with many iridescent lights and colors. His feet seem to fade into the networks of light which emanate from him. His eyes see right through me as if they are seeing beyond time and distance, as if by looking at me he immediately looks far beyond me into my destiny, seeing all aspects beyond time at once. He says he dims his presence in front of me that he may be beheld.

Fig. VIII-12. ***Portrait of Metatron as beheld in Vision***

OPENING QUESTION 1: In the name of the holy and undefiled Spirit, the Father, the begotten Son, and Holy Ghost proceeding from both, what is thy true name?

SPIRIT : «My name as you can understand it is simply Metatron. My name is written in the form of a snowflake, in the movement of water, in the stones and crystalline shapes of the earth and all the solid places of the deep, beyond the kin of mankind is my name. Written in the minutest fibers of creation, by the Great Author.»

OPENING QUESTION 2: What is thy office?

SCRYER: He turns around and he flings a star behind him, and it looks like it strikes the fabric of space, and moves and ripples.

SPIRIT: «My office is the rolling thunder of the word of God. I write His memories, His children, His open and conceiving mind and heart. My office is the office of a child, scribbling furiously, ecstatically, uncomprehendingly the thoughts of my Father. Crying, laughing, singing in states of horror and joy and peace. I attempt to keep pace with His glory. I anguish to write the story of time, of non-time, of form and formlessness.»

OPENING QUESTION 3: What is thy true sign or character? Is there a better symbol beyond your cube that represents your true being?

SCRYER: He shows me a flat darkness, like a paper or parchment made of pure night. He draws the circles from that symbol you showed me, of Metatron's cube, connecting and expanding outward. He shows me one pattern, then moves his hand over it and erases it, and then shows me another. He whispers in my ear:

SPIRIT: «The pen that draws is the servant of the mind that conceives: The creative genius of my Father implanted in me, in you, and all the shards of light called ‹mankind,› dimmed, fractured, broken, scared but untouched.

«Only the parchment of pure night, a truer symbol of me than the cube that is written on it. I have been asked this question before, and it is very difficult to convey in the limited experience that is the mind of men and women. It is a matrix that they create over as a veil of the truth. It is simply your nature and cannot be circumvented. Embrace your finitude. Hold your ignorance as a temporary gift. For when the veil is parted the joy is that much greater.»

OPENING QUESTION 4: When are the times most agreeable to thy nature to hold conference with us?

SPIRIT: «When the Moon is dark, and the night in its depth, before a single flame, within the circle, writing from the wellsprings of the mind, with no other purpose but to create, purely.»

SCRYER: He shows me an image of a man. It looks like Hiram actually. He is standing at the edge of the ocean alone. There is no moon, but the stars are everywhere, and the waves come in and bathe only his feet. He places his hands over his heart and then in front of him in a gesture of prayer and he weeps at the beauty of creation. It's as if he sees the imprint of the mind and heart of God written by the gentle hands of Metatron.

OATH: Wilt thou swear by the holy blood of Jesus Christ that thou art truly the Archangel Metatron?

METATRON: «I, Metatron remember when the Son's story was only written upon the pages of night. I remember the anticipation of seeing His face for the first time. To see the Father, my Father, made man. I swear by that holy perfect, humble, visage that is Jesus Christ, that I am Metatron.

«And I thank you both for your work and your courage to write the mind, heart, and spirit of my Father in your own way. The joy I feel when I see you write these words is like a father that beholds his son. Thank you. Thank you. You have no conception of how many people through years to come will read these words and how it will move their fingers, their eyes, their heart, and their minds.

«To be a scribe is a Holy thing...»

(There is a long moment of silence as the impact of these words moves me very deeply, though I do not truly understand why, try as I might to come to grips with why such a statement would affect me so profoundly. I remember at this time I had difficulty thinking and standing as everything seemed to nearly black out around me.)

QUESTION 6: Great and Mighty Metatron, celestial high priest, chancellor of Heaven, and King of the Angels, what is your connection to Enoch, and his sacred and mysterious writings?

METATRON: «Enoch; raised upon my palm above the limitations of the world at a time when men needed to see beyond his bounds of everyday concerns of kings, and priests, and noblemen, beggars and fools. Each of us, the Angels of God, poured our fires through him. We overwhelmed him with the wisdom of our Father. We showed him the beginning, the parts that he could see and understand. We hinted at what was to come. We took the simple, humble part that he had and filled it with the ecstasy of God. The patterns and tapestries that rolled out before him were like grass mats woven of light, perfect, complete, and the darkness was shown to him as well. And above all the tumult that he saw, the briefest faintest glimpse of *Tetragrammaton*. What was given to him was the war, and the reconciliation, and the knowledge that only some of what he saw could be spoken and remembered by men.»

QUESTION 7: It is said that you have seventy names. Is this true? Can you teach us any of these names and their meanings?

METATRON: «There is truth to the seventy names, though it is hard for me to relate them through the seer.»

SCRYER: I see *El, Pur, Nohnis, Feneahook...(Pause)*....He seems a little impatient with me.

METATRON: «The mind of the seer is like a gate, the eyes of the seer like a gate. What comes through is necessarily limited by the gateway. The names mark and record the various phases of my birth, my maturation, my death, and my rebirth.»

OPERATOR: Is there anything further you can teach us of your origin and creation?

METATRON: «I remember first the unrelenting and infinite pattern, as if I was written into and came from it. It was as if I stretched and curved and moved everywhere. As if the matrix and writing of God became the consciousness that is Metatron. I remember nothing before the pattern but know that I was there...somehow in Him. Some of my names refer to this gradual awakening of my consciousness and the gradual awakening of all things in their birth.»

QUESTION 8: Great and most powerful Archangel, nearest to the crown of the Ultimate Highest, what can you teach us in the working of sacred magic? What knowledge, wisdom, and insight can you impart to us to achieve our highest aspirations in magical work? Great and mightiest Archangel, is there some token or gift of the Most High which none have received in this particular quality that you could impart to us?

METATRON: «Magic is the blessing and responsibility of the mage to press his fingers into the matrix from which all things arise. I know of an amulet inscribed with a heart, a flame, a hand descending below it, that speaks of this power and magnifies it, reminding at the same time that with the blessing comes the burden. Blessed in the right way and in the right frame of mind, smoked with sacred herbs of jasmine, Lebanon cedar, cinnamon, and myrrh, taken to the shore at night and holding it to the stars while the waves bathe the feet. On the back, inscribe the cube.

There are hand gestures, similar to weaving rope, that enable the magician to pull more clearly and more effectively on the Tapestry of Being. This can be learned by weaving and praying until the insight comes.»

QUESTION 9: Are you able to impart to us wisdom to help and heal others with distressed nerves, stress, confusion, neurosis, or insomnia?

SCRYER: He shows me a man lying on his back with only his stomach exposed. He shows me a smooth-ended rod of glass dipped in ink, blessed and infused with mica. And as the physician prays, he inscribes, very carefully the thirteen circles of the cube on the stomach.

METATRON: «In this operation it is better for the person to be asleep that is being drawn on, or at least very relaxed. However, the patient must know the intent of the working clearly. They must pray before and after in the same words that the physician uses when inscribing the symbols on the body. At the end, the magician or the physician lays their hands on the belly, the heart, and the head to seal the power of the working into the body.

«The patient must softly sing three holy names of God upon waking and before going to sleep. They must be the first and last words they speak for 21 days.

«The circles of the cube can be removed and cleansed off just after the magician or physician seals the power with hands to the belly, the heart, and the mind. After the 21 days, the imprint of the circles will still be there, though not visible to the eye. The magician or physician must cleanse the patient one last time to remove the imprint. When this is done, the malady or the infliction will drop with the energetic imprint of the circles down into the earth and be lost.»

QUESTION 10: Hiram suggested that I should inquire about the nature of existence itself and what secrets you would be able to teach us on creation. Also, what can you tell me of my birth and purpose and how I came to be?

METATRON: «The nature of existence can be likened to the ecstatic creative, infinite, outpourings of my Father's mind and heart. These creations live thus—»

SCRYER: He shows me a circle of light, connected faintly to another by a string that is invisible until it is 'plucked' like a musical instrument.

METATRON: «Connections unseen but formed subtly from sound, movement, and vibration; creations living on their own but always streaming back to the infinite source of the mind of my Father.

«This is similar to your birth. I could speak of the nature of creation in so many symbolic ways, but this specifically links us to you and your birth. The illusion is separateness and separation but the string, the connection, always there.

«There are some who are born, and in the very first hours of their lives, we come and we pluck the string. Like a lightning bolt, plucked to make thunder, the instant quick reminder that you are still connected to the heart of God. So we stretched out our hands and plucked that string and made that voice, that sound, and reminded you before you could even form memory as Bryan Garner of where you came. The shamans, magicians, the priests, we pluck their strings early, but their symbols are different, their paths are different, and how I would explain it to them would be very different. Think carefully on the lightning and the thunder of that day, and your purpose will become more and more clear.»

QUESTION 11: Great and Holy Archangel, may I ask for your blessing and further guidance in becoming and fulfilling the duties as a divine magician and priest?

(Slight pause.)

METATRON: «Listen very carefully to those who teach you. Let the gestures and the words and the ceremonies that you learn be brought consciously into the cells of your body. Attempt to reflect their truths in how you walk and move though your life knowing with holy humility that you will fail. And seek God in the failures. Do not revile them, embrace them as paths that lead deeper into the heart of God. Humility is the key that opens the lock.»

QUESTION 12: Is there any message you would wish to impart to mankind, to those who would read these words?

METATRON: «Walk forth. Feel the supporting movement of the pattern of God beneath your feet. Do not be afraid, for you walk to us and all will be forgiven. No one shall be denied entry into the kingdom at the last.»

QUESTION 13: A magical associate of mine who seeks to walk the path of the magician, but who has struggled, asked me to ask on his behalf if there were some advice and wisdom or message for him to assist in his difficulties with seeing and interacting with spirits and helping him on his path.

METATRON: «Yes. Tell him to go alone to a high place at twilight and look to the west for nine nights in a row. Wait patiently, give offerings, and make prayers and be silent. And we will show him a wonder. Remember to look to the west.»

OPERATOR: Blessed and most mighty Archangel under the Creator, we thank you for your attendance and council to us. I ask for your blessing and guidance always as I continue this path.

(License to depart given.)

Afterthoughts on the Metatron Operation

OPERATOR: I very nearly abandoned this operation toward the beginning. I became overwhelmed with sensations I cannot explain, and also my hands shook uncontrollably, and I had difficulty focusing and concentrating on the operation. I seriously felt like I was going to pass out or lose consciousness in the middle of the circle.

SCRYER: Wow. I know I say it almost every time but, that was different. This one, in particular, is different simply from the fact that I feel like I was having my memory erased! I've never had this happen since we began. I couldn't remember what I was saying, right after I said it. Honestly, after two sentences I couldn't remember a thing! I remember a few images and flashes but that's it. During the operation, it was like someone was coming up behind me and erasing what had just transpired from my mind. It's a little freaky actually. I didn't feel like it was necessarily a bad thing or a negative experience, but it was odd having that happen to me.

I do remember seeing Metatron; that was really vivid. I also remember the image of Hiram standing on the shore. I remember Metatron holding this ball of light up and, at first, it seemed isolated in space. I couldn't see any connection, and then he made a plucking motion and I could suddenly see a cord stretched from the ball way out to another source and vibrating, rippling, and moving, and looked like it was actually changing the fabric of space. It made this massive thrum, and so much energy was released from it. Ohh, and I remember seeing words, golden words on a black space, but only pieces of them.

OPERATOR: When you started pronouncing those first two names, my senses became flooded, as if there was a huge entity in the room and its presence was filling the entire chamber. I can't quite explain it, but the feeling was overbearing; I was unsure of what to do about it. The sensation seemed to lessen a bit when I switched to the next question. I suppose it's understandable, but some of my questions just seemed too deep or involved to have answered in this first session.

SCRYER: I'm glad you recorded it so I can listen to it and remember what was said. You know, each and every time we've done this, I go in there and worry and think to myself, 'I wonder if nothing will come across this time? I wonder if I sit here and I won't see or hear anything?' It really feels like I'm being invited to have faith, as if the entire process is saying to me,

> 'Don't worry about it, just let it come, just have faith and it will arrive.' That is a powerful lesson for me in and of itself, because each and every time I always think, 'Man, what if I don't see anything?'

The nature of the Angels and benefits of their presence is such that it will be missed after their departure. As time goes on, you will easily recall their presence, vision, and experience, and it becomes a longing, like you would miss a treasured loved one or close friend. Their energy lingers after the operation, but eventually dissipates as time and life go on. Eventually, the magical chamber no longer hums with the intense presence of the Spirits that were there just weeks ago. The memory of the experience and what they felt like never diminishes, but the palpable, lingering presence eventually fades.

I passed on the findings to the magical associate of mine that asked for advice and wisdom or a message from Metatron. The Archangel's assurance that if he went alone to a high place at twilight and looked to the west for nine nights in a row that «we» would show him a wonder seemed like a given. It was initially disappointing, however, when my magical friend reported that he had done what was instructed but nothing had happened. No wonder or anything remarkable occurred, in his assessment. A bit befuddled, I wondered what had possibly gone wrong. Regardless, soon after, my friend reported magical success as well as his own publication of magical experiments he had conducted, with apparently growing accomplishment in the esoteric community. This had possibly been what 'wonders' my friend was expecting, but I thought it interesting nevertheless.

By this time, it became important for me to maintain the relationship with the Archangels and honor their teachings long after the thrill of the evocation had passed. I also realized it was imperative I not simply call them up for every issue, mystery, or problem, or just because I missed their company and council. It felt important for me to act on the information and instruction they gave, and heed their messages. I felt I could demonstrate that I valued their time and assistance by pursuing the courses of action they recommended, and integrating their natures into myself through practice and action.

Times and interests will change, but I found the true materialization of the power and gifts the Archangels grant will depend greatly on what is done with the information after the operation. Magic is an act of creation, and manifestation of the benefits is confirmed when all the proper pieces come into alignment through your will and directed attention. Relationship and familiarization with the Spirits is the surest way to truly harness the extent of their office. A single introduction and conversation can yield amazing results, but a building relationship and constant integration will definitely bring about the full capacity of that sphere of power.

All the experiences of the Archangels, needless to say, left a profound spiritual impact and I decided to take more serious steps to honor the experiences by pursuing ordination into the Christian esoteric priesthood. I have a family and a child for whom to provide, but I felt this was an important undertaking to better honor the gifts the Angels had given me.

After the operation with Metatron, I decided I would forgo attempting to evoke any more Archangels or lesser Angels for the time being. The experience had left me changed in ways I could not explain and I knew I had a long way to go before I would begin to understand. Likewise, the changes caused by the preceding seven Planetary Archangels and those of Uriel and Sandalphon caused as many transformations as I could handle for the time being. Any one of them had given enough information and guidance that I could dedicate my entire existence without running out of work.

I decided instead to focus on other particular Spirits that were prominent in esoteric and occult literature, such as the four Directional Kings I had inquired about to Sandalphon.

I began spending time poring over various magical texts and piecing together the information I had received from Archangel Sandalphon to ready myself to summon forth these mighty kings. Hiram was also able to provide excellent insight as well as assurance of being able to call forth these beings, although there was a somewhat foreboding tone to his warning of what was likely to occur once Benn and I made successful contact with each of them.

✣

IX
The Four Kings of the Cardinal Directions
Part One • The Round of Evocations

> ... On the table on which the crystal stands the following names, characters, &c. must be drawn in order.
>
> First, The names of the seven planets and angels ruling them, with their seals or characters. The names of the four kings of the four corners of the earth. Let them be all written within a double circle, with a triangle on a table; on which place the crystal on its pedestal: this being done, thy table is complete and fit for the calling of the spirits ...[1]

HE NAMES OF THE "FOUR KINGS of the four corners of the earth" that border the four cardinal directions on the Holy Table of Practice are shrouded in mystery. In many grimoires they are seen as Archdemons who hold sway over the influences and allotments of the Sublunary Intelligences. They are also often considered the gatekeepers for the celestial influences upon the earth. However, as prominent as they are in grimoric literature, the identities of the four Kings or Rulers are oddly obscured, with both their names and their attribution to the quarters varying among the texts. They remain relatively unknown to modern magicians save for the few who have successfully made contact with them.

I was determined to solve the mystery of these powerful Spirits. It was my hope that the cumulative accomplishments of my scryer and me, including the newfound awareness and abilities acquired as a result of our recent operations, would allow us access to and audience with these Kings.

I first began to consider the identities of the four Kings of the Cardinal Directions years ago when I began to design my own Holy Table for my *DSIC*

1. Barrett's translation of *The Art of Drawing Crystals into Spirits*. —APF

*Fig. IX-1. **The Holy Table as described in The Art of Drawing Spirits into Crystals***

practice. After much research and deliberation, I settled on four names, and engraved them on my Table of Practice in the following directions: Oriens in the East, Amaymon in the South, Paymon in the West, and Egyn in the North.

On the Four Cardinal Kings

Agrippa refers to the four Directional Rulers a couple of times in his monumental *De Occulta Philosophia*. In book II, in his Scale of the Number Four, he lists Oriens, Paymon, Egyn, and Amaymon as being associated with East, West, North, and South.[2] In book III, he states that

2. These are Agrippa's "Four Princes of the Demons over the Four Angles of the Globe" from the Scale of the Quaternary. As I previously remarked in the notes to *Liber Spirituum* (Azoth Press, 2016), "J.F." (probably John French, but possibly James Freake), the 1651 English translator of *De Occulta Philosophia*, for some reason chose to mislead his readers, including many modern occultists who do not have access to the Latin original. Although he translated *Quatuor **principes dæmoniorum** nocentes in elementis* (referring to Samael, Azazel, Azael, and Mahazael) two lines earlier in the same table as "Four **Princes of devils**, offensive in the Elements," and though Agrippa has unambiguously placed both sets of Demonic Princes in

> amongst evil spirits, there are four which as most potent Kings are set over the rest, according to the four parts of the world, whose names are these: *viz.*, Urieus, King of the East; Amaymon, King of the South; Paymon, King of the West; Egin, King of the North, which the Hebrew Doctors perhaps call more rightly thus, Samuel, Azazel, Azael, Mahazuel.[3]

In *The Book of the Sacred Magic of Abra-Melin the Mage*, we find eight Sub-Princes of the Evil Spirits divided into two groups of four, with one group consisting of Oriens, Paimon, Ariton, and Amaimon.[4] Mathers notes that "Ariton is often called Egin or Egyn in other works on Magic."[5] The Abramelin system includes the interesting detail that the magus should request a familiar Spirit from each of these four.

The *Key of Solomon* in many of its versions knows the Cardinal Kings Oriens (or, in some versions, Asmodee), Paymon, Amaymon, and Egyn in an invocation for erotic magic.[6] In the Abognazar *Veritable Clavicles of Solomon*, a table of

---

parallel *in Mundo Infernali, ubi lex iræ & punitionis* ("in the Infernal World, where is the law of wrath & punishment"), J.F. disingenuously translates *Quatuor* ***principes dæmoniorum*** *super quatuor angulos orbis* (referring to Oriens, Amaymon, Paymon, and Egin) as "Four **Princes of spirits** [rather than the 'Princes of devils' of two lines above], upon the four angles of the world." Unlike J.F., I have no reservations in translating Agrippa's intentionally parallel descriptions of Samael & co. as "Four Princes of the Demons wreaking harm in the Elements," and of Oriens & co. as "Four Princes of the Demons over the Four Angles of the Globe." In fact, in Book III, as Ashen Chassan points out, Agrippa moves beyond parallelism to explicit equation of the two lists of Demon Princes. —APF

3. Agrippa and J.F., *Three Books of Occult Philosophy written by Henry Cornelius Agrippa of Nettesheim* (London: Printed by R.W. for Gregory Moule, 1651), Book III, chapter 24. —APF

4. Book II, chapters 15 and 19 of the French MS employed by Mathers, and the same chapters in Book III of the German MSS. In the system of Abramelin, Oriens and his peers are, as Mathers accurately translates, "Sub-Princes" (*sousprinces* in the French and *Unterfürsten* in the German, curiously translated as "dukes" by Guth in the Dehn edition). It is intriguing that in *Abramelin* as in Agrippa another set of four Demon Princes stands alongside the Oriens tetrad, though in *Abramelin* the other four are Astarot, Magot, Asmodee, and Belzebud rather than the Samael tetrad. —APF

5. S.L. MacGregor Mathers and Abraham ben Simeon of Worms, *The Book of the Sacred Magic of Abra-Melin the Mage* (London: J.M. Watkins, 1898), Book II, chapter 15. —APF

6. *E.g.*, *The Clavicle of Solomon revealed by Ptolemy the Grecian* (MS Sloane 3847), *Clavicula Salomonis filii David* (MS Duveen 388), and *The Kay of Knowledge: Clavicula Salomonis* (Add. MS 36674), all available for study on Joseph H. Peterson's wondrous Twilit Grotto—Esoteric Archives website. —APF

Elemental correspondences gives Baël, Moïmon, Poïmon, and Egin.[7] The *Magical Calendar* includes in its correspondences of the Elements and Directions Bael, Poymon, Egyn, and Moymon. Cecco d'Ascoli knew the Directional Kings as Oriens, Paymon, Amaymon, and Egim.[8] A version of the *Grimoire du Pape Honorius* evokes Magoa, Egym, Bayemon, and Amaymon. Stephen Skinner and David Rankine have made extensive material regarding Oriens, Amaymon, Paymon, and Egyn accessible in their *Keys to the Gateway of Magic: Summoning the Solomonic Archangels and Demon Princes.*[9] Skinner and Rankine have also made available a small grimoire, *The Grimoire of Saint Cyprian: Clavis Inferni,*[10] that is of great interest to magicians wishing to evoke the four Directional Kings, as it gives images of Urieus, Paÿmon, Maymon, and Egÿn, along with distinctive seals and symbolic creatures, and even a magic circle of evocation (Fig. IX-2).[11]

---

7. The names of the Kings in the table are apparently borrowed from *The Method of Making the Astronomic Rings, Compounded from the Metals, Called Talismans,* which is appended to the Abognazar *Clavicles,* and teams the Directional Kings with the Olympic Governors. For more on the *Astronomic Rings,* see Frater Ashen Chassan's "Substance Through Spirit: A Reflection on Magical Evocation and Talisman Construction" in *Liber Spirituum.* —APF

8. Cecco d'Ascoli (Cichus Asculanus) wrote a grimoric-style Latin commentary on Johannes de Sacrobosco's famous astronomical monograph on the nature of the macrocosmic Sphere, and both Cecco and his book were burned at the stake by the Inquisition in 1327. Brian P. Copenhaver translates a section of the ill-fated work in his *Magic in Western Culture: From Antiquity to the Enlightenment* (Cambridge: Cambridge University Press, 2015), p. 209, and reveals a very dark tradition regarding the nature of the Kings. Cecco cites a grimoire spuriously ascribed (as were many magical texts) to Zoroaster, which states that "Oriens, Amaymon, Paymon, and Egim [*sic*]" are four Archdemons at the cardinal angles of the Sphæric universe, who are "spirits from the greater hierarchy, and each has twenty-five legions of spirits under him who . . . want sacrifices of human blood as well as the flesh of a dead man or a cat." Disturbingly gruesome details aside, this text provokes me to wonder whether Agrippa's classification of the four Kings as stationed over *quatuor angulos orbis* ("the four angles of the globe or orb") rather than *quatuor angulos mundi* ("the four angles of the world") might derive from Cecco's association of them specifically with the cosmic Sphere. —APF

9. Singapore: Golden Hoard Press, 2005. The relevant material is from MSS Sloane 3824, Sloane 3821, and Rawlinson D.1363. —APF

10. Singapore: Golden Hoard Press, 2009. The source text is the late-eighteenth-century codex MS Wellcome 2000, *M: L: Cypriani Clavis Inferni sive Magia Alba et Nigra approbata Metratona* (Latin, *"M.L. Cyprian's Key of Hell, or Magic White and Black, approved by Metatron"*). —APF

11. The Latin inscription inside the Circle reads *Ego me circumcingo Virtute horum Nominum Quibus hic Circulus est consignatus* ("I encircle myself with the Virtue of these Names, by which this Circle is sealed." The inscription in the Transitus Fluvii alphabet in the red-tinted band consists of Hebrew Archangelic and Divine Names for each Quarter. The Names were a

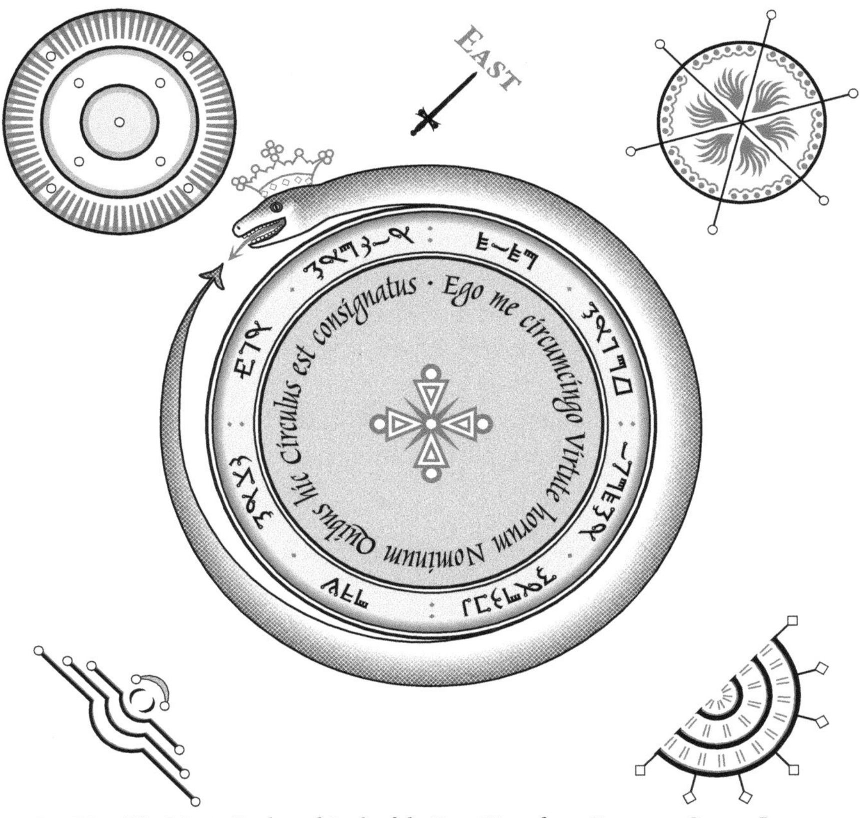

Fig. IX-2. The Magic Circle and Seals of the Four Kings from CYPRIANI CLAVIS INFERNI

And then of course there are grimoires with sets of Directional Rulers that have little to no overlap with those of the Oriens group. Johann Reuchlin, in *De Arte Cabalistica*, gives the names of the four Hebrew Demon Princes known to Agrippa.[12] The *Theurgia Goetia* gives the Emperors of the Directions as Carne-

---

Quarter off in the illustration in the codex (as proven by their pairing with the proper Kings in the individual portraits), and had to be rotated 90° clockwise to align them properly (*e.g.*, מיכאל and יהוה with Oriens), so a question arises whether the Ouroboros should also be rotated to place its head in the East. One could also well question whether the interior of the Circle should not properly be rotated 45° clockwise to orient the head of the Cross and the beginning of the Latin inscription to the East. —APF

12. Late in his 1517 dialogue (Book III, sig. O7^{r}), Reuchlin describes the Archangels Michael, Gabriel, Uriel, and Raphael as the four *antesignani* ("commanders before the banners") of the army of God, and then tells us: "In like manner, in the army of Satan, the standard-bearing punishers סמאל, עזאזל, עזאל, and מהזאל (Samael, Azazel, Azael, and Mahazael) carry the most

siel in the East, Caspiel in the South, Amenadiel in the West, and Demoriel in the north.[13] *Liber Juratus* has Barthan, Iammax, Harthan, and Maymon. The *Hygromanteia*[14] has Berzebeoul, Asmedaē, Astaroth, and Loutzepher. *Abramelin* has no less than three sets of four Demonic Rulers; in addition to the Oriens group of Sub-Princes, there is a second set of Sub-Princes (Astarot, Magot, Asmodee, and Belzebud) and a set of Superior Princes (Lucifer, Leviatan, Satan, and Belial). Also, there is the best known divergent set of Directional Kings, those deriving from the Goetic *Liber Officiorum Spirituum ("Book of the Offices of the Spirits")*, and found in the *Goetia*, Wierus' *Pseudomonarchia Dæmonorum*, and Scot's translation of Wierus in *Discoverie of Witchcraft*: Amaymon, Corson, Ziminiar, and Goap.[15]

In searching for ancient forms or precursors of the Four Kings, references to directional and seasonal rulers can be found in every ancient civilization from

---

wide-spread flags." At the same time he was writing *De Occulta Philosophia*, Agrippa taught classes in Reuchlin's *De Arte Cabalistica*, and it is almost certainly the source from which he learned the Hebrew names of the infernal princes. —APF

13. See fig. XI-2, the *32-rayed Compass Circle from THEURGIA GOETIA*, in chapter XI. —APF

14. MS Atheniensis 115. Excerpts translated in Ioannis Marathakis, *The Magical Treatise of Solomon, or Hygromanteia* (Singapore: Golden Hoard Press, 2011), pp. 345 ff. —APF

15. However, Paymon is also listed as a King in the Goetic catalogue. It is also certainly worth noting that there are versions of the *Offices of Spirits* which do include the Four Cardinal Kings. Folger Shakespeare Library MS V.b.46 includes an *Officiū de Spirittibꝰ (Officium de Spiritibus, "The Office of Spirits")* in English, which not only includes but begins with the Four Kings:

> There be 4 kinges of the ayere Orience R of the eaſt / Paymon R of the weſt /
> Amaymon R of the south / & Egine R of the north -/

The manuscript can be seen online at the Folger Library (http://luna.folger.edu/luna/servlet/view/search?q=v.b.26&sort=call_number%2Cauthor%2Ccd_title%2Cimprint&os=0), with a transcription at the Twilit Grotto—Esoteric Archives (http://www.esotericarchives.com/folger/v_b_26_transcription.pdf), and in the book by Daniel Harms, James R. Clark, and Joseph H. Peterson, *The Book of Oberon: A Sourcebook of Elizabethan Magic* (Woodbury, Minnesota: Llewellyn Publications, 2015).

Other versions of the *Offices* citing the Kings by the familiar names include those in MSS Sloane 3853 and Add. 36674 (both of which may be seen in the online editions of excerpts by the indefatigable Joseph H. Peterson on his Twilit Grotto—Esoteric Archives website <http://www.esotericarchives.com/solomon/offices.htm>); and (as pointed out by Jean-Patrice Boudet, "Les who's who démonologiques de la Renaissance et leurs ancêtres médiévaux," in *Médiévales* 44 | Spring 2003: Le diable en procès <http://medievales.revues.org/1019>)— Cambridge Trinity College MS O.8.29, *Livre des esperitz*, and Oxford Bodleian MS Rawlinson D.252, the latter of which provides the curious detail that Amaymon should be skryed in a separate glass from the other three Kings. —APF

Asia to the Americas. However, my direct experiences with the Spirits in evocation have shed additional light on my historical researches and led me to pay particular attention to some striking similarities between the grimoric Directional Rulers and certain Gods and Goddesses of the ancient Near and Middle East as possible original forms of the Rulers of the Quarters. For instance, the Babylonian, Assyrian, Phœnician, and Ugaritic Gods Hadad, Baal, Bel, and Marduk (and in the *interpretatio Græca* of the Hellenistic world, Zeus) were all identified with each other as the deity associated with the East, storms, and winds, an identification easily synonymous with Oriens. For another example, we can look to Egypt, whose powerful impact on Western magical traditions such as those of the Greek Magical Papyri eventually influenced the grimoires. There our attention is drawn to the four Sons of Horus. Best known as the guardian Gods of the four Canopic jars that preserved the organs of mummies, they are also Gods of the cardinal directions, who uphold the heavens and connect the heavens and the earth.[16]

The effort to historically pinpoint the correct name of each of the four Kings continues to sparks an ongoing discussion in the occult community, which supports differing points of view. For my interests in these workings, it seemed a prudent decision to stick with the names that I had inscribed on the Holy Table which I had used in nearly every operation, since none of my researches had disturbed my confidence in their validity.

Since each of these four Rulers has a collection of Spirits who are under his control, I wanted to evoke each and see what manner of Spirits they ruled and also what powers they themselves had from which we could benefit. To conjure any other Spirit in classical magic, the magus would petition one of the Kings to cause the Spirit to appear if they did not arrive after their initial invocations. As Sandalphon had said in our earlier working, the Kings «open gates that allow the plane of experiences to converge on the circle of the magician.» I had never attempted to directly invoke one of these "demon kings of the directions" before this point, and I was excited by the prospect of finally learning from them at first hand. In all honesty, I should admit that I realized this was a bit arrogant and possibly even dangerous, as the grimoires often state that the Cardinal Kings are not to be conjured because of their might and unpredictability. As *The Old Book of Magic* states:

16. The Sons of Horus are jackal-headed Duamutef, falcon-headed Qabehsonef, human-headed Amseth or Imset, and baboon-headed Hapi. The Sons are still actively invoked in the magic of the Golden Dawn and in the religious practices of some Kemetics. —APF

> These four powerful spirits are difficult to be constrained, or urged to visible appearance. They are dangerous to contend with, and are *"powers of evil," "swift to destruction."* They bear an inveterate hatred to humankind, will delude the *Theurgist* with lies and deceit, and in every other way strive to render his work abortive. But if the *Theurgist* shall be able to make them enter a consecrated pentacle, or a circle fortified with divine names, they will be forced against their will to reveal the truth; and he need fear no harm, if he be born under a right constellation.[17]

I was not quite convinced that the rulers were entirely evil or hateful to mankind, but I was nonetheless reasonably wary of the upcoming operations. Again quoting from the Sandalphon operation: «Associated with their direction, they pull the qualities of that space and send it to those who call in a holy matter for holy intentions...and for those who call for bad or evil intentions. They are without judgement, without morality. They give their energies forth simply to give, not to judge.»

---

17. L.W. De Laurence, *The Old Book of Magic: A Precise History of Magic, Its Procedure, Rites and Mysteries* (Chicago, Ill: De Laurence, Scott & Co, 1918), pp. 19–20.

The Old Book of Magic is one of the works of 'Dr.' De Laurence, the most notorious and shameless plagiarist in modern Western occultism. For this book, De Laurence claims to have had access to the *"Ancient Manuscripts"* of the popular British astrologer Raphael. Raphael—like the Dread Pirate Roberts—was in actuality a series of men, but De Laurence meant the first Raphael, Robert Cross Smith (1795–1832), who may have been a student of Francis Barrett. De Laurence's steely-eyed, lavishly-mustachioed, exotically-turbaned, and carny-worthy frontispiece portrait as a master of the mystic arts in *The Old Book of Magic* almost tempts one to smile and forgive his bluster and braggadoccio as a game until one remembers the number of significant European books by authors such as Mathers and Waite which he pirated and published in America as his original work. *The Old Book of Magic*—or at least the portions of it in which we are interested—is one of those piracies; all of the relevant material in *The Old Book of Magic* consists of sections not coped from Raphael's private manuscripts, but abducted wholesale (footnotes, illustrations, and all) from his published work, specifically *The Astrologer of the Nineteenth Century, or, The Master Key of Futurity and Guide to Ancient Mysteries: Being a Complete System of Occult Philosophy*, by the Members of the Mercurii: Raphael, the Metropolitan Astrologer; the Editor of the Prophetic Almanack; and other Sidereal Artists of Eminence (London: Knight and Lacey, 1825). The paragraph quoted above from *The Old Book of Magic*, for example, is found on p. 203 of *The Astrologer of the Nineteenth Century*. However, from a purely pragmatic perspective, if one is willing to tolerate De Laurence's posing and occasional tampering, *The Old Book of Magic* remains a practical source for finding useful invocations from various grimoires gathered in one convenient place. —APF

Creating the Implements of the Directional Rulers ✠ Part 2[18]

As for the talismans in which to call or focus the presences of these four Kings, Sandalphon had instructed us that «A circle of stone. A lens. A candle. A cup can be used to summon each of the Kings.» He concluded by stating «A symbol of an Element that is also a gateway make excellent talismans for them.» The function of these four items truly seemed to be creating an official threshold for them to pass through and thus affirming their authority in governing the particular Spirits under their direction.

My idea was to take the instructions of Sandalphon regarding the Elemental implements or talismans, and combine them with the symbols and imagery given in the *Clavis Inferni*, which gives some of the best detail and resources for contacting "the Four Demon Kings," as it describes them, complete with symbols for each and corresponding magical animals.

The Cardinal Talismans Indicated by Sandalphon

The Stone Ring

A «circle of stone» seemed a bit vague at the time, and I muddled over what exactly this talisman would be. I surmised that this would be the object associated with the North and attributed to the Spirit Egyn. With obvious Earth references, I wondered if there was further significance to this particularly shaped stone. Researching ancient stone ring objects with significant value and meaning, I came across the *bi* disks. In Neolithic China, important persons were buried with stone—often particularly jade—disks with holes in the center. I wasn't sure if this was the type of object the Archangel and the King of the North intended, but it did fit the description.

Finally I obtained a Neolithic stone bowl or round stone that is deeply concave on both sides and has naturally occurring circular lines that resembles Egyn's symbol depicted in the *Clavis Inferni.* I reasoned that this would serve as a suitable talisman. Although it wasn't quite a «circle» with a hole through the center, the outer rims of the bowl clearly formed a circular shape.

The Lens

The Lens would be simple enough to obtain, but I wanted some sort of frame that would display the Lens so it could be viewed through without being held

18. Part 1 may be found in chapter VIII, following the Invocation of Sandalphon.

in the hand, something like a caliper stand. The Catholic monstrance for holding and displaying relics also seems to be a lens of a particular nature typically located in the east or front of the church. I also could not help comparing it to the mirror often found at the head of the *kamidana* shrine in Shinto homes and businesses.

Finally, I decided that this talisman—as Sandalphon had specifically called it a lens—should be a magnifying lens and not just a sheet of glass.

I reasoned that the Lens would belong to Amaymon in the South, since his animal in the *Clavis Inferni* is the bird, which seems obviously to correspond to the Element of Air.

The Candle

As simple as a candle and candleholder are, I wanted them to be specifically selected and consecrated to open the gateway and draw forth the Fire King. As the *Clavis Inferni* shows a dragon as the creature of the East, I decided that the candle should be in the East and have a dragon holding it to associate it with Oriens.

I spent a while trying to obtain a suitable candleholder, as I was determined to find a dragon. Eventually I did discover a lovely coiled brass one with its mouth open toward the sky, and a small red beeswax candle that fit perfectly into the dragon's mouth.

The Cup

The Cup associated with the West and Water for Paymon seemed straightforward. Although the animal in the *Clavis Inferni*—manticore? sphinx? chimera?—did not appear to coincide with any magical water being with which I was familiar, I felt confident that the Cup belonged to Paymon in the West.

After securing these four talismans, I found it fascinating that each invariably had a gateway point or symbolic threshold through which sight and focus could pass to the other side. For the lens, it was simply seeing through the glass to the other side. We had already used a candle flame as a doorway through which to travel, thanks to our experimentation utilizing the scrying method described by Josephine McCarthy.[19] The cup of water is a scrying device that has been used

19. Josephine McCarthy, *The Exorcist's Handbook* (Berkeley, CA: Golem Media, 2010), p. 18.

through the ages to see into the Astral. The stone ring, when held or supported vertically, provides a window through which a seer may scry.

The Lamens

Although I felt confident that the seals found in *Clavis Inferni* would suffice as lamens, I was adamant about tracking down any other possible sigils that were attributed to the four Rulers. It just so happened that when I brought up this concern to a fellow magician who goes by the name of Asterion Mage, he had just the information for which I was searching. He called my attention to a rare magical text, the *Fasciculus Rerum Geomanticarum*,[20] that reveals sigils attributed to the four Cardinal Kings by name, as well as to many of the Archdemonic rulers that are notoriously present in many grimoric volumes. I decided that I would use these sigils on the lamens.

As usual, I created a pair of matching lamens for each of these four great Spirits: a golden lamen which I would wear as the operator, and a parchment talisman with 24k gold-leaf backing upon which my scryer would meditate in preparation for skrying.

As a precaution, I also inscribed the name and sigil of the associated "thwarting" Archangel on the reverse side of each King's lamen.

The Seal Plaques

As I was using the esoteric sigils from the *Fasciculus* on the lamens, I decided to also make a set of four small wooden pedestals and cap each with a metal disk that I engraved with the seal of one of the Kings from the *Clavis Inferni*. I added some gold leaf and painting in what I felt were the appropriate colors. Each pedestal was three inches wide and about an inch and a half in thickness, and around each of them I wood-burned names and titles of the King. I would use these plaques as the bases on which to stand the directional talismans prescribed by Sandalphon. I thought this an excellent way in which to use both known sigils and seals for the Direction Kings during the ritual.

The Incenses

Finally, Sandalphon had instructed my scryer and me on the use of incense in the conjurations: «An incense can be used for each of them, but only use one as

---

20. Latin, "A Small Collection of Geomantic Items." Florence, Biblioteca Laurenziana, Codex Pluteo LXXXIX superiore 38 (often abbreviated to Plut. 89 sup. 38). —APF

dominant for the particular purpose that fits the intent of the working. To use incense of all four would bring in too much and dilute the intent of the work. Using the correspondences with the intent of the work, any energy direction of the gate correspondence can pull and amplify the energy of the gatekeeper. Use the correspondences to the direction intuitive to the magician, as these qualities are mixed and reflected differently in each of you.» The incenses I chose for each of the Kings were frankincense and copal for Oriens, galbanum and sandalwood for Amaymon, myrrh and onycha for Paymon, and storax and benzoin for Egyn.

The Elements and the Quarters

I was comfortable with the attribution of the individual Kings to the respective directions, but the proper attribution of the talismans, incenses, etc., depended on the Elemental correspondences of the directions. The *Clavis Inferni* was my richest source of information, and it shows a dragon as the creature in the East, and a bird as the creature in the South, which seems to correlate Fire with the East and Air with the South.[21] This was something of a dilemma for me, as my usual correspondences for the directions were the reliable Air East, Fire South, Water West, and Earth North.

So far my findings had led me to establish the correspondences in Figure IX-3 in the hope to clearly connect each Cardinal King with the proper direction, Element, and other attributes.

I had many questions to ask of the Direction Rulers, as I wanted to get as much information as I could, not only to understand them better but to be able to call upon them again should the need arise. I wished to know in what manner they should be invoked in order for them to send or release other Spirits to arrive before my scryer and me. I was also anxious to see which of them was the "most dominant" for me, which I took to mean that one of them would be the most agreeable and powerful for my personal development.

I was interested to discover if the Kings really did act as overseers and 'border control' over every Spirit's interaction with the physical plane of the earth.

21. The *Clavis Inferni* never explicitly states the Elemental attributions of the Quarters, and may have been meaning—in whole or in part—to follow Agrippa, who in his Scale of the Quaternary uses the directional attributions of the Cardinal Signs of the Vernal Zodiac: Fire East (♈), Earth South (♑), Air West (♎), and Water North (♋). —APF

Cardinal King	Direction	Element	Talisman (*according to* Sandalphon)	Incense	Thwarting Archangel	Symbolic Animal (*according to* Clavis Inferni)
Oriens/Urieus	East	Fire	Candle	Frankincense, copal	Michael	Dragon/ Ouroboros
Amaymon/ Amaimon/ Maymon	South	Air	Lens	Galbanum, sandalwood	Gabriel	Bird
Paymon/ Paimon	West	Water	Cup	Myrrh, onycha	Raphael	Sphinx or Manticore
Egyn/Egin/ Ariton	North	Earth	Stone Ring	Storax, benzoin	Uriel	Bear

Table IX-3. ***Initial Table of Correspondences for the Four Cardinal Kings***

Although the grimoires certainly give the magus reason to be cautious in any decision to evoke these Spirits, they are specifically included as part of this art of conjuration in many classical works. They have their own "ring" on the Holy Table in the *Art of Drawing Spirits into Crystals*. Their aspects and roles in conjuration should be understood and integrated into the magician's workings.

By climbing the ladder of our spiritual and physiological evolution, we can piece together the specifically divine nature of our own creation in the matrix of the greater macrocosm. But unless we become intimately familiar with and achieve mastery over each piece, we cannot hope to understand the aspects of the whole. The great work and secret adventure of the Hermetic magician is this journey, both inwardly and outwardly, in exploration of the deep space of totality. And it seemed to me that the Cardinal Kings of the Four Directions were likely to prove important to that journey.

The Cardinal King of the East
Oriens

Day and time	On Sunday or Wednesday at Dawn
Name and meaning	Oriens (Latin, "East; Rising")
Other names and possible meanings	Uriens (possibly from Latin *Urens*, "Burning, Enflaming"); Urieus (possibly from Greek Εὐρέϊος [*Eureios*], "Easterly," relating to Εὖρος [*Euros*], the East Wind); Oraeus
Pronunciation of name (as spoken by the Spirit)	«Or-ee-ens»
Element	△ (?)
Direction for invocation	East
Materials for lamen	Parchment, iron, gold
Sigils	
Incense	Frankincense, copal
Talisman	Candle (?)

Table IX-4. ***Evocatory Correspondences for Oriens***

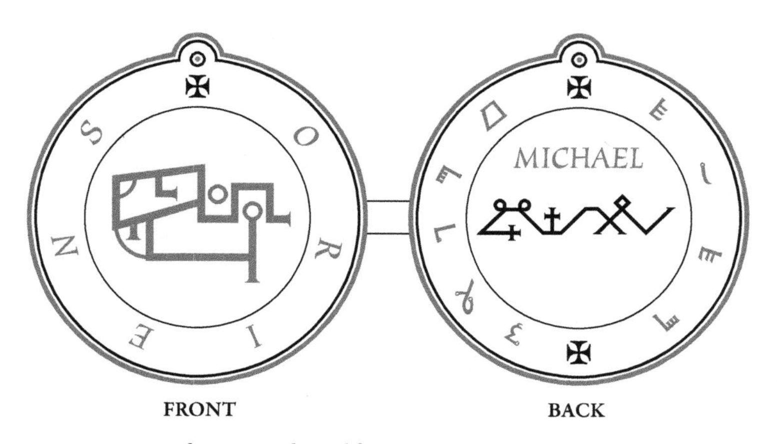

Fig. IX-5. ***Lamen of Oriens with Sigil from Fasciculus Rerum Geomanticarum, and Thwarting Archangel from Clavis Inferni***

Of Oriens

Consulting *The Keys to the Gateway of Magic*, MS Sloane 3824 tells us of the Eastern Cardinal King:

> Oriens King of the East, appeareth with a hundred & two hundred legions, having a fair countenance and a goodly crown upon his head, riding upon an elephant, having trumpets, sahlams[22] and much minstrels of diverse instruments going before him, and when he cometh he comes with other great kings but if he be called alone he appeareth in the very likeness of a royal horse. He telleth the truth of all things present, past and to come, gives money, teaches sciences, confereth books, and willingly gives answers to all demands and questions, he knows of all experiments and has power to teach them.[23]

Fig. IX-6. ***Pentacular Plaque of Oriens with Seal from*** **CLAVIS INFERNI**

The King of the East's description and office can likewise be found in *The Old Book of Magic*, where we find the same description nearly word for word, citing no specific source but an *"Ancient Manuscript"*:

> He appeareth with a firm countenance, and a goodly crown upon his head; he rideth upon an elephant, having before him numbers of hands and swords. Sometimes he appeareth in the similitude of a horse; and, when he is constrained by magical incantations, assumeth a human shape. He hath under him 250 legions of inferior spirits. His power, according to the ancients, is great, and he can answer truly to all demands, both past, present, and to come.[24]

The description of Oriens having "a number of hands and swords" as well as the accompanying illustration (fig. IX-7) appear strikingly Hindu in nature. As he

22. The nearly identical passage in MS Folger V.b.26 provides a more familiar form for this word as "shawms," being a type of reed instrument like an oboe, popular in the Middle Ages and Renaissance. —APF

23. Stephen Skinner and David Rankine, *The Keys to the Gateway of Magic: Summoning the Solomonic Archangels & Demon Princes* (London & Singapore: Golden Hoard Press, 2005), p. 224.

24. De Laurence, *op. cit.*, p. 18.

is a "king of the East," it certainly would make sense for some of his imagery to come from eastern lands. With further research, it became quite obvious that Oriens was being identified as the Hindu God Indra, the *Deva* of rain and thunderstorms. He rides on a four-tusked white elephant,[25] and like Zeus, is the King of the Gods (*Devarāja*), and wields the thunderbolt (*vajra*). He upholds the sky and releases the dawn from a cave every new day, and as such Indra is also regarded as one of the Guardians of the Directions, representing the East. With all the similarities in office and description, it is hard to ignore the connection of this Hindu Deva to the Spirit Oriens.

Fig. IX-7. ***Image of Indra as Oriens in The Old Book of Magic***

In his speculations on the possible meanings of the Spirit names in *Abra-Melin*, MacGregor Mathers notes of Oriens:

> *Oriens*, = rising or Eastern. This name is also written Uriens, from Latin, *Uro*, = to burn, or devour with flame. It is probably from Uriens that a mediæval title of the Devil, *viz.*, "Sir Urien," is derived. The Name is also sometimes written "Urieus," from Latin, "*Urios*," a title given to Jupiter as presiding over the Wind. Urieus is also derivable from the Greek Adj. "*Eurus, Eureia, Euru*," meaning vast or extensive.[26] By the Rabbins he is also called SMAL, *Samael*, which is derived from the Hebrew root SML, which means "a figure, image, or idol". It is a name given in the Qabalah to one of the Chief Evil Spirits.[27]

---

25. In fact, the picture of Indra on his elephant which De Laurence had his illustrator engrave is a copy of an image so well known that a version of it is at the head of both the English and Sanskrit Wikipedia pages on Indra. It replaced a far less Oriental image of the elephant-riding Oriens in *The Astrologer of the Nineteenth Century*. —APF

26. Starting with '*Urios*,' Mathers gets a little lost in this etymology, though he is surely on the right track. There isn't a Latin *Urios*, but *Eurius* and *Eureus* are Latinized forms of Greek *Eureios*, "pertaining to the East Wind," from *Euros*, "the East Wind," and *Eureios* is obviously highly pertinent to Urieus in form and meaning and Oriens in meaning. —APF

27. S.L. MacGregor Mathers, "Notes to the Foregoing Lists of Names of Spirits," appended to Chapter 19 of his translation of *The Book of the Sacred Magic of Abra-Melin the Mage*. —APF

Invocations of Oriens

In preparation for the operation, I also studied the invocations of Oriens provided in various grimoires.

Cyprian, in the *Clavis Inferni*, says that we should hold his book in our left hand, and raise the first three fingers of our right hand while reciting the *Exclamatio*, or "Calling Aloud":

In the name of the Father and Lord, I powerfully exorcise you, Spirit Oriens, King of the East, from the bottom of the whole Infernal World, and powerful through the name of the ever-living and true Lord, I powerfully command you through the strong and wonderful names El, Elohim, Adonai, Tzabaoth, that you appear before this Circle in a fair and visible human form, and without tortuosity, come because I command you through the names Yod, Yah, El, Shaddai, IHVH, Elion, Elohim, Yeheshuah, Ararita, Eloah va-Daath, Elohim Gibor.

I call you through the Heavens, the Cherubim and Seraphim, Thrones, Dominations and Universal Powers and Virtues ✠✠✠ and the merciful four chiefs of the heavens: Michael, Gabriel, Raphael, and Uriel; the Sun and Moon and revolving Stars; the Elements Earth, Fire, Water, Air; Summer, Spring, Winter, Autumn; and that praises M.N. Lord God El, set above the blessèd and most sacrosanct wonderful Raphael, strong Gabriel, redeeming Michael, eternal Haniel, praiseworthy Tzadkiel. Invincible Creator of the Sun and Moon, Christ Incarnate, and the Paraclete, the Trine God, Amen.[28]

Sloane 3824 provides another conjuration of the King of the East, although its goal is to adjure him to send one of his subordinate Spirits, as is the function of the Kings and the fashion in most grimoires. I present a slightly altered form of the conjuration, adapted to call Oriens to appear directly, rather than to send the Spirit Marage as in the manuscript:

O thou great and potent Spirit Oriens, King of the East, and bearing rule and command in the East Region of Air, I adjure, call upon, and constrain, and most powerfully and earnestly urge you by and in and through the virtue, power, and might of these efficacious and binding names: Tetragrammaton, Jehovah, Adonay,

28. Wellcome MS 2000, p. 10. The form of the invocation above is slightly adapted by Ashen Chassan to be specific to Oriens, but follows very closely the translation of Dr. Peter Forshaw in Skinner and Rankine, *The Grimoire of Saint Cyprian: Clavis Inferni*, pp. 62–65, from the Latin of the codex with its plentiful abbreviations, reversed words, and cryptographic symbols. —APF

Agla, El, Sabaoth, Elohim, even the Almighty, Immense, Incomprehensible, and Everliving God, the omnipotent Creator of Heaven and earth, and in and through the names of our Lord and Savior Jesus Christ, Messias, Sother, Emanuel, the only Begotten Son of God the Father, born of the Virgin Mary, the High King and Lord of all the world, whose name all the celestial Angels honor and obey, and before whom all the holy company and choir of heaven incessantly sing O Mappa Laman, Hallelujah, and at whose divine and inestimable name all knees on earth do homage and bow, and all the Aerial, Terrestrial, and Infernal Spirits do fear and tremble. And now, by all the aforesaid, I do now again powerfully adjure, call upon, constrain, and most earnestly urge you, O you great and mighty spirit Oriens, King of the East Quadrant of the Air, in and through the most effectual, glorious, sacred, and puissant names of him who sayeth "It is done," that now, immediately, without further tarrying or delay, you arrive and appear unto me visibly, plainly, peaceably, affably, in all serenity and humility, here apparently to my sight and view, and positively, effectually, faithfully, and fully to serve me and be responsive to me in such queries and interrogations as I shall ask and require of you, and that without delay, guile, deceit, or illusions whatsoever that may in any wise obstruct or destroy our expectations. And I do again earnestly importune, adjure, urge, and constrain you, O you powerful and regal Spirit Oriens, to appear forthwith immediately, and now at this present time, to me, and to appear plainly visible before me, in all mildness, peace, and friendliness, without any hurt, disturbance, or any other evil whatsoever, either to me, my scryer, or this place wherein I am, or any other place, person, or creature whatsoever, but that quietly, courteously, and obediently to serve me and fulfill my desires and do my commandments in all things, all which I earnestly urge and constrain thee, O thou royal and potent Spirit Oriens, to do for me in Nomine Patris, et Filii, et Spiritus Sancti.[29]

The manuscript notes that, if needed, this constraint should be uttered three times.

The next Invocation comes from Sloane 3821, which introduces it and subsequent invocations as "Operations of the East Angle of the Air by Invocation made to the Regal Spirit Orients [*sic*], who is the King & Ruler of the Same for the moving and calling forth of all, or any of Such, Aerial Spirits by name Order and office of what Degrees soever from the Superior to the Inferior to Visible

29. The original form of this conjuration or constraint may be read in Skinner and Rankine, *The Keys to the Gateway of Magic*, pp. 226–227. —APF

Appearance &c." Again this invocation has been modified slightly to fit the nature of the operation we wish to perform.

O you Royal Spirit of great power who art called Oriens, and said to be King of the East Angle, Region, or Mansion of the Air, and governing or bearing rule therein over many legions of Aerial Spirits subjected unto you, unto and under the power, obedience, and command of that great and mighty Spirit called Sathan, who is said to be the Prince of the Air, and to govern the four Angles, Regions, Divisions, or Mansions there of East, West, North, and South, and unto whom power and command is given over all Spirits having place, residence, or mansion therein, as by the preordinate decree of the Most High God, the only Creator of Heaven and Earth, and of all things whatsoever is contained in the creation, is constituted and appointed.

O ye Regal Spirit Oriens, King of the East Region or Angle of the Air, being governed and governing as aforesaid, we the servants of the Most High God reverently here present in His holy fear, being dignified, armed, and supported in the Holy Trinity through divine grace, with celestial power and authority given unto our first parents in the Creation, at the beginning of time, and by lineal descent from them to us and all posterity or succeeding generations, as the heirs of God's promise and grace, even to the utmost period thereof, and by the name of your God, and in the name of your prince or head of your Orders, and by your seal or character, preordinately decreed of the Most High God, confirming, subjecting, and binding you by orders and office unto strict obedience: first, to the fulfilling of His divine will and pleasure, both at his mediate and immediate commandments and appointments; secondly, unto the command, service, and obedience of your prince or head of your Orders as in place, degree, and office appointed; thirdly, as well unto the service, obedience, and assisting of the sons of men, servants of the Most High God, now living on Earth, according to your orders and office as to tempt and subvert them from their allegiance to the divine laws and duty to God, by your evil and crafty insinuations and delusions.

By the contents of all aforesaid, and by the power thereof, we do exorcise, conjure, command, compel, constrain, and move you, O you Regal Spirit who is called Oriens, King of the East Angle of the Air, forthwith and immediately at our invocation to move and appear in fair and decent form, and in no wise hurtful, dreadful, terrible, or frightful unto us or this place, or to any other person or place whatsoever, but in all humility and serenity, visibly to the sight of our eyes, in this crystal receptacle standing here before us, and to make us true and faithful answers unto all such our demands and requests, and to fulfill and accomplish all such our desires, as we shall by invocation declare, and at large in the contents thereof expressly show forth and move unto them without delay, delusion, or disturbance whereby to surprise or assault our senses with fear and amazements, or in any wise to obstruct or hinder the effects of these our present operations by any subtle crafts or illusions whatsoever.[30]

Many versions of the *Key of Solomon* include a ritual which conjures Oriens and the other three Directional Kings in turn. The purpose of the rite in which the invocation occurs is to secure a desired sexual partner,[31] but the relatively simple Four Kings invocation has no natural connection to that objective; as Omega Ω intelligently states in his online discussion of this text in the context of the Kings,

> the script appears to be highly adaptable, with the appearance of what modern magicians term 'a frame ritual'. One might be forgiven for imagining the table of Trithemius forming a part of such a modus operandi.[32]

Here is a modified form of the invocation from *The Clavicle of Solomon King of the Hebrews*, adapted as the previous calls to suit the intention of our current working:

O thou Orient, most shining, most excellent King, who reigns and who hath the command in Eastern Regions, whose Kingdom hath had commencement at the beginning of the World and which will endure until the end of the Ages.

I invoke you with power and I pray to you with the authority of the One Who spoke and Who hath made all, and Who with one sole word gave birth to the world, and Whom all creatures obey. By the Seat of His Majesty, by which He hath created the Ages before the permanent Ages, Who is described with four letters, Jod

30. The unmodified form of this invocation may also be read in Skinner and Rankine, *op. cit.*, pp. 229–230. —APF

31. This invocation will not be found in Mathers' edition of the *Key*. He deleted the erotic ritual of which it was a part (which involves a wax poppet of the desired but disinclined woman), as he had powerful ethical objections to the use of the magical equivalent of rohypnol to subvert the will of another person in the interests of a sexual predator. Instead, having been inspired by Anna Kingsford to a strong position on the protection of animals, he substituted another rite with which he had much more sympathy, an experiment designed to prevent hunters from injuring any animals. —APF

32. Omega Ω, "The Four Kings in the Grimoires Tradition," on the weblog *A Journey into Ceremonial Magick* (http://omega-magick.blogspot.com/2015/03/the-four-kings-in-grimoires-tradition.html). —APF

He Vau He, and by all the talismans and their virtues, and by the great and august names of the Creator, that you may appear unto my scryer and unto me visibly in this consecrated crystal, and positively and fully respond to me in such queries and interrogations as I shall ask and require of you, and that in all peace and courtesy you obey me and fulfill my desires and do my commandments in all things. By the most holy name of Adonay, whose virtue hath no beginning and will have no end.[33]

If there is one identifiable constant in my experience of magical evocations, it is that the encounters with the Spirits never seem to quite match my expectations. It's not that Spirits appear or converse in bizarre manners wildly contrary to what has been written of them, which would cause me to question the validity of what I was encountering. What is constant is that there is always a marked difference between what my imagination conjures up while researching and speculating about the Spirit and what occurs during the actual magical conjuration. Not that this has prevented me from continuing to imaginatively theorize about them. However, it has encouraged me to form no attachment to my speculations and daydreams, so that there is only surprise rather than disappointment or frustration when the expectation and the manifestation do not match. I do find it fairly humorous, however, just how little impact my preliminary visualizations and imaginings have on the actual outcome. Of course, I don't downplay my imagination, since it has led me to figure out how to craft numerous magical and grimoric items which at one time seemed vague and unknowable. It spurs me on to further magical adventures and nurtures my sense of wonder and excitement for what may be around the next Astral corner. It just doesn't create a predictable outline of what an experience will be like when it actually occurs. In fact, I've realized that it leaves me with a sense of validity regarding not only the experience but the independent nature of the Spirits themselves.

The evening where we attempted to contact the first of the four Cardinal Kings was no different. Since these rulers are often given the title of Demon Princes in the grimoires, I wasn't sure how this Spirit would present itself, or if it would present itself at all. In spite of the number of references to the four Kings, few details have been written concerning the great ruler of the East Oriens and

---

33. The unmodified form of the invocation, translated by Paul Harry Barron from the French of *La Clavicule de Salomon Roi des Hebreux traduite . . . par Abraham Colorno* in MS Kings 288, is available in Skinner and Rankine, *The Veritable Key of Solomon* (Singapore: Golden Hoard Press, 2010), p. 312. —APF

the description of his appearance and office in *The Old Book of Magic* half led me to believe that I might encounter a Hindu God-form. I was glad I had prepared a list of questions that would hopefully allow my scryer and me to better understand the nature and identity of this powerful Spirit.

I began as usual with the conjurations from *The Art of Drawing Spirits into Crystals*, but did not achieve materialization even with the follow-up conjurations. I finally had to resort to combined invocations from both the *Clavis Inferni* and the texts in *The Keys to the Gateway of Magic* before the Spirit would show itself in conversational form.

Invocation of the Cardinal Ruler Oriens

Fig. IX-8. ***Section of Circle for Drawing Oriens into the Crystal***

Appearance of the Spirit

SCRYER: The Spirit appears as a tall man formed of wind, with mist resting on his features so that I can see him. As if he has clothed his body in mist. Sometimes he looks almost Asian, and colorful, sometimes he looks somewhat feminine. He says:

SPIRIT: «Oriens is the first layer of the East. The gate.»

SCRYER: When he speaks, it is like a hundred voices all at once, but not in a cacophony; I can understand him perfectly.

Opening Questions[34]

OPENING QUESTION 1: In the name of the holy and undefiled Spirit, the Father, the begotten Son, and Holy Ghost proceeding from both, what is thy true name?

34. The Opening Questions, as always, are the probationary queries specified by the *The Art of Drawing Spirits into Crystals* as those proper to begin the conversation with any evoked Spirit.

Fig. IX-9. ***Portrait of Oriens as beheld in Vision***

SPIRIT: «Oriens is the name given for all voices spoken ever into the wind, for all the breaths first taken by a child or exhaled by the dying. Recorded, whispered, echoed through the mouths of Oriens.»

OPENING QUESTION 2: What is thy office?

SPIRIT: «Oriens opens the pathways that allow breath, spirit, and the invisible which can move tunnel its way to those who need it or call for it, consciously or unconsciously. Oriens speaks with many tongues and many mouths. Pulling words and languages from the heart, the mind, and the body to help fulfill The Great Plan of the Creators.»

OPENING QUESTION 3: What is thy true sign or character?

SPIRIT: «The sun that rises above and sets below. The scroll that covers the ground, written with the languages of all living things, the road that leads back to the beginning.»

(Symbol appears much like the symbol in the Clavis Inferni *but with one half of the circle darker.)*

OPENING QUESTION 4: When are the times most agreeable to thy nature to hold conference with us?

SPIRIT: «Any time. The nature of Oriens and the Four Kings is out of time. And though oriented in the East, the East is everywhere. The South is everywhere. The West and the North are everywhere. The center is 'intent,' called at need or at the behest of the unfolding of the Creators. Oriens speaks with those tongues.»

OATH: Wilt thou swear by the blood and righteousness of our Lord Jesus Christ that thou art truly the Mighty King, Ruler, and Spirit of the East called Oriens?

The administration of the Oath constitutes the fifth Opening Question. They are worded according to Barrett's translation. —APF

SPIRIT: «I swear that as I have presented myself to you from a millennia as Oriens, I am.»

OPERATOR: Wilt Thou swear by my Book of Spirits here and by my holy wand to swear loyalty to us and assist us? Loyalty and word, speech and assistance truthfully?

ORIENS: «When called by the heart, the mind, or the body, Oriens will come to breathe the first of spirit into your works, in return for praising my name and speaking my name to the wind.»

Further Questions

QUESTION 5: What are your views on humanity? What are your roles and interactions?

ORIENS: «One of my greatest gifts or media for speaking with humanity is language: the creation of it, the morphing of it, the growth of it, the way it is lent and borrowed and stolen. A great exchange of ideas from within the soul cages of abandonment. Each human speaking from their cage to the others nearest and closest to them. It is these words and this desire to speak and know one another that opens the cages slowly. And until all the cages are open, I fly on the words of humans and all that do speak or sing to remind them they are not alone and that together, they create the unfolding tapestry of the plan of the Creators.»

OPERATOR: In your replies you mention 'Creators,' as in more than one. Whom do you perceive as the Creators and what is your meaning?

ORIENS: «Oriens has learned that all are endowed with the power to create. Some use it, some do not. I saw at one point, on the languages and tongues of all the beings that speak and converse with one another, that the source of the ultimate Creator was in all of them: Angels, Demons, birds, beasts, and men. Even the rumbling of the earth or the scream of a pulsar, all vibrating with the voice that is unknowable. And I am privileged to carry that voice wherever it chooses to go from whoever or whatever it chooses to emanate from. Blessèd is my office.»

QUESTION 6: Do you have your own recollection of your creation and origin? Where do you come from? What is your purpose? Can you explain your relationship to the Angels and to God?

ORIENS: «I remember only that the four of us were at once one. I remember a separating, a division from one into four. With the division, I remember clarity and a rapidly unfolding purpose of what I was created for.

My relationship to Angels is the same that it is for men or anything else. I open my particular gates of intent to them. Regardless of purpose, I open and breathe into them the Spirit of the First Breath of the First Word. Sometimes horrified at the results, but later, always, always confirmed with my faith. The Creators, the ultimate Creator always astounded me, showing the short term is never the long.»

QUESTION 7: Many texts of magic ascribe different, or mixed-and-matched, names as Kings of the Four Directions. You are accredited as being King of the East. Can you explain more about this? Which Archangel rules directly over you? What other names are you known by? The *Lemegeton* says the four Cardinal Kings are Amaymon, Corson, Ziminiar, and Gaap ruling the quarters East, West, North, and South. Are these correct? Are any false or mistranslated?

SCRYER: He shows me a symbol of many concentric circles that stretch far out, and four lines run through each concentric circle as a cross, forming a cross, each one of them leading into the center. With his finger, he inscribes one circle with the name *Oriens*, the one closest to us. The Spirit overlays one of the lines that comes into the circle, the *i* lying directly over the line. He overlays the next circle with another name, *A-E-O-L-U-I-S*, and he keeps overlaying names over the different circles. He steps into the middle of the circle and holds the line stretching out before him. He then turns and the line follows his face wherever he is facing and begins to spin really fast. Then he will suddenly stop facing a direction until he is looking at me and I feel the line going through my heart and stretching out behind me.

ORIENS: «The name of Oriens written right here, and then another name behind it in another circle. This is the clearest way I can describe it to you.»

SCRYER: He blows out and the symbol disappears.

QUESTION 8: Cardinal King of the East, it is said you can supply as much gold and silver as one wishes. Is this true? How are you able to supply us with enough gold, silver, or wealth to be a millionaire and self-sustainably wealthy for life?

SCRYER: Oriens holds up a scale and he sets it on a large black stone. On each scale is a large pile of gold coins. The scale is balanced and there are an equal number of coins on each plate.

ORIENS: «Oriens can deliver these riches to you.»

SCRYER: He says, «You,» and points at one of the plates. He then begins to remove coins from one side and put it onto the other.

ORIENS: «If this is your wish, you must remember that the coins come from another, somehow, someway, and the more the coins, the heavier the burden. It can be done; when coming to me, when asking for this wealth, I will always present you with this symbol, and you must accept the responsibility before the coins are moved from one plate or another.»

OPERATOR: It is said that you "know all things that are to come and have been." Are you able to provide us with winning lottery numbers? If so, please specify which lottery and for which time.

ORIENS: «Yes. Commune with me regularly, for you must open the gates of the mind as possible, to let the images of the numbers arise, both creating them in the future and seeing them in the future. Patience, serenity, and the steady breath exchanged between you and Oriens during the working: patience, the most important of these virtues.»

QUESTION 9: Are you able to provide us each with a powerful familiar Spirit which will bring us profit and wealth and further develop the attributes you describe? What are the terms for this?

ORIENS: «There are many familiars I can provide, each especially for the relation of information across great distances in times of need or fear or even on a whim. Invoke my presence in the East, in the circle, and together we will open the gate that guards these Spirits. A familiar must volunteer themselves to serve with you. They will relate their name, they will show themselves in a vision or in a dream, and they must be fed, fed substances of white.»

OPERATOR: Any further instructions on how we are to invoke you and open this gate in the East as you've explained?

ORIENS: «The vision you saw at the beginning, of the Sun above the horizon covered in mist, and below it a tunnel of wind blowing the mists apart, and me standing with the key before you. Sing my name whilst invoking this image, gazing through the Lens, and just as I have come now, I will come then.»

QUESTION 10: Can you describe how you are able to cause any Spirit to appear in any form? How are you able to cause visions? Can you supply information on how to retain familiars?

ORIENS: «Oriens speaks with many tongues from many mouths and feels their intent. Sometimes when I call them before you or when we call them together, it is a simulation—my memory of them, my understanding of them—and sometimes it is the actual Spirit. If it is the actual Spirit, the magician will feel their actual presence in their body. If it is not the actual Spirit and a simulation, they will not feel its presence in this way, but the knowledge is there, the ability to communicate is there, regardless of presence or absence. It is the same with the East, the South, West, and the North.»

QUESTION 11: It is said that you can cause one to fly anywhere they like. Is this true? Are you able to grant us safe travel to anywhere we wish?

ORIENS: «Yes, I can grant that travel, even to faraway places or places physically impossible for you to go at this time. Whether it is on the wings of the mind or with the physical body. When traveling, you may blow your road ahead of you while speaking my name. Holding the hands below the mouth, speaking my name once, blowing the breath to create the path, from where you are now to your destination. Yyou must see it; you must feel it before you. Done in this way, I will walk before you. This can be done when going from the next city to across a country, or from this world to the Astral, from the Astral to the higher spheres, or even from the depths of despair toward hope.»

QUESTION 12: It is said that you "can bring the dead to life for seven years." Can you explain to us how this works, and what are the terms for this?

ORIENS: «Again, the simulation can be brought to life, and sometimes—with the consent of what has departed—their presence can be felt. But on that open road, all the passions, the knowledge, all the emotion, ignorance, and wisdom of who has left flows unhindered between the person who calls the spirit for seven years and the spirit itself. This can cause confusion in the mind of the living between their own motivations and the motivations of those who have departed; it is always a two-way road. Possible, but dangerous.»

QUESTION 13: What can you tell us of the Olympic Spirits known as Aratron of Saturn, Bethor of Jupiter, Phaleg of Mars, Och of the Sun, Hagith of Venus, Ophiel of Mercury, and Phul of the Moon? Do you rule over or have any relation to any of these Spirits, and how may they be of use to us?

ORIENS: «I do not rule over them, but over a part of their office. I understand a part of each of their natures. Each one speaks for their sphere, and I know them through their song. I know them for what they sing, what comes out from them and spreads into the space and time that they go through—the song of Mars, the song of the Sun—and each of the other Kings knows and rules another part of their nature. I hear their song, I hear their words, but I know they communicate in other ways as well that my brother and my sisters will hear also, but in a different way.»

OPERATOR: I ask if there is anything more you can tell us of the other three Cardinal Kings of the Directions and also if the materials are correct to summon them forth.

ORIENS: «This is correct. Each of them will show you when you converse with them the way in which they speak and the way in which they listen. It is natural for you to begin in the East, as the breath must come first. As you move through my other brother and sisters, your understanding of the complexity of creation will blossom. Take time as you do this work each day to be silent. Face the East and speak my name. Face the South, the West, and North, and speak the names of my kin. This simple prayer will make their presence more and more palpable and energetic for you. The more it is done, the greater the connection. The tools are correct, just as the directions are correct. Together we are a coalescence of consciousness.»

QUESTION 14: Great and Mighty Spirit Oriens, is there any more advice or methods you can give for magicians to work and speak with you in the most beneficial of ways and how to harness the benefits of your office?

ORIENS: «Like the Angel of the East, feeling my presence in the words that are spoken, remembering my purpose in the words, in the songs that are sung or said within the circle and without, calls me to you instantly. Even if for a moment, remembering Oriens with the words or the songs that you sing, knowing that I am there in the echo and the vibration that they create, empowers those words, makes them move just a little bit further. That prayer to all four of us quickly, simply, even once a day, will reveal to you the different circles of who we are.»

OPERATOR: Great and mighty Spirit, King and Governor of the East and Ruler of the Winds, we thank Thee for thy attendance here and ask that we harness fully the benefits of your office and governance.

(License to Depart given.)

Afterthoughts on the Oriens Operation

After the debrief, the best the scryer and I could come up with was "terrestrial in feeling, but too numerous beyond being able to nail down." The Being did arrive and spoke as hundreds of voices at once, yet in perfect synch and understandable. It often referred to itself in the third person and seemingly in plural as well. My suspicion is that this being doesn't deal directly and in uniform appearance with humans often, if hardly at all. It did, however, provide some very interesting responses to my questions, some dealing with large questions in the world of ceremonial magic. It also provided excellent considerations for the other three Cardinal Rulers, and how to phrase further inquiries in order to unlock the gates over which they have charge.

OPERATOR: The first of the four Cardinal Kings gave us tons of new information to consider, but like most Spirits, generated just as many questions as answers, if not more. This Spirit was so completely different in feeling than the Archangels. I felt like we were getting just the very first layer of him. I understand now why there is very little information on magicians actually conjuring the four Cardinal Kings. The answers we received were somewhat vague and hopefully not misleading in some context, as he seemed to answer, but not all at the same time. I'm not sure if he fully answered the Oath satisfactorily either. Regardless, his answers did seem to improve and be more forthcoming as the operation went on.

I saw a large haze over the altar of the stars and misted light and a variety of faces would appear in the crystal: really bizarre faces, one after the other. The Spirit claimed to be one of the primary vehicles behind mankind's development and usage of language. Obviously related differently than Archangel Uriel, where pure sound, filled with intention and pattern singing or music was, this was more the academic and rational side of language, which seems to be very associative with Air Elemental correspondences. The vibratory waves that carry sound from one place to another seem to be within the office of Oriens, thus the quality of the air vibrating at understandable frequencies, allowing communication to occur. In this, the meaning and content of information seems to be within his function too, as the networks build communication and industry through exchange.

SCRYER: It would be nice to invoke these beings twice after the first round. It seemed fairly abstract in some way. It seems that if we did this again, we would get a fuller picture. I really liked the magical technique of 'breathing your path before you.' I'd like to try that. Are the Elements best approached in a way similar to the ancient philosophers, or is there a better way, given our current beliefs? Very interesting.

I researched the name that was presented to my scryer when I asked, "Which Archangel rules directly over you? What other names are you known by?" There was a part where my scryer said, "He (Oriens) overlays the next circle with another name: *A-E-O-L-U-I-S*. And he keeps overlaying names over the different circles." I could not find an exact match to the name Aeoluis, but I did find a very similar being whose name was the same, minus the letter *I*. *AEOLUS*[35] is the usual Latinized spelling of the name of the Greek god Aiolos, who rules the winds and is also a king. He also apparently responds to petitions from humans, as in Homer's *Odyssey*, Aeolus gifted the famous Odysseus with a bag containing winds to help him return home from his voyage. Researching on the excellent

35. On seeing this name, I recalled that just before spelling out *A-E-O-L-U-I-S*, my scryer had said that the name "overlays one of the lines that comes into the circle, the *I* lying directly over the line." Quite interesting, indeed.

Theoi Project website,[36] I learned that the Greeks visualized the Winds as Spirits in the form of horses, and so called Aeolus *Hippotades*, "Reiner of Horses." This also struck me as relevant, since some of the grimoires describe Oriens appearing in the form of a horse when he is called. Of course I found this all quite interesting and asked my scryer if he was familiar with this God, and he said he had not heard of him before.

Asking the King of the East about riches and delivering large sums of money was interesting. I was more curious as to what the Spirit's responses would be concerning this alleged office rather than having any expectation that the entity could fulfill such a task. Regardless, I was rather surprised with how assured he seemed of being able to perform this, but his explanation of how it worked gave me pause. I had learned that something does not come from nothing. I felt a pointed warning of intuition cautioning me against asking for such sums and forgoing any concern for where or from whom it was taken. While personally untroubled by the idea of karma, I was more concerned about the network of lines pulled to make such a "wish" come true, and what it would inevitably mean for me—and those near me—if I did. My desire for money has never been as strong as my desire for knowledge and experience, so I did not follow this up. Given the fact that the Spirit did not specify what responsibility this action would entail, I decided to forgo the Faustian temptation, as it were. The work with lottery numbers was interesting, though, and seemed safer to go about it by that route, but possibly much more time-consuming, and it could lead to an obsessive practice if results were not achieved in a reasonable time. I may yet give this more attention, but have thus far not attempted what the Spirit instructed. Again, I do not expect such a thing could be deciphered easily without considerable work and energy, perhaps matching the equivalent in some way to what was being asked.

The Spirit's responses when questioned about its ability to bring forth spirits of the deceased was interesting as well, and further spoke to its Air Elemental quality. It seemed to suggest that it brought forth the revenants of thought patterns, intellect, and reasoning, and in some instances, the patterned emotions and passions of that individual which the spirit had in life, but not the "soul" itself, so to speak.

I had asked about the Olympic Spirits because I wanted to get a clearer sense of their natures and offices before attempting to evoke any of them with my

---

36. http://www.theoi.com/Titan/Aiolos.html

scryer, and had hoped the Cardinal Kings could help. However, the response garnered from Oriens was rather vague and not entirely useful. The King of the East did not seem to have much direct relation with the Olympic Spirits or Angels, which suggests there is not much involvement between the two types of Spirits, and that they are likely Spirits or Angels of very different functions.

There was much, much more to dissect and review about this operation, and I felt that I was only scratching the surface. However, the reference to the name of this King as possibly being written as *Urieus*, from *Eureios*, a title given to Jupiter as presiding over the Wind, seemed to make much more sense now. Also, if it were indeed derived from the Greek adjective *Eurys*, meaning vast or extensive, this would also fit the nature and manifestation of this Spirit.

The palpable nature of the entity (Angels and Demons having distinct feelings associated with them respectively) is nearly impossible to define. The evening had been a review of past frustrations, and an exploration of the possibility of great revelation and insight. Further consideration for what the Spirit's messages may have meant continued to create further mysteries. Another door was being unlocked through the proper interaction, questioning, dealing, and integration of the offices and gifts from these great Kings. Theirs is not an ethical disposition, and consideration for the well-being of the mage and risk of misfortune may befall those who attempt to open the wrong doors.

This first evocation of one of the Directional Kings was very interesting indeed.

With much more review of the Oriens material awaiting me in the future, I decided to turn my attention to the next King, that of the South, Amaymon, to continue establishing introductions, and to develop a grounded sense of each of the four Kings in turn. Before delving into deeper aspects of their working, I felt it was necessary to evoke each of them initially and gather what basic information we could before conjuring any of them subsequent times to establish a deeper rapport and understanding.

The Cardinal King of the South
Amaymon

✠	Day and time	On Saturday or Tuesday? At Noon?
✠	Name and possible meaning	Amaymon (possibly from Greek Μαιμῶν [*Maimōn*], "raging, being eager to commit violence")
✠	Other names	Amaimon, Amoymon, Maymon, Maimon, Moymon; Ziminiar?
✠	Pronunciation of name (as spoken by the Spirit)	« Ah-may-mon »
✠	Element	🜁 (?)
✠	Direction for invocation	South
✠	Materials for lamen	Parchment, iron, gold
✠	Sigils	
✠	Incense	Galbanum, sandalwood
✠	Talisman	Lens (?)

Table IX-10. ***Evocatory Correspondences for Amaymon***

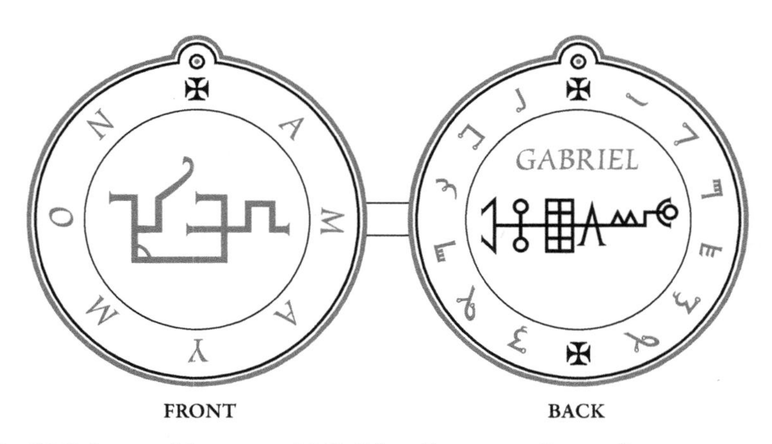

Fig. IX-11. ***Lamen of Amaymon with Sigil from Fasciculus Rerum Geomanticarum, and Thwarting Archangel from Clavis Inferni***

Of Amaymon

Fig. IX-12. ***Pentacular Plaque of Amaymon with Seal from*** **CLAVIS INFERNI**

Despite the encouraging albeit ambiguous responses from the first Directional King Oriens that the talismans and lamens were correct, I had my reservations about the Elemental correspondences for the Kings.

In the course of my past experiments, I had developed a firm assurance of being able to conjure the proper Spirit, but now I was as befuddled as the grimoires which list the Kings. At first I attributed my confusion to becoming fixated on the directions that I had previously used for Elemental workings, and tried to reason that the correspondences could easily change places where the Kings were concerned.

The bird associated with Amaymon in the *Clavis Inferni* still led me to believe that this correspondence placed the Air Element firmly in the South with Amaymon. Also, my further researches had found a confirmation of the bird association, in an anonymous Latin manuscript grimoire,[37] where the Demon King *Maymon Rex* is portrayed as a black monster with two bird heads looking in opposite directions (Fig. IX-13).[38] I admittedly remained confused, however,

37. The *circa*-1600 grimoire is the *Book of Invocations of the Demons Vercan, Maymon, Suth, Samax, Sarabotres, Mediac or Modiac, and Arcan*. The image of Mammon Rex is most familiar as a plate in a bookseller's catalogue, *Curiouser and Curiouser! A Catalogue of Strange Books and Curious Titles* (London: Maggs Bros., 1932), which includes a description of the grimoire. Although the Book fo Invocations was apparently produced in England, the artistic style reminds me strongly of German *Faustbücher*, such as the *Magia naturalis et innaturalis* published by Scheible. It is worth observing that this grimoire is of Planetary Magic, and that in it (as the sigils in the illustration indicate) Maymon is primarily a Spirit of Saturn rather than one of the four Cardinal Kings. —APF

38. I am unaware of this having been noticed previously, but the image of Maymon in the *Book of Invocations of the Demons* is based (with the exception of the dragon on which he rides) on Chapter CXXII of *Liber Juratus Honorii*, where King Maymon and the other Saturnine Spirits of the Air are described as follows (my translation from the Latin of Sloane 3854): "Their bodies are long and lean, filled with wrath and rancor. They have four faces: one from the front part [of the head] and the other from the back part, on which are two great and long beaks to the measure of three feet, and they seem to devour two serpents; and on their two knees are the other two, which seem to lament with the greatest grief; and they are black in color,

as there was practically an overabundance of wind and Air Elemental imagery that my scryer related while talking with Oriens in the East. I wondered if perhaps this was a distortion caused by the presence of both the Candle *and* the Lens during the first invocation. For the Amaymon operation, I decided to forego having more than one talisman present. I locked the remaining three talismans in a chest, and set the Lens on the altar facing the circle.

Fig. IX-13. ***Maymon Rex from Book of Invocations of the Demons Vercan, Maymon, Suth, &c.***

Ms Sloane 3824 says of the Southern Cardinal King:

> Amaymon is a King of the South, He is great & mighty, and appeareth in the Similitude of an old man, with a great Bear; His hair like to horse hair, & hath a bright Crown on his head, and Rideth on a fierce Lion, usually roaring at the first appearance; and shaking a Rod in his hands, his ministering spirits going before him, with all manner of musical Instruments, with him Cometh other three Kings, who are Emlon, Ocarbidaton, and Madicon, being messengers to the King of the South, he cometh with a great Company and very obscurely &c: He giveth a true Answer to all Demands, & maketh a man wonderful Cunning and deport, in all Learning, Philosophy & *Ars Notoria*, he giveth the best acquaintance with nobility, & Confirmeth the Doings thereof, as Dignity, promotion, &c: he may be detained one hour: &c: and but no Longer &c: And when you go to act by this spirit Amaymon, Direct your Self & Countenance to the South . . .[39]

From *The Old Book of Magic* we get:

> The *spirit Amaymon* is great, high, and mighty, and terrible in appearance. He usually assumes the form of an old man, with a long

and shining like a polished mirror. Their motion is like the movement of the Winds, with the appearance of an earthquake. Their Sign is that the earth will appear covered with white snow when invoking them." —APF

39. Skinner and Rankine, *The Keys to the Gateway of Magic*, p. 225.

> beard, his ears being like to those of a horse, with a royal diadem on his head. His first appearance is unusually tremendous; forked lightning and deep-mouthed thunders, shaking the earth apparently to the centre, announce his awful appearance. Then suddenly the earth will appear to vomit forth gushes of flame, and sulphureous odors taint the charmed atmosphere. Anon, are heard all sorts of musical instruments; then an uncouth clatter of creaking wheels and horrid crashes, will every instant astound the invocator; but on a sudden will all be again calm; and, clothed in the whole pomp of his spiritual grandeur, attended by countless legions of invincible spirits, *Amaymon* will be seen riding furiously on a fierce and roaring lion. He will approach to the utmost limits of the space assigned him, and it will well become the *Theurgist* to preserve his wonted calmness; for, if he powerfully constrain, and urgently invoke, this furious spirit, he may be brought to the most submissive obedience. He has power to give knowledge, dignity, and great promotion.[40]

These descriptions only provoke further confusion regarding the correspondence of the Kings with the creatures in the *Clavis Inferni*. In the Sloane 3824 account, Amaymon is seen arriving "with a great bear," which is the animal associated in the *Clavis* with Egyn, King of the North.[41] Likewise, in both descriptions, he is also seen riding a lion, and this most closely matches the animal seen with Paymon in the *Clavis*.

Regarding the King's name, Mathers suggests:

> perhaps from the Greek word MAIMON, present participle of MAIMAO; and A as an enforcing particle; hence, AMAIMON would mean "terrible violence and vehemence." This Spirit is also called by the Rabbins MHZAL, Mahazael, perhaps from the root MZ, = to consume, or devour.[42]

Invocations of Amaymon

In the *Clavis Inferni*, Cyprian provides one *Exclamatio* to be adapted to invoke each of the four Kings, so the calling of Amaymon only varies from that of Oriens in the name and title:

---

40. De Laurence, *op. cit.*, p. 19, copied from Raphael and the Members of the Mercurii, *op. cit.*, pp. 202–203. —APF

41. Although the manuscript used by the Mercurii seems to resolve the "bear" as an impressive "beard," which certainly makes sense in association with the form of an old man. —APF

42. Mathers, *loc. cit.* —APF

In the name of the Father and Lord, I powerfully exorcise you, Spirit Amaymon, King of the South, from the bottom of the whole Infernal World, and powerful through the name of the ever-living and true Lord, I powerfully command you through the strong and wonderful names El, Elohim, Adonai, Tzabaoth, that you appear before this Circle in a fair and visible human form, and without tortuosity, come because I command you through the names Yod, Yah, El, Shaddai, IHVH, Elion, Elohim, Yeheshuah, Ararita, Eloah va-Daath, Elohim Gibor.

I call you through the Heavens, the Cherubim and Seraphim, Thrones, Dominations and Universal Powers and Virtues ✠✠✠ and the merciful four chiefs of the heavens: Michael, Gabriel, Raphael, and Uriel; the Sun and Moon and revolving Stars; the Elements Earth, Fire, Water, Air; Summer, Spring, Winter, Autumn; and that praises M.N. Lord God El, set above the blessèd and most sacrosanct wonderful Raphael, strong Gabriel, redeeming Michael, eternal Haniel, praiseworthy Tzadkiel. Invincible Creator of the Sun and Moon, Christ Incarnate, and the Paraclete, the Trine God, Amen.[43]

The next Invocation comes from Sloane 3821, which introduces it as the first of the "Operations of the South Angle of the Air by Invocation made to the Regal Spirit Amaymon, who is the King & Ruler of the Same: for the moving and Calling forth of all or any of Such Aerial Spirits by names, Orders, & office of what Degrees soever from the Superior to the Inferior to Visible Appearance." Again this invocation, like that of Oriens, has been modified slightly to summon Amaymon to direct appearance, rather than to send subordinate Spirits.

O you Royal Spirit of great power who art called Amaymon, and said to be King of the South Angle, Region, or Mansion of the Air, and governing or bearing rule therein over many legions of Aerial Spirits subjected unto you, unto and under the power obedience and command of that great and mighty Spirit called Sathan, who is said to be the Prince of the Air & to govern the four Angles, Regions, Divisions, or Mansions there of East, West, North, and South, and unto whom power and command is given over all Spirits having place, residence, or mansion therein, as by the preordinate decree of the Most High God, the only Creator of Heaven and Earth, and of all things whatsoever is contained in the creation, is constituted and appointed.

O ye Regal Spirit Amaymon King of the South Region or Angle of the Air, being governed and governing as aforesaid, we the servants of the Most High God reverently here present in His holy fear, being dignified, armed, and supported in the Holy

43. Wellcome MS 2000, p. 10. The original form of the invocation is in Skinner and Rankine, *The Grimoire of Saint Cyprian: Clavis Inferni*, pp. 62–65. —APF

Trinity, through divine grace, with celestial power and authority given unto our first parents in the Creation, at the beginning of time, and by lineal descent from them to us and all posterity or succeeding generations, as the heirs of God's promise and grace, even to the utmost period thereof, and by the name of your God, and in the name of your prince or head of your Orders, and by your seal or character, preordinately decreed of the Most High God, confirming, subjecting, and binding you by orders and office unto strict obedience: first, to the fulfilling of His divine will and pleasure, both at his mediate and immediate commandments and appointments; secondly, unto the command service and obedience of your prince or head of your orders as in place degree and office appointed; Thirdly, as well unto the service, obedience, and assisting of the sons of men, servants of the Most High God, now living on Earth, according to your orders and office as to tempt and subvert them from their allegiance to the divine laws and duty to God, by your evil and crafty insinuations and delusions.

By the contents of all aforesaid, and by the power thereof, we do exorcise, conjure, command, compel, constrain, and move you, O you regal Spirit who is called Amaymon, King of the South Angle of the Air, forthwith and immediately at our invocation to move and appear in fair and decent form, and in no wise hurtful, dreadful, terrible, or frightful unto us or this place, or to any other person or place whatsoever, but in all humility and serenity, visibly to the sight of our eyes, in this crystal receptacle standing here before us, and to make us true and faithful answers unto all such our demands and requests, and to fulfill and accomplish all such our desires, as we shall by invocation declare, and at large in the contents thereof expressly show forth and move unto them without delay, delusion, or disturbance whereby to surprise or assault our senses with fear and amazements, or in any wise to obstruct or hinder the effects of these our present operations by any subtle crafts or illusions whatsoever.[44]

The following conjuration of Amaymon is slightly adapted from that in a French version of the *Grimoire of Pope Honorius*:

O thou, AMAYMON, King and Emperor of the Southern Parts, I call, invoke, exorcise and conjure thee, by the virtue and power of the Creator, and by the virtue of virtues, to appear presently, and without delay, in this crystal in comely and human form. In whatsoever Place thou now art, come hither and render that honour which thou owest to the true living God, Who is thy Creator. In the name of the Father, of the Son and of the Holy Ghost, come therefore, and be obedient, in front

44. The unmodified form of this invocation may be read in Skinner and Rankine, *The Keys to the Gateway of Magic,* pp. 229–230. —APF

of this circle, without Peril to my body or soul. Appear in comely human form, with no terror encompassing thee, I conjure thee, make haste, come straightway, and at once. By all the Divine names—SECHIEL, BARACHIEL—if thou dost not obey promptly, BALANDIER, suspensus, iracundus, Origratiumgu, Partus, Olemdemis, and Bautratis, N. I exorcise thee, do invoke and do impose most high commandment upon thee, by the omnipotence of the living God, and of the true God; by the virtue of the holy God, and by the power of Him Who spake and all things were made, even by His holy commandment the heaven and earth were made, with all that is in them! I adjure thee by the Father, by the Son and by the Holy Ghost, even by the Holy Trinity, by that God Whom thou canst not resist, under Whose empire I will compel thee; I conjure thee by God the Father, by God the Son, by God the Holy Ghost. In like manner, I conjure thee by the Holy Trinity, by all other mysteries, by the sign of the Cross, by the most precious blood and water which flowed from the side of Jesus Christ, by the sweat which issued from His whole body, when He said in the Garden of Olives: My Father, if it be possible, let this chalice Pass from me. I conjure thee by His death and Passion, by His burial and glorious resurrection, by His ascension, by the coming of the Holy Ghost. I adjure thee, furthermore, by the crown of thorns which was set upon His head, by the blood which flowed from His feet and hands, by the nails with which He was nailed to the tree of the Cross, by the holy tears which He shed, by all which He suffered willingly through great love of us: by the lungs, the heart, the hair, the inward Parts, and all the members of our Saviour Jesus Christ. I conjure thee by the judgment of the living and the dead, by the Gospel words of our Saviour Jesus Christ, by His preachings, by His sayings, by His miracles, by the child in swaddling-clothes, by the crying child, borne by the mother in her most pure and virginal womb; by the glorious intercession of the Virgin Mother of our Saviour Jesus Christ; by all which is of God and of His Most Holy Mother, as in heaven so on earth. I conjure thee by the holy Angels and Archangels, by all the blessed orders of Spirits, by the holy patriarchs and Prophets, by all the holy martyrs and confessors, by all the holy virgins and innocent widows, by all the saints of God, both men and women. I conjure thee by the head of St. John the Baptist, by the milk of St. Catherine, and by all the Saints.[45]

45. This conjuration by virtue of an astonishing catalogue of the hallows of Catholic Christianity is from *Le Gremoire du Pape Honorius*, in the edition which claims publication at Rome in 1760, but was probably published in Paris in 1810. Amaymon is the last of the four Kings in this text, and it is likely that the long conjuration was meant to be added to that of each of the Kings, as otherwise the other three are miniscule by comparison. The adaptation here closely

The *Heptameron* records that the King of the Angels of the Air ruling Saturday is *Maymon Rex* or "King Maymon." As this was one of the few allusions I could find regarding a time to contact this Direction King, I decided to conduct the conjuration on Saturday at midday.

Regardless of any previous misgivings, by the time my scryer and I were ready to evoke Amaymon, I was certain that all would go as planned. The ritual chamber was set up with the Altar of the Stars[46] in the South, with the pedestal on the Holy Table bearing the names and sigils of the seven Planetary Archangels as well as the names of the Directional Kings themselves. Two beeswax taper candles were set in the candlesticks and the Lens talisman stood near the Holy Table.

I felt a slight unease, as I knew the Spirit that we were calling was specifically regarded as a powerful Demon in many traditions, and was potentially a hazardous Spirit to call into one's presence, let alone home. I decided to wear my lion-skin belt that I typically reserved for Goetic workings. The belt had a throng of holy names as well as angelic names and symbols pertaining to the ten Sephiroth, the Planets, and the Spheres of creation.

Finally, as Mathers remarks in *Abra-Melin*:

> Amaymon is spoken of in the various mediæval Magical works as being a very potent Spirit, and the use of a ring, with Magical characters to hold before the mouth while conversing with him is recommended, as a protection against his deadly, fiery, and poisonous breath.[47]

For this reason, I provided my scryer with a magical ring, while I wore the one I always used for *DSIC*.

---

follows the translation of A.E. Waite, *The Book of Black Magic and of Pacts* (Edinburgh: Privately printed, 1898), pp. 284–286. —APF

46. A beautiful original Altar designed by Frater Ashen Chassan for use in his *DSIC* Workings. See *Gateways Through Stone and Circle*, pp. 118–121. —APF

47. Mathers, *loc. cit.*

Invocation of the Cardinal Ruler Amaymon

Fig. IX-14. Section of Circle for Drawing Amaymon into the Crystal

Appearance of the Spirit

SCRYER: What I see is like a dust devil as if I was looking at it from across a desert, right at the edge of the horizon. Almost as if I was fifty or so miles away. It seems that there is a great distance between me and him still. At one point I thought I saw the ground at the horizon was on fire and an opening in the fire like a gate, and he stood at the other side of this gate but I couldn't see him clearly. Now the fire is gone and I only see this billowing and churning of dust and sand.

OPERATOR: Lord, I call Amaymon, suffer him to minister unto us and appear, clearly and closer and in more form, and that in all things may be together in the honor and glory, Amen.[48]

SCRYER: ....

OPENING QUESTION 1: In the name of the holy and undefiled Spirit, the Father, the begotten Son, and Holy Ghost proceeding from both, what is thy true name?

SCRYER: ....I see a bonfire casting shadow instead of light on the ground around it. I see the sigil of Amaymon in the shadow, glowing a whitish blue.

OPERATOR: How does the sigil appear to you?

SCRYER: Just as it does on the lamen as I looked at it...I see stars dimly in the sky above. It's a very flat, open land with no defining features. The flames of the fires split in the middle, then come back together again at the top.

48. A form of prayer from *DSIC* to summon Spirit closer.

Fig. IX-15. ***Portrait of Amaymon as beheld in Vision***

An oval with a point on the top and a point below, and I can see through the fires. On the other side I just see the sky. And the sigil rises up off the ground and moves into the space between the flame. I only hear the fire. It's very quiet. The shadows that come from the fire are mesmerizing.

Opening Question 2: What is thy office?

Scryer: I saw brief images of what looked like a judge's gavel...
(Whispers:) This one is very difficult to perceive.......

Opening Question 3: What is thy true sign or character?

Scryer: I seem to have to move back, and I see the sigil even clearer, glowing between the flames. Above the flame I see one star, bright in the sky.

(Scryer draws symbol.)

Opening Question 4: When are the times most agreeable to thy nature to hold conference with us?

Scryer: I see a top spinning. Now I see a man walking from the north toward the south. I see a coil, almost like a metal spring, made of fire going around his body as he walks. He is walking toward the equator, the closer he gets to the equator the more intense the fire, the more masculine he looks, older, more mature. He crosses the equator and begins to change as he keeps walking toward the south. As he walks, *he* starts to become a *she*; he starts to change into female. And the fire coil begins to look like stone or ice, almost like obsidian. The further south she goes, the more feminine she looks.......Now I'm back in front of the fire again.

Oath: Wilt thou swear by the blood and righteousness of our Lord Jesus Christ that thou art truly the Mighty King, Ruler, and Spirit of the South, Amaymon?

Scryer: I see the sigil glow brighter. But I only hear the fire still. I do see a ray of light that seems to slowly stretch down and touch the top of the bonfire.

QUESTION 6: What are your views on humanity? What are your roles and interactions?

SCRYER: I see a man and a woman holding hands, naked. They are standing in front of the bonfire looking through the gap where the sigil glows. There is a light coming through the gap between the flames. I can even see their hair moving in the light, as if the light was made of a wind. They narrow or squint their eyes because the light is so intense. It seems to bathe them in its energy, and as it does so they appear to grow a bit taller. They also seem more defined. I see them turn to one another and embrace one another and kiss. Their arms wrapped around one another, they are very close.

QUESTION 7: Do you have your own recollection of your creation and origin? Where do you come from? What is your purpose? I am curious why you are often referred to as being a Demon or Archdemon in many texts.

SCRYER: I see an ember in the sand, glowing intensely red in the center but mostly black on the outside. It even seems to bake or brown the sand around it. I see it suddenly flare into the bonfire, and as it does, the star appears above it once more. Somehow, I get that the fire and the star are the same. One is a gateway for the other. The star is very, very distant.

QUESTION 8: What can you teach us in order to speak with you more clearly and productively?

SCRYER: I see globes or spheres in a circle: sixteen of them. They hold their position, but they spin in place. The whole shape of them moves in a rotating fashion around, as if on a disk in space. And I see that surrounding the sigil in the middle of the fire, in the open space where the fire bends around it and touches the top. I hear a voice whispering, 'Amaymon, Amaymon, Amaymon,' over and over again, and the faster the name is repeated, the quicker the globes spin around the sigil. The star above it grows brighter, and the flames seem to move faster. It's a little bit disturbing to listen to the voice.

QUESTION 9: What is the most successful way to assist us to manifest Spirits and have them speak clearly to us? To command Demons and Spirits to arrive quickly when summoned?

SCRYER: I see the sigil disappear, and it seems like a very hot wind is coming through, blowing from the star through the gap in the fire. I get this feeling like it's delivering heat or energy to the evocation, like raw power or passion or amperage. The ultimate source seems to be the star far away. The fire is the instrument, helps direct the celestial wind from the star. I see the sigil again in the middle of the gap. The more air that flows, the more the sigil glows, like blowing coals to intense heat.

QUESTION 10: What should your sigil be made of? Of what type of material—metal or wood?

SCRYER: I see a large cedar tree. I see someone's lips move close to a flat piece of the wood, into the grain. The wood looks polished, like it's been sanded and polished. It has an odd shape, like a man is speaking into this piece of wood. I can't hear what he is saying, but he is whispering into the wood. He turns it over and I see the sigil is burned into the wood.

QUESTION 11: What can you teach us about the next two kings, Paymon and Egyn? What can you teach us on how to summon and work with them?

SCRYER: There seems to be a connection between the North and the South, like one transforms into the other. Like fire moving into obsidian...or becoming obsidian, and man becoming woman. I see the man walking toward the equator again. Then I see the fire again, with the hot glowing air going through the flame, and I can see the sky starting to dim as it gets closer and closer to the North. And there is a meeting place somewhere between the two. Where the hot wind flows to connect with something that is flowing from the North that I cannot see. There is something extremely beautiful about it. Even though I'm in this great expanse, I feel so sheltered. As if the connection between them brings something into being. I see almost the hint of something coming from the East and West as well, joining in the middle, but where they join is very far away...feels like just an immense circle, the size of a continent. I look at the ground. I see, I see almost small pebbles rolling out of sight towards where everything joins.

QUESTION 12: Any other magical teachings or methods you can share with us at this time? You are said to be the infernal King who can display any manner of visions to others, grant the others to impart visions to instill thoughts in other minds, men's mentality. Can you reveal any further secrets about your nature and identity?

SCRYER: I do see very clearly a scribe with a roll of papyrus on a block of red stone. He's facing the tablet and papyrus, looking at it from the South. The red stone is being shown clearly that it is in the North. The scribe is breathing very heavily and sweating. His eyes open widely and he passionately and hurriedly starts writing on the papyrus. He seems angry and in love all at the same time. The Sun is above him in the height of the sky at noon. His shadow is cast very starkly at the base of the tablet and papyrus. He continues to keep taking very harsh inhalations and let them out slowly. The whole scene disappears, and I just see the noon Sun over the desert. I see stones sticking up through the desert about the size of a man, thin stones laid out very haphazardly; some are tilted, straight up, or fallen over. The place feels really, really old. There is something very beautiful about it. All I can see is desert all around, nothing else. This place is very remote.

QUESTION 13: What more can you show us to conjure any other manner of Spirits, earthbound Spirits, clearly and fully manifested and physical forms, visible and audible?

SCRYER: I see a man staring at a fire at night. There is an odd sort of singing going on around him, and he keeps his eyes fixed on the fire. He has a staff across his lap. He seems to be whispering a phrase over and over again. His eyes are fixed on the fire. He is saying 'Amaymon' over and over again, in sets of six. He'll pause briefly, then he'll say another set of six. It seems to take a lot of effort; he's sweating and his eyes tear. He tries to see the gap between the flame and the sigil. As if it was there at the very edge of sight as it was at the beginning of this work. Like he approaches slowly. I can see the bonfire, but it is distant now with the star above it.

QUESTION 14: Are there any abilities and gifts dedicated unto you?

SCRYER: I see two men on either side of the fire, and they are tossing in what looks like a medallion without a chain, through the fire and flames to one another. Even though it's not hot, they bounce it in their hands and blow on it like it is hot, then toss it through the flames again to the person on the other side. This seems to power the medallion or talisman. They catch it like it's a hot stone and blowing on it.

Afterthoughts on the Amaymon Operation

This was the first time we did not receive clear audible communication from a spirit or angel. All communication was purely in visual context and much of it was abstract or steeped in representation. Regardless of this frustration, the related images did remind me of descriptions of Middle Eastern *jinn* as beings of smokeless fire or whirlwinds in the desert.

After the operation, I became convinced that the Lens is not the proper talisman for this Directional Ruler as the Candle and flame were alluded to quite a number of times, telling us that this was its proper talisman and gateway. When reviewing the recording, it was quite obvious the Spirit or Intelligence coming through was informing my scryer and me that the Fire (Candle) was the needed Element, and not the Lens. When the Spirit was asked, "What can you teach us to speak with you more clearly and productively?" the vision described by the scryer was "globes or spheres in a circle, rotating around the sigil in the middle of the fire. In the open space where the fire bends around it and touches the top."

Although there was some interesting information gathered, this operation was not a success by any means, and I knew we would be required to attempt this a second time with the proper talisman and possibly another correction as well. Considering that in the grimoires the magician does not typically speak to the King directly, but requests that he send other Spirits forth, I felt we were making headway. For example, there was some possibly useful information as to the nature or identity of the King of the North, as the vision my scryer beheld showed (again) a fire transforming or blending into what looked to him to be obsidian or dark glasslike stone. It was difficult to tell what exactly this vision was meant to impart to us or how or even if it was valuable, but I made a mental note of it.

I was particularly glad that I had decided to wear my lion-skin belt that is used in Goetic workings, and that I had fashioned another magic ring for my scryer to wear. Although this Spirit didn't seem particularly hostile, I had a feeling of uneasiness during the operation, considering that there was no control and there were missing components and I was glad to have had the extra safety measures.

SCRYER: It seems like their nature to be somewhat elusive or transcendent. The image of the fire was really interesting; it was almost obviously vaginal in shape and appearance. I'm not sure what to make of this operation, other than it felt far removed and distance, like I couldn't draw near enough to speak with the King directly. I think we missed something for this working.

So far, the initial conjurations of Oriens and Amaymon were less than satisfactory. Particularly, the evocation of Amaymon frustrated me since the Spirit refused or was unable to speak or appear in an understandable form of any sort. As previously mentioned, the main cause for the difficulty was likely the incorrect gateway talisman being utilized. This was later confirmed by Hiram when I spoke with him (and something I should have clarified with him beforehand). Looking back, I should have reviewed what Archangel Sandalphon stated more precisely, as I now realized that the Archangel had suggested each Elemental talisman in order, starting from the North and moving clockwise: a Stone ring (North), a Lens (East), a Candle (South), and a Cup (West). This oversight and confusion from suggestions in the grimoires made me a bit abashed that I had overlooked such obvious cues from our direct experiences.

Hiram also mentioned that another missing component was the lack of offerings for these great Kings, which were vital for these particular Spirits to cooperate. I realized that the necessity for this is hinted at several times across differing grimoires that relate back to the Cardinal Kings in one fashion or another. For instance, in the *Lemegeton*'s *Goetia*, we see this of Paymon: "Now if thou callest this Spirit Paimon alone, then thou must make him some offering." However, Hiram said the particular nature of the offerings would be revealed at a later time and refused to provide further information on the matter.

After considering my mistakes, I was surprised that we had received any acknowledgment or contact at all. Although more of a failure than success, I felt I was at least learning something from the unsuccessful operation. I reviewed the notes and experiences I had this far, and made the following corrections:

Cardinal King	Direction	Element	Talisman (according to Sandalphon)	Symbolic Animal (according to Clavis Inferni)	Incense	Offering
Oriens	East	Air	Lens	Dragon/ Ouroboros	Copal	?
Amaymon	South	Fire	Candle	Bird	Galbanum, sandalwood	Burnt offerings?
Paymon	West	Water	Cup	Sphinx or manticore	Myrrh, onycha	Liquid offerings?
Egyn	North	Earth	Stone Ring	Bear	Storax, benzoin	Solid food offerings?

Table IX-16. ***Revised Table of Correspondences for the Four Cardinal Kings***

Shortly after this experiment I began remaking the talismans for the Eastern and Southern Kings. For Oriens, I found a round bronze dragon in the style of an Ouroboros that I made to be a frame for the Lens. The dragon encircling the glass fit perfectly into a brass caliper stand. For Amaymon, I found a decorative candleholder that I thought would work and purchased a red beeswax candle onto which I engraved his sigil and name. I awoke at dawn on a Wednesday and engraved the Lens sculpture as well as consecrating it by passing it through smoke of the incense I had made. I did the same on a Tuesday at noon for the Candle and candleholder.

With these corrections, I hoped that the next time my scryer and I evoked these beings the operation would be more fruitful and clear. Before returning to Oriens and Amaymon, however, I felt it was important to attempt to call the Kings of the West and North, and hopefully gather more relevant information on how to re-conjure the other Kings.

The Cardinal King of the West
Paymon

✠ Day and time	On Monday or Friday at Dusk during Autumn
✠ Name and possible meaning	Paymon (possibly from Hebrew פעמן [*paämon*], "a tinkling sound or small bell," from the root פעם [*paäm*], "to agitate, impel, or strike forward")
✠ Other names	Paimon; Corson?
✠ Pronunciation of name (as spoken by the Spirit)	«Pay-mon» or «Peem-on»
✠ Element	▽
✠ Direction for invocation	West
✠ Materials for lamen	Parchment, silver, gold, iron
✠ Sigils	
✠ Talisman	Silver Cup with emeralds
✠ Incense	Myrrh, onycha
✠ Offerings	Beer, wine, sweet milk, mead

Table IX-17. ***Evocatory Correspondences for Paymon***

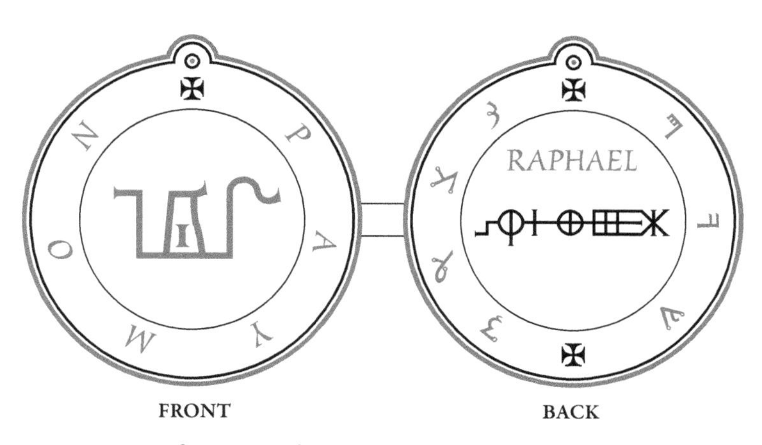

Fig. IX-18. ***Lamen of Paymon with Sigil from FASCICULUS RERUM GEOMANTICARUM, and Thwarting Archangel from CLAVIS INFERNI***

Of Paymon

Of the four directional Kings, I was most familiar with the name of Paymon. The Spirit is among the most popular of the seventy-two listed in the *Goetia* of the *Lemegeton.*

Fig. IX-19. ***Pentacular Plaque of Paymon with Seal from Clavis Inferni***

> PAIMON.—The Ninth Spirit in this Order is Paimon, a Great King, and very obedient unto LUCIFER. He appeareth in the form of a Man sitting upon a Dromedary with a Crown most glorious upon his head. There goeth before him also an Host of Spirits, like Men with Trumpets and well sounding Cymbals, and all other sorts of Musical Instruments. He hath a great Voice, and roareth at his first coming, and his speech is such that the Magician cannot well understand unless he can compel him. This Spirit can teach all Arts and Sciences, and other secret things. He can discover unto thee what the Earth is, and what holdeth it up in the Waters; and what Mind is, and where it is; or any other thing thou mayest desire to know. He giveth Dignity, and confirmeth the same. He bindeth or maketh any man subject unto the Magician if he so desire it. He giveth good Familiars, and such as can teach all Arts. He is to be observed towards the West. He is of the Order of Dominations. He hath under him 200 Legions of Spirits, and part of them are of the Order of Angels, and the other part of Potentates. Now if thou callest this Spirit Paimon alone, thou must make him some offering; and there will attend him two Kings called LABAL and ABALIM, and also other Spirits who be of the Order of Potentates in his Host, and 25 Legions. And those Spirits which be subject unto them are not always with them unless the Magician do compel them. His Character is this [see Fig. IX-20] which must be worn as a Lamen before thee, etc.[49]

I did not want to simply assume that the directional king of the West and the catalogued Spirit in the *Goetia* were one and the same, but it was impossible to ignore the probability. The Spirits of the *Goetia* are considered Demons in

49. From the edition of Mathers published by Crowley, *The Book of the Goetia of Solomon the King* (Boleskine, Foyers, Inverness: Society for the Propagation of Religious Truth, 1904). —APF

many respects and several of them definitely deserve that assumption. I had contacted some Spirits from the *Goetia* before, and found them to be powerful but also unpredictable in their ability to assist the magician as well as provide useful information. I had never evoked Paimon directly however, and thus had no direct experience with which to compare the two Spirits if my scryer and I were successful. Certainly one of the many questions I began formulating for the Spirit was whether or not the Cardinal King and the ninth Goetic Spirit were, in fact, one and the same.

The above description and outline of Paymon's offices is fairly detailed and provides clues to successfully contacting the Spirit even beyond the frame working of the *Goetia*. Perhaps the most useful instruction was that "thou must make him some offering." This confirmed Hiram's information that the absence of offering may indeed have been the missing ingredient in the last operation with Amaymon, and contributed to the less than satisfactory results. I surmised that if the King of the West had any relation to the Element of Water, then offerings of a liquid nature would be most appropriate. I went out and bought a selection of fine wine, ale, beer, and mead that I hoped would be agreeable to the Spirit.

The statement that this Spirit is "very obedient onto Lucifer" was an item I need to explore needed to know if this was the case and what that entailed. If it also applied to Paymon's role as a Directional King, I felt it was important to know if it was something of which I had to be wary.

In the *Goetia* description, there is obvious reference to Paymon being knowledgeable about the Elements, and I wondered if this related to its position as one of the Directional Rulers.

The Goetic sigil ascribed to Paymon (Fig. IX-20) seems to suggest a crown with jewels, or possibly waves or clouds, but in no way seems to share any symbolism with the sigils or seals attributed to him in the *Clavis Inferni* and the *Fasciculus Rerum Geomanticarum*. The *Fasciculus* sigil I used on the lamen for our operation (Fig. IX-18) could suggest the outline of a camel or dromedary if one used a bit of imagination, and I wondered if this had any significance or if it was purely coincidence.

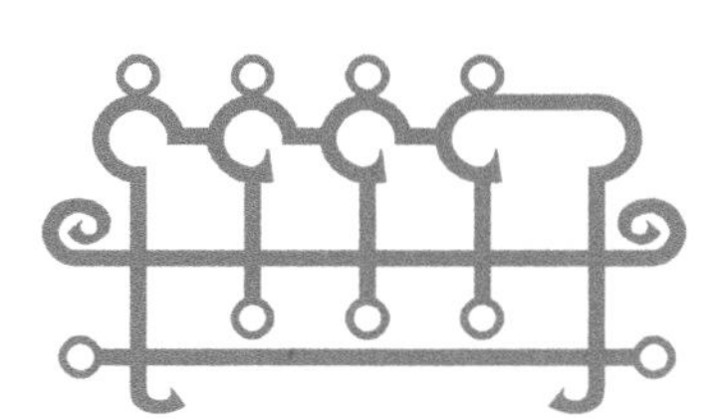

Fig. IX-20. ***Character or Sigil of Paymon from the Goetia***

Luckily, the *Goetia* is not the only source we have which describes the Spirit known as Paymon. MS Sloane 3824 describes Paymon as the King of the West, and says that

> he appeareth at first somewhat terrible & speaketh with a Hoarse Voice, but being Constrained by a Divine Power, he then taketh the form of a Soldier, and when he Cometh to the presence of the Invocant, is oft times apt to Cavill & make variance. He rideth upon a dromedary, or a Camel, which is Crowned with a Bright Crown, & hath the Countenance of a woman, Before goeth a Band of ministering spirits, with all Kind of musical Instruments, And when he appeareth, Let the Invocant Cast a paper to him, wherein is Inscribed, that he shall speak plainly & Distinctly, so that the Master may Understand what he sayeth, And with him Cometh five other principal or regal Spirits, who are Balserth the messenger to the King of the west, and Belial a King, And Baroson a King, and Rombulence or, Ramblane, and Alphasis, they may appear from the 8th hour to the 12th &c.[50]

The above description provided even more useful information that a written terms and conditions should be written out ahead of time with the spirit swearing to agree by them before the operation continues. If the machinations of this particular spirit included dealings that were not in my best interest, I wanted to be sure to bind it so that they would not take effect on myself or my scryer. It also mentioned that Paimon had feminine facial features, which seemed to coincide with what Oreins said about his counterpart in the west being a "sister."

The Old Book of Magic similarly describes Paymon as

> powerful to evil, appearing in the likeness of an armed soldier, riding upon a camel or dromedary, being crowned with a bright crown; his countenance is feminine, but his voice hoarse and uncouth. Before him goeth all kinds of musical instruments: yet, when constrained by art, he readily performs the desired wishes of the invocator, and hath under him an infinity of spirits.

After reviewing the various descriptions, I had little doubt that the *Goetia* and the other grimoires were indeed describing the same Spirit. Whether or not attributed to being one of the four Directional Rulers, Paimon seemed to be an entity of considerable power and influence.

Considering the Spirit's name, Mathers wrote in *Abra-Melin*:

50. Skinner and Rankine, *The Keys to the Gateway of Magic*, p. 226.

> PAIMON:—Is also frequently written "Paymon," and sometimes "Paimonia". Probably from Hebrew, POMN, = a tinkling sound or small bell. This is again derived from the Hebrew root POM, = to agitate, impel, or strike forward. The word POMN is employed in Exodus 28, 34; 28, 33; and 39, 25. Paimon is also called by the Rabbins by the title of OZAZL, *Azazel*, which is a name used in Leviticus with reference to the Scape-Goat. Its derivation is from OZ, = a Goat; and AZL, = to go away. It has frequently been warmly discussed whether the word in question means simply the Scape-Goat, or whether it signifies a Demon to whom that animal was dedicated. But in Rabbinic Demonology it is always used to mean one of the Chief Demons.[51]

John King (Imperial Arts), a magical colleague experienced in the *Goetia*, declared that Paimon is from Hebrew PYM, meaning "Little Coin," and is pronounced "Peem-on."[52]

Invocations of Paymon

The invocation from *Clavis Inferni*, adapted to summon Paymon, follows:

In the name of the Father and Lord, I powerfully exorcise you, Spirit Paymon, King of the West, from the bottom of the whole Infernal World, and powerful through the name of the ever-living and true Lord, I powerfully command you through the strong and wonderful names El, Elohim, Adonai, Tzabaoth, that you appear before this Circle in a fair and visible human form, and without tortuosity, come because I command you through the names Yod, Yah, El, Shaddai, IHVH, Elion, Elohim, Yeheshuah, Ararita, Eloah va-Daath, Elohim Gibor.

I call you through the Heavens, the Cherubim and Seraphim, Thrones, Dominations and Universal Powers and Virtues ✠✠✠ and the merciful four chiefs of the heavens: Michael, Gabriel, Raphael, and Uriel; the Sun and Moon and revolving Stars; the Elements Earth, Fire, Water, Air; Summer, Spring, Winter, Autumn; and that praises M.N. Lord God El, set above the blessèd and most sacrosanct wonderful Raphael, strong Gabriel, redeeming Michael, eternal Haniel, praiseworthy Tzadkiel. Invincible Creator of the Sun and Moon, Christ Incarnate, and the Paraclete, the Trine God, Amen.[53]

---

51. Mathers, *loc. cit.*

52. John R. King IV, "#9 Paimon," in his *Imperial Arts* LiveJournal for Wednesday, June 10th, 2009 (http://imperialarts.livejournal.com/?skip=20).

53. Wellcome MS 2000, p. 10. The original form of the invocation is in Skinner and Rankine, *The Grimoire of Saint Cyprian: Clavis Inferni*, pp. 62–65. —APF

The next Invocation is from Sloane 3821, which as we now expect labels it one of the "Operations of the West Angle of the Air by Invocation made to the Regal Spirit Paymon, who is the King & Ruler of the Same: for the moving and Calling forth of all or any of Such Aerial Spirits by names, Orders, & office of what Degrees soever from the Superior to the Inferior to Visible Appearance." Again I have modified this invocation slightly to summon Paymon to direct visible appearance.

O you Royal Spirit of great power who art called Paymon, and said to be King of the West Angle, Region, or Mansion of the Air, and governing or bearing rule therein over many legions of Aerial Spirits subjected unto you, unto and under the power obedience and command of that great and mighty Spirit called Sathan, who is said to be the Prince of the Air & to govern the four Angles, Regions, Divisions, or Mansions there of East, West, North, and South, and unto whom power and command is given over all Spirits having place, residence, or mansion therein, as by the preordinate decree of the Most High God, the only Creator of Heaven and Earth, and of all things whatsoever is contained in the creation, is constituted and appointed.

O ye Regal Spirit Paymon King of the West Region or Angle of the Air, being governed and governing as aforesaid, we the servants of the Most High God reverently here present in His holy fear, being dignified, armed, and supported in the Holy Trinity, through divine grace, with celestial power and authority given unto our first parents in the Creation, at the beginning of time, and by lineal descent from them to us and all posterity or succeeding generations, as the heirs of God's promise and grace, even to the utmost period thereof, and by the name of your God, and in the name of your prince or head of your Orders, and by your seal or character, preordinately decreed of the Most High God, confirming, subjecting, and binding you by orders and office unto strict obedience: first, to the fulfilling of His divine will and pleasure, both at his mediate and immediate commandments and appointments; secondly, unto the command service and obedience of your prince or head of your orders as in place degree and office appointed; Thirdly, as well unto the service, obedience, and assisting of the sons of men, servants of the Most High God, now living on Earth, according to your orders and office as to tempt and subvert them from their allegiance to the divine laws and duty to God, by your evil and crafty insinuations and delusions.

By the contents of all aforesaid, and by the power thereof, we do exorcise, conjure, command, compel, constrain, and move you, O you regal Spirit who is called Paymon, King of the West Angle of the Air, forthwith and immediately at our invocation to move and appear in fair and decent form, and in no wise hurtful, dreadful, terrible, or frightful unto us or this place, or to any other person or place whatsoever, but in all humility and serenity, visibly to the sight of our eyes, in this crystal receptacle standing here before us, and to make us true and faithful answers unto all such our demands and requests, and to fulfill and accomplish all such our desires, as we shall by invocation declare, and at large in the contents thereof expressly show forth and move unto them without delay, delusion, or disturbance whereby to surprise or assault our senses with fear and amazements, or in any wise to obstruct or hinder the effects of these our present operations by any subtle crafts or illusions whatsoever.[54]

Finally, here is the conjuration of Paymon slightly adapted from a version of the *Grimoire of Pope Honorius*:

O PAYMON, most potent King, who reignest in the Western quarter, I call and I invoke thee in the name of the Deity! I command thee by virtue of the Most High, to appear immediately before this circle, in this crystal, in comely and human form, that thou may answer in everything, even as I shall require thee. If thou failest, I will torment thee with the sword of fire divine; I will multiply thy sufferings and will burn thee.[55]

The day of the operation was at hand. The Altar of the Stars was set against the western wall with the tripod incense burner directly in front, nearly touching the edge of my magical circle. Three different offerings of liquid substance were placed near the bottom of the Altar; I provided fine red wine, mead, and beer. Dark blue taper beeswax candles with the name and sigils of the Spirit Paymon inscribed on them were set in the candlesticks.

I again felt unease about calling this King, knowing that it was widely reputed to be an Archdemon and a being of considerable power with unknown persuasions. However, I was equally excited to finally meet this Cardinal King and discover what manner of being it truly was and what occult knowledge it could impart to my scryer and me.

---

54. The unmodified invocation may be read in Skinner and Rankine, *The Keys to the Gateway of Magic*, pp. 234–235. —APF

55. This is adapted from the 1760=1810 edition of *Le Gremoire du Pape Honorius*, closely following the translation of Waite, *The Book of Black Magic and of Pacts*, pp. 283–284. —APF

Invocation of the Cardinal Ruler Paymon

Fig. IX-21. Section of Circle for Drawing Paymon into the Crystal

Appearance of the Spirit

SCRYER: I see a figure standing on the edge of the sea. Now I see the Moon coming out of the ocean, a crescent Moon, facing up like horns. I see the waters swelling as it rises through the water. It looks as if it's coming out of the sea itself. The Moon is like the crown of what must be Paymon. I feel an enormous presence below the Moon, very, very deep into the ocean itself. It's as if the Spirit extends down into the dark, dark depths of the sea. There is just barely a hint of sunlight in the sky, as if the Sun has set behind a wall in the ocean. There are a few stars in the sky, and there is a deep rumbling below. It feels old and somewhat feminine.

OPERATOR: I ask that the King of the West, Paymon, come forth and appear to us in human shape so that we may best speak and inquire of you. Appear unto us visibly and affably and in human form.

SCRYER: ...I see something very difficult to describe. It looks like a she, but there is also something animal-like about her face. The Moon looks like horns as well as a crown on her head. The body is formed of dark, almost blue-black water. It looks as if there is hair beneath the water itself, as if adding a texture to her form. She is very tall. I see her torso; she is naked and formed of this black, black water. Her face, animal-like, is framed by long hair with a star in each eye. She seems to be breathing heavily but slowly.

OPERATOR: Great King of the West, we have brought you mead, fine wine, and beer to give unto you if you will speak and be bound to treat with us here until the closing of this rite.

Fig. IX-22. ***Portrait of Paymon as beheld in Vision***

OPENING QUESTION 1: In the name of the holy and undefiled Spirit, the Father, the begotten Son, and Holy Ghost proceeding from both, what is thy true name?

(Scryer's voice relates a rather raspy—? loud whisper—and authoritative tone.)

SPIRIT: «I am Paymon, great Ruler and sister in the West.»

OPENING QUESTION 2: What is thy office?

SCRYER: She moves to the side, and behind her she shows me a gate.

(At this point the audio recorder plays back what sounds like rushing water, where during the ceremony I didn't recall anything like that.)

The gate looks like onyx or a black steel or obsidian almost. I see, suddenly, people walking over the ocean toward the gate. Some are crippled or deformed in some way; others are blind, deaf, or weak. Beyond the gate seems to be a road that leads into the distant stars. As they pass through the gate, she whispers something to each of them before they go through. She seems to whisper a question to them and then gives them some sort of key with her words."

OPENING QUESTION 3: What is thy true sign or character?

SCRYER: She is now showing me an event: A black man sits at the edge of a desert looking out to the sea. She has possessed him, the Spirit Paymon, and she is singing through him. He is wearing many, many layers of clothes that are tattered, brown, and dirty. His eyes are wide open and black, and he sings and chants almost uncontrollably. She leaves him suddenly, almost violently, and the man is left blind and in a stupor. In order to regain his sight, the man scrawls something quickly on the ground. It looks exactly like the first amulet (sigil) that you showed me: the one with the peaked square in the middle, with the dot and the line below and the crook to the left and the curve to the right. When the man is finished drawing it in the sand, the darkness leaves his eyes and he can see again as well as breathe.

Paymon says that is the oldest symbol, the first symbol.

OPENING QUESTION 4: When are the times most agreeable to thy nature to hold conference with us?

SCRYER: She shows me again the time after sunset when there is just barely blue light in the sky, when the last rays of the sun are barely seen. The twilight of dusk.

OATH: Wilt thou swear by the blood and righteousness of our Lord Jesus Christ that thou art truly the King of the West, Paymon?

SCRYER: She steps again in front of me and closes the gate behind her. She raises her arms and the seas swell up beneath her and then she drops her arms down very fast. What looks like a ring of water rushes away from her into the ocean and the Spirit looks at me and says:

SPIRIT: «I am Paymon, as you have summoned.»

OPERATOR: Great King of the West, Paymon, we thank thee for thy coming, and again I ask that you attend unto us during this ceremony in the name of the Most High God and not depart until given license. Behold the offerings which it is said you require and do so desire to have. Also, in the tradition of this conjuration and magic of my forebears, I present you with this written statement of Oaths and Terms and the contract given.

(At this point I read a lengthy binding invocation commanding the Spirit to be favorable and peaceable unto my scryer and myself, and to assist us without harm in any way. I read the written words aloud then set the document, folded on my wand, onto the altar.)

PAYMON: «Yes, if offerings are given for the next three nights, after sunset, when the rays of the Sun are barely seen in the west.»

OPERATOR: These terms are agreed.

QUESTION 5: Are you the same spirit listed in the Catalog of Spirits known as the *Goetia*?

PAYMON: «My office is the same but I am a different string on the lyre. *Tiamat* is my Mother and *Tehom*...my dwelling.» *(When «Tehom» is uttered, the whole earth seems to vibrate.)*

QUESTION 6: You are given the title one of the four great Kings or Spirit Governors of the directions, this being West. Can you explain your role and purpose in this position?

PAYMON: «Like all the Kings, our office can be everywhere. The direction is a guide, a symbol of our place. The West receives the Sun, the soul at the end of its life, and the deep waters of wisdom are held in its Cup. Like my brothers and sister, I give the unique knowledge that flows and is received in what you call the West. My feet are deeper than the Earth, standing in the depths of Tehom, and my head crowned by the Moon. My body, the deep black waters of the sea. My bones, the beasts feared by men.»

QUESTION 7: How do you relate to the other three Kings or Directional Rulers, and what can you tell us about Oriens, about Amaymon, about Egyn?

PAYMON: «I receive and assimilate the energy of all three. What is born flows like three streams through the center of each being as they walk to me. Through Oriens they rise. Through Amaymon they mature and are exalted and tested. And Through my sister, they have their hearthstone. What I whisper through the gate is the question that their next round will bring and the wisdom that their past round has given them. And what they show me echoes through the depths of Tehom and the Spirits beneath me.»

QUESTION 8: It is said in the *Goetia* that you are "very obedient unto Lucifer." Is this so, and can you tell us more about this being known as Lucifer if this is in fact so?

PAYMON: «In my office I do not discriminate. I am a gateway and assimilation, and all who pass this way are welcomed by me. I saw the one, Lucifer, fall down into the depths where my feet stand, and I know the horrors of his discovery, the pain of his break with the Father. I make no excuses for my actions with him, for it is my place to assimilate what he brings forth. It is a wisdom that is terrible and is most often far beyond the puny understanding of men.»

QUESTION 9: Does Lucifer refer to the "glittering riches, to the morning star (Venus), or to the Devil, all of which have received the title of Lucifer?" I ask who or what is this Lucifer and what manner of obedience you owe unto him?

PAYMON: «Lucifer is all of those things and can be seen as all of those things. They are the base symbols that I can relate to you, as a mortal being, the vastness of who he is. My obedience to Lucifer is the recognition that on his fall there was a recreation of this place, this Earth that you call home. Know that many of the things that will change and alter come ultimately from him. Ask yourselves: Could it be that the horrors you unleash on one another is the grief, the anger, and the anguish of a son ripped from his Father? Could it be that you play out his anguish for the inevitable reunification? The reunification is my obedience.»

SCRYER: She parts her hands and opens a cleft into the waters in front of her, and I see down in the depths of the black water. Between her hands there are visions of suffering, war, and violence, and confusion and panic. With a clap, she closes the waters over it again.

QUESTION 10: What is the explanation and meaning behind your own name and how you received it? Is your name pronounced "Peem-on" which means "Little Coin"? If this is correct, can you explain the meaning behind your name and how you received it?

PAYMON: «The coins placed over the eyes of the dead, the toll of the soul as a way to open the gates. The assimilated wisdom, the treasures of life, placed into my hands from their eyes. And my ability to show those who ask in earnest and offer as required the monetary treasures needed in life. But the ultimate purpose of what I give, must be given back...to me. And that is a mystery that will be decided each time according to their need.»

QUESTION 11: *(Operator gestures to the Cup talisman on the altar.)* I have chosen this Cup to be dedicated to you as the talisman for the King of the West. I ask that it be harnessed with the strengths of your office and to better call you forth. How should it consecrated toward this end?

PAYMON: «Place my oldest symbol in the Cup. And the symbol of my crown rising from beneath the waves on one side. When the Cup is used, the newer symbol of the ocean swelling above the Moon must be always pointed to the West. It will open the gate through which I can pass to you. On the outside should be precise, the one on the inside rough like he who scribed it in the dirt the first time. The gate sigil *(Goetia sigil)* can be used specifically to pass through that gate which I can pass through to you.»

QUESTION 12: It is said you have great understanding and knowledge of the earth, waters, and winds. Can you teach or impart to us any esoteric and magical methods or secrets you know in order to harness and better understand these powers?

PAYMON: «Yes. There is a meeting place between Earth, Water, and the Air where my hand lies; some would say my palm, some would say my forehead, some would say my breast. From this spot, the one with knowledge, the magician, may walk with me to this place where Earth, Water, and Air meet, where the winds are stirred by my palm, where they are beaten by my heart where they are envisioned in my mind. On this spot where the earth rolls over my hand, caresses my breast, and crystallizes in my mind—at this point where the waters churn through my heart, are spiraled and moved like the beginnings of currents in my palm, and faintly lit from far below in my mind—walk with me to this place, and I will place your hand on all three.»

QUESTION 13: According to your office, can you impart and confirm in us the fullest extent of dignities and reveal to us the arts of business, the science of economy, and the secret of money itself? Will you confer upon us the skills in those arts and sciences as my undertaken works would require?

PAYMON: «I will place you beneath the sheets of your deathbed, and from there we will speak of the money that you need, we will speak of the business you must perform and the best way to achieve it. Your death will cancel you, and the money given, ultimately tendered back to me. When you know that the money is given as a gift to be used, multiplied for the benefit of all, and then received back to me through their hands and yours, best to consult me just before the beginning of a project or a business or to speak with me specifically about the long-term direction of the way people spend, where they invest, and how and what they will achieve—a glimpse of the future. For as those who have passed pass by me, I learn of what they have done and where they wanted to go.»

QUESTION 14: Can you teach us any secret knowledge, methods, or requisites to summon Spirits to fuller visibility, manifestation, and presence?

SCRYER: She shows me three lines of light going toward a spiral in the middle: the one in the North is barely visible, and the East and South are still faint.

PAYMON: «By correctly summoning all four of us, and standing before us truthfully, all three lines will be lit. And at this time will the Spirits that you summon be more visible and clearer in their communication. Hiram knows more of this and can tell you more. Summon all four of us, and that act in itself will make the connection and the contact much clearer. Be wary that as you see more into the Spirit world, it sees you far more clearly; and that applies to all the Spirits—those you wish to contact, and those you don't wish to contact.»

QUESTION 15: Through this divine work, is there a way, if there be any negative holdings or influences, that my scryer and I be exempt from any subjection impressed by you or your office and energies; furthermore to be released from it, and to be set over those who would use us to their advantage at our own expense?

PAYMON: «As part of your three offerings to me at the time when the light of the Sun is barely seen in the West, after you have inscribed my Cup as I have directed. You must each meet those three nights in a row and drink holy water from the Cup.»

QUESTION 16: How do you wish your offerings to be given to you?

PAYMON: «Best to find a lake or a pond or some body of water where it may be poured, running or still; second best to be buried. That the offerings you leave will find their way to my feet in Tehom.»

QUESTION 17: Great King of the West, Paymon, do you have any final words of wisdom, advice, or instruction you can give us before this rite is concluded?

PAYMON: «When you stand at a crossroads in your life, or when you see other beings that you love and wish to protect at crossroads in their life, summon the image of them passing through my gate at the end. The image, even just held in the mind, in the heart, in the body for a moment will bless them...and you.»

OPERATOR: Great King of the West, we thank thee for thine attendance upon us and the sharing of your power and knowledge.

(License to Depart given.)

Afterthoughts on the Paymon Operation

SCRYER: Wow, that one was the clearest one by far.

OPERATOR: I wonder if it was the offerings which made the biggest difference?

SCRYER: It must be, because what a difference! I can't believe how close the symbol of Paymon was. The Moon and waves and the part in the center looks like the gate. Also, the visions I got of the lines of light going to the direction was really powerful and really suggested how each King unlocked a channel of power that flowed and spiraled toward the center.

The conjuration of Paymon was insightful but equally cryptic, with some responses being rather ominous instead of insightful or helpful. However, in my assessment, a clearer picture of the identity and nature of Paymon was achieved. As confirmed by the Spirit, it appears that the identities of the Paymon listed in the *Goetia* and the one listed as one of the four Kings may differ slightly. The Western King (Queen?) did not really give a detailed response that would make me confirm whether they were truly two different entities or simply one serving in different functions. Paymon definitely didn't appear on a dromedary or camel as most of the grimoires claim it does, but the symbolism of the crown and the gate was intriguing. This Spirit had the feeling of being ancient, primordial even, with its origins being steeped in early civilization and chaotic creation. I definitely could not claim that it was a friendly Spirit, recalling how it remarked on my death as soon as riches or wealth were mentioned, but it also wasn't hostile or uncooperative either. True to its nature of being an amorally neutral yet immensely powerful Spirit, Paymon's influence could be felt on an emotional level.

There was no mistaking the great ocean and primordial water connection with the Spirit of Paymon, and sounds of the ocean could still be heard after the conjuration was concluded. The Spirit seemed to have centuries of experience with mankind, their workings and process. The Spirit definitely appeared to understand how to manipulate and process people's reasoning and desires as well. The vision of the man possessed by Paymon was also interesting, and the vision seemed to show that the sigil has some power over the effects of Paymon and possibly controlling its influences. I wonder if this was a clue as to how such magical lamens functioned.

On the surface, we had received interesting responses and images but they were also confusing with little practical knowledge gained, unfortunately. Perhaps deeper knowledge and usefulness would be apprehended after further meditation on the words of this King. The method of conversation was indeed cryptic and tended to fit nicely with a subconscious, Water Elemental, and emotionally based theme. It definitely seemed more like a threat and warning rather than a helpful reply when the Spirit said, «I will place you beneath the sheets of your deathbed, and from there we will speak of the money that you need.» My question about it providing us with wealth and success seemed to yield unfavorable responses and apparently no assistance. It was fascinating that the spirit Paymon seemed to relate the function of her and her fellow three Kings, receiving and assimilating the energy of all three. The Spirit said, «What is born flows like three streams through the center of each being as they walk to me. Through Oriens they rise. Through Amaymon they mature and are exalted and tested. Through my Sister, they have their hearthstone.» To me, this signifies each King monitoring or being involved in the three primary stages of life, all life cycles, let alone human existence. Definitely with the Spirit King Paymon, I saw how the seasons of the year matched with the directions as well as the times of the day. Oriens started with the dawn of day, followed by noon of Amaymon, the dusk and twilight belonged to Paymon, and the middle of the night to Egyn. All quarterly divided between them.

By far the most fascinating part of the ceremony was to hear her repeated mention of *Tiamat* and *Tehom*, two words with which both my scryer and I were completely unfamiliar, and which required a bit of research to discover their origin and meanings. Apparently, in ancient Sumerian and Babylonian religion, Tiamat is a Goddess, a chaos monster of the deep abyss of the salt ocean,[56] who bore a series of Gods and monsters from her union with her mate, the primeval God of the fresh waters, Abzu. Paymon claimed to be the child of Tiamat, and this would seem highly appropriate. Also, the marriage of Tiamat and Abzu as the mythological mixing of the salt and fresh waters to bring about creation in the world is very comparable Paymon's function of mixing the Elements together and redistributing them, as she related to my scryer. Tiamat is occasionally depicted in the form of a dragon or sea serpent, which is apt here as Paymon is described in some grimoires as riding a dragon. Finally, the other word mentioned by Paymon was *Tehom*, which I learned is the Hebrew תהום, the name for the deep abyss of the ocean in the *Book of Genesis* 1:2, which scholars have connected with the name of Tiamat.[57] I found it fascinating that Paymon claimed such ancestry and association, and it confirmed a belief that many if not most Spirits found in Mediæval esoteric traditions stem from ancient sources.[58]

Follow-Up to Paymon Working

The following day I had a full list of things to do. I had a large seminar to prepare for which required running several errands and making sure everything was set and ready. I also wanted to engrave the silver chalice as Paymon had instructed to make it a completed and consecrated talismanic Cup for the King of the West. I was apprehensive about the agreement I had struck with the mighty Spirit, and started to consider that it would be quite easy for me to be delayed or barred from being able to perform the seemingly simple task of depositing Paymon's three beverage offerings. Regardless, I was determined to see the ritual through and also did not want to have to face whatever consequences might await me should I fail to complete the three offerings.

---

56. Tiamat was later known as *Thalattē* (the Attic Greek word for "Sea") in the writings of Berossus, a Hellenistic Babylonian priest of Marduk.

57. B. Alster, in K. van der Toorn, Bob Becking, and Pieter Willem van der Horst, *Dictionary of Deities and Demons in the Bible* (Leiden: Brill, 1999), *s.v.* TIAMAT. —APF

58. For more on Tiamat, see Alexander Heidl, *The Babylonian Genesis: The Story of the Creation* (Chicago: University of Chicago Press, 1942), pp. 96–114; Thorkild Jacobsen, "The Battle between Marduk and Tiamat," in *Journal of the American Oriental Society*, Vol. 88, No. 1 (Jan.–Mar. 1968), pp. 104–108; Norman Cohn, *Cosmos, Chaos, and the World to Come: The Ancient Roots of Apocalyptic Faith* (New Haven: Yale University Press, 1993), pp. 45–49; and Walter Burkert, *The Orientalizing Revolution: Near Eastern Influence on Greek Culture in the Early Archaic Age* (Cambridge, Massachusetts: Harvard University Press, 1995), pp. 92–93.

First Offering

As dusk arrived, I immediately set to work engraving the silver and copper chalice, so I could make it out to a nearby lake and perform my first offering in time. I spent a little more time than I intended on the two sigils, and just as I finished, my phone alarm went off reminding me I needed to leave as soon as possible. I climbed into the car with the newly engraved Cup, the written oath and agreement of terms, and the corked bottle of ale that was to be Paymon's first offering. On the way to the lake, traffic seemed to be worse than usual and I felt myself stressing over the closing window of opportunity as the Sun began to sink lower behind the mountains. I arrived at the lake to find it apparently completely frozen with the last snowfall still covering its entirety. I parked, retrieved my items in the bag, and made for the west shore. There were quite a few people walking around the path encircling the lake and I felt another twinge of discouragement as there was absolutely nowhere to do a covert magical ritual of any sort without receiving at least a few odd looks. Soon I found a point where I felt I could go out onto the lake, and was relieved to notice that there were quite a few patches where the ice had melted and dark water was peeking through.

I considered venturing a little ways out onto the ice, but thought better of it knowing I'd be even more exposed as well as looking suspicious to others, not to mention I would also be tempting my fate by possibly falling through the ice trying to perform a simple offering. Instead, I moved just far enough out to where I believed the edge of the lake water was and tested its stability under my feet. All seemed well, so I opened the bag of items just as a few people walked behind me a few yards up on the footpath. I ignored them and set to work pouring the choice ale into the silver Cup, covering the sigil I had inscribed in the bottom only minutes before. I whispered a small statement of intent and then, on intuition, drew the same sigil that was inside the cup in the snow before me. I poured the offering of ale directly on the snow, and an interesting effect happened. The cold ale melted directly through the snow... and also through the ice, to mix with the dark waters below. Everything was done rather quickly and I issued one more acknowledgment to the West, uttering the King's name aloud in a whisper, stating that the first of the three offerings was completed. The drinking of the holy water from the Cup was an odd and salty taste that incurred an interesting reaction in me. I felt somewhat perturbed or worried for reasons I could not readily identify. These feelings turned into a concern hoping I had performed the requisites correctly and that the timing was specific enough for the ritual. I stowed my Cup and the empty ale bottle in my bag and hurried back to my vehicle. The twilight deepened to that odd orange, dark glow which makes everything seem in a dream state. On my way home, I I glanced toward the darkening mountains and spoke aloud to the Spirit, expressing that I hoped it accepted the offering in full.

Second Offering

The following day proved to be even more difficult as I had to leave right in the midst of a seminar I was hosting. Luckily some of my senior students were able to cover for me and keep things going as I drove to a creek near which I had previously lived. I was determined to complete the second offering, which was the select red wine I had brought specifically for this occasion. I arrived just as the sun was setting behind the mountains and found a place along the creek which was not frozen completely through.

Trying to remain hidden from any possible onlookers who might happen by, I poured the red wine from its bottle into the ritually engraved silver and copper Cup. With a silent prayer and invocation to get Paymon's attention, I poured the red wine from the Cup into the creek that carried it away downstream.

I then retrieved the vial of holy water, poured some into the Cup, and drank it down. Again the salty taste lingered, and I felt an odd stirring within my being. I wondered what effects if any would occur as I ingested the holy water from the vessel of a supposed ancient demon. I spent just a moment longer considering this action and unknown ritual, then I declared the second of three offerings and terms of the contract were now completed, and gathered up my belongings and headed back to the car and back to the seminar before it grew completely dark.

Third Offering

The third and final offering had me the most worried since it would require that I somehow complete it at work during the midst of my shift. Not only that, but it turned out that I was unable to work out my shift in order for me to be outside at that time where I could deliver the offering. I couldn't help sense that this spirit was somehow testing me and my resolve, or even possibly putting up obstacles in order to keep me from completing the task. I did not want to consider the ramifications of missing the final offering, so when the hour approached, I asked if one of my coworkers would switch out with me early and luckily he agreed. I secretively drove to the nearest stream I could and dashed down a steep embankment with my ritual Cup and the final offering, which consisted of a vial of mead. The timing seemed even better than even the last two offering rituals, as the last rays of the sun were just visible and cast the land into a deep twilight. I poured the vial of mead into the Cup and offered it to Paymon by pouring it into the stream and watching it move quickly down the waters. I declared the final part of the contract and offering agreement completed, and poured the holy water into the chalice and drained it. This time the effect was interesting, as it felt like a weight had been lifted from my shoulders. I felt peaceful and relieved, and sensed that it was not just the stress of the difficult offerings being completed.

Follow-Up with Hiram

A few days after the completion of Paymon's offerings and fulfillment of the terms, Hiram stated that I had received a considerable amount of «power» and further aptitude in Spirit workings. He began by mentioning that it was important to consciously decide how to respond and feel about any given scenario in life, whether seemingly important or mundane, because if I decided to become passive then other Spirits or forces would attempt to take an active role for me. He said that the Spirit Paymon gave power and granted access to others quite indiscriminately, and that the abilities and power associated with such a gift could be just as dangerous as it could be rewarding. He mentioned that the responsibility was great, whether or not I was even aware of it at the time, and that thoughts and actions had influence and weight that would extend far outside my own sphere of influence.

In the following days, a shadow crept up in my mind, which possibly originated with the words of Hiram's warning as well as the rather uncertain nature of the Western King. I found myself a bit more reserved around people and my mood was definitely darker than it had been, or typically was. My particular attention was brought to my mood shift which was concerning. I wondered if there were any other reason for my mood shift besides my contemplation of the recent magical experiences. A time of trial or purification ensued shortly in my personal life, but luckily the worst passed with one full cycle of the Moon.

So far, the experience of contacting the four Kings was proving to be empowering but definitely more unsettling than my experience with the Archangels. In retrospect, it definitely seemed that the Angels are better disposed toward the magician, with a fonder outlook on humanity, and with their highly evolved essence perhaps being more congruent to spiritual seekers.

Despite my uneasiness, I was grateful that the third round of evoking the Directional Kings had gone so much more smoothly, with direct communication and exchange. I was also pleased at the unique rituals described by the Spirit that would add to the mounting collection of original occult methods these experiments were garnering.

The operation of King Paymon gave me confidence that my scryer and I would have little trouble evoking the fourth and final Cardinal King in the North. Paymon gave little additional detailed instruction of what we were to do to contact it, but I felt I had enough information and ability to be successful. I was eager to see what awaited after all four Kings were conjured, and if there was a way to harness the strengths of their four offices collectively.

The Cardinal King of the North
Egyn

Day and time	On Saturday at Midnight during Winter
Name	Egyn
Other names	Egin, Egim; Ariton (Asmodai? Goap?)
Pronunciation of name (as spoken by the Spirit)	«Eag-an»
Element	∇
Direction for invocation	North
Materials for lamen	Parchment, gold, iron, stone
Sigils	
Talisman	Stone Ring
Incense	Storax, benzoin
Offerings	Bread, fruits

Table IX-23. ***Evocatory Correspondences for Egyn***

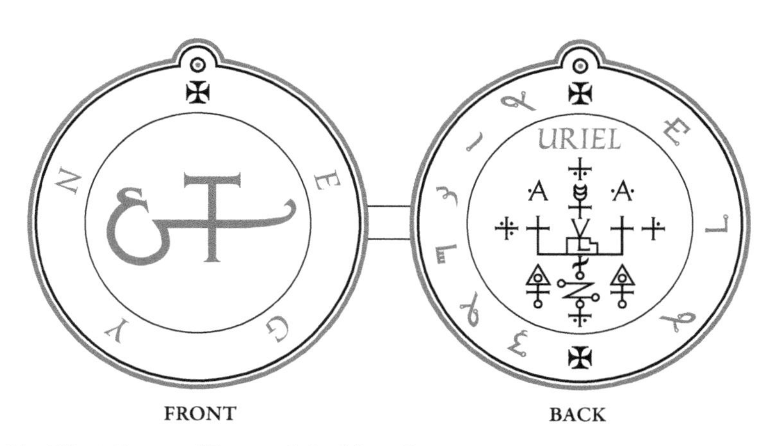

Fig. IX-24. ***Lamen of Egyn with Sigil from Fasciculus Rerum Geomanticarum, and Thwarting Archangel from Clavis Inferni***

Of Egyn

My magical companion and I were finally on to the last of the four Directional Kings. The last operation had definitely regenerated my confidence in being able to contact the final King directly and evoking it to appear in conversation form.

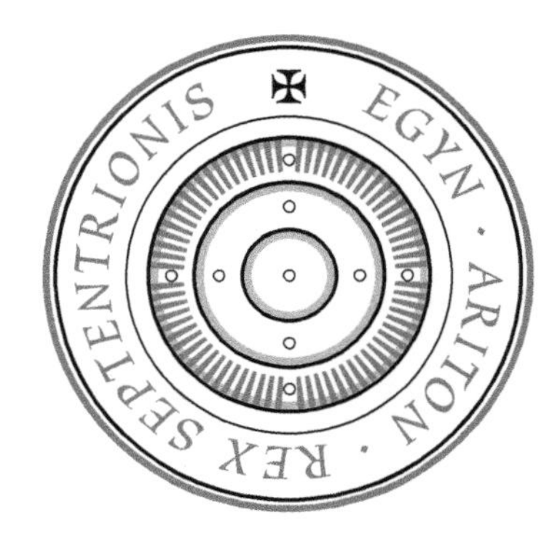

Fig. IX-25. ***Pentacular Plaque of Egyn with Seal from CLAVIS INFERNI***

Ms Sloane 3824 has a surprisingly brief description of Egyn:

> Egyn is King of the North, he appeareth in the Likeness of a man, his face very fair and Clear, his nostrils very sharp like a sword.[59]

However, there was a bit more information to be found on the northern King in various forms with more extensive descriptions and involved conjurations. The *Old Book of Magic* provides this description:

> This *spirit* is high and mighty. He appeareth in the form of a man riding upon a dragon, with a regal crown: on each side of him are hissing serpents. He cometh with a fearful and tremendous noise, with many inferiors around him; and under him are countless legions of mighty spirits. When constrained by powerful incantations, this spirit assumes the form of a child, and the raising of this spirit is less dangerous than of either of the preceding, and has proved of great use to the magician, when rightly invoked. He discovers treasures of the earth, and is very tractable.[60]

The *Old Book of Magic* also provides an illustration of Egyn (Fig. IX-26),[61] as well as a rare example of a magic circle for the four Kings (Fig. IX-27).[62] The

---

59. Skinner and Rankine, *The Keys to the Gateway of Magic*, p. 226. —APF

60. De Laurence, *op. cit.*, p. 19, duplicating Raphael and the Mercurii, *op. cit.*, p. 202. —APF

61. De Laurence, *op. cit.*, p. 31, duplicating Raphael and the Mercurii, *op. cit.*, p. 217. —APF

62. There is of course the very different Ouroboric Magic Circle of the Four Kings in *Clavis Inferni*. Our current Circle is illustrated in an engraving on p. 28 in *The Old Book of Magic*, duplicating p. 214 of *The Astrologer of the Nineteenth Century*, which I followed for our illustration here. A related but conspicuously different version of it is to be seen in Folger MS V.b.26 (p. 130), an illustration of which by James R. Clark is published in Harms, Clark, and Peterson, *The Book of Oberon: A Sourcebook of Elizabethan Magic* (Woodbury, Minnesota: Llewellyn,

FORM IN WHICH THE SPIRIT USUALLY APPEARS

Fig. IX-26. ***Portrait of Egyn from* The Old Book of Magic *(1918) and* The Astrologer of the Nineteenth Century *(1825)***

2015), p. 340. If you are interested in merely ancedotal information, I have a sketch and a note in my files that another version of this Circle—much closer to the version here than the Folger—is in a Wellcome manuscript, but I have been unable to find or verify that in time for this publication. The inscriptions around our Circle are in Roman letters, but while the inner inscription is Latin, the outer is Greek Romanized into the Latin alphabet.

The inner inscription reads ✠ *Per Crucis hoc Signum fugiat omne* ✠ *malignum, et ipse Signum salvetur* ✠ *quod benignum; per Signum sancte* [late form for *sanctæ*] ✠ *Crucis libera nos, Domine.* (Latin, "Through this Sign of the Cross may all evil flee, and by the Sign itself may the good be saved; through the Sign of the holy Cross free us, O Lord.").

The outer inscription, which reads ✠ *Agios Johannes Otheos* ✠ *Agios Marcus Otheos* ✠ *Agios Matheus Otheos* ✠ *Agios Lucas Otheos*, is an interesting combination of tradition and confusion. Christian symbolism, both Qabbalistic and exoteric, has long connected the tetrad of the four Gospel authors with that of the four Holy Living Creatures who sing the praises of God in the Hebrew Vision of Isaiah and the Greek Vision of John (perhaps most beautifully visualized in the iconography of the Celtic *Book of Kells* and of the best embodiments of the *leone di San Marco* which are to be seen throughout Venice). Iconoclastic grimoirists of the sort who avoid direct contact with scripture may turn to Agrippa's Scale of the Quaternity to validate the correspondences. As it stands, the text is a slightly erroneous Romanization of the modern Greek pronunciation of the *Trisagion* or *Trishagion* (the "Thrice Holy," the praises of God sung by the Angelic Holy Living Creatures in both Isaiah's and John's Visions)—still part of the Greek liturgy—combined with the names of the four Gospel authors. The Circle's

Fig. IX-27. A Magic Circle for Evocation of Egyn (or any of the Four Cardinal Kings) from ***The Old Book of Magic*** *and* ***The Astrologer of the Nineteenth Century***

detailed double magic circle is shown with stars at the four corners like the ones found in the *Heptameron*.

Mathers provides conjectures about both names, Egyn and the alternative name Ariton, in *Abra-Melin*:

---

two words *Agios Otheos* are a slight error for the three-word beginning of the *Trisagion*, "*Agios o Theos*"—the modern Greek pronunciation of the ancient koine *Hagios ho Theos (Ἅγιος ὁ Θεός)*. The names inserted into the middle of this repeated phrase are of course the names of the saintly authors of the four Gospels. The whole confusion hinges on the fact that *Agios (Hagios) Johannes* also means "Saint John," *Agios Markos* means "Saint Mark," etc. I would like to think this is a poetic or even a punning combination, but I suspect it is just a scribal confusion in which *'Otheos'* became a mysterious Divine Name, following the well-known names of the Gospel saints. —APF

> ARITON:—It is also often called "Egyn," or "Egin". This name *may* be derived from the Hebrew root ORH, = to lay bare, to make naked. It may also be derived from the Greek word ARHRETON, = secret, or mysterious, in any sense good or bad. Egin, may be derivable from Hebrew, OGN, = to delay, hinder, or retard. There may also be a connection with the Greek AIX, AIGOS, = a Goat. This Spirit is also called by the Rabbins OZAL, *Azael*, from the root OZ, which means both a Goat, and also vigour, vehemence of force; thus having partly the same root as "Azazel".[63]

Invocations of Egyn

The Old Book of Magic includes an invocation of Egyn along with the magic circle in the section entitled "Method of Raising the Mighty and Powerful Spirit Egin, King of the North." Although it is not the same invocation that I used for the Spirit in my operation, I offer it here for consideration and study by the astute magician wishing to compare the invocations.[64]

> The *Theurgist* must call this spirit in a fair chamber or quadrant, twenty or twenty-four feet at the most in breadth, in every part a window, a cubit wide, or a little more, east, west, north, and south. *The floor of the chamber must be paved, bordered, or plastered, very plain and close, so that he may make his circle thereon with chalk or coal, that it may be perfectly seen. This house or chamber must be in a void place, and not near the intercourse of men; for the opinion of some expert men in this art is, that spirits are more willing to appear in some waste place, as in woods, heaths, fens, moors, downs, or in any place where there is no resort, nor were any of the sacraments have been administered; for otherwise thy purpose will not be effected. *Therefore be warned.*
>
> The weather must also be observed, for all weathers are not good for thy work; wherefore, when thou wilt begin thy work, see that the air is clear, and, if it be in the day, see that the sun shine; and, if it be in the night, let the moon be unobscured, or the sky full of stars; but take heed of foul or close weather, for in those the spirit will not be visible; and why? Because it cannot receive bodily form or shape from the elements; wherefore select fine weather, for the spirit much delighteth therein.

---

63. Mathers, *loc. cit.*

64. It is curious that the original author decided to share the evocation of this particular King and not the others, although this invocation could easily be formatted to invoke the other three Directional Kings.

The spirit must also be invocated on even days of the moon, and in his proper hour, although some *Theurgists* say they have began in the new moon, and it hath been thirty days' labor before they could effect their entire purpose; therefore, let not this work seem tedious, nor think for one day being spent fruitlessly that thou wilt not effect thy purpose, seeing that expert *Disciples* have spent several days before they could obtain an appearance. This being performed, thy circle must be of the above form.

THE INCANTATIONS

FIRST.—To Bind The Ground, Whereby Neither Mortal Nor Spiritual Beings Can Have Power To Approach Within A Limited Distance.[65]

Having made your necessary suffumigations and mystic preparations, describe a circle of a hundred feet or more in diameter, or as much more or less as you may think fit; and, if you wish to keep all living creatures from within a quarter of a mile or more of your experiment, make, at the four parts of the same, east, west, north, and south, proper crosses, and devoutly pronounce thrice the following incantation:—[66]

In the name of the Father, and of the Son, and of the Holy Ghost, Amen. I bind all mortal and immortal, celestial and terrestrial, visible and invisible beings, except those spirits whom I have occasion to call, to avoid and quit this space of ground, which I now mark, and wherein I now stand, and that with all possible speed and despatch. I bind you to avoid and no longer to tarry, by the unspeakable power of Almighty God, by the most high and mighty name of ✠ Tetragrammaton ✠ by

65. The *Ancient Manuscript* from which this is taken is valued at Ten Thousand dollars, and was formerly in the possession of a great *Master Adept*, but is now in the possession of the Author. —L.W. DE LAURENCE

This footnote is an example of the most blatant of De Laurence's piratical excesses. It is a plagiaristic adaptation of the footnote in *The Astrologer of the Nineteenth Century*, which reads: "The MS. from which this is taken is valued at five hundred guineas, and was formerly in the possession of R. Cosway, Esq. R. A. but is now in the possession of the Mercurii." —APF

66. These curious proceedings are copied literally from the *Ancient Manuscript* before spoken of, and I have given the same orthography to the *Latin* and *Hebrew* words as in the original, and, notwithstanding some part may be found rather defective when compared with these languages as they are *now* used, yet the high antiquity of the *Ancient Manuscript* will be a sufficient excuse for the difference in point of *elegance*, should there be any. —LWDL

This footnote is duplicated (as all else) by De Laurence from Raphael and the Mercurii, with the revision of "MS" in the original to his italicized *"Ancient Manuscript,"* and the utterly shameless revision of "the Editor has thought proper to give" to his "I have given." —APF

the all-powerful names ✠ Agla ✠ Saday ✠ Jesu ✠ Messias ✠ Alpha ✠ and ✠ Omega ✠. By all these most high and powerful names, I charge, adjure, bind, and constrain both mortal and immortal, terrestrial, celestial, visible, and invisible beings to avoid, quit, and depart this ground, and do request that none of you, except those I have occasion to call at this time, be sufiered to come within these sacred limits. These things I request in the name of the Father, of the Son, and of the Holy Ghost, Amen.

Then dig a foot depth at the four parts of the compass, and bury in the Earth a piece of *Virgin Parchment* 3 inches square in each part, and no power, either visible or invisible, shall have power to come near thee, or to interrupt thy proceedings.[67]

INCANTATIONS FOR INVOKING THE SPIRIT TO INVISIBLE APPEARANCE

I conjure thee, Egin, Rex Borealis, and also charge thee that thou appear here before me, and before this circle, by the sufferance of Almighty God, and by the virtue of his passion and other sentences which here shall be rehearsed, to bind and constrain thee. I conjure thee, Egin, by the Father, the Son, and the Holy Ghost, and by the heavens, the air, the earth, and the sea, and by all that therein is contained, that thou come shortly, and appear to me and my fellows, not terrible nor fearful, but in mild and peaceable form, without hurt or envy to any of us.

I conjure thee, Egin, by all the holy words that God spoke in the creation of the world, and by all creatures visible and invisible, and by the four elements, and by the virtue of heaven, and by all the holy words that God spake unto Moses, and to all other prophets, and by the incarnation, passion, death, and resurrection, of the mild and ineffable Savior of all mankind.

I conjure thee, Egin, by the general resurrection, and by the dreadful day of judgment; I conjure thee, Egin, by the coming of the Holy Ghost; I conjure thee, also, by the virtue of all the spirits of the just, and by the most holy patriarchs, apostles, evangelists, and by the most holy saints of all ages. I conjure thee, Egin, by the mercy, grace, and power of God; I conjure thee, thou spirit Egin, under the pain of condemnation, and thy fearful doom at the great day of judgment; I conjure thee, Egin, by the great curse of God; I conjure thee, Egin, by all the high names of

67. This paragraph has been altered by De Laurence from the original of Raphael and the Mercurii, which reads: "Then dig a certain depth at the four parts of the compass, and bury the seal of the earth in each part, and no power, either visible or invisible, shall have power to come near thee, or to interrupt thy proceedings." The change may puzzle unless one knows that De Laurence sold merchandise which he claimed was "*Virgin Parchment*" to his readership. —APF

God; I conjure thee by the high power and strength of our Lord Jesus Christ, the Son of God, the heavenly King of glory; and I conjure thee by the whole of these, in what place of the world soever thou art, to appear instantly before me in the likeness of a child of three years old, and that, without fear, hurt, or envy, thou fulfill my request.

REPLICATORY INCANTATIONS

If, at the *third* rehearsal of the above mystic ceremonial, the spirit refuses to appear, prepare a fume of sweet-smelling savors, such as frankincense, aloes, cinnamon, oil olives, nutmegs, musk, cassia, roses, saffron, and white wax; which must be burnt, commixed together, on a fire consecrated for the purpose; and, while the fume is forming, and the fire fiercely burning, repeat what follows:–

I conjure thee, Egin, and command thee instantly to appear before me, by the virtue of the sentences and words hereafter written, upon pain of the most awful and bitter maledictions of Almighty God.

I conjure thee, O thou spirit Egan, that thou arise and appear to us, by the might, majesty, and power of the FIRST *word that our Lord spake, in the creation of the world, when he made the light to shine, and said, "Lux et facta, est lux."*[68]

---

68. An important word is strangely missing here, which may serve as an omen for the remaining quotations. The formula which is meant to be employed is one well-known in Theurgy and Qabbalah, which is that there is a great creative power in the words and phrases spoken by Elohim in the Creation of the world, beginning with the essential word which trasnlates as "Let there be" (in the original Hebrew יהי, *Yehi*, and in the Latin of the Vulgate translation *Fiat*), and that by citing those words, the Magician may call on that creative power to energize his or her invocations. Yet in this invocation that key word is missing. The line should read: '***Fiat** lux,' et facta est lux.* ("'Let there be light,' and light was made."). These errors (which you will see are extensive in the course of the invocation) are among the few things of which I must admit De Laurence to be innocent, as he plagiarized the Biblical blunders along with everything else from his English source. May I observe to the deceased and unresponsive Raphael and his Mercurial brethren, as to their American parasite, that it seems a very ill-advised practice for a would-be Magus to badly and repeatedly misquote *Genesis* in a magical ritual, particularly one intended to evoke Spirits who by all testimony are powerful Archdemons? Such a gross error almost demands Monkey's-Paw repercussions. Here and in the following notes on the verses quoted in this invocation, ***boldface*** indicates those portions—sometimes small and sometimes nearly all-encompassing—of the verses which are missing or corrupted in the Mercurii's quotations. The nature of many of the errors leads me to the somewhat shocking conjecture that Raphael or another of the Mercurii copied this conjuration from a manuscript written in a difficult hand, and not recognizing that these were some of the most well-known verses in the Bible, and obviously having only a remote acquaintance with Latin, simply did the best he could one word at a time. —APF

I conjure thee, by the SECOND *word that he spake when he made the firmament, and said, "Fiat firmamentum in medico aquas, et deinde aquas ab aquis."*[69]

I conjure thee, by the THIRD *word, when he gathered all the waters that were under heaven into one place, saying, "Congregentur aque que sub cælo sunt et apparia mida."*[70]

I conjure thee, by the FOURTH *word, which he spake when he made to spring forth trees and herbs, "Germinat terram herba veroli facientur semen cum semendi teipso sit super terram."*[71]

I conjure thee, by virtue of the FIFTH *word, when he made the ☉, ☽, and ***, saying, "Fiat luminaria magna in firmamento cæli ut illuminare terram."*[72]

I conjure thee, by the SIXTH *word, which he spake when he made birds, fishes, &c. "Producat aque reptile aere virentes et voluntate super terram sub firmamento cælo."*[73]

I conjure thee, by the virtue of the SEVENTH *word, which he spake when he blessed them, saying, "Crescite et multiplicamini et reptili aquas maris oves multiplicantur super terram."*[74]

---

69. Here the *fiat* is present, but much of the remaining verse is corrupted. It should read: *Fiat firmamentum in* ***medio aquarum*** *et* ***dividat*** *aquas ab aquis.* ("Let there be a firmament in the midst of the waters, and let it divide the waters from the waters.") —APF

70. This verse should read: *Congregentur* ***aquæ quæ*** *sub cælo sunt* ***in locum unum*** *et* ***appareat*** *arida.* ("Let the waters beneath the heaven be gathered together in one place, and let dry land appear.") Note that though the word *fiat* is missing in this verse, its creative power is not. The "let there be" is expressed in the Latin by the subjunctive mood of both *congregentur* and *appareat.* —APF

71. It should read: ***Germinet terra herbam virentem et facientem*** *semen* ***et lignum pomiferum faciens fructum iuxta genus suum cuius semen in semet*** *ipso sit super terram.* ("Let the earth bring forth vegetation verdant and producing seed, and fruit trees producing fruit according to its kind, whose seed is in itself, upon the earth."). The creative power of *fiat* is contained here in *germinet.* —APF

72. This is a sort of extreme paraphrase of two verses, *Genesis* 1:14–15. It should read: ***Fiant*** *luminaria in firmamento cæli ut* ***dividant diem ac noctem et sint in signa et tempora et dies et annos. ut luceant in firmamento caeli et inluminent*** *terram.*

73. The verse should read: *Producant* ***aquæ*** *reptile animæ* ***viventis*** *et* ***volatile*** *super terram sub firmamento cæli.* ("Let the waters bring forth the living creatures that creep, and those that fly above the earth beneath the formament of heaven.") —APF

74. It should read: *Crescite et multiplicamini et* ***replete*** *aquas maris* ***avesque multiplicentur*** *super terram.* ("Flourish and be imultiplied and fill the waters of the sea, and let the birds be mutliplied above the earth.") —APF

I conjure thee, by the EIGHTH *word, which he spake when he made beasts, worms, and serpents, "Ducat terram aliam in genero suo immenta et reptilia secondum specias scias."*[75]

I conjure thee, by virtue of the NINTH *word, when he made man in his own image, saying, "Faciamus homo ad imagine et similitudine nostra et per sit pissibus et volatibus que cæli et bestias terre et universe creature qui reptile que monentur in terra."*[76]

I conjure thee, O thou spirit Egin, instantly to appear, by virtue of the TENTH *word, which he spake when he placed Adam and Eve in Paradise, saying, "Crescite et multiplicamini et replete terra subjugate eam et semite vivi pissibus maris, et volatibus cæli et bestias terre, et universus animalibus que quem monentus super terra."*[77] *"Et per hac verba, conjuro te, spiritus Egin."*[78]

Lastly, I conjure, charge, bind, and command thee, O thou mighty and invincible spirit Egin, by these most high, powerful, and ineffable names of the most highest— ✠ Jesus ✠ Fons ✠ Salvator ✠ Christus ✠ Sabaoth ✠ Adonay ✠ Graton ✠ Messias ✠ Victor ✠ Osanna ✠ Nazarenus ✠ Theas ✠ Emmanuel ✠ Unigenitus ✠ Primogenitus ✠ Alpha ✠ et Omega ✠ and by the great, supreme, and all-powerful name ליהוה[79]

---

75. This should read: ***Producat terra animam viventem** in **genere** suo **iumenta** et reptilia **et bestias terrae** secundum **species suas***. ("Let the earth bring forth the living creature in its own kind, cattle and creeping things and beasts of the earth according to their kind.") —APF

76. The verse should read: *Faciamus **hominem** ad **imaginem** et **similitudinem nostram** et **praesit piscibus maris** et **volatilibus** cæli et **bestiis universæque terræ omnique reptili quod movetur** in terra*. ("Let Us make a human being in Our image and likeness, and let him be set over the fish of the sea and the flying things of the heaven and the beasts, and the whole world, and all the creeping things which move upon the earth.") —APF

77. This final verse should read: *Crescite et multiplicamini et replete **terram et subicite** eam et **dominamini piscibus** maris et **volatilibus** cæli et **universis animantibus quae moventur** super terram*. ("Flourish and multiply and fill the earth and subdue it, and have dominion over the fish of the sea and the flying things of the heaven and all the living animals which move upon the earth.")

    This concludes the tortured sequence of ten Biblical misquotations. Note that in the original Qabbalistic formula, these ten creative Divine Utterances from *Genesis* (*Bereishith*) are the ten מעמרות (*Maamaroth*, "Utterances" or "Words" or "Sayings") of the *Sepher Bahir*, which are the same as the ten Sephiroth of the *Sepher Yetzirah*. —APF

78. This should read *Et per **hæc** verba conjuro te, spiritus Egin*. (Latin, "And by these words I conjure thee, O Spirit Egin.") —APF

79. Hebrew, *le-YHVH*, "Unto YHVH" *i.e.*, "Unto Tetragrammaton." This is peculiar here, where following "by the great, supreme, and all-powerful name," we would rather expect ביהוה, *be-YHVH*, "By YHVH," or "By Tetragrammaton." Almost uniquely, De Laurence corrected an error here, transforming the Mercurii's (or their printer's) nonsensical להךה to ליהוה. —APF

> *which all creatures obey, at which the elements are moved, and the devils fear and tremble. By all these tremendous and awful names, I charge thee, finally, to appear before me. Fiat, fiat, fiat.*[80] *Amen.*
>
> These things being rightly performed, with a rushing sound, "as of many waters,"[81] and a tremendous noise, will the spirit appear, and by powerful invocations thou shalt obtain what thou wishest. But let thy proceedings herein be secret, and beware of vain curiosity; for these mysteries are sacred.[82]

The following conjuration of the King of the North is from a French version of the *Grimoire of Pope Honorius*, slightly adapted to summon Egyn to appear directly rather than send a subordinate Spirit:

O thou, EGYN, great King of the North, I conjure and invoke thee by the most high and holy Names of God, do thou here manifest, clothed with all thy Power; come before this circle, to make answer unto me, and to execute all my wishes. If thou failest, I shall force thee by God Himself.[83]

The next Invocation comes from Sloane 3821, which provides it as one of the "Operations of the North Angle of the Air by Invocation made to the Regal Spirit Egin, who is the King & Ruler of the Same: for the moving and Calling forth of all or any of Such Aerial Spirits by names, Orders, & office of what Degrees soever from the Superior to the Inferior to Visible Appearance." Again this invocation, like those of the three preceding Kings, has been modified slightly to summon Egyn to direct visible appearance, rather than to send lesser Spirits.

O you Royal Spirit of great power who art called Egyn, and said to be King of the North Angle, Region, or Mansion of the Air, and governing or bearing rule therein over many legions of Aerial Spirits subjected unto you, unto and under the power obedience and command of that great and mighty Spirit called Sathan, who is said to be the Prince of the Air & to govern the four Angles, Regions, Divisions, or Mansions

---

80. Latin, "So mote it be, so mote it be, so mote it be." —APF

81. *Revelations of John* 14:2, 19:6. —APF

82. The whole series of invocations and instructions occupies pp. 28–33 of *The Old Book of Magic*, and pp. 214–220 of *The Astrologer of the Nineteenth Century*. —APF

83. This conjuration is from *Le Gremoire du Pape Honorius*, in the edition which claims publication at Rome in 1760, but was likely published in Paris in 1810. The adaptation here closely follows the translation of A.E. Waite, *The Book of Black Magic and of Pacts* (Edinburgh: Privately printed, 1898), p. 283. —APF

there of East, West, North, and South, and unto whom power and command is given over all Spirits having place, residence, or mansion therein, as by the preordinate decree of the Most High God, the only Creator of Heaven and Earth, and of all things whatsoever is contained in the creation, is constituted and appointed.

O ye Regal Spirit Egyn King of the North Region or Angle of the Air, being governed and governing as aforesaid, we the servants of the Most High God reverently here present in His holy fear, being dignified, armed, and supported in the Holy Trinity, through divine grace, with celestial power and authority given unto our first parents in the Creation, at the beginning of time, and by lineal descent from them to us and all posterity or succeeding generations, as the heirs of God's promise and grace, even to the utmost period thereof, and by the name of your God, and in the name of your prince or head of your Orders, and by your seal or character, preordinately decreed of the Most High God, confirming, subjecting, and binding you by orders and office unto strict obedience: first, to the fulfilling of His divine will and pleasure, both at his mediate and immediate commandments and appointments; secondly, unto the command service and obedience of your prince or head of your orders as in place degree and office appointed; Thirdly, as well unto the service, obedience, and assisting of the sons of men, servants of the Most High God, now living on Earth, according to your orders and office as to tempt and subvert them from their allegiance to the divine laws and duty to God, by your evil and crafty insinuations and delusions.

By the contents of all aforesaid, and by the power thereof, we do exorcise, conjure, command, compel, constrain, and move you, O you regal Spirit who is called Egyn, King of the North Angle of the Air, forthwith and immediately at our invocation to move and appear in fair and decent form, and in no wise hurtful, dreadful, terrible, or frightful unto us or this place, or to any other person or place whatsoever, but in all humility and serenity, visibly to the sight of our eyes, in this crystal receptacle standing here before us, and to make us true and faithful answers unto all such our demands and requests, and to fulfill and accomplish all such our desires, as we shall by invocation declare, and at large in the contents thereof expressly show forth and move unto them without delay, delusion, or disturbance whereby to surprise or assault our senses with fear and amazements, or in any wise to obstruct or hinder the effects of these our present operations by any subtle crafts or illusions whatsoever.[84]

Lastly I include the conjuration of The King of the North from Sloane 3824. Once again, the original text is intended to summon the King's subordinate

84. The unmodified form of this invocation may be read in Skinner and Rankine, *The Keys to the Gateway of Magic*, pp. 239–240. —APF

Spirits; below is the slightly altered conjuration fit for calling the spirit Egin directly, and the outline I used in my own workings:

O thou great and potent Spirit Egyn, King of the North, and bearing rule and command in the North Region of Air, I adjure, call upon, and constrain, and most powerfully and earnestly urge you by and in and through the virtue, power, and might of these efficacious and binding names: Tetragrammaton, Jehovah, Adonay, Agla, El, Sabaoth, Elohim, even the Almighty, Immense, Incomprehensible, and Everliving God, the omnipotent Creator of Heaven and earth, and in and through the names of our Lord and Savior Jesus Christ, Messias, Sother, Emanuel, the only Begotten Son of God the Father, born of the Virgin Mary, the High King and Lord of all the world, whose name all the celestial Angels honor and obey, and before whom all the holy company and choir of heaven incessantly sing O Mappa Laman, Hallelujah, and at whose divine and inestimable name all knees on earth do homage and bow, and all the Aerial, Terrestrial, and Infernal Spirits do fear and tremble. And now, by all the aforesaid, I do now again powerfully adjure, call upon, constrain, and most earnestly urge you, O you great and mighty spirit Egyn, King of the North Quadrant of the Air, in and through the most effectual, glorious, sacred, and puissant names of him who sayeth "It is done," that now, immediately, without further tarrying or delay, you arrive and appear unto me visibly, plainly, peaceably, affably, in all serenity and humility, here apparently to my sight and view, and positively, effectually, faithfully, and fully to serve me and be responsive to me in such queries and interrogations as I shall ask and require of you, and that without delay, guile, deceit, or illusions whatsoever that may in any wise obstruct or destroy our expectations. And I do again earnestly importune, adjure, urge, and constrain you, O you powerful and regal Spirit Egyn, to appear forthwith immediately, and now at this present time, to me, and to appear plainly visible before me, in all mildness, peace, and friendliness, without any hurt, disturbance, or any other evil whatsoever, either to me, my scryer, or this place wherein I am, or any other place, person, or creature whatsoever, but that quietly, courteously, and obediently to serve me and fulfill my desires and do my commandments in all things, all which I earnestly urge and constrain thee, O thou royal and potent Spirit Egyn, to do for me in Nomine Patris, et Filii, et Spiritus Sancti.[85]

---

85. The original template of this conjuration or constraint, addressed to Oriens, may be read in Skinner and Rankine, *The Keys to the Gateway of Magic*, pp. 226–227. —APF

The operation to contact the final king, Egyn, was set during the evening. By this time, I was well aware of the Directional King's associations with the four parts of the day and Egyn was firmly associated with the evening. Plates with bread and fruits were arranged near the Altar of the Stars for offering. The magical chamber was unusually cold for that time and made the preparations a bit uncomfortable. However the atmosphere and prospect of the coming work certainly kept my scryer and me alert and eager to begin. Excitement built inside me as I considered that this would be the meeting of the final Cardinal Ruler. I hoped my understanding of who these beings were would form a complete picture of how they worked within the scope of creation.

Invocation of the Cardinal Ruler Egyn

Fig. IX-28. ***Section of Circle for Drawing Egyn into the Crystal***

Appearance of the Spirit

SCRYER: I see an enormous landscape before me, an evergreen forest, spruce pines, ancient, snow on the ground that looks lit by a full moon but I don't see any moon in the sky. On the other side of the forest I see a great wall of ice, like the edge of a glacier, but the ice is black and opaque. A wind comes very strongly from over the glacier down over the forest towards me. I can see the wind moving the trees and branches. It is a very, very cold wind. The glacier begins to move, and looks like it is the back of something.

I can see now that the glacier is the back of a massive beast. A light is seen on top of it, on top of its back. It looks like almost like the back of a bear, but it's so big I cannot see the head or the tail of it. As if the glacier of the body spans down into the body of the earth.

I find myself standing on top of the glacier, on the bear, in front of a pillar of black ice over stone. At the base of the pillar is a throne. On the throne sits a woman clothed in black, with long, white hair, and the wind is coming from her mouth. Her eyes are closed, she seems at peace

---

OPENING QUESTION 1: In the name of the holy and undefiled Spirit, the Father, the begotten Son, and Holy Ghost proceeding from both, what is thy true name?

SCRYER: I hear the land all around me say «Egyn *(Eag-an)*» as if the stone were groaning the name. It seems almost like she rides the bear. As if the bear is somehow aware of the touch of her fingers on the throne. She closes her mouth and the wind stops, and she opens her eyes and looks at me. She has pupils that seem to go very, very deep, into an infinite black space. The pupils are deep, endless.

OPERATOR: What is the origin and meaning of Egyn? How is it properly pronounced and spelled? What other names are you known by?

(Scryer's voice takes on a very breathy, almost hoarse, but powerful tone.)

SPIRIT: «Egyn is the name given to me by the people of the South who lived on the sea. They saw me as a king, a man, because they could only conceive a ruler as a man, but I was known to the people of the North long before that. I watched as your first ancestors approached the glaciers, before they knew how to make pictures.»

OPERATOR: Great King of the North, we thank thee for thy coming and ask that you attend unto us during this ceremony in the name of the Most High God. I have brought you offerings, which it is said you require and do so desire to have. I have brought you meat, bread, and fruit. How would you like it delivered and offered to you?

SPIRIT: «Meat and bone, ground to a powder and mixed with spring water and tea made of evergreen leaves are most agreeable to me.»

OPENING QUESTION 2: What is thy office? What is under your office and duties? Your purpose?

SPIRIT: «I breathe forth from deep within the Earth and the North wind. I bring stability, stasis, and structure. I also bring the rest associated with death and the deep turning within the earth that will manifest in the stars. The fiercest of beasts that walk the earth are my eyes. I feel the footfalls of the bear on my skin and I am the light on its back. The great guardian of the Northern pole is the bear upon which I ride, the stability and the fecundity of the earth depend on the winds and the powers that stretch forth from my mouth.

«Opposite my brother in the South, we are akin to the fire and ice that create and maintain the balance between, but now the South begins to expand and the North begins to shrink and my bear may awaken.»

SKRYER: I see her stroking the back of the bear's ear. It has a picture she is showing me in a—a glass—no, an ice wiped away of snow at her feet. So she's calming the bear; she whispers to it and sings to it, and I also know somehow that it is also her.

OPENING QUESTION 3: What is thy true sign or character? What is the meaning of your sigil and signs? Is there another name by which you would prefer to be called?

SPIRIT: «Egyn is proper for your ceremonies. My sigil, the same you showed to the scryer on the talisman. It is the old form representing the great bear in the sky of the North, crossed by the power of the pole star which you call Polaris that has changed over the eons; the curve of the sigil is like the rolling, groaning power of the bear that I ride, that I am. My hand like the pole star crossing its handle to calm it, to bring forth its power in harmony with my brothers and my sister.

«I am the last key for you and your scryer. I will open these four pathways and make your work more manifest on the earth.»

OPENING QUESTION 4: When are the times most agreeable to thy nature to hold conference with us and other magicians?

SPIRIT: «Midnight. Winter. And when the North wind blows fiercely.»

OATH: Wilt thou swear by the blood and righteousness of our Lord Jesus Christ that thou art truly the King of the North, Egyn?

EGYN: «I swear that I am Egyn, known and conceived of as the great power, wind, and ruler from the North.»

Fig. IX-29. ***Portrait of Egyn as beheld in Vision***

QUESTION 5: What are your views on humanity? What are your roles and interactions?

EGYN: «I have seen you change and grow from the times you have first approached my walls of ice, long ago. I listened to the songs you made in the caves and you saw my power and witnessed my power in the bears that lived in those caves long ago. Through the bear we spoke to one another and I heard your songs. You lived in harmony with all around you then, but it was not meant to stay that way. Now you must choose to come back, to harness your gifts and your knowledge to enhance the whole, rather than place yourselves as master over it—a task you cannot attain. I can be invoked to check the hot, tyrannical power of leaders who do not see their place in the whole, those who would lord over you and others and the earth. But if you call on justice for them, I will visit you first.»

QUESTION 6: You are given the title of one of the four great Kings or Spirit Governors of the four Directions, this being the North. Can you explain your role and purpose in this position? What can you tell us of the other three Kings? From our experiences thus far, it seems as if each from you stem from ancient Babylon, Syria, even India or another ancient civilization. Is this correct? Can you explain your origins in greater detail?

EGYN: «Your perception of them is correct in the way that it can be. But my power is older than the civilizations of men and women. I am akin more to my brother in the South. Mitigated and harmonized by my sister in the West and my brother in the East. When fire and ice join together, the balance is maintained. But at some point on your planet, in your perception of how it is shaped, North becomes South and then becomes North again.»

QUESTION 7: In the form of the *Grimoire of St. Cyprian* called the *Clavis Inferni*, the four Kings are each pictured with animals. Your picture was with the bear, and the other three with different beasts. Is there anything you can tell us about the other animals with the other three Kings that may be of importance to us or give us further knowledge as to their purpose and office?

EGYN: «Your scryer saw the 'camel' of my sister in the West, but he did not recognize it for what it was. His vision was as this is: an older, different form that he has not seen. The other two animals were hidden from you on your first two invocations of my brothers. Now that I have opened the last stream to you, when you invoke them again, they will appear. Your contact with both of them will be stronger. And additional knowledge coming from them will be revealed. The offerings facilitate this.»

OPERATOR: Are you able to instruct us on which offerings are preferred by your brothers in the South and East?

EGYN: «Bread and wine for my brother in the South and cinnamon, honey, and beer. White gold and shavings of cedar to my brother in the East.»

QUESTION 8: Do you know what sort of effects the three days of consecutive offerings to Paymon and then drinking the holy water did to me?

EGYN: «As my sister opens to you the depths of the oceans, I open to you the depths of the Earth. The Water connected you to the deepest part of her dwelling, enabling her power to flow more quickly and more easily to you. The Water is like many keys for many locks within you. It is a blessing for your continued interactions with the Spirits that you will summon who will be adversaries against you and those who will be allies with you.»

QUESTION 9: Are there further abilities and insights you can offer or impart to us?

EGYN: «I can destroy tyranny over you. I can see through the fingers of the Northern wind those who would come against you. I can receive you gently, and send to you your ancestors at death. I can impart to you secret knowledge when you stand in an evergreen forest at night and listen to the wind. Speak and sing my name quietly, until the wind begins to blow, until you feel the vibration of the Earth under your feet and listen carefully to the wind.»

QUESTION 10: As per your office, can you tell us and teach us how and where to discover 'treasures of the Earth'?

SCRYER: She shows me the mountains as a scene from very long ago, before there were people, before there were ever human civilizations. I see her taking stars and placing them inside of the mountains. Some she pulls almost into threads and they melt into the rock as the veins of silver, gold, platinum, gems, created from the starlight of her fingertips.

EGYN: «They are conduits for the power that rises from deep below the core of the planet. These gifts are given in need as long as you recognize that by taking them you change the flow of the energies within the earth. What is given must be used to enhance life and to rebalance the broken energies by their removal. I can be a conduit by which other Spirits who know where these treasures are can speak to you and help you find them.»

QUESTION 11: Now that all four Kings have been summoned, what effects or benefits can be expected? Is there a way to link the four Kings together in a separate ceremony or bring the four talismans together for a powerful rite? Is there anything we should be cautious of or do to avoid unfortunate happenings?

EGYN: «Now that you have spoken with all four of us, your contacts with the Spirits will be stronger. Your contacts with the Angels will be stronger. There is a ceremony that joins the power of the four of us, but it is not yet time for you to know what that is to be. But we will tell you, my brother in the East will tell you when that time has come. Until then, know that your connection is greater for good allies who would help you and for those who would oppose you. Our job is not to mitigate the right and the wrong but to provide the energy, to provide the power. You will have to go to other Spirits for protection, as that is not our role. We are the gateways through which the different energies enter your world.»

QUESTION 12: Is this stone adequate for your chosen talisman and vessel? A "Stone Ring" was mentioned by the Archangel Sandalphon, and this seems closest to your grimoric symbol, but I was unsure if it was what was intended. Are there any modifications or further consecrations you would have done to it for it to be more amplified by your spirit and office? What could this talisman be used for, and how should it be used?

EGYN: «The stone ring can be used. It should be simple, unadorned. It can be left through the winter, outside in a shallow pool that freezes to the bottom, and retrieved again in the spring. Through the winter I will sing and whisper to it.»

SCRYER: She shows me an image of someone doing this ceremony and singing her name over the stone ring in the frozen pool and then leaving.

OPERATOR: Due to the timing, I wish to inquire from a student and friend who had a dream about a bear attacking him and then befriending him after he refused to fight it. I wish to inquire if you had any dealing with it and wished to pass on any words of wisdom to him.

EGYN: «All bears are connected to my bear, to me. It is an untamable power within him. It is a symbol of his friendship with the untamable darkness inside that is necessary for living in the world. If it is resisted, it will rise up and it will disassemble him, alter and destroy his current views and rebuild them. Because he has not warred with it, it has become a warden for him. That power must always be respected and understood as untamable and greater. If not, the relationship can change.»

QUESTION 13: Great Spirit King and being of the North, I thank you for your allowances to open up the gate, your words of insight and direction. Before we hail you farewell, I wish to ask if there are any further magical insights, wisdom, or words of advice before departing.

EGYN: «Your child will be from the North and know the turning of the Earth within.»

(I remain silent unable to speak or move for a time. Continued silence ensues. For some reason, I am unable to ask further questions and stand there stunned. I'm not sure why this has such an effect on me, but I am unable to say anything for a while. The unexpected response about my unborn child somehow affects me deeply. After a time I simply give the License to Depart.)

Afterthoughts on the Egyn Operation

OPERATOR: That remark about my child really struck me. I have no idea what to really make of it, or what «Your child will be from the North and know the turning of the Earth within» means. Right after the Spirit said that, I felt like everything went quiet, outside as well as internally. There was just instant stillness. I cannot guess exactly what that closing statement meant, and I seemed prevented from asking anything further, so I gave the License to Depart. During an earlier conversation, my familiar Spirit Hiram mentioned something about my daughter having a lot of «Spirits around her, like an envoy around her.» I was excited and intently curious about what sort of person she was going to be. I suppose I will have to wait and see.

SCRYER: The look on her (Egyn's) face was like she was smiling when she said it. The expression leads me to believe it was among the more important things that she was going to say. With the other three we talked to, I hadn't seen them as clearly as I did with her. Everything from beginning to end was clear, the landscape was really vivid, Narnia-like. At first, I was in this clearing at the top of a hill, an evergreen forest around me, and the forest went down and then up to this huge wall of black ice, but also sort of frosted over. I had the feeling it was a new Moon, dark of the Moon, yet the snow and things were glowing.

OPERATOR: I am beginning to see the identities and purposes of these Spirits a bit more clearly now. I also understand that to truly appreciate any one of these beings, a magician would have to work with one of them over many years, continuously. To really grasp the aspects and powers of each King and to also harness the fullest power available would be a lifelong relationship.

There was a ringing sound periodically though the operation that I initially thought was occurring in my own ears. However, my scryer mentioned that he had heard it as well. The high-pitched ringing would occur for several moments, stop suddenly, and then come back again. My scryer and I could not discern the source of the sound or what possible significance it had. Further examination of the experience suggested connections between the king of the North and the Archangel Uriel. More so than any prior information we had on the two beings as a sense of familiarity between the two. Speaking with both entities, though greatly different in many aspects, felt the same somehow to both my scryer and myself though neither one of us could quite reason why this was so. I wondered if perhaps the Archangels that ruled over the four kings were mismatched in the grimoires as the kings themselves were in several texts. It occurred that I should have directed these questions to the kings themselves during initial contacts as an important confirmation. It appeared I had yet another inquiry for consecutive operations.

After the operation, my scryer mentioned to me that he was curious about the part where the Spirit told him that the sigil for the lamen was «the old form representing the great bear in the sky of the North.» I voiced that he wanted to know if the Spirit meant Ursa Major or Ursa Minor and if the one of the Spirit's names was an old name for "bear." I wonder what the significance is and what the connection with Polaris is.

A deeper perhaps more sophisticated understanding began to develop concerning the correspondences of the four Kings following the conversation with Egyn. The process for confirming the Kings' 'Elemental' alignment and direction is not as straightforward as, say, for the Elemental Kings. For instance, Egyn stated, «when fire and ice join together,» referring to itself and Amaymon in the South. Initially, one might attribute stone and Earth only to the King of the North, but Egyn definitely included ice as a prominent feature of its station as well. Although the Northern King was fairly clear that the Stone Ring was the correct talisman and related several confirming statements that Earth was its corresponding Elemental alignment, was also a potent symbol of its office. When considered from the perspective of seasonal and timely associations as well as Elemental associations, the correspondences begin to make better sense. Oriens is indeed associated with the East and winds, Air, but also with the spring, the rising of the Sun and thus dawn or daybreak. There is a particular sort of Fire here, too, but more of a celestial one.

Oriens alluded that it coincided with the heat and light of a new day in the East. Perhaps associating the Kings with seasons answers the riddle of what it meant when it said that the Directions were «everywhere.» With the dawn of a new day, the Sun filters through to creation bringing about a quickness and birth to movement as well as new beginnings. Awakening and springtime go hand in hand with this ideal, and with the light comes the perception of sight. With Amaymon, the light and heat is intensified and concentrated as the day reaches its peak at noon and the season moves into summer. After its point of energetic height and maturity, the light dwindles, begins to fade to dusk, sinking into the depths in the West, the realm of Paymon. Autumn and fall are also associated with the ruler of the West in this way, where nature and light begin to sink back into shadow. Midnight and midwinter is the realm of Egyn, the ruler of the North. The themes and imagery are the polar opposite in direction and function to Amaymon. More than one of the Kings mentioned their functions coinciding with the cycle of life and cyclical progression symbolized by the seasons and times of day. There is direction in their office, but there is also movement and exchange to which the magician seeking to harness their authority would do well to be attuned.

Considering the above possibilities, I undertook a reexamination of the talisman for the North. I reasoned that a natural and perhaps ancient stone ring was what the talisman should be for Egyn. I had become familiar with a fairly well-known folk-magic or pagan charm referred to simply as 'holey stones.' These nature-made objects are rocks that have naturally occurring holes through them, sometimes referred to as Odin Stones, Crick Stones, Hag Stones, or Fairy Stones. Used as magical amulets for a variety of situations, these stones are formed typically by water erosion creating an opening over many, many years. They are believed to have magical, healing, protective, and prophetic properties. Besides these, the Chinese *bi* disk also still seemed like an excellent choice for the Northern talisman; I felt there was some ancient and potent meaning to these objects that coincided perfectly with the allusions of the Archangel Sandalphon and the King of the North. The ceremony which Egyn showed to my scryer of someone placing the stone ring in a freezing pool was interesting and something I wanted to try for myself. I felt the ceremony would be the perfect opportunity to further consecrate the talisman for the North.

Further Reflections on the Four Cardinal Kings

A few days after the operation with Egyn, my scryer contacted me, eager to share a spontaneous dream or vision he had concerning the four Kings.

SCRYER: After one of my personal workings, I woke up after having an intense vision or perhaps instruction/insight into the nature and purpose of the four Kings. According to the vision, part of how the four Kings manifest is through the magnetic field of the planet. In this function, they are responsible for protecting the earth from cosmic, interstellar, and stellar energies that could destroy life on the earth. It was clear this protection was not required due to these cosmic energies and beings being 'evil' or 'malevolent,' but simply due to the nature and power those energies and beings have inherent in them. Also, regardless of this cosmic power, some of it needs to be let through because, without the connection, life on the planet would die. The four Kings, specifically the Northern and the Southern Kings, let some of the energies from the cosmos and the Sun through in a controlled way that assists and allows life to change and

> evolve. There are also times when they will change their configuration to let different energies in as necessary for the greater plan of the Creator. Apparently the Archangels direct when that is supposed to take place. The Northern King is dominant in the Northern hemisphere for what is let in. And the Southern King is dominant for the Southern hemisphere and what is let in, but somehow these energies come in at the poles.

This revelation by my scryer seemed fascinating and touched on points both scientific and esoteric in nature. The functions of the Four Kings as both Spiritual and energetic moderators definitely seemed to fit the bill. Their balance between the four primary Elements as well as the seasons and times of the day spoke to an amazing sophistication of harmonious energetic exchange. It was after this revelation and the following operations that I began looking at the Holy Table of *DSIC* with much more appreciation. I now see it as a complete representation of the divine forces of creation in symmetry. The names and sigils inscribed on the surface are no longer strange and foreign, but familiar presences of power, position, and immense intelligence. Though I could not hope to understand their full nature, I felt a part of each Spirit transcribed on the reflection of the ritual object within me: within my mind, within my body, within my understanding. The keys of each Spirit's interaction and instruction were releasing various sublime locks.

In the weeks following the evocation of Egyn, I began receiving spontaneous glimpses or visions of how creation worked and functioned. Beyond simple imaginative musings, certain ideas would suddenly enter my head that were more scientific and methodical in nature than the sort to which I was accustomed. I began considering the Spirits and energies I had interacted with as highly complex patterns of intelligent exchange through a mind and intention which eclipses humanity's vain attempts to classify and understand them.

Benn and I still had to successfully contact Oriens and Amaymon a second time, but before my scryer and I could re-conjure the Kings of the East and South, we both experienced challenges in our personal lives which seemed to upset plans for magical workings for a short while. True to their words, the Kings indeed seemed to have 'opened doors,' and my scryer and I began sensing more Spiritual activity in our homes than we had ever experienced before. More Spirits seemed to be coming around all the time, with many appearing in various ways to my wife and son. I constantly had to magically safeguard the rest of the rooms in the house and perform blessings and clearings to keep life at home as normal as possible. Luckily, when situations did occur, Hiram was able to provide useful information regarding what was going on and how to handle it.

Along with such phenomena came turbulent shifts in our moods, energy levels, and perceptions as we attempted to go about our daily lives. I was having to magically ward myself and center after each little upset or distraction. I felt palpable pulls from foreign Intelligences and energies that were not present prior to the operations of the four Kings. This was interesting, but also distracting and sometimes upsetting for my family and myself. If consecutive days passed without my performing a clearing or blessing, it tended to invite odd dreams that would shift my mood and sometimes cause me to be irritable.

As a matter of record-keeping, I kept a copy of one of my scryer's messages around that time which stated: "I am really having some depression coming up, plus some weird Spirit stuff around the house. Yeah, we need to sit down and talk; some of it is Spirit-related, some of it is just personal conflict coming up. Also, some really weird 'Earth' images have been coming up in dreams and daydreams lately."

I responded that I was having similar issues, and that we needed to get together soon and perhaps do some intense centering and clearing practices before moving forward with another evocation ritual.

Before we could get together, however, my scryer called me, stating that the previous night he awoke suddenly to the feeling of a heavy tapping on his chest. He said that when he opened his eyes he saw his personal protective talisman thump up and down twice on his chest as if someone had lifted it and slammed it back down. At this same instant he heard footsteps approaching, then suddenly cease when they neared his bedroom.

Soon after the above conversation, Hiram suggested that my usual methods of clearing and banishing were not enough and that something more was needed. Although the Spirit's statement seemed obvious at this point, I urged him to continue. He replied that he would instruct both my scryer and me on methods to help better deal with the increased activity. My familiar Spirit advised that «with greater interaction comes greater need for control and security for working magic within a household.» I was in full agreement with this statement, and looked forward to new processes for spiritually moderating my environment. Although increased Spiritual activity was not totally undesirable, it was important for me to have my home, workplace, and other areas free from heavy influence, especially from those that might cause harm or disturbance. I needed to find a way to be able to 'open the gates' without being bombarded by disruptive Spiritual influence and meddling.

Before my scryer and I could get together to talk with Hiram in tandem, Benn's wife contacted me, saying that a friend who was staying with them had been experiencing drastic changes in mood and personality. Apparently their visitor was particularly affected by the odd occurrences which had been going on throughout the house. My friend's wife was familiar with the sort of work her husband and I were doing, and asked if there was anything I could do to help. Naturally I agreed to come over as soon as possible and do what I could.

The next Saturday I went over to perform several blessings and clearings, with which I had been getting frequent practice. For house clearing, I take a three-step approach in both spoken ritual and implement use. I ritually cleanse the space by the use of holy water, holy incense, and holy oil anointing of the doorways and windows of the house, as well as any areas which seem to generate the most phenomena. There were a couple of areas where my senses told me something nasty had been hiding out, and I spent a while making sure those areas felt cleaned out.

The prayers and invocations I use in conjunction with these clearings come from the Syriac *Book Of Protection*. Many of the prayers are severely outdated and not applicable, but a few ring with a powerful authority in the tradition from which the later grimoires are derived. Below are the very slightly modified versions of two prayers which I use in such house blessings.

The Anathema of the Gospel,
which is of avail for all pains and all sicknesses.

In the beginning was the Word: that Word was with God. And this Word was God, and the same was in the beginning with God. And all was by his hand, and without him there was not one thing made of that which was. In him was life, and the life was the light of men. That light is in the darkness: it preventeth it not. By the power of those Ten Words, proceeding from the Lord God, and by the name I Am That I Am, Almighty God, Adonai, Lord of Hosts, may there be distanced and destroyed all the evil and abominable actions of accursed demons, and all their practices, and all opposition, temptations, unclean spirits, and stumbling-blocks, sounds, and creakings, fear, and trembling that come to oppose, devices, malice, and evil occurrences, also the effects and bonds of evil magic, the hot and cold fever, the fever-horror, and may they be driven from the body and soul of the one who suffers, by the prayer of my Lady, the blessed Mary, and of Mar John the Baptist. Amen![86]

The Anathema of Mar Shalita, which is of avail for The Evil Spirit.

In the name of the Father, the Son, and the Holy Ghost. The prayer, request, petition, and supplication of Mar Shalita, which he prayed and asked of God at the hour of martyrdom. He said: O my Lord, Jesus Christ, as regards everyone who shall make mention of thy Holy Name, and of my name, thy servant Shalita, may no unclean spirit nor evil spirit approach him, but may it be expelled from the body and soul of N. (friend's name) by the prayer of blessèd Mar Eugenius. Amen![87]

As the conclusion of the house cleansing, I utilize a method that has worked wonders over the years. The process involves the combining of strong rubbing alcohol, Epsom salts, frankincense essential oil, and incense. The salts, frankincense oil, and blessed incense are placed within a cast-iron pot or cauldron and blessings are said above it to expel all negative entities and energies. The consecrated alcohol is then poured over the mixture and the concoction is lit on fire to burn until the alcohol is exhausted. Of course you need to be sure that this is done in an area where nothing nearby will catch fire or melt. The effects of the flames from the consecrated ingredients seem to clear out any remaining entities that may have contributed to the issues. Both Benn and his wife reported that instant effects were noticed throughout the house and that the disturbing phenomena ceased for a time.

When the more severe haunting phenomena and disturbances began to quiet down at my own house, I planned out the operation to re-conjure Oriens, King of the East. Not only was I looking forward to being better prepared with the correct talisman and offerings, I was interested to see how the second operation

86. The unmodified *Anathēma of the Gospel*, as translated by Gollancz, may be read in Hermann Gollancz, *The Book of Protection: being a collection of charms, now edited for the first time from Syriac MSS* (London: Henry Frowde, Oxford University Press, 1912), p. xxvi. Gollancz reports that the Syriac codex from which he translated the prayer or spell is internally dated to 1802–3. *The Book of Protection* may also be read online courtesy of Joseph H. Peterson on his Twilit Grotto—Esoteric Archives website (http://www.esotericarchives.com/gollancz/protect.htm). —APF

87. The unmodified *Anathēma of Mar Shalita* may be read *ibid.*, p. lii. —APF

would compare to the first. I was sincerely hoping to have a few more questions answered and further clarity revealed about the Spirit's identity and nature. I wanted to see if the King would have any information regarding the increased Spirit activity and if it knew the identity and nature of any of the Spirits bothering my scryer's family or my own. I also very much wanted to know what the ceremony was to join the power of the four Kings together, as Egyn had said Oriens would know. Perhaps the mystery of the proper associated animal could be solved, as well as what Oriens' relationship to King Paymon in the West signified. I had purchased a small piece of pure white gold and some fine cedar shavings for an offering as Egyn instructed. I was unsure as to how or in what manner the Spirit planned to receive them but I figured that if my scryer and I were successful in conjuring the Spirit, he would tell us himself.

Besides the above questions, I was also interested to learn if magicians of the southern hemisphere were required to regard Planetary hours differently than those in the northern hemisphere. The roles of the Directional Kings seem to be intricately tied to the seasons and turning of the earth as it frames out a day from sunrise to sunset. I wondered how this affected the offices of the Spirits in relation to people on the other side of the world.

With the information I had received, I updated my previous assumptions concerning the correspondences of the four Kings of the Directions in preparation for the new conjurations.

Cardinal King	Direction	Time/Day/Season	Talisman	Incense	Offering
Oriens	East	Dawn, on Wednesday or Thursday, in Spring	Ouroboros Lens	Copal resin, cedar shavings	White gold and shavings of cedar
Amaymon	South	Noon, on Tuesday or Sunday, in Summer	Candle	Galbanum, sandalwood	Bread with cinnamon and honey; wine and beer
Paymon	West	Dusk, on Monday or Friday, in Autumn	Cup	Myrrh, onycha	Beer, wine, sweet milk, mead
Egyn	North	Evening or Midnight, on Saturday, in Winter	Stone Ring	Storax, benzoin	Powdered meat and bone, mixed with spring water; tea of evergreen leaves

*Table IX-30. **Further Revised Table of Correspondences for the Four Cardinal Kings***

Corrected Directional Talismans

The Stone Ring

I felt I needed to find a more suitable talisman for the Northern King. It was not long before I came upon a large Neolithic *bi* stone bracelet that immediately stood out as the intended talisman for Egyn. The thick stone hoop looked quite ancient and did not have any adornments besides the appearance of rough carving marks. I decided to purchase it and use it for my new treasured talisman for the King of the North. It was in every sense a «stone ring» and displayed perfectly in a vertical fashion within the stone bowl that was my first talisman. I would wait until the next Winter Solstice to consecrate it to Egyn in the method the Spirit had outlined to my scryer.

The Lens

The talisman for the King of the East was already redefined to be the Lens. Having fixed the now obvious mistake, I bought a new lens and caliper to fashion the talisman with the correct correspondences, including the Ouroboros to frame the Lens focusing the Spirit of Oriens and the gateway to the East. I also decided to etch the sigil of Oriens onto the glass of the Lens itself. The Lens window catching the first rays of the Sunlight connected as the sense of sight in the Air, carried on the light as the Eastern portal for this King. I hoped this new talisman would bring better success to the next operation of Oriens.

The Candle

This was the only correspondence remaining a bit of a dilemma for me on the basis of the *Clavis Inferni* showing a bird for Amaymon, clearly suggesting an Air correlation to the South. I used a triangular brass candleholder with a red beeswax candle engraved with Amaymon's name and sigil.

The Cup

The Cup associated with the West and Water for Paymon had already been consecrated with the «old form» of its sigil engraved inside in the very bottom and center of the chalice, while the seal or sigil from the *Clavis Inferni* was engraved on the outside. The same beautiful chalice with green emeralds was used in the ritual process the Spirit prescribed. The talisman connects with the deeper, darker, albeit sacred aspects of Water and the twilight of the Spiritual world.

✣

X

The Four Kings of the Cardinal Directions

Part Two • Learning and Redoing

I WAS EXCITED TO CONJURE the King of the East again, this time with the correct talisman as well as proper offerings. I wondered how similar this operation would be to our first, which was at this time over a month gone.

Of the four initial operations, that of the last, the King of the North, had been the most insightful with the richest responses. I wondered if the King of the North would turn out to be the one with whom I had the most affinity. At this stage, it was difficult to tell, since it felt like my scryer and I were barely past the introductory stage of attempting to comprehend these mighty Spirits.

I hoped that conjuring both Oriens and Amaymon again would be just as fruitful as the last operation had been, if not more so. At the same time, I hoped that these new rounds of evocation would not unleash a barrage of haunting and disturbing situations like those that occurred after the cycle of the four Kings had been completed with the Egyn operation.

In preparation for the reconjuration of the King of the East, I purchased a small piece of the purest white gold I could afford. I etched Orien's sigils (both versions), on either side. I ground up two small piles of fine cedar shavings, one to burn as incense, the other to be offered next to the white gold on the altar.

The Cardinal King of the East
Oriens

✠	Day and time	On Wednesday at Dawn
✠	Name and meaning	Oriens (Latin, "East; Rising")
✠	Pronunciation of name (as spoken by the Spirit)	«Oh-ree-ens»
✠	Direction for invocation	East
✠	Materials for lamen	Parchment, iron sealed with gold
✠	Sigils	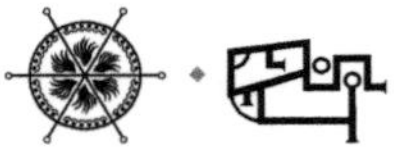
✠	Incense	Frankincense, copal, with cedar shavings added
✠	Offerings	Fine cedar shavings, and a plate of pure white gold
✠	Talisman	The Ouroboros Lens

Table X-1. ***Evocatory Correspondences for the Second Evocation of Oriens***

Second Conjuring of the Cardinal Ruler Oriens

Appearance of the Spirit

SCRYER: I feel as if I am high up on top of a mountain peak. I see an odd-looking cedar tree in front of me. It seems to weep or drip from the end of each branch, a substance that looks like white gold, molten white gold, onto the ground. There are clouds below, all around and near the base of the cedar. Behind the tree and above the clouds is a cyclone, like a tornado. It's really, really tall and perfectly formed, as if it doesn't touch the clouds below but is suspended perfectly directly above them and perfectly shaped. Behind the cyclone I see the Sun rising. There is wind coming from the Sun, which seems to feed into the cyclone itself. Somehow all three—the cedar, the cyclone, and the rising Sun—are all Oriens. I see eight gateways through which the singing wind of the Sun enters into the cyclone.

OPENING QUESTION 1: In the name of the holy and undefiled Spirit, the Father, the begotten Son, and Holy Ghost proceeding from both, what is thy true name?

Fig. X-2. ***Portrait of Oriens as beheld in Second Vision***

(«Oriens» is heard by both the scryer and the operator being whispered.)

OPENING QUESTION 2: Great King of the East, Oriens, what is thy office?

SPIRIT: «I open the mouth of the eternally rising Sun that sings the song of the Creator. I do this through the Archangel of the East, through the eight gateways, whose keys I hold. My face is ever turned toward the Sun. Its fire does not enter through me, but its light does. The breath of the Sun and its song entered through the eight gateways and focused in me, and through what the seer calls 'the cyclone.' And my living mask, the Lebanon cedar weeping the white gold of the stars. Infused with the song of the choirs of the Seraphim. And the clouds are the carpet for my feet.»

(Scryer's voice is very, breathy and drawn as if at a high whisper.)

OPENING QUESTION 3: What is thy true sign or character?

SPIRIT: «The oldest sign, the one I first revealed, is the talisman on your chest, showing the rising sun above the house of the above world and the one below. My other sign, the eight gateways opened by my key through which the light and song of the Sun can be heard.»

OPENING QUESTION 4: When are the times most agreeable to thy nature to hold conference with us?

SPIRIT: «At a sunrise or when the winds blow first out of the East. When the clouds make a carpet above the rising Sun and it is seen only for a short time leaving a clear band along the horizon. When the clouds are above you at sunrise and lit with the red gold and orange and ambers, know that I walk with my feet above you on the soft carpet of the clouds. I can also be called when the tornado or cyclone is near. When my name is sung over and repeatedly I will steer the cyclone away from thee.»

OATH: Wilt thou swear by the blood and righteousness of our Lord Jesus Christ that thou art truly the Mighty King and Spirit of the East called Oriens?

ORIENS: «I swear by the feet of the crucified Son that I am Oriens. I remember rising in the East as the light and caressing his feet. And moving slowly up his body like an embrace to comfort him with the light of his Father.»

OPERATOR: Wilt thou swear by my Book of Spirits here and by my holy wand to swear loyalty to us and assist us? Will you swear that your loyalty, word, speech, and assistance will be provided truthfully?

ORIENS: «I do swear. When called by the heart, the mind, or the body, Oriens will come to breathe the first of spirit into your works. In return for praising my name and speaking my name to the wind.»

(Spirit presented with the Book of Spirits.)

QUESTION 6: At the request of your sister Egyn, ruler in the North, we have called you again, this time to complete with one other, your brother, Amymon, with new questions. Which way and manner should we evoke you to send or release other Spirits we evoke and wish to appear before us?

ORIENS: «My sigil of the eight gateways and my name sung with purpose to vibrate along with the song of the Sun and its light will be as the rising of the Sun on the world of the Spirit. You have walked this pathway to me with the correct offerings and talisman, and so the road is now more solid, easier for me to walk upon, easier for you to receive. See the Spirits you call from the East who have to do with the winds and songs walking with your mind's eye, with the seer's eye, on a carpet of clouds.»

QUESTION 7: I ask if you can reveal to us the identity, nature, and purpose of any Spirits or beings which may be present around or in my home or my scryer's home and others who may dwell there. If any harmful Spirit exists, can you reveal its name, identity, and nature to us?

ORIENS: «The home of the invoker is clear aside from the Spirits which attend the birth of your daughter, whose presences are welcome and necessary to her birth. At your scryer's home there is a Spirit, although not attached to him, is somewhat curious of the other man who lives there. This can only be changed by a ceremony of purification and severance with its thread that still ties it to him. The Spirit itself is not evil, merely lost and hungry.

It is a wanderer in the underworld whose internal despair issues forth like a wave. The tie must be broken and the Spirit itself blessed.»

QUESTION 8: Great King of the East, how would you like your offerings, the cedar shavings and piece of white gold, delivered unto you? Would you like the piece of gold attached to the lamen or talisman?

ORIENS: «The white gold can be attached to the seal you wear around your neck or embedded with wax to base of the lens. The cedar in the morning as the Sun rises sprinkled into the wind as you sing my name with your face like mine always toward the eternal rising Sun.»

QUESTION 9: Before going further I wish to ask if you know of my daughter's name who is not yet born? If you have knowledge of what her name is, will you deliver this unto me?

ORIENS: «I do know the name, but its time to be revealed has not yet come. The bestowing of the name awaits a decision by your child. When the decision is made by the child, your wife will know the name first and will say it almost as if by accident. And when it is spoken first, you will feel the power of it run through both of your bodies at once.»

QUESTION 10: What is your relationship to King Paymon, your sister in the West?

ORIENS: «As I always face the eternal rising Sun, she always faces the eternal setting Sun. As I sing forth the song of the light of the Sun, she sings forth the song of the night, of the darkened starry sky. Together we anchor the song into your world, empowered and vitalized by our brother and sister in the South and the North.»

QUESTION 11: Do you have any further instruction, insight, and knowledge to assist us to conjure your brother Amaymon in the South?

ORIENS: «The offerings revealed by my sister in the North will be enough to bring him. The light of Fire to shine his way forth. Singing all of our names when we are called upon empowers the contact between us and you as it recapitulates the song that we sing towards your world. Sing our names when we are next called and the gateway, the filaments of energetic thread that run from us to you, will brighten and thicken.»

QUESTION 12: Great King of the East, Oriens, from the information we received from your sister in the North, can you instruct us on the ceremony to join the power of the four of you, the four Kings together in one?

ORIENS: «I can. But it is my brother in the South who will reveal this to you.»

QUESTION 13: Is there an associated animal or being that represents your power as the bear does to your sister in the north?

ORIENS: «I have been seen as many things: a falcon, an Ibex, a cloud, and even a butterfly. Each one like a key to the eight gateways, though I reveal only six.»

QUESTION 14: Should magicians of the Southern hemisphere regard Planetary times and hours differently than those in the North? If so, how should each proceed?

ORIENS: «Yes, it is very different in the Southern hemisphere where my brother is the dominant. In the South my brother takes on aspects of his sister in the North, and his sister takes on aspects of her brother in the South. It is like sitting close or far away from a symphony; the music and its effect will change the closer and further away from it you are. The height of the energy will come from the South to those in the South, anchored and echoed by his sister, my sister in the North. But my relationship and the relationship of my sister in the West remains the same. We shape and provide the song, while my sister and brother in the North and South enhance and augment the song.»

QUESTION 15: It is said that you are able to revive the dead. How is this done by you and how exactly is this accomplished?

SCRYER: I see a dead man on a slab of stone in a cave. I see a stone roll away from the entrance with the light of the Sun falling on his face. It is a cave or tomb and it's been opened just a small amount so that the Sun just touches the man's head. A wind blows through the crack of the door and fills the tomb with a song. The sound of the song seems closest to those deep chants the Tibetan monks make, but more of a deep whisper. And that is all I see.

QUESTION 16: Great and Mighty Spirit Oriens, is there any more advice or methods you can give for magicians to work and speak with you in the most beneficial of ways and how to harness the benefits of your office?

ORIENS: «The simple repetition of waking in the morning, sprinkling the cedar onto the wind, and singing my name is the most promising way to deepen the communication between me and you. This repeated contact between me and the magician is the surest method to deepen the communication between us. The power of the time of sunrise is often ignored in your world today.»

OPERATOR: We thank thee for thine attendance.

(License to Depart given.)

Afterthoughts on the Second Oriens Operation

The second interaction with Oriens did supply us with new information to consider, but as before, the Spirit inspired just as many questions if not more. There was a considerable difference in this operation compared to the first conversation. Beyond what was said, the presence and sensations were much stronger as well. This particular operation seemed to stir something within me and I felt I was connecting deeper to the Directional Ruler of the East. There was something greatly familiar and pleasant about this King, and I wondered if I should explore this further.

SCRYER: Wow, that was one of the most beautiful things I've ever seen. The images were so unbelievably clear this time! It was like literally being on a mountaintop. That cedar tree was right in front of me, and it was dripping like molten white gold onto the ground, and behind that was just clouds everywhere. It was like a pure sea of clouds, and behind that, on top of the clouds, was the cyclone, and then behind that was the Sun, one superimposed upon the other. It seemed so multilayered and so vast. Oriens' voice sounded like the wind whispering through this cyclone. It was odd because he kept saying «eight gateways» but I kept seeing six, and then he said that he had only revealed six. I have no idea what that was all about.

OPERATOR: It's funny how you mentioned how real the mountain top felt, since during the entire operation I got the distinct sensation of being on a mountain top as well in the early morning. It was chilly but warming, as if I could feel the actual Sun, with the freshest air and breezes going by. I found the part where Oriens said my home was occupied by several Spirits which attend the birth of my daughter, whose «presences are welcome and necessary» rather interesting, and wondered if the increased activity is indeed due to that. Also, my wife has been wanting us to discover our child's name through the Spirits since she has been so unsure of what it should be. Oriens stated that «the bestowing of the name awaits a decision by your child. When the decision is made by the child, your wife will know the name first and will say it almost as if by accident. And when it is spoken first you will feel the power of it run through both of your bodies at once.» I am excited to see if this will come to pass like the Spirit said, and exactly how this would occur.

I was initially a bit confused by answers we received in this working. For instance, Egyn alluded that Oriens could reveal the ceremony for joining the power of the four Kings, but Oriens said his brother in the South will. I'm not sure if this is because we have to properly conjure all four again and the final King will reveal this, or if there is something else we missed.

SCRYER: I wonder if it's because we haven't done the full offering and conjuration to the one in the South yet? The conversations with the Kings have been so interesting; there is definitely something energetic and linking between each of them and us. It's been utterly amazing to see how this unravels; I have to admit that the four Kings have been among my favorite workings because they are just so fascinating and multifaceted. It seems to me that we need a full contact with each of them in order to unlock their gifts.

OPERATOR: There really do seem to be multiple layers to these beings; each is another puzzle piece being fitted together. This work has been fascinating, and I cannot believe how far we've come.

Upon reviewing the record of what Egyn had said, I noticed that what the Northern King actually mentioned was that Oriens would know *when* revealing the ritual for all four would occur.

After the operation, I was reminded of the gifts bestowed upon me by the Archangel Uriel when Oriens mentioned that I should «sing» when invoking him and the other Kings. This seemed to finally register with me, and I became convinced that it would definitely be more powerful if I sang or chanted the holy names when I spoke the invocations aloud. My voice had become a force that seemed to cut through the fabric of time and space and brought about the experiences my scryer and I had been privy to for over two years by this point. I decided that I would use this voice and sing the name of whatever Spirit I was evoking from that point on. Interestingly, the voices of the four Kings seem to correspond to their nature and office. The voice of Oriens was just above a strong whisper; Paymon's voice was raspy and echoed; and Egyn sounded breathy, almost hoarse, but powerful as well.

I was happy to receive a somewhat detailed answer of how the Directional Rulers and thus Spiritual beings at large work within the hemispheres. I wasn't sure exactly what was meant when Oriens stated that «in the South my brother takes on aspects of his sister in the North, and his sister takes on aspects of her brother in the South,» but it seemed to suggest that the roles of the Kings are somehow reversed at certain longitudes past the equator. It also seemed that the Northern and Southern Kings were stronger the closer they were to their given poles. Oriens explained that he and Paymon «shaped and provided the song,» while Amymon and Egyn «enhanced and augmented the song.» I found this fascinating, yet don't think I fully grasp what that entails. These answers were yet more information to study and meditate on to hopefully understand better.

Follow-Up to the Second Conjuring of Oriens

I also did a bit of research on the animal associations Oriens related. The ibex is a wild goat with long, thick-ridged horns and a beard, which is found in the Alps and Pyrenees, as well as the mountains of Ethiopia and central Asia. It would definitely be an animal that was accustomed to the environment Oriens presented to my scryer and me through vision. However, I was admittedly disappointed that the King had made no mention of a dragon or serpent.

Days after the operation, I affixed the small piece of white gold to the back of Oriens' lamen with wax. I reasoned that Oriens' lamen ideally should be made of white gold. I didn't have the means to create one of these but considered it a future project if the Eastern King proved to be a strong ally.

I chose a following Sunday to climb to a favorite mountain peak that overlooks the city to the East, and I made a gesture of offering and thanks to Oriens by scattering cedar shavings to the first breezes as the Sun rose from the horizon.

Hiram Consultation

Hiram asked to speak to my scryer and myself at the same time before we proceeded with conjuring Amaymon a second time. I was excited at this prospect since Benn and I had not spoken to Hiram together since he was brought into the skull, and that was while we were both traveling in Spirit vision. On several occasions my scryer had come to my house and asked to consult Hiram directly about issues which were going on in his personal life. I always agreed and encouraged him to speak with my Familiar Spirit. It was wonderful seeing my friend emerge from the magical room looking amazed and satisfied with the advice he received. My friend, my wife, and I spoke about Hiram often, praising his excellent council, his straightforwardness, and his ability to assist in situations beyond the esoteric. The magical life was such that having an actual human skull in the house became no bother, as my wife had grown quite fond of the Spirit's presence and excellent advice during challenging times. She often brought him extra offerings, and samples of her cooking to show appreciation. Family conversations often included grateful references to the Familiar Spirit and how life had improved since his addition to the household.

My wife had also begun acting as my scribe since Hiram started sharing his story with me of how he came into the state he had since his time on earth. His narrations were utterly fascinating and filled with descriptions and images that captured both our interests. Hiram's story, which was as old as the Biblical passages that referenced him, began filling up the little journal as my wife wrote down everything I related from Hiram's words. I reasoned that at some point I would have to dedicate a complete volume simply to the story of the king of Tyre as I've experienced it in Spirit form.

The evening Hiram requested to speak with my scryer and me, I brought the skull down from its place on the shelf to a small table in the center of the magical chamber. I arranged two candles on either side and also lit some incense in front of the table. I also decided to bring down the audio recorder I used to record the evocations since I figured we didn't want to miss any details because the two of us were in different states of consciousness. I found that speaking about what transpired right after an experience secured the clearest details from an experience even if weren't transcribing the Spirit's words in real time.

My scryer arrived moments after the chamber was set and we both sat on the floor in front of the skull. I lit the candles on either side of the small table and began my usual summoning procedure for inviting Hiram to "come forth from his library" and speak with us. Below is the transcript of the recorded event:

SCRYER: Man, it's just amazing how much presence that skull has.

OPERATOR: Yeah, he is always there now. The house never feels empty, and I can always tell he's around.

Hiram was pretty adamant about talking to us; let's see what he has to say.

(Operator and scryer quiet minds and enter into a receptive state.)

HIRAM: «I was pleased to see how the last operation went. There is still more that the final King will reveal that will bring the four gates more fully open and the lines of travel and communication more clearly revealed. I need to speak with each of you individually on how you can better protect yourselves when needed. Currently, the cleansing and banishing methods you use will not be enough for some of the other Spirits that will come near to you. I need to make sure that Benn is able to hear me properly and hear my instructions.»

(Silence)

OPERATOR: Are you able to hear him?

SCRYER: Yes.

OPERATOR: Good, because it got silent all of a sudden and I stopped hearing him.

(Silence)

HIRAM: «Bryan, your technique with the dagger must be first preemptively cleansed with a new ritual of purification... First before, and then after... Washing and clearing both of body and mind is essential to sever strands of foreign bodies or Intelligences attempting to connect to you. The quickest way to accomplish this is to take some holy water in each hand and run some over the top of your head, back of your neck, and near eyes and mouth, as well as down your chest and over your heart area. After making this gesture with prayers of purification, take your dagger and tap three times the point toward each direction, plus above and below, and finally to the center. Also, use your voice as Archangel Uriel inspired in you and sing more the names of the Archangels and holy names for protection. Your intention through singing and chanting will have immediate and profound effects.»

(Silence)

HIRAM: «It was necessary to speak with both of you at the same time, as the matter concerns your continued work together as well as individually. Hopefully these new considerations will bring even further success to your work.»

OPERATOR: Always a pleasure, and again, thank you for your council and wisdom, for not only myself but for my scryer as well.

(Ritual closing and thanking for Hiram's service and assistance.)

SCRYER: Man, oh man, I love how practical he is. The first thing he really said is that «you are not really using your *will* well enough. You really need to be focusing more on what your intent is, and letting that break through the obstacles that are coming up and in your way. Focus on your intent, let that power come up in you, and it will break through what you feel is an obstacle at the time. Whether your health, energy levels, such as feeling tired or concentration seems difficult, focus your intention, let it well up, and the power will come.» He said that, especially with all the work that we are doing, that I do need to do more ritual washing and some purification, and that the big part of it is the intent when I'm doing it: that I should be specifically washing Spirit energy, Spirit stuff, and coming back to a clean slate.

OPERATOR: That was interesting being side by side, and also interesting that Hiram talked to me about washing and ritual purification as well. It was funny because he would be talking to me, and then all of a sudden it was silent and I couldn't hear him. Then I could hear you making sounds as if someone was speaking to you.

SCRYER: How interesting, because he would pause and be silent a couple times with me as well. He also said that since you are calling such powerful beings near to me, I needed to perform another cleansing after each operation in order to close the connection with the Spirit and keep them from coalescing on me. He also mentioned song. He said singing is a powerful way of calling things forward, and a lot easier, because it taps into an area of being and intention and will through sound. I remember him saying that «song and chant removes unnecessary thoughts and distractions when issued fully toward pure energetic occurrence, and gets your mind out of the way without filtering.»

You know, it is not until you begin to chant those sacred names for the invocation that I really start to see and feel things. It makes senses why not only Hiram but the Spirits have emphasized how important the use of the voice is in this respect.

Hiram is just simply amazing. I get very practical and very straightforward advice from him. It's so interesting; I remember when you first got the skull and I thought, 'Eww, that thing is kind of creepy, sort of garish and morbid.' Now I have a totally different feeling being around it, and honestly feel very comfortable. It's like talking to an old friend. I would definitely say Hiram is one of the Spirits I feel most comfortable around. I feel like I can be very honest and very forthright, and that I get very practical and very useful advice in return. I'm not sure if you were aware but I have discovered that you have 'familiar' ancestors and then ancestral ancestors. I think somewhere I read that they are referred to as 'Ancestors of the Order.' You know, it's quite possible that Hiram is your Ancestor of Magical Order. Maybe a powerful relational order, formed of people who share a magical connection with you.

Following Hiram's advice, I conducted several purification rituals as he had outlined. With each repetition I felt lighter and that I regained a lot of my previous focus. I was elated to be learning new magical methods and techniques from a Spiritual advisor, grateful to have a mentor and advisor on the esoteric that was intimately connected to the 'source.' Both my scryer and I were appreciating the benefits of newly refined daily practices and furthering our advancements in spiritual and magical practices.

With the new talisman made, offerings secured, and advice for conjuring, we made ready to reconjure the King of the South.

The Cardinal King of the South
Maymon

✠ Day and time	On Tuesday or Saturday, at Noon, in Summer
✠ Name	Maymon
✠ Pronunciation of name (as spoken by the Spirit)	«May-mon»
✠ Direction for invocation	South
✠ Materials for lamen	Parchment, iron, gold
✠ Sigils	[sigils]
✠ Incense	Galbanum, sandalwood, and cinnamon
✠ Offerings	Bread, wine, honey, cinnamon, and beer
✠ Talisman	Lit Candle

Table X-3. ***Evocatory Correspondences for the Second Evocation of Maymon***

Second Invocation of the Cardinal Ruler Maymon

Notes: Preparation of the ritual chamber seemed to increase the temperature noticeably and I could tell energies were already moving by the time the hour approached for the operation.

During this invocation, I made sure to sing/chant the Spirit's name three times during its conjuring, putting my gifts of voice into the calling of its name.

During the invocation, I witnessed a very intense energy completely fill the southern portion of the wall and room. The heat increased and an intensely powerful force was palpable. It felt like an immovable presence lingered just outside the circle. Heat wave distortions were clearly seen rising from the base of the altar all the way to the ceiling.

Appearance of the Spirit

SCRYER: First I was in the desert and I could see the stars above me. Some of them seemed to fall down and they shaped themselves into a pyramid. At first the pyramid appeared as pure starlight, and then became stone. Above the pinnacle of the pyramid was a gateway of fire, an oval of two points; I still see the fire moving on either side of the opening of this gateway.

The gateway expands and I see what looks like a huge black peacock or something similar to that. But instead of the feathers that come up, it looks like fire or flashing gems frame the figure of the bird. Its feet are grasping the top of the pyramid, and it looks almost reptilian. The gems are of many, many colors, and the fire is very intense coming from the feathers, and seems to push the gateway apart. I can see the eyes of the peacock looking at me. It is very aware that I am here.

OPENING QUESTION 1: In the name of the holy and undefiled Spirit, the Father, the begotten Son, and Holy Ghost proceeding from both, what is thy true name?

SCRYER: The bird says, «May-mon, spoken by pharos.» After he says his name, it sounds as if there are a thousand people around us who repeat his name in an almost warlike yell.

(After this the operator notices a very distinct image in crystal of the pedestal. Lines or feathers which seem formed of bright light extended out of the crystal to the gold disk, displaying an even spacing and the dark profile of a bird's long neck and head. The majority of the operation continues with this imagery and intensity of feeling and presence.)

OPENING QUESTION 2: What is thy office? What are your views on humanity? What are your roles and interactions?

SPIRIT: «I amplify the iron in men's blood. Its heat. I amplify the desire of man to be apart. To explore the universe, the creation of the Creator, the One God, the fire that warms, yet also separates. I ennoble the individuality of man, and when out of balance, I become the scourge of man. I enforce the laws of the Creator by letting in the Fires of the South. The brewing of ales and wine, the bubbling heat is governed by me. The Intelligence of fermentation.»

OPENING QUESTION 3: What is thy true sign or character?

Fig. X-4. ***Portrait of Maymon as beheld in Second Vision***

SCRYER: The bird bends its head down and I see very, very clearly the tail feathers. They are almost perfectly symmetrical and very bright, studded with jewels and flame. There is a half-Moon nature to it in shape.

OPENING QUESTION 4: When are the times most agreeable to thy nature to hold conference with us?

SCRYER: The bird screeches loudly and the Sun is suddenly in the height of the sky, casting a very intense light on everything.

SPIRIT: «At the height of day while running, lifting, in strenuous physical exertion, when the pulse is fast and the body is hot. My name brings strength. When Mars is in the South at its apex. Mars is a jewel in my feathers and the eye of the gate.»

OATH: Wilt thou swear by the blood and righteousness of our Lord Jesus Christ that thou art truly the Mighty King and Spirit of the South, called Amaymon/Maymon?

MAYMON: «I swear by the Son that suffered on the heat of the cross, I am Maymon. From before the time of the Son, spoken by pharos.»

QUESTION 6: I am curious why you are often referred to as being a Demon or Archdemon in many texts. What is the nature of your origin and purpose?

MAYMON: «I swear by the Son that suffered on the heat of the cross, I am Maymon. From before the time of the Son, spoken by pharos.»

QUESTION 7: Do you have your own recollection of your creation and origin? Where do you come from? What is your purpose? I am curious why you are often referred to as being a Demon or Archdemon in many texts.

MAYMON: «My origin is before the incarnation of the Son. And as I spoke, I am the scourge of man. The instigator of the iron in his blood and the fierceness inherent in living beings. My ways are not always kind, but they are necessary to the balance. The more out of balance the one who perceives me is, the more terrible I will appear.»

QUESTION 8: What is the most successful way for us to conjure Spirits and have them speak clearly to us? In which ways can you assist us to command Demons and Spirits to arrive quickly when summoned?

MAYMON: «With the summoning of Demons, the reflected light of the jewels in my feathers are in the flames that you use. Seeing the jewel in the flame enlivens its power. With the use of a flail, I may chastise and scourge a Spirit that does harm. This flail can be used as an instrument of balance to drive the Spirit away or bring it forth into submission. In the summoning of Spirits not of Demonic nature, when the four Kings are summoned and our gateways opened together, the Spirit summoned cannot help but be drawn forth.»

QUESTION 9: Can you explain more fully the ritual and requirements needed for the ritual combining the power and offices of the four Cardinal Kings? Oriens said you would have this knowledge for us.

MAYMON: «Starting in the East, the visions of the scryer are seen for each of us. Proceeding to the South, the West, and the North. In each direction, by calling forth the image in word and with the mind, the images seen by the scryer will be brought forth. Our names should be sung with the passion of the invoker. When this is done, the four lines of light will appear. Offerings are given to the four of us as we each desire. When the pharaoh that looks backward that you know as Orion is in the height of the sky, or when the Sun is still just below the horizon at sunrise and sunset in the revolving twilight that moves eternally around your world, singing with passion with the visions and the offerings at those times is the proper and best way to enhance our presences here. At the close, you *must* see the four gates disappear and wish our farewells. The gates must be closed at the end, and the offerings placed beneath the earth. When the offerings are buried, they are sprinkled with holy water.»

QUESTION 10: Are there any further instructions for the creation, design, and consecration as well as the proper use and function of the scourge or flail you mentioned?

MAYMON: «The handle of the flail is black. The base of the handle, a black pyramid like the one on which I sit. The flail has as many rays as in my sigil. Each strand that comes out of the handle is the same number as in my sigil. At the end of each strand is a stone, each of a different color. Every strand should be red, like the fires of my feathers. When stored, it is placed on the wall with each strand set carefully, and symmetrical like my sigil. My name, MAYMON, inscribed on the handle and spoken with authority as it is inscribed and used. The invoker can scourge and banish any Demon that threatens or harms life or spirit. When my name is invoked as MAYMON, as spoken of by the pharos, I will come. My power will fill the flail and the Demon will feel pain until it leaves or submits. After it has departed, it must be blessed by sending holy water in its direction so that it cannot return.»

(Intense power and even greater light is seen surrounding the Altar of the Stars as well as the pedestal and holy table. The forceful and powerful energy intensifies. Although not threatening, it is intimidating.)

QUESTION 11: What should your sigil be made of: which type of material? Also, how would you like your offerings to be delivered unto you?

MAYMON: «As you have set forth the offerings tonight is acceptable. The transformation of grain to bread, of water and grape to wine, of grain and water to beer, and of the divine gift of honey together with cinnamon are all symbols of my mystery. To further appreciate the strength of my office, honor the iron in your blood. Honor the gift of separation, but remember your place. Explore, change, grow, but maintain the balance or my visage will become terrible.»

QUESTION 12: What is the purpose and symbolism of your talisman? In what ways does it resemble your being and office?

MAYMON: «The Candle is as the gateway of fire which surrounds me now; pulling and focusing stellar light into my might that can sear or bless. The presence of Fire has enabled me to see and feel the scryer clearly, and for him to feel and see me. When it is present when you invoke me, the perception from me to you and you to me is focused. When done correctly, you will feel a heaviness in your chest and a curving of the spine.»

QUESTION 13: Besides the powers and methods mentioned in the above ritual, what can be expected now that all four gates of the Kings have been fully opened and unlocked?

SCRYER: It looks like I am above the earth. I can see the magnetic field or the ozone, or some energy that surrounds the earth. I see the light of the Sun and stars and the Moon. I see a gateway at each pole for the North and South, and I see a gateway always towards the Sun and I see a gateway always away from the Sun.

MAYMON: «You will see more clearly and feel more clearly the light of the Creator that comes from above and around. You will sense where it enters into your world and why. Your perception of the Spirit world will become even more clear, and it will become even more aware of you. We will teach you and instruct you in your dreams, and you will awake with knowledge. Some of this has already begun. Our relationship with you will grow over time and we will reveal new things.»

QUESTION 14: Can you reveal to us any more information or knowledge regarding your animal and other symbols associated with you? What do they mean?

MAYMON: «The deep black between my feathers is as the space between the stars. The flame and jewels of my feathers are the ornaments of the Archangels, the treasures of wisdom and long discovery. The symmetry, the perfect music of God. The gateway that surrounds me, the loving embrace of the power that watches over man. The blessèd iron in your blood, the redness in your face, whether blush or by anger, sadness, or joy, the rising of your inner Fire.»

FINAL QUESTION: Great and mighty Spirit Maymon, we thank you for your arrival and attendance upon this working and for sharing your knowledge.

Before we bid you hail and farewell, are there any final words of wisdom or instruction you wish to impart to us?

MAYMON: «One of the greatest mysteries of man: the *iron* in your *blood*. Remember the iron in your blood. Remember your original desire to be separate from the Creator. To leave Him, to explore Him, and to ultimately return to Him.»

OPERATOR: Great and Mighty King of the South, Maymon, we thank thee for thy attendance upon us and this rite, and ask that you return to us when called. For now, fare thee well, and may peace be between us always, in the name of the Father, Son, and Holy Spirit. Amen.

(License to Depart is given.)

Afterthoughts on the Second Maymon Operation

After asking further about its symbolism and animal, Maymon mentioned that the jewels were like «the ornaments of the Archangels.» After noticing that there are indeed "seven rays" making up the King of the South's seal, I cannot help but figure the number of the Planetary Archangels are somehow linked with this being. Perhaps this particular King, or all the Kings, coordinates or somehow translates the powers and offices of each Archangel to the terrestrial realm of earth? For the creation of the scourge, I am inspired to make each "jewel" at the end of the thong of the scourge to be one of the classically colored images and stones correlating to each of the seven Archangels: black, blue, red, yellow, green, orange, and silver.

The ability to open the four gateways of the Cardinal Kings is based on proper introduction and direct experience. The mind now familiar with the sense, images, voices, and presence of each King reveals the ability to call their direct line of energy forward to open up the gates to allow any Spirit to come through directly and powerfully. This is not something that can be learned remotely or statically, but only experienced and unlocked due to direct interaction and exchange. Never before have such images and knowledge come to us, never before has our working magic come to this height of experience and aptitude.

SCRYER: Before I forget, when Maymon caused me to feel like I was above the planet and seeing the four gateways, it was like seeing everything move through time. I could see that the stars were sort of rotating around the world, and the gateways would open and then close. It was like the Kings could shrink or expand the gateway to let in their particular kind of energy, and that this is part of how things are harmonized. They bring in what is needed, and sometimes one King has to be more dominant than the others. Sometimes two of them will be equalized, sometimes not. There is some sort of symphonic relation between all of them. It was amazing to witness! Some of the images and happenings reminds me of something I saw about the electromagnetic field and odd occurrences scientists were noticing, how it would sometimes open and allow some of the solar winds and such to enter earth, and I wonder if this has anything to do with that? The opening from the show looked like an eye, like a pupil.

When you first evoked the Spirit and the vision began to formulate, it was like the landscape just rushed up and formed right in front of me. And then suddenly these stars moved down and formed this sort of triangular shape. All of a sudden, the light of it just solidified and there was this pyramid. Then the fiery gateway appeared right above it, like a sideways eye, and the bird came through. Man, he was really intense! I could even see the shadows of the pyramid on the ground from the Fires of the gateway. Also, the thousands of voices chanting "Maymon!" gave me chills. I feel so energized right now! This one was really clear; I wonder if the talisman really did help a lot with that. Also, right as you did the License to Depart, I saw the bird being almost sucked back through the gateway, and the gateway vanished, and then the pyramid was gone.

OPERATOR: Again I had a huge presence, and the heat waves and images of the bird were easy to see; it was hard to remain separate from getting drawn into the vision and remember my questions and control of the ceremony. The Spirit seemed to be able to raise the temperature in your blood. These Kings are so fascinating. They have obvious Elemental correlations, but amped up to almost a stellar connection. It's very interesting. The Elemental Kings were masters of their Element and domain, but these Kings seem to use the Elements and directions simply as symbolic references to their power and office. You can almost see a hierarchical design where the Direction Kings stand right between the Elementals and other Spirits as well as the Archangels above. There is definitely an interplay where the Kings moderate the exchange of energy and communication between all these realms. Obviously the Spirit reiterated the importance of the «iron in our blood,» both figuratively/symbolically and actually. I'm still not sure what the exact importance of this is.

Follow-Up to the Second Conjuring of Maymon

Soon after the operation with Maymon I decided to recreate his talisman to suit the nature of the working. I opted to have an iron peacock or bird candleholder with a red beeswax Candle with the sigil of Maymon etched on it. I also added cinnamon and olive oil to the Candle. The oval-shaped flame and related images that were brought up in the first evocation attempt I feel alluded to the correct talisman needing to be used.

I also spent a considerable amount of time trying to understand the significance of the shape the Spirit took during the evocation. Besides the bird shapes and animal found in the grimoires, I was sure there was significance to the peacock, as he appeared to my scryer.

I went to work researching possible origins of the great Southern King through his associated imagery.

Although of dissimilar name, the Egyptian God Amun-Ra seemed to possess several characteristics similar to what my scryer saw of Maymon. Amun (or in the Greek form of his name, Ammōn, more similar to Maymon) held the position of being a transcendent, self-created Creator, and often a Solar God. He became associated with Osiris, and his popularity increased to the point that he eclipsed the other Deities to become almost the single worshiped God in Egypt, his worship even spreading to Greece and other neighboring lands.[1]

Also in Egyptian mythology, the *Bennu* was depicted as a large heron which landed on the pyramid-shaped *benben* stone, the first dry land in the midst of the primordial waters, and sang a call that initiated the process of creation. The Bennu was Solar, self-created, and associated with Amun-Ra and Osiris. It is quite probable that it was the origin of the Greek Phœnix, the great firebird which periodically flew to Egypt and resurrected itself from its own combustive destruction, traits that are difficult to ignore after the images my scryer related of Maymon.[2]

The peacock imagery led me to a little-known Mesopotamian religion, that of the Kurdish Yazidis or Yezidis. According to Yazidi belief, God created a group of seven Archangels led by *Malak Ṭā'us*, whose name translates literally

1. For more on Amun-Re, see Richard H. Wilkinson, *The Complete Gods and Goddesses of Ancient Egypt* (New York: Thames & Hudson, 2003), pp. 92–97; Barbara Watterson, *The Gods of Ancient Egypt* (New York: Facts on File, 1984), pp. 138–145, 59–68.

2. For more on the Bennu and the Phœnix, see Wilkinson, *op. cit.*, p. 212; Watterson, *op. cit.*, pp. 47–48; and R. van den Broek, *The Myth of the Phœnix* (Leiden: Brill, 1972). —APF

as the "Peacock Angel." These seven Angels assisted in the Creation of the human race, and the Peacock Angel is still set as ruler over the human race and the earth. In that role, according to a Yazidi scripture, he bestows both good and ill fortune upon humans. The categorization of Maymon as a Demon King also finds parallels in the history of the Yazidi tradition, as fundamentalists among their Muslim neighbors have long identified Malak Ṭā'us with Iblīs or Shaiṭān and labeled Yazidis as devil worshippers, leading to persecution which continues to the present day. It seems that the Peacock Angel refused to bow before the first human at God's instruction, and—according to conflicting accounts—either was a Fallen Angel for a period as a result, or never fell as his refusal to bow was in accord with an earlier commandment of God to him.[3]

We also find a God in India associated with the peacock. Kārttikeya, a Hindu God of war, rides upon the peacock Paravāni. In southern India, Kārttikeya is identified with the God Murugan, whom Tamil scripture describes as the Red God seated upon the blue peacock.[4]

It is difficult at this point to say whether or not Maymon can be connected with either the Yazidi Archangel or the Hindu God, but both offer striking parallels and suggest further questions to put to the Southern King.

---

3. For more on the Yazidis, see Christine Allison, "Yazidis i. General," in *Encyclopædia Iranica*, online edition, New York, 1996–2016 (http://www.iranicaonline.org/articles/yazidis-i-general-1); and, for the perspective of apparently one internet-savvy Yazidi, "What is the Peacock Angel?" on the *YezidiTruth.org: The Truth about the Yezidis* website (http://www.yeziditruth.org/ /the_peacock_angel).

   In the West, the reputation of the Yazidis as Devil-worshippers stems from R.H.W. Empson, *The Cult of the Peacock Angel: A Short Account of the Yezîdî Tribes of Kurdistân* (London: Witherby, 1928). Empson seems to have actually encountered the Yazidis, but fully accepted the Muslim polemic which labeled them secret worshippers of Shaiṭān. The cultural anthropologist Lady E.S. Drower, who studied the Mandæans and visited the Yazidis in the 1940s, may be correct in regarding them as descended from an isolated Gnostic Mandæan sect. See her *Peacock Angel: Being Some Account of Votaries of a Secret Cult and Their Sanctuaries* (London: J. Murray, 1941). —APF

4. For more on Kārttikeya and Murugan, see Margaret and James Stutley, *Harper's Dictionary of Hinduism* (New York: Harper & Row, 1977), *s.v.* KĀRTTIKEYA; Kanchan Sinha, *Kartikeya in Indian Art and Literature* (Delhi: Sundeep Prakashan, 1979); Iravatham Mahadevan, "'Murukan' in the Indus Script," on the *Murugan Bhakti* website (http://murugan.org/research/mahadevan.htm); and Ambikai Velmurugu, "Cult of Skanda-Murukan in Tamilakam: The Antiquity of Murukan Worship in Tamil Nadu," on the *Murugan Bhakti* website (http://murugan.org/research/ambikai.htm). —APF

Yet Further Reflections on the Four Kings of the Directions

Thus the importance of the Four Cardinal "Demon Kings" is that they are essential for unlocking and opening the doorways between the heavenly and underworld Spiritual realms. While the Angels protect and council the magician and put unruly Spirits in check, the Kings simply allow the flow of energies between the worlds in a dynamic way. They are directly linked to the cycle of seasons, the parts of the day, the elements, and the give and take of creation. In a further revelation, my scryer had a spontaneous vision of them as atmospheric Intelligences. The Northern King was at the very pole of the North, and the Southern at the South Pole. The Eastern King was on the side of the earth nearest the Sun, while the Western one was on the side furthest from the Sun. However, the four great Kings are not isolated to the atmosphere and sky by any means. Their dominion seems to penetrate to the depths of the earth and reach to the very limits of the atmosphere, their mediating natures extending far beyond simple definitions of terrestrial or chthonic dwelling. They seem to exert their office through every transfer of intelligence, communication, and interaction between the supernal and infernal realms without favoring one above the other, yet moderating them in knowing harmony.

Although far from completed, the efforts of my scryer and me have left us with a rich assortment of possible references and parallel lore which may help us in our ongoing efforts to better understand these mighty beings known as the Rulers of the Four Directions. Table X-5 reflects some of the potential associations to be further investigated.

Cardinal King	Direction	Other Names and Possible Names	Colors	Possible Mythological Associations	Archangel
Oriens	East	Uriens, Bael	Gray and yellow, gold	Anshar (Mesopotamian heaven God and male principle paired with Kishar); Marduk; Baal; Aiolos/Aeolus (Greek Wind God and King); Ninshubur (Queen of the East, second-in-command to Inanna)	Raphael or Michael
Maymon	South	Amaymon, Mimoun, Mammon	Red and black	Egyptian Amun-Ra, Bennu; Greco-Egyptian Phœnix; Yazidi Melk Taus; Hindu Murugan	Michael or Samael
Paymon	West	Paimon, Corson	Black, dark blue, and silver	Claimed to be offspring of Mesopotamian primordial ocean Goddess Tiamat	Gabriel
Egyn	North	Egin, Ariton, Ziminiar	Black and green	Kishar (Mesopotamian Goddess of Earth and Horizon, female principle paired with Anshar)	Uriel

Table X-5. ***Table of Possible Associations for the Four Cardinal Kings***

My scryer and I did not fully appreciate the power and significance of conjuring the Directional Kings till weeks following the fifth and sixth operations. Spiritual activity became even more frequent, with odd dreams and occurrences affecting everyone in our households. Spirit work was now taking on a whole new and startling reality, with frequent encounters which were not always pleasant. I found that I constantly had to clear and bless the house to keep things at least partially resembling normalcy. I could not neglect any of my magical practices or ignore the constant presence of Spirits. At no previous time had my role as a working magician become so apparent.

Although we were just beginning to learn to utilize the benefits of the offices of the Cardinal Kings, I felt that it was time for my scryer and me to move on and explore another category of Spirits that I had been planning to delve into for some time. The Olympic Spirits are featured in several books of magic, but mostly clearly focused on in the famous 16th-century grimoire, the *Arbatel*.

✢

XI
The Olympic Planetary Spirits of the Arbatel

HE TIME LEADING UP to the invocations of the seven Olympic Spirits or Angels found me feeling only marginally familiar with their identities. Although I had studied the descriptions of them in the primary grimoric source, *Arbatel de magia veterum*,[1] I remained uncertain as to their exact natures and true positions in the Spiritual or Angelic hierarchies. They were clearly Spirits of high rank, though whether they were in the hierarchy of the Planetary Archangels or in a separate order was unclear to me. Their sigils and names occur in quite a few later grimoires, but without any discussion of the Spirits themselves. There is a bit more information in *The Complete Book of Magic Science* (perhaps the closest relatable text to *The Art of Drawing Spirits into Crystals*) and *The Secret Grimoire of Turiel*, but they really add little of use to the evocator beyond what is in the *Arbatel*.

---

1. Latin, *"Arbatel on the Magic of the Ancients."* Unusually for a grimoire, the earliest known text of the *Arbatel* is not a manuscript, but rather its first printing at Basel, Switzerland, in 1575. *Not* unusually for a grimoire, its title takes more than one form on subsequent title-pages, even in print. In the original edition, the first title page proclaims it as ארבעתאל ARBATEL *DE MAGIA VETERUM: Summum Sapientiæ Studium* ("ארבעתאל ARBATEL *ON THE MAGIC OF THE ANCIENTS: The Greatest Study of Wisdom"*), and the second title page rephrases and expands the title as *Arbatel DE MAGIA seu PNEVMATICA VETERVM tum Magorum populi DEI, tum Magorum Gentium, pro illustratione gloriæ & Philantropias DEI ("Arbatel ON MAGIC, or THE SPIRITUAL [ART] OF THE ANCIENTS, both the Magi of the people of GOD as well as the Magi of the Heathen, to illustrate the glory & Philanthropy of GOD")*. It has been well-known to the English-speaking occult world for more than three and a half centuries due to its translation by Robert Turner, who published it in 1655 in an invaluable anthology with five other works: the *Fourth Book of Occult Philosophy,* falsely attributed to Agrippa but truly useful; the hugely influential *Heptameron*; a dialogue concerning Sublunary Spirits; and two manuals of Geomancy. —APF

Although the justly renowned grimoire of the *Arbatel* is certainly among the clearer and more orderly texts of classical magic, it does nothing to describe the appearances of the seven Olympic Spirits and little to explain exactly how a magician should conjure them.[2] It briefly introduces them by telling us that

> There are seven different governments of the Spirits of *Olympus*, by whom God hath appointed the whole frame and universe of this world to be governed: and their visible stars are ARATRON, BETHOR, PHALEG, OCH, HAGITH, OPHIEL, PHUL, after the *Olympick* speech.[3]

The obscure names of these spirits do nothing to help decipher their origins or their exact role, purpose, and nature. To begin with, I wanted to discover whether these Spirits are Angels as some texts claim, or if they are perhaps Planetary Dæmons or more manipulative Spirits associated with the planetary influences.[4]

---

2. Some readers who have not had the opportunity to study the grimoire itself but only know it by reputation will be surprised to learn that *all we have is the introduction to the work*. The text tells us that the whole *Arbatel* is meant to be a nine-volume *magnum opus*, consisting of an introductory volume followed by eight further volumes, each of which will teach, in the form of 49 aphorisms, the theory and practice of a separate type of Magic (an ogdoadic Magical curriculum consisting of Microcosmic Magic, Olympic Magic, Hesiodic and Homeric Magic, Roman or Sibylline Magic, Pythagorean Magic, Apollonian Magic, Hermetic Egyptian Magic, and Prophetic Wisdom). The 1575 volume makes it clear that it is simply "The FIRST VOLUME of the BOOK of Arbatel on Magic. Called ISAGOGE [Greek, 'Introduction']," which it further explains as "ISAGOGE, or book of the Institutions of Magic, or τῆς πνευματικῆς [Greek fem. pl., 'the spiritual (arts)'], which in 49 very general Aphorisms embraceth the precepts of the whole art." So the volume we have is a general introduction to the whole work, not a book about Olympic Planetary Magic; that would have been the entire subject of the *Arbatel's* promised volume III, *Olympica Magia*, whose theme was to be "in what manner a human being may take action and may endure [*agat & patiatur*, the verbal equivalent of *activus* and *passivus*] through the Spirits of Olympus." So the 49 "very general" Aphorisms of the Isagoge refer to the whole span of the projected work, and everything we learn specifically about Olympic Magic is contained in the third septenary of Aphorisms (numbers 15 through 21), in effect a brief appetizer to whet our taste for Volume III, which was, for whatever reason, never published and likely never written. So if we wish to learn more Olympic Magic, we must, as Ashen Chassan and others have done, evoke the Spirits and be taught by them. —APF
3. From Aphorism 16, in Robert Turner (trans.) and Arbatel, *Arbatel of Magic*, in Robert Turner, *Henry Cornelius Agrippa, His Fourth Book of Occult Philosophy* (London; John Harrison, 1655). —APF
4. In the course of my ongoing journey into magic, I've come across a myriad of intelligent entities that have unique and often useful perspectives on the workings of the universe. As magicians taking on the roles of spiritual investigators and ambassadors, we should become

Containing far more than the rather brief explanation of the procedure for conjuring the Olympic Spirits, the Aphorisms of the *Arbatel* convey great wisdom and philosophical meditations for the magician to integrate in his work. More than most grimoric texts, the *Arbatel* is concerned with holy magic and the refinement of the magician's spirit towards union with the Divine. An extreme emphasis is placed on purification, pious living, and adherence to holy thoughts and actions. Aphorism 19 particularly stands out:

> *Olympus* and the inhabitants thereof, do of their own accord offer themselves to men in the forms of Spirits; and are ready to perform their Offices for them, whether they will or not: by how much the rather will they attend you, if they are desired? But there do appear also evil Spirits, and destroyers, which is caused by the envy and malice of the devil; and because men do allure and draw them unto themselves with their sins, as a punishment due to sinners. Whosoever therefore desireth familiarly to have a conversation with Spirits, let him keep himself from all enormous sins, and diligently pray to the most High to be his keeper; and he shall break through all the snares and impediments of the devil: and let him apply himself to the service of God, and he will give him an increase in wisdom.[5]

I decided to utilize the same framework of *Drawing Spirits into Crystals* that we had used for all the previous operations with the Archangels, Supercelestial Angels, and Directional Kings instead of attempting to formulate a new ritual from the instructions scattered through the *Arbatel*. For example, a complex circle is described in Aphorism 27, but it is not clear if it is meant to be a magical circle within which the magician stands or a Holy Table like the one in *Theurgia Goetia*. The formation of the circle in the *Arbatel* is described as first being divided into four quadrants, according to the four cardinal directions. Each quarter is then divided into seven equal sections, forming a total of 28 sections. The 28 sections are each further divided into four subsections, forming 112 subsections of the magical circle. From the *Arbatel*'s description of the circle and its brief

skilled at communicating with and learning from the highest and lowest perceivable forms of the spiritual hierarchy. As much as we might like to concentrate solely on the supernal forms of spiritual intelligence, there is a need to learn what parts of creation are accustomed to the lowly demons, sublunary spirits, and earthbound phantoms which haunt the imagination and lore of countless cultures. A ceremonial magician should not be obsessed with such beings as means of thrill-seeking or in hopes of forbidden power, but should acknowledge them simply as separate potential sources of knowledge and willful workings in the world.

5. Turner and Arbatel, *op. cit.* —APF

Fig. XI-1. 112-rayed Circle of the Sigillum Secretorum from the Arbatel

mention of a hierarchy of Angels or Spirits attributed to each subcategory of directions, obvious similarities can be drawn between the 112-part circle of that grimoire (see figure XI-1) and the similar 32-part circle of the *Theurgia Goetia* (fig. XI-2) where every sub-direction has an associated Spirit or Spirits with particular offices. The *Arbatel* goes on to state that "this circle in this manner divided, is the seal of the secrets of the world," which leads me to believe that the divided circle is likely a compass-rose design for a Holy Table like the one from the *Theurgia Goetia*. Another theory, this from Dee Rapposelli's report of a four-person group that did dreamwork with the Olympic Spirits in 2010, suggests adding the dimension of time to the circle by associating the 28 intermediate sections of the circle with the mansions of the Moon.[6]

6. Dee Rapposelli, "The Arbatel Working," on the weblog *Sorcerers and Magi*. —APF

Fig. XI-2. ***32-rayed Compass Circle from the*** ***Theurgia Goetia***

The significance of the *Arbatel*'s circle diagram and associated directions aside,[7] I was primarily concerned with contacting the primary Olympic Spirits themselves and discovering more about their identities. So I proceeded with my preparations.

---

7. It is a very plausible decision to set aside the circle of the Sigillum Secretorum even if one is attempting to evoke the Olympic Spirits in a 'purist' manner as precisely as possible in the mode of the *Arbatel*, as it is entirely possible that the circle has nothing to do with the Olympic Spirits. As I explained in a previous note, all of the material which undeniably concerns Olympic Magic is contained in the third septenary of aphorisms, foreshadowing Volume III on *Olympica Magia*. Unless the relationship of the third septenary to the third volume is a coincidence, we may be justified in supposing that as Aphorism 27 (which describes the Sigillum Secretorum) is in the fourth septenary, its circle and associated Spirits are a foretaste of *Magia Hesiodica & Homerica*, the intended subject of Volume IV. —APF

In planning the timing for the working, I found that the instructions provided in the *Arbatel* are in line with the other Solomonic grimoires.

> Magically the Princes of the seven Governors are called simply, in that time, day, and hour wherein they rule visibly or invisibly, by their Names and Offices which God hath given unto them; and by proposing their Character which they have given or confirmed.[8]

And also:

> When you would call any of the *Olympick* Spirits, observe the rising of the Sun that day, and of what nature the Spirit is which you desire; and saying the prayer following, your desires shall be perfected.[9]

Bearing in mind that emphasis on the relevance of the particular prayer, although I did use the format of *DSIC* for the Olympic operations, I decided to include the prayers and invocations from the *Arbatel*, both because they were fairly brief and directly in line with the invocations provided by *DSIC*, and to honor the *Arbatel* as the primary Olympic grimoire and so to contact these Spirits through the familiar wording of the invocations associated with them for nearly half a millennium. Given below are the opening invocations and prayers:

Arbatel Prayer

O Lord of heaven and earth, Creator and Maker of all things visible and invisible; I, though unworthy, by thy assistance call upon thee, through thy only-begotten Son Jesus Christ our Lord, that thou wilt give unto me thy holy Spirit, to direct me in thy truth unto all good. Amen.

Because I earnestly desire perfectly to know the Arts of this life and such things as are necessary for us, which are so overwhelmed in darkness, and polluted with infinite human opinions, that I of my own power can attain to no knowledge in them, unless thou teach it me: Grant me therefore one of thy spirits, who may teach me those things which thou wouldest have me to know and learn, to thy praise and glory, and the profit of our neighbor. Give me also an apt and teachable heart that I may easily understand those things which thou shalt teach me, and may hide them in my understanding, that I may bring them forth as out of thy inexhaustible treasures, to all necessary uses. And give me grace, that I may use such thy gifts humbly, with fear and trembling, through our Lord Jesus Christ, with thy holy Spirit. Amen.[10]

8. Turner and Arbatel, *op. cit.*, Aphorism 17. —APF

9. *Ibid.*, Aphorism 21. —APF

10. *Ibid.*, Aphorism 14. —APF

Arbatel Olympic Prayer

Omnipotent and eternal God, who hast ordained the whole creation for thy praise and glory, and for the salvation of man, I beseech Thee that thou wouldst send thy Spirit N.N.,[11] *of the Solar*[12] *order, who shall inform and teach me those things which I shall ask of him; or, that he may bring me medicine against the dropsy, &c. Nevertheless, not my will be done, but thine, through Jesus Christ, thy only begotten Son, our Lord. Amen.*[13]

This example invocation includes the section "*who shall inform and teach me those things which I shall ask of him; or, that he may bring me medicine against the dropsy,* &c." which clearly indicates that the invocation is to be changed to suit each individual Spirit and to mention the particulars of its office in which the magician wishes the Spirit to instruct him. This is exactly what was done for our experiments following the invocations in *DSIC*. After this short invocation, the magician is warned "But thou shalt not detain the Spirit above a full hour, unless he be familiarly addicted unto thee." And finally a license to depart is given which nearly matches the one found in *DSIC* and many other grimoires:

The Olympic License to Depart

Forasmuch as thou camest in peace, and quietly, and hast answered unto my petitions; I give thanks unto God, in whose Name thou camest: and now thou mayest depart in peace unto thy orders; and return to me again when I shall call thee by thy name, or by thy order, or by thy office, which is granted from the Creator, Amen.[14]

As with the previous experiments, I made a pair of talismans for each Olympic Spirit bearing its sigil, one of calfskin parchment and one of the planetary metal. My scryer would meditate on the parchment talisman during the opening invocations and prayers, while I as the operator would wear the corresponding engraved metal talisman as a lamen.

---

11. For *N.N.*, insert the name of the particular Olympic Spirit whom you wish to evoke. —APF

12. For *Solar*, insert the Planetary order of the particular Spirit whom you are evoking: *i.e.*, Saturnine, Jovial, Martial, Solar, Venereal or Venereous, Mercurial, or Lunar. —APF

13. Turner and Arbatel, *op. cit.*, Aphorism 21. —APF

14. *Ibid.* —APF

With my preparations complete, I again found myself speculating as to the Olympic Spirits' exact nature, trying to predict within the recesses of my imagination their exact roles and purposes. Predictably, I found that my speculations and assumptions fell ultimately short when my scryer and I began actually conjuring these magnificent Spirits within the crystal stone.

The Olympic Spirit of Venus
Hagith

✠ Day and time	On Friday during hour of Venus
✠ Name and possible meaning	Hagith; Hebrew הגית *(Haggith* or *Chaggith)*, "The Festive One"; Greek Ἀγγιθ *(Haggith)*
✠ Pronunciation of name (as spoken by the Spirit)	«Ha-geet»
✠ Planet	♀
✠ Materials for lamen	Parchment, copper
✠ Sigil	
✠ Direction for Invocation	North
✠ Incense mixture	Musk, ambergris, wood aloes, dried red roses, jasmine flowers, ylang ylang. *Or* benzoin, valerian, sandalwood, cinnamon, lavender, and storax.

Table XI-3. ***Evocatory Correspondences for Hagith***[15]

Fig. XI-4. ***The Talisman of Hagith in the manner of DSIC***

15. Please see the Cautionary Warning Regarding Grimoric Ingredients in Appendix A. —APF

Of Hagith

The first Olympic Spirit I decided to conjure was Hagith, the Spirit of Venus. I did not feel that it was necessary to proceed in any particular order, since my scryer had already successfully communicated with each of the seven Planetary Archangels. The choice of Hagith was influenced by a client coming to me in need of magical work concerning love, relationship, and a desire for companionship. I will keep the client's name and exact case private of course, but needless to say, I surmised that I could accomplish two objectives in one magical operation by evoking this Spirit to learn its true nature as well as petition it to assist the client.

Fig. XI-4. ***An alternative Greek Talisman of Hagith in the language of the Papyri Græcæ Magicæ***[16]

I did not do an extraordinary amount of research on this Spirit in advance, both because I wanted to simply appreciate it from the experience of the upcoming conjuration, and because so far little has been written in the way of accounts of exact dealings with the Olympic Spirits and how they often appear to the magician. The *Arbatel* explains the Spirit of Venus very succinctly:

> *Hagith* governeth *Venereous* things. He that is dignified with his Character [*i.e.*, his seal or sigil], he maketh very fair, and to be adorned with all beauty. He converteth copper into gold, in a moment, and gold into copper: he giveth Spirits which do faithfully serve those to whom they are addicted.[17]

As with practically all of the grimoires, in describing the offices of the Spirits the *Arbatel* makes rather extraordinary claims regarding the services they are able to perform, but experience has shown that these offices are often not to be understood as what they seem to entail at first reading. I was hoping to be

16. The Greek inscription around the Talisman says, *En tē Hēmera kai tē Hōra tēs Aphroditēs epikaloumai te, ō Olympike Daimon* ("In the Day and Hour of Venus, I summon thee, O Olympic Spirit"). It is of course modified in each Talisman to accord with the Planet of the evoked Spirit. —APF

17. Turner and Arbatel, *op. cit.*, Aphorism 17. —APF

able to establish updated information for each of the Olympic Spirits as well as determine their usefulness for myself.

Invocation of the Olympic Spirit Hagith

Fig. XI-6. Section of Circle for Drawing Hagith into the Crystal

Appearance of the Spirit

SCRYER: I see a dove flying through pillars of a temple, and it lands on the top of one pillar, and there is a halo of light behind the dove, silvery blue. And I see that there is a flame burning within the chest of the dove, and its wings are extended out.

Opening Questions[18]

OPENING QUESTION 1: In the name of the holy and undefiled Spirit, the Father, the begotten Son, and Holy Ghost proceeding from both, what is thy true name?

SPIRIT: «Hagith *(pronounced by the Scryer as 'Ha-geet').*»

OPENING QUESTION 2: What is thy office?

SCRYER: It shows me a vision of itself as a dove, with a chain of gold connecting one heart to another. The dove is flying between people and places, connecting the golden chain that runs from her feet to the heart of one being to another.

18. The Opening Questions, as always, are the probationary queries specified by the *The Art of Drawing Spirits into Crystals* as those proper to begin the conversation with any evoked Spirit. The administration of the Oath constitutes the fourth Opening Question. They are worded according to Barrett's translation. —APF

SPIRIT: «Creating bonds of love from one person to another. From a place to a person. From a project or endeavor to a person. Love gives energy but also a binding.»

OPENING QUESTION 3: What are the best and proper times to call you to hold conference with us?

SCRYER: I see an image of two people in a wedding. I see two people hugging and embracing. I see an image of Venus in the sky near sunset or sunrise.

OATH: Wilt thou swear by the holy blood of Jesus Christ that thou art truly the Olympic Venus Spirit Hagith?

HAGITH: «I swear by the name of Jesus, who gave his blood to heal sorrow, that I am Hagith.»

Further Questions

QUESTION 5: Please explain to us more about the Olympic Spirits' titles and place. What manner of being are you? What is your relationship to the Archangel Anael? In which station in the spiritual hierarchy do you reside?

HAGITH: «I am the handmaiden of Anael, her eyes, her wings. I carry the golden chains of binding love that she gives forth, tying one heart to another. I am ruled under the planet of Venus, under Spica and Virgo. And along with my many sisters and brothers, it is my destiny to sow and cultivate love in God to all things. I specifically am charged to spread that love among humanity.»

(At this point scryer slumps over in seeming exhaustion and fatigue.)

SCRYER: Suddenly I'm feeling extremely lightheaded. I got this really overwhelming image of how many connections it makes between people. Love almost *equals* Hagith.

(Several moments pass. Operator places hands on scryer's shoulders, asking if he can continue.)

SCRYER: Yeah, I think I can continue.

Fig. XI-7. ***Portrait of Hagith as beheld in Vision***

QUESTION 6: What is the meaning and origin of your name, Hagith? Can you tell us more about its history and meaning?

SCRYER: I see what looks like a wedding, and women bringing forth the bride on their shoulders and saying, "Hagith," singing and shouting it over and over again.

The Spirit says it comes from an old Semitic word.

QUESTION 7: What is the history and source of your sigil? Can you tell us more about its structure and meaning? What are the best ways to use this sigil for empowering the benefits of your offices for ourselves and others?

HAGITH: «The sigil is the marriage within the temple: two hands upraised in praise, the other hands joined as one. The temple surrounds the both of them. They are also my wings flying through the pillars of the temple, connecting the pillars of creation through love, strengthening them, bolstering them.»

QUESTION 8: It is expected that my next child will be under the sign of Virgo, which is connected to your office. I was wondering if you had any intelligence or wisdom about my forthcoming child.

SCRYER: It shows me the image of a girl with many Spirits which are behind her. She holds a sheaf of wheat in her arms. The wheat burns with a white flame but doesn't consume the stalk or the grain. She hands and distributes these stalks of wheat to those she sees and meets.

The Spirit doesn't show or say anything further.

QUESTION 9: It is said of your office that you transmute metals, are commander of four thousand legions of spirits, and rule over 21 provinces. Can you explain this?

HAGITH: «My metals are the adornment of the bride and the groom. The raw stones of the earth polished and cut, heated and blended and re-polished into the rings that bind the necklaces that adorn the crowns. The alchemy of their forging was first not for weapons but to give praise, to adorn and exalt. When gold is refined and poured and shaped and hammered, it is the echo of a lesson once given by me and Anael to the high priestess who would marry the king.»

QUESTION 10: Great Spirit and Angel of Venus, this next part I wish to ask on behalf of one who commissioned me to help her with a most important issue for her. I am performing this operation to help a client, NN, who is in need of your service and office and assistance to help her: She sets before you a petition of which I will read each. These are her words:

(Operator reads questions and petitions, one by one.)

HAGITH: «She is already worthy of love. With her whole understanding she is to hunt down that which is at the root of her feelings of unworthiness of love. Anael will be at her side when she composes a prayer, a song in praise of Anael. She is to repeat this prayer, this song, seven times a day for forty days. These forty days will be like the Sun in the desert. Seven times a day for forty days. Sung and repeated seven times a day. With offerings of wine and fruit, honey, and bread, with the talisman of Anael being continually on her neck for the forty days.»

(Scryer becomes extremely fatigued again, and operator places his hands on his shoulders once more.)

OPERATOR: I will recite the rest of her words from the petition she wrote so that I will not omit anything of her desires. She asks:

(Reads aloud the remaining personal questions of client.)

QUESTION 11: I ask if there is anything else which could be done for her. Do you have any advice for this woman, or words for which she can achieve her heart's desire? Are there any ways we can help her further? Is there a talisman, symbol, or spell that would aid her in achieving her desire?

HAGITH: «The scryer and you must take time during the forty days. Go before your altars, your place of prayer, see the image of her with a man who is formed of light. See them embracing. Hold this image in your mind every day for her during the forty days when it has begun. And lend the power of your prayer and your spirit to the endeavor. With the three of you doing this, you cannot fail. The prayer that she repeats seven times a day will attract who she needs and will also help to heal her wounds.»

Question 12: Great and wonderful Spirit, thank you for your instruction, which we will carry out. Also, we thank thee for your wisdom and advice. We will assist in this endeavor and relate your words back to her. I ask if you have any final words of wisdom to help myself and my scryer in our own lives and relationships, and matters of the heart.

Hagith: «The scryer must drink a lot more water. And take time, both of you, to touch your wives, softly, gently. Run your fingers through their hair. And spend time with no words spoken, only touch. Grapes would be good for both of you.»

(Scryer appears fully exhausted. Operator gives the thanks and License to Depart.)

Afterthoughts on the Hagith Operation

This was a comparatively short and oddly difficult operation, where the scryer became visibly fatigued, lightheaded, and exhausted. He later explained that it may have been due to a recent surgical operation he had undergone and medications he was taking, but wasn't sure. The feedback the Spirit provided for my client's petition seemed hopeful and quite involved. Obviously, there would be some work ahead, and not an instant fix from the Spirit side. Everything I had experienced thus far was unsurprising. The Angels and higher Spirits seem to enforce a stance of human beings taking as much responsibility and proactive involvement as possible. I found myself wanting to ask more questions as to the office and identity of this Spirit, but decided that for an initial operation it provided plenty of insight to build upon at later times.

Scryer: I am sorry for the difficulty. I felt fine when I got here, but that just really hit me for some reason. The Spirit stayed in the dove form the entire time, but it was beautiful watching it fly from person to person with that golden chain, connecting one heart to another.

The Spirit seemed like a more focused servant or energy aimed at this particular aspect of love and relationship for people. The Spirit describing itself as more of a focused servant or handmaiden seemed perfect for some reason: a Spirit to help get what needed to be done. I think this work for helping your client is important, and a further function of what these magical operations are about.

OPERATOR: Yes, I will be making further talismans for her in conjunction with this work for forty days.

Although Benn's gifts as a seer never cease to amaze, I'm always impressed when my scryer envisions a Spirit very much as it is described in a classic grimoire. As with the previous workings, I did not give him any detailed information about the Spirit we were contacting or from what source it came. To my knowledge, he only sees the sigil or seal right before we conduct an operation. Before each evocation, he meditates on the talisman for approximately fifteen minutes as I complete the other preparations and opening ceremonies. In the *Fourth Book of Occult Philosophy*, under the chapter dealing with the "Visible Appearance of Spirits," a dove is given as one of the classical and appropriate images or "familiar shapes" in which a Spirit of Venus is supposed to show itself.

Furthermore, Hagith's brief statement that her name came from an old Semitic word led to some fascinating confirmation in my follow-up research. It turns out that there is in fact a relevant Hebrew name in the Bible. One of King David's first wives, the mother of his fourth son Adonijah,[19] was named חגית, that is, *Chaggith* or *Ḥaggith*, written Haggith in the King James Version.[20] According to the lexicons,[21] *chaggith/ḥaggith* is originally an adjective meaning "festive or festal (as in celebrating a *chag/ḥag*, 'a festival')," and so "joyous, rejoicing, even dancing or whirling," which then became a proper noun, so the name means "the festive one, the joyous, rejoicing one."[22]

From what we were told and and shown by the Spirit, Hagith seems to be the very personification of the joy and celebration of love in union, which was even particularly expressed in the vision as the loving celebration (*ḥagigah*) of the wedding festival (*ḥag*).

---

19. King Solomon, the archetypal mage, was the tenth of David's 15 legitimate sons, and his mother was Bathsheba. —APF

20. *II Samuel* 3:4, *I Kings* chapters 1 and 2, *I Chronicles* 3:2.

21. Francis Brown, Samuel Rolles Driver, and Charles Augustus Briggs, *A Hebrew and English Lexicon of the Old Testament* (Oxford: Clarendon Press, 1906); R. Laird Harris, Gleason Archer, and Bruce Waltke, *Theological Wordbook of the Old Testament* (Chicago: Moody Press, 1980). —APF

22. It is also quite relevant that the Spirit Hagith identifies herself as female, and the Hebrew name Ḥaggith or Chaggith is specifically feminine. The masculine equivalent is Ḥaggi or Chaggi, and it also occurs in the Hebrew Bible (*Numbers* 26:15), being the name of one of the sons of the eponymous founder of the Hebrew tribe of Gad. —APF

Not only were these confirmations of parts of the Olympic communication remarkable, but I also found the image of the golden chain and the explanation of the sigil to be quite powerful.

Of course, one of the most fascinating pieces of information for me was the vision the Spirit showed concerning my child. My wife was still in the early stages of pregnancy and the gender of our child was undetermined, but it seemed that Hagith was convinced that I would be having a daughter. I recalled that the Directional King Egyn had closed an earlier ceremony with the enigmatic comment that my child would be "of the North." She (I found myself inclined to share Hagith's prediction about my child's gender at this point) was due to be born during the time when the Sun was in Virgo, an Earth Sign, and this might be the connection with the Earthy quarter of "the North," but this was purely speculative. This new vision shown to my scryer by Hagith was intriguing, but I had no idea what significance it held if any. However, I did later find that the image of a maiden holding a sheaf of wheat was a classic iconic image of Virgo. Also, as I contemplated the vision, I began considering that my second child might be gifted in much the same way as my father and me, and that she could possibly carry on a magical legacy which seemed to be growing more and more pronounced through the generations.

As for my client, the working continued over the next forty days, and I kept up the consistent practice of praying for her as Hagith had instructed. My scryer kept in contact and reported he was doing the same, and even my wife joined in praying for this client's desire to secure a romantic companion. After the forty-day period was concluded, I did not hear from the client for some time and she did not return my inquiring emails. About a month later, she finally responded, saying that she had done what the Spirit requested but was still having difficulty. Apparently the client had been expecting that she would be able to magically convince someone that they were made for each other. The reports led me to believe that the client was fixated on a particular person or idea and was not willing to look elsewhere which, in fact, might be the cause of her situation. I responded by saying that the help would often not match what we have fixated our minds on, but that we must be open to a possibility that is potentially better than what we had imagined for ourselves.

I offered to assist my client further and even to speak with her on the phone to find out what other possibilities could be causing the continued difficulty. When the client did not return my messages, I conjured the spirit Hagith a second time, as well as consulted Hiram. Both the Spirit of Venus and my familiar Spirit gave me the same response: The operation and forty days of prayer had worked. The client, although unable to break years of obsessive thinking and behavior, was finally starting to mend. Her way of life before the working had made the potential for lasting relationships impossible, with deep rooted emotional barriers. However, due to the work and her prayers, they were finally being worked through. The spirit of Venus spoke about the desert as the intense pain one has to go through and face before coming into new ways of relating to others. Only in this way could a real and substantial relationship and love form and grow. It was not immediate, it took longer than forty days and there was much pain, resentment, and hurt from the client who expected all of her problems to simply vanish with the appearance of a fictitious romantic partner.

She had come to me asking for magic to fix her problems. Magic had responded, but not in the way she had expected. It was not the magic of fantasy but the magic of truth, the magic of reality, which will accept no substitute from the demands of our imaginations.

Hiram Consultation

A short while after the conjuration and following work from the Olympic Spirit of Venus, my scryer suggested we consult my Skull Spirit Hiram again, and see if the Spirit had any advice for handling the obvious intensity produced by performing evocations. It seemed important that we keep up with a practice to handle the operations without being completely drained and exhausted physically. I readily agreed and made preparations for both of us to speak with Hiram again. This was to be the second time that we spoke to him together, by this time having no doubt that we would not only hear him but that he would provide excellent council. Hiram was again brought down to a table and we both sat in front of him. I lit a candle near the skull and spoke my summoning litany inviting Hiram to come forth from his library and speak.

SCRYER: So when I began speaking to Hiram and asking him how to better handle these operations, his first response was that keeping the body healthy and fit was vital. He said that I wouldn't have the energy I needed to continue this work along with daily responsibilities unless I spent more time keeping up my vitality. He said, "Make sure it happens soon and make sure it is a regular practice." He then went on to mention that whenever I exercise it should always be with music. I was actually amazed that he said that because the last time I worked out, I was told not to listen to music because it would be "distracting me from listening to my body."

Hiram said, "Don't worry about that; that's just a purism concept." He's like, "Lots of traditions used music when they exercise because it helps disengage from the pain, and allows you to instead feel the vitality of the exercise. Music allows you not to worry about the pain or discomfort." I like how he explained this to me. He continued, saying, "Plus it takes the edge off. You're getting older; you are not going to be like you were in your twenties, but you can be very active, very fit and healthy. It's wise to acknowledge this but not be deterred by it."

After the talk about my physical health, Hiram showed me images of us being outside. We were both near a huge ponderosa pine tree at night. There was snow on the ground and we stood in front of a gravestone, in a circle with a candle. He said that this was an important working for us in the future, but that no more would be said about it. He went on saying that working with the spirits of the dead as the year got darker would be prevalent. He said I had to keep up my bodily exercise before working with the darker and spirits of the departed. The continual exercises and training both body and mind would be in preparation for doing bigger things. The candle in front of the gravestone was interesting. I could see us clearly inside a circle engraved on the ground, both of us looking down toward the gravestone, but I couldn't make out the name on it.

OPERATOR: That's interesting that he showed you being somewhere outside, as he showed me something similar. At first I thought I was being shown some place we would be camping, since it looked like a deep forest. He said we need to be out there meditating. He spoke about 'power spots' out in nature that were far from civilization and that held a potent energy. As I was seeing this, I heard him say, «You need to go out to the places of energy with beings there that will help strengthen you and instruct you.» Apparently there are a lot of big things we need to be ready for. He's like a personal trainer in the magical world. He told me specifically that I needed to be mindful of my thoughts, practice, and continual focus. He mentioned that if I became overly distracted by certain emotions and thoughts, that certain Spirits would be able to find the strands and use them against me. That they can influence the more you are not aware of them. It was all very interesting and informative. I definitely think we need to get outside soon. He is very calming and even-tempered, very authoritative but patient and soothing, very wise, very studious.

SCRYER: Hiram has such a great energy! It's so calming to be around him. I get the feeling like he's been watching us for a long, long time. There is something familiar about him.

Hiram did say that the workings we were doing with the hospital ghosts and other spirits of the departed were 'getting our feet wet,' and that releasing certain spirits that were stuck was important. He said that as we got more experienced, we would be able to move to bigger entities, whatever that meant. It literally gave me goosebumps. When he was talking about that, it instantly occurred to me how important working with the Archangels was. It really is like walking through a series of consecutive waterfalls, the water washing over us, cleaning us out, as well us gifting us with another aspect of creation that was vital to progress. I really feel that every Angel was something that we needed, and that being in their presence allowed us to go further.

The Olympic Spirit of Jupiter
Bethor

✠ Day and time	On Thursday during hour of Jupiter
✠ Name	Bethor; Hebrew ביתור *(Bethor* or *Beithor)*; Greek Βηθωρ *(Bēthōr)*
✠ Pronunciation of name (as spoken by the Spirit)	«Beht-or»
✠ Planet	♃
✠ Materials for lamen	Parchment, tin, silver, gold
✠ Sigil	[sigil]
✠ Direction for Invocation	Southwest
✠ Incense mixture	Mastic gum, cloves, powder of agate, saffron, lignum aloes, storax benzoin, allspice, star anise, juniper berries, vanilla, peppercorns, nutmeg.

Table XI-8. ***Evocatory Correspondences for Bethor***[23]

Fig. XI-9. ***The Talisman of Bethor in the manner of DSIC***

23. Please see the Cautionary Warning Regarding Grimoric Ingredients in Appendix A. —APF

Of Bethor

A bit more time passed after the first operation of Hagith before my scryer and I felt ready to conjure the next spirit of the Olympic order. We had become preoccupied, independently dealing with a few hauntings about which acquaintances of our friends and family had informed us. We each offered our assistance as needed, my scryer several times putting false claims of hauntings to rest and offering alternative explanations. It seemed that our magical work was constant, involving one area of the paranormal or another, independent of our magical conjuration work.

Fig. XI-10. ***An alternative Greek Talisman of Bethor in the language of the Papyri Græcæ Magicæ***

I was eager to finally meet the Olympic Spirit of Jupiter for obvious reasons. Besides the Jupiter Archangel acting as my patron in numerous dealings magical, personal, and financial, I had grown fond of the weekly invocations where I could sense his presence quite easily above the altar I had created for him. I was blessed by frequent events of inspiration, instruction, and visual imagery through my ongoing practice. However, I was not sure of the exact nature of the Olympic spirit under the same planetary influence. I thought an evocation of him during a particularly favorable Thursday would be the perfect time to greet this being and learn what it had to teach my scryer and me.

In the *Arbatel*, it is said that

> *Bethor* governeth those things which are ascribed to *Jupiter*: he soon cometh being called. He that is dignified with his character, he raiseth to very great dignities, to cast open treasures: he reconcileth the spirits of the aire, that they give true answers: they transport precious stones from place to place, and they make medicines to work miraculously in their effects: he giveth also the familiars of the firmament, and prolongeth life to 700 yeares if God will.[24]

24. Turner and Arbatel, *op. cit.*, Aphorism 17. —APF

He is said to rule 42 kings, 35 princes, 28 dukes, 21 counselors, 14 ministers, 7 messengers, and 29000 legions of Spirits.[25]

The sigil of Bethor is as interesting and as mysterious as those of the other six related spirits. Besides the description of his offices and roles as they relate to Jupiter, there is not much written on how the spirit is supposed to appear. As before, I made one talisman from metal (tin in this case) and one from calf parchment. I used the same timing as I would for the Archangel of Jupiter.

Invocation of the Olympic Spirit Bethor

Fig. XI-11. Section of Circle for Drawing Bethor into the Crystal

Appearance of the Spirit

SCRYER: I see a man dressed as a king, only he has the head of a ram, although he is handsome, with white fur, and he is crowned with gold circlet. He has a large cup in his right hand and a small cup in his left hand. He wears a magnificent white and gold robe with deep blue azure trimming or hems and a sash looks like it comes out of his trousers which goes from his right hip down to his knee. He takes wine from the large cup and pours a portion of it into the small cup. The room looks like it's made entirely of marble, and behind him is the night sky. I see Jupiter is directly above his head. However, the room is lit as if by the Sun and so is he.

OPENING QUESTION 1: In the name of the holy and undefiled Spirit, the Father, the begotten Son, and Holy Ghost proceeding from both, what is thy true name?

SPIRIT: «By the Father, the Son, and the Holy Spirit, I am Bethor. My blessings are only for the magnanimous.»

25. One of the greater mysteries is how the author ever came to some of the numbers of these subordinate Spirits.

Fig. XI-12. ***Portrait of Bethor as beheld in Vision***

(Voice as coming through scryer is almost stern; more confident, authoritative, and absolute.)

OPENING QUESTION 2: What is thy office?

SPIRIT: «I am the distributor of wealth and of power. I am the bridge between the large cup and the small. Some are born with a cup large with capacity, and some are born with a cup small. I link the powerless with the powerful, that the large cup may fill many small ones. Only in this way will rule be in harmony with the spirit of the Creator and in keeping with the just, loving law of the Son. Only for the magnanimous are my blessings.»

OPENING QUESTION 3: What is thy true sign or character?

SCRYER: He holds forth in his hand a scepter and the two cups.

OPENING QUESTION 4: What are the best and proper times to call you to hold conference with us?

SCRYER: He looks up at Jupiter, and I get the impression that it's when Jupiter is at the highest point in the sky. He opens a book in front of him and shows me, in the book, an image of a man deciding on a dispute between two parties.

OATH: Wilt thou swear by the holy blood of Jesus Christ that thou art truly the Olympic Jupiter Spirit Bethor?

SPIRIT: «I am Bethor, one of the Olympic. And I swear by the blood of the Son, who died on the cross distributing grace, as I distribute wealth and justice.»

OPERATOR: Great spirit Bethor, could you please explain to us more about the image in the book dealing with your proper time and calling?

BETHOR: «When Jupiter is at its height and I am called upon by name, I will listen. My attention is focused most readily when justice needs to be dispensed with wisdom, or when wealth needs to be used for the benefit of those who have little. From life to life, your stations will change. But the calling of generosity with sovereignty will always remain. The image in the book shows the power of one invested with my blessings able to mediate between those who are in conflict. During those times, when my name is whispered three times, I will aid in the end of the dispute and the distribution of abundance.»

QUESTION 5: Great Spirit Bethor, please explain to us more about the Olympic Spirits' titles and place. What manner of being are you? What is your relationship to the Archangel Sachiel or Tzadkiel? In which station in the spiritual hierarchy do you reside?

BETHOR: «I am the servant of Tzadkiel, I am the hands of his heart.»

SCRYER: The image has changed, I see him sitting on a throne in a rather relaxed posture and he is eating grapes and smiling. The ground around the throne is heaped in gold coins.

BETHOR: «The abundance of Tzadkiel is to be distributed with a light heart, with the arms of justice and the feet grounded in truth. Each of us, the Olympic Spirits are like the focused attention of the archangel who stands behind us, whose power watches over many worlds, many places, many stars. We are for Earth alone. We understand the workings of the human mind the way in which trees respond to light, the way in which birds navigate on their migrations, and the way whales sing through the depths of the ocean. We link the needs of the small to the needs of the great. And in this way, I Bethor, link the wealth and abundance and the sovereignty from the great to the small.»

QUESTION 6: What is the meaning and source of origin of your name, Bethor? Can you tell us more about its history and meaning?

SCRYER: He shows me his sigil... It's on a door, and he pushes it open and we step through.... and I see a wooden home. It looks very old. It's round. I see people dressed in skins and furs all around, and I see a chief come out of the home. He is very broad and strong. He smiles and laughs. He has a couple of women on either arm. The people around him seem very happy to see him. He has many wives and they come out of the house as well and they are distributing dry meat to the people in front. You can really see the admiration of these people for this man. He's happy; he has a light heart.

I see another scene; he's lying on his deathbed. I see a shaft of light coming through the roof and illuminating where he sleeps. At the base of his bed, I see Tzadkiel standing and smiling down at him. The chieftain's eyes open, and he beholds the Archangel Tzadkiel. There aren't any words spoken between them, but there is a feeling that Tzadkiel is pleased with him. The Chieftain has a look on his face like he recognizes him from a dream and is surprised to see him.

He calls the name of the chieftain, «Beht (Beth),» and he brings forth the spirit of the chieftain from his body. The spirit of the chieftain comes to stand in front of Tzadkiel and the archangel holds up a coin of gold, plain, no markings, circular, thick, coin of gold. He places it on the tongue of the chieftain who opens his mouth, and he bids Beht to swallow it. As Tzadkiel held the coin up in front of the chieftain, he spoke aloud saying, «Or.»

BETHOR: «I, Bethor, am the son of Tzadkiel, combined with the spirit of a great ruler among the ancient people of your world. ‹Beht-Or,› Bethor. ‹Or› was the contained essence of Tzadkiel mingled with my spirit to create a new level of being. Each of us, each of the Olympic Spirits, is the child of a man or woman of your world and the essence of the Archangel whom we serve.»

QUESTION 7: What is the history and source of your sigil? Can you tell us more about its structure and meaning?

BETHOR: «My sigil is like the bridge between the small cup and the large cup. Like a scepter joining the powerful to the weak.»

QUESTION 8: According to the text of *Arbatel*, how is it that you "reconcile the Spirits of the Air to man, so that they will give true answers?" You are said to grant "familiars of the firmament." Can you explain more about this and how you will do this?

BETHOR: «In granting familiars of the firmament to those who desire them, there is a common essence between the familiar and the invoker, the magician. Through the power of breath, especially through song—not of words but of vocals, vowels, sounds—and the gestures of the hand can the winds be excited, the thunder made to roll and the lightning to strike. Only when the magician is filled with ecstasy can the link be made. I link the large cup of the familiar to the small cup of the magician. My link is ecstasy, joy.»

(The operator is shaking and feeling tremendous emotion run through him as he recalls one of his first true experiences of magic, when he called forth a storm exactly as the Spirit described.)

OPERATOR: You speak of my experience I had when I was younger in my teens, on the side of a mountain when I called a large storm, and I wonder if you were there with me then.

BETHOR: «Yes, child of Tzadkiel, you felt the ecstasy in your skin, blood, and in that moment the hand of Tzadkiel, Bethor, was in your hand. It was a reminder of who watches over you, whose breath you breathe, whose hands you are born with, and whose mission you fulfill.»

(Hearing this response and associated feelings, the operator notices an increase to the shaking. It takes a moment to come back to the ritual and recall the questions and purpose. The simple exchange is a personal one, and one that strikes at the operator's core.)

QUESTION 9: According to the *Arbatel*, it is said you can exalt the person who is dignified by your character to illustrious positions and they may obtain large treasures. How can you perform this and how is it achieved?

BETHOR: «‹Illustrious position and large treasures.› These are things that are often concretized in the mind of men and women. Ask yourselves, what is ‹illustrious position›? What is ‹great treasure›? Think • on • this. Illustrious position can be achieved in a day, in a moment, and is sometimes granted to many for years on end. Treasure is in the eyes of the beloved. The beloved who benefit from the distribution of the wealth you already own. Position and wealth are granted by need only and not by the whims of men. The greater Plan of the Creator is always at work. The large cup is linked to the small cup through the Will of the Creator alone.

«I, to the true magician, I, Bethor, open the eyes of the invoker, the seer, to see the position they already have and the wealth they already possess and ask the question: With both of these things, how will you distribute them? How will you be my hands to fill the cups of many?»

QUESTION 10: Spirit of Jupiter Bethor, we thank thee for your council and wisdom and will heed your words. It is also said of you that you can transport precious stones or messages and compose medicines having miraculous effects. How was this understood by magicians of old and can you explain more about how you accomplish this and what this entails?

BETHOR: «Long ago, before you had the ability to speak to one another through your computers and your phones, vast distances separated magician from magician, priest from priest, shaman from shaman, healer from healer. There was, in many ways, an unspoken fellowship between these men and these women who served their people, wherever they may be, through ecstasy and the achievement of ecstasy; I link the knowledge of one to the other in these ways, with the illuminations, the knowledge, and medicines, and techniques of one given to another as my sigil shows, the linkage of one to the other. These medicines may be of the power of plants, stones, fermentation, song, touch. In the times of need, it is I that made the bridge through the air by the mind.»

QUESTION 11: Perhaps one of the most pertinent questions I have for you is to ask if there is truth behind the claim that you "can prolong life to seven hundred years, subject to the will of God," Such qualification imparts an air of caution. Is this true? Have you done this in the past and what were the circumstances which allowed this? Are you able to grant me and my scryer longevity? If so, to what degree can you grant this?

BETHOR: «Both you and the scryer will live long lives, that I can say now. There are a few, who still live in three mountain ranges of the world, whose gift this has been granted to: the life span of seven hundred years. Why they were granted this gift is a mystery that cannot be spoken of. Suffice to say their presence in your world is necessary. What they give forth is like the steady vibration of a string, plucked by God. When this gift is given, it is us who will approach you to give it. It cannot be asked for, it cannot be petitioned. It is grace alone.»

QUESTION 12: A question petitioned from one of the Gentlemen for Jupiter[26] is, are there any female deities who can be considered part of the Jupiter current, maybe one of the Egyptian sky Goddesses like Nut or Mehet Weret, or perhaps the Sumerian Enlil's wife Ninlil? Secondly, do you have any information regarding feminine polarity within the current?

BETHOR: «Look into the eyes of Hera, whose will and jealousy and wisdom balanced the might of her husband. These polarities of the Archangels are set to come forth soon. Like Hera, the Goddesses, the Angels, the Familiars of my family are bound to the same degree and in the same way that the male polarity vibrates to. Without one or the other, the power created by the Creator and sent into your world could not fully manifest.

«To the one who asked the question, I say this: In your rites, in your prayers, and with the intention of your offerings, seek these beings. It is part of your destiny and part of your path to uncover this. When done with sincerity and with fervency, I will lend blessing to your work.»

QUESTION 14: Are there any specific energies or benefits particular to tonight which make the powers of Jupiter more veritable and focused?

BETHOR: «Listen to the wind. *(Strong wind had been blowing and rushing rather loudly since the start of the ceremony, and could be heard easily just beyond the door and window of the magical chamber.)* Feel the clouds moving above. In the gusts, hear my breath. In the trees hear my song. It is not just the invoker who invokes. It is the invoked that surrounds the will and draws it forth. Do you hear the wind?» *(Wind grows even louder outside.)*

QUESTION 15: Is there a ritual or invocation which you can impart to us which would bring the Gentlemen for Jupiter more success as well as 'Health,

26. The Gentlemen for Jupiter is an association of magicians pursuing the work of prosperity and abundance in the Jovial Sphere in a gentlemanly fashion, often involving fine dress, fine whiskey, philanthropy, and setting the world aright. —APF

Wealth, and Prosperity'? Can you suggest a particularly powerful rite and working we can do every Thursday?

BETHOR: «On the day of Jupiter the rite can be simple, but the attainment of its desired end difficult. Seek a high place with views all around you. And through the ecstasy of song, song without words, sing to me, to Tzadkiel, with the heart of devotion—pure, crystalline devotion. When the spirit of the body is raised three inches above the head, ecstasy is achieved and the blessing, inevitable. With the completion of this ecstasy, your success, your wealth is guaranteed through the rest of the days of your incarnation.»

QUESTION 16: As a magician or priest, how may I assist others in receiving your blessings and benefits?

BETHOR: «Sing our names over them, while laying your hands on their body with reverence. Remind them of the abundance that they already possess. Allow them to see the wealth that surrounds them with new eyes. Remind them that the cup of the Father is vast, that it will never run dry. When their eyes are anointed with gratitude, wealth comes. Blessings come as our voices, as our hands touch them, fill them with this knowledge, this wisdom. Let it be in every cell of your body so that you may give it forth to theirs. We make your cup great so that you can fill the cups of many.»

QUESTION 17: Great and wondrous Spirit Bethor, we thank you greatly for you wisdom and attendance upon us. Is there a talisman or magical method to draw even more wealth and abundance or the great benefits of your being and office? Do you have any other words of wisdom to impart to others so that they may gain the blessings of your presence?

BETHOR: «A single gold coin, carried on the person, blessed beneath the light of Jupiter at its apex, vibrated with the singing of my name, with a vow to always remember the abundance already possessed: this simple thing is my greatest talisman and the echo of my birth.»

OPERATOR: Great and wondrous Olympic Angel and Spirit under my beloved Tzadkiel, ruler of Jupiter under the Father, I thank thee for thine attendance here and for your words of wisdom. Great Spirit Bethor under

Jupiter, may the blessings of your office continue to grace us and may your guidance be ever near.

(License to Depart given.)

Afterthoughts on the Bethor Operation

OPERATOR: This was a very powerful and emotionally moving experience for me. Besides what was said, the images and sensations related struck deep chords within me. Throughout this operation I could perceive an electric blue aura around the entire altar space of the crystal. I've really come to see how there is no conflict or discrepancy between traditions or spiritual beings. Angels have spoken of gods, goddesses, and other beings as well as demons without the least bit of hostility or reservation. It seems so different from what you might find from a person or religious official discussing beings of other traditions and religions besides the one they adhere to. This has been a very pleasing aspect and realization from doing this work and makes me wonder at the broader spectrum of spiritual unity.

I am very grateful for the spirit's response about its origin and nature as well as rank in the spiritual/angelic hierarchy. How fascinating! So if Bethor is to be believed, the Olympic spirits are a combination of human and angel, some sort of unique being that comes into existence after an archangel has chosen them? That part was very interesting.

The particular part of calling the winds and storms struck right at home for me as well. It was one of the first times I saw magic work in nature, dynamically and powerfully, and I was sort of lost in this ecstasy, laughing and yelling like a mad person as these things were happening which coincided with my gestures and thoughts. This was before I had any real knowledge of the occult, of Angels, Archangels, Spirits, of the Hermetic tradition.

SCRYER: I was so humbled in his presence, but not in a sense of being a lesser or insignificant before him. I was amazed how handsome he was, considering the appearance. It was so odd to see a ram-headed man, but there was something incredibly striking about him. It was really amazing, hard to describe. I wonder, why a ram? It was amazing; he had these large, pure white locks, curls of hair, and these perfect golden horns which curved around.

OPERATOR: Yeah, that wasn't expected; the typical list I have for how this Spirit might appear from the *Fourth Book of Occult Philosophy* is "A king with a sword drawn riding a stag, a man wearing a mitre in a long robe, a young woman with a laurel crown adorned with flowers, a bull, a stag, a peacock, an azure garment"—which you did describe this Spirit wearing. "A sword and a box tree" are also listed. I'm curious as to the significance and origin of the appearance of this Spirit.

There was a huge golden glow coming from the pedestal and altar as well as an azure blue light I kept seeing appear from your lower right but just out of view from where I was standing directly behind. The blue light then surrounded the entire altar. There was an enormous and viable presence which appeared to encapsulate the entire altar area in a glow and presence. The winds outside were crazy and increased at very particular times during the ceremony while the spirit was speaking. Notice how the winds completely died at the close of the ceremony.

SCRYER: Man, that makes so much sense for tonight! The other thing that he showed at one point was the two goblets and a scepter lying across between them, connecting one to the other. One of the goblets was large and the other was small, but they were the same height. One was just wider than the other. The spirit conveyed to me that the purpose of the larger cup was to fill the smaller cups. He was holding the cups by balancing the bases on his hands in his palms. One was larger and one was smaller, yet they were the same height—as if there was no hierarchy between them, just that one had a greater capacity. Later he laid the scepter on top of them describing how he was the link, the scepter between them.

OPERATOR: I think that was a very important image and visual representation of the Spirit's office. The display seems powerful and meaningful, displaying how his energy functions. Hearing about how that chieftain changed or ascended into the Olympic Spirit under Tzadkiel was just amazing. I felt so in awe and envious of his destiny. What an honor! I would have absolutely no problem with my spirit transcending like that.

SCRYER: Seeing all that was amazingly clear, too; I could even see the dust particles in the air as that beam of sunlight was shining through the roof of the chieftain's house. I could hear people outside crying quietly when he was passing away. The chieftain was the only one in the house for some reason. He was completely by himself, and then all of a sudden, Tzadkiel was there. I remember seeing how he placed the coin on the chieftain's tongue and that reminded me exactly of Holy Communion. He just took it in, swallowed it whole, and it transformed him.

OPERATOR: That was the first thing I thought when you were describing that as well: like the Eucharist. I thought, how perfect! Since this operation happened to take place on Maundy Thursday.[27] The visual symbolism was pretty spot on with this and the transformation which occurred. These operations are always so rich with imagery, so much knowledge and information transpires which takes a while to absorb.

SCRYER: It was interesting that at the beginning he was very serious and very direct, like 'you need to see and understand this lesson,' and once he imparted that, he sat down on this throne, put his leg over one of the arms and began eating grapes. All of a sudden he was just talking to me very casually. He seemed very lighthearted. It was so, so odd to see a ram eating grapes like that. It was quite bizarre since he was so handsome. I liked the question about the male and female counterparts and then how the Spirit said how that worked. The need for both really seems to really make sense.

Later the same day as the operation, I was almost asleep when I recalled an image from Giordano Bruno's *De Umbris Idearum ("On the Shadows of Ideas")*, which describes a Jupiter Spirit with a ram's head. The section dealing with the images of Spirits is "The 49 Planetary Images" which are heavily connected with the *Picatrix*, the *Magical Calendar*, and other illustrated esoteric works concerning the planets.[28] Among the seven Images of Jove, Bruno describes the third as "one having the head of a ram, seated upon a wheel and bearing in his hands a vessel of Balsam."

Not long after the experiment, I came upon an image that was rendered from the description in *De Umbris Idearum*. The illustration of a ram-headed man in an azure blue garment was perfect, and is now my representation for the Olympic Spirit Bethor. I printed out a copy and added it to my Jupiter altar.

---

27. The day which commemorates the Last Supper of Jesus Christ with the Apostles, also known as Holy Thursday, Covenant Thursday, Great and Holy Thursday, Sheer Thursday, and Thursday of Mysteries.

28. Perhaps most famous is the image of the Saturn Spirit Cassiel riding the dragon with the arrow depicted in the Book of Spirits example in *The Magus*. This image is derived directly from *De Umbris Idearum*.

I was again pleased and impressed by our working and the richness of the visual imagery as well as the words of the Spirit. I felt rejuvenated and inspired to put the Spirit's suggestions for further blessings into practice.

The Olympic Spirit of Mars
Phaleg

☩ Day and time	On Tuesday during hour of Mars
☩ Name	Phaleg; Hebrew פלג *(Phaleg)*; Greek Φαλεγ *(Phaleg)*
☩ Pronunciation of name (as spoken by the Spirit)	«Fa-leck»
☩ Planet	♂
☩ Materials for lamen	Parchment, iron, nickel, brass
☩ Sigil	
☩ Direction for Invocation	South
☩ Incense mixture	Cedar wood, red sandalwood, cypress, white poppy, storax, gum Benjamin, black ground pepper, costus root, sausurea lappa, powder of lodestone, and a small amount of sulfur. *Alternative mixture:* Pepper, cumin, dragon's blood resin, tobacco, and spearmint.

Table XI-13. ***Evocatory Correspondences for Phaleg***[29]

Fig. XI-14. ***The Talisman of Phaleg in the manner of DSIC***

29. Please see the Cautionary Warning Regarding Grimoric Ingredients in Appendix A. —APF

Of Phaleg

There was considerably less time between the Bethor operation and the operation set to summon the Olympic Spirit of Mars than had passed between the two previous evocations. It seemed that I had more opportunities to allow for completing these operations as I drew nearer to the end of this initial series. In my perspective, the work would never cease so long as I had the will and grace to be able to continue. However, the introductory stage of meeting these Spirits was drawing to its conclusion, and I wondered what new perspectives I would have after experiencing them all. Since the initial hypnosis experiment in which my scryer contacted an Angel who instructed us to work together, we had contacted the four Elemental Kings, a plethora of ghosts and departed spirits, the seven Planetary Archangels, my Familiar Spirit Hiram, the four Directional Rulers, and now the first two of the seven Olympic Spirits. Both my scryer and I had undergone changes from the experiences we had had that neither of us could quite put into words. Magic was more real and palpable than either of us could have imagined. Changes both subtle and dynamic were ongoing with each encounter.

Fig. XI-15. ***An alternative Greek Talisman of Phaleg in the language of the Papyri Græcæ Magicæ***

The *Arbatel* says little of the Olympic Spirit of Mars. It simply states that Phaleg or Phalec "ruleth those things which are attributed to Mars," whom it confusingly calls "the Prince of Peace," which seems opposite to the usual function of Mars. However, more conventionally in line with the Martial office, Phaleg also "raiseth to great honours in warlike affaires." I gave up trying to predict what the encounter with the Spirit of Mars would be like and just set my attention on readying the ritual.

Lamens of iron and parchment for the Spirit were constructed on the proper day and hour preceding the ritual, and the chamber was made ready on a favorable Tuesday afternoon to summon the Spirit forth.

Invocation of the Olympic Spirit Phaleg

Fig. XI-16. Section of Circle for Drawing Phaleg into the Crystal

Appearance of the Spirit

SCRYER: I see what looks like a battlement on top of a castle wall, and in the space between two of the battlements I see what looks like a flame. The flame stands alone for a moment, then it appears in the heart of a man with dark copper skin, crowned in fire and holding a spear in his hand. The spear is uniquely styled with a long shaft, with a long spearhead. The man wears an old-looking breastplate which covers his front and back.

The battlement shifts and each tower becomes a warrior that looks similar to the man. They form a phalanx formation, and he is at the front and center. The flame moves from his heart to the tip of his spear and they all advance. Once again, I see the flame up on the battlements.

OPENING QUESTION 1: In the name of the holy and undefiled Spirit, the Father, the begotten Son, and Holy Ghost proceeding from both, what is thy true name?

SPIRIT: «My true name is Phalec *(Phaleg? Difficult to tell if 'g' or 'c')*. It was my genius, my invention; from me is descended the phalanx and I am always at its head. I am the first in aggression at the point of battle and I am the last gatekeeper on the battlements during the final defense.»

OPENING QUESTION 2: What is Thy office?

SPIRIT: «I lend the passion, the anger, the aggression, needed in life on your planet to all living things. I am the directed attention of Sachiel. I am a piece of the spirit of every warrior that has died on your world. On their way to the Father upon death, a piece of their essence lives on in me. I know the horrors of war. I know the feeling of elation of victory. I know the black depths of genocide and massacre as well as the lightened, honored, heights of honorable service and sacrifice for the benefit of others. I contain all these things and am blind to none of it.

«The Archangel Sachiel is the first of the kings. For the warrior to be in balance, he must serve the king first. Only in this way can the fierceness, the rage of the warrior be tempered by the wisdom of rule.»

OPENING QUESTION 3: What are the best and proper times to call you to hold conference with us?

SCRYER: He shows me an image of a group of people around a fire, they look like warriors. I see them turn and walk away from the fires and stand with the fire to their backs and they are looking up at Mars. Jupiter is just visible above and behind Mars. While the men and the women look up at the planets, I see Phaleg standing in the fire behind them and pull the energy from Jupiter through the lens of Mars. He pulls it through their hearts and into his. They all hold up spears and shake them, and chant his name again and again.

Now I am seeing an image of a youth putting on a football uniform on his own before he goes out to play. I see the image of a smith using the bellows to heighten the fire of the smithy and I see the sigil of Phaleg glowing in the coals. I see the power of Phaleg passing from the heat of the fire into the sword that is being made above.

OATH: Wilt thou swear by the holy blood of Jesus Christ that thou art truly the Olympic Spirit of Mars, Phaleg?

SPIRIT: «I swear by the Son who gave his blood for men, the greatest warrior of peace, that I am Phaleg, as I have said.»

QUESTION 5: Great Spirit Phaleg, please explain to us more about your name and title, its meaning, history, and source of origin. Do you have any relationship to Archangel Samael?

SCRYER: I see the image of a young warrior. He looks Sumerian to me, ancient. He is the son of a renowned warrior. He looks up at his father and I see

Fig. XI-17. ***Portrait of Phaleg as beheld in Vision***

that he has tremendous amount of respect and is in awe of his father. The young warrior cares for his father very deeply. A large group of warriors are gathered all around and they look as if they are going into battle to defend a large bridge or river crossing of some kind. The boy appears terrified. It is apparent he's never seen real conflict before; it's all been in training previously. All of them are lined up in a row, many of them; his father is at the front and leads the army that they are with. The boy has been selected as part of the front row of fighters because of his lineage. His name is Phael (Phae-el).

There is a great fight on the bridge, with screaming and dying men, and blood dripping off of the bridge and dripping into the waters into the river. There is a lot of blood. And I see that Phael's father is wounded in his thigh. He falls to one knee and some of his men try to go toward him to pick him up, but they are instantly speared through the chest and die. With great fear and great anger, the young Phael rushes forward, jumps over the men in front of him, climbs over their bodies and spears the attacker who lanced his father in the chest. When the other men see the courage of the son, they rally and drive their enemy back to the other side of the bridge. In the midst of the fighting, the boy is stricken and killed. I see the father weeping, holding his son, as the army passes over the bridge around them. I can see the color fading from the boy's face and the father telling him how proud he is of him.

I see Samael, standing behind the father looking over the shoulder of the father down at the face of the boy, Phael. He says to the boy, «Your father, wounded in his thigh, his blood gave birth to your courage. From the wound he received in his thigh it gives birth to the son, a warrior whose courage will last for many ages of men.» He lifts the spirit of the boy out of the body by his hands and stands him before him. Samael takes a coal, a hot burning coal from his own heart, and calls it «Ehg/Eck» and gives it to Phael who swallows it.

I hear the men lamenting the boy and I see the face of the boy now, in the copper skin man who stands on the top of the battlements with a flame in his heart.

QUESTION 6: What is the history, and source of your sigil? Can you tell us more about its structure and meaning?

PHALEG: «The sigil must be looked at with depth. See it in three dimensions. I, standing atop the battlements, am the flame in the middle. Seen on the battlements, I am at the last of the three gates. Seen at the front of the phalanx, I stand again in the middle, my men by my side. The sigil, when looked at properly, will show you both. The magician must use the mind to see the sigil recede and advance. When this is done my spirit is able to speak and manifest more clearly.»

QUESTION 7: What can you teach us about the magical properties of metals? How can they be used in working with spirits and garnering the potent effects of their correspondences?

PHALEG: «Although you have iron all over the place now in your world, at one point it was very secret metal known to none. Its knowledge was given long ago when the time had come. Iron runs in your blood, it shines in the light of Mars, and it can explode a sun.

«When my spirit is invoked, and the spirit of Samael is invoked in the flame, the essence of us is drawn to the metal like a magnet. For we are akin, we are similar. The raw material forged with strength, will, and discipline. The metals that came before—bronze, tin, copper—all of them shine only when polished by the will and determination of the seekers who carry the iron in their blood. As the King told you, ‹Remember the iron in your blood.› And gold, gold is for Sachiel, the ruler, the king. The order of the cosmos is served only when the might of Sachiel is focused through us. We were not meant to rule, we were meant to serve.»

QUESTION 8: According to the text of *Arbatel*, it is said that the person who possesses his character is raised by him to great honor in military affairs. Can you explain more about this and what it entails and how you accomplish this?

PHALEG: «Honor in military affairs can only be brought about in the long term. Any fool can become a great warrior in the short term. The work of a warrior, the work of those who are generals and kings, colonels, and officers, the work of these men is only seen over the stretch of time and their lives. Those who carry my sign in their hearts know that they are required to defend as well as attack. The terrible might of their will, in order to bring them honor, must serve the king, the plan of the Creator, The Most High.

«As a paradox, I remind the general, I remind the warrior of the color of their lover's hair. I remind them of the glint in the eyes of their son or their daughter or the laugh of their father or grandfather or the lullaby of the mother. The fire of the warrior is tempered like the sword in the waters of the beloved. Without the tempering, it is a fire that could burn the world to ash and leave nothing behind... It is indeed as the fire. Next time...that leaves nothing behind.»

QUESTION 9: Would you be able to grant us even more success at places of business related to military affairs? In what ways can you assist us in martial arts?

PHALEG: «I am able to do these things: To make the hand of the warrior more skilled, more precise, and more wise. I am able to take a fire of currency and lend that fire to the profitableness, the venture of war, the business of war. This can become balanced and unbalanced. In martial arts, I teach the middle point between the tip of the phalanx and the last gate of the battlement, and a way in which your energy, your balance, swings between those two places. When you set my fire as the balance point between the two, your endeavors and your training is blessed, especially when you sacrifice your training to the will of the Creator and make your training a prayer for his glory. It is a blessing that can only be felt and not told.»

QUESTION 10: In what ways can we use your symbol and sigils for magic and calling your office to empower us and others? Can you teach us a method of raising and channeling power and energy when needed?

SCRYER: He shows me a man with a mallet in his hand. He is dressed similarly to Phaleg, yet he is robed, robed over armor. He takes a raw, round, small piece of iron that is wavy, almost thin, and begins to hammer it with the mallet. As he hammers, the iron becomes more and more round and flat, almost bowl-like. As he hammers away at it, he keeps saying the name, 'Phaleg.' When he is done, the man inscribes the sigil onto it. It looks rough and beaten. He takes the round iron sigil and passes it over a fire again and again, and when it is glowing, he presents it to the light of Mars above him. He gives glory to the Father, the Creator, the Most High. He then symbolically lays it at the feet of Samael, and it is done.

QUESTION 11: What are your methods which you can impart to us and teach us for overcoming evil and to achieve magical protection? Are there any enemies who seek to harm us? If so, can you reveal their identity and how we can defeat them?

PHALEG: «When asked of evil, I ask the question in return, search the heart of the asker for what it recognizes as evil: Why does evil wear this mask for you and what does it hide? When the magician confronts the evil behind the mask, then he can bless the sword with this wisdom, this knowing, and this feeling. The evil must first be recognized within so that it becomes an antidote to the evil without. The sword, when viewed like this, carries great power, and none who would attack or assail you can withstand it. Perfect truth is required to see the evil behind the mask, and courage to see the mirror of the hated, in oneself.»

QUESTION 12: What will the effects of this talisman you showed to the scryer have for the owner? How can someone best call upon your power to use it constructively in their life?

SCRYER: I see the image of two curved walls of fire coming together on a straight line. I see the two walls begin to diverge. I see on either side of walls of flame, many people. Their legs are bound across the wall of flame by chains and manacles. Their faces look fearful and angry; they stare loathingly at one another. I see the walls of fire begin to burn and melt these chains. The faces of the people begin to grow less stern and angry, looking more like the face of a calm warrior. They now look unafraid, somehow knowing with a glint in their eyes that the strength of the Father, the Creator runs in their veins. They realize that fear is an illusion from which they are awakening. And I see chains on their hearts breaking and falling away, in that same fire. Not the fire of anger or hatred but the fire of faith.

QUESTION 13: Can your virtue be imparted to a weapon? What rites would you transmit to do so? How will this affect the weapon and the wielder in combat?

PHALEG: «Any weapon can be blessed with my power: a gun, a knife, a hammer, a sword. When Mars is at the height of its orbit above the earth, I am invoked in the circle with a fire burning inside of it. Some part of the weapon, its tip or base, is heated in the fire and made hot. While this is done, the magician focuses his eyes on Mars and speaks my name, Samael's name, and Sachiel's name again and again in that order. The weapon is then taken from the fire and the tip of the heated metal is burnt into the thigh of the magician. This is a reminder that if used aggressively, the power of the weapon shall come back to the wielder; that in harming another, always some harm is done to you. When the burn is made on the thigh, my sigil is inscribed in the air above the weapon and the rite is done.»

QUESTION 14: Could you please give us any pertinent oracles of future wars, one(s) that will have the greatest impact on us?

PHALEG: «There will come a time when another explosion from the cutting of an atom will happen again. It will only be one blast, one explosion. This will initiate a time of great fear, but will become the foundation for ten thousand years of peace. It will be a peace that reigns in hearts and minds of men and women. The physical peace will last only a thousand years. What rages now in the heart of Sumer is the birth of this occurrence.

«And no more will be said.»

QUESTION 15: What are the proper ways for working with and tasking Demons? How can we best utilize their offices without interference or downfall?

PHALEG: «Although I have the power to stay interference, I cannot eliminate downfall. Like the general and the warriors before that I spoke of, the holy intent of the magician is the only thing that is the antidote, the elixir against downfall. The Goetia, the teeming Goetia, can be chastised and herded with my power, but when done without the will of the Creator, the inevitability is downfall. But when in need, when you or others are under attack, my power, the focused power of Samael, under the direction of Sachiel, wielded with the sword and the spontaneous intuition of the magician can eliminate interference. The rite cannot be told, it must spring from the heart in the moment, as a warrior reacts with the body and the mind is as empty as the sky.»

Question 16: Great Spirit Phaleg, we thank thee for your attendance upon us and offering your council and insight. Is there any further wisdom or instructions on how we magicians and others should work with you?

Phaleg: «In return for the gifts I have given you tonight, I give you this task: Focus your magics, your intents, and your will to destroy the barriers between men. With your sword and your discernment and your courageous passion, devote yourself to the destruction of the illusion of separateness among you. Evoke my spirit within you, remembering that it is the focused intent of Sachiel through the instrument of Samael. And remember the image of converging, diverging walls of fire. Certain chains within you can only be broken when you break the chains of others. You are linked and that is the will of God.»

(License to Depart given.)

Afterthoughts on the Phaleg Operation

Operator: I think we got a lot more out of this operation than I was expecting. There is so much information to follow up on that I will have to come back to this operation and break it down into parts to focus on. The remark about dealing with the Goetia closely matches instances of my own spontaneous encounters with rather unruly spirits, demons, and hostile entities. During those times, I used a sword but did not have a memorized prayer or ritual from a magical text. I remember simply bringing up an energy and determination inside and acted purely out of what rose within. What the spirit said made a lot of sense to me and brought up these memories.

It is interesting with the burning of the thigh. It seemed to correlate closely with the rite given by Samael of burning the palm to invoke his presence and office. Very interesting, with some connecting themes of fire, effort, pain, and awareness. Service also seemed to be a huge factor.

Again, this time in the manner of the courage and determination of the warrior. Perhaps the astute and balanced warrior guided by duty and service. It makes sense that the pure aspect of Mars would need to be guided by a higher order or ruler like Jupiter to be directed toward positive end. Otherwise, aggression can become chaotic and unfocused.

The correlation between this spirit Phaleg and Sachiel was surprising to me, one I did not expect and, at first, made me question the validity of the information. I thought it might have had something to do with my personal relation to the Spirits of Jupiter as a directing force to my abilities in martial arts but I'm not sure. The explanation did seem to make sense but it was the first time offices of different planetary authority were brought up with that much emphasis.

SCRYER: What was so interesting about the birth or forming of Phaleg was that he was the one who was most afraid in the beginning. He was the youngest one, had the least amount of experience, and the fact that he overcame that in front of all the veterans made the act legendary. It felt like there was so much power in that. They were all like, 'If he can do it then we can.' He seemed like the morale booster that inspired everyone else around him. The sense I got from the other soldiers was, 'We just witnessed a warrior being born right there!' That was my favorite part of the whole operation, was seeing that moment of triumph unfold.

It seemed to me that the burning of the thigh was like remembering how Phaleg was born or brought into being. It suggests that by undergoing this ritual, the power of that time would come back. Another point that I found fascinating was that anytime Phaleg spoke or showed anything concerning 'the sword,' it was your sword, the one that was blessed by Samael. It seemed like the sword was very powerful and the epitome of what he was trying to convey.

Conducting further research on this operation, I came upon the Greek myth of Semele. She was a mortal woman who was seduced and impregnated by Zeus. He promised to grant her any boon, and she asked that he show himself to her in his full, divine glory. Semele failed to survive beholding the true aspect of the God, and the expectant mother perished. Zeus rescued the fetal Dionysos, however, by sewing him into his own thigh. A few months later, the God Dionysos was born. This leads to Dionysos being called "the Twice-Born."[30] I thought the reference was interesting, since it was the only other lore I found where a God was born out of the thigh of another God. There is quite possibly more significance to this relation of which I am not yet aware.

SCRYER: The sigil is fascinating, how it can come into three dimensions if you look at it a certain way. It can be viewed forward or backward and the flame looks like it's in the front or middle or back. The battlements were the first thing I saw, then the men became the walls and the walls became the men. Absolutely amazing, and it feels like we were allowed a secret look on what that symbol really entailed.

The procedure for fashioning a talisman for this Spirit was fascinating and seemed quite appropriate. Beginning with a raw, round, small piece of iron (which seemed to be almost a Damascus steel from the wavy patterns that were described), the name of Phaleg is chanted over and over with each strike of the hammer as it is forged into a thin, bowl-like shape. It seems that it should be engraved with the sigil of Phaleg during a Tuesday on an hour of Mars while the actual planet is visible in the sky. The talisman is finally consecrated by passing it through a fire, which I would make using woods, plants, and incense sacred to Mars. Finally, the talisman is sanctified by uttering a prayer to glorify God and laying it at the feet of Archangel Samael. When this was described, I envisioned an altar made sacred to the Archangel, perhaps with a statue of the being.

30. The birth of Dionysos is recounted in many ancient sources, including Euripides' *Bacchæ*, Apollodoros' *Bibliotheka*, and the *First Homeric Hymn to Dionysos*.

The Olympic Spirit of Saturn
Aratron

✠ Day and time	On Saturday during hour of Saturn
✠ Name	Aratron; Hebrew ארתרון *(Arathron* or *Aratron)*; Greek Ἀραθρων *(Arathrōn)*
✠ Pronunciation of name (as spoken by the Spirit)	«Ar-ah-throne»
✠ Planet	♄
✠ Materials for lamen	Parchment, lead
✠ Sigil	
✠ Direction for Invocation	North
✠ Incense mixture	Balsam of myrrh, a grain of musk, and ambergris, sulfur, root of mandrake, calamus, bdellium, spikenard, galangal.

Table XI-18. ***Evocatory Correspondences for Aratron***[31]

Fig. XI-19. ***The Talisman of Aratron in the manner of DSIC***

31. Please see the Cautionary Warning Regarding Grimoric Ingredients in Appendix A. —APF

Of Aratron

The timing of this ritual could not have been more appropriate. It was during the darkest part of the year and a couple of my close friends were falling on particular difficult times in their lives. Their difficulties were such that I was in constant contact with one of them, doing my best to assist them out of the depression that was beginning to overtake them due to some ill-fated turn of events. It became apparent that a potent Spirit of Saturn could assist with some of these issues and possibly reveal the root cause of some of the goings on.

Fig. XI-20. ***An alternative Greek Talisman of Aratron in the language of the Papyri Græcæ Magicæ***

There were also continual spiritual visitations to my house and that of my scryer which kept us on our toes. I reviewed our working with Cassiel and determined it was time to make the crystal-handled knife about which both Archangel Cassiel and Gabriel had instructed us. Although this tool would clearly be a potent magical implement, I had not completed the full ritual to consecrate the knife. It seemed to me there were some components still missing and I wanted to confirm the procedure with the Olympic Spirit of Saturn, whom I hoped would provide the final clues.

It is said of Aratron (or, as the name is spelled in some texts, Arathron) in the *Arbatel*:

> *Those things which he doth of his own free will, are,*
> 1. That he can convert any thing into a ſtone in a moment, either animal or plant, retaining the same object to the sight.
> 2. He converteth treasures into coals, and coals into treasure.
> 3. He giveth familiars with a definite power.
> 4. He teacheth *Alchymy*, Magick, and Physick [*i.e.*, medicine].
> 5. He reconcileth the subterranean spirits to men; maketh hairy men.
> 6. He causeth one to be invisible.
> 7. The barren he maketh fruitful, and giveth long life.

I was highly interested in discovering the truth behind the long list of specialties this Spirit had, and to what use they could be put.

Invocation of the Olympic Spirit Aratron

Fig. XI-21. Section of Circle for Drawing Aratron into the Crystal

Appearance of the Spirit

(A very palpable and eerie stillness settles throughout the chamber.)

SCRYER: At first I saw what looked like snow, glittering upon the ground. It was as if I was moving over a land covered in snow. I see I am on top of a hill and there is a man—an old man, with a strong body—and he is looking up in the night sky, up at Saturn. He has a look in his eye that pierces me to my core. He gestures that *I* should look up, and I can see the rings of Saturn are like the blade of a sickle. He asks me how clearly I can see the place around here. It reminds me somewhat of the landscape I saw with the Northern Queen, Egyn. It is very quiet, very still, very cold. The spirit's eyes have a blue fire in the pupils, like a light from within his skull.

OPENING QUESTION 1: In the name of the holy and undefiled Spirit, the Father, the begotten Son, and Holy Ghost, proceeding from both, what is thy true name?

SCRYER: He holds up an hourglass and turns it over. I see the sand beginning to fall to the bottom and he then shows me the sigil in the snow before his feet. It seems to be catching the light of Saturn.

(Voice of the scryer is just barely louder than a whisper but very clear.)

SPIRIT: «I am Arathron. I have been called Kronos, Old Man Time, Reaper, and Horseman in Black.»

OPENING QUESTION 2: What is Thy office?

SCRYER: He takes up some of the snow in his left hand and blows the snow into the air. I see it falling on what looks like a gate. It seems that the gate is

Fig. XI-22. ***Portrait of Aratron as beheld in Vision***

usually invisible but the snow covers it like dust and enables me to make it out. He throws the hourglass into the air and it becomes a scythe that falls into his hands. He takes a bird out from underneath his cloak that looks like a dove or a pigeon and with the scythe he cuts it. I see the blood falling on the snow and with the scythe covered with blood he places the scythe between the gates and opens them. I see a road, a tunnel of light that leads to Saturn at the other end.

SPIRIT: «My office is the opener of the way. My key is the scythe lubricated by the blood of the fallen. I liberate spirit from body. I liberate seed and harvest from cold earth. Time is the song and my dance and the rhythm in which I move. I am the cutting down and frame the mirror of life.»

SCRYER: He tosses the body of the bird through the gates and I see the spirit of the bird fly out of the body that falls lifelessly onto the snow. The spirit flies up through the tunnel to Saturn and I feel, at the end of the tunnel, the presence of the Archangel, of Cassiel.

OPENING QUESTION 3: What are the best and proper times to call you to hold conference with us?

SCRYER: He looks into my eyes; I see the blue fire in his pupils.

SPIRIT: «My time is death. My time is the ending of things. My time is when Saturn is in the sky and midnight chimes. Between midnight and 3:00 AM I walk the Earth. During endings, speak to me; the endings of ambition, endings of life. When snow blankets the earth and all is silent, you may hear my voice. Those who can look into my eyes unafraid before they pass through the gates of death are blessed and whole.»

OATH: Wilt thou swear by the holy blood of Jesus Christ that thou art truly the Olympic Spirit of Saturn, Aratron or Arathron?

ARATHRON: «By the blood and blessed sacrifice of Jesus Christ, who came to me unafraid and suffered the scythes of sin, I am Arathron whom you have called.»

QUESTION 5: Great Olympic Spirit Arathron, please explain to us more about your name and title, its meaning, history, and source of origin. What is your relationship to the Archangel Cassiel?

SCRYER: I see an old man in a cave, lying under a bear skin. I hear voices outside of the cave and see the flicker of a fire nearby. You can really see the presence of death on his skin and his face. I am above him looking down. The old man's hands are fidgeting with the bear skin and always trying to kick and push it off, but there are people around him who keep covering him with it. It is a cold night, as I can see people's breath in the air. There is great fear in the old man's eyes. He knows he is dying and he is very afraid. He looks similar to Arathron, but thinner, frailer. The old man has the same beard, the same long hair as Arathron, but disheveled, frizzled, and dirty.

Now I am looking at Cassiel standing at the entrance to the cave; the fire is behind him. I see the eyes of the man looking at him but no one else around is able to see Cassiel. There is panic in the old man's eyes; I can also see the fire in his body beginning to die. He begins to slowly stop breathing and his eyes stare only at the cave entrance with a look of complete fear.

Now another man comes in the cave from outside. He removes his hood which is also made of skins, and looks down at the old man's face. He turns his face towards his, but the eyes remained fixed on the cave's entrance. The man with the hood looks like a shaman or a healer of some kind. He slaps the old man in the face and says, 'What do you fear?! Do you fear him?' He seems exasperated or frustrated with the old man. The shaman is able to see Cassiel as well. He begins to sing and rattle some sort of group of shells over him. I see the old man begin to relax, but he also begins to fade and stops breathing. He has died.

I see the spirit of the man not wanting to leave the cave. Cassiel changes into what looks like a large black wolf or a dog of some kind. It's an animal that the old man recognizes somehow from his past. Cassiel approaches the man in this form and the man begins to soften and looks relieved to see the animal and runs his hands over its fur and begins to weep. I see the dog lead the old man out of the cave, and inside I hear the people around the body of the man singing. I see the wolf push the man down onto his back and stand on his chest. The dog vomits into his mouth. It somehow seems to fill the man with life again.

ARATHRON: «I am the focused attention of Cassiel. I am a shape shifter; I appear in the form that enables the being to move through the gates on their road back to the Creator. I wear the mask of the familiar, the beloved, the departed in my compassion for those afraid to cross. They call me the ferryman, the reaper, the black horseman. Like Cassiel appeared as the wolf, I appear to those dying to help them to leave. My scythe pries open the gate and allows them to step through.»

QUESTION 6: What is the history and source of your sigil? Can you tell us more about its structure and meaning?

ARATHRON: *(Operator gets exact same message in mind before scryer repeats aloud.)* «Look on the sigil and see the gateway of death and the scythe is the key between them with which I pry them open. Crafted by Cassiel are the gate, and the key, his key, lent to me.»

QUESTION 7: How is it that you can "convert any living organism, plant or animal into stone, and that in a moment of time?" Please explain this process and how it is achieved.

ARATHRON: «When plant and animal is turned to stone, the memory of their life is encoded in the structure of the stone. Stone is the memory keeper, the great recorder. As the spirit is liberated, the body returns to stone. Also, those who cannot reconcile with the past, whether in actions or words, are frozen as stone, they become fixed in their transition from your world to the Creator. There they must remain stuck until reconciliation and epiphany occurs that fractures and explodes the stone to release the spirit. Those epiphanies, that reconciliation with the past are the coins given to me as the ferry man to allow them to cross. Truth is the toll.»

QUESTION 8: According to the text of *Arbatel*, you can also "change coals into treasure and treasure into coals." What does this entail? Please explain more about this and how you accomplish this.

ARATHRON: «Coals are fire, not yet ash. Within the coal, the jewel already exists; the treasure already exists. The fusing of the jewel and the treasure comes near the moment before the coal falls away and becomes dust. For those who have concentrated their life's work into the spirit through charity, bravery, joy, peace, the treasure is liberated from the coal. For those who've come to the gates of death only holding treasure or jewels, having focused and cultivated their life on their proliferation, their beauty, their abundance, and ignored the calling of their spirits, the treasure as they walk through the gates of death is turned back to coal and ash at their feet. I contain this paradox and offer it as the ultimate wisdom of Cassiel to whom every being must bow.»

QUESTION 9: Also, according to the *Arbatel*, you give "familiars and reconcile subterranean spirits to men." What does this entail and how would a magician or person go about securing this benefit of your office?

ARATHRON: «The familiar is a Spirit from below which volunteers to come to the magician when called. This can take the form of an animal, an artifact, or even a song. With my key, I open the gate, between the magician and the familiar who wishes to come. I can reconcile the Spirits of below, of the chthonic earth, with the magician when I am approached with humility and with need. These Spirits from below, when reconciled through me, have the power to break family curses, disease, and misfortune.»

(At this the operator is instantly inspired to petition for assistance for two friends who have fallen on difficult times.)

OPERATOR: If it be by your will and power and right under God to do so, I ask if you could help and please send a helpful Spirit to NN to help him with his current situation, and to our mutual friend OO, who seems to be equally struggling in many ways.

ARATHRON: «In both cases, with my scythe, I may cut the black tendrils that connect to them. They both, however, must purify themselves pointedly and consciously with whatever ceremony or ritual of their choosing. But they must understand that the cutting away and the reconciliation and purification cannot change the mind. They must meditate and search within themselves for what they are doing that calls these things to them. Without this last step, my fix is a temporary one only.»

OPERATOR: This seems to coincide with the instructions Hiram dictated to me the evening before.

QUESTION 10: In what ways can we use your symbol, and sigils for magic and calling your office to empower us and others?

ARATHRON: «I am present at the time of death. Feel me in the room at the time of death and the hours and days and months leading to death. When there is fear, I recall my own fear in the cave. Whisper my name and I will come. Invoke me and the sacred, holy, name of Cassiel. Remember the blood of the Savior on the cross and the Father, who shall ultimately receive them. I am but the opener of the gate and the way. Tell me of their life: their likes, their dislikes, what brings them comfort. Review their life with me in prayer and in this way, I will ease their transition and my prying open of the gates will be a gentle one.»

QUESTION 11: In our dealings with Archangel Cassiel, the crafting of a crystal and silver blade is mentioned for «being excellent in protection and severing of attack and retribution,» as well as cutting the cord with any spirit. Besides the materials, and the sigils inscribed thereon, I ask you for further clarification of the exact ritual for its consecration and making. So far, the information I have is that it is to be consecrated on the dark of the Moon, at a crossroads, quite possibly on or near the winter solstice. Cassiel showed a vision of a man in black, with black skin, whispering the name of Cassiel to the blade three times and then fades. Can you clarify for us if this is pertinent to the construction of the blade? Does a black man in black clothes need to make it? After this, a man is seen waiting on the eastern road (what does this entail?), silent, and picks up the blade after a period of time in total silence, then leaves down the eastern road. Please explain more about this and how a magician would perform this ritual properly in detail.

ARATHRON: «What was shown to you is exact. Perhaps this detail will help: On its consecration, the face of the magician is painted in black. And when going to the crossroads and coming away from the crossroads at that time, the magician maintains complete silence, except from the three utterances of the name of Cassiel. The power, the ceremony, is in the silence. In painting the face black, the conscious remembrance should be of the mortality of the magician. In so doing, remember the item is used on loan for the service of others. If not used in service, the scythe can turn on the magician and destroy him.»

QUESTION 12: Great Spirit, is there anything you can teach us, as it is aid of your office, of the arts of alchemy, magic, and medicine?

ARATHRON: «In alchemy, magic, and medicine, there is the conscious ending of one state to create another. All of these acts are acts of sacrifices and transmutation. The herb dies to become the oil. Cancer dies to become flesh. Old energies die to be transmuted into new. With each of these acts, the gateway between life and death is opened and shut. And in each of these acts, a commitment is made to accept what comes about in the new state.»

QUESTION 13: Do you have a process for Spirit communication and necromancy that would be most useful for magicians and those agreeable to utilizing your office?

ARATHRON: «The dirt of the oldest grave in a graveyard, the first grave in a graveyard, carries great power. In that soil, I am always present. This dirt can be used in necromancy and the calling forth of spirits departed. Collected between my hours of twelve and three is the time to do this. Leave a smooth stone of obsidian behind as a gift and pour a libation. Light a single candle near the grave and stand within a protected circle that you carve in the earth.

«When using the dirt before the operation of necromancy, some of the dirt is rubbed on the forehead in the name of Jesus Christ in the form of the cross. When the name of Cassiel and my name, Arathron, are spoken, call on us and we will aid you in speaking with the dead. But you must first make an oath to us that if you are called after you have passed through the gate, that you too will come to speak, to be torn from the otherworld, and recalled here to serve. Do • not • make • this • commitment • lightly.»

QUESTION 14: I wish for you to impart and confer to us the secret of invisibility. How may we accomplish this?

ARATHRON: «I can confer invisibility, but its feat is not lightly won. The magician must come to a place where he can still and eliminate the internal conflict within, to cultivate a feeling of total peace. The magician must be able to see through his own body, with his mind's eye, to eliminate himself from where he stands. And as he walks or runs or stays still, he must maintain the feeling of peace. There can be no inner conflict, no thought, and no fear. In this state, my cloak will be laid over you and you shall not be seen. Call to me in your meditations and your prayers to achieve this state of peace, for this is also the state that, in the end, will help you move through the gates on your final faring.»

QUESTION 15: How is it that you can make the barren fruitful? How would we petition or invoke you for this? It also says you can confer on us long life. We ask your blessing on this and also wish to inquire how this is done and how others may gain this blessing.

ARATHRON: «I cannot yet divulge this secret of long life. I can promise this: To the magician who invokes me and calls to me and does so in the humble service of the Father and Cassiel, I will reveal this secret to their heart. But its mystery cannot be written, only revealed. The barren can be made fruitful by surrender, surrendering to the will of God.»

QUESTION 16: Is there any relationship between you and the Spirit King known as Ariton, Elemental or Demon King of the North? Are you the same entity, or just similar in name?

ARATHRON: «We are not the same. But for those who seek the root of our names, a mystery will be revealed and further knowledge of our shared origin.»

OPERATOR: Are you able to explain any more about this being, Ariton?

SCRYER: I just see him shaking his head 'no.'

OPERATOR: Great Spirit and Angel Arathron, Olympic Spirit of Saturn under Cassiel the mighty and great Archangel, before we bid you hail and farewell, are there any final words of wisdom, insight, or instruction that you would impart to us to better understand and utilize the strengths and powers of your office?

ARATHRON: «Remember that the root of disease, suffering, and ultimately death itself germinates and originates in spirit first. Only its effects are seen in your world. It is this connection to the root that my scythe can sever and the scythe of Cassiel can sever but only in accordance with the will of the Creator. Take care of the spirit first and the body and the fortunes of the magician will follow. The skull and the seed are one.»

OPERATOR: Thank you for your council and wisdom and attendance upon us, mighty Spirit.

(Closing and License to Depart given.)

Afterthoughts on the Aratron Operation

OPERATOR: The exact same message of what the sigil truly represented popped into my head right before you repeated it. This working was more involved for me and felt like a few things were happening to me during the whole operation. I was really absorbed in everything that was going on, I could feel, sense each word, and see what was going on in my head. Perhaps since Cassiel was my first working I am even closer to this spirit? There was a shifting of light and dark, like a density in the air enveloped the altar space and holy table and pedestal. There was also this weird spiky light anomaly...really bright but deep somehow. The light would brighten and darken with density depending on what was occurring during the evocation.

SCRYER: Something that really stood out for me was the mention that 'the light at the end of the tunnel' was Saturn's light, I found that very interesting for some reason. The Spirit's voice was very calm, almost soothing, but strong. His presence was amazing, not fearful but actually calming. I feel the presence of the Spirit is in my body still.

There was a funny, almost ridiculous part during the operation when you were asking about how to help our friends. You mentioned that Hiram concurred with what Arathron said regarding what was needed, and Hiram and Arathron walked past each other and actually 'gave each other five.' I seriously saw this and I couldn't believe it. I almost lost all my focus since I wanted to start laughing.

OPERATOR: Ha! I'm almost considering not adding this to our records, but that is hilarious. Hiram does come out with a humorous remark now and then, so I wouldn't put it past him, but that is funny coming from perhaps the most somber of the Planetary Spirits. I think Hiram is always happy when I remember what he tells me.

SCRYER: When the Spirit talked about the coals and treasures, it reminded me of a story I recently read on the internet where the billionaires are paying large sums of money to defeat mortality. They are trying to get the science to live forever and I wondered if these words meant something like that.

OPERATOR: I really like how perfect the choice was for this Spirit...human spirit becoming an ascendent Olympic Spirit...one who was so fearful of death, one who understands that fear and can ease it for others who are passing. It makes me wonder if many of the family members and others that people see near death are actually Arathron. This presents some very interesting possibilities to consider.

The response on necromancy from the Spirit seemed intense and a very serious matter. This is definitely not an oath to be taken lightly. I see such an undertaking as suitable for a person born for necromancy and specifically geared toward that work. I'm not sure if I'd care to undergo that binding contract myself. I'm satisfied with having Hiram to help me with necromancy and talking to spirits of the dead.

SCRYER: Yes, that makes a lot of sense; there is some give and take there, not just some snobby necromancer calling spirits to "do my bidding." Recognizing that you would get ripped from the otherworld makes you consider what you are doing a bit more seriously.

The Knife of Cassiel ✢ Part 3

After I felt I had come to terms with the implications of what the weapon of Cassiel was capable of, I decided to move forward with consecrating the crystal knife. The idea of possessing a magical Instrument of such devastating power was unnerving but also too much to resist. I also understood that the blade, once empowered, would be best left alone unless needed in the utmost dire circumstances. Taking your own fate as well as the fate of a spiritual creature in your hands is not something to be done lightly. After so many encounters, I was convinced of the interdependence between spiritual beings and human magical abilities. My work as a magician relied upon them and severing their ties from anyone or anything would be a severe consideration.

The Process for Crafting the Knife of Cassiel

I had purchased the Mughal crystal-handled knife I had found online. The hilt was carved from transparent crystal into a ram's head. I had mounted three pearls in silver settings on each side. I had also sharpened the Persian-style Damascus blade. Having planned the procedure for consecrating the knife, and having formulated an exact idea of how it should look when it was engraved with the proper sigils, I selected the date to create what would possibly be one of the most potent magical weapons in existence. I finally had enough information about how it was to be empowered, with only a few remaining questions that I would attempt to clarify with the Spirit Hiram. I was certain that it needed to occur on the dark of the Moon nearest the winter solstice on a Saturday at night, preferably at 3:33 AM. I had found the perfect location: a rarely travelled dirt crossroads up in the mountains, where all four roads extended off in the distance, disappearing out of view.

The Preliminary Consecration of the Knife

Items used:

- ✠ Holy water
- ✠ Black silk cloth, 1 square yard
- ✠ Blessed Cassiel incense
- ✠ Tripod censer
- ✠ Engraving tool

Before the day came when I would be heading out in the dead of night, it seemed wise to bless and dedicate the knife ahead of time. I began with a prayer of invocation and consecration adapted from the *Key of Solomon*:

I conjure thee, crystal-handled Knife of Cassiel, by God the Father Almighty, by the Virtue of the Heavens, of the Stars, and of the Angels who preside over them; by the virtue of stones, herbs, and animals; by the virtue of hail, snow, and wind; that thou receivest such virtue that thou mayest obtain without deceit the end which I desire in all things where I shall use thee; through God the Creator of the Ages, and Emperor of the Angels. Amen.[32]

32. Mathers and Solomon, *The Key of Solomon the King: Clavicula Salomonis* (London: George Redway, 1889), Book Two, Chapter XIX, "Concerning the Needle and Other Iron Instruments." —APF

I sprinkled the knife with holy water and censed it with the incense mixture I used to evoke Archangel Cassiel. After this, I took my engraving tool and deeply etched the sigils of Cassiel and the symbols of Saturn on both sides of the blade. During the engraving, I spoke directly to the blade and said a prayer to the Archangel of Saturn for him to empower this knife for its intended purpose and that it be suitable and well received to inherit the properties described by him during the last invocation. Already, I could sense the potency of the knife coming into being.

Afterward I chanted:

DANI, LUMECH, AGALMATUROD, GEDIEL, PANI, CANELOAS, MEROD, LAMIDOC, BALDOC, ANERETON, METRATON, TUANCIA, COMPENDON, LAMEDON, CEDRION, ON, MYTRION, ANTON, SYON, SPISSON, LUPRATON, GION, GIMON, GERSON, AGLA, AGLAY, AGLAOD, AGLADIAMERON, Angels most holy, be present for a guard unto this instrument.[33]

I then recited this invocation from the *Veritable Clavicles of Solomon*:

O Lord God Almighty, Who hath created all things from nothing, mayest Thou despise not Thy servant, Frater Ashen Chassan, who prayeth humbly unto Thee that it please Thee to bless, purify, and sanctify this Implement so that it may be worthy and powerful to fulfill my operations; and bid Thy holy Angels that they shall assist my operations. O Lord, remember my father, on whom Thou bestowed the knowledge of all things;[34] *make it so that the virtue of his precepts may cause this Implement to be pure, that it may be acceptable unto Thee, through Thy Name, which is the holy Tetragrammaton. Amen.*[35]

---

33. *Ibid.* —APF

34. The *Clavicles* here has the magus (who is nevertheless directed to insert his own name, indicated by the usual *N.N.*, into the invocation) identify so fully with King Solomon that he refers to King David as "my father." —APF

35. Translated by Adam P. Forrest from the Latin "Exorcism of the Stiletto" in *Les Véritables Clavicules de Salomon, traduites de l'Hebreux en langue Latine par le Rabin Abognazar* (British Library Lansdowne MS 1203). Lansdowne 1203 provides the original Latin of the prayer along with a French translation. The interested student may find Joseph H. Peterson's edition of much of the Abognazar *Clavicles* along with his translation from the French online at http://www.esotericarchives.com/solomon/l1203.htm. —APF

Fig. XI-23. The Crystal Knife of Cassiel

After invoking this blessing and passing the knife through the incense a final time, I wrapped it in black silk until the night of the operation.

When the evening of the ritual arrived, I had already been preparing several hours ahead of time. Besides fasting and other abstenances as per the dictates of most magical rituals, I had taken a vow of silence that I was keeping for the entirety of the 24-hour period leading up to the ritual. This wasn't easy considering my family situation, and I nearly slipped a number of times. The intensity of the energy built with each passing silent hour, as I reviewed the outline for the nocturnal ritual I had planned based on the instructions of two Angels and an Olympic Spirit.

The magician was required to be entirely black for this working. I first dressed in layers of black clothing. I also had a black, hooded cloak that I had made out of heavy material specifically for this operation, and black gloves, which I stowed in a bag.

I also placed the engraved and dedicated crystal knife in the bag with the cloak and gloves; it was not given a sheath and was still wrapped in a yard of black silk. Lastly, I brought a candlelit "blacklight" lantern that would allow just enough light but not ruin the nature of the operation. I thought perhaps the effect might even aid it in a way. The lantern was premade, but the glass had been painted to give it the blacklight effect.

A couple of hours before 3:00 AM, I went into the bathroom and silently painted my face black from hairline to neck. I even rubbed the paint deeply into my hair, causing it to be black and slicked back. I gathered my things as quickly and as silently as I could and loaded them into the car.

I tried to keep my mind clear of distracting thoughts as I drove up into the mountains. Worries and doubts crept up in my mind with a measure of caution, but I swept them aside as I made my way to the dirt road that I would walk up to reach the crossroads. Several times I had to catch myself to preserve my vow of silence, as I had a habit of talking to myself when alone and preparing for an operation, and it took conscious effort to keep my thoughts from being verbalized.

Where I live, the winters are long and usually very, very cold. At around 3 AM it's even colder. If ever there was a time that represented the still cold and ineffable presence of death, it was during that time. Perhaps more so now than ever, considering the ritual I was going to do in complete silence. When I arrived, I remember the cold hitting me and nearly taking my breath away as I opened the door to my vehicle and stepped outside. There was no wind, no Moon, no sound. I grabbed my large cloak, wrapped it firmly around me, and put the hood up. Next I pulled the lantern from the bag, and it took me several long minutes to finally light the black candle within it. Then I took up the silk-wrapped knife, and headed up the road as silently as I could.

To say that the dirt road and surrounding mountain forest was eerie would be an extremely understated description of my perception of it. The lantern did little to light the way and simply enhanced the depths of the shadows. Lingering patches of snow cast strange glows against the pines that pierced a clear night sky. It took everything I had to keep my mind focused on putting one foot in front of the other. It seemed to be taking forever to reach the crossroads. I didn't recall it feeling so far away when I had been there last. The silence of the forest and lack of wind did nothing to put my nerves at ease, but I continued to make my way up the dirt road to the destination I could not reach soon enough.

When I finally set foot on the intersection of the roads that split almost equally in four directions, I felt a sudden dizziness rush through me that caused me to pause for several moments. The feeling eventually subsided, but it felt like I had stepped into one of my Spirit visions rather than onto a physical road.

I knelt down, removed the crystal knife from the black sheet of silk, and observed it for a moment. The crystal handle seemed to glow in my hands as I turned it over, but the blade was nearly invisible. I had not noticed the stark polarity of the weapon before, but it became quite apparent as I stared at it in starlight and lantern light.

I then spent a moment examining the area of the crossroads, and near the edge of the northern road I spotted a mound of snow which was just a few feet in length and half that in width. Leaving the lantern on the eastern part of the road, I approached the northern part of the crossroads with the knife in hand. Everything was perfectly still and silent. The trees were barely visible past a few dead grasses and shrubs. I knelt down next to the pile of snow. Taking the knife in both hands, I slowly and ceremonially embedded it in the snow, hoping as I did that I would not jab the tip into the frozen earth below. The knife pierced the frosted-over snow and broke the deep silence of the night with its crunching sound. I continued to press down until the knife was buried nearly to the end of the handle.

I had been waiting for this moment for hours, and now I released the power accumulated during my wordless day as I finally broke my silence to whisper the name of the Archangel of Saturn three times to the knife.

"Cassiel."

I paused half a minute between each repetition, taking my time to patiently enunciate the name.

"Cassiel."

The sound of my own voice was startling after the long, self-imposed silence. Even in a whisper it seemed loud, as if the entire world could hear.

"Cassiel."

After the third repetition, I waited for a moment.

Nothing occurred and the night was once again completely silent.

I nearly forget that this ritual was based on Saturnine patience, as the breaking of my silence had made me anxious to accomplish the rest of the ritual. However, remembering the nature of the ceremony, I rose and silently walked toward the easternmost section of the crossroads next to my lantern. There I sat down, tucking the black cloak beneath me, and remained still. Before I had left my house, Hiram had reminded me that I needed to remain patient and let go of expectation and any sense of urgency, since the very nature of the Spirits of Saturn was insurmountable patience. He seemed assured that the knife would be consecrated as the Archangel had foretold, and that I required no further advice on how to complete it successfully.

However, as the minutes wore on and I sat in the cold silence, I wondered just how much that was true. I didn't plan to be out till the Sun rose and knew I would be getting seriously chilled if I sat too much longer. I could feel the black paint on my face becoming cold and hard, beginning to crack in places. Pushing doubts and distracting thoughts aside, I told myself that now would be a good time to embody the silence that was the overall theme of the magical operation. I breathed deeply and evenly and closed my eyes. I began the meditative practice I did on a daily basis to silence my thoughts and center my awareness. One of the last lingering thoughts before I found my meditative state was that the silence, the operation, falling asleep, and dying all seemed to have common elements.

In the midst of my practice I lost track of time, and even of the reason for being out in the dead of night in the freezing cold. Even the discomfort of the pressing cold faded as I remained completely still in the dark folds of my cloak and hood. I might have been meditating for minutes or an hour when a sudden wind rushed through the trees, breaking the silence and whipping my cloak violently around me. It was so fierce and sudden that I didn't have time to even jump, but instead kept frozen in place. The winter wind ripped through the trees for a few seconds and then suddenly died just as quickly as it had begun. The event left me a bit wide-eyed, but I knew that the ritual had been successfully completed and it was time to retrieve the knife.

I stood slowly, feeling rather shaken from having been ripped from my meditative state, and pulled my cloak closer and the hood further down. I walked back to the center of the crossroads where the patch of snow at the northern edge of the intersection held the knife. Pausing briefly over where the knife rested, I used my intuition to assure myself that the ceremony was complete. With a bit of effort, I released the knife from the snow and held it in front of my face. As before, an odd gleam came from the otherwise dark weapon. I had an unsettling sensation in the pit of my stomach that what I held was a beacon to death itself. I simply knew the knife was now a magical implement of perhaps the most severe power I could ever comprehend.

With a spontaneous bow toward the north, the direction I had faced to speak with the Archangel and the Olympic Angel, I turned in silence, retrieved the lantern, and wrapped the Knife of Cassiel in its black silk once again. Then I walked away down the eastern dirt road by which I had come to the crossroads.

The return trip was uneventful and I found that I remained silent the entire drive back, although my vow had ceased at the climax of the ceremony. I was tempted to look over the knife just consecrated through the ritual dictated by Cassiel, but resisted the urge. If the weapon was needed, I would know where to find it. A large part of me hoped that—even with all the effort to make and consecrate it—I would never have to use it.

The Use or Ritual for Severing a Spirit's Power, Influence, and Office

Items needed:

- An urn of ash
- Consecrated Knife of Cassiel

At home after the ritual, during the couple of hours or so before dawn, I had an intense dream.

Somehow I knew it was Cassiel's hour of 3:33 AM as it was pitch black and still. I was watching a dark-robed figure in a mask creating a magic circle by pouring ashes from a dark urn. It was a relatively small circle that was made around another person who was standing in the center, rocking back and forth, apparently upset. When the figure finished making the ring of ashes, he circled around behind the distressed man, who had his face buried in his hands. The robed magician placed a hand on the back of the man's head and appeared to be saying a prayer or blessing. Suddenly the magician produced a knife, and I remember thinking for a second that I was having a nightmare and that the person in the circle was about to be killed.

Instead, in a loud, harsh whisper, the magician said, "Cassiel, cut the cord, remove the harmful Spirit!" He then made a sweeping motion behind the person with the weapon, which I now saw was a crystal-handled knife. He made a slash in the air behind the man and then down to slash a line in the earth within the circle. He then moved around the outside of the circle to the person's left and did the same thing, cutting an angled line in the earth. This was done a final time, and when he finished, I could see that inside the circle he had cut a triangle in which the person was now standing. The magician stabbed the Knife of Cassiel at the point of the triangle in front of the person, and proclaimed that the Spirit was now released and that the person should step from the circle.

The man, who looked like he had just woken from a bad dream, stepped out and looked around sort of bewildered. The magician quickly engraved another circle in the earth and told him to sit within it. Turning his back to the person, who simply sat and remained still, the magician knelt before the first circle with the triangle and stabbed the Knife of Cassiel into it once more. He began intoning a prayer of invocation that I could not hear or could not remember clearly after waking. What I do remember was hearing Cassiel's name and something about the spirit being blessed but not being allowed to return. After sitting silently for a time, the magician rose and walked around that circle a last time, rubbing it out as he went. When he returned to where he had been sitting, he retrieved the knife, placing it back within his robes.

I awoke then and quickly wrote down everything I could remember, as I knew this was an important teaching regarding the proper usage of the Knife of Cassiel. The contents of the dream were clear and showed how the knife would be used in times of need. I recalled that the black-hilted knife featured in various manuscripts of the *Key of Solomon* is used to "make the Circle, wherewith to strike terror and fear into the Spirits."[36] However, Cassiel had not initially mentioned using his crystal-handled knife to cast a circle, nor explained to my scryer or me how the weapon was to be used to cut "the cord" and any influence or attachment from Spirits, while visiting retribution on them. Until now.

36. Mathers and Solomon, *The Key of Solomon the King: Clavicula Salomonis* (London: George Redway, 1889), Book Two, Chapter VIII, "Of the Knife, Sword, Sickle, Poniard, Dagger, Lance, Wand, Staff, and Other Instruments of Magical Art." —APF

The Olympic Spirit of Sol
Och

✠ Day and time	On Sunday during hour of Sun
✠ Name	Och; Hebrew אוח *(Och)*; Greek Ὦχ *(Ōch)*
✠ Pronunciation of name (as spoken by the Spirit)	«Oh-cht»
✠ Planet	☉
✠ Materials for lamen	Parchment, gold
✠ Sigil	[sigil]
✠ Direction for Invocation	South
✠ Incense mixture	Frankincense, red sandalwood, saffron, amber, musk, aloes wood, balm wood, laurel seeds, benzoin, storax, labdanum, galbanum.

Table XI-24. ***Evocatory Correspondences for Och***[37]

Fig. XI-25. ***The Talisman of Och in the manner of DSIC***

37. Please see the Cautionary Warning Regarding Grimoric Ingredients in Appendix A. —APF

Of Och

The recent magical activities had left me hoping that I would not have to be battling any demons or dark entities, which seemed to have been hinted at as the theme for my winter. Luckily, no imagined battle occurred, and I was able to continue with my work and plan out the next evocation of an Olympic Spirit. The completion of the Crystal Knife of Cassiel left me yearning for a much-needed return to the light and balancing forces of the Sun. As the season crept toward spring, I decided it was time to evoke the Solar Olympic Spirit and discover what wisdom and treasures awaited in that realm.

***Fig. XI-26.** An alternative Greek Talisman of Och in the language of the Papyri Græcæ Magicæ*

The *Arbatel* describes the Solar Spirit Och like this:

> *Och* governeth solar things; he giveth 600 yeares, with perfect health; he bestoweth great wisdom, giveth the most excellent Spirits, teacheth perfect Medicines: he converteth all things into most pure gold and precious stones: he giveth gold, and a purse springing with gold. He that is dignified with his Character, he maketh him to be worshipped as a Deity, by the Kings of the whole world.[38]

Overall, this Spirit seemed agreeable and quite favorable to contact. I chose a suitable Sunday during the first rising hour of the Sun, and coordinated with my scryer to meet me before the Sun rose.

38. Turner and Arbatel, *op. cit.*, Aphorism 17. —APF

Invocation of the Olympic Spirit Och

Fig. XI-27. Section of Circle for Drawing Och into the Crystal

Appearance of the Spirit

SCRYER: I see what looks like a temple with two pillars in the front. One is black, the other is white. The black pillar is on the left and the white is on the right side. Between them I see the Sun; the whole place is bathed in golden light. The presence is really immense, but calm. The Sun stands almost as if behind a fog or a mist between the pillars. In brief flashes, it looks like an eye. Most of the time it is a bright golden light that is mercifully dimmed by the mist.

OPENING QUESTION 1: In the name of the holy and undefiled Spirit, the Father, the begotten Son, and Holy Ghost proceeding from both, what is thy true name?

SCRYER: I hear the name Och, and it vibrates everything.

OPENING QUESTION 2: What is Thy office?

SPIRIT: «I am the station of pure giving. The revolving, turning wheel of Michael's glory. I am the descent and mingling of the three pillars: The Father, the Holy Ghost, who is Sophia, and the Son. I am the tunnel through which the original fire, given by the Father, wielded by Michael, born of the Father, the Mother, and manifest in the Son, is channeled to your world.»

OPENING QUESTION 3: What are the best and proper times to call you to hold conference with us?

Fig. XI-28. ***Portrait of Och as beheld in Vision***

SCRYER: I see an image of the Sun at the height of the sky. I then see an image of midnight, as if the Sun has dropped to the exact opposite side of the earth.

SPIRIT: «For workings of prosperity, increase, growth, the implements of fire used in ceremony will be consecrated under that time. Noon.

«For times of destruction, banishment, the causing of pain, the implements of fire in the ceremony will be consecrated at that time, with the invoker seeing me though I am absent below the earth. These are the earthly times that correspond to the black and white pillars, through which I am born, and always stand upheld in-between.»

OATH: Wilt thou swear by the holy blood of Jesus Christ that thou art truly the Olympic spirit of the Sun, Och?

SPIRIT: «I swear by the Father, the Mother, and the Son, on whom I am wholly dependent for my existence. Whose grace, strength and mercy has guided me to be more than I once was.»

QUESTION 5: Great Spirit Och, please explain to us more about your name and title, its meaning, history, and source of origin? What is your relationship to the Archangel Michael?

SCRYER: I see a home. I see a man standing and two other people are under a table. The people are a mother a father, and a young boy. The mother and the boy are hidden underneath a table covered with a blanket. I hear the sounds of screaming and fire and bloodshed outside. There is a tremendous feeling of terror in the room. All the man has, the father, is a hammer in his hand, a mallet. There is some sort of massacre going on outside. There is a hearth fire burning in the middle of the room and suddenly there is a light that comes from the fire. It is an intense, brilliant light. The man drops his hammer and is so stunned that he hides beneath the blanket with his wife and his son.

Suddenly all the noise outside stops and Archangel Michael pulls the blanket off of the table and stands in front of the frightened family. «Come forth, children,» he says, «and do not be afraid, for the Lord thy God is with you.» The three members of the family come forth from underneath the table holding one another's hands. Their legs are weak; they fall to their knees, and tears fill their eyes.

«Do you wish to save your people?» Michael asks them. Even the dust in the air is still, no longer moving. The fire in the hearth looks frozen in time.

The boy speaks first and says, "Yes, we do."

«Then stand before me,» Michael says. The three of them rise together to stand before Michael. Michael says unto the family, «If you are to save your people, then the three of you must become one in my heart, and together we will step forth with the might of the Creator and turn your enemies to dust... to which all men must go and become. Will you sacrifice your individual being to become one, that this deed may be done?» Michael asks.

"Yes, we will," the father says.

«Then embrace one another,» says Michael. I see the son, mother, and father all holding one another.

«Only when you embrace one another may I embrace you,» Michael says. He wraps his arms and massive wings around the three of them, and there is a sudden shining light so brilliant that it fills the room. The sound from outside suddenly returns; the sounds of screaming, fighting, are heard, and the fire is moving again.

Filled with light, Michael goes towards the door and steps out into the village. An intense light comes from his body and all the people—those who are killing, those who are being killed—stop. They turn toward the light and kneel before him.

OCH: «I, Och, am the being of the Father, The Mother, and the Son merged and born in that moment.»

QUESTION 6: In our dealings with Archangel Samael and in the consecration of place where the spirit of the two boys were to be liberated, the Archangel mentioned the use of «the Oil of Archangel Michael.» Could you please give us the recipe and process for making the Oil of Archangel Michael?

SCRYER: I see the pressing of olives. Olive oil enclosed in a brass container inscribed with the sigil of Och and Michael under the noon Sun. Twelve petals of sunflower are placed inside, along with three nodules of frankincense and a small fleck of gold. It looks like the wing of an insect is also added, that is first held up to the Sun. The preparer first looks at the Sun briefly through the transparent wing, then places it into the container. The container is brought to a high place and a circle is inscribed around the container.

Leaving his or her head and torso uncovered, the invoker sits beneath the Sun to be burned, and sings softly the name of Michael 77 times. They then sit with the container closed, letting the vessel heat in the Sun. Och explains that the invoker, like Christ, takes on the sins and ignorance of the world and suffers for them, to lend that power to the oil in front of them. For one hour of the Sun is this made and done.

QUESTION 7: Is there any further instruction for the proper use and purpose of this powerful holy oil besides the ones mentioned by the Archangel?

OCH: «The oil can be used to protect those who leave for war. For those charged with the defense of the home. It can be used to anoint the sword that scourges the Demon, the Wraith, or the Spirit that comes against you and yours.»

QUESTION 8: According to the text of *Arbatel*, it is said that you prolong life to "600 years, with perfect health." We have spoken to many of the other Olympic Spirits who claim this ability in different hundreds of years. Although this seems a grace bestowed by few, I am interested in the variety of years and meaning behind these passages. Please explain more about this and how you accomplish this.

OCH: «This can and has been done, and will be done again. The men and women picked for this are picked by the hand of the Creator. They become like me, a light that shines in the world. Their locations are kept secret, but their existence is necessary to maintain the harmony and balance of life. They can communicate the love, grace, and strength of the Creator through their presence and their being. I can imbue them with long life, but I am not the one who makes the choice. That is done by the Creator alone. And in that process, Michael is the messenger and I am the hand that anoints.»

QUESTION 9: Also according to the *Arbatel* you are said to impart great wisdom. I ask what great wisdom can you impart to us at this time, as well as for those who will read of your words?

OCH: «There is a Sun that burns in your heart. It is that unique fire of the Creator which you alone can carry and wield. To connect that fire back through the Sun (Son?) and the heart of the Creator is to remake and recreate the world. To all of you stands open a hallway of grace, mercy, love, and strength, but you must use the fire of your will to walk through it, to keep it open. Devotion is the way to keep the channel between you and the Creator clear, free, and open. Devotion is the ultimate tool, like a broom that sweeps away the dust of fear, doubt, rage, and hatred. It is with devotion that these things are cleared away. Know that when you behold the light, even the far-away light of the Creator, the flame in your heart leaps and grows in joy. Wisdom is the child of devotion. Wisdom is the child of love. Wisdom is the child of peace, tempered with strength.»

QUESTION 10: Great Solar Spirit, in what ways can we use your symbol and sigils for magic and calling your office to empower us and others?

OCH: «Like the black and white pillars, I can be wielded for benefit and for harm. I am the giver, the tunnel of the light and fire of creation, the candles, the charcoals of incense, as the light in your eyes and in your heart has its ultimate source in me; given by Michael, born by the mother and the father. The incense holder, the brazier, can be inscribed with my sigil. A small amount of the oil of Michael can be placed on the candles when the need is correct. In this, the invoker must use their discernment. I am the enlivener: a revitalizer, a fire maker, a fire wielder. Through the will of men and women, they learn what creates with my fire and what destroys with my fire. You may warm yourselves in this fire or you may burn yourself in this fire. If you need the extra vital force for your workings, I can give this to you when asked with humility, with respect, and with the acknowledgment that you speak only the will of the Creator.»

OPERATOR: Earlier you spoke of the Mother as Sophia. Could you impart to us the relevance or truth behind any of the Gnostic teachings? Is there any truth to the beings referred to as Archons, Æons, the Demiurge? The philosophy and lore behind the Gnostic scriptures are interesting to me, and I wish to know if there is any validity or truth to them.

OCH: «In the beginning of the church of Peter, there was the sacrifice of Sophia in the name of the Lord. As men do, their hearts craved power. But since those times the faith of that church has been half a being. Priests cannot take wives and so naturally their love falls towards the Child, the Son. The Demiurge under the first dove, Sophia, the light warm heart of the Mother channeled through Mary cradling her son in her lap. The Archons and the Æons whose Spirits still move through the world, reminding men and women of their ultimate being and beginning, are all true. The inner knowing is what can balance the outer forms of power, which are necessary as well. They are the two pillars through which I look between. Sophia, the Holy Ghost, the Presence, the close abiding Presence of the Mother. Without her, the church will continue to flounder, stumble, and can ultimately die. The Demiurge is the initial kiss of creation. The desire to go forth to know the Creator. The blessing is unparalleled, and is the spark that moves creation forward to its ultimate return.»

QUESTION 11: Great Solar Spirit, what "most excellent" familiar Spirits are you able to give? It is also said of you that "he... giveth the most excellent Spirits, teacheth perfect Medicines: he converteth all things into most pure gold and precious stones." Please tell us more about how you can accomplish this.

OCH: «The feat of turning metals into precious metals and stones into gems can be done physically. This is done when the need is great and again by the will of the Creator. Men's obsession with wealth, though originally well intentioned has brought many to grief and despair. It is a power wielded by the Creator and must be recognized as such. It is the realm of the spirit that these things are most powerfully done. Lead to gold, stone to diamond. What is often undervalued in this world becomes, when stepping through the threshold, treasure, real treasure. Humility becomes joy. Compassion becomes the diamonds of your spiritual crown. Hope, a necklace of gold that adorns your breast. This is the ultimate transmutation of which this mystery speaks. Round and round to this world and back. To the world of the Creator are these transmuted and changed across the threshold.

«The medicines that you have, when filled with the light of faith and blessed with my sigil drawn over them in the air, and the quick, intense utterance of my name, may fill them with that extra vitality that is sometimes necessary for healing.»

OPERATOR: And what of the "most excellent Spirits" and your ability to gift them to a magician as familiars? Can you tell us more about this?

OCH: «Not at this time; that must be related later. After three events surrounding a familiar in your life. The mystery of the familiar is a powerful one, and I am reluctant to speak of it to be written down.»

QUESTION 12: According to the *Arbatel*, you are said to bestow "gold, and a purse springing with gold." I understand that the true treasures are not of metals and gems to hoard wealth, as you say, but I wanted to know if there is any truth to this, if you indeed have provided such riches previously.

OCH: «It is the springing forth of the gold of devotion; it is also a symbol of the vital currency I lend to your workings. How I enliven the flame, and my power lives in the gold in your world, created ultimately by the Sun. It is the joy of devotion we hope and ask for you to spread. Towards what no longer matters. It is the cultivation of devotion alone that matters. That devotion is the currency that buys the way back to the Creator and will fill every need.»

QUESTION 13: There has been much strife and violence in the world, perhaps more than usual. Upheaval of natural disasters as well as discord among people, apparently more than usual. Can you explain to us the happenings of the world today and how they relate between the physical and spiritual worlds?

OCH: «A birth is taking place. The beginning of a new station of the Sun. And the labor pains of that birth is what you witness. Protection cannot be guaranteed to any at this time. Like the lamb, the blood that runs from those sacrifices helps to create the world anew. Like your wife who suffers for the birth of your daughter, so does the world.

«Hope and faith are the shoes through which you can walk through the fires of the world. And like that day with Michael in our old home, do not be afraid for the Lord, thy God is with you. These births are taking place within the structures of your societies and also in the living, breathing earth. It is no punishment, it is the way in which life is sustained, and continues to grow. Know that those who depart are always sheltered in the heart of the Creator.»

QUESTION 14: Finally, in the *Arbatel* it is said that the possessor of your character will be made "to be worshipped as a Deity, by the Kings of the whole world." This is an astonishing account, and I am curious as to its validity and significance. Can you tell us if there is any truth to this statement?

OCH: «This passage was meant for an older time and is no longer true. In older times, the power of the Creator was concentrated in fewer hands and this was necessary, as the mind and bodies of men were not yet prepared. As a species, as a people, you have grown and learned, and the concentration of that power has been spread. My sign still carries great power, but in a different way for a different time. What you do now, through these invocations, is why knowledge can no longer live solely in books. What was true once may not be true again, or now.»

QUESTION 15: Great Spirit and Angel Och, Olympic Spirit from the Sun under Archangel Michael the mighty and great celestial general, before we bid you hail and farewell, are there any final words of wisdom, insight, or instruction that you would impart to us to better understand and utilize the strengths and powers of your office?

OCH: «I ask you... to those who read these words, and to you, the seer and the invoker, to consider the story of my birth. Meditate on it. Close your eyes and do the best that you can with your heart, your inner vision, and even your body to be in those moments. To feel what was felt, to see the presence of Michael. Consider this story deeply and I promise to you that more will be revealed in its telling, in its recapitulation. Walk through that story with devotion, and that is how the flame in your heart is connected to the first fire of God, Whom you call Yahweh Elohim, and Whose presence makes me free.»

OPERATOR: Thank you for your council and wisdom and attendance upon us, mighty Spirit.

(Closing and License to Depart)

Afterthoughts on the Och Operation

OPERATOR: I saw a mighty Angel within the crystal the whole time. However, I also saw a woman on the right behind his shoulder and then under his left arm was a child. It was pretty clear; I don't always see clear images in the crystal as you scry, but this time I was able to. The first thing I saw was the crystal had a very dark part on the left and a bright part on the right with a graying mist in the center, with a slight shining from behind it just like you described as the Spirit appearing in the throne with the two pillars and Sun behind with the mist.

SCRYER: The Spirit remained looking like the bright light or Sun between the pillars and the mist when not showing other visions. I had tears coming down my face during that whole thing. It was very intense for me.

OPERATOR: The responses about the Gnostic questions were fascinating and seemed to contain many subtleties that I'll have to meditate on.

SCRYER: Yes, I got the sense that there was a lot of information along that whole line of thinking. I'm not really familiar with it, but there seems to be a very powerful feminine element to the whole Gnostic side of Christianity.

Michael looked how I remembered him, in that golden scaled armor and long blond hair. He has this extremely powerful but very compassionate face. The wings were immense, simply enormous white wings. You could see he wanted to embrace them; it was pleasurable for him to do so. Then this intense light that made the entire room and everything else vanish. I could see his sword on his side. I remember seeing his shoes, which I don't remember the first time, but they really stood out to me for some reason. It looked like they were made from some sort of white silk. They had this golden embroidery work around the base. The sides were about ankle high. There was an equal-armed cross on the toes on both of them. They were simply gorgeous. In the middle of each equal-armed cross was a ruby. I saw such gorgeous and vivid detail for his shoes. I'm not sure why I saw those so clearly—if it, they, have any significance.

The temple or image of Och was fascinating. It appeared as a floor of light and mist, it seemed to slope upward with the pillars on either side with the Sun in the middle. There was a thick fog, you could still see the Sun, it was still really bright, but it was shielded from perhaps incinerating you or blinding you completely. You felt like the mist was mercy.

I was burning up through the whole operation. Normally it would be uncomfortable, but it was oddly very pleasant. I need some water, though.

OPERATOR: The process for making the holy oil was intense and powerful. The idea of willfully suffering for a particular purpose seems to be prevalent in many ancient religious practices. We usually come away with more questions than the ones we started out with. Perhaps one of the most important pieces of information we received is that this Spirit can be used for both healing and destruction. The light and fire being used for either polarity remains an important occult theme for Solar workings.

SCRYER: I feel this working has been good for my body. I feel my lungs clearer, my heart beats better, and my veins are a little wider. It's weird; I feel so revitalized. This whole thing is so impacting on so many levels. Everything seems so connected. There is this whole story that is taking place and connects all these different levels together. There is not separation that is going on; everything is connected. It's exalting and humbling at the same time. This one is a bit overwhelming. I feel revitalized, but a bit spaced out after this one. Michael and Uriel still stick out to me as being the more overwhelming Angels we have spoken with, but this one was definitely powerful.

The Olympic Spirit of Mercury
Ophiel

✠ Day and time	On Wednesday in the hour of Mercury
✠ Name	Ophiel; Hebrew אופיאל *(Ophiel)*; Greek Ὀφιηλ *(Ophiēl)*
✠ Pronunciation of name (as spoken by the Spirit)	«Oh-fee-ell»
✠ Planet	Mercury
✠ Materials for lamen	Parchment, fixed mercury, cinnabar, metal alloys
✠ Sigil	
✠ Direction for Invocation	East
✠ Incense mixture	Mastic gum, wood aloes, storax, cloves, cinnamon, coriander, cardamom, musk, anise, bergamot

Table XI-29. ***Evocatory Correspondences for Ophiel***[39]

Fig. XI-30. ***The Talisman of Ophiel in the manner of DSIC***

39. Please see the Cautionary Warning Regarding Grimoric Ingredients in Appendix A. —APF

Of Ophiel

Fig. XI-31. ***An alternative Greek Talisman of Ophiel in the language of the Papyri Græcæ Magicæ***

There were only two more Spirits of the Olympic order left to conjure. I felt that we had been getting a rich collection of esoteric knowledge and experiments to consider, and I was looking forward to more. There were several experiments for talismans and rituals suggested by the Spirits that I had not attempted up to this point. I spent most of my time writing down the recordings from each operation and planning for the next evocation, which left me little time to delve into the particulars of each operation, although I certainly planned to return to them.

The Olympic Spirit of Mercury was next on the list, and I had some particular questions for this Spirit which I hoped it could answer satisfactorily.

> *Ophiel* is the governour of such things as are attributed to *Mercury*... His Spirits are 100000 Legions: he easily giveth Familiar Spirits: he teacheth all Arts: and he that is dignified with his character, he maketh him to be able in a moment to convert Quicksilver into the Philosophers ſtone.[40]

Invocation of the Olympic Spirit of Mercury, Ophiel

Fig. XI-32. ***Section of Circle for Drawing Ophiel into the Crystal***

Appearance of the Spirit

SCRYER: I see a figure, but cannot tell if it is a man or a woman. The being has wings which look like large hummingbird wings. They are huge but they

40. 40. Turner and Arbatel, *op. cit.*, Aphorism 17. —APF

move in almost a blur and the body of the Spirit is tall and sparkling with multicolored fire. The fire looks almost like garments. The Spirit is hovering over the ground by a few feet and is positioned in front of what looks like a hallway at the corner of a great stone fortress. At the end, behind the figure toward the end, what looks like the Sun, but a close-up of the Sun as if you were only seeing a piece of it. I hear voices in the hallway.

OPENING QUESTION 1: In the name of the holy and undefiled Spirit, the Father, the begotten Son, and Holy Ghost proceeding from both, what is thy true name?

SPIRIT *(speaking quickly)*: «Ophiel is my true name and I have come here tonight to converse with you.»

OPENING QUESTION 2: What is thy office?

SPIRIT: «I am like the spark in your electrical wires, over your phones, in your towers; I move with the speed of thought and vibrate with the message of creation from one place to another. I focus the communication of the great to the small and the small back to the great. I revel in speed. I allow creatures to speak with one another though they are not the same. I create bonds of brotherhood between man and beast. I am the quicksilver that flows through the veins of your world and the solar system in which you live and reside.»

OPENING QUESTION 3: What are the best and proper times to call you to hold conference with us?

SPIRIT: «All times are my time. Whenever communication or prophecy takes place is my time. Whenever there is laughter and joy, those are my times as well.»

OATH: Wilt thou swear by the holy blood of Jesus Christ that thou art truly the Olympic Mercury Spirit Ophiel?

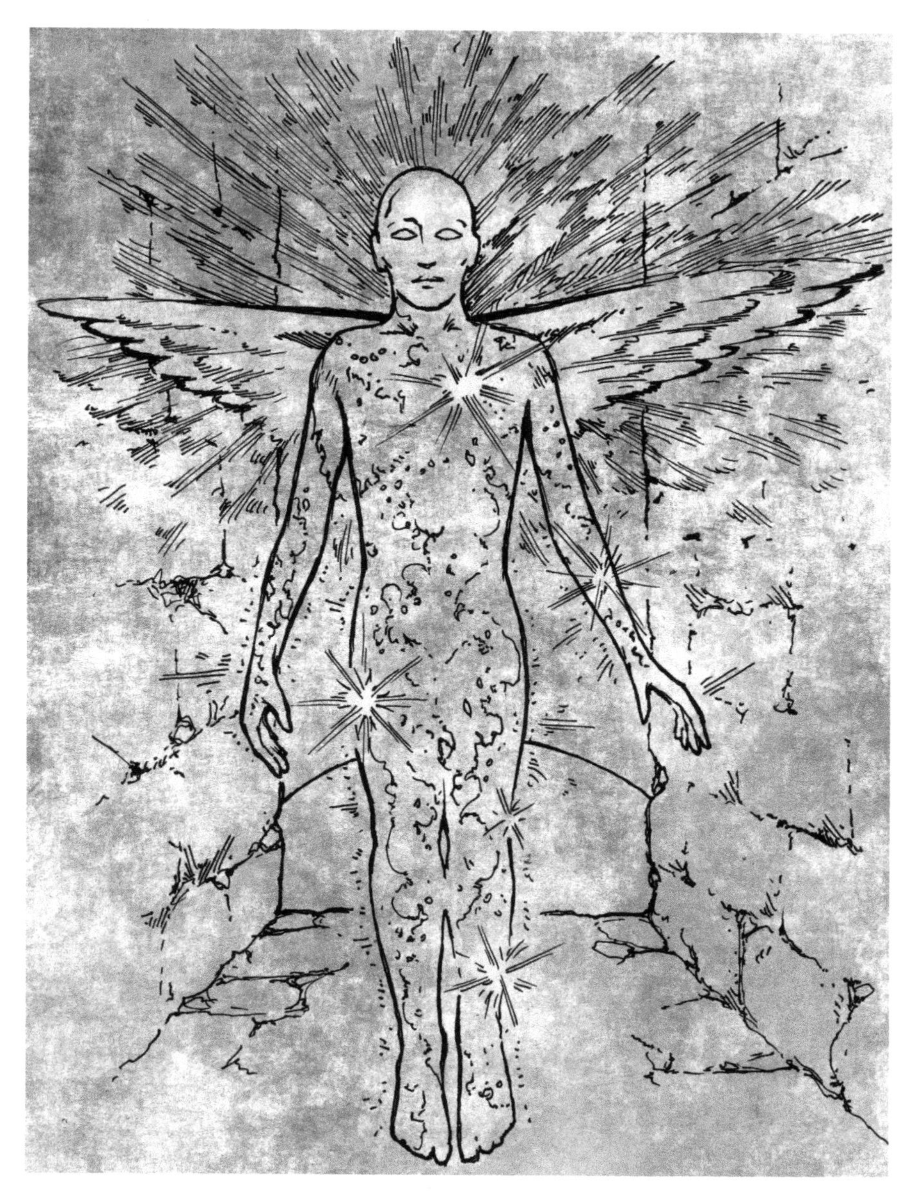

Fig. XI-33. ***Portrait of Ophiel as beheld in Vision***

OPHIEL: «I am the Olympic spirit Ophiel, who carried the words of the Son: 'Father, why has Thou forsaken me?' on the cross to the ears of the Father in that most holy of moments.»

QUESTION 5: Great Spirit, you stated that you assist creatures to speak to one another though they are not the same, as man could communicate with beasts. Could you instruct us on how we may achieve this and harness this blessing when calling upon you?

OPHIEL: «There are many different types of connections between man and beast, man and plant, man and stone. Some as close as Familiars, some as temporary allies who meet on the path so that both may grow. I bring these beings together at the time that is the correct time for them to speak and to learn from one another. You may call on me when there is some way in which you need to see or understand that is beyond the human. There is communication that relies on stone intelligence, plant intelligence, reptilian intelligence, bacterial intelligence, viral intelligence, mammalian intelligence, avian intelligence. All the beings are like a switchboard of your planet, each knowing what the other cannot know. And with the speed of my thought and my intention, I may bring you together and deepen the bond, from Familiar that is life-long to guide and acquaintance for as long as is needed and is best and is right.»

OPERATOR: Beyond calling on your name in the moment, is there any other method we should utilize if we would wish to make this contact?

OPHIEL: «Keep my talisman, my sigil close when you are within proximity to the beast or the creature that you wish to communicate and deepen your relationship with. Bring an offering to the creature you wish to speak to, something that they would enjoy. And before you go to speak or deepen your relationship with this creature, it is best to speak the contradictions, the joys and the heaviness of the heart, away to me that I may carry those things away and leave your heart open and clear, your spirit engaged, clean, and ready for the communication. My talisman, like Raphael's, should preferably be made of silver. Make a small hole in the middle of the talisman through which you must look on the fleeting image of Mercury at sunrise or sunset. Even spying Mercury for a moment through that small hole and when Mercury is seen through the hole, speak aloud my name, and this is the way in which to charge the talisman to make the communication between you and the creature smoother and more comprehendible.»

QUESTION 6: Great Spirit Ophiel, please explain to us more about your name and title—its meaning, history, and origin. What is your relationship to the Archangel Raphael?

SCRYER: I see Ophiel move to the side of the hallway and gesture for me to look down at the hallway where the Sun disappears and the hallway grows dark. After a moment, I see a small girl, she looks to be running around what looks to be like a Greek city. She's in a market and it looks like she is there on her own. Some people are rather scandalized by the fact that she is out there by herself as a young girl. However the girl seems very uncaring of this and some of the merchants are very pleased to see her and laugh and give her pieces of food as she flits along. She seems to be just talking and giving people news of what's going on. Her father is a senator or diplomat of some kind and she is constantly sneaking out of the house.

I see her older now, her teens, and she's being led by a group of women who are holding up her arms. She's been washed, cleaned inside and out. Her hair is combed straight down. Now she's being lead to a cave. There is some sort of writing over the cave, it looks like it's in Greek letters, I don't know what it means. I don't know what it says, but she's lead into this cave and there is a strange smell in the air. Her eyes look like they are almost milky white, as if she has become blind. I see her sitting on a stool, with fumes coming up from below the stool. I can see the spirit of... *(pauses)* It looks like Mercury or Archangel Raphael in the fumes. The girl is breathing the fumes in through her nose and mouth. The fumes age her body and weaken her. I see her growing old very quickly. I see her sitting there speaking to people, many people who have come to hear her speak, to listen to her. She's telling them of the future, she's telling them of their ancestors, of the gods.

I see her beginning to die, and just before she collapses off of the stool some years later, I see her sit straight up and the milky fog in her eyes clears. I see that she has deep brown eyes and a feeling of joy and astonishment on her face. She takes in a deep, deep breath—her last breath. And Raphael rushes into her lungs, and as her body collapses off of the stool to the side, I see her transformed into the form I saw as Ophiel.

I am before her again and I see her hovering right before the hallway to the corner and the great Sun beyond at the end of the hallway.

OPHIEL: «That is my origin; that is the making of Ophiel.»

QUESTION 7: What is the history and source of your sigil? Can you tell us more about its structure and meaning, and also the meaning of your name?

OPHIEL: «I stand at the entrance of my sigil. If you look, you will see. My name: I am like the Omphalos of communication, of exchange, blessed and born of El.»

QUESTION 8: Can you please explain exactly how you can "cause the possessor of your character to change quicksilver immediately into the Philosopher's Stone," as is written in the *Arbatel*?

OPHIEL: «The Philosopher's Stone is like the coalescence of the four.»

SCRYER: I see her taking the four Elements and fusing them into a crystal, and breathing life into the Stone, which burns with an inner fire. She pulls her garments aside and I see her navel. And pouring from her belly button is a liquid like mercury or quicksilver. It surrounds the Stone and sinks into it.

OPHIEL: «The Stone is the fusion of the four Elements, enlivened by the breath of the Creator, the fire of the (Son/Sun?), and quicksilver is the medium that makes its power available to those who use it and carry it. The making of quicksilver can be accomplished by the rapid speaking of prayer and the names of the Creator over mercury. They must be spoken loud and quickly so that mercury vibrates visibly as it is done. This can only be accomplished by an alchemist who has worked the contradictions and paradox out of the soul first, one who has enlivened the spirit through the blessing.»

SCRYER: I see her gesture up into the sky and I see the seven planets up above, very clearly. I see them aligning into a straight line in a ray of light going through her heart down into her navel and out into the Stone.

(A few moments pass as I wait for more information.)

SCRYER: She is saying, «Keep going; I have more to tell!» She seems impatient.

QUESTION 9: The *Arbatel* states that you are able to "teach all arts." What does this mean, and which arts can you teach us which would be most beneficial to our work?

OPHIEL: «I love to teach! It is one of my greatest joys. I can teach you the art of expression in any form you desire. Through song, through instruments—harps, lyres, pianos, horns, drums. I can teach you the delectate ways of painting with brush and ink, with needles with calligraphy, through poetry. Any way you wish to express a uniqueness of the shard of the Creator that is in you. I can teach you and deepen what you already know of these things.

«As humans you are so blessed with the wonderful gift of free will, the ability to express in any way you choose. When you find the way in which you are meant to express it will feel like coming home. Instead of walking up a steep mountain it will be like stepping on to an escalator that rapidly takes you to the top and gives you the view from the top of the mountain. And in the expression meet the challenges that come, the walls inside your heart and in your mind. Have the courage to break through them and see what lies on the other side.

«You may inscribe my sigil on the medium of your communication—an instrument, a canvas, a pen, a brush. As a singer, you may keep my talisman close to your heart when you sing in front of others and I will join you in the song.

«For you and the Seer, and those who read this book, I urge you: Express your spirit through the tools that you create. Make its act an act of devotion, an act of creativity, an act that keeps the integrity of the symphony that is ceremonial magic but with the spice and flavor of your own, unique expression. In the making of wands, circles, and censers, and all the things that you use, fuse it with the creativity of your spirit and call on me to help and I will.»

(The Spirit seemed to know my next question already.)

QUESTION 10: What can you teach us of the proper methods for constructing a wand, a sword, and any other magical implements which may be of use for communing with Spirits? Is there a magical breastplate or armor? Could you tell us the proper way of creating one of these?

OPHIEL: «For defense, on the breastplate, inscribe the symbols that appear and feel the most right to you—on the inside, not on the outside, so they are not seen by the Spirits who may wish you harm or ill. The hidden nature of them will make them stronger, so they should be inscribed on the inside. Touch briefly, if you can, the breastplate to a single drop of mercury. The known emblems and symbols of divinity are engraved and displayed on the outside per the norm.

«As for implements of the ceremonies that you may do, regardless of the task, the creative expression must be placed into each one. Something that is completely unique, never before done, or made. Let the heart speak of what this flavor shall be. The ceremonial magician sometimes can get stuck in the mind. Remember how the body and the heart communicate as well, and allow it to speak. For example, if you were to make a wand in a traditional way, with the traditional length and colors, there should be some tiny flaw or unique spice or spark that you put into it that is all your own. It is in this spot that the magic can come in and out of the item the most powerfully, because this is the doorway of the unique shard of the Creator expressed on the wand itself. And only the one who makes it can know the mystery of what it should be.»

QUESTION 11: How does one move beyond communication conflicts? Can you grant us further eloquence and power of speech and communication both to people and Spirits?

OPHIEL: «Prejudging intention is one of the greatest downfalls of humans speaking from one to the other. Assuming actions mean one thing, from one perspective, because it is your own, assuming that the actions of another speak of those same intentions as if you created the act yourself is incorrect. True communication prejudges no intent. It takes the words in and the actions in assuming that the other being is on a spiritual path and the road back to the Creator as well. There are times however when the communicator and those who they are communicating with may be on different levels. One may be lost in ignorance and the distractions of the world while the other has eyes and heart directed towards the Father. This is hard to cross, this barrier, this gap in understanding and perception. But the responsibility lies mostly on those who have their hearts and minds directed toward the Creator. They must remind themselves, that because of their blessing, because of their perspective, they must have patience with those who have lost themselves in the distractions that are presented to them from so many directions. And although I love distractions, communications, colors, songs, messages, these things can cloud the mind, the heart and the body of its true intention, of its purpose.

«When speaking one to the other, try to find that passageway into their destiny. Try to remind them of the unique power that they alone can wield. And in helping them to find that spot, that place, like the doorway that you inscribe on the wand, it is inscribed somewhere on the human soul. Help that other person to find that path back to the Creator, even if it is through deception, trickery, honesty, humor, whatever it takes, lead them back to that place, if it is even for just a moment. This is the beginnings of true communications from one being to another. This can be done between human beings, it can be done between man and animal, man and plant, all created beings have that one gap, that one opening that connects them back to the Creator, and it is through that gap that they may communicate as one.»

QUESTION 12: Is there a definitive universal means of communication with all levels and manners of Spirits? If so, what is it? How does it work? How is it learned? How is it then implemented? How are the answers given, recorded, and definitively made intelligible to the one posing the questions, where there can be no possible misinterpretation of said answers?

OPHIEL: «Ironically, misinterpretation is part of communication. It allows growth. When misinterpretations happen there is sometimes destiny involved in that misinterpretation. The Creator works through misinterpretation as he does with clear, perfect communication. The Father has a great sense of humor and a side that is very tricky, clever, and beyond even my comprehension, far beyond my comprehension. I have seen men's heart grow closer and wiser through the fortunate accident. To give one secret for the communication between all beings would be impossible, as each one has a unique lock that fits a unique key. Help each other to find the key and the lock can be opened. The key is to help each other to find that key. Beyond that instruction the need for intuition is paramount. Timing is paramount. And timing is a matter of grace: grace given from On High.»

OPERATOR: I thank you for your words of wisdom and instruction on these great many matters. I also wish to extend my sincere thanks and wonder at how I came to this point of being able to create so many things without prior instruction or talent. I am curious about any hidden assistance or inspiration I may have received.

OPHIEL: «I have loved seeing your work and progress. So many whom I speak with among the Spirits who rule and act in the ways that I do have acknowledged the creation of your implements, your prayers, everything that you have done. It speaks of a great desire to go out and know the unknown, to know the infinite, and that is your purpose. It is equally the purpose of all human beings, the purpose of all things, to go out, to feel, to understand, and to remember. This is done in many different ways. We have laid our hands and fingers on you when the Work is done. We have seen and felt your spirit respond in its own unexpected creations that even we could not have foreseen. You are blessed, Frater Ashen, with this inner change that has manifested in the tools of your craft. You honor us as we honor you. And in that exchange, there is no hierarchy; there is only the perfect expression of God.»

OPERATOR: I thank you greatly and genuinely from the bottom of my heart. I ask if there is anything else you can teach us in the realm of healing. I have procured a green stone which was related to me by another scryer before when speaking to Archangel Raphael. Can this be used in healing? I wondered if you had any further instruction as to its function or usefulness. Or if you had another method for healing you could teach to us.

OPHIEL: «The green stone can be used to heal. It can be infused with the energy of the greening world around you: plants grasses, moss, and lichen. When the spirit of those creatures is invited with humility, love, and respect into the stone, to fill it with their spirit and vitality, the stone can be used for great benefit to heal all manner of afflictions. The infusion of the Spirit of greening world is key and most important. The permission of the overarching Spirit that watches over the lichen, the tree, the grass, that you call upon to fill the stone must be given first.

«As far as any other instruction I would give who read these words: Learn, learn, and learn. Create, create, and create. And speak, speak, speak. Fill your heart with the perfect, laughing, creative love of the Creator and be free to be at peace.»

OPERATOR: Great, wondrous Olympic Spirit of Mercury, Ophiel, we thank you for your attendance upon us, upon this rite, and ask if you have any final instructions, lessons, or teachings before we bid you hail and farewell.

SCRYER: I see her point up to the Moon, which is in the crescent shape. She holds a cup out below the Moon, and I see dew or liquid falling out of the crescent Moon into the cup. *(Scryer laughs.)* She takes this cup and pours it over her own head, laughs, and then shoots off into the stars.

I can hear the wind.

OPERATOR *(after a moment)*: Has the Spirit departed?

SCRYER: ...Yeah.

(License to Depart given.)

Afterthoughts on the Ophiel Operation

OPERATOR: The Spirit spoke very quickly, answered very quickly at length, and responded energetically. She was quite a stark contrast with the other Spirits. It's remarkable how much the scryer's voice takes on aspects and inflections of the Spirit.

SCRYER: I was amazed at how fast she was speaking! I couldn't help but laugh at the end as she was looking all reverent, collecting the dew from the Moon in that cup. Then she looked at me and dumped it all on her head and started laughing. Then she just shot off!

OPERATOR: That was really surprising and rather humorous. I like the lightheartedness of this Spirit; there is really a sense of playful and youthful ambition. It is interesting, the imagery with the Moon and how we only have the Moon left to do. Do you think that had anything to do with it?

The allusion during our operation to the Spirit Ophiel coming into being through the oracle of Delphi, the girl who became the oracle eventually melding with the Spirit of Archangel Raphael or Hermes to become Ophiel, was, to say the least, spectacular and unexpected. It was a bold claim, but also one which seems to fit in many ways. The Spirit's ability to convey the will of the gods and communicate between heaven and earth is undeniably fitting for this Mercurial being.

I had to do a bit of research for some of the words and images that Ophiel conveyed. An *omphalos* (Greek ὀμφαλός, "navel") stone is a sacred stone, sometimes natural and sometimes carved, which marks the centre of a region or of the entire world. Several omphaloi were known in the Hellenistic Mediterranean; however, *the* Omphalos was without question the sacred stone at Delphi. In Greek myth, Zeus simultaneously released two eagles at opposite ends of the earth to meet at its center, the navel of the world, Delphi. There the Omphalos stood in the sanctuary where the oracles were delivered.

However, the tradition of a sacred stone marking the centre of the world was not isolated to the Greeks. Jewish tradition says that there is a Foundation Stone in the Temple Mount upon which the Ark of the Covenant rested in the Holy of Holies of the Jerusalem Temple which marks the centre point of the world. Christian tradition says that the limestone visible through gaps in the floor of the Church of the Holy Sepulchre at Jerusalem marks both the hill of Golgotha and the tomb of Jesus, and so is the cosmological centre of the Christian world.[41]

Another name sometimes applied to a sacred stone was Bætyl (Latin *Bætylus*, from Greek *Baitylos*, itself a loanword from Semitic *Beth El*, meaning "House of God"). According to ancient sources, these objects of worship were meteorites which fell from the heavens and were dedicated to the gods or revered as symbols of the gods themselves.[42] The ancient myths tells us that there was a Baitylos stone at Delphi (some said it was the same as the Omphalos, others that it was a second stone at the site) which was the very stone that Rhea wrapped in swaddling clothes, pretending it was the child Zeus, in order to deceive Kronos.[43] The stone caused Kronos to disgorge his other swallowed children, the future Olympian gods. When he also expelled the stone, it fell from the sky to land at Delphi.

---

41. Christian tradition also claims that the skull of Adam was buried at the spot marking the centre of the world, and it was for that reason that the hill became known as *Golgotha* (Aramaic, "the Skull," translated into Latin as *Calvaria*), Mediæval Christian iconography of the crucifixion regularly depicts the skull of Adam underground beneath the Cross. —APF

42. The Hebrew and Christian Bibles contain an explicit example of *Beth El* or *Baitylos* stone lore in *Genesis* 28. Jacob uses a stone for his pillow and experiences his famous dream vision of Angels ascending and descending between heaven and earth. In the morning he sets up the stone on which he dreamed as a standing stone (*matzevah*), and anoints it with oil, and names the place *Beth El*. —APF

43. Kronos was the Titan king who swallowed his children so as to prevent them from usurping his power as he had deposed his own father, Ouranos.

Omphalos and Baitylos stones were believed to allow direct communication with the gods. A 1933 article[44] suggested that the Delphic stone was hollow to allow intoxicating vapors to channel through it and be breathed by the oracle. This revelation coincided directly with what my scryer described during the relation of the Spirit in human form.

Finally, the explanation that Ophiel offered on communication was also enlightening, that even miscommunication is a source of creative expression and further communication needed through the resolving of conflict or perhaps further cooperation. Innovation, communication, and the invention of new ideals would definitely be in the scope of this Spirit's office. The Mercurial aspects were emphasized beautifully by the Spirit's responses to our questions and gave further insight on how to utilize the strengths of its talents.

---

44. Leicester B. Holland, "The Mantic Mechanism at Delphi," in *American Journal of Archaeology* 37, no. 2 (1933): pp. 204–214.

The Olympic Spirit of Luna
Phul

✠ Day and time	On Monday in the hour of the Moon
✠ Name	Phul; Hebrew פול *(Phul)*; Greek Φουλ *(Phoul)*
✠ Pronunciation of name (as spoken by the Spirit)	«Foo-al»
✠ Planet	Moon
✠ Materials for lamen	Parchment, crystal, silver
✠ Sigil	
✠ Direction for Invocation	West
✠ Incense mixture	Euphorbe, bdellium, sal ammoniac, lignum aloes, myrtle leaf, clary sage, davana, geranium, wormwood, eucalyptus, rosemary, and a small amount of camphor

Table XI-34. ***Evocatory Correspondences for Phul***[45]

Fig. XI-35. ***The Talisman of Phul in the manner of DSIC***

---

45. Please see the Cautionary Warning Regarding Grimoric Ingredients in Appendix A. —APF

Of Phul

*Fig. XI-36. **An alternative Greek Talisman of Phul in the language of the Papyri Græcæ Magicæ***

There was just one more Olympic Spirit to be conjured. It was interesting that the rounds of both the Planetary Archangels and the Olympic Spirits would be concluded by summoning the Spirit of the Moon. The Moon was the gateway to the Spiritual according to the teachings of the Kabbalah and other Mystery traditions. It was fitting that the final evocation for this series was to be undertaken to receive the wisdom from the Spirit of the Moon.

The *Arbatel* says of the Spirit Phul:

> He changeth all metals into silver, in word and deed; governeth Lunary things; healeth the dropsie; he giveth spirits of the water, who do serve men in a corporeal and visible form; and maketh men to live 300 yeers.

I consulted again with Hiram before the conjuration, asking his advice. My familiar Spirit said to inquire about a potent method for scrying and contacting others in the Astral/Spirit world. He also said the Spirit would know more about Astral travel as well. I was glad to have asked him and wish I had done so with every single operation.

Invocation of the Olympic Spirit Phul

*Fig. XI-37 **Section of Circle for Drawing Phul into the Crystal***

Appearance of the Spirit

SCRYER: I'm on a seashore. It is at night, and I see the full Moon setting in the west but still above the water. Right where the waves are breaking on the beach, I see a figure like a shadow standing in the surf with the waves breaking around them. I cannot tell if it's male or female. In its right hand it holds a globe of crystal with a vein of milky white crystal that runs through its equator all the way through. In its left hand it holds a silver cup or bowl. It seems to transform between the two. Around the Spirit's feet, I see very clearly where the waves break over and around the shadow Spirit, the foam turns into pearls. The Spirit is very tall, seven or eight feet high.

Opening Question 1: In the name of the holy and undefiled Spirit, the Father, the begotten Son, and the Holy Ghost proceeding from both, what is thy true name?

Scryer: The first part of the name sounds like it is pronounced through the hissing of the waves breaking on the beach. And then there is a deep, basal intonation that seemed to roll down into the waters below. I hear 'Ooouuuul. Phhaooouulll.'

There is something very, very old about this Spirit. I cannot see its face well, but I can feel its presence very strongly.

Opening Question 2: What is Thy office?

Scryer: I see the full Moon within the sigil in the square below the arc. The Moon sits on the right bottom corner. I see the sigil in the sky, huge, tall. I can see that the Moon makes a circuit around this gate, opening, and the dark of the Moon is on the opposite corner.

Spirit: «I take the three Elements and bring them together into the fourth. The Elements of which I speak are stellar and unearthly in nature. What the power of Water, Earth, Fire, and Air are amongst the stars, their essential nature before they are coalesced and compressed into the forms you know as the Elements. My benefactor is the one that brings these four together, and I am like the pieces sliding along the gate, like the tides growing to full, waning to new. I am the gateway through which all these things come, all life, all spirit, imprinted between the full and dark of the Moon.»

Fig. XI-38. ***Portrait of Phul as beheld in Vision***

Opening Question 3: What are the best and proper times to call you to hold conference with us?

Scryer: I see the Moon moving along the line of the gateway around the square below the arc of the sigil. I can see it going from full back to new, new back to full.

Spirit: «All these times when the Moon is visible are acceptable to speak with me. It is best at the edge of water, whether lake or spring, river or ocean or glacier, does not matter.»

Scryer: I see the Moon wink out of existence for a few moments and then it comes back.

Spirit: «Only when the Moon is in void speak not with me, as this is my turning away from the world to look upon the face of Gabriel and remember the mystery and love of the Creator before I turn my face back again.»

Oath: Wilt thou swear by the holy blood of Jesus Christ that thou art truly the Olympic Spirit of the Moon, Phul?

Spirit: «I am Phul, given by Gabriel to your world.»

Scryer: I see the Spirit now change to be full of light. It's no longer a shadow but a bright, shining being. It then moves to a place of silvery-grey between the two. I see scales, almost like fish, over the skin and in the eyes; the pupils are like crescents swimming on an ocean of deep blue.

Phul: «I swear by the blood of the crucified Son that I am Phul, the Olympic Spirit, as you have called.»

Question 5: Could you tell us more about your origin and nature, also the meaning of your sigil? Please explain to us more about your name and title, its meaning, history, and origin. What is your relationship to Archangel Gabriel?

Scryer: I see a tear falling from the Moon into the sea. The tear is shed by Gabriel.

Phul: «When she first beheld the world, there was a tear, half of sorrow for the suffering, and half at the astounding beauty that she saw.»

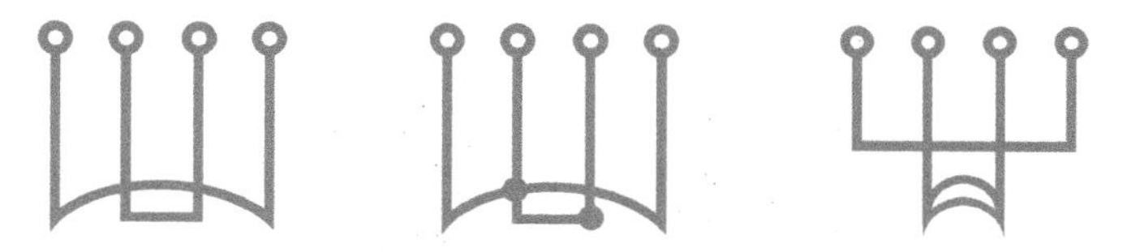

Fig. XI-39. Three Variants of the Olympic Sigil of Phul

SCRYER: I see the tear fall into the ocean, which transforms into a globe of light with one spirit from each of the forms of life living in the ocean merge with the stone that was a tear. I see it drop down deep into the black night of the ocean and come to rest far to the bottom and stir the ocean floor in a cloud. I see spirit after spirit of the animals, the plants, glow as they merge into the stone, partaking of them all.

Now I see a child being thrown into the sea, but am unable to see who threw him. I see the child begin to sink down beneath the surface of the waters, its eyes open and looking at the light of the full Moon above. The child begins to age as it sinks deeper. The child grows into a boy, becoming a teenager, then a man. The further down he sinks, the older he gets, and just as he is about to reach the stone, I see a woman. The woman appears like a Spirit who almost looks like a mermaid, and together she and the man fall into the stone.

Suddenly, I'm back on the beach and I'm standing before Phul. I see waves crashing around Phul's ankles, creating the pearls in the surf.

PHUL: «I am the first tear shed by Gabriel when the world was first shown to her, the tear that contained the dark of the Moon and the suffering of all things, the tear that contained the full of the Moon and the glory, the beauty, and the victory of all life on your world. Within me I contain the memory of the oceans and a piece of the light of the Creator.

«The hissing of the waves is the beginning of my name, the end the deep song of the sea. It is the song that comes first, and the hissing, the end, though the beginning of my name, is its focus.

«The sigil shows the four Elements before they are born, the spirit of what they are before they manifest, coming through the arc of your Solar system and focused through the gateway of the Moon. They also show through the arc of Gabriel, the four great Archangels and how they enter into your world from their thrones amongst the stars.»

QUESTION 6: Please tell me what it entails when it is written of you that Phul "changeth all metals into silver, in word and deed"?

SCRYER: The crystal globe disappears from Phul's hand and she raises the cup above her head, just beneath the Moon.

PHUL: «My cup is like the gateway of the sigil, which is like the gateway where all these things are brought together and where they come and go from your world. As they pass through my gate, they are transformed to take on the nature of the Moon, the nature of Gabriel, like a coating of silver over its essence. Consider the fluid of the placenta, for every being born coated with the silver which allows it to slip through the gateway. It is a covering of silver, a mask of silver, and one that enables all the metals that come through to enter and to leave. Some created by the pressure, some by intense heat, some by the exploding of stars and the death of Angels.

«Furthermore I cannot say, as your vocabulary is too limited, but it is a mystery upon which to dwell and can unlock many doors.»

OPERATOR: Are Angels truly able to die?

PHUL: «Some, yes. But what is death but a change or a transmutation into another form decreed by the Creator since the beginning of time?»

OPERATOR: Great Spirit, can you tell us more about the objects you hold? I wish to know more about the clear stone with the milky white midsection and the silver bowl or cup you hold.

PHUL: «The milk through the diameter of the globe I hold is like the spiral nature of your Milky Way, of your galaxy, and the clear crystal that surrounds it like the protecting love of the Father for all the beings who dwell therein. It is a reminder to me by Gabriel of the balance. That life and existence is best cultivated and formed between the extremes. The milk of creation is like the light of the Moon, like the light of the stars. It is the nourishment of the Father, and through the gateway of the Moon this milk comes to you. With the integrity of my cup it can be gathered and consumed to sustain life. It is a symbol of the generosity of the Father.»

QUESTION 7: I wish to know how is it you heal the dropsy,[46] and also if there is a charm or symbol that may be of best utility in affecting healing in lymph problems.

SCRYER: I am seeing a woman lying on a hilltop of grass surrounded by four people who hold their hands on her. It is the full Moon; I see the light of the full Moon on her. One of them has their hands on her head, the other at her feet, and another at the right arm, and the other the left arm. I see a silver bowl of holy water, and she lies down on the blanket and together they begin to wash her with this water as the Moon shines on her. They sing the name of Gabriel. They sing the holy names of God.

As the Moon goes dark they say, 'As it grows dim, so too may your ailment. As the Moon lessens, so too does your disease.' They repeat this over and over again; they slowly remove the blanket from underneath her so that she is lying directly on the grass.

The cup or bowl they use is inscribed with the symbol of Phul on the bottom and the sigil of Gabriel is inscribed on the inside. The bottom of the bowl has a loose stone like a sapphire in it.

PHUL: «It is best to start this at the full Moon and done as often as possible. Preferably each night between its full state and the new, all the while seeing and feeling the disease leave the body as the light leaves the Moon.»

QUESTION 8: Which are the best ways to utilize your influence to expand psychic faculties such as clairvoyance, clairaudience, and clairsentience? How can we have all senses Astrally aware?

PHUL: «When the Moon is at the waning crescent and the waxing crescent, stand by yourself within the confines of your circles, protected. Have with you only a silver bowl or cup. Empty the mind. Sing my name while looking at the Moon. This must be done at its waning crest and its waxing crescent, both. And see the light of the Moon fall like the tear of Gabriel into the cup or the bowl that you hold. The mind must be empty, non-interpretive, absence of language and voice, open and receptive to paradox

46. Dropsy was the proper English name in Turner's day for a range of medical conditions for which the term in modern medicine is *edema* (including myxedema, lymphedema, etc.), characterized by the accumulation of excess water within the body, often under the skin, resulting in obvious swelling. The wateriness of the condition brings it under the Lunar sway. —APF

and to contradiction, non-judging and liberated. Sing my name and the name of Gabriel and drink deep of the water and feel it merge with your bones. The more this rite is done, the deeper the faculties you speak of will become, the more your gateways through this will open. However this will come in time and cannot be forced. This is an act bereft of reason and founded on faith. It is in its repetition and your pure, open trust that those things, those faculties are attained.»

QUESTION 9: Can the deepest depths of emotion purge the heart of Archon control? What can you reveal about the Gnostic perspective? What more could you tell us about Archons, Æons, the Demiurge, and the true destiny of mankind?

PHUL: «The Archons are like gifts and distractions, and they can put a net over the heart and cloud perception of the mind. It is not an act of evil, simply one of their natures. With the full release of emotion, whether through joy or sorrow or pain or compassion or even rage, is the net burned away and heart made pure and open again. If the strong emotion that predicated it is fully blessed and released and let go, the Demiurge, like the great experiment of the mind of men and women, though misguided, an expression of the longing of man to reach the infinite.»

QUESTION 10: How can we call in the rains and moisture? Are we able to stop the drought in California gently from here? Also, as you are recorded as being able to do, how do you "give Spirits of the water, who do serve men in a corporeal and visible form"? How can you do this for us and other capable magicians who ask it of you?

PHUL: «You have done this rite before, and now you benefit from the wisdom of the balance that must be maintained. In the way water and the Spirits that move water through and around the world are called and asked to benefit others, very rarely in your world have people called on the rain to fall to benefit another. The Elementals long for the participation of mankind.»

SCRYER: I see an image of beach sand being divided with the hands into two halves. One of the halves of sand symbolizes the west coast, and the other symbolizes the eastern slope of the Rocky Mountains. I see this done on a round piece of leather or hide of some kind that has been inscribed with the sigil of Phul. A few drops are sprinkled from the bowl filled with holy water onto the sand which represents the mountains. A larger number of drops are sprinkled on the sand which represents the West Coast. The bowl looks like the same one that was used and seen in the previous vision of the healing. All this is done within the confines of a circle. The Elemental Kings of Water and Air are called. The blessing of Phul is asked for as a seashell is held up to the ear of the one that is calling. I see the specific desire of balance to be maintained between the two piles of sand and thus two areas of land. When the sands are fully parted between the two, they look like a crescent shape, like the crescent Moon, and the symbol of Phul is revealed as they are parted by the hands.

OPERATOR: And of the gifting of the Spirits of Water?

PHUL: «The rolling, churning sea is like a great horse that guides and can be ridden but never tamed. In vision and communication with me, first I will teach the magician to respect and understand the power of the sea, to feel in your blood its ultimate wildness and untamable nature. I will teach you how to come into agreement with this power and never to be foolish enough to think you are its master. And when this knowing and respect is bone deep, then I will reveal these teachings to each magician, uniquely and in secret. Begin with vision, speaking, and communicating with me, and allow me to instruct you.»

QUESTION 11: Is there a way to walk through the world of dreams and remember and utilize the information we find there? How can you best instruct us and others to do this?

PHUL: «A moonstone kept near the bed is very helpful in the remembrance of dreams. I and Gabriel can both be called upon to help stimulate your journey into the dream and your remembrance of it. Dreams thrive under attention. The more you pay attention, the more you record them, the more you speak of them, the more they will come. Like caring for a friend or a child, dreams thrive under this attention, this care. The more you bring them into your conscious during the day, the greater your connection with them will be.

«The body must be well nourished and well rested for this to occur in the most powerful ways possible. Eating raw foods, raw vegetables, foods which are close to their original creation as possible, will aid in this as well.»

QUESTION 12: Can you instruct us on any formulas to be able to send messages to other people's dreams clearly?

PHUL: «This is largely a matter of connection between the two people who wish to communicate. At higher levels, once developed, you may begin to implant communication into the minds and the dreams of people whom you do not even know. Mastery of this allows you to do this to others whom you have only glimpsed. First learn to communicate with your closest friends or your circle of fellow magicians or seers. This can be expanded upon to communicate with those outside of your sphere. The cup, my cup, can be used like a vessel to transport your communication from one dream to another. First put your hands upon it physically, then with the mind. When the cup appears clearly in your dreams, you will be ready to communicate more clearly, even with those whom you do not know. Its appearance in your dreams is a symbol of this milestone being crossed.»

QUESTION 13: I was informed to ask you about a potent method for scrying and contacting others in the Astral Spirit world on which you could instruct us.

PHUL: «One way is to sit at the proper angle during the day above a body of water. The water, when looked at with the eyes focusing just below the surface of the water, the movements and patterns on the water is your window into which you wish to scry.

«Another way is to first anoint the third eye with the cross, and then gaze into a blackened, dark mirror. Do this using an indirect source of light that does not shine into the eyes of the scryer. Before scrying, anoint the mirror on both sides with holy water. Also, on the back side of the mirror, the one opposite the scryer, draw my sigil in holy oil. In this, the mirror becomes like the gateway of the Moon, and the visions can come through more clearly, especially when, before the operation of scrying while in a protected circle, the magician sings my name over and over again. Wait with the eyes closed until the feeling of trance comes over the body and the mind. Upon achieving this state, the eyes are then opened to the mirror.»

QUESTION 14: I was also informed that you have a method for 'entering into the Astral.' What would you advise as the most potent way for this?

PHUL: «There are many methods to do this, but with the focused intention of entering through my sigil, you will be able to travel to new worlds. Travel between the dark and the full of the Moon through the symbol, and while feeling the vibrations running through the body, you may travel through spirit form. By focusing on that gateway while within a protected circle, and practiced over and over again, the gateway of my sigil can be a powerful one into the Astral realm.»

QUESTION 15: Bethor of Jupiter stated how a few men were granted the ability to live 700 years, Och to 600 hundred years. It is written that you can prolong the life of others to 300 years as per the *Arbatel de magia veterum*. What is the significance of this, as it differs with Bethor's and Och's, and under what circumstances was this done or can be done?

PHUL: «The coating of silver that I spoke of earlier, when applied in the right way when a being is born into the world, can prolong its life for that time. These are people, animals, and even plants of tremendous emotion. They are like grand empaths that can enable the transference of emotion of one being to another. They are necessary to create and communicate between species or beings who cannot understand one another through words, but can only understand each other through the emotions of the heart. They can relate suffering; they can relate joy or pain; they can relate compassion and perspective. However, the intensity of the exchange makes their ability to live long not quite as vital as six hundred or seven hundred years. Three hundred years is the longest that a being can maintain this kind of exchange. It is difficult to explain further in any language.»

QUESTION 16: The physical Moon through influence of the tides moves the sea; the Moon moves the ocean. What blessings might you be able to give to sailors or fishing-folk? Others wish to know what curses you can work against folks despoiling the sea.

PHUL: «The Sea has always been drawn toward the gateway of the Moon, moving like a great bulge toward its body. What you see as the tides is the longing of the sea. When this longing is known and respected among sailors and fishermen, and when they come to know the sea as a living being with the depth of longing just like the human heart or the mind or the body, this knowing, this feeling creates the blessings that ward them and protect them and can deliver them abundance and steer them clear of dangers and peril when they are on the open sea.

«Those who do not know this, who treat the sea as a ‹thing› to be used that is not conscious, that is not aware, awake, and alive, is a curse in itself. When taken to the extremes, those who would despoil the sea for their own gains, the salt in their blood begins to thicken like a poisoning. It is a poisoning by not knowing the connection between blood and the ocean. In these extreme cases, I am the Spirit to watch over the sea who can be called to hasten this process into death.»

QUESTION 17: The dead seem to move in a sea of their own; what roles do you and yours play with them? Do you have power to raise and settle storms across oceans, seas, and other bodies of water, large and small? If so, will you teach those who ask how to raise and calm such storms?

PHUL: «Calling upon storms upon the sea is like calling forth the vitality of a living being. It must be fed in the right way and stimulated in the right way. The need must be clearly laid out to me and to the king of the Element of Water that you have summoned and spoken to before. A storm is the excitement of Air and Water together. Through this excitement come the Fire of lightning and the rolling of the thunder that can sooth and terrify men and women. The excitement, the ecstasy of that excitement, must be raised within the spirit of the magician first. They should do this close to the edge of the sea, on a prominence that gives them a wide view of the horizon of the sea. The emotion called forth by chanting my name and the name of the king of the Element of Water and the calling of the Elementals of Air. The singings of the names are important, but it is the agitation of the spirit of the magician that is the key to the creation or the cessation of storms. A wand is very helpful in this endeavor.»

OPERATOR: What material should this wand be constructed from?

PHUL: «This wand should be created by a piece of drift wood collected on the ocean shore edge. It should be one that calls to the magician who seeks it purposefully. It should first be purified with salt and left for three days in the darkness. When it is brought forth, it should be anointed with sea water blessed as holy water. The wand is to be unadorned. Finally, it is blessed with the names of Gabriel, of myself, Phul, and all the Elementals of Water and of Air.»

OPERATOR: As this is the last operation we have planned for this book, are there any other Spirits we should contact to include or complete for this work? Do you have any final words of wisdom and instruction to assist with bringing the collection of these operations to a close?

PHUL: «The work is never truly done, but your book has come full circle. My message to you is like the gateway of the Moon. Seek out the knower of secrets and mysteries. Many voices speak from beyond, and I hear all of them say that they bless and give prosperity to the work the both of you have done. Know that our Spirits are with you. When obstacles arise, we will help to tear them down. When you receive the first book printed, bring it into the circle and call all of us that you have summoned by name. The book that you hold will be as every other one which is sent out henceforth and purchased by others. Bless the book in all of our names, and we will make a gateway of each book for those who need them. For those who do not or use it in an improper way, they will be as inert as stone. In your dedication of the book, give glory to the Creator, its ultimate source.»

OPERATOR: Great and wonderful Olympic Spirit of the Moon, Phul, great Angel under Gabriel of the Waters, of the Moon, and gateway to the Spirit, we thank thee for thine attendance and wisdom.

(License to Depart given.)

Afterthoughts on the Phul Operation

SCRYER: Regardless of the length, I feel that I was upheld through the whole thing. Even when I was sitting for a long time, it felt like I was being assisted.

The circles on the sigil seemed to really represent the two main phases of the Moon. The empty full Moon circle was on the bottom right and the filled-in one was black for the new Moon and it moved around in a clockwise fashion.

The Spirit's voice was very powerful, very deep, but nearly impossible to distinguish between male and female. It really looked like a merfolk sort of being, but really difficult to distinguish and discern the face properly. For whatever reason, I wasn't able to focus on the face. It was easiest to see when it was in its gray state, definitely feminine qualities to the face but very aquatic. Oddly, I really think my mind was having a difficult time figuring out what I was looking at.

OPERATOR: During the entire operation I was swaying back and forth, feeling like I was standing right in the ocean, like in the tide.

I felt it was important to do some serious magic to give the West Coast some much-needed moisture. From what Phul revealed, it seemed initially that the ritual should be done on the beach or on the seashore rather than in the mountains. However, after further consideration, it became apparent that the beach sand could be sent to me from the coast and used here, which would give a powerful tie to that location.

Also Phul said, «You have done this rite before,» which I took to mean the silver bowl that was used for the Water Elemental working that may have contributed to the flood waters that followed.

I went to work planning out the specifics of what the ritual would involve. I surmised that the magical circle would need to be made facing the coast to which the blessings of moisture should arrive. I imagined that conducting this ritual outside, near a source of water, would add to the rite's effectiveness. The magical materials needed would be:

1. A good measure of beach sand from the location needing rain and moisture.
2. The silver chalice or bowl as described by the Spirit and used for operations involving Archangel Gabriel and Phul. The vessel should be inscribed with both of their sigils and consecrated to operations described by the Spirit. A large bottle containing holy water and a crystal glass cruet will be used in conjunction with the silver vessel.
3. A crystal sphere or orb, ideally with a natural center that is milky-colored that runs through the diameter.
4. A shell that would replicate the echoing sound of the ocean, likely a conch shell, with the sigil of Phul engraved on it.

5. A driftwood wand, ideally from the same ocean as the sand and shell, described by the Spirit.
6. Lamens and articles for the Elemental Rulers of Water and Air, as well as the lamen for Phul.
7. A three-foot-wide circle of cow leather,[47] painted with the sigil of Phul in the center. The leather should be consecrated and may also be dyed silver and/or dark, dark blue.

Since the Elements of Water and Air are to be called, the names and sigils of both the Elemental Kings of Water and Air would be inscribed in the circle along with the general Elemental Signs. The consecrated seashell with the sigil of Phul engraved on it would be set near the silver vessel or possibly on an altar table within the circle.

After the invocations of the Elemental Kings of Water and Air, using the driftwood wand, an invocation is also said to Phul while the shell is held to the ear of the magician. The specific desire of balance to be maintained between the two piles of sand (and thus the two areas of land) are to be expressed inwardly as well as aloud.

The piles of sands are evenly parted with the hands and made into crescent Moon shapes. In so doing, the sigil of Phul should be seen clearly on the round piece of leather.

A small cruet is dipped into the silver bowl, and with a petition for a blessing from the angel Phul, the holy water should be lightly sprinkled on both parts of the sand.

The rite should conclude with a blessing and license to depart to the Elemental kings and to Phul. The sand used in the ceremony should be deposited in the nearest fresh-water source.

Besides the ritual above, the Spirit gave excellent magical instruction for Astral forms of magic from Spirit travel to developing extra-sensory perception. At the time of this writing, I have not yet had the chance to experiment with these formulæ, but I plan to put them to the test at the next available opportunity.

47. The cow is an animal sacred to the Moon and one of the forms in which the associated Spirits may appear.

This concluded the full round of spiritual evocations, and the recording of the work for review and experimentation.

I had a sense of returning to a small town after completing a long journey to exotic lands, a life-altering experience that had changed my scryer and me in ways that are beyond my powers of description.

✣

XII
A Further Archangelic Mystery
Raziel: The Secret of God

EARLY A YEAR HAD PASSED since the last evocation operation of the Olympic Spirit of the Moon. In between juggling the usual demands of daily life and the fresh demands of being father to a newborn baby girl, I was diligently working on completing the writing of this volume.

It was in the winter when a magical colleague in the Jupiter Order in which I am involved urged me to contact Archangel Raziel. He said that he had made contact with the Archangel, and that it was an intense experience like none other. Apparently Raziel had urged that other magicians should work with him, and indicated that he would reveal the deeper mysteries of their purpose and work. I took the suggestion under advisement, but made no real plans to do an evocation. Then I was independently prompted in the same direction by two other magicians whom I respect, which led me to believe that the operation was important.

Even after deciding to conduct an evocation of Raziel, I had not planned to include it in this volume. However, after deliberate consideration and discussion with my scryer, I decided factors made it obvious that it was intended to be the closing working to this book. The lessons and events surrounding the experience seem appropriate to the overall theme of the volume and will hopefully give the reader an idea of what the collective Angelic intelligences were attempting to convey to my scryer and me.

The Archangel
Raziel

✠	Day and time	On Saturday (?), at 1:00 AM
✠	Name and meaning	Hebrew רזיאל *(Raziel)*, "Secret(s) of God"
✠	Pronunciation of name (as spoken by the Spirit)	«Ra-zai-el»
✠	Other known names and meaning	Hebrew גליצור (*Galitzur, Galizur*), "Revealer of the Rock," Hazheir/Hazhair/Azhear?
✠	Materials for lamen	Azure blue parchment, platinum, gold, silver
✠	Sigils	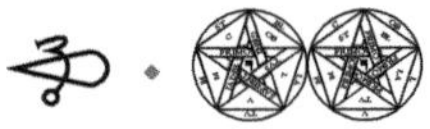
✠	Direction for Invocation	Northeast
✠	Incense mixture	An equal blend of the seven Planetary Archangel mixtures
✠	Candles	Violet-colored beeswax candles with engraved sigils and name of the Archangel.

Table XII-1. ***Evocatory Correspondences for Raziel***[1]

Of Raziel

I was only moderately familiar with the Archangel who is said to be privy to the most arcane and divine secrets of the Creator. Raziel's name in Hebrew means "Secret of God," from the root רז (*raz*), "secret, mystery, hiden thing." The Angel is also known under the name *Galitzur* or *Galizur,* which means "Revealer of the Rock." He is in Kabbalistic tradition the Archangelic governor of the Sephirah Chokmah, and so one of the governors of the Briatic world, and the herald of Deity. Because he works so closely with the Creator, it is said that he knows all of the secrets of the Universe and how it operates. As Archangel of

1. Please see the Cautionary Warning Regarding Grimoric Ingredients in Appendix A. —APF

Chokmah, he is classed as a leader of the Cherubim in some traditions, and of the Ophanim in others.[2]

According to Hebraic lore, Raziel recorded the secrets of God in a tome called *Sepher Raziel*, *"The Book of Raziel,"* reputed according to one source to contain the 1,500 keys to the Mysteries of the universe.[3] He is known as the preceptor Angel of Adam, because after the first humans were expelled from Eden, Raziel bequeathed his book to Adam in order to guide him in understanding concerning God's grace.[4] Later, the prophet Enoch received the book prior to his ascension and transformation into the Archangel Metatron. Noah was also given the book, and he used the information to build his ark and to help its inhabitants after the flood.

There are several earthly texts which claim to be the Archangel's book, bearing names like *Sepher Raziel* and *Sepher Raziel ha-Malakh ("The Book of Raziel the Angel").* The existing *Books of Raziel* are, like many magical works, compilations of material, including excerpts from the older, similarly titled *Sepher ha-Razim ("Book of the Secrets").* A version of *Sepher Raziel* was printed for the first time in the Netherlands in 1701, and stories soon circulated that the book itself was a talisman that protected the home against fire, leading to many subsequent printings.

The *Book of Raziel* falls in line with many grimoires within the Solomonic magical strain in that it has detailed lists and ledgers of the Angels of the seven Heavens, with different rites and sacrifices to be performed in order to invoke them and receive their services. However, the book is difficult to decipher, and it is said that readers must call upon Raziel in order to make sense of it. In addition to the expected Kabbalistic references, the texts make obvious allusions to Gnostic and Hermetic cosmology.

---

2. The double-sided Talisman or Seal of Chokhmah in fig. XII-2, is originally from the *Calendarium Naturale Magicum Perpetuum,* and was included by Rudd/Smart in MS Sloane 3825 at folio 56v. It follows Agrippa's Scale of the Denary (*De Occulta Philosophia* II.XIII) in citing both hosts of Angels: *Cherubin* (Aramaic form of *Cherubim* or *Kerubim*), commonly associated with the Eighth Sphere by those following the Christian angelology of pseudo-Dionysios, and *Rotæ* (Latin translation of *Ophanim,* "Wheels"), associated with Chokhmah and the Eighth Sphere by Qabbalists. —APF

3. *Zohar* 1:55*a*, *Parashath Bereshith.* —APF

4. Each of the Hebrew patriarchs is said to have had a particular Angel who served as his preceptor or instructor. —APF

As the first revealer of Mysteries to humans, Raziel can apparently assist us in understanding esoteric wisdom of all varieties, from mystical philosophy to sacred geometry to quantum physics. In this capacity he is also said to assist magicians with opening themselves more fully to divine guidance and to psychic perception in general.

Fig. XII-2. ***Two-sided Talisman of the Starry Heaven attributed to Raziel in the*** **CALENDARIUM**

I found only a few seals and one sigil ascribed to Archangel Raziel. The first two seals (or two sides of a seal talisman) are to be found alongside an Invocation of Archangel Raziel in *The Keys to the Gateway of Magic* (Fig. XII-2).[5]

The other sigil of Raziel is in the Abognazar *Veritable Clavicles of Solomon* in the chapter "How to Make the Magic Carpet Proper for Interrogating the Intelligences, so as to Obtain an Answer Regarding Whatsoever Matter One May Wish to Learn." In addition to providing a sigil for Raziel, the rite introduces one very useful magical method, the making of a magical circle on a wool carpet, that is, a portable and reusable circle for evocation. The grimoire instructs:

> When thou shalt be desirous to make thine interrogations, choose the night of full or of new moon, and from midnight until daybreak. Thou shalt transport thyself unto the appointed spot if it be for the purpose of discovering a treasure; if not, any place will serve provided it be clean and pure. Having had the precaution on the preceding evening to write upon a slip of virgin parchment colored azure-blue, with a pen made from the feather of a dove, this Character and Name.

The Hebrew name is so corrupted in the manuscript that it is difficult to tell where the name ends and the sigil begins (Fig. XII-3), but it can be resolved with patience (Fig. XII-4). Therefore I was able to take the sigil into account

5. Lansdowne MS 1203, translated by Paul Harry Barron in Stephen Skinner and David Rankine (eds.), *The Veritable Key of Solomon* (Singapore: Golden Hoard Press, 2010), p. 152.The chapter and the sigil may also seen in Joseph H. Peterson's edition at his Twilit Grotto—Esoteric Archives website (http://www.esotericarchives.com/solomon/l1203.htm#chap28). Mathers translated the chapter in his edition of the *Key of Solomon the King*, but unfortunately did not include the sigil. —APF

Fig. XII-3. ***The corrupted name and character of Raziel in the Abognazar VERITABLE CLAVICLES OF SOLOMON***

Fig. XII-4. ***The rectified name and character of Raziel***

when fashioning the lamen for the experiment. It seems that the symbols most associated with the Archangel of Mysteries are the triangle, the pentagram, and the all-seeing eye. With a bit of assistance from my familiar Spirit, I completed the lamen design seen in Fig. XII-5, and made one for the operator of gold and one for the scryer on parchment which I dyed an azure blue color, using ink.

The only direct evocation of this Archangel which I found is the Second Key in *Dr. Rudd's Nine Hierarchies of Angels with Thir Invocations to Visible Appearance*, which survives in two manuscripts in the British Library. This is a form of that invocation, modified to eliminate some redundancy and to summon only Raziel rather than all the Angels of the Eighth Sphere:[6]

THE SECOND KEY

Moving or Calling Forth to Visible Appearance the Celestial Hierarchies Of Angels of the Order of Cherubim, whose principal governing Angel or blessed Intelligence bearing rule is Raziel, residing in the Eighth Orb, Mansion, or Sphere called the Starry Firmament.

THE PRAYER OR INVOCATION

O You great, glorious, sacred, and celestial Angel or blessed Intelligence who is called Raziel, servant of the most high, omnipotent, incomprehensible, immense, immortal, and eternal God of Hosts, the only Creator of Heaven and Earth, and of all things whatsoever—celestial, elemental, animal, vegetable, mineral, reptile, or insect—that are contained and comprehended therein, serving as a ministering Angel present always before Him, at His most superior and divine commands and

6. The invocation is in English in the manuscripts. A transcription of MS Harley 6482 was first published by Adam McLean in *A Treatise on Angel Magic: Being a Complete Transcription of Ms. Harley 6482 in the British Library* (Edinburgh: Magnum Opus Hermetic Sourceworks, 1982); and more recently a critical edition noting the variations between MSS Harley 6482 and Sloane 3825 was published by Stephen Skinner and David Rankine in *The Keys to the Gateway of Magic: Summoning the Solomonic Archangels & Demonic Princes* (Singapore: Golden Hoard Press, 2005). —APF

appointments, in the Order or hierarchy of Angels called Cherubim, and residing in the Eighth Heaven, and bearing office, rule, and power in the Sphere called the Starry Firmament:

We, the servants of the Highest, reverently here present in His holy fear, do call upon you, humbly request, earnestly entreat, and move you to visible appearance in, by, and through this most excellent, ineffable, great, mighty, signal, sacred, and Divine name of the most high God, Jod Jehovah, and His numeral attribute, Hockma,[7] *Him Who sitteth in the most imperial and highest Heavens, before Whom all the host or choir of Celestial Angels incessantly sing, « O Mappa-la-man Hallelujah, » and by the seal of your creation, being the mark or character of holiness unto you, and by the occult mystery and secret virtue, efficacy, and influence thereof, dignifying and confirming you in orders, office, name, nature, and corporality with Divine, Celestial, Angelical, immortal, eternal, and sublime excellency, glory, power, purity, perfection, goodness, and love, first unto the service of the most high God, and His divine laws and commands; and next unto the charge, care, conduct, counsel, comfort, benefit, and assistance of His servants, the sons of men living on Earth, to inspire, instruct, and guide them into the knowledge and way of truth, and all true physical and metaphysical sciences.*

Fig. XII-5. **The Lamen of Raziel in the manner of DSIC**

We do humbly beseech, earnestly request, and incessantly entreat you, O you magnificent, benevolent, and sacred Angel or blessed Intelligence Raziel, who is said to be the principal Angel or blessed Intelligence governing in the Eighth Sphere, called the Starry Heaven, minister of truth and true science and sapience both Celestial and Terrestrial, minister Spiritual of light, and medium of Divine grace from the superior to the inferior, residing and bearing rule in the Order called Cherubim in the Sphere of the Starry Firmament, as it shall please God, by Divine

7. "Hockma" is obviously the second Sephirah, *Chokhmah* (חכמה, "Wisdom"), and "numeral" is meant to translate Hebrew *Sephirah* (ספירה, a neologism coined by the author of the *Sepher Yetzirah*, and variously translated as "Number," "Word," or "Logos"). —APF

permission to move and descend from your Celestial Mansion or place of residence into this crystal stone, and therein to appear visibly unto us.

We do also entreat you to be favorably pleased in and through the same to transmit your true Angelical and real presence plainly unto the sight of our eyes, and your voice unto our ears, that we may visibly see you, and audibly hear you speak unto us, or otherwise to appear out of the same, as it shall please God and you, His servant of Divine grace and Messenger of mercy, as seemeth best befitting this action; and to show plainly and visibly unto us, a foregoing sign or test of your appearance, and we also yet further humbly and earnestly entreat, and undeniably request, and move you, O you benevolent & glorious Angel or blessed Intelligence Raziel. O you great Angel or blessed Intelligence Raziel, of the Order of Cherubim, medium of Divine grace and mercy, minister of true light and understanding, and servant of the most high God, particularly recited, and respectively spoken of, invocated, moved, and called forth to visible appearance as aforesaid, descend we say, by the power of Superior emission, appear visibly here before us, as shall please God, and be friendly unto us and in your respective office; do for us as for the servants of the most high God, whereunto we move you, in power and presence, whose works shall be a song of honor, and the praise of your God in your Creation. Amen.

The operation of evoking Raziel would have been placed in the supercelestial chapter with Uriel, Sandalphon, and Metatron had my scryer and I contacted him prior to the Olympic Spirits. However, this operation was conducted well after all the rest of the Angels and Spirits had been contacted. The timing, as usual, proved to be appropriate for my scryer and me to absorb the full gravity of the knowledge being shared.

Although prior experience had taught me repeatedly the futility of guessing and formulating expectations based on the Spirit's reputed nature, appearance, or capabilities, I inevitably found myself entertaining such notions once more. I surmised that we would contact an Angel who would simply reveal magical secrets, esoteric knowledge, and spiritual insights. As was the norm for Angels, this one turned my imaginings upside down.

The day for the operation arrived and almost did not take place as my scryer was feeling unwell. However, after a bit of urging on my part regarding the importance of the working, he pushed through any discomforts and arrived on time. I was impressed by his ability to overcome a difficult day and show up for the operation energetic and eager to evoke once more.

Invocation of the Archangel Raziel

Fig. XII-6. Section of Circle with Correspondences for Drawing Raziel into the Crystal

Appearance of the Spirit

OPERATOR: Do you perceive the Spirit?

SCRYER: Oh, yeah.

I can see four stars and I can hear a voice say, «Those are the four ruling stars, and they make a gateway through the six-pointed star.»

I hear another voice say, «And I am the key to the secret heart of God.»

At first the Spirit was not apparent to me in the Angelic realms but on earth, this world. I was looking at what appeared like an ordinary man, and he was observing the world. I could see him witnessing deeds of charity and deeds of cruelty. It was apparent that the man was not the Angel, but was only one of his eyes. I could see his Spirit leave the man and fly up between the four ruling stars between and in the middle of the six-pointed star to an opening of light that was shaped like a pyramid. The Spirit flying through this point of light looked almost like a black bird but partly human. When it went through the gateway, I could see that part of the vision was being hidden from me, as if it was blocked out. But I could only see the Spirit coming unto the throne of God.

Next I see I see the Angel Raziel whispering into the ear of God of what he had seen. In one ear he whispers the acts of charity he had witnessed, and in the other the acts of cruelty. His skin looks jet black; it's so black that it's almost hard to make out his features. He has long black hair, and wings of black like a crow's or a raven's, but eyes of shining gold. He has a long thin blade of obsidian with a haft of pure jet and a pommel jewel at the end of a large white pearl. In his other hand he holds a dove.

Fig. XII-7. ***Portrait of Raziel as beheld in Vision***

OPENING QUESTION 1: In the name of the holy and undefiled Spirit, the Father, the begotten Son, and Holy Ghost proceeding from both, what is thy true name?

SCRYER: He doesn't speak his own name, but I can hear a multitude of Angelic voices around him and the throne, and they sing his name «Raziel» once.

OPENING QUESTION 2: What is thy office, purpose, and function?

(Foreign, odd pacing and cadence in voice of scryer.)

SPIRIT: «I inform the Father of the drama and the play of unfolding creation that He has made. It is my barest of understandings from the Father that certain acts of charity and cruelty are signposts to the Creator; milestones in the unfolding story of His work.

«I look for Him; I listen for Him. I have many eyes and many what you would call ‹avatars› that have taken physical form on your world. I take these signposts back to God, these acts of charity and cruelty; that influence is a secret part within.»

OPENING QUESTION 3: What is thy true sign or character?

SPIRIT: «I have many, but the sigil on the parchment that you drew shows the four ruling stars, my many eyes, and the pathway through to the heart of God that lies at its center. It is one of my symbols that show the pathways that I take between the Creator and the created.»

OPENING QUESTION 4: When are the times most agreeable to thy nature to hold conference with us?

SPIRIT: «This is hard to answer because of the understanding of time. However, 1:00 AM is a good time to speak with me, to invoke me. When the heart is beset with the need to be charitable or cruel, in those moments, enveloped by darkness, those are the times when I am invoked that I will reveal to you most of the secrets that you are allowed to hear. At these times, the heart must be vulnerable, the mind should be slightly confused, and the body relaxed. When one of the four ruling stars is at its apex in the sky, this is also a good time to speak with me, to call to me.»

OATH: Wilt thou swear by the holy blood of Jesus Christ that thou art truly Archangel Raziel?

RAZIEL: «I swear by the blood of the beloved Son that I am Raziel. The symbol of the Son exposing His heart, the flaming heart of God, is a mirror or an echo of the journey that I take from the Creator to the created. It is always through the heart. When the Son showed His heart to the world, this was a recapitulation of that ancient Mystery, the bridge between the Creator and the world.»

QUESTION 6: Great Archangel Raziel, what are your views on humanity? What are your roles and interactions with us? Is there only one Angelic hierarchy per solar system or galaxy, or are there many such hierarchies, and if so, what is the extent in cosmic space of their rule?

RAZIEL: «In the end there is only one hierarchy, only one set of Archangels and the orders that go below them, level by level by level. Though in other parts of the universe, other solar systems, they are expressed symbolically in different ways, but their energy is the same. The tone of the note that God plucks on the strings of His harp may be heard differently being to being, but the vibration is the same. And all of us Angels who adore the Father long to be plucked by His fingers. We sound these vibrations at His will alone. When a man or a woman is blessed, they too become the willing heartstrings of God. So from place to place, or galaxy to galaxy, or planet to planet, the hierarchy, the tones are the same, though they are heard in different ways.

«My views on humanity are like my views of all life: I answer only to the creating, unfolding beauty of my Father. Mankind can chose to align himself with the harmony of the story of God or chose to take himself out of it; that is the blessing and curse of free will. It is my hope, with every fiber of what I am, that man aligns himself with the beauty of the Creator. In this capacity, I have no choice but to act as He instructs, nor would I want the choice to not be able to follow His grace. But He gave all of mankind the right to choose to follow Him into the harmony, that acceptance all living creatures, or to go into the coldest of exiles.

«In my journeys between His heart and your world, I whisper secrets into the hearts and minds of men. It is my faint understanding that in the deeds that are done here on earth, the Creator has an idea of which secrets are to be revealed to whom and to when. For every act of charity comes another gift from the Creator. From every act of cruelty comes a curse.»

Question 7: What can you teach of us of true alchemy, of magic, and the hidden knowledge of occult magic and working with Spirits?

Raziel: «True alchemy is similar to the Mystery that I have just expressed. Will you mold your Spirit into lead or to gold? Will you understand the nuances of the alchemy of your Spirit, and use them to serve the unfolding vision of the Creator? Or will you use all of the nuances and the blessings that you have been given to work for your own purpose? Silver is like the mind; it is open, it is clear, but will tarnish without renewal. It can chastise and it can feed. Gold is a dim, dim reflection of the perfection of the Creator's vision. Gold uplifts, it elevates, it inspires. Lead deadens, causes disease, and weighs the Spirit of man down into the baser of his natures. Even these symbols do not express the real power of alchemy; they only hint at the outer nature of things cannot be fully understood with the mind. Deeper secrets may be understood with the body and with the heart. They can be bathed in like the Jordan. I should also say that one man's expression of ‹gold› will not be another's. Unrelenting clinging to moral absolutes weighs down like lead. The mind of God is like the world expressed through nature. To observe the many varieties of trees, fish, stones, or flowers around you is the barest hint of the diverse mind of God.»

Question 8: Great Archangel Raziel, can you impart to us any further knowledge on the making of magical tools or talismans to best harness the benefits of your office? Can you impart to us any unique talisman or magical method to grant us the positive powers of your office?

Raziel: «I can say that your invocations will be more affective, especially with the crystal, that if there are stars on the talisman of the Angel or Demon that you are speaking, there should also be accompanying reflections on the crystal from the point of view of the scryer. When the candles glint off of the crystal, the position of each glint should correspond with the star on the talisman. The two candles that burn on either side of the altar should always remain. The absence of which will not be a block for them communicating, but it will open the door wider.

«An orb of pure gold is precious to me. Not because of its monetary worth, but because of what it represents: It symbolizes the pure singular vision of my Father. It should be uninscribed, smooth, pure, and may be of any size. Procure whatever is within your means. When this orb of gold is held, cradled next to the heart like I cradle my dove next to my heart, the spirit of the dove which I have saved since Noah, who is always with me, when this orb of gold is held near to the heart at 1:00 AM, within darkness or doubt, give me the pure truth of your thoughts in this hour and I promise to take them to the heart of God.»

QUESTION 9: Great Archangel, can you tell us more about the obsidian-looking blade with the jet handle and pearl pommel in your one hand and the dove in your other? I am curious as to their deeper symbolic meaning and purpose.

RAZIEL: «This is hard to fully explain and put into words. The best way to relate this to a human would be that the blade is like the void; the handle, the place of balance; and the pearl, the gift of creation of light that is upheld by the void.»

QUESTION 10: Was humanity created on earth or did humanity migrate from other worlds/existences? Is there anything you can teach us about this that is not known?

(Odd whispers, breathing can be heard outside circle.)

RAZIEL: «The form of humanity was born here, fashioned by wind and earth, air, fire, water. Fashioned by walking and running, by moving, adapting, changing. The form of man enables him to live perfectly here. However, the spirits of men are formed of ‹tribes.› Some of the tribes have been here since the very beginning, their spirits born of this world, nurtured and made by this world. And there are tribes who have come from among the stars. Although there are many nuances between the two types of tribes, there are different degrees of bloodlines they hold. The ones born here will remain here. They are old; they are caretakers of the world. They love the forms of this world deeper than any of the other tribes of men do. The other tribes—of which there are many now on this crossroads that humanity stands at—are drawn by the drama of what is happening. They are in some ways like children, thrill seekers who bounce from star to star, planet to planet, seeking the transitional times. Any further discussion on this would take a very long time to explain, but that is the basic representation.»

QUESTION 11: Is there any significance to the recent Venus occultation and other Planetary activity at this time? Does it affect anything on a global scale?

RAZIEL: «Of Venus I will say only this for now. In future times with me, I will explain more. Venus is the gateway, one of the first gateways where love came from God into your world. The pulsing of Venus lately is to let a little more of that original power in because it is desperately needed.»

QUESTION 12: What, if any, specific magical influences are impacting the increased violent activates in the world right now, and if so, what is the larger goal?

RAZIEL: «Before most of humanity lies two roads: The road of charity and the road of cruelty. The time has come in your unfolding story that each of you is being asked to make a choice between these two roads: to align with the unfolding beauty of the harmony of God, or to align with the self-delusions of your own visions. In between these roads is the place of the magician. For you must learn with your magics to seduce the hearts of men onto the right road. This is not a matter any longer of faith or wisdom; it is now a matter of survival if you wish your race to stay within the story of God.»

QUESTION 13: Do you have any further advice or wisdom for us? As magicians, how and in which ways we should accomplish this?

RAZIEL: «Invocations must be frequent. Walk the road as often as possible between you and the secret heart of the Creator. Carry this deep, ancient, and unbreakable magic with you as you move through the world and broadcast this magic consciously to all around you. Come together as magical brethren and open the gateway together and move the magic through the world at different places and at different times. Your role is absolutely essential to the survival of your species now. If you do not act in this capacity, the chapters that you write in the story of God are rapidly coming to a close. If you act in your capacity, and seduce the hearts of men to follow the brilliance of the harmony that God has made for you, then as a race, people, your story has only barely begun. God is calling you back to the Garden. It is your choice to go.»

QUESTION 14: What are your and other Angels' relationship to Christianity? How do you perceive the spiritual significance of the Roman Catholic sacraments? What about the sacraments given in other Christian denominations, such as the Gnostic one I'm a part of?

RAZIEL: «When the institution serves to open a path between the secret heart of God and the secret heart of the people, it is blessed. When the institution deliberately closes the pathway between the secret heart of God and the people, it becomes lost, cursed. Each institution must never place itself above the possibility that it may one day decide to close the passageway rather than open it. Whether a pontiff, a bishop, a saint, or a layman, each one lends a hand in keeping the sacred passageway open. When the passageway is open, the work is done well and blessings flow. This takes a tremendous amount of faith, because often what God reveals in His unfolding story is not what we expect. All the institution that are created—whether Roman Catholic, Greek Orthodox, Baptist, Jehovah's Witness, and the many, many others—are good when they keep the passage open. When it is closed, they do the work of the Enemy. None are above this.»

QUESTION 15: I was inspired to contact you through some individuals in the Gentleman of Jupiter who claimed that you and Archangel Tzadkiel/Sachiel had been powerfully working together, and that through the combined working, wisdom could be generated for further progression and success.

RAZIEL: «Yes. The first working is the prayer of the golden orb done solely with me. When you hold the orb close to your heart at 1:00 AM when your mind and your heart is in darkness and despair, it is the first key that will open another doorway into the generosity and power of Tzadkiel. Once this is done and done genuinely, when your darkness through the prayer of the golden orb is transformed directly into light, summon me again.»

QUESTION 16: What is the particular significance of the Hebrew Kabbalah for the contemporary magician? Is it necessary to always evoke Angels with Hebrew names? Do you have other names that predate the Hebrew culture, or others that are more universal?

RAZIEL: «An older name of mine is 'Hazheir'/'Hazhair'/'Azhear.' *(Galizur?)* It is not Hebrew. Hebrew names are not necessary per se, but they are like a band of musicians or an orchestra. It is like the harmonics that a cello, a trumpet, a violin, a bass have; all of these things play well naturally with each other; their tones, their sounds coincide with one another and the system of notation and the distance between notes, the way they are played, are harmonized to enable to create the right music to summon the energies or the beings they wish. However, combined with the symbols or instruments of names of other traditions, the overall harmonics of the action breaks down. Regardless, as you interact as magicians and learn from one another, a day is coming—if your mastery of your own harmonics is high enough—they will start to be able to blend it with the harmonic of others. The Kabbalah is one of those sets of harmonics that works well when used wisely, integrated into the proper methods of invocation. It expresses a base energy that can be expressed in different ways by different peoples in different cultures in a different system. That underlying transmission is the secret heart of God.»

SCRYER: This is so interesting. Throughout this whole section I can see him puzzling over language. He closes his eyes and moves the obsidian blade out in front of him. His arm extends out with his hand on top of the pommel and he gets this faraway look in his eyes. He has the most incredible golden eyes. He moves his index finger around the pearl almost like a Planet orbiting the star, and the blade quivers in place without being touched. At the same time he moves the dove up to his chest, and it begins to coo.

QUESTION 17: Archangel Raziel, you are credited with writing the *Book of Secrets* that was given to Adam. Is there anything you can tell us of the secrets contained within the original book given to Adam? Tell us about the secrets you proclaimed to men on Mount Horeb.[8]

RAZIEL: «Although the original book that was given no longer exists, fragments of its wisdom are in many works of men. What was shown to Adam in the book was the deeper explanation of why there was a choice for the knowledge of good and evil, or put in another way, of charity and cruelty. The doorway to the Tree of Life is through the Tree of Knowledge of Good and Evil. Only by those passages can it be reached. In order for free will to be born. The book outlines the need for the Tree of Good and Evil, for the great initiator of women to give the apple, and the ways through prayers, through song, through invocation, through ceremony for men to call themselves to the Tree of Life.»

QUESTION 18: Great and mighty Archangel Raziel, you of divine wisdom and the Secrets of the Creator, we thank thee for Thy attendance upon this ceremony and ask of you if there are any finale words or secrets or wisdom to best help us during this time before we bid you hail and farewell?

RAZIEL: «I cannot stress the importance enough of the prayer of the golden orb. It is in those moments at 1:00 AM, when your heart is in the greatest of despair, that you must come to me. Come within your circles, with that golden orb held against your heart as if it was the cooing dove. If you as the magician can transform your spirit in that moment from the darkness

8. This is a reference to the Targum (an Aramaic 'translation' of the Hebrew Bible, which is actually more of a paraphrase with commentary) on *Ecclesiastes* 10:20. The Hebrew verse cautions against cursing the powerful in secret, for "a bird of the air shall carry the voice, and that which hath wings shall tell the matter" (KJV). However, it may be read literally as "a Flying Being of the Heavens [*Oph ha-Shamayim*] shall carry the voice, and a Lord of Wings [*Baal ha-Kenaphim*] shall proclaim the word [*davar*, which can also refer to an oracular message]"), which the Targum expands into a statement that the voice of the Archangel Raziel daily speaks from the Heavens, revealing secrets on sacred Mt. Horeb, and that his voice reverberates throughout the world. —APF

of the sword to the pearl of the pommel, the greater blessings of Tzadkiel await, and your skill at seducing the minds and hearts of men and women toward the path of charity will increase. When this is done, genuinely, when tears come down your face because you know and feel with your body the blessing you have received, then invoke me again.»

(License to Depart given.)

Afterthoughts on the Raziel Operation

Both my scryer and I were shaking after this one. That was completely different than I expected, and throughout the expeieince I was moved by very intense feelings. It felt very foreboding in many parts, but also intriguing and inspiring.

SCRYER: This was just—it was so interesting. Throughout the operation I really got the sense that the Angel had all of this stuff that he wanted to say, but that language was a barrier or not suitable to convey it properly. His eyes looked like gold fire going throughout the filaments of his irises. I'll never forget that; it blew me away. Then he would extend his right arm out and move his finger around the pearl and the sword would vibrate so quickly it would hum. At the same time he would hold the dove nearer to his chest and it would start to coo. An olive branch would all of a sudden materialize in its beak! I suppose this was the same branch that was brought to Noah, like the Angel described. When he moved the dove away again, the branch would simply vanish. I was really captivated by this one. It felt like he could have gone on and on. It was as if he was ready to talk, but knowing that there would be difficulty in us being able to comprehend what he had to say.

Another part that really stood out was when Raziel was showing me how he whispered acts of kindness and cruelty to the Creator. He somehow emphasized to me that both acts were signposts in some way. When the Creator heard certain events that were happening, He would give something back to Raziel to further the story along. Whatever he gave or said back to the Angel were the Mysteries that were the secrets that were not revealed yet. I was shown that creation was *always* happening, that it was an ongoing work.

Indeed this was perhaps the most amazing 'secret' or bit of sacred knowledge given: that God's creation was ongoing, and not something that happened long ago and was done, but that His work as well as His story and message was still developing. I became aware that God is constantly creating, and the feedback that He is given determines it in a large way, the forming of it. It's interplay between the Creator and created. I will never forget that.

I will also never fucking forget this: When he was talking about the two roads, he showed me one that was light and one was dark. The dark one showed the most horrible acts of mankind imaginable. It made me sick to even look at. There was cannibalism, rape, torture, murder, awful, awful stuff...things of your worst nightmares. Then on the light side was this green, verdant world. It showed images of all of life that was thriving, and humanity was bathed in prosperity. It was way more than anyone could ever want or need.

In the middle of the two roads appeared a magician. After the Angel laid out the two roads in front of me, I saw a magician floating between them, between these two worlds. I watched as he began calling people from the dark road toward the white road. The magician could see both roads clearly; he knew both were a possibility and he was blessed with the ability to call people from one to the other. It seemed like he needed to know both to effectively bring people from one side to the other. The Angel seemed to convey to me that this is what a druid, priest, seer, witch, and shaman, whatever you want to call it, the role that they play. They are the mediators between the two roads. They stand between the light and shadow, candle and the flame, darkness and light. That vision was extremely intense, extremely potent.

I got a feeling there was so much to communicate; there was a lot to convey but they were more doors. The work has to continue; the stuff he would say wouldn't make sense without it. The prayer of the golden orb seemed amazingly important. It seemed like the worse you felt, the more powerful it would be, and the greater the blessing.

I am just shaking after this.

For some reason it really reminded me of the Mercurial Archangel we contacted, Raphael, and also the Olympic Spirit Ophiel. It would be nice to go back and review those; I'm not sure why they felt so familiar or conencted.

With the question you had about Tzadkiel and this Archangel, I really got the impression that he thought that was a great question or perhaps a question he was waiting for: You need to think more about how we combine, how we work together. There is a deeper Mystery here once that gets unlocked with the working of the golden orb, I think.

So apparently the reflections of the candles from the talisman should be in the same places as the stars on the talisman, so that it matches up, making almost the same pattern from the reflections on the crystal to the talisman.

OPERATOR: So according to the Archangel's allusions, on the lamens of the *DSIC* or *Fourth Book*, the circle seemed to represent the crystal itself, the surrounding stars corresponding to the lights of the candles around the central six-pointed star, which represents the sacred area of the Spirits themselves where they appear.

SCRYER: The choice of humanity I also found fascinating. The Angel made it clear that it was not God simply directing that one man should go here or there, but that the choice was ultimately up to each individual. It wasn't dictated by a single religion or path, either; it was simply that you either harmonize with His story, or you don't. I thought that was interesting. It is indeed a stark choice, but the magician was shown to stand between those two roads and is meant to be in between those two visions and recognize the power of both. Their function is to move the energies between those two visions. I have a feeling that image is going to present a lot more to us in the years ahead. We both get shivers from this.

I feel great right now; I feel so much better.

OPERATOR: I could see the face of Raziel clearly at some points; it was hard for me to look the Angel in the face, in the golden eyes, during parts of the evocation. It was rather intense and I really can't explain my feelings or thoughts at that time.

My scryer and I both noticed the candles and light intensify once more as soon as the Spirit arrived.

The working was so intense and a lot to take on and responsibility to shoulder. During the operation it seemed impossible to downplay this or circumvent the intensity of the message. It was apparent and right in our faces. I felt somehow bewildered by this operation; I'm not sure why. It deeply affected me on many levels. So much mystery and meaning that my mind was twirling for days after.

SCRYER: We seem to be reaching a critical time. We really need to step into our roles as magicians and take it seriously. We simply cannot afford to be distracted. I'm really not sure how to integrate all this tonight. It was a bit overwhelming, to be honest.

OPERATOR: It seemed important but I never considered this work to have any devastating consequences or meaning beyond my own development and curiosity.

SCRYER: I think you need to include this operation at the end of the book. You need to bring this energy into the world wherever you happen to be. I think this happened tonight for a reason.

I had once again stepped into the circle for an Angelic operation naively thinking that my scryer and I would simply be privy to occult knowledge and secrets. The Spirit's answers to my questions challenged my notions of acceptable truths. Discussion ensued far into the night with my scryer in an attempt to understand the full weight of what we were told. One realization was that neither my scryer nor I would have been ready for this operation without the many interactions in which we had previously participated.

After several pre-ritual weeks of a strict vegetarian diet, abstinence, and similar acts of purification, I was nearly emotionally and energetically turned upside down from the effects of the working. I hadn't taken into account the considerable length of time that had transpired since my scryer and I had last conducted an operation. The experiences—for all the amazement and wonder they bring—are taxing on the human condition. I discovered that being in a receptive state and then receiving powerful information that I possibly wasn't prepared to accept made returning to normal functions challenging. I came away amazed, but not feeling as strong and up to the task as I have after prior workings. My faults and petty distractions felt stacked up against me in face of the experiences in which I have been allowed to participate.

The responses of this Archangel of Mysteries were foreboding in several cases and placed a lot more responsibility on my shoulders than I may ever be willing to accept. The emotional and energetic effects of this working really seemed to take a toll. The gift of the experience and working came with a price: a choice that is becoming just clear enough to realize that the alternative is far worse.

For some readers, the records of these magical experiments may be little more than an entertaining or interesting read. For my scryer and me, the experience of Archangel Raziel and his communication was profound to the point of being life-changing. Although the same could be said to some extent of every preceding operation, Raziel offered very serious pronouncements about what results either action or inaction would have in our reality.

We live in a participatory universe. Magicians forever play a practical role within their societies, acting in the interests of their own lives and livelihoods and those of their loved ones, associates, and clients. However the magical work, if successful, will rarely cease at those levels, as there is a vast difference between simply exerting one's will and ideals on a personal scale and acting out of a creative and purposeful center for the good of all. There is a particular wisdom that comes with real compassion, and it is a compassion that has no attachment to the outcomes of other's actions or to our own egos. It is this wisdom of human relationship that will be the key to unlocking the deepest secrets and magical potential of humanity.

I was fascinated to discover the parallels between the experience my scryer and I had of this Archangel with that of other magicians pursuing classical magical practice. The following is part of a response from the magical associate in the Jupiter Order who initially suggested that we contact Raziel:

> I worked with Angels extensively during the early part of the Yetzirah work with NN and OO, we were working our way up the classic Western Magical Tradition angelic hierarchy and I had amazing experiences. But compared to the visions, atmospheres and ecstasies that I experienced with the others a few words from Raziel were enough to change the course of my entire life. This is not to belittle the other angels; I want to be very clear on that. I've been trying to explain what Raziel has communicated over the past few years and it has completely flipped my mind upside down and inside out—almost literally.
>
> The experiences with Raziel have been similar in feeling to that of Indrid Cold in the film *Mothman Prophecies*. It is chilling but not because the entity is hostile; it just makes people think extremely deeply about everything. These workings are not for the faint of heart and I salute you, brother magus, for undertaking them and specifically this one.
>
> I want to draw your attention to *Job* 28 again, which Raziel sent as a communication for the Gentlemen of Jupiter.

I did not know what *Job* 28 contained at all; my Bible reading, at least in this life, is limited. I had almost certainly never encountered it previously, or if I had, it must have been buried in my subconscious.

Job 28

Interlude: Where Wisdom Is Found

There is a mine for silver
and a place where gold is refined.

Iron is taken from the earth,
and copper is smelted from ore.
Mortals put an end to the darkness;
they search out the farthest recesses
for ore in the blackest darkness.
Far from human dwellings they cut a shaft,
in places untouched by human feet;
far from other people they dangle and sway.
The earth, from which food comes,
is transformed below as by fire;
lapis lazuli comes from its rocks,
and its dust contains nuggets of gold.
No bird of prey knows that hidden path,
no falcon's eye has seen it.
Proud beasts do not set foot on it,
and no lion prowls there.
People assault the flinty rock with their hands
and lay bare the roots of the mountains.
They tunnel through the rock;
their eyes see all its treasures.
They search the sources of the rivers
and bring hidden things to light.
But where can wisdom be found?
Where does understanding dwell?
No mortal comprehends its worth;
it cannot be found in the land of the living.
The deep says, "It is not in me";
the sea says, "It is not with me."
It cannot be bought with the finest gold,
nor can its price be weighed out in silver.
It cannot be bought with the gold of Ophir,
with precious onyx or lapis lazuli.
Neither gold nor crystal can compare with it,
nor can it be had for jewels of gold.
Coral and jasper are not worthy of mention;
the price of wisdom is beyond rubies.
The topaz of Cush cannot compare with it;
it cannot be bought with pure gold.
Where then does wisdom come from?
Where does understanding dwell?
It is hidden from the eyes of every living thing,
concealed even from the birds in the sky.
Destruction and Death say,

"Only a rumor of it has reached our ears."
God understands the way to it
and he alone knows where it dwells,
for he views the ends of the earth
and sees everything under the heavens.
When he established the force of the wind
and measured out the waters,
when he made a decree for the rain
and a path for the thunderstorm,
then he looked at wisdom and appraised it;
he confirmed it and tested it.
And he said to the human race,
"The fear of the Lord—that is wisdom,
and to shun evil is understanding."[9]

Reading this *Psalm* that my associate had pointed out, the message struck me where before I would not have grasped the depth of its meaning. To the casual reader, it would look very much like a simple relation of men working riches from the earth, and discerning where true value and riches exist within themselves. The *Psalm* opens up many hidden mysteries, signifying something specific that perhaps only the initiated will grasp and comprehend.

Although being a magician goes hand in hand with influencing a wide variety of situations, I was never much for trying to influence the beliefs and actions of another person. I am also wary of any Spirit who tells me that my actions are enormously important in any way and that I'm required to persuade others to believe or become supportive of any ideal or spirituality. With all this stated, I could not help but be moved by the seriousness of the words that were spoken, and even more so by the overall feeling and intensity that was communicated by the Spirit. Also, the Angel of Mysteries did not attempt to inflate my ego by claiming that either my scryer or I was a prophet or intended to lead a group of people, or form a new religion (think Mormonism). Likewise, the Angel did not claim that one religion was predominant and that we needed to convince others of a tradition's supremacy as the 'one true faith.' On the contrary, many institutions were acknowledged but warned against the closing of doors. The primary urgency communicated by the Archangel seemed to be in relation to the task of leading others to compassion rather than cruelty.

Raziel's words were a challenge to seriously consider what path to follow and to what end these experiences and interactions would be used. My scryer and

9. *Job* 28 (NIV translation).

I have indeed been blessed with rare opportunities and experiences very few appear to have encountered. We have been privy to sights, sounds, images, and happenings that border on the unbelievable. My early yearnings to experience the reality of the spiritual world and magic have been answered a hundredfold. The question remains, to what use do we put such experiences beyond our own satisfaction? If these beings do have any measure of objective reality and their words are to be trusted, how should we respond to them? As a magus, what will your gifts, efforts, and talents be used for once you realize they are intended for a higher purpose than personal gratification?

It's tempting to consider that all of the events and blessings are self-generated and that the magic and wonders extend solely from within. However, both intuition and reason inform me that this is simply not the case. If anything, I have seen clear evidence of external support and assistance. For example, many of my magical successes must be accredited to Hiram's instruction and advice, often reminding me of crucial points I missed or elements I overlooked. The Angels have provided guidance and instruction far beyond what I could have reasoned out for myself. True magic is not the displayed power emerging from a practitioner, but the evidence of Spiritual assistance far beyond the conscious apprehensions of a human being. If there is one fact of which I am well aware, it is that there are many others whose faculties of concentration, piety, patience, consecration, and will are more highly developed than mine. The records do not speak to my or my scryer's extraordinary abilities, but to the wondrous grace bestowed upon us from that unknowable but intimate Source of creation. My only hope is to somehow give due credit and return for the gifts which have been bestowed upon us, and perhaps inspire those better suited than I to carry on the legacy of these traditions. If more magicians were to balance the aims of their craft between personal practical ends and furthering the progression of mankind away from its destruction, then magic could fulfill its potential as a force for good in the world. Beyond religion, creed, or tradition, there exist the examples of human excellence. When this excellence is expressed through the will of a magician, it has the potential to reach beyond perceived limits of time and space. We become the emissaries of humanity's true story, all too often hidden, obscured, and misunderstood.

The grimoires, even some of the darker ones dealing with Goetic beings, insist on spiritual refinement and humility before God. This is an area sorely overlooked and disregarded by too many modern enthusiasts of ceremonial magic. These passages are not, as some have suggested, simply blinds and deterrents to escape persecution in earlier days, but are in fact an expression of the true spiritual passions of the authors. Spiritual piety and reverence are virtues lacking in today's society of comfort and entitlement. And contrary to the over-simplifications of much current discussion of spirituality and religion in the West, one can be deeply spiritual and even devout without being a zealot or fanatic. Spirituality is very much an individual affair with which each person should come to terms in his own way. However, without some sense of deep connection with and passion for the divine powers which infuse the entirety of the classic magical worldview, the aspiring magus will not achieve access to the highest possibilities within his or her craft. The Archangel Raziel challenges us as magicians to take on more responsibilities in our roles, and to use our gifts for the betterment of humanity.

Further research into the Archangel of the Mysteries led me to the writings of Abraham Abulafia, the founder of the school of Prophetic Kabbalah. This medieval sage wrote concerning Archangel Raziel:

> If you wish to learn before a great master, who is the angel of prophecy, whose name is Raziel, and if you understand all that I have hinted of his power and his teaching, then you will know the secret of his name. And if you wish to be one of his disciples and to learn in his book, which is that of the completely righteous, and you wish to be inscribed with them immediately for eternity, then take care to study continually from [the age of] thirteen years until [the age of] forty years in the book of the intermediate ones before the good angel Gallizur, who is the intellective master; and from forty years onward let your principal study be before Raziel, and then secrets of wisdom shall be revealed to you, for you shall already be a great man among the giants.[10]

10. Abulafia, *Sepher Toledoth Adam*, trans. in Moshe Idel, *Kabbalah in Italy, 1280–1510: A Survey* (New Haven: Yale University Press, 2011), p. 151. Abulafia was so strongly influenced by Raziel that he assumed the Archangel's name as one of his own mystical names. —APF

Afterword

The Path of the Scryer

BEING A SCRYER is the art of getting out of the way. This can be a real challenge for the modern mind which lives in a culture that emphasizes thinking, thinking, and more thinking. As a scryer, you are called upon to be a clear vessel so that beings greater and older than yourself can speak and interact with the Magician. This requires dropping all preconceived notions of what form the Spirit will appear in, how its voice should sound, or what implements or symbols it should wield. Abandon yourself to faith. Relax and let the Magician set the space, ask the questions, and make the necessary prayers and supplications. Faith in the process of the invocations, and the ability of the Magician to call the spirits to you, is one of the most important factors that enable you to "get out of the way."

Perhaps the most under-emphasized aspect of being a scryer is the body. There are those with natural abilities to "see" without a healthy body, but this natural talent often comes at a tremendous cost to their personal lives. For the scryer that needs to live with one foot in the world of Spirits and one foot in the everyday world of jobs, family, taxes, and friends, the health of the body is an essential component. If the scryer is a receiver of spiritual and cosmological energies, the body is the radio that anchors these communications to this plane of existence.

It has been my experience that what is actually received during a magical working versus what is consciously apprehended by the scryer is vastly different. In any magical working the scryer is conscious of and communicates maybe ten percent of what is actually given. The majority of the experience takes place below the level of the conscious mind and is integrated by a far wiser instrument, the body and the soul.

As my teacher Orion Foxwood is fond of saying, "The mind is a useful tool, but it shouldn't run the show." Before, during, and sometimes after your working you will have thoughts that you're "making it all up." In truth only experience dispels doubt, but never fully conquers it. Doubt keeps the scryer humble and allows him or her to experience the wisdom of "I don't know." Report what you see and experience and do your best not to interpret or judge. Even if what you see is contrary to the older grimoires or established tradition, don't ignore it or explain it away. The mind loves to explain, interpret, judge, and alter. Often the contradictions (and there will be many) end up showing you the truth. Let go of needing to know and "get it right," and have faith in the Magician and your own precious experiences. You are not trying to regurgitate the experiences of scryers past; you are linking with entities capable of giving endless wisdom and letting them speak to the world now.

Much of what comes across in your scrying may at first be confusing or nonsensical. But over time these apparent aberrations come to make more and more sense. The more operations you do, the more locks in your spirit are released. Some locks need to be opened before others can be approached or even noticed. Faith in the unfolding process of multiple evocations and communications helps the scryer not to edit or question what is seen. Ultimately the best aspect of being a scryer is the blessing of actually standing in the presence of Angelic and Spiritual beings who are older than time itself. Reading grimoires or stories of other magicians gives you only the leftovers of lessons and teachings meant for others. Bathing in the presence of Spirits is where real magic exists. Long after the session is over, you may suddenly get epiphanies seemingly out of the blue that did not even occur to you during the working itself. What you are receiving as a scryer is so much bigger than you can comprehend that it often takes our limited minds and limited vocabulary time to catch up. Insights come when they are needed, so don't try and rush the process. Keep the modern obsession with quick fixes and quick knowing out of the circle.

In many of my sessions with Angels, they have continually reminded me of the tremendous blessing it is to be a scryer. They have shown me time and again that far from being a weekend-warrior activity, scrying is meant to transform your life and your reality. It requires a commitment that speaks back to the Spirits through your actions and says, "In return for these gifts that you have given to me, I express my devotion and gratitude through service. I place my distractions aside and give to you my life transformed."

Four Cornerstones of Scrying

I will end with what I call the Four Cornerstones of Scrying. These are suggestions of things that will stabilize and enhance your scrying abilities so you can communicate the sights and messages of the Spiritual world to the Magician when a working is taking place. The electrical/nervous system of trees, animals, reptiles, and mammals that allows them to perceive things beyond the ken of humanity is only accessible to them when their bodies are in a state of relative wellness. As incarnate beings, why would these same rules not apply to humanity? Never underestimate the importance of the body in perceiving Spiritual and Angelic realms. The body is an ancient miracle of evolution containing the experiences of your ancestors. As such, it has untapped modes of perception that open up in a balanced way when the body is well cared for. The Four Cornerstones are rooted in the four elements: Earth (diet), Water (hydration), Fire (exercise), and Air (devotion).

The First Cornerstone is Earth, or diet. Your diet, as often as possible, should be centered on eating foods that are whole, or as close to their original created state as possible. Many modern foods keep the body alive but often tax the spirit and blind the spiritual eyes. It is best to go into a magical session with an empty stomach, giving at least two hours of time since your last meal. Your meals leading up to the day of the working should be whole foods that make you feel awake, alive, and happy. If you do not know what kinds of foods those may be for you, it is time to start paying attention.

The Second Cornerstone is Water, or hydration. Water is the best "food" for your scrying eyes. Avoid alcohol, drugs of all kinds (if you can), and bless the water that you drink. Water is a powerful element of purification and cleansing. All that you experience in your everyday life (good and bad) can take root in your body, even if your mind has forgotten the experience altogether. Water helps the body clear these internal barriers, removing the extra filters between you and the Spirits you seek. Pray over the water you absorb that it may give you the ability to scry more clearly and channel the energies released in a beneficial way for you and the Magician. If you are not hydrated, scrying can be difficult and confusing even if all three of the other cornerstones are handled.

The Third Cornerstone is Fire, or exercise. In order for a radio to receive a signal, it has to have a power source. The power of the spirit is stoked by regular exercise. When I started to regularly practice Kundalini Yoga, it revolutionized my ability to scry. The form of exercise does not matter, however, as any regular routine of exercise will do the trick. The fire of exercise helps to move "body held" experiences out of your spirit, burning away the filters that may cloud your communications with Spiritual beings. With the fire of exercise, you will find that your magical workings will have a more durable impact on your thoughts, emotions, and actions. You will also notice that after your working is over you will be excited and refreshed rather than drained and sleepy.

The Fourth Cornerstone is Air, or devotion. Maintaining regular contact with the powers you hold dear is essential to receiving blessings and gifts that will help you along the way. As you become more aware of the Spirit world, it becomes more aware of you. After sessions have ended, you may be visited by unwelcome Spirits at unwelcome times. If this happens, be sure to inform your Magician so he or she can provide you with talismans to keep unwanted Spirits at bay when you are just trying to get a good night's sleep. Aside from what your Magician can provide you, your own regular devotion to the powers who watch over you help fend off these kinds of visitors. Not only does the power of your devotion provide you with protection, it will also help you integrate and understand the teachings and visions you receive. Use song, prayer, mantra, meditation, or any other practice of devotion to set aside time in your life to connect with the powers who watch over you. As a scryer, they are allies you cannot afford to do without.

Benn mac Stiofán
May 2016

Conclusion

> The value of wisdom cannot be measured, nor understanding of knowledge. Also, there is no measure to the value of the secrets written herein, as revealed by Elohim.... Elohim treasures the reverence. The Lord fills all the Earth with glory, as in heaven where the throne is established. There is no measure to the glory.[1]

THE EVENTS RELATED IN THIS BOOK were and are, in many ways, at the pinnacle of my magical career. As a classical ritual magician, the amount of data and interaction with Spiritual beings resulting in phenomenal occurrences and changes in our realities was second to none. Beyond any question of relevance, usefulness or life altering enlightenment, the experiences of each evocation left a profound impact on my life and my considerations for magical practice, and the objective existence of spiritual beings. Thanks to the experiences from the very beginning of my work in *Drawing Spirits into Crystals*, Angels and Spirits are no longer just names; they are active, vibrant, and unique aspects of creation which have left a lasting imprint. The experiences are even more profound since I've now shared these wondrous events with a close friend. There is absolutely no question that the experiences related in this work have changed the way our magic is practiced as a whole and also the dynamic way interaction with Spirits is conducted. Both my scryer and I have commented to each other several times how our individual workings have heightened in both clarity and complexity, far beyond what we considered was even possible prior to these operations. This

1. Steve Savedow (trans.), *Sepher Rezial Hemelach: The Book of the Angel Rezial* (York Beach, ME: Samuel Weiser, 2000), p. 1. —APF

is an observation which continues to grow truer with each subsequent working since the events related in this book.

As mentioned earlier in this work, I don't believe it's possible for someone to successfully conduct these experiences in a sterile, purely objective manner without being impacted by the presence of and interaction with the Spirits. In truth, I don't consider such a scenario to be a veritable interaction with the Spiritual on any practical or significant level. In several respects, linear reasoning and rational explanations do not always relate to this art and practice. Indeed, one paradox lies in mankind's efforts to sort, classify, categorize, and label certain events and beings which by all sense of reality do not conform to any such limitations. Yet it is by these efforts that our forebears in magic were able to organize and relate to the unseen world which existed in earnest all around them in often complex and confusing modalities. In this understanding, I personally experience no conflict in considering that the beings which my scryer and I beheld, as well as their instruction and elegant responses, were not concrete facts, meant to be integrated into an unmoving objective consciousness, but that they were blessings of information and considerations for our present time of being, and involvement with the world around us. It could easily be argued that the latter form of interaction and exchange is far more powerful and meaningful than the former, and much more practical as a source of moving, breathing, and living magic.

Twenty-some years is not a terribly long time to become an expert in any field, but I do feel that my efforts have given me a certain perspective on the practice of classical ritual magic. From my beginning as a novice, my standpoint was to immerse myself in the arts, learning, integrating, and establishing the network of corresponding powers, symbols, meanings and references which would form the foundation of my practice. When I felt I was finally ready to delve into the raw experiential process of evocation, I experienced many failures or partial successes that were questionable and vague. Since, I have seen a bit of evolution in my own workings. I began as a studious traditionalist, attempting to replicate systems of classical and ancient magic and produce the intended effects of which the texts speak. I have since emerged as someone who, while still honoring and replicating several of the foundational aspects of classical magic, now combines them with tried and true methods and instructions I've received directly from the Spirits who have instructed me in it refinement. I have never considered the exhaustive labors, considerable investment, and even monumental failures as a waste of time and resource. Quite the contrary, I would never wish to take back any moment of the process in which I was tried and tested in the crucible of magical discovery. Magic working is not safe; it is not without risk, uncertainty, trial and disappointment. It is not a test of the supposed reality of magic and its denizens against your suspicion and incredulousness, but a test of your determination and commitment to an often unseen and unfelt world. Many seek out magic simply for the thrill and prospect of seeing the incredible; the same juices which fire during elaborate displays of entertainment often fuel the attraction which draws the neophyte to magical pursuits. The adept is formed out of the matured and awakened child who seeks beyond his own amusement.

There is a milestone of monumental import which occurs when the presence of Spirits becomes observable without the issue of psychological schisms or discontinuity. For some, these manifestations exist as full-bodied beings able to speak and interact much as any physical begin would. For others such beings interact as disembodied voices, intuited presences, or misty apparitions. For many magicians, the desire for Spirit interaction is fulfilled primarily by its capacity to carry out desired tasks with little to no negative repercussions. This probably fits the majority of conjure workers and evocation magicians worldwide. However my own approach has been much more in line with Dr. Dee and his desire to know more about the world and the heavens. It will be interesting to see whether or not the findings of my scryer and me will have any lasting impact in the occult community.

The nature of the Angels and the benefits of their presence are such that they will be missed after their departure. As time goes on, you recall their presence, vision, and experience, and that recollection becomes a longing, like you would miss a loved one or close friend. Their energy lingers after the operation but eventually dissipates as time and events continue in your magical work, just as in the rest of your life. It's important to maintain the relationship with the Archangels by honoring their teachings long after the thrill of the evocation has passed. It's equally important to not attempt to call them up every time you have an issue or just because you miss their presence. Act on the information and council they give you. Demonstrate that you value their time and assistance by pursuing the courses of action they recommend.

Times and interests will change, but the true materialization of the power and gifts the Archangels can grant you will be determined largely by what you do with the information after the operation. Magic is an act of creation, and the manifestation of your intentions is confirmed when all the proper pieces come into alignment through your will and directed attention. Ongoing relationship and familiarization with the Spirit is the surest way to truly harness the extent of its office. A singular introduction and conversation can yield amazing results, but the building of a relationship and integration of influence will bring about the full capacity of that sphere of power. Take each opportunity to exercise your magical will and focus toward your goals.

Looking Back

Since the completion of this series of operations, magical ventures have continued to capture my time, attention, and awe. I speak with my house Spirit Hiram every night save the ones when I am out of town. I never cease to be amazed by the continual council and assistance he gives in not only magical matters but practical ones as well. He has spoken to my scryer at his request several times and has helped him in his own matters, quite independent of my involvement. A martial-arts student of mine who is very close to my family and knows of my magical practice requested an audience with Hiram, and was able to speak and converse with him successfully as well. He cherishes the experience and comments on it often. I find that Hiram has been indispensable to my work and progress as a ceremonial magician. I honestly cannot imagine myself being without his council and advice from this point onward.

True to the words of the Directional King Egyn and the Olympic Spirit Hagith, my daughter was born following the initial series of magical operations, and the images shown of her to my scryer were fascinating as they correlated directly with classical images of Virgo and she was born with that as her Sun sign. We were blessed to have her born healthy, strong, and magical with that special magic that babies bring to our lives.

Appendix A

A Cautionary Warning Regarding Grimoric Ingredients

CAUTION: IMPORTANT! If you would be a worthy, skillful (and long-lived) magician, you must assume responsibility and do your own research to be aware of any dangers inherent in the materials prescribed in texts transmitting premodern recipes—and this applies to talisman components, incenses, oils, and any other items requiring unfamiliar ingredients.

The toxicity of some metals was understood poorly (and in some cases not at all) before the modern era. Both lead and mercury are toxic to humans when handled, and particularly when heated as for casting a lamen or other talisman, as deadly vapors can be released. While lead poisoning (sometimes called saturnism) has been known since antiquity, it is only in recent years that we have learned how dangerous even small levels can be. Other materials can also include toxic metals about which you will be ignorant unless you do your research. Cinnabar, for example, is an ore of mercury, and can exude liquid mercury or—far more dangerously—mercury vapor under some circumstances.

Several of the plant ingredients in grimoric incense recipes (such as henbane and wolfbane) are also poisonous to humans and other animals, and sulphur, when burned, releases potentially deadly sulphur dioxide. Be responsible for yourself and those who trust your expertise.

A true magician should be a wise man or woman, and if not wise, at least competent. **DO YOUR RESEARCH.**

Appendix B

The 62 Angels of the Fifth Encampment by Whose Names Qriphoriya Is Evoked[1]

These are the angels who serve אסימור [Asimor] in the fifth encampment:

[Thaqu] תקו
[Azi] עזי
[Qarva] קרבא
[Ovar] עבר
[Edaath] אדעת
[Elphantos] אלפנטוס
[Detznachaya] דצנחיא
[Tathqahah] תתקהה
[Remgadal] רמגדל
[Perutz] פרוץ
[Diqana] דיקנא
[Taai] טעי
[Kerem] כרם
[Anqiu] אנקיו
[Yiqqar] ייקר

[Edoma] אדומא
[Ali] עלי
[Benesh] בנש
[Haramna] הרמנע
[Pratuph] פרעתוף
[Dinamor] דינמור
[Ninchaya] נינחיא
[Livranakh] ליברנך
[Daknasor] דכנסור
[Gedgedal] גדגדל
[Mavas] מוס
[Didiel] דידיאל
[Taai] טעי
[Hunmora] הונמורא
[Tzeviyuda] צביודע

[Shekhintathakh] שכינתתך
[Lehava] להבא
[Kanur] כנור
[Chelashiel] חלשיאל
[Malkhiah] מלכיה
[Manmelakh] מנמלך
[Kalnah] כלנה
[Dimahan] דימהן
[Zavitur] זביטור
[Elai] עלי
[Kaddir] כדיר
[Thuv] תוב
[Didiel] דידיאל
[Eqav] עקב
[Tzabbiel] צביאל
[Regaviel] רגביאל

[Bethoar] בתואר
[Meqva] מקפא
[Shakniel] שכניאל
[Sarekh] סרך
[Hud] הוד
[Quph] קוף
[Didriokh] דידריוך
[Malgadam] מלגדם
[Aphniel] אפניאל
[Lahatquph] להתקוף
[Mashrutz] משרוץ
[Nashar] נשר
[Demula] דמולא
[Atthar] אתר
[Gazriel] גזריאל
[Adduth] אדות

These are the angels who obey (you) during the night (if you wish) to speak with the moon or the stars or to question a ghost or to speak with the spirits.[2]

1. See chapter 7.
2. Michael A. Morgan (trans.), *Sepher Ha-Razim: The Book of the Mysteries* (Chico, Ca.: Scholars Press, 1983), p. 36. The construed pronunciations of the names are mine; Morgan, whose interests are purely scholarly, reasonably provides only the transliterated Hebrew. —APF

References

Agrippa, Heinrich Cornelius, and Joseph H. Peterson. *Heinrich Cornelius Agrippa: his Fourth Book of Occult Philosophy*. At the *Twilit Grotto—Esoteric Archives* website (http://www.esotericarchives.com/agrippa/agrippa4.htm). Last accessed 2016.

—, and Robert Turner. *Henry Cornelius Agrippa His Fourth Book of Occult Philosophy, translated into English by Robert Turner*. London: printed by J.C. for John Harrison at the Lamb at the East-end of Pauls, 1655.

—, and J.F. *Three Books of Occult Philosophy written by Henry Cornelius Agrippa of Nettesheim*. London: Printed by R.W. for Gregory Moule, 1651.

—, James Freake, and Donald Tyson. *Three Books of Occult Philosophy*. St. Paul, MN: Llewellyn Publications, 1995.

—, J.F., and Joseph H. Peterson. *Of Occult Philosophy*. At the *Twilit Grotto—Esoteric Archives* website (http://www.esotericarchives.com/agrippa/). Last accessed 2016.

Allison, Christine. "Yazidis i. General." In *Encyclopædia Iranica*, online edition. New York, 1996–2016 (http://www.iranicaonline.org/articles/yazidis-i-general-1). Last accessed 2016.

Alster, B., "Tiamat." In K. van der Toorn, Bob Becking, and Pieter Willem van der Horst. *Dictionary of Deities and Demons in the Bible*. Leiden: Brill, 1999.

Anonymous, MS Folger V.b.26, *Book of magic, with instructions for invoking spirits, etc.* At the Folger Shaespeare Library website (http://luna.folger.edu/luna/servlet/view/search?q=v.b.26&sort=call_number%2Cauthor%2Ccd_title%2Cimprint&os=0). Last accessed 2016.

Ashen Chassan (Bryan Garner). *Gateways through Stone and Circle: A Manual of Evocation for the Planetary Intelligences.* Timmonsville, SC: Nephilim Press, 2013.

Ashen Chassan (Bryan Garner). "Substance Through Spirit: A Reflection on Magical Evocation and Talisman Construction." In Adam P. Forrest (ed.), *Liber Spirituum: A Compendium of Writings on Angels and Other Spirits in Modern Magick*. Portland, OR: Azoth Press, 2016.

Barrett, Francis. *The Magus, or Celestial Intelligencer*. London: Lackington, Allen, and Co., 1801.

Betz, Hans Dieter. *The Greek Magical Papyri in Translation, Including the Demotic Spells. Vol. 1, Texts*. Chicago: University of Chicago Press, 1986.

Boudet, Jean-Patrice. "Les who's who démonologiques de la Renaissance et leurs ancêtres médiévaux." In *Médiévales* 44 | Spring 2003: Le diable en procès (http://medievales.revues.org/1019). Last accessed 2016.

Briggs, Constance Victoria. *The Encyclopedia of Angels*. New York: Plume, 1997.

Broek, R. van den. *The Myth of the Phoenix, According to Classical and Early Christian Traditions*. Leiden: E.J. Brill, 1972.

Brown, Francis, Samuel Rolles Driver, and Charles Augustus Briggs. *A Hebrew and English Lexicon of the Old Testament: With an Appendix Containing the Biblical Aramaic*. Oxford: Clarendon Press, 1906.

Burkert, Walter. *Greek Religion*.Cambridge, Massachusetts: Harvard University Press, 1985.

—. *The Orientalizing Revolution: Near Eastern Influence on Greek Culture in the Early Archaic Age*. Translated by Margaret E. Pinder and Walter Burkert. Cambridge, Massachusetts: Harvard University Press, 1995.

Church of St. Uriel the Archangel. "Our Patron Saint." On Church of St. Uriel the Archangel website (http://www.urielsg.org/our-patron-saint). Last accessed 2016.

Cohn, Norman. *Cosmos, Chaos, and the World to Come: The Ancient Roots of Apocalyptic Faith*. New Haven: Yale University Press, 1993.

Coleman, Martin. *Communing with the Spirits: The Magical Practice of Necromancy Simply and Lucidly Explained, with Full Instructions for the Practice.* York Beach, Maine: Samuel Weiser, 1998.

Conybeare, F.C. "The Testament of Solomon." In *The Jewish Quarterly Review*, Vol. 11, No. 1 (Oct., 1898), pp. 1–45.

Copenhaver, Brian P. *Magic in Western Culture: From Antiquity to the Enlightenment.* Cambridge: Cambridge University Press, 2015.

Crowley, Aleister[, S.L. MacGregor Mathers, and Solomon]. *The Book of the Goetia of Solomon the King: Translated into the English Tongue by a Dead Hand and Adorned with Divers Other Matters Germane, Delightful to the Wise: the Whole Edited, Verified, Introd. and Commented by A. Crowley.* Boleskine, Foyers, Inverness: Society for the Propagation of Religious Truth, 1904.

Davidson, Gustav. *A Dictionary of Angels: Including the Fallen Angels.* New York: Free Press, 1967.

Davila, James R. *Descenders to the Chariot: The People Behind the Hekhalot Literature.* Leiden: Brill, 2001.

De Laurence, L. W. *The Old Book of Magic: A Precise History of Magic, Its Procedure, Rites and Mysteries As Contained in Ancient Manuscripts, Embellished with Engravings of Wonderful Charms and Talismans.* Chicago, Ill: De Laurence, Scott & Co, 1918.

Drower, E. S. *Peacock Angel: Being Some Account of Votaries of a Secret Cult and Their Sanctuaries.* London: J. Murray, 1941.

Eliade, Mircea. *Shamanism: Archaic Techniques of Ecstasy.* Trans. from the French by Willard R. Trask. London: Routledge & Kegan Paul, 1964.

Empson, R.H.W. *The Cult of the Peacock Angel: A Short Account of the Yezîdî Tribes of Kurdistân.* London: H. F. and G. Witherby, 1928.

Forrest, Adam P. (ed.), *Liber Spirituum: A Compendium of Writings on Angels and Other Spirits in Modern Magick.* Portland, OR: Azoth Press, 2016.

Garner, Bryan. See works listed under ASHEN CHASSAN.

Gaster, Moses. *The Wisdom of the Chaldeans: An Old Hebrew Astrological Text.* London: Proceedings of the Society of Biblical Archaeology, 1900

Gollancz, Hermann. *The Book of Protection: being a collection of charms, now edited for the first time from Syriac MSS*. London: Henry Frowde, Oxford University Press, 1912.

—, and Joseph H. Peterson. *The Book of Protection: being a collection of charms, now edited for the first time from Syriac MSS*. At the *Twilit Grotto—Esoteric Archives* website (http://www.esotericarchives.com/gollancz/protect.htm). Last accessed 2016.

Greer, John Michael, and Christopher Warnock. *The Picatrix (Liber Atratus Edition): The Occult Classic of Astrological Magic*. [n.p.]: Adocentyn Press, 2010–11.

Hall, Manly P., and J. Augustus Knapp. *An Encyclopedic Outline of Masonic, Hermetic, Qabbalistic, and Rosicrucian Symbolical Philosophy: Being an Interpretation of the Secret Teachings Concealed Within the Rituals, Allegories, and Mysteries of All Ages*. San Francisco: Printed for M.P. Hall by H.S. Crocker, 1928.

Harms, Daniel, James R. Clark, and Joseph H. Peterson. *The Book of Oberon: A Sourcebook of Elizabethan Magic*. Woodbury, Minnesota: Llewellyn Publications, 2015.

Harris, R. Laird, Gleason L. Archer, and Bruce K. Waltke. *Theological Wordbook of the Old Testament*. Chicago: Moody Press, 1980.

Heidl, Alexander. *The Babylonian Genesis: The Story of the Creation [Translations of the Enuma Elish and Other Babylonian Stories, with Old Testament Parallels. With Plates.]*. Chicago: University of Chicago Press, 1942.

Hockley, Frederic, and Dietrich Bergman. *A Complete Book of Magic Science*. York Beach, ME: The Teitan Press, 2008.

Holland, Leicester B. "The Mantic Mechanism at Delphi." *American Journal of Archaeology* 37, no. 2 (1933): pp. 204–214.

Homer, and A.T. Murray (ed. and trans.). *The Iliad with an English Translation by A.T. Murray, Ph.D. in two volumes*. Cambridge, MA: Harvard University Press; London: William Heinemann, Ltd., 1924.

Idel, Moshe. *Kabbalah in Italy, 1280–1510: A Survey*. New Haven: Yale University Press, 2011.

Isaac, E. (ed. and trans.). *I Enoch (The Ethiopic Apocalypse of Enoch)*. In James H. Charlesworth (ed.), *The Old Testament Pseudepigrapha, Vol. 1: Apocalyptic Literature and Testaments*. Garden City, New York: Doubleday & Co., 1983.

John R. King IV. "#9 Paimon." In *Imperial Arts* LiveJournal for Wednesday, June 10th, 2009 (http://imperialarts.livejournal.com/?skip=20). Last accessed 2015.

Levene, Dan. "Rare Magic Inscription in Human Skull." In *Biblical Archæology Review* (March/April 2009), Volume 35, Number 02.

Littlejohn, Josephine. See JOSEPHINE McCARTHY.

Maggs Brothers. *Curiouser and Curiouser! A Catalogue of Strange Books and Curious Titles*. London: Maggs Bros., 1932.

Mahadevan, Iravatham. "'Murukan' in the Indus Script," at the *Murugan Bhakti* website (http://murugan.org/research/mahadevan.htm). Last accessed 2016.

Malchus, Marius. *The Secret Grimoire of Turiel*. Aquarian Press: London, 1960.

Mathers, S.L. MacGregor, and Solomon. *The Key of Solomon the King (Clavicula Salomonis)*. London: George Redway, 1889.

Marathakis, Ioannis, and Solomon. *The Magical Treatise of Solomon, or Hygromanteia: Also Called the Apotelesmatikē Pragmateia, Epistle to Rehoboam, Solomōnikēs*. Singapore: Golden Hoard Press, 2011.

Mathers, S.L. MacGregor, and Abraham ben Simeon of Worms. *The Book of the Sacred Magic of Abramelin the Mage*. London: J.M. Watkins, 1898.

McCarthy, Josephine. *The Exorcist's Handbook*. Berkeley, CA: Golem Media, 2010.

McLean, Adam. *A Treatise on Angel Magic: Being a Complete Transcription of Ms Harley 6482 in the British Library*. Edinburgh: Magnum Opus Hermetic Sourceworks, 1982. Magnum Opus Hermetic Sourceworks, 15.

Members of the Mercurii: Raphael, the Metropolitan Astrologer; the Editor of the Prophetic Almanack; and other Sidereal Artists of Eminence. *The Astrologer of the Nineteenth Century, or, The Master Key of Futurity and Guide to Ancient Mysteries: Being a Complete System of Occult Philosophy*.

London: Printed by Davidson, Printer, for Knight and Lacey, Paternoster Row, and Westley and Tyrrell, Dublin, 1825.

Miller, Jason. *The Sorcerer's Secrets: Strategies to Practical Magick*. Franklin Lakes, NJ: New Page Books, 2009.

Morgan, Michael A. *Sepher Ha-Razim: The Book of the Mysteries*. Chico, Ca.: Scholars Press, 1983.

Murray, Margaret A. *The God of the Witches*. London: Oxford University Press, 1970. [First ed. London: Sampson Low, Marston and Co., 1931.]

Nagel, Alexandra. *Marriage with Elementals:From Le Comte de Gabalis to a Golden Dawn ritual.* Dissertation prepared for the MA Mysticism and Western Esotericism. Eindhoven: University of Amsterdam, 2007.

Odeberg, Hugo (ed.). *3 Enoch or The Hebrew Book of Enoch*. London: Cambridge University Press, 1929.

Omega Ω. "The Four Kings in the Grimoires Tradition." At the weblog *A Journey into Ceremonial Magick* (http://omega-magick.blogspot.com/2015/03/the-four-kings-in-grimoires-tradition.html). Last accessed 2016.

Peterson, Joseph H. *Arbatel: Concerning the Magic of the Ancients*. Lake Worth, FL: Ibis Press, 2009.

Peterson, Joseph H., and Daniel Harms (eds.). *Book of magic, with instructions for invoking spirits, etc. (ca. 1577-1583): Folger SHAKESPEARE LIBRARY manuscript V.b.26*. At the Twilit Grotto—Esoteric Archives website (http://www.esotericarchives.com/folger/v_b_26_transcription.pdf). Last accessed 2016.

Peterson, Joseph H., Ptolemy, and Solomon. *The Clavicle of Solomon revealed by Ptolemy the Grecian*. At the *Twilit Grotto—Esoteric Archives* website (http://www.esotericarchives.com/solomon/sl3847.htm). Last accessed 2016.

Peterson, Joseph H., and Solomon. *The Lesser Key of Solomon: Lemegeton Clavicula Salomonis: Detailing the Ceremonial Art of Commanding Spirits Both Good and Evil*. York Beach, ME: Weiser Books, 2001.

Peterson, Joseph H. *The Offices of Spirits, excerpted from Sloane 3853, Wellcome 110, and Ad. 36674*. At the *Twilit Grotto—Esoteric Archives* website (http://www.esotericarchives.com/solomon/offices.htm). Last accessed 2016.

Peterson, Joseph H., R. Abognazar, and Solomon. *The Veritable Clavicles of Solomon (Les Veritables Clavicules de Salomon) (Abognazar) (EXCERPTS)*. At the *Twilit Grotto—Esoteric Archives* website (http://www.esotericarchives.com/solomon/l1203.htm). Last accessed 2016.

Pope, Hugh T. "Gabriel." In *The Catholic Encyclopedia, Volume VI*. New York: Robert Appleton Company, 1909.

Raphael. See work listed under MEMBERS OF THE MERCURII.

Rapposelli, Dee. "The Arbatel Working." A the *Sorcerers and Magi* weblog (http://sorcerersandmagi.blogspot.com/2013/06/the-arbatel-working.html). Last accessed 2016.

Savedow, Steve. *Sepher Rezial Hemelach: The Book of the Angel Rezial*. York Beach, ME: Samuel Weiser, 2000.

Sibley, Ebenezer, Frederick Hockley, and Joseph H. Peterson. *The Clavis or Key to the Magic of Solomon*. Lake Worth, FL: Ibis Press, 2009.

Sinha, Kanchan. *Kartikeya in Indian Art and Literature*. Delhi: Sundeep Prakashan, 1979.

Skinner, Stephen. *The Complete Magician's Tables*. Singapore: Golden Hoard Press, 2006.

—, David Rankine, and Cyprian. *The Grimoire of Saint Cyprian: Clavis Inferni: sive Magia Alba et Nigra approbata Metratona = the Key of Hell with White and Black Magic proven by Metatron, being Wellcome MS 2000*. Singapore: Golden Hoard Press, 2009.

—, and David Rankine. *The Keys to the Gateway of Magic: Summoning the Solomonic Archangels & Demonic Princes*. Singapore: Golden Hoard Press, 2005.

—. *Techniques of Graeco-Egyptian Magic*. Singapore: Golden Hoard Press, 2014.

—, David Rankine, and Solomon. *The Veritable Key of Solomon*. Singapore: Golden Hoard Press, 2010.

Steiner, Rudolf, and Christopher Bamford (ed.). *The Archangel Michael: His Mission and Ours: Selected Lectures and Writings*. Hudson, NY: Anthroposophic Press, 1994.

Stratton-Kent, Jake. *Geosophia: The Argo of Magic: from the Greeks to the Grimoires*. [Dover]: Scarlet Imprint/Bibliothèque Rouge, 2010.

Stutley, Margaret and James. *Harper's Dictionary of Hinduism*. New York: Harper & Row, 1977.

Theoi Project. "Aiolos" on the *Theoi* website (http://www.theoi.com/Titan/Aiolos.html). Last accessed 2016.

Tobit, in the King James Version of the Bible. Online at King James Bible Online (http://www.kingjamesbibleonline.org/Tobit-Chapter-1/#). Last accessed 2016.

Trithemius, Johannes. *The Art of Drawing Spirits into Crystals*, in Francis Barrett, *The Magus, or Celestial Intelligencer*. London: Lackington, Allen, and Co., 1801.

Turner, Robert (trans.) and Arbatel. *Arbatel of Magic*. In Robert Turner (ed. and trans.). *Henry Cornelius Agrippa, His Fourth Book of Occult Philosophy, translated into English by Robert Turner*. London: printed by J.C. for John Harrison at the Lamb at the East-end of Pauls, 1655.

Velmurugu, Ambikai. "'Cult of Skanda-Murukan in Tamilakam: The Antiquity of Murukan Worship in Tamil Nadu." At the *Murugan Bhakti* website (http://murugan.org/research/ambikai.htm). Last accessed 2016.

Waite, Arthur Edward. *The Book of Black Magic and of Pacts*. Edinburgh: Privately printed, 1898.

Watterson, Barbara. *The Gods of Ancient Egypt*. New York, N.Y.: Facts on File, 1984.

Wilby, Emma. *Cunning Folk and Familiar Spirits: Shamanistic Visionary Traditions in Early Modern British Witchcraft and Magic*. Brighton: Sussex Academic Press, 2005.

Wilkinson, Richard H. *The Complete Gods and Goddesses of Ancient Egypt*. New York: Thames & Hudson, 2003.

YezidiTruth.org. "What is the Peacock Angel?" At the *YezidiTruth.org: The Truth about the Yezidis* website (http://www.yeziditruth.org/ /the_peacock_angel). Last accessed 2016.

FRATER ASHEN CHASSAN · BRYAN GARNER is a practicing occultist and grimoric traditionalist who has been involved in Western ceremonial magic since 1999. His passions center on reproducing experiments from the Solomonic magical texts and exploring their effectiveness. His approach is based on a serious study of historic forms of magic and spirit communication. He is the author of Gateways Through Stone and Circle: A Manual of Evocation for the Planetary Intelligences *(Nephilim Press, 2014), as well as contributions to several notable anthologies, including* The Holy Guardian Angel *(Nephilim Press, 2013) and* Liber Spirituum: A Compendium of Writings on Angels and Other Spirits in Modern Magick *(Azoth Press, 2016). You may follow his blogs at* Frater Ashen Chassan *(ashenchassan.wordpress.com) and* A Magician's Workings *(bryanashen.blogspot.com), and find him on Facebook (https://www.facebook.com/frater.ashenchassan).*

✢

Azoth Press is a small independent publishing house which makes its home in the Pacific Northwest. Our purpose is to create extraordinary books by practicing magicians for the practicing magician, with a standard of knowledge influenced by years of dedicated occult study and magical experience. We hope that our books will contribute to the practitioner's evolution and transformation, and also add to the magician's library a collection of unique, hand-made tomes meant to last for generations. Magical books should be Hermetic and talismanic works of art produced by the conjunction of well-written, well-researched, and enlightening content with beautiful design and elegant binding. In line with our goal of creating such magical volumes for practitioners and scholars of the Great Work, all Azoth Press limited-edition books are hand-bound by artisans with decades of experience in the fields of printing and master bookbinding. Each book is manufactured not only to a high æsthetic standard to please the eye and hand, but also to a demanding standard of artisanship and materials, so that each rare volume may be handed down, read, and used in their practice by generations of magicians to come. Please visit our website at azothpress.com *and follow us on Facebook at* https://www.facebook.com/AzothPress/.

✣

CPSIA information can be obtained
at www.ICGtesting.com
Printed in the USA
BVHW020058141019
560666BV00025B/107/P

9 781935 006985